Teaching and Research Aptitude

For UGC-NET/SLET

PAPER - I

Teaching and Research Aptitude

For UGC-NET/SLET

PAPER - I

Atlantic Research Division

PUBLISHERS & DISTRIBUTORS (P) LTD

Published by

ATLANTIC

PUBLISHERS & DISTRIBUTORS (P) LTD

7/22, Ansari Road, Darya Ganj,
New Delhi-110002
Phones : +91-11-40775252, 23273880, 23275880, 23280451
Fax : +91-11-23285873
Web : www.atlanticbooks.com
E-mail : orders@atlanticbooks.com

Branch Office
5, Nallathambi Street, Wallajah Road,
Chennai-600002
Phones : +91-44-64611085, 32413319
E-mail : chennai@atlanticbooks.com

Printed in India at Nice Printing Press, A-33/3A, Site-IV, Industrial Area, Sahibabad, Ghaziabad, U.P.

Preface

The book covers the general paper (Paper-I) on Teaching and Research Aptitude for UGC-NET/SLET. It has been designed to cover the entire syllabus of the general paper with the objective of assessing the teaching and research capabilities of the aspirants of lectureship and research through UGC-NET/SLET. It will be very helpful in improving the cognitive abilities of the candidates, including comprehension, analysis, evaluation, and understanding the structure of arguments and deductive as well as inductive reasoning. It will also be helpful in improving general awareness and knowledge of sources of information. The questions relating to the interaction between people, environment and natural resources and their impact on quality of life have been properly dealt with in this book.

Utmost care has been taken to cover all possible types of questions asked in the general paper. Six model test papers, based on the style and contents of the original papers set in the UGC-NET/SLET, have been included in this book to test the level of preparation of the students. At the end of this book, previous years' papers with answers have been provided to familiarize the students with the pattern of the questions asked in the UGC-NET/SLET.

Since, general paper is common to all the students appearing for the UGC-NET/SLET, irrespective of their principal subjects, this book will be useful to each and every student pursuing a career in teaching and research.

Atlantic Research Division

General Instructions

About the NET

The National Educational Testing Bureau of University Grants Commission (UGC) conducts National Eligibility Test (NET) to determine eligibility for lectureship and for award of Junior Research Fellowship (JRF) for Indian nationals in order to ensure minimum standards for the entrants in the teaching profession and research. The Test is conducted in Humanities (including languages), Social Sciences, Forensic Science, Environmental Sciences, Computer Science and Applications and Electronic Science.

The Council of Scientific and Industrial Research (CSIR) conducts the UGC-CSIR NET for other Science subjects, namely, Life Sciences, Physical Sciences, Chemical Sciences, Mathematical Sciences and Earth Atmospheric Ocean & Planetary Sciences jointly with the UGC. The tests are conducted twice in a year generally in the months of June and December. For candidates who desire to pursue research, the Junior Research Fellowship (JRF) is available for five years subject to fulfillment of certain conditions. UGC has allocated a number of fellowships to the universities for the candidates who qualify the test for JRF. The JRFs are awarded to the meritorious candidates from among the candidates qualifying for eligibility for lectureship in the NET. JRFs are available only to the candidates who opt for it in their application forms.

The test for Junior Research Fellowship is being conducted since 1984. The Government of India, through its notification dated 22nd July, 1988 entrusted the task of conducting the eligibility test for lectureship to UGC. Consequently, UGC conducted the first National Eligibility Test, common to both eligibility for Lectureship and Junior Research Fellowship in two parts, that is, in December 1989 and in March, 1990.

NET Schedule

UGC conducts NET twice a year, i.e., in the months of June and December. The notifications announcing the June and December examinations are published in the months of March and September respectively in the weekly journal of nation-wide circulation, viz, Employment News.

NET Results Declaration Schedule

The result of June, UGC-NET is declared generally in the month of October. Similarly December, UGC-NET result is usually declared in the month of April. The UGC-NET results published in the Employment News are also available on UGC website.

UGC-NET in Objective Mode from June, 2012 Onwards

1. The UGC-NET will be conducted in objective mode from June 2012 onwards. The Test will consist of three papers. All the three papers will consist of only objective type questions and will be held on the day of Examination in two separate sessions as under:

Session	Paper	Number of Questions	Marks	Duration
First	I	60 out of which 50 questions are to be attempted	50 × 2 = 100	1¼ Hours (09.30 a.m. to 10.45 a.m.)
First	II	50 questions all of which are compulsory	50 × 2 = 100	1¼ Hours (10.45 a.m. to 12.00 Noon.)
Second	III	75 questions all of which are compulsory	75 × 2 = 150	2½ Hours (01.30 p.m. to 04.00 p.m.)

2. The candidates are required to obtain minimum marks separately in Paper-I, Paper-II and Paper-III as given below:

Category	Minimum marks (%) to be obtained		
	Paper-I	**Paper-II**	**Paper-III**
General	40 (40%)	40 (40%)	75 (50%)
OBC	35 (35%)	35 (35%)	67.5 (45%) rounded off to 68
PH/VH/SC/ST	35 (35%)	35 (35%)	60 (40%)

Only such candidates who obtain the minimum required marks in each Paper, separately, as mentioned above, will be considered for final preparation of result.

However, the final qualifying criteria for Junior Research Fellowship (JRF) and eligibility for Lectureship shall be decided by UGC before declaration of result.

3. The syllabus of Paper-I, Paper-II and Paper-III will remain the same.

4. The candidates will be allowed to carry the carbon printout of OMR Response Sheets with them on conclusion of the examination.

5. There will be no negative marking.

UNIVERSITY GRANTS COMMISSION NET BUREAU

PAPER-I

SUBJECT: GENERAL PAPER ON TEACHING AND RESEARCH APTITUDE

The main objective is to assess the teaching and research capabilities of the candidates. Therefore, the test is aimed at assessing the teaching and general/research aptitude as well as their awareness. They are expected to possess and exhibit cognitive abilities. Cognitive abilities include comprehension, analysis, evaluation, understanding the structure of arguments and deductive and inductive reasoning. The candidates are also expected to have a general awareness and knowledge of sources of information. They should be aware of interaction between people, environment and natural resources and their impact on quality of life. The details are given in the following sections:

NOTE : (i) Each section gets equal weightage : five questions and 10 marks from each section.

(ii) Whenever pictorial questions are set for the sighted candidates a passage followed by equal number of questions should be set for the visually handicapped candidates.

I. Teaching Aptitude

- Teaching: Nature, objectives, characteristics and basic requirements;
- Learner's characteristics;
- Factors affecting teaching;
- Methods of teaching;
- Teaching aids;
- Evaluation systems.

II. Research Aptitude

- Research: Meaning, characteristics and types;
- Steps of research;
- Methods of research;
- Research Ethics;
- Paper, article, workshop, seminar, conference and symposium;
- Thesis writing: its characteristics and format.

III. Reading Comprehension

- A passage to be set with questions to be answered.

IV. Communication

- Communication: Nature, characteristics, types, barriers and effective classroom communication.

V. Reasoning (Including Mathematical)

- Number series; letter series; codes;
- Relationships; classification.

VI. Logical Reasoning

- Understanding the structure of arguments;
- Evaluating and distinguishing deductive and inductive reasoning;
- Verbal analogies: Word analogy—Applied analogy;
- Verbal classification;
- Reasoning Logical Diagrams: Simple diagrammatic relationship, multidiagrammatic relationship;
- Venn diagram; Analytical Reasoning.

VII. Data Interpretation

- Sources, acquisition and interpretation of data;
- Quantitative and qualitative data;
- Graphical representation and mapping of data.

VIII. Information and Communication Technology (ICT)

- ICT: meaning, advantages, disadvantages and uses;
- General abbreviations and terminology;
- Basics of internet and e-mailing.

IX. People and Environment

- People and environment interaction;
- Sources of pollution;
- Pollutants and their impact on human life, exploitation of natural and energy resources;
- Natural hazards and mitigation.

X. Higher Education System: Governance, Polity and Administration

- Structure of the institutions for higher learning and research in India; formal and distance education; professional/technical and general education; value education: governance, polity and administration; concept, institutions and their interactions.

SAMPLE QUESTIONS

I. Teaching Aptitude

1. Which one of the following is the main objective ofteaching?
   (a) To give information related to the syllabus
   (b) To develop thinking power of students
   (c) To dictate notes to students
   (d) To prepare students to pass the examination

Key: (b)

2. Which one of the following is a good method of teaching?
   (a) Lecture and Dictation
   (b) Seminar and Project
   (c) Seminar and Dictation
   (d) Dictation and Assignment

Key: (b)

3. Teacher uses teaching aids for
   (a) Making teaching interesting
   (b) Making teaching within understanding level of students
   (c) Making students attentive
   (d) The sake of its use

Key: (b)

4. Effectiveness of teaching depends on
   (a) Qualification of teacher
   (b) Personality of teacher
   (c) Handwriting of teacher
   (d) Subject understanding of teacher

Key: (d)

5. Which of the following is not characteristic of a good question paper?
   (a) Objectivity
   (b) Subjectivity
   (c) No use of vague words
   (d) Reliable

Key: (b)

II. Research Aptitude

1. A researcher is generally expected to:
   (a) Study the existing literature in a field
   (b) Generate new principles and theories
   (c) Synthesize the ideas given by others
   (d) Evaluate the findings of a study

Key: (b)

2. One of the essential characteristics of research is:
   (a) Replicability (b) Generalizability
   (c) Usability (d) Objectivity

Key: (d)

3. The Government of India conducts Census after every 10 years. The method of research used in this process is:
   (a) Case study (b) Developmental
   (c) Survey (d) Experimental

Key: (c)

4. An academic association assembled at one place to discuss the progress of its work and future plans. Such an assembly is known as a
   (a) Conference (b) Seminar
   (c) Workshop (d) Symposium

Key: (a)

5. An investigator studied the census data for a given area and prepared a write-up based on them. Such a write-up is called:
   (a) Research paper (b) Article
   (c) Thesis (d) Research report

Key: (b)

III. Reading Comprehension

Read the following passage and answer the question Nos. 1 to 5

The Constitution guarantees every citizen the fundamental right to equality. Yet after 50 years of independence, just one perusal of the female infant mortality figures, the literacy rates and the employment opportunities for women is sufficient evidence that discrimination exists. Almost predictably, this gender, bias is evident in our political system as welL In the 13th Lok Sabha, there were only 43 women MPs out of a total of 543; it is not a surprising figure, for never has women's representation in Parliament been more than 10 per cent.

Historically, the manifestos of major political parties have always encouraged women's participation. It has been merely a charade. So, women's organisations, denied a place on merit, opted for the last resort: a reservation of seats for women in parliament and State Assemblies. Parties, which look at everything with a vote bank in mind, seemed to endorse this. Alas, this too was a mirage.

But there is another aspect also. At a time when caste is the trump card, some politicians want the bill to include further quotas for women from among minorities and backward castes. There is more to it. A survey shows that there is a general antipathy towards the bill. It is actually a classic case of doublespeak: in public, politicians were endorsing women's reservation but in the backrooms of Parliament, they were busy sabotaging it. The reasons are clear: Men just don't want to vacate their seats of power.

1. The problem raised in the passage reflects badly on our
   (a) Political system
   (b) Social behaviour
   (c) Individual behaviour
   (d) Behaviour of a group of people

Key: (b)

2. According to the passage, political parties have mostly in mind
   (a) Economic prosperity (b) Vote bank
   (c) People' welfare (d) Patriotism

Key: (c)

3. "Trump Card" means
   (a) Trying to move a dead horse
   (b) Playing the card cautiously
   (c) Sabotaging all the moves by others
   (d) Making the final jolt for success

Key: (b)

4. The sentence "Men just don't want to vacate their seats of power" implies
   (a) Lust for power
   (b) Desire to serve the nation

(c) Conviction in one's own political abilities
(d) Political corruption

Key: (a)

5. What is the percentage of women in the Lok Sabha
(a) 10 (b) 7.91
(c) 43 (d) 9.1

Key: (b)

IV. Communication

1. Informal communication network within the organisation is known as
(a) Interpersonal Communication
(b) Intrapersonal Communication
(c) Mass Communication
(d) Grapevine Communication

Key: (d)

2. TV Channel launched for covering only Engineering and Technology subjects is known as
(a) Gyan Darshan (b) Vyas
(c) Eklavya (d) Kisan

Key: (c)

3. In which state the maximum number of periodicals are brought out for public information:
(a) Uttar Pradesh (b) Tamil Nadu
(c) Kerala (d) Punjab

Key: (c)

4. The main objective of public broadcasting system i.e. Prasar Bharti is
(a) Inform, Entertainment & Education
(b) Entertain, Information & Interaction
(c) Educate, Interact & Entertain
(d) Entertainment only

Key: (a)

5. The competency of an effective communicator can be judged on the basis of:
(a) Personality of communicator
(b) Experience in the field
(c) Interactivity with target audience
(d) Meeting the needs of target audience

Key: (d)

V. Reasoning (Including Mathematical)

1. Which one of the following belongs to the category of homogeneous data:
(a) Multi-storeyed houses in a colony
(b) Trees in a garden

(c) Vehicular traffic on a highway
(d) Student population in a class

Key: (a)

2. In which of the following ways a theory is not different from a belief?
   (a) Antecedent-consequent
   (b) Acceptability
   (c) Verifiability
   (d) Demonstratability

Key: (b)

3. The state—"Honesty is the best policy" is
   (a) A fact (b) An value
   (c) An opinion (d) A value judgement

Key: (d)

4. Which one is like pillar, pole and standard?
   (a) Beam (b) Plank
   (c) Shaft (d) Timber

Key: (a)

5. Following incomplete series is presented. Find out the number which should come at the place of question mark which will complete the series: 4, 16, 36, 64?
   (a) 300 (b) 200
   (c) 100 (d) 150

Key: (a)

VI. Logical Reasoning

1. The following question is based on the diagram given below. If the two big circles represent animals living on soil and those living in water, and the small circle stands for the animals who both live on soil and in water, which figure represents the relationships among them.

(a) 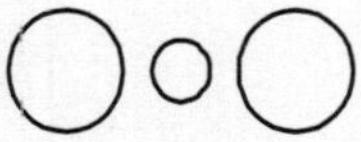 (b)

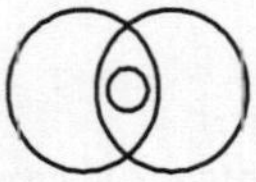

(c) 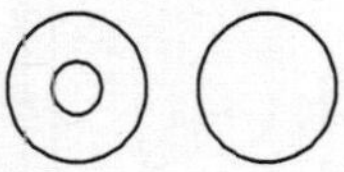 (d)

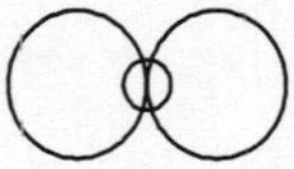

Key: (d)

2. Of the following statements, there are two statements both of which cannot be true but both can be false. Which are these two statements?
   (i) All machines make noise
   (ii) Some machines are noisy
   (iii) No machine makes noise
   (iv) Some machines are not noisy

(a) (i) and (ii) (b) (iii) and (iv)
(c) (i) and (iii) (d) (ii) and (iv)

Key: (c)

3. In the following question a statement is followed by two assumptions: (i) and (ii). An assumption is something supposed or taken for granted. Consider the statement and the following assumptions and decide which of the following assumptions is implicit in the statement.

Statement: We need not worry about errors but must try to learn from our errors.

Assumptions: (i) Errors may take place when we are carrying out certain work.
(ii) We are capable of benefiting from the past and improve our chances of error-free work.

(a) Only assumption (i) is implicit
(b) Only assumption (ii) is implicit
(c) Either assumption (i) or (ii) is implicit
(d) Both the assumptions are implicit

Key: (d)

4. The question below is followed by two arguments numbered (i) and (ii). Decide which of the arguments is 'strong' and which is 'weak'. Choose the correct answer from the given below: (a) (b) (c) (d).

Should the press exercise some self-restraint?

(i) Yes, they should not publish news items which may incite the readers to indulge in wrong practices.
(ii) No, it is the responsibility of the press to present the truth irrespective of the consequences.

(a) Only the argument (i) is strong
(b) Only the argument (ii) is strong
(c) Neither argument (i) nor argument (ii) is strong
(d) Both the arguments (i) and (ii) are strong

Key: (a)

5. Study the argument and the inference drawn from that argument, given below carefully.

Argument: Anything that goes up definitely falls down. Helicopter goes up.

Inference: So the helicopter will definitely fall down.

What in your opinion is the inference drawn from the argument?

(a) Valid (b) Invalid
(c) Doubtful (d) Long drawn one

Key: (d)

VII. Data Interpretation

Four students W, X, Y, Z appeared in four papers, I, II, III and IV in a test. Their scores out of 100 are given below:

Students	Papers			
	I	II	III	IV
W	60	81	45	55
X	59	43	51	A
Y	74	A	71	65
Z	72	76	A	68

Where 'A' stands for absent

Read the above table and answer below mentioned questions 1 to 5.

1. Which candidate has secured between 60-65% marks in aggregate?
   (a) W (b) X
   (c) Y (d) Z

Key: (a)

2. Who has obtained the lowest average in aggregate?
   (a) W (b) X
   (c) Y (d) Z

Key: (b)

3. Who has obtained the highest average?
   (a) W (b) X
   (c) Y (d) Z

Key: (a)

4. In which paper the lowest marks were obtained by the candidates?
   (a) I (b) II
   (c) III (d) IV

Key: (b)

5. Which candidate has secured the highest percentage in the papers appeared?
   (a) W (b) X
   (c) Y (d) Z

Key: (d)

VIII. Information and Communication Technology (ICT)

1. ICT stands for
   (a) Information common technology
   (b) Information and corrnnunication technology
   (c) Information and computer technology
   (d) Interconnected technology

Key: (b)

2. Computer can
   (a) process both quantitative and qualitative information
   (b) store huge information

(c) process information and fast accurately
(d) All of the above

Key: (d)

3. Satellite Communication works through

(a) Radar (b) Transponder
(c) Receptor (d) Transmitter

Key: (b)

4. A computer is that machine which works more like a human brain. This definition of computer is

(a) correct (b) incorrect
(c) partially correct (d) None of the above

Key: (a)

5. Information and communication technology includes

(a) E-mail (b) Internet
(c) Educational television (d) All of the above

Key: (d)

IX. People and Environment

1. It is believed that our globe is warming progressively. This global warming will eventually result in

(a) increase in availability of usable land
(b) uniformity of climate at equator and poles
(c) fall in the sea level
(d) melting of polar ice

Key: (d)

2. In which parts of India groundwater is affected with arsenic contamination?

(a) Haryana (b) Andhra Pradesh
(c) Sikkim (d) West Bengal

Key: (d)

3. Sunderban in Hooghly delta is known for

(a) Grasslands (b) Conifers
(c) Mangroves (d) Arid forests

Key: (c)

4. Sardar Sarover dam is located on the river

(a) Ganga (b) Godavari
(c) Mahanadi (d) Narmada

Key: (d)

5. Which one of the following trees has medicinal value?

(a) Pine (b) Teak
(c) Neem (d) Oak

Key: (c)

X. Higher Education System: Governance, Polity and Administration

1. Which one of the following is not considered a part oftechnical education in India?
   (a) Medical (b) Management
   (c) Pharmaceutical (d) Aeronautical

Key: (a)

2. Which of the following is a Central University?
   (a) Mumbai University (b) Calcutta University
   (c) Delhi University (d) Madras University

Key: (c)

3. Identify the main principle on which the Parliamentary System operates:
   (a) Responsibility of Executive to Legislature
   (b) Supremacy of Parliament
   (c) Supremacy of Judiciary
   (d) Theory of Separation of Power

Key: (a)

4. The reservation of seats for women in the Panchayat Raj Institutions is:
   (a) 30% of the total seats
   (b) 33% of the total seats
   (c) 33% of the total population
   (d) In proportion to their population

Key: (b)

5. Match List I with List II and select the correct answer from the code given below:

   List I (Institutions)
   (1) Indian Veterinary Research Institute
   (2) Institute of Armament Technology
   (3) Indian Institute of Science
   (4) National Institute for Educational Planners and Administrators

   List II (Locations)
   (i) Pune (ii) Izat Nagar
   (iii) Delhi (iv) Bangalore

Codes:	(1)	(2)	(3)	(4)
(a)	(ii)	(i)	(iv)	(iii)
(b)	(i)	(iv)	(ii)	(iii)
(c)	(ii)	(iii)	(i)	(iv)
(d)	(iv)	(iii)	(ii)	(i)

Key: (a)

Contents

1

Teaching Aptitude

1. On the basis of political background, the process of education can be classified in
   (a) Three categories
   (b) Four categories
   (c) Two categories
   (d) Five categories
2. If majority of students in your class are weak you should
   (a) not care about the intelligent students.
   (b) keep your speed of teaching fast so that students comprehension level may increase.
   (c) keep your teaching slow.
   (d) keep your teaching slow along with some extra guidance to bright pupils.
3. If some parents complaint about you to the principal, then
   (a) you would not take notice of it.
   (b) you would abuse the parents.
   (c) you would tell real situation to the principal.
   (d) None of the above.
4. The main duty of a teacher is
   (a) to stimulate and guide student's learning.
   (b) to provide remedial aid and diagnostic aid wherever required.
   (c) to teach only the prescribed curriculum.
   (d) to ensure that all students belong to same social group.
5. The definition based on Autocratic system is supported by
   (a) H.C. Morrison
   (b) N.L. Gage
   (c) John Brubacher
   (d) None of the above
6. If some of your pupils misbehave with you in the college campus you must
   (a) report to the principal.
   (b) report to their parents.
   (c) improve their behaviour by your own character and scholarship.
   (d) mobilize other teachers against these guys.
7. The functions of a teacher are in the order of
   (a) guiding the child, helping him towards progress and evaluation.
   (b) checking homework, guiding him and assigning further task.
   (c) Both (a) and (b).
   (d) None of the above.
8. Why do teachers use teaching aid?
   (a) To make teaching fun-filled
   (b) To teach within understanding level of students
   (c) For namesake
   (d) To make students attentive.
9. N.L. Gage is associated with the definitions of teaching based on
   (a) Democratic system
   (b) Autocratic system
   (c) Laissez-faire system
   (d) None of the above

10. Maximum participation of students is possible in teaching through
    (a) lecture method
    (b) discussion method
    (c) audio-visual aids
    (d) textbook method

11. The teachers should study educational philosophy because
    (a) they lack philosophy.
    (b) they may improve their work by classifying their philosophy.
    (c) they follow wrong philosophy.
    (d) they are incapable of following their own philosophy.

12. The primary cause of teachers failure in maintaining discipline is due to teacher's lack of
    (a) a constructive programme of meaningful things to be learnt and done.
    (b) competence.
    (c) knowledge of educational psychology.
    (d) knowledge of the subject.

13. Generally the political system of a country has great influence over teaching because
    (a) Political leader keeps the education under his influence.
    (b) Politics determines the value system of education in a country.
    (c) It satisfies the vested interests of political leaders.
    (d) Political leaders fulfil their ambition by keeping education under their own subordination.

14. A teacher who is not able to draw the attention of his students should
    (a) evaluate his teaching method and improve it.
    (b) resign from the post.
    (c) find fault in his pupils.
    (d) start dictating.

15. A teacher in the class is
    (a) a director of the group.
    (b) the president of the group.
    (c) a leader and guide of the group.
    (d) All of the above.

16. The main drawback of current tests is that
    (a) they are not equally fair to persons of different backgrounds.
    (b) they measure performance rather than quality.
    (c) they are unreliable.
    (d) None of these.

17. If some students fail in the examination it is the fault of
    (a) the teacher
    (b) the principal
    (c) pupils themselves
    (d) textbooks

18. If back-benchers are always talking in the classroom a teacher should
    (a) let them do what they are doing.
    (b) punish them.
    (c) ask them to sit on the front benches.
    (d) None of the above.

19. As a teacher you are going to show historical places of a city to your students. Father of a student does not send his child with you. In this situation, you would
    (a) leave this child and would go with others.
    (b) try to know why his father was hesitant to send his child.
    (c) convince his father by telling the importance of such educational and cultural trips.
    (d) None of the above.

20. The best way to improve the professional status of teaching is
    (a) fixing salaries.
    (b) enforcement of high standards.
    (c) sponsoring of state conventions.
    (d) publication of journal.

21. John Brubacher is influenced by
    (a) Educational process
    (b) Educational philosophy
    (c) Teaching method
    (d) Teaching system without interference

22. A teacher
    (a) should introduce the lesson before he starts teaching.
    (b) should have command over his language.
    (c) should have command over his subject.
    (d) All of the above.

23. In the past, the secondary school teaching held more prestige than elementary education because
    (a) the subject-matter was at a higher level of difficulty.
    (b) the secondary school teaching was paid high.
    (c) the secondary school teachers had a higher training level.
    (d) All of the above.

24. Teaching is a mutual influence which aims at to bring change in the other individual's behaviour. This notion is expressed by
    (a) Gage (b) Ryans
    (c) Amidon (d) Morrison

25. The teaching can be interpreted as
    (a) the influence of a mature person on a less mature person.
    (b) an interactional process.
    (c) a process helping in learning.
    (d) All of the above.

26. If a teacher is not able to answer the question of a pupil he should
    (a) say that he will answer after consultation.
    (b) rebuke the pupil.
    (c) say that the question is wrong.
    (d) feel shy of his ignorance.

27. In our present society, where values are deteriorating, the excellent education will be which
    (a) enables one to earn in an easy manner.
    (b) exaggerates the competition in the society.
    (c) works for re-establishment of human and cultural values.
    (d) deaccelerates the social-change in the society.

28. Attitudes, concepts, skills and knowledge are products of
    (a) Learning (b) Research
    (c) Heredity (d) Explaining

29. The teaching is not possible at all in case of
    (a) two individuals having similar expertise in a specific area or subject.
    (b) it is not to be happen in a classroom.
    (c) it is not based on definite curriculum.
    (d) All of the above.

30. Arrange the following teaching process in order.
    (i) relating the present knowledge with the previous knowledge
    (ii) evaluation
    (iii) reteaching
    (iv) formulating objectives
    (v) presentation of materials
    (a) (i), (ii), (iii), (iv), (v)
    (b) (ii), (i), (iii), (iv), (v)
    (c) (v), (iv), (iii), (i), (ii)
    (d) (iv), (i), (v), (ii), (iii)

31. While teaching in the class one of your students pointed out sharply your mistakes. What will you do in such a condition?
    (a) You leave the class for the day.
    (b) You scold the child and angrily resist him.
    (c) You feel sorry for committing a blunder.
    (d) You will not show any emotion.

32. Learning implies something in the individual
    (a) developing within.
    (b) occurring within.
    (c) required.
    (d) absorbed by.
33. The process of giving direction to individuals (for learning) and also guiding them for some other purposes is called teaching. This statement was given by
    (a) Amidon
    (b) Ryans
    (c) World Book Encyclopaedia
    (d) Morrison
34. Use of telecast materials
    (a) enhances concentration and learning.
    (b) reduces the burden of the teacher.
    (c) increases retention power.
    (d) All of the above.
35. Trial-error learning differs in man and animals chiefly in that man plans greater dependence upon
    (a) symbolic manipulation
    (b) overt activity
    (c) avoidance of insight
    (d) None of the above.
36. Which one of the following is not related with teaching process?
    (a) Interaction process
    (b) Vocational process
    (c) Continuous process
    (d) Social process
37. If students are not able to follow, you should
    (a) give them prompt
    (b) make the matter easy
    (c) illustrate with examples
    (d) All of the above
38. One of your colleagues is living in your locality but you have no affinity with him, the reason may be
    (a) his selfishness
    (b) his religious faith
    (c) his social rejection
    (d) his miserable behaviour and rural background
39. The critical factor needed to make teaching a true profession is
    (a) improved school buildings.
    (b) better spirit among the professionals.
    (c) discipline of its own members.
    (d) an improved salary scale.
40. How can you define teaching in relation to following phrases?
    (a) It is a face-to-face interactional process between two individuals.
    (b) It is a purposful process.
    (c) It is a remedial process.
    (d) All of the above.
41. Micro teaching is useful to students of
    (a) primary classes only
    (b) junior classes only
    (c) 10 + 2 classes only
    (d) Both higher classes and primary classes
42. If a girl student is attracted towards you beyond the ethical limits then how would you control your own emotions?
    (a) You will try to calm down her emotions, as she is passing through the adolescent stage.
    (b) You will take advantage of the situation and will exploit her.
    (c) You will like to repress her intentions through strict measures.
    (d) You will communicate this matter to her parents for help.
43. Language is best thought of as
    (a) an instinctive process.
    (b) a nomenclature for cataloguing experience.
    (c) a process of personal enhancement.
    (d) a tool for solving problems.

44. The teaching can be a
(a) measurable product
(b) therapeutic method
(c) remedial method
(d) All of the above

45. If remarks are passed by students on you, as a teacher, you will
(a) punish them.
(b) expel them from the college.
(c) take revenge while evaluating internal test copies.
(d) be impartial at the time of evaluation.

46. While delivering lecture if there is some disturbance in the class, then a teacher should
(a) keep quiet for a while and then go on.
(b) punish those causing disturbance.
(c) not bother of what is happening in the class.
(d) All of the above.

47. The elementary school level of modern day education in Indian context can be best described as
(a) student-centred.
(b) teacher-centred.
(c) curriculum-centred.
(d) research-centred.

48. The teaching is a tripolar process because it consists of
(a) Child - Teacher - Curriculum
(b) School - Teacher - Child
(c) Child - Book - Study
(d) Child - Parents - Principal

49. Maximum participation of students is possible in teaching through
(a) lecture method
(b) discussion method
(c) textbook method
(d) audio-visual aids

50. If a group of students enter your room and abuse you and behave violently with you, at that time how would you control your emotions?
(a) You will feel ashamed among your teaching community.
(b) You will react in similar tone and try to assault them physically.
(c) First you will try to pacify their emotions, then ask politely about their behaviour.
(d) You will report the case to the principal with recommendation of punitive measures.

51. The function of the school as an agent of society is
(a) to make children vocationally competent.
(b) to make the children understand environment.
(c) to prepare child for life.
(d) to teach the children to read and write only.

52. The communication in teaching is going on between
(a) Teacher and taught
(b) Teacher and principal
(c) Student and parents
(d) Senior and junior students

53. Which of the following is the most important single factor in underlying the success of beginning a teacher?
(a) Scholarship
(b) Communicative ability
(c) Personality and its ability to relate to the class and to the pupils
(d) Organisational ability

54. The main role of education according to Plato was
(a) to develop the power of contemplation.
(b) to strengthen the state.

(c) to develop the personality of each individual.
(d) All of the above.

55. The term 'gang' according to education represents
(a) male-group only.
(b) female-group only.
(c) social phenomena.
(d) terrorists.

56. The teaching is treated as improvement process because it is related to
(a) the self-improvements in a teacher.
(b) the desirable improvements in child's behaviour.
(c) the improvements in the institution.
(d) the improvements in Human material.

57. The greatest important cause of failure in beginning for a teacher lies in the area of
(a) interpersonal relationship
(b) verbal ability
(c) knowledge of the teacher
(d) tight handling of the students

58. Suppose you are asked by your friends to take the membership of the teachers union. How could you take decision in this situation?
(a) You will de-affiliate yourself from the colleagues instead of hostility with the management.
(b) You will have faith in unity so you will accept the membership.
(c) You will give priority to social relations, therefore, you will accept the offer.
(d) You will try to avoid the issue.

59. The term continuous process is interpreted as
(a) The process going on everywhere, all the time.
(b) Lifelong process.
(c) The process going on from cradle to grave.
(d) The process going on at home, all places and every time.

60. John Locke's phrase of *tabula rasa* means
(a) free education
(b) Tal and Ras
(c) mind itself is a result of the process of evolution
(d) All of the above.

61. While helping children to make educational plans it is unfair for them to
(a) select all subjects from one particular field.
(b) plan the programmes ahead.
(c) choose a subject of lesser interest.
(d) take typing with college preparatory subjects.

62. The characteristic of an excellent teaching is
(a) exchange of desirable informations
(b) adoption of democratic ideals
(c) directiveness
(d) All of the above.

63. An effective teaching means all of the following except
(a) a teacher teaches with enthusiasm.
(b) a teacher finds fault in his students.
(c) a teacher puts emphasis more on teaching than on class control.
(d) a teacher is interested in making the subject matter understood rather than on completing the course.

64. A career course should be aimed at
(a) obtaining from every student a realistic self-appraisal.
(b) securing from every student a choice of his life's work.
(c) developing the ability to make intelligent choice of jobs.
(d) None of these.

65. Which one of the following is not a quality of a good teaching?
(a) It creates emotional instability.
(b) It remedies children's difficulties.
(c) It eliminates student's problems in a classroom.
(d) It enriches student's potentialities.

66. The field of education is permeated by conflicts and misconception because
(a) problems in education call for subjectivity of interpretation.
(b) problems encountered in teaching are not amenable to rigorous scientific investigation.
(c) there are not good teaching methods and procedures.
(d) teachers are not worthy of doing rigorous scientific investigation.

67. Kindergarten (KG) system of education means garden of small kids which is indebted to
(a) Plato (b) Froebel
(c) Dewey (d) Spencer

68. To educate according to nature means
(a) to return to the nature as opposed to artificiality.
(b) to educate according to the law of nature of human development.
(c) to study natural laws and apply them to the educational process.
(d) All of the above.

69. The foundation of a good teaching in Indian circumstances is
(a) Democratic values
(b) Enrichment of students potentialities
(c) Teacher—a philosopher and a friend
(d) All of the above

70. The introduction of career courses in schools and colleges aims at
(a) developing the ability to make the intelligent choice of jobs.
(b) providing professional knowledge to students.
(c) increasing G.K. in students.
(d) All of the above.

71. The major responsibility with which the school personnel have been entrusted is that
(a) it harmonizes the needs of the child and demands of the society for the benefit of both.
(b) it prepares the school programme according to the need of the child.
(c) it makes the child able to get job.
(d) All of the above.

72. In teaching, if nothing has been learned, nothing has been
(a) Assigned (b) Studied
(c) Learned (d) Taught

73. On the basis of teaching objectives in how many categories it can be divided?
(a) Cognitive - Affective - Conative
(b) Philosophical - Psychological and Cultural
(c) Spiritualistic - Physical and Mental
(d) None of the above.

74. The most appropriate meaning of learning is
(a) personal adjustment.
(b) modification of behaviour.
(c) inculcation of knowledge.
(d) acquisition of skills.

75. Meaning of the phrase—any two students are not alike is
(a) the students differ in their familial and social status.
(b) the students differ in their physical makeup.
(c) the students differ in their mental makeup.
(d) All of the above.

76. Cognitive objectives are related to
   (a) Mental abilities
   (b) Physical abilities
   (c) Psycho-motor abilities
   (d) All the above abilities

77. A democratic society is one which
   (a) respects the enlightened individuals.
   (b) follows the principles of equality, freedom, fraternity and justice.
   (c) believes in equal educational opportunity.
   (d) All of the above.

78. What is the criteria, on the basis of which you will select a monitor in your class?
   (a) On the basis of physical makeup.
   (b) On the basis of personal preference.
   (c) On the basis of superiority in the class.
   (d) On the basis of democratic ideals.

79. The mental abilities includes
   (a) Memory, Reasoning, Thinking and Creativity
   (b) Interest, Attention and Feelings
   (c) Dynamism
   (d) Psycho-motor Abilities

80. The famous sayings (spare the rod and spoil the child) in modern classroom serves our purpose in a
   (a) effective manner.
   (b) better way.
   (c) worst way.
   (d) exclusive manner.

81. The meaning of 3H in education is
   (a) Head - Heart - Hand
   (b) Heart - Hurt - Hat
   (c) Headmaster - Head office - Head clerk
   (d) None of the above

82. The sense of Appreciation and Values are composed by
   (a) Affective domain
   (b) Cognitive domain
   (c) Psycho-motor domain
   (d) All of the above

83. The education aims at the fullest realisation of all the potentialities of children. It implies that
   (a) they should provide suitable opportunities and favourable environmental facilities which are conducive to the maximum growth of children.
   (b) teachers and parents must know what children are capable of and what potentialities they possess.
   (c) it is necessary that their attitudes are helpful, encouraging and sympathetic.
   (d) All of the above.

84. A scheduled caste student is treated by other classmates as untouchable and so he lives in isolation. How will you adjust him in a better way in the class?
   (a) By preaching.
   (b) By putting examples by his own deeds.
   (c) By justifying the plight of down-troddens.
   (d) By showing fear of legal actions.

85. The term Psycho-motor can be interpreted as
   (a) The mind has greatest speed in the world.
   (b) The mental thinking is dynamic in nature.
   (c) The mental abilities are expressed in actual behaviour.
   (d) General psychological concept.

86. An effective teacher adopts the norms of the
   (a) democratic society
   (b) laissez-faire society
   (c) autocratic society
   (d) all of the above according to the situation

87. The greatest, important cause of failure in beginning for a teacher lies in the area of
(a) interpersonal relationship
(b) knowledge of the teacher
(c) verbal ability
(d) tight handling of the students

88. Suppose you are a teacher, then how would you like to behave with your students?
(a) Laissez-faire
(b) Democratic
(c) As the conditions permit
(d) Autocratic.

89. All the muscular activities and expressed human behaviour is included in the behavioural domain of
(a) Affective teaching
(b) Cognitive teaching
(c) Psycho-motor teaching
(d) None of the above

90. While dealing with juvenile delinquents a teacher should
(a) play them with filthy sex jokes.
(b) talk with them frankly and guide and channelize their potentialities in constructive ways.
(c) complain to the principal against them.
(d) None of the above.

91. How will you demonstrate your impartial behaviour?
(a) By maintaining high self-esteem and egoistic behaviour.
(b) By making own behaviour more balanced and fair.
(c) By assaulting the teacher.
(d) By criticising the teaching community.

92. For the discipline in classroom the essential element is
(a) the dignified cadre of the teacher.
(b) the seriousness of the teacher.
(c) the idea and scholarly personality of the teacher.
(d) the well preserved personality of the teacher.

93. The teacher is generally teaching at
(a) Uniform level
(b) Multi-levels
(c) Tri-level
(d) Quadrate level

94. TV is superior to radio as teaching aid because it
(a) is costly.
(b) invites two senses—hearing and vision simultaneously leading to more accurate form of learning.
(c) is generally liked by pupils.
(d) All of the above.

95. A teacher in the class should keep the pitch of his voice
(a) high enough
(b) moderate
(c) low
(d) sometime low and sometime high

96. The formal discipline theory of education is the outcome of
(a) Genetic psychology.
(b) Structural psychology.
(c) Functional psychology.
(d) Faculty psychology.

97. There are existed three types of teaching levels which are as following:
1. Reflective level
2. Understanding level
3. Memory level

The correct sequence of all these levels is
(a) 1, 2, 3 (b) 3, 2, 1
(c) 2, 3, 1 (d) 3, 1, 2

98. The major responsibility with which the school personnels have been entrusted is that

(a) it harmonizes the needs of the child and demands of the society for the benefit of both.
(b) it makes the child able to get job.
(c) it prepares the school programme according to the need of the child.
(d) All of the above.

99. While the teacher was delivering the lecture, a student helped the teacher to solve the problem. The student was
(a) an evaluative listener.
(b) an emphatic listener.
(c) an information listener.
(d) a realistic listener.

100. The relationship of memory level of teaching is related with the students' behaviour pertaining to
(a) Recall (b) Recognition
(c) Understanding (d) Both (a) and (b)

101. The best educational programme is one which is according to the
(a) need of the child.
(b) ability of the child.
(c) interest of child.
(d) all of these along with the need of the society.

102. Which of the following is the most important single factor in underlying the success of beginning a teacher?
(a) Communicative ability
(b) Scholarship
(c) Personality and its ability to relate to the class and to the pupils
(d) Organisational ability

103. Teaching on TV is considered to be a superior mode of instruction than classroom because
(a) teaching materials can be filmed for reuse.
(b) very large classes are made possible and thus it is economically advantages.
(c) experts for teaching a difficult topic can be arranged and others can be benefited from them.
(d) All of the above.

104. Which one of the following level of teaching is least adopted by a teacher?
(a) Understanding level
(b) Memory level
(c) Thinking level
(d) Evaluation level

105. While delivering lecture if there is some disturbance in the class, then a teacher should
(a) keep quite for a while and then go on.
(b) not bother of what is happening in the class.
(c) punish those causing disturbance.
(d) All of the above.

106. You have children. You are a teacher. How would you like to behave with your students in comparison to your children?
(a) Just like own children.
(b) Repressed treatment.
(c) Equal treatment is not possible to all the students.
(d) It is better to lend them a free hand.

107. Which of the following teacher, will be liked most by you?
(a) A teacher of highly idealist philosophy.
(b) A loving teacher.
(c) A teacher who is disciplined.
(d) A teacher who often amuses his students.

108. The teacher should do the favourable efforts in order to raise the teaching upto the thinking level in a class of
(a) Gifted students
(b) Normal students
(c) Mentally retarded students
(d) All sections without discrimination.

109. On which of the following statements there is consensus among educators?
(a) Disciplinary cases should be sent to the principal only when other means have failed.
(b) Disciplinary cases should never be sent to the principal's office.
(c) Disciplinary cases should be totally neglected in the class.
(d) None of the above.

110. Some of your colleagues are busy in cracking filthy jokes during their leisure in college. You are also a member of that group but unable to stop them. What would you do to avoid it?
(a) You advice your colleagues to mind their languages while cracking jokes in college.
(b) You persuade them not to waste their leisure time in filthy jokes.
(c) You change the groups or live in isolation because you don't relish it.
(d) You remind them of their noble profession.

111. Among the following teachers, whom you will like the most?
(a) One who uses motion picture as a last resort.
(b) One who uses chart and maps.
(c) One who uses board occasionally.
(d) One who uses film projector along with the proper use of the board.

112. Which one of the following is not associated with Memory?
(a) Learning (b) Recall
(c) Recognition (d) Evaluation

113. Classroom discipline can be maintained effectively by
(a) knowing the cause of indiscipline and handling it with stern hand.
(b) providing a programme which is according to the need and interest of the pupils.
(c) by putting on fancy clothes in the classroom.
(d) None of the above.

114. The best educational programme is one which is according to the
(a) ability of the child
(b) need of the child
(c) interest of child
(d) All of these along with the need of the society.

115. Among the following statements, which is the correct one?
(a) Teacher can be assisted by computer aided instruction.
(b) Face to face teaching and on-line teaching are equally effective.
(c) On-line teaching is more effective than face to face teaching.
(d) Teacher can be replaced by computer aided instruction.

116. When a student get mastery over Memory level, the learning of a student should be automatically converted into
(a) Understanding (b) Thinking
(c) Imagination (d) Synthesis

117. Who among the following is a good teacher? The one who
(a) keeps on updating his information.
(b) makes difficult subject matter easy for students.
(c) say that I do not know everything.
(d) All of the above.

118. Teaching is a continuum which spreads from Memory level to Thinking level. The essential connecting link between these two levels is called as

(a) Evaluation Level
(b) Understanding Level
(c) Moral Level
(d) Creativity Level

119. In the final analysis, teaching must be thought of mainly as a process of
(a) asking questions and evaluating the learning.
(b) directing the activities of the pupils.
(c) hearing the recitation of pupils.
(d) All of the above.

120. Education officers often speak of the tone of an institution. This concept of 'tone' refers to
(a) the disciplinary measures adopted by an institution for avoiding classes.
(b) the organisational and supervising set up of the institution.
(c) the healthy atmosphere of the institution from the sentimental point of view.
(d) the programmes and activities planned by the institution.

121. On the basis of Nature, the teaching is classified as
(a) Descriptive - Diagnostic - Remedial
(b) Assertive - Interrogative - Explanatory
(c) Psycho-motor - Affective - Cognitive
(d) All of the above.

122. In the words of Mahatma Gandhi himself, basic education is
(a) a struggle for freedom to be inculcated in children.
(b) education through crafts, throughout.
(c) training and observation by teachers.
(d) education through crafts is creative for children.

123. The necessity of Diagnostic teaching is being felt when
(a) The students are unable to follow some difficult concepts.
(b) The students are unable to explain some facts.
(c) The students are disinterested in studying.
(d) The students are gifted.

124. The male students of your class are annoyed with you on the pretext you have been easily approached by the girl students and do a favour to them (girls). In such an embarrassing situation how would you like to control them in the class?
(a) You will tell the male studenls that girls have no option except to depend on the school teacher for their academic assistance.
(b) You will justify that most of the female students are more sincere towards their studies than male students.
(c) You will communicate to the male students that it is difficult for you refuse the request made by female students.
(d) None of the above.

125. One will be more successful as a teacher, if
(a) he is trained in teaching.
(b) he belongs to the family of teachers.
(c) he can organise his teaching material systematically and coveys the same effectively.
(d) he belongs to the family of teachers.

126. The remedial teaching is given to
(a) The backward students in particular subject.
(b) The weak students.
(c) The gifted students.
(d) Both (a) and (b)

127. How competent a teacher is, can be judged on the basis of

(a) length of service.
(b) personality of teacher.
(c) publication of books.
(d) meeting needs of students.

128. The Remedial teaching has been identified through
(a) Achivement test given to a student.
(b) Continuous assessment of the student in a class.
(c) Unsuccess of the student in a class.
(d) All of the above.

129. A teacher is expected to do all except
(a) participation in community activities
(b) help pupils to solve their problems
(c) taking interest in politics
(d) sponsor clubs and other school affairs

130. Which one among the following commitments is not used to assess the teacher's professionalism?
(a) Commitment to the religion and castes.
(b) Commitment to the parents and community.
(c) Commitment to the profession and students.
(d) Commitment to the colleagues and employer.

131. The fundamental aim of Diagnostic teaching is
(a) To diagnose the subject-related difficulties of the students
(b) To develop weaknesses in students
(c) To assume students' weakness in some subjects
(d) To develop the spirit of imitation in students

132. In order to develop rapport with your pupils you should
(a) guide them
(b) behave them in a democratic way
(c) have communicative ability
(d) All of the above.

133. A mentally retarded student attends your lecture and sits in a deaf and dumb manner. What will you do?
(a) Make your lecture very simple and spare some extra time for him.
(b) You pressurise the student to leave the class.
(c) You do not like to spoil majority for the individual.
(d) You do not support him at all.

134. A new teacher is misbehaved in the class. He will deal with the students by
(a) changing his class after consultation with the Principal.
(b) applying punitive measures.
(c) improving his qualities and expressing it before them in a good way.
(d) giving them a threat of expulsion.

135. In context of Educational activities, the categories of teaching are
(a) Presentation - Demonstration - Action
(b) Presentation - Statement of aim and Introduction
(c) Thinking - Meditation and Adidhyasan
(d) None of the above.

136. Verbal guidance is least effective in teaching
(a) Attitude (b) Concept and facts
(c) Relationship (d) Skills

137. If a girl student requests you to collect her posts at your address what would you like to do in this case?
(a) You will permit her because you have some attachment with her.
(b) You will never give her your own address, suspecting a foul play.
(c) You would not give permission as it is against your own principles.
(d) You will permit the girl to collect the posts at your address because as a teacher, you should do it.

138. The teaching can be categories as following in relation to educational organisation
(a) Formal - Informal - Nonformal
(b) Formal and Informal
(c) Formal and Nonformal
(d) None of the above.

139. A teacher meeting his students for the first time should
(a) start teaching without caring the students' likes and dislikes.
(b) develop rapport with the class.
(c) give a broad outline of the whole subject.
(d) Both (b) and (c).

140. In which among the following, Education should bring a permanent change?
(a) Only in bad habits
(b) Behaviour and thought
(c) Habit of children
(d) Both (a) and (b).

141. The significant agency of Formal Education is
(a) Family
(b) School
(c) Newspaper
(d) Television

142. Before starting instruction a teacher should
(a) know the existing knowledge of his students and their background knowledge.
(b) be aware of the environmental variables acting on the mind of the pupils.
(c) be competent enough to arouse the curiosity of his pupils.
(d) All of the above.

143. The students who keep on asking questions in the class
(a) should be encouraged to find answers independently.
(b) should be encouraged to participate in the classroom discussion.
(c) should be advised to meet the teacher after the class.
(d) should be encouraged to continue questioning.

144. The identification of formal teaching is
(a) fixed place
(b) fixed time-table
(c) fixed aim
(d) All of the above.

145. Observable behaviours which a teacher can use in the class to bring home to the pupil an idea or point is technically called
(a) teaching skills
(b) communication facilities
(c) demonstration
(d) None of these

146. Use of telecast materials
(a) enhances concentration and learning.
(b) increases retention power.
(c) reduces the burden of the teacher.
(d) All of the above.

147. The most important single factor in underlying the success of a teacher is his
(a) personality and his ability to relate to the class and to the pupils.
(b) organisational ability.
(c) scholarship.
(d) communicative ability.

148. The Informal mode of teaching is required for
(a) illiterates—to make them literate
(b) neo-literates
(c) drop outs from school
(d) All of the above.

149. Quality of education in a school/college can be measured through
(a) infrastructural facilities available.
(b) manpower, teachers and principal available.

(c) students' achievement.
(d) All of the above.

150. Teachers who are enthusiastic in the classroom teaching
(a) simply dramatise to hold the student's attention.
(b) often lack proficiency in the subjects which stays hidden under their enthusiasm.
(c) involve their students in the teaching learning process.
(d) All of the above.

151. A teacher can become popular among students by
(a) arranging periodical tour programmes.
(b) giving tips while teaching.
(c) helping them personally.
(d) maintaining good social relations.

152. Which one of the following is the independent variable in teaching process?
(a) Teacher (b) Curriculum
(c) Student (d) Principal

153. Which of the following statements regarding motivation is correct?
(a) Freewill, intellect and reason are the motivating factors according to Plato.
(b) Inborn, unlearned tendencies, called instincts are the motivating forces according to James Burt.
(c) Curiosity and level of aspiration are the motivating factors according to Berlyne.
(d) All of the above.

154. Which among the following is the least important aspect of the teacher's role in the guidance of learning?
(a) The provision of continuous diagnostic and remedial help.
(b) The provision of encouragement and moral support.
(c) The development of insight into what constitutes an adequate performance.
(d) The development of insight into what constitutes the pitfalls and dangers to be avoided.

155. The student is treated as a dependent variable in teaching process because
(a) The student follows the teacher's advice.
(b) The student learns according to teacher's teaching.
(c) The student makes teacher a fool.
(d) The student is pressurized by the teacher.

156. Democracy in the classroom is best reflected through
(a) allowing student's freedom to the observance of classroom rules and regulations.
(b) allowing the class to decide the curricular experiences of the classroom.
(c) allowing the maximum participation of all the students in classroom activities.
(d) None of the above.

157. Which among the following is an odd statement?
(a) Knowledge is static.
(b) One way interaction prevails in classrooms.
(c) Majority of teachers use lecture method.
(d) Most of the classrooms are poorly equipped.

158. The basic function of the variables in teaching process is
(a) Diagnostic (b) Remedial
(c) Evaluation (d) All of the above

159. The professional requirements of a teacher as explained in the UNESCO publication is/are

(a) mastery over the subject and competency for teaching.
(b) Innovativeness in approach and teaching strategies.
(c) justice to the profession.
(d) All of the above.

160. Diagnostic work consists of
(a) The previous behaviour (Entry behaviour) of the students.
(b) Analysis of the constituents of the textbook.
(c) Both of the above.
(d) None of the above.

161. Effective teaching means
(a) Love, cooperation, sympathy, affection and encouragement given to students
(b) Corporal punishment given to students at the time of moral offences
(c) Individualized instruction and open classroom discussion
(d) Both (a) and (c).

162. Which is the basic responsibility of a teacher in diagnostic teaching?
(a) Determining the students' entry behaviour.
(b) Collection of students individual behaviour related informations.
(c) To do Job-analysis.
(d) All of the above.

163. All of the following statements regarding a teacher are correct except that he is/he
(a) a friend, guide and philosopher.
(b) teaches what the students do not know.
(c) the leader of the class.
(d) changes his attitudes and behaviour according to the need of the society.

164. The Remedial work in teaching is related
(a) To make teaching-skills more practical
(b) To organise feed-back procedures
(c) Both of the above
(d) None of the above

165. Drop outs are more likely to be
(a) unemployed.
(b) vulnerable to the requirement of public assistance.
(c) engaged in antisocial behaviour.
(d) All of the above.

166. If a principal of your college, charges you with the act of negligence of duties, how would you behave with him?
(a) You would take revenge by giving physical and mental agony to him.
(b) You would neglect him.
(c) You would take a tough stand against the charges.
(d) You would keep yourself alert and make his efforts unfruitful.

167. A teacher's most important challenge is
(a) to make students do their home work.
(b) to make teaching-learning process enjoyable.
(c) to maintain discipline in the classroom.
(d) to prepare the question paper.

168. The continuum of teaching is hypothesized from
(a) conditioning to indoctrination.
(b) behavioural change to change in beliefs.
(c) change in general learning to complete change in faith.
(d) All of the above.

169. Teacher's professionalism means
(a) the extent to which a teacher subscribes to a professional code.
(b) a teacher has to teach for the sake of getting salaries.
(c) a teacher must have completed professional teachers training course before his appointment.
(d) All of the above.

170. When your friend seeks your assistance to get his ward's admission in the school, how would you extend your cooperation to him?
(a) You would extend all types of support as you have intimate relationship.
(b) You would not help him.
(c) You would put forward some lame excuse.
(d) None of the above.

171. The Discussion method can be used when
(a) the subject is easy.
(b) the subject is difficult.
(c) the subject is very difficult.
(d) None of the above.

172. The main steps of teaching continuum are given as following in a jumbled form
1. Indoctrination 2. Instruction
3. Training 4. Conditioning
The correct sequence of the teaching continuum is
(a) 4, 3, 2, 1 (b) 1, 2, 3, 4
(c) 2, 3, 4, 1 (d) 3, 2, 1, 4

173. You are a teacher of literature. A chapter of a book deals with a biography of a scientists and his works. In this situation, what would you do with this chapter?
(a) You would ask the students to read themselves.
(b) You would request the Science teacher, to teach this chapter to the students.
(c) You would consult other book concerning with the scientist and then you would teach the lesson to students.
(d) Any one of them.

174. Effectiveness of teaching depends on
(a) personality of teacher.
(b) qualification of teacher.
(c) subject understanding of teacher.
(d) handwriting of teacher.

175. Through conditioning the change in behaviour occur in
(a) Dogs and cats (b) Human infant
(c) Adult individual (d) All of the above

176. The first important step in teaching is
(a) planning before hand.
(b) organizing material to be taught.
(c) knowing the background of students.
(d) None of the above.

177. If a student wears some odd dress and attends your class, you will
(a) ask the student to not to attend the class.
(b) make a joke on him.
(c) communicate him not to wear such clothes.
(d) not give any attention on it.

178. Which among the following is supplementary teaching material?
(a) Taper recorder
(b) 16 mm film projector
(c) Functional model of wind mill
(d) All of the above.

179. The pioneer of conditioning is
(a) Pavlov (b) Skinner
(c) Gestalt (d) Thorndike

180. Suppose you are an ambitious teacher. You have high ideals for classroom teaching but your hard labour goes in vain. The reason underlying this problem may be
(a) your teaching level is above the ability level of students.
(b) individual differences among students make your efforts futile.
(c) Both of the above.
(d) None of the above.

181. Classroom discipline can be maintained effectively

(a) by putting on fancy clothes in the classroom.
(b) providing a programme which is according to the need and interest of the pupils.
(c) knowing the cause of indiscipline and handling it with stern hand.
(d) None of the above.

182. Four classification of students can be done on the basis of their learning. Which among the following seeks meaning and reasoning for learning?
(a) Common sense learner
(b) Analytic learner
(c) Innovative learner
(d) Dynamic learner.

183. The training can be imparted to
(a) Bodily muscles
(b) Lower class of Animals
(c) Workers
(d) All of the above.

184. If a student becomes unconscious in the class what will you do first?
(a) Rushing to the principal's office and convassing for help impatiently
(b) Telephoning student's parents and waiting for them
(c) Giving first aid to him and trying to contact any nearby doctor
(d) Making arrangement to send him to his home

185. If you invite your personal friends and colleagues in your son's birthday party, the procedure of it will be
(a) only personal invitation will be extended to most dear ones.
(b) only a specific group of teachers will be invited.
(c) extend invitation to all the teachers without any distinction.
(d) You would invite all the personnel of the school.

186. Majority of students in a large class are found dozing. There may be something wrong with
(a) the teaching process.
(b) the time of instruction.
(c) the students concerned.
(d) the content taught.

187. Instruction can be imparted to
(a) Within the classroom
(b) On the Assembly ground
(c) Universally everywhere
(d) At no where

188. If you come across to teach a blind student along with the normal students what type of behaviour you are expected to exhibit?
(a) Take care of him with sympathy.
(b) Don't give any extra attention because majority of students may suffer.
(c) Arrange the seat in the front row and try to keep your teaching pace according to him without making the other students suffer.
(d) None of the above.

189. Teachers should study educational philosophy because
(a) they do not have their own philosophy.
(b) they do not know it.
(c) philosophy is the backbone of all disciplines.
(d) they may improve their work by clarifying their own philosophy.

190. A teacher is effective if he/she
(a) repeats explanations for each student.
(b) provides a variety of learning experiences.
(c) explains everything in the class.
(d) answers all questions raised by students.

191. Indoctrination can be done through
(a) Brain washing
(b) Complete change in one's ideology

(c) Complete change in one's faith
(d) All of the above

192. A newcomer teacher who is maltreated in his class will deal with the students by
(a) applying punitive measures.
(b) improving his qualities and expressing it before them in a good way.
(c) changing his class after consultation with the principal.
(d) giving them a threat of expulsion.

193. Which among the following gives more freedom to the learner to interact?
(a) Use of film
(b) Small group discussion
(c) Lectures by experts
(d) Viewing country-wide classroom programme on TV.

194. Which of the following objective is associated with instruction?
(a) To enhance behavioural changes and habits in a child.
(b) To enhance behavioural changes and skills in a child.
(c) To transmit the knowledge.
(d) To change the beliefs and develop values.

195. If a child is a backbencher and is unable to watch the blackboard clearly. As a result he stands, sees and sits repeatedly. What inference will you draw regarding the case?
(a) The child is of short height as compared to his classmates.
(b) The blackboard is under shining effect of light.
(c) The child has defective-vision.
(d) Both (a) and (c).

196. There will be better communication in a lecture if a teacher
(a) reads from prepared notes.
(b) prepares the notes well in advance and uses them as a guide.
(c) talks extempore.
(d) talks extempore drawing examples from other disciplines.

197. The distinction between moral and ethical instruction could be made as follows.
(a) Ethics stress knowledge and morals emphasize performance.
(b) Morals are long-standing but ethics are slow in change.
(c) Ethics are fast changing but morals are slow in change.
(d) The morals emphasise knowledge and ethics stress performance.

198. In stage of Indoctrination the form of knowledge is
(a) Abstract
(b) Typical skills
(c) Typical habit formation
(d) Concrete knowledge

199. A child may have hearing impairment if
(a) he speaks loudly unusually.
(b) he comes nearer to the speaker during conversation.
(c) he generally says, "Please repeat" to the teacher.
(d) All of the above.

200. As one of the methods of teaching the teachers are recommended to adopt the problem method. The precaution to be observed in this method is to see that
(a) the problem starts with some life experience of the pupil.
(b) problems are suggested by teachers at the end of the lesson.
(c) the problem starts with a school subject itself.
(d) the problem is of the teacher and not of the pupil.

201. High level action-oriented knowledge is associated with
(a) Conditioning (b) Training
(c) Knowledge level (d) Instruction

202. One remarkable principle of the Montessori schools of the young children is that, there is no place for fairy tales in the curriculum. What do you think of the reason behind this?
   (a) Such tales are beyond the comprehension of young children and create fear in them.
   (b) Their tales conform children and hinder in adjustment to the real world.
   (c) They do not contain anything of interest to young children.
   (d) They make children too imaginative and abstract rather than real.

203. The learning of Laws and Principles can be carried out through
   (a) Instruction (b) Indoctrination
   (c) Training (d) All of the above

204. Suppose you are teaching in a minority college where casteism and narrow mindedness victimize you, for better adjustment there you should
   (a) uplift the humanistic values beyond these narrow wall and develop scientific temper in your students.
   (b) be submissive there and save your job at all costs.
   (c) rebel against such attitudes as it is against the norms of the Indian society.
   (d) None of the above.

205. Many experienced teachers go into a classroom and embark straight away upon a lesson. As a beginner to the teaching profession you will
   (a) do as the student's like.
   (b) make a written note of your preparation.
   (c) adopt the same procedure.
   (d) None of the above.

206. Which one of the following teaching continuum would you like to accept, in case of you are interested to teach at level of understanding?
   (a) Training (b) Instruction
   (c) Conditioning (d) Indoctrination

207. If a high caste teacher adopts a discriminatory attitude toward a low caste students his behaviour is
   (a) correct according to his religion.
   (b) against the national spirit, and need of the hour.
   (c) not against the constitutional provisions.
   (d) not against the code of teacher's professionalism of UNESCO.

208. Before starting instruction a teacher should
   (a) be aware of the environmental variables acting on the mind of the pupils.
   (b) know the existing knowledge of his students and their background knowledge.
   (c) be competent enough to arouse the curiosity of his pupils.
   (d) All of the above.

209. In view of teaching in school, which among the following would you favour?
   (a) Students knowledge more important than its application.
   (b) Discipline is more important than learning.
   (c) Methods are more important than learning.
   (d) Subject matter is more important than method of teaching.

210. What will you do in order to develop positive attitude among children?
   (a) Teaching at Indoctrination level
   (b) Only Instruction
   (c) Only Conditioning
   (d) Only Training

211. If a student is constantly rubbing his eyes and is unattentive during blackboard work he is having
(a) adjustment problem
(b) hearing problem
(c) visual problem
(d) All of the above.

212. A teacher can guide students very much efficiently, because
(a) students obey teacher's orders.
(b) he is the boss of the students.
(c) students fear him.
(d) he understand's student's psychology.

213. Discipline in classroom can be maintained effectively by
(a) providing a programme which is according to the need and interest of the pupils.
(b) by putting on fancy clothes in the classroom.
(c) knowing the cause of indiscipline and handling it with stern hand.
(d) None of the above.

214. If Signal learning is associated with conditioning, the multi discrimination of concepts is associated with
(a) Training (b) Instruction
(c) Indoctrination (d) All of the above.

215. If you are irritated and show rashness because of the inadequate behaviours shown by others what do you think about your own behaviour
(a) it is justified because behaviours are echo lime.
(b) your behaviour is not good because elders have the right to behave you in this way.
(c) your behaviour is also the sign of maladjustment and so try to control youself when you are maltreated.
(d) None of the above.

216. Teacher's primary responsibility is
(a) implementing policies.
(b) planning educational experiences.
(c) keeping students records.
(d) All of the above.

217. The effective constituent of Formal education is
(a) Instruction (b) Indoctrination
(c) Training (d) Conditioning

218. To stop malpractice of mass-copying in the examinations, what will you do?
(a) You will give punishment to student and his parent.
(b) You will give severe punishment to students.
(c) You will try to give moral education to the students.
(d) You will rusticate the students forever from the school.

219. In a calssroom teaching, overhead projector is superior to short circuit TV because
(a) pictures in it may be shown in a desired sequence and with a minimum of lost motion (material).
(b) it is cheap and self-devised.
(c) it is easy to use.
(d) information presented through it is easily retained.

220. Training helps in
(a) development of skills
(b) development of good habits
(c) formulation of artificial behaviour
(d) human development

221. If a student absents from the classes for a long time,
(a) you will try to know the cause of his absence.
(b) you would be neutral and would not show any interest in it.

(c) he would be absent due to some personnel reasons.
(d) It is not duty of teacher.

222. Evaluative listening's main purpose is
(a) to accept or reject an idea given to the listener.
(b) to evaluate the speaker's credibility and personality.
(c) Both of the above.
(d) None of the above.

223. The stage of teaching is
(a) Preparatory stage
(b) Interactional stage
(c) Post teaching-readiness stage
(d) All of the above.

224. A teacher exploits students in your school. In this situation, you will
(a) not interfere in this matter.
(b) report the matter to the principal.
(c) guide the teacher please stop this activity.
(d) go on satyagraha against the teacher.

225. Out of the following statements no two can be true at the same time, but both can be false. Identify the same
I. motivated students succeed in examinations.
II. irregular students fail is examinations.
III. some intelligents are irregular.
IV. intelligent students succeed in examinations.
(a) I and II (b) II and III
(c) III and IV (d) I and IV

226. Which one of the following process is completed in pre-active phase of teaching?
(a) Formulation of objectives of teaching.
(b) To take judgement about the content (subject-matter).
(c) To make sequential arrangements for presentation.
(d) All of the above.

227. What should every teacher do to make the teaching more effective?
(a) Analyse responses of students.
(b) Publish his/her writings.
(c) Keep him/herself abreast of development in the area in his/her subject.
(d) Discuss with colleagues.

228. Which one of the following process is not associated with pre-active phase of teaching?
(a) To seek judgement about the teaching tactics and procedures.
(b) To develop the tactics for specific content.
(c) To ask the evaluation-related questions from the students.
(d) To organise the presentation in a sequential manner.

229. Observable behaviours which a teacher can use in the class to bring home to the pupil an idea or point is technically called
(a) teaching skills
(b) demonstration
(c) communication facilities
(d) None of the above.

230. When meaningful learning takes places?
(a) When the new content being taught is related to the previous knowledge of the students.
(b) When students raise questions and get them clarified.
(c) When students are interested in the topics taught.
(d) When explanations are given within the reach of the students.

231. Which one of the following is associated with interactive phase of teaching?
(a) To realise the shape and size of the class.
(b) Diagnosis of the students.

(c) Action and its reaction.
(d) All of the above.

232. Quality of education in a school/college can be measured through
(a) manpower, teachers and principal available.
(b) infrastructural facilities available.
(c) students' achievement.
(d) All of the above.

233. Play therapy is included in the study of children in order to
(a) make the education more centralised to activities.
(b) make the process of education joyful.
(c) understand the inner motives of the children and complexities in them.
(d) highlight the importance of play activities in education.

234. In the Interactive phase of teaching Action-Reaction step is concerned with
(a) Selection of stimuli
(b) Presentation of stimuli
(c) Application of tactics
(d) All of the above.

235. An effective teacher is expected to
(a) reduce the anxiety level of students to moderate level.
(b) encourage the students to make initiative.
(c) to make students feel that education is their need.
(d) All of the above.

236. The immediate after the pre-active phase of teaching the next phase is having concerned with
(a) Evaluation.
(b) Scholastic achievement of the students.
(c) Selection of excellent evaluation procedures.
(d) None of the above.

237. Knowledge of psychology is must for a educational philosopher, because
(a) psychology acquaints the philosopher with the world of reality in his theorising.
(b) psychological principles arise out of philosophical maxims.
(c) the questions of 'why' and 'what' in philosophy is purely psychological at the root.
(d) psychology is after all a branch of philosophy.

238. The significance of teaching activities is
(a) The teachers know each and everything about their class at the time of entering and leaving a class.
(b) The teachers can improve in their teaching methodology to a certain extent.
(c) The adequate knowledge of teaching variable to the teachers.
(d) All of the above.

239. A teacher's most precious item is his
(a) Job (b) Pay
(c) Pride (d) Student's faith

240. Regarding the teacher's control in the education of children, the following is the main difference between the Herbert and Dewey.
(a) Dewey favours teacher control, but Herbert is against it.
(b) Herbert is in favour of teacher control while Dewey cannot agree with him.
(c) Herbert favour normal steps, but Dewey gives more importance to teacher control only.
(d) Both are in favour of imparting knowledge through teacher control.

241. Why boarding schools are considered to be better than the day schools?
(a) They are helpful in freeing parents from their responsibilities.

(b) They are meant for homeless and parentless children.
(c) They save the trouble for children to walk to school from homes.
(d) They help children in their social development.

242. A teacher is the leader both *de jure* and *de facto*. He is the authority before the students, and so it is his right to lead. While assuming leadership of the students, he should follow some important principles
(a) preparation and planning
(b) creating right atmosphere in the class
(c) providing opportunities
(d) All of the above.

243. The term 'problem child' is used for a child in school, when
(a) he suggests useful approaches to teachers when they are explaining any problem.
(b) he is able to solve the problems of other children.
(c) he behaves such that it becomes a problem for the teacher to understand him.
(d) he is able to solve the problems of other children.

244. The relationship between teaching and learning is
(a) Teaching-learning—the addition of these two processes makes learning more effective.
(b) The more significance of learning theories in the development of teaching theories.
(c) Teaching is a purposive process which reaches at adequate learning.
(d) All of the above.

245. How should a teacher behave with the students?
(a) Father like (b) A friend like
(c) General (d) Elder like

246. Who among the following is a good teacher?
(a) One who teaches well.
(b) One who cooperates well with the principal.
(c) One who reads a lot.
(d) One who publishes lots of research papers.

247. The psychological forces of teaching according to Gagne are
(a) The forces changing behaviour
(b) The forces changing learning conditions
(c) Cognitive forces
(d) All of the above.

248. If a teacher has to establish his credibility in evaluating answer scripts he must be
(a) Lenient (b) Strict
(c) Objective (d) Prompt

249. The supplementary teaching material among the following is
(a) television.
(b) functional model of windmill.
(c) tape recorder.
(d) All of the above.

250. A serious minded teacher as a rule
(a) allows the mistakes to be committed and explains how to minimise those mistakes.
(b) takes all precaution so that students never commit mistakes.
(c) never allows any mistakes on the part of his students.
(d) should mildly punish students who commit mistakes.

251. Among the following of subjects, which can develop better teaching methods in a teacher?

(a) Philosophy and Psychology
(b) Sociology and Philosophy
(c) Psychology and Sociology
(d) All of the above.

252. In Robert Gagne's stratification of learning conditions, on its basis at extreme ends are lying
(a) Stimulus-Response-Verbal level Relationship
(b) Stimulus-Response and Problematic learning
(c) Stimulus-Response and Principle learning
(d) Stimulus-Response and Multi Discriminationing conditions

253. Teachers should not demand from their pupils something which is beyond their stage of growth. If they do so, they only cause
(a) anger among pupils
(b) frustrations, heighten tension and nervousness in children
(c) encouragement to students to learn more
(d) None of the above.

254. If a student visits his teacher to share his problems with him, in such a condition the teacher should
(a) suggest him to discuss with his parents.
(b) contact the student's parents and solve his problems.
(c) warn him to never visit his house.
(d) extend reasonable help and boost his morale.

255. In Gagne's level of learning conditions, the complex phases are
(a) Stimulus-Response Relationship-verbal level Relationship
(b) Multi-discriminatory conditions
(c) Concept-Principle and Problematic learning
(d) None of the above.

256. Students differ greatly in their susceptibility to anger due to heredity, health status and environment and to the way they are dealt with by adults. As a teacher, how will you try to direct his attention towards some thing else?
(a) Grown up children should be taught a problem-solving behaviour in coping with situations that provoke anger.
(b) Anger should be used into socially acceptable channel.
(c) They must be taught how to express anger so as to avoid disapproval.
(d) All of the above.

257. Consider yourself as an ambitious teacher. Your hard labour goes in vain despite of your high ideals for class-room teaching. The results of the students was not satisfactory. The reason behind this is
(a) the teaching has no access to students.
(b) your egoistic teaching behaviour is beyond student's own level.
(c) downfall in the educational level of the students.
(d) individual differences among the students.

258. In how many categories Gagne has classified the learning conditions?
(a) 8 (b) 9
(c) 10 (d) 12

259. What will you do as a teacher if the students do not attend your class?
(a) Keep quiet considering the present attitude of students.
(b) Blame the students for their absence.

(c) Think of using some interesting methods of teaching.
(d) Know the reasons and try to remove them.

260. Suppose you have no idea about a child having some hearing problem. What should be your duty towards the child?
(a) You become neutral because it is not your headache.
(b) You report to teachers, parents and principal to send him to a special school.
(c) You send him to specialist for treatment.
(d) Recognise the child and manage accordingly.

261. The simplest form of learning conditions according to Gagne's classification is
(a) Signal Learning
(b) Principle Learning
(c) Concept Learning
(d) All of the above

262. Ancient Indian teachers applied some psychological principles in educating the young child from pre-school age to adolescence. They recognised the role of
(a) convent system of schooling.
(b) sense and perceptions in learning and teaching.
(c) *Gurukul* type of schooling.
(d) None of the above.

263. Suppose a teacher has acute stammering problem but he wins the favour through sycophancy. Therefore he goes to any extent to seek favour from the administration. The other colleagues have great jealousy with him, because he climbed all the progressive ledder through that quality. How would you like such a person in your company?
(a) You criticise and abuse him.
(b) You will treat him as your best friend.
(c) You treat him like your 'guru' as he is the most successful teacher.
(d) You tell him the difference between right and wrong things, to enhance his moral courage.

264. Signal learning is associated with
(a) Pavlovian conditioning
(b) Skinnerian conditioning
(c) Both of the above.
(d) None of the above.

265. Language is a
(a) instinctive development
(b) system of symbols for effective communication
(c) medium to express experiences
(d) medium for self-enhancement

266. The stimulus-Response is related with
(a) Operant conditioning
(b) Classical conditioning
(c) Gestalt principles
(d) None of the above

267. An individual's ability to learn is
(a) Absorbed (b) Acquired
(c) Occurring within (d) Developed

268. Programmed Instruction took its birth from
(a) Classical Conditioning
(b) Operant Conditioning
(c) Stimulus-Response Learning
(d) Both (b) and (c).

269. It is said that teacher is a 'Friend, Philosopher and Guide', because
(a) he transfuses the high values of the humanity into young ones in the classroom.
(b) he has to play all these vital roles in context of the society.
(c) he is the great reformer and patriotic saviour of a nation.
(d) None of the above.

270. You want to get a job in the profession of teaching. How would you do so?
   (a) By any means as job conditions are very difficult.
   (b) By seeking political support.
   (c) By giving bribery for your appointment in village or town school.
   (d) By exalting your excellence in national level competition.

271. The types of Chain learning are
   (a) Verbal and non-verbal learning.
   (b) Quantitative and Qualitative learning.
   (c) Problematic and Cooperative learning.
   (d) Positive and Negative learning.

272. Collective psychology of the whole period is a theory which
   (a) can explain all phases of historical development.
   (b) means psychological approach of data collection.
   (c) means the psychology of the whole society.
   (d) All of the above.

273. Suppose you are a newly appointed teacher and going in the class for the first time. How will you start?
   (a) Give the class a broad outline of the subject.
   (b) Begin with the first lesson without delay.
   (c) Divide your class into, terms for discussion, group project, etc.
   (d) Concentrate on identifying potential troublemakers and leaders of the classroom mischief.

274. The verbal learning is mostly used in
   (a) Language teaching
   (b) Science teaching
   (c) Drawing teaching
   (d) None of the above.

275. It is popularly said that any two students are not alike. This means
   (a) each and every student differ in their physical and mental set up.
   (b) they differ in their familiar and social status.
   (c) they are different in their mental set up.
   (d) All of the above.

276. Among the following classifications of work, teaching would come under
   (a) Skilled (b) Managerial
   (c) Clerical (d) Professional

277. Discriminating learning is comparatively related with
   (a) Understanding level
   (b) Reflective level
   (c) Knowledge level
   (d) Memory level

278. Our present higher secondary curriculum is based on the premise that a number of courses in our scheme of studies have identical elements. This statement is based on the
   (a) theory of Identical Component
   (b) theory of Mental Faculty
   (c) theory of Formal Discipline
   (d) theory of Generalisations

279. The primary responsibility of the teacher is to adjust with
   (a) the principal (b) the teacher
   (c) the children (d) the community

280. Which one of the following stage begin after mastery over discriminating learning?
   (a) Concept learning
   (b) Principle learning
   (c) Problem-solving learning
   (d) All of the above.

281. Suggestion helps in the development of in formation, moral behaviour, aesthetic

sense and character traits. Which of the following is the chief source of suggestions which mould the life?

(a) Teachers
(b) Pupils of same age
(c) Elders
(d) None of the above.

282. As the agent of the society the primary function of the school is

(a) to prepare the child for life.
(b) to maintain social stability.
(c) to develop in children an adequate level of vocational competence.
(d) to provide children with an understanding of their environment.

283. The resultant of the principle learning is

(a) two or more than two chains.
(b) two or more than two learning conditions.
(c) two or more than two teaching variables.
(d) None of the above.

284. The primary task of a teacher is

(a) to teach the prescribed curriculum.
(b) to stimulate and guide student's learning.
(c) to provide diagnostic and remedial aid wherever desired.
(d) to promote habits of conformity to adult demands and expectations.

285. Among the following which one is the most important factor which leads to the success of a new teacher?

(a) His attitudes and outlook on life.
(b) His competence in the area of his academic preparation.
(c) His personality and ability to relate to the class.
(d) His verbal facility and organisational ability.

286. Problem-solving learning is directly related with

(a) Reflective level
(b) Memory level
(c) Understanding level
(d) None of the above.

287. As a new teacher the first professional responsibility you must meet is to

(a) change the curriculum in the light of your training.
(b) co-operate with your fellow teacher inspite of differences.
(c) ascertain and follow the procedures of your predecessor.
(d) None of the above.

288. How many constituents has been put forth by Cronbach on the basis of teaching principles?

(a) 7 (b) 8
(c) 9 (d) 10

289. A teacher can establish rapport with his class by

(a) becoming a figure of authority.
(b) impressing students with knowledge and skill.
(c) playing the role of a guide who desires to help the pupils.
(d) becoming a friend to the pupils.

290. Below are given the Cronbach's principles of learning in a jumbled form

1. Condition
2. Reactions to Fear
3. Characteristics of the students
4. Interpretation
5. Goal
6. Action
7. Result

What is the correct sequence among them?

(a) 1,3,5,4,6,7,2 (b) 1,2,3,4,5,6,7
(c) 1,3,5,7,2,4,6 (d) 1,2,5,6,4,3,7

291. Which one of the following is a product of learning?
(a) Intelligence (b) Maturation
(c) Skills (d) Forgetness

292. The best education programme is one which looks at
(a) the ability of the child.
(b) the need of the child.
(c) the interest of the child.
(d) All of the above along with the need of the society.

293. In 'Situation', Cronbach includes
(a) Content-teacher
(b) Student's learning material
(c) Learning objectives
(d) All of the above.

294. Which of the following explains the mental growth most suitably?
(a) A growth pattern runs parallel to the physical growth.
(b) It is an erratic pattern.
(c) It is not an erratic pattern.
(d) A uniform rise to the middle teens and gradual levelling off during middle twenties.

295. By which method it is possible to make the maximum participation of students in teaching?
(a) Discussion method
(b) Audio-visual aids
(c) Textbook method
(d) Lecture method.

296. 'Interpretation' in the words of Cronbach means
(a) The learning objectives of students.
(b) Evaluation of students.
(c) Previous experiences of students.
(d) Discipline of the students.

297. Verbal guidance is most effective in
(a) Concepts (b) Attitudes
(c) Relationships (d) All of the above

298. What should you do, if the students are not able to follow?
(a) Make the matter easy
(b) Give them prompt
(c) Illustrate with examples
(d) None of the above.

299. Post-teaching stage is related to
(a) to define behavioural change in its actual (real) form by a teacher.
(b) selection of appropriate procedures of Evaluation.
(c) to bring strategic change in teaching on the basis of obtained results.
(d) All of the above.

300. Teachers are regarded as the builders of the nation. They are performing an onerous task. Their salary is not commensurate with the service they render. Promotion and salary increment of teachers should be on the basis of periodic evaluation of their merit efficiency. The proposition
(a) cannot be implemented by the educational Institutions.
(b) is not justified.
(c) is sound proposition but should be put into effect gradually.
(d) None of the above.

301. If a teacher comes across ideas difficult for others to understand, he should
(a) explain it to others only at a cost, be it money or favour.
(b) keep this understanding to himself which would ensure him a special status.
(c) rather not explain it to a person who obviously does not wish to spend much time on it.
(d) be happy and look forward to explain it to others.

302. The significance of teaching activities is that

(a) The teacher gets all desirable guidance within the classroom and out of it.
(b) The teacher integrate the process of teaching with that of learning.
(c) The teacher makes effective the process of from memory level to reflective level.
(d) All of the above.

303. There is a debate as to whether teaching is a true profession or not. The most critical factor needed to make teaching a true profession is
(a) discipline of its own members.
(b) a longer period of training.
(c) better spirits among teachers.
(d) a longer period of learning.

304. Which among the following is the least important in teaching?
(a) Maintaining discipline in the class
(b) Punishing the students
(c) Drawing sketches and diagrams on the blackboard if needed
(d) Lecturing in impressive ways.

305. Which one of the following is showing a similarity between instruction and teaching?
(a) Both are student-centred
(b) Both are content-oriented
(c) Both are having feed-back, reinformcement and content
(d) None of the above.

306. There are so many definitions of learning. Which of the following is most adequate?
(a) The modification of behaviour.
(b) The acquisition and organisation of knowledge.
(c) The development of skills.
(d) All of the above.

307. What is the main purpose of evaluative listening?
(a) To evaluate the speaker's credibility and personality.
(b) To accept or reject an idea given to the listener.
(c) Both (a) and (b).
(d) None of the above.

308. The correct alternative in the following is
(a) Teaching consists of instruction in itself
(b) Teaching includes learning in itself
(c) Teaching includes evaluation in itself
(d) Teaching includes harmonious development of the student in itself

309. The objective of guidance at the college stage is
(a) to assist students to get employment immediately.
(b) to assist the students in acquiring knowledge about other vocations available after the university education.
(c) to assist employer to select prospective employees.
(d) All of the above.

310. Which of the following methods will be the best to make the students learn by heart, the poem you are teaching?
(a) Alternate reading of lines and whole stanzas one after the other.
(b) Ask them to memorise each line, one at a time and combine all the memorised lines in the memory.
(c) Ask them to read the poem aloud instead of silently looking at the book.
(d) Read the whole stanza fully every time and repeat this whole reading till they learn it by heart.

311. Which one of the following is most fundamental of the guidance activities and should be executed first?
(a) Selection of the learning activities
(b) Determination of material

(c) Determination of objectives
(d) Selection of study material

312. Which is the best method of teaching second language according to the modern linguistics?
(a) Grammar translation method
(b) Audio-lingual method
(c) Audio-visual method
(d) Direct method

313. In the above question the diagnostic function of teaching is related to
(a) Analysis of teaching problem
(b) Determination of students' entry behaviour
(c) Knowledge of content analysis and of individual differences
(d) All of the above

314. The most common cause of the nervous instability amongst teachers is
(a) Worry
(b) Quarrelsome behaviour
(c) Fatigue
(d) All of the above.

315. What was the method usually adopted by the government schools of India in earlier times to teach English as a second language?
(a) Audio-visual method
(b) Audio-lingual method
(c) Grammar translation method
(d) Direct method

316. The Remedial function of teaching includes
(a) selection of teaching skill, tactics, and principle, etc.
(b) organisation of feed-back procedure.
(c) remedy according to diagnosis.
(d) All of the above.

317. Which one of the following satisfactions helps our children from infancy onwards to adolescence, equipped them with a sense of achievement, recognition and independence?
(a) Affectionate, warm, security giving satisfactions.
(b) Self-enlarging, ego-building adequacy giving satisfactions.
(c) They gain satisfaction and love through close physical contact.
(d) None of the above.

318. In which of the following statements there is consensus among educators?
(a) Disciplinary cases should never be sent to the principal's office.
(b) Disciplinary cases should be sent to the principal only when other means have failed.
(c) Disciplinary cases should be totally neglected in the class.
(d) All of the above.

319. Who had communicated that learning is modification in one's behaviour through experiences?
(a) Ciates (b) Guilford
(c) Hunter (d) Garrett

320. Radio is used in small scale for teaching purpose. Which of the following is not a reason for it?
(a) Many teachers are not alert to its possibilities.
(b) The evidence relative to its effectiveness is too inconclusive.
(c) Teachers training school have not been sufficiently energetic in the field.
(d) None of the above.

321. On what order is the functions of a teacher?
(a) Checking homework, guiding him and assigning further task.
(b) Guiding the child, helping him towards progress and evaluation.
(c) Both (a) and (b).
(d) None of the above.

322. The teaching in a country is exclusively influenced by
   (a) Socio-political conditions
   (b) Socio-economic conditions
   (c) Socio-psycho conditions
   (d) Socio-legal conditions

323. The maladjustment among teachers is
   (a) exceedingly prevalent amongst lady teachers.
   (b) relatively non-existent.
   (c) of greater incidence.
   (d) of average incidence.

324. The purpose of asking questions from the students in between the lecturers is to
   (a) learn which one of the student is the brightest one.
   (b) learn whether students are understanding the lecturer or not.
   (c) assist the students.
   (d) know whether the students are giving full attention to the lecture or not.

325. In automatic system of a country the teacher's position is
   (a) Powerful (b) Liberal
   (c) Political (d) Pitiable

326. Equal educational opportunity means
   (a) equal opportunity to have the type of education which one is suited for.
   (b) equality of educational standards for each child.
   (c) equal opportunity for all children to have access to education.
   (d) All of the above.

327. How should a teacher be to prove bis credibility in evaluation of answer booklets?
   (a) Very much regular
   (b) High handed
   (c) Dutiful
   (d) Impartial

328. What should be desired from teaching in democratic set up?
   (a) Teacher and taught mutually influence each other to a great extent.
   (b) Teacher holds all the powers repress the taughts.
   (c) Teaching should be according to democratic principles.
   (d) Sometimes taughts have given due opportunities in order to learn from them.

329. The teacher should understand the crudeness of the child instincts and try to sublimate these. He should improve it through
   (a) modifying each instinct.
   (b) the repressed instincts may appear in undesirable forms and hinder the growth of the child.
   (c) a network of activities to provide ample opportunities for the sublimation of the instincts.
   (d) All of the above.

330. Which among the following statements is not suitable for the teachers?
   (a) They are not interested in moulding themselves.
   (b) They really take interest in students.
   (c) They are very much enthusiastic about such tasks as are done by teachers.
   (d) They are capable of guiding students and maintaining discipline.

331. In ancient times, which type of education was most prevalent?
   (a) Moral (b) Religious
   (c) Vocational (d) All of the above

332. What is teaching?
   (a) Art of interpersonal influence.
   (b) Guidance or direction of learning.
   (c) Arrangement of contigencies of reinforcement.
   (d) All of the above.

333. The general aim of education is to foster the mental development of children. Traditionally, emphasis of education was on mastery of subject matter, acquisition of facts and information through deliberate memorisation. Along with these attributes, modern education also aims to provide
(a) vocational education.
(b) verbalism and theoretical knowledge.
(c) useful curricular and co-curricular activities in the form of projects, and to encourage the use of discussion and other socialised teachings.
(d) All of the above.

334. The most important characteristics of good teaching is
(a) genesis of self-motivation for learning.
(b) based on democratic principles.
(c) progressive in nature.
(d) All of the above.

335. Teaching is being affected by
(a) Classroom (b) School
(c) Society (d) All of the above.

336. Characteristics of all informal and formal communications are
(a) Unstructured (b) Same
(c) Structured (d) Different

337. Teaching topology includes
(a) Training—Instruction— Conditioning —Indoctrination
(b) Training—Conditioning—Instruction —Indoctrination
(c) Training—Indoctrination—Instruction —Conditioning
(d) None of the above.

338. The objectives of mental health in education can be achieved, if the following principles are observed in the curriculum.
(a) The child's need, interest and experiences, individual differences in learning capacity should form the central factor.
(b) It should be dynamic and possible of revision so that it may be in harmony with changing social conditions.
(c) It should be flexible and adjustable to the needs of pupils at every stage.
(d) All of the above.

339. McDonald's concept of teaching includes the elements
(a) Curriculum—Instruction
(b) Curriculum—Teaching
(c) Curriculum—Learning
(d) Curriculum—Instruction

340. The major duty entrusted to the teaching community is
(a) to adjust his/her pupils to conform to the demands of society.
(b) to change human nature to conform to social expectations.
(c) to teach students how to adjust themselves to social demands.
(d) to harmonise the needs of the child and the demands of society for the benefit of both.

341. On the basis of Objectives of Education, the teaching can be classified to
(a) Cognitive, Affective and Psychomotor
(b) Mercury, Understanding, and Reflective Teaching
(c) Autocratic, Democratic, Laisser-faire
(d) Presentation, Demonstration and Action

342. To educate according to nature means
(a) to come back to nature as opposed to mechanical life.
(b) to educate in accordance with the law of nature of human development.
(c) to study natural laws and apply them to the educational process.
(d) All of the above.

343. Diagnostic functions of teaching do not include
(a) Analysis of teaching problems
(b) Entering behaviour of pupils
(c) Task-Analysis
(d) Judgemental process of teachers and students

344. Indoctrination brings changes in one's
(a) Behaviour
(b) Beliefs and values
(c) Biases
(d) Biological composition

345. Which one is not the objective of the special education?
(a) To develop motivational patterns in the handicapped that will produce achievements.
(b) To pursue those curricular matters that strategically determine effective living for specific type of handicapped children.
(c) To develop a realistic self-concept in handicapped children.
(d) None of the above.

346. Phases of teaching are
(a) 2 in numbers (b) 3 in numbers
(c) 4 in numbers (d) 5 in numbers

347. Learning of social roles consists of an internalisation of the expectation concerning the various roles and of applying these expectations to oneself. If the social roles are learned effectively, the individual becomes
(a) attains higher social adjustments
(b) a good member of the group
(c) a good member of the group and attains higher social adjustments
(d) None of the above.

348. Which one of the following is not included in pre-active phase of teaching?
(a) Determining objectives
(b) Curriculum judgement
(c) Development of strategy
(d) Diagnosis of the students

349. The period of adolescence is known as a period of stresses and strains. It is the most difficult and the awkward period, and marks the re-awakening of the repressed sex-impulse. Which type of behaviour is unwanted?
(a) Attitude of independence
(b) Sympathetic understanding
(c) Silence and hush-hush policy
(d) None of the above.

350. Which one of the following is having highest order of learning?
(a) Signal learning
(b) Stimulus-Response learning
(c) Chain learning
(d) Problem-solving learning

351. Problem-solving type at _____ of learning occurs.
(a) memory level
(b) understanding leve
(c) reflective level
(d) knowledge

352. How can absenteism in the class be minimised?
(a) By punishing the students.
(b) By telling students that it is bad to be absent in the class.
(c) By ignoring the fact of absenteism.
(d) By teaching the class effectively and regularly.

353. Primarily the development of child is depend on
(a) Parents (b) Environment
(c) School climate (d) Society

354. The Law of Similarity of Heredity proposes

(a) Like begets like
(b) Like does not beget like
(c) As the parents are their children are having little bit similarity with them
(d) Cannot say.

355. What norms an effective teacher adopts?
(a) Norms of the democratic society
(b) Norms of the autocratic society
(c) Norms of the laissez-faire society
(d) None of the above.

356. Generally when it is witnessed that the child is somewhat different from his parents, it can be interpreted through the Genetic law of
(a) Similarity
(b) Difference
(c) Regression
(d) Germ Plasm continuity

357. Play-way technique's important principle in education is that
(a) learning should take place under disciplined conditions.
(b) opportunities for self-expression should be selective under guidance and supervision.
(c) authoritarianism is a must for speedy learning and adaptation.
(d) children should learn on their own responsibility.

358. The origin place of behavioural instincts in children is
(a) Heredity (b) Environment
(c) School (d) Neighbourhood

359. Who among the following teachers is most desirable?
(a) One who is a moralist and preaches morals to students all the time.
(b) One who comes to teach regularly but does not care to know what the students are learning.
(c) One who just knows enough of his subject but motivates his students a lot to learn.
(d) One who comes to the class on time, but does not mind students coming late in the class.

360. The bodily organisation of the child is influenced by
(a) Generation tree (b) Parents
(c) Diet (d) Grandparents

361. Who among the following types of children is having maximum physical capacities?
(a) Athletic (b) Aesthenic
(c) Viscerotonic (d) Somatotonic

362. In the final analysis, teaching must be thought of mainly as a process of
(a) directing the activities of the pupils.
(b) asking questions and evaluating the learning.
(c) hearing the recitation of the pupils.
(d) None of the above.

363. Who among the following scientists have proved that the children are influenced from their parents' size, shape and health?
(a) Karl Pearson (b) John Watson
(c) Kretschmer (d) Galton

364. The discrimination witnessed among the various human species is the resultant of
(a) Heredity (b) Environment
(c) Both of these (d) None of these

365. As a teacher in a minority college, you have become victim of narrow-mindedness, what should you do for better adjustment there?
(a) Be submissive there and save your job at all costs.
(b) Uplift the humanistic values beyond these narrow wall and develop scientific temper in your students.

(c) Rebel against such attitudes as it is against the norms of the Indian society.
(d) All of the above.

366. The children's instincts are called
(a) Emotional tendencies
(b) Cognitive tendencies
(c) Innate tendencies
(d) Action tendencies

367. Generally the instincts are witnessed in
(a) Children
(b) Animals
(c) Man and Animals
(d) Cannot say

368. If you are with the teachers who are cracking filthy jokes, but you are unable to stop them you should
(a) instruct them to mind their language while passing leisure time.
(b) be critical and remind them for the nobility of their jobs.
(c) live in isolation or change the group.
(d) persuade them decently not to waste their time in filthy jokes.

369. The chief characteristics of instinct is
(a) Purposiveness (b) Intelligence
(c) Empirical (d) Real

370. The 'Escape' instinct expresses in the state of
(a) Hunger (b) Difficulty
(c) Fear (d) None of these.

371. On the basis of the study of instincts, one can explain
(a) Nature of children
(b) Intelligence of children
(c) Character of children
(d) Tendencies of children

372. The student can be trained in social behaviour through
(a) Curriculum
(b) Social and cultural programmes in school
(c) Discipline
(d) Classroom teaching

373. If a low caste student is discriminated by a high caste teacher, then the behaviour of the teacher is
(a) not against the code of teacher's professionalism of UNESCO.
(b) correct according to his religion.
(c) against the national spirit, and need of the hour.
(d) not against the constitutional provisions.

374. The behaviour, based on realisation of other persons feelings is generally called
(a) Sympathy (b) Love
(c) Pity (d) Affection

375. The development of the abilities related with learning in children takes place through
(a) Creative tasks
(b) Self-expression
(c) Co-operative works
(d) Self-analysis

376. The primary stage of promoting the learning in a child is
(a) Imitation (b) Conditioning
(c) Motivation (d) Instinct

377. The 'Play' of children in the technique commonly applied by the psychologists in
(a) Teaching
(b) Making foods for children
(c) Learning
(d) Distracting attention of children

378. Expecting on a effective teacher is to
(a) make students feel that education is their need.
(b) encourage the students to make initiative.

(c) reduce the anxiety level of students to moderate level.
(d) All of the above.

379. When a child imitating elderly behaviour through role modelling, then it is called
(a) Constructive play
(b) Mock play
(c) Emotional play
(d) Intellectual play

380. What type of the development is possible among children through games?
(a) Feelings of mutual respect
(b) Co-operation and adjustment
(c) Social qualities
(d) All of the above

381. The first important step in teaching is
(a) organising material to be taught.
(b) knowing the background of students.
(c) planning before hand.
(d) All of the above.

382. The propounder of the teaching methods based on play is
(a) Froebel (b) Hurlock
(c) Skinner (d) Pavlov

383. The children's learning is affected most by
(a) Motivation
(b) Interest
(c) Intellectual abilities
(d) Physical organisation

384. Which one of the following is the main characteristics of childhood?
(a) Realistic point of view.
(b) Comparatively slow developmental process.
(c) Intensity of learning.
(d) All the above.

385. The major difficulties in adolescence arises due to
(a) Ego
(b) Anger
(c) Group feelings
(d) Physiological changes

386. Within the classroom, the factor which is affecting most of the students' learning is
(a) discipline of the class.
(b) psychological environment of the class.
(c) social environment of the class.
(d) economic environment of the class.

387. What will be your first step if a student becomes unconscious in the class?
(a) Telephoning student's parents and waiting for them.
(b) Giving first aid to him and trying to contact any nearby doctor.
(c) Making arrangement to send him home.
(d) Rushing to the principal's office and convassing for help impatiently.

388. Generally in a state of mental fatigue a person can experience
(a) Mental weakness
(b) Attentional passivism
(c) Anxiety
(d) All of the above.

389. Which one of the following measure do you want to employ for focussing students' attention in the class?
(a) Change in content
(b) Relaxation through exercise
(c) Observing silence
(d) All of the above.

390. What does effective teaching mean?
(a) Corporal punishment given to students at the time of moral offences.
(b) Individualised instruction and open classroom discussion.
(c) Love, cooperation, sympathy, affection and encouragement given to students.
(d) Both (a) and (c).

391. The duration of Infancy is
(a) Birth to 2 years
(b) Birth to 6 years
(c) 10 to 15 years
(d) 5 to 7 years

392. Which one of the following is the main factor influencing child's development?
(a) Heredity (b) School
(c) Parents (d) Friends

393. How can the quality of education in schools be measured?
(a) By the student's achievement
(b) By infrastructural facilities available
(c) By manpower, teachers and principal available
(d) None of the above.

394. When the children shows the feelings of self-possession on the objects
(a) 5-8 years (b) 2-5 years
(c) 6-12 years (d) 10-14 years

395. The period of teenage is
(a) 13 to 19 years (b) 12 to 16 years
(c) 7 to 15 years (d) 14 to 18 years

396. The area where the teacher-made tests cannot be pertinent is
(a) Attitudes (b) Interests
(c) Intelligence (d) Personality

397. In Indian climate the period of adolescence is
(a) 12 to 18 years (b) 14 to 18 years
(c) 10 to 15 years (d) 11 to 16 years

398. In which of the following stages of development do you feel highest rate of impulses in one's life?
(a) Adolescence (b) Infancy
(c) Childhood (d) Adulthood

399. You are teaching a subject or a topic to your students. At the end of a unit you test their achievement. Which of the following would be called the dependent variable?
(a) The test that you prepared.
(b) The subject that you teach.
(c) The background of your students.
(d) The response of your students.

400. Generally it is observed that the child is making contacts with
(a) Homosexual children
(b) Heterosexual children
(c) Both of the above.
(d) None of the above.

401. Which of the following period is generally termed as the 'period of conflicts' in one's developmental stages?
(a) Childhood (b) Infancy
(c) Adolescence (d) None of these.

402. "The adolescence is that state when a child is moving towards maturity". This statement is given by
(a) Stanley (b) Jersild
(c) Hurlock (d) None of these.

403. Training for a democratic mode of life can be performed by the school in a better way through
(a) moral and religious education by specialists.
(b) secular education and social functions in the schools.
(c) practicing students' government in schools.
(d) teaching the principles of democracy as an integral part of the curriculum.

404. "Adolescence is the stage of struggle, storm and strain." This statement is propounded by the famous psychologist named
(a) Brevur (b) Jersild
(c) Stanley Hall (d) Skinner

405. Which type of help can be extended to an adolescent through guidance?
   (a) To take the right decision.
   (b) To control the emotions.
   (c) To develop insight into physiological disturbances.
   (d) All of the above.

406. If students do not understand what is taught in the classroom, the teacher should feel
   (a) terribly bored.
   (b) pity for the students.
   (c) to explain it in a different way.
   (d) that he is wasting time.

407. What is the purpose of giving guidance to an adolescent according to Crow and Crow?
   (a) Health related areas
   (b) Sexual development related areas
   (c) Mental stability
   (d) All of the above.

408. The term motivation is derived from
   (a) Motum (b) Motif
   (c) Motion (d) Motive

409. Among the following in which mode should a teacher give his lecture?
   (a) Elongated tone
   (b) Precise and low tone
   (c) Moderate tone
   (d) Precise and high tone.

410. Which one of the following is the adequate measure to motivate a learner?
   (a) Punishment (b) Praise
   (c) Criticism (d) Penalty

411. Internal motivation is
   (a) Positive
   (b) Negative
   (c) Both the above.
   (d) None of the above.

412. The essential role of the teacher in a classroom is to
   I. give information.
   II. develop learning competencies.
   III. prepare them for writing answers.
   IV. motivate the students to learn.
   (a) I and III (b) I and II
   (c) III and IV (d) II and IV

413. A learner may get adequate motivation through
   (a) Ambition
   (b) Good school
   (c) Stories of the great persons
   (d) Value education

414. Who said it "Motivation is an art to generate interest in a student".
   (a) Thomson (b) Taylor
   (c) Skinner (d) Thorndike

415. Good teaching is best reflected by
   (a) pin-drop silence in the class.
   (b) attendance of students.
   (c) number of distinctions.
   (d) meaningful questions asked by students.

416. The principle of instinct based on motivation is proposed by
   (a) Adler (b) McDougall
   (c) Nunn (d) Freud

417. The development of human behaviour is based on
   (a) Heredity (b) Environment
   (c) Both of these (d) None of these.

418. What is the main aim of classroom teaching?
   (a) To develop inquiring mind
   (b) To give information
   (c) To help students pass examinations
   (d) To develop personality of the students.

419. From whose bodily traits are determined the child's bodily traits?

(a) Traits of the mother.
(b) Traits of the father.
(c) Both of the above.
(d) None of the above.

420. If the skin colour of parent is dark then the possibility of their offspring will be
(a) Dark coloured child
(b) White coloured child
(c) Any colour either (a) or (b)
(d) All the possibilities are uniform in nature

421. A teacher who believes in the realistic philosophy of education would
(a) allow full freedom to students in learning, following a non-interference policy.
(b) support strict control and supervision to make children understand human race and culture.
(c) oppose supervision and interference of the teacher with the interests of students.
(d) not allow control and pressure on the students to learn what they want to learn.

422. Which one of the following plays a determining role in the sexual development of the child?
(a) Heredity (b) Environment
(c) Both of these (d) None of these.

423. "Give me a child, I can develop him as I like." This statement gives emphasis upon
(a) Environment (b) Heredity
(c) Both (a) and (b) (d) None of these.

424. Which teacher students should prefer?
(a) The one who gives important questions before examination.
(b) The one who clear their difficulties regarding subject-matter.
(c) The one who are themselves disciplined.
(d) The one who dictates notes in the class.

425. "Hereditary and Environment are not indicating towards a concrete thing but towards abstract thing." This statement is put forth by
(a) Davis (b) Galton
(c) Watson (d) Kelley

426. Which one of the following psychological construct is determined through heredity?
(a) Intelligence (b) Sex
(c) Personality (d) Learning

427. Suppose you want to teach your students to develop factual knowledge of a subject which of the following methods would be suitable opinion?
(a) The source method.
(b) The heuristic method.
(c) The demonstration method.
(d) The lecturer method.

428. Which one of the following psychological construct is influenced by environment?
(a) Intelligence (b) Physical growth
(c) Nature (d) All of the above.

429. Which one of the following generation tree was studied to support the effect of heredity on it?
(a) Kallickok (b) Edwards
(c) Jux (d) All of the above.

430. It is said that teachers should adopt methods so that their pupils do not feel that teachers are always necessary for learning. Which of the following devices would substitute the teachers?
(a) The programmed learning method
(b) The discussion method
(c) The seminar method
(d) The experimental method.

431. Which one of the following argument is presented against the influence of heredity?
(a) Heredity has the limited effect
(b) Effect of environment on intelligence

(c) Effect of environment on physical characteristics
(d) All of the above.

432. Who had given this conclusion that child's intellectual development is the result of Heredity's 80 percent contribution and 20 percent environmental contribution?
(a) Davis (b) Yerks
(c) Garrett (d) Henry

433. How would there be a better communication in the lecture given by the teacher?
(a) If the teacher talks extempore.
(b) If the teacher prepares the notes well in advance and uses them as a guide.
(c) If the teacher talks extempore drawing examples from other disciplines.
(d) If the teacher reads from prepared notes.

434. Who said it that "Heredity gives us potentialities to grow but its development is possible only in environment"?
(a) Landis and Landis
(b) Crow and Crow
(c) Young
(d) None of the above.

435. Which one of the following is termed as central agency of human society?
(a) Family (b) School
(c) Neighbourhood (d) Social class

436. To make one's teaching more effective, the teacher should depend most on his
(a) Feedback (b) Teaching aids
(c) Knowledge (d) Management

437. The best agency of family's socialization is
(a) Traditions (b) Cultural values
(c) Discipline (d) All of the above.

438. The important agency giving adequate contribution in child's language development is
(a) Family (b) School
(c) Mass media (d) Magazines

439. Teacher should himself
(a) be a example before students.
(b) be talkative.
(c) be taller.
(d) None of the above.

440. Which one of the following is the main factor in social development of a child in school environment?
(a) Curriculum
(b) Co-curricular activities
(c) Discipline
(d) Community feelings

441. What would you assume when you perceive an isolated child in your class?
(a) He is pray of frustration and conflicts.
(b) He has inadequate socialization.
(c) He is day-dreaming.
(d) He is delinquent.

442. What does a unit means in teaching of any subject?
(a) The post of a presentation requiring demonstration.
(b) A topic which may require several lessons to be completed.
(c) A part of lesson plan such as introduction of assignment.
(d) The portion covered by the teacher in the class period.

443. The important role is played by the following to produce the effect of social stratification on the children
(a) Parents (b) Teacher
(c) Friends (d) Any person

444. The direct proportion of the child's socialisation process is
(a) Social development
(b) Mental development
(c) Motor development
(d) All of the above.

445. The most sensible idea about teaching and research is
   (a) they interfere with each other.
   (b) they cannot go together.
   (c) they are two entirely different kinds of activities.
   (d) they are two sides of the same coin.

446. Which one of the following is the most important factor in the social development?
   (a) Social commitment
   (b) Balanced personality
   (c) Social adjustment
   (d) Social traditions

447. Pre-schooling plays of children can be classified as
   (a) Self-centred plays
   (b) Object-centred plays
   (c) Both the above
   (d) None of the above.

448. What is the key to effective classroom discipline?
   (a) Providing a programme with inbuilt means for the satisfaction of pupil needs.
   (b) Developing close personal friendships with the group leaders.
   (c) Making an example of the leaders of any classroom mischief.
   (d) Inspirit respect by remaining cold and aloof to pupils in and out of the classroom.

449. The stage of beginning of socialisation process is
   (a) Infancy (b) Childhood
   (c) Adulthood (d) Senile stage

450. At what stage the social behaviour of the child exhibit stability?
   (a) Before three years
   (b) 3 to six years
   (c) 6 to twelve years
   (d) After twelve years

451. Which among the following is not an aspect of learning?
   (a) The elimination of errors.
   (b) The sensitisation of nerve fibres.
   (c) Cue reduction.
   (d) The accumulation of knowledge.

452. In which of the following stages the concept of sex has been developed in children?
   (a) Infancy (b) Childhood
   (c) Adolescence (d) None of these.

453. Which one of the following points of views is suited to behaviourists in context of socialisation of a child?
   (a) Environment-oriented
   (b) Escapism-oriented
   (c) Instinctive
   (d) Based on heredity

454. The most valid criterion, on the basis of which it can be judged whether teaching is a profession, is the teacher's
   (a) observance of professional ethics.
   (b) love for children.
   (c) observance of professional ethics.
   (d) broad and thorough knowledge of subject matter.

455. During the process of socialisation the child perceived
   (a) The society (b) The self
   (c) The family (d) The school

456. The main reason of socialisation of boys and girls separately is
   (a) the differences in their bodily organisations.
   (b) the variations in their role modelling.
   (c) the cultural conflicts.
   (d) the social prejudices.

457. Which among the following would least qualify as an essential aspect of the process of learning?

(a) Response to stimulation.
(b) The reinforcement of a response.
(c) An obstacle to the attainment of the goal.
(d) Insight into means-end relationship.

458. In what capacity a senior student should work in a group of juniors?
(a) A friend (b) A model
(c) A guide (d) A colleague

459. Suppose a child used to quarrel with his siblings and family-members. What will you do in order to get rid of him from this bad habit?
(a) You will declare public punishment for this act in school assembly.
(b) You will try to search the chance to capture him in any school's quarrelling so that you will get an opportunity to dishonour and reject him openly.
(c) You will talk to him in isolation and ask in detail about such sort of behaviour.
(d) You will demoralising him by giving the examples of some other good students of his class and the school on whom the school feel proud.

460. If nothing has been learned in teaching, nothing has been
(a) Examined (b) Taught
(c) Studied (d) Observed

461. When a child exhibits aggressive behaviour in the presence of newcomers at home, what would you suggest to the parents of such a child in order to give some remedy?
(a) The parents have badly neglected the child during his rearing, therefore they must pay for it.
(b) The parents should attempt to know about his child's basic problem and find some remedy accordingly.
(c) The parents should consult a counsellor in order to remedying child's problem in real sense.
(d) The parents should penalize the child for showing such a behaviour, gradually child may modify his behaviour.

462. Sometimes a few students admitted in primary schools are developing the habit of theft and they run away with their classmates' books, copies, pen or lunch boxes, etc. What would you like to do for improving such a behaviour of a child?
(a) When you catch first time give him stern warning.
(b) When you catch second time give him physical punishment.
(c) When you catch third time give him a note of rustication.
(d) Whenever you catch him keep vigilant eyes on him and his activities, ask thoroughly and call his parents immediately to take the action.

463. What is the main argument against teachers' strike?
(a) Teachers contract should not be violated.
(b) Salaries have risen faster than the cost of living.
(c) Teachers' strikes generally have been unsuccessful.
(d) None of the above.

464. Which one of the following is the most effective method of modification in children's behaviour?
(a) Reward (b) Punishment
(c) Blame (d) Rustication

465. Suppose a child is creating a scene after seeing anything of his preference like eatables or toys in the main market places which causes shame to parents in such a public places. What efforts would you

like to make in order to modify his behaviour?

(a) You become angry and giving a severe punishment to the child.
(b) You will satisfy the child immediately and making positive efforts to modify his behaviour.
(c) You will satisfy each and every wish of child and admire his nature.
(d) You will do all possible efforts to bring favourable changes in his behaviour.

466. Under which terms we should think of our work, as a teacher?

(a) Discipline pupils
(b) Child growth and development
(c) Systematic drill
(d) The mastery of subject matter.

467. What would you like to do to modify the behaviour of a stubborn child?

(a) His total neglect.
(b) His desire's satisfaction.
(c) Efforts to advise him in a harsh manner.
(d) During normally in a normal giving him advice not to show such a behaviour.

468. What would you like to do in order to inculcate healthy study practices (habits) in adolescent?

(a) You will tell them the life stories of Noble laureates of the world.
(b) You will engage yourself in regular studies in order to influence the children.
(c) You will motivate them from their childhood to develop study habits in a regular manner.
(d) You will not take care of all his studies at all due to your own tough engagements and engage a tutor for him who can look into his study problems.

469. The term intra-individual differences refers to

(a) differences among the various traits in a given individual.
(b) differences in a given trait between two or more individuals.
(c) differences in a given trait between two more than two individuals.
(d) differences in a given trait in a given individual associated with errors of measurement.

470. The trait of honesty in students can be developed through

(a) giving group punishment to such students in a school's public places like school assembly, etc.
(b) highlighting their morale by telling moral stories related to the greatmen of the world.
(c) adopting all pious and honest measures in your personal life to create an example.
(d) giving rewards to such students who have demonstrated this trait in their life.

471. The reason of making mid-day meal arrangement by the government in primary schools is

(a) the poor child can take required nutrition and get balanced diet.
(b) the child can reduce their fatigue and the teachers also can regenerate their energies for further teaching.
(c) the child and teacher both satisfy their appetite and begin with teaching-learning work-afresh.
(d) the child can feel liberated from all disciplinarian measures during these hours.

472. Seggregation into special classes for the educable is generally recommended for approximately the lowest per cent of the general school population

(a) One-fourth (b) Two
(c) Five (d) Ten

473. Which of the following fact is not appears to be correct in terms of the motivation?
(a) Motivation is the internal state of the individual.
(b) The motivated activities are goal oriented.
(c) The motivated behaviour is continued till realization of the goal.
(d) The motivated behaviour has a predetermined goal.

474. Which of the following elements is not associated with the cycle of motivation?
(a) Need (b) Food
(c) Drive (d) Incentive

475. Which one of the following demonstrate the correct relationship between drive and need?
(a) Compensatory to one-another.
(b) Uniform in nature.
(c) Drives comes first and need afterwards.
(d) Both are parallel to one another.

476. The development of desirable person's characteristics is largely a matter of
(a) social pressures.
(b) habit-formulation.
(c) motivation.
(d) inherited pre-dispositions.

477. Which one of the following depicts the correct sequence of the constituents of motivational cycle?
(a) Need ⇒ Incentive ⇒ Drive
(b) Incentive ⇒ Drive ⇒ Need
(c) Drive ⇒ Need ⇒ Incentive
(d) Need ⇒ Drive ⇒ Incentive

478. What is the second name given to innate motives?
(a) Physiological motives
(b) Biological motives
(c) Acquired motives
(d) Both (a) and (b).

479. When a student can no longer recall material he had learned sometime back, one can assume that
(a) he had never learned it.
(b) he repressed it.
(c) it was lost as a result of the interference of subsequent learnings.
(d) the neural connections involved faded as a result of disuse.

480. The McDougall's explanation of the instinct is
(a) Innate (b) Acquired
(c) Both (a) and (b). (d) None of these.

481. McDougall has enumerated three basic elements of instinct. Which one of the following is not included in them?
(a) General energizing aspect
(b) Action aspect
(c) Goal directedness
(d) Impetus aspect

482. Which of the following best explains the phenomenon of forgetting?
(a) The passage of time
(b) The phenomenon of reminiscence
(c) The phenomenon of interference
(d) Repression.

483. The origin of frustration in students occur due to
(a) Conflicts among motives
(b) Lack of incentives
(c) Personal disability
(d) None of the above.

484. Who among the following Psychologists have given the concept that the child has specific emotion at the time of birth?
(a) Watson (b) Hull
(c) Lewin (d) Robinson

485. Which of the following procedures would be best from the stand point of efficiency

of acquisition for a given degree of long-term retention?

(a) A high level of over-learning.
(b) Reviews spaced progressively further apart.
(c) Trial and error.
(d) Cramming.

486. Which of the following factors is responsible for emotional development of the child according to contemporary psychologist?

(a) Maturity and economic status
(b) Environment and maturity
(c) Maturity and learning
(d) Learning and environment

487. Maturity and Emotional Development are directly proportional to each other. This concept is put forth by

(a) Goodenough (b) Sermon
(c) Hull (d) Bridges

488. Purposeful group learning in the class-room generally begins with

(a) intelligent trial and error activity.
(b) motives and a clarification of objectives.
(c) hypothesis and generalisations.
(d) delegation of responsibility to the members.

489. Which age group of children is being studied by the famous psychologist Bridges to derive her emotion related concepts of its development?

(a) 2 months to 24 months
(b) 1 month to 18 months
(c) Birth to 24 months
(d) Birth to 18 months

490. Recitation in learning appears most profitable when introduced

(a) at the beginning of the learning period.
(b) uniformity throughout the learning period.
(c) toward the end of the learning period.
(d) only as preparation for the testing period.

491. Which of the following is not a type of sentiments?

(a) Simple sentiments
(b) Complex sentiments
(c) Concrete and Abstract sentiments
(d) Value-related sentiments

492. According to Valentine sentiment is

(a) the organised nature of emotional tendencies and feelings.
(b) condensed feelings.
(c) acquired tendencies.
(d) None of the above.

493. Which one of the following denotes sentiment of an infant towards his mother?

(a) Love (b) Joy
(c) Affection (d) Pity

494. Verbal guidance is least effective in the learning of

(a) Attitudes (b) Concepts
(c) Facts (d) Relationships

495. Which one of the following is not one characteristic of sentiment?

(a) Acquired in nature
(b) Mental structures
(c) Concrete in nature
(d) Self-realised

496. Which one of the following is not a Play method?

(a) Winetkka Plan (b) Basic Education
(c) Dalton Plan (d) Watson Plan

497. Heredity is associated with

(a) Genes
(b) Physical structure
(c) Mental level
(d) Physiology

498. The Laws of Heredity are laid down by

(a) Gregor Mendal (b) John Hilton
(c) Lamarck (d) Neil's Bohr

499. Development of a child is influenced and can be exhibited through the equation
(a) D = H × E (b) D = H – E
(c) D = H + E (d) D = H ÷ E

500. In the following list of the aspects of the guidance of learning activities, which is the most fundamental and should occur first from the stand point of time?
(a) Determination of methods of evaluation.
(b) Determination of methods of presentation.
(c) Determination of objectives.
(d) Selection of the learning activities.

501. The importance of Heredity for a teacher is
(a) The knowledge about an individual.
(b) The knowledge of innate capacities.
(c) The development of Educational planning.
(d) All of the above.

502. The knowledge of child's environment helps as
(a) guessing the process of socialisation.
(b) analysing the future possibilities.
(c) creating healthy scheme environment.
(d) All of the above.

503. In order to give effective guidance to the learning of a skill, the instructor must necessarily be able
(a) to execute the skill with a high degree of perfection.
(b) to execute the skill with a higher degree of perfection than the person he is trying to instruct.
(c) to develop in the student's insight into the nature of the skill to be learned.
(d) to foresee and forestall the development of bad habits, the occurrence of plateaus.

504. Who had putforth the concept of instinct first of all?
(a) McDougall (b) John Watson
(c) Gregar Mendal (d) Robert King

505. The instinct in corresponding with its emotional reaction 'wonder' is
(a) Curiosity (b) Sex
(c) Combat (d) Escape

506. A teacher today, is least expected to serve as
(a) a director of many activities.
(b) an able publicist of the school.
(c) an encylopaedia of knowledge.
(d) a committee member and consultant.

507. Which one of the following characteristics is not associated with Instincts?
(a) Emotional affiliation
(b) Universally present in all living beings
(c) Pragmatic its approach
(d) 3-D pictures and can be visualised

508. The Educational significance of the instincts is in
(a) Motivation
(b) Interest-making
(c) Promoting creativity
(d) All of the above.

509. A most important task in teaching
(a) making assignments and hearing recitations.
(b) directing pupils in development of experiences.
(c) scoring test papers and giving outgrades.
(d) making monthly reports and keeping records.

510. Emotions are influencing human behaviour by its

(a) Organisation
(b) Empowerment
(c) Global-directness
(d) All of the above.

511. Condensed and stabilised form of emotion can be casually termed as
(a) Sentiments (b) Instincts
(c) Innate spirits (d) Motivation

512. What is play?
(a) An Innate tendency
(b) Free and self-motivated exercise
(c) Enjoying and exciting mechanism
(d) All of the above.

513. The most important function of the teacher is to
(a) maintain a order.
(b) impart subject-matter.
(c) teach problem-solving techniques.
(d) guide pupil's growth.

514. Theory of play associated with exhaustion of emotions is
(a) Theory of surplus energy
(b) Anticipation theory
(c) Instinct theory
(d) Catharsis theory

515. Educational importance of play has extended its utility in
(a) teaching and learning.
(b) making educational access.
(c) making children tiny giants of knowledge.
(d) spoiling children's development.

516. The group rules for the classroom should be established by
(a) Principal
(b) Pupils
(c) Pupils and teacher
(d) Teacher

517. Play of a child are
(a) Purposeless activity
(b) Developmental activity
(c) Enjoyable activity
(d) Therapeutic activity

518. Proximo-distal direction of development explains the nature of development
(a) from centre to periphery.
(b) from top to bottom.
(c) from inner organs to outward organs.
(d) from internal organs to external organs.

519. Which stage of development is called unique stage of development?
(a) Infancy stage
(b) Childhood stage
(c) Adolescent stage
(d) Adulthood

520. Which of the following best reflects democracy in the classroom?
(a) Allowing children to sit where they want and work with whom they please.
(b) Allowing children freedom to the observance of classroom rules and regulations.
(c) Allowing the class to decide the curricular experience of the classroom.
(d) Allowing the maximum participation of all the students in classroom activities.

521. Infancy is termed as the most important period of human life because
(a) It is formative stage of human life.
(b) It is the only enjoyable period in human life.
(c) it is making foundation for whole life.
(d) It is delicate stage of development.

522. Adolescent stage is termed as most difficult stage of human life done to the reason that
(a) Awkward physique
(b) Difficulty in social adjustment
(c) Sex attraction
(d) All of the above.

523. The best statement of the position of the teacher in the classroom is that he is
(a) the chairman of the group.
(b) the superiror of the group.
(c) one member of the group.
(d) the director of the group.

524. After the age of 2 years a child, shows the emotion of distress in the form of
(a) Fear (b) Disgust
(c) Anger (d) All of the above

525. 'Delight' has its further specifications as
(a) Elation and Affection
(b) Joy and Elation
(c) Love and Elation
(d) All of the above.

526. Political responsibilities make demands upon many people. Teachers should
(a) take a firm stand on political issue and support their side in any way, they can.
(b) refuse to take a stand.
(c) accept civic responsibilities, but refuse to be drawn into fractional disputes.
(d) never mention politics in class.

527. According to State and National Codes, it would not be unethical for teachers to
(a) promulgate private religious views in the classroom.
(b) tutor members of their classes privately for pay.
(c) apply for a specific position that is not vacant.
(d) refuse to sign a contract which displease them.

528. Which of the following elements has minimum role in effective teaching?
(a) Planning of teaching
(b) Organisation of teaching
(c) Teaching aids
(d) Teaching related feelings

529. Planning of teaching is not related with
(a) Analysis of Task
(b) Identification of teaching objectives
(c) Writing of learning objectives in behavioural terms
(d) Class management

530. The initials PTA refer to what organisation?
(a) Progressive Teacher Association
(b) Parent Teacher Association
(c) Private Tutors Association
(d) Principal Teacher Administration

531. Analysis of task is related with
(a) the learning activities of the students.
(b) the expected learning behaviour of the students.
(c) the learning conditions.
(d) the formulation of criterion for expected performance and all the above.

532. The advantage of analysis of task is
(a) to familiarize a teacher with teaching work.
(b) to familiarize a teacher with learning activities of the students.
(c) Both of the above.
(d) None of the above.

533. In present times, the prestige level of teachers is recognised by the general public as
(a) above that of professional worker.
(b) on a par with the professional class of workers.
(c) on a par with the wage earner or labour.
(d) somewhere between wage earner and professional worker.

534. During content analysis a teacher focuses upon
(a) The topic
(b) The sub-topic

(c) Content elements
(d) All of the above.

535. The skill analysis is not related with
(a) The functions performed during teaching period by a teacher.
(b) Asking questions.
(c) Conducting experiments.
(d) Explanation and diagnosis.

536. It is generally agreed that
(a) each educational group should have its own independent organisation.
(b) administrators and teachers should have separate professional organisation.
(c) any professional organisation should include several leaves leadership.
(d) All of the above.

537. The objectives of cognitive domain are
(a) Knowledge - Understanding - Experiment
(b) Analysis - Synthesis - Application
(c) Both of the above.
(d) None of the above.

538. The pioneer of the classification of objectives in cognitive domain is
(a) Bloom B.S. (b) Skinner B.F.
(c) Terman M.R. (d) Guilford G.

539. Primary responsibility for the teacher's adjustment lies with
(a) the children.
(b) the principal.
(c) the teacher himself.
(d) the teacher's parents.

540. The objectives lying at the ends of psycho motor Domain are
(a) Stimulus-Habit formation
(b) Manipulation-Habit formation
(c) Stimulus-Naturalisation
(d) None of the above.

541. The person who had given classification of Affective Domain is
(a) Krathwohl (b) Binet
(c) Raymont (d) Munroe

542. Modern Indian education at the Elementary school level can best be described as being
(a) curriculum-centred.
(b) project-centred.
(c) pupil-centred.
(d) subject-centred.

543. The cognitive objective is related to
(a) Brain (b) Heart
(c) Hands (d) Talks

544. The most complicated classification of Educational objectives which, is still in vogue belongs to
(a) Affective Domain
(b) Cognitive Domain
(c) Psychomotor Domain
(d) All of the above.

545. The primary goal towards which the modern school is oriented is that of the development on the parts of its students of
(a) adequate behaviour.
(b) socially acceptable behaviour.
(c) personal adequacy and independence.
(d) a sound system of ethical values.

546. The major sources of content analysis are
(a) The study of authentic books
(b) To keep vigil on students needs
(c) To satisfy students educational needs
(d) All of the above.

547. Which one of the following is not the characteristic element of a textbook?
(a) Positive reactions of the students when they learn about the element.
(b) To guess the position of different elements with the help of students behaviour.

(c) To identify behavioural changes on the basis of the reactions of the students towards elements.
(d) To expert from the students that they gain expertise in elements.

548. The field of education is permeated by conflicts and misconceptions largely because
(a) the problems encountered in teaching call for subjectivity of interpretation.
(b) there are no best teaching methods and procedures.
(c) the problem encountered in teaching are not amenable to rigorous scientific investigation.
(d) education has first to be practical and only secondarily to be scientific.

549. Which one of the following arrangement is against the content's elements?
(a) From known to unknown
(b) From simple to complex
(c) From concrete to abstract
(d) From knowledge to darkness

550. The Educational Objectives can be differentiated with Instructional objectives on the basis of
(a) Nature (b) Part and whole
(c) Time (d) All of the above

551. "To develop feelings of National Integration in students"—This objective can be classified under the category of
(a) Educational objective
(b) Teaching objective
(c) Specific objective
(d) National objective

552. The teacher's major contribution towards the maximum self-realisation of the child is best affected through
(a) constant fulfillment of the child's needs.
(b) strict control of classroom activities.
(c) sensitivity of pupil needs, goals and purposes.
(d) strict reinforcement of academic standards.

553. The source of educational objective is
(a) Social philosophy
(b) Psychological principles
(c) Politics
(d) Economic policies

554. The cognitive objectives are related to
(a) Informations, knowledge and facts
(b) Interest, attitudes and values
(c) Training of physical skills
(d) All of the above.

555. The primary task of the teacher is
(a) to teach the prescribed curriculum.
(b) to stimulate and guide student's learning.
(c) to ensure that all students belong to socially acceptable peer groups.
(d) to promote habits of conformity to adult demands and expectations.

556. The title of the famous book written by Bloom on Educational objectives is
(a) *Taxonomy of Educational Objectives: Cognitive Domain*
(b) *Taxonomy of Instructional Objectives: Cognitive Domain*
(c) *Taxonomy of Affective Objectives*
(d) None of the above.

557. The learning points included under the knowledge objective are
(a) Knowledge of specific facts
(b) Generalisation
(c) Atomic analysis of the content
(d) To take external/internal judgements

558. Educational Psychology should provide prospective teachers with
(a) insights into the various aspects of modern education.

(b) principles, insights and attitudes as points of departure for effective teaching.
(c) research procedures by means of which to evaluate current teaching procedure.
(d) rules of thumb to deal with everyday classroom situation.

559. The Comprehension included
(a) Translation (b) Interpretation
(c) Extrapolation (d) All of the above.

560. Analysis is related with
(a) analysis of elements.
(b) to explore the mutual relationship existed between two elements.
(c) to analyse a principle.
(d) All of the above.

561. Teachers who are enthusiastic in the classroom teaching
(a) often lack proficiency in the subjects which stays hidden under their enthusiasm.
(b) simply dramatise to hold the students attention.
(c) involve their students in the teaching learning process.
(d) All of the above.

562. Evaluation is the topmost category of knowledge objective which is meant
(a) Qualitative and quantitative interpretation of the fact
(b) Self-judgement
(c) Examination
(d) None of the above.

563. Knowledge plus Comprehension form
(a) Application (b) Skill
(c) Analysis (d) Synthesis

564. Factual informations are collected through
(a) Knowledge and Comprehension
(b) Understanding and Analysis
(c) Experiment and Evaluation
(d) Synthesis and Analysis

565. When you start teaching a new topic to a class, the foremost precaution to be observed would be to
(a) prepare the teaching matter as thoroughly as possible.
(b) see that what is important is impressed upon the class first.
(c) create the feeling among students that the new topic has logical relation with what they knew before.
(d) None of these.

566. The basis of conceptual formation is
(a) Comprehension and Analysis
(b) Analysis and Synthesis
(c) Evaluation and Analysis
(d) Extrapolation and Analysis

567. Which one of the following alternative denote the best contribution of Bloom's taxonomy in examination system?
(a) To formulate objective based examination it has refuted the importance of textbooks.
(b) To write the objectives in the format of programmed learning.
(c) To give more emphasis on psycho-motor domain in present day examinations.
(d) All of the above.

568. For writing on the Blackboard, which of the following methods would be correct for a teacher?
(a) Writing the matter first and than asking students to read it.
(b) Putting a question to students and then writing the answer as stated by them.
(c) Writing fast and as clearly as possible.
(d) None of the above.

569. Which one of the following 'Action verb' is not related with knowledge objective?
(a) To recall (b) To enlist
(c) To identify (d) To explain

570. The verb 'To Interpret' reflects its taxonomic position as
(a) Knowledge objective
(b) Understanding objective
(c) Application objective
(d) Analysis objective

571. Which one of the following is an odd statement?
(a) Majority of teachers use lectures method.
(b) Most of the classrooms are poorly equipped.
(c) Knowledge is static.
(d) None of the above.

572. If you are interested to develop in your students the 'ability to forcast' then you would like to give emphasis upon
(a) Application Aspect
(b) Analysis Aspect
(c) Synthesis Aspect
(d) All of the above.

573. The three 'Action verbs' viz., to listen; to accept; and to show interest—are related with
(a) responding stage of affective domain.
(b) reaction stage of affective domain.
(c) valuing stage of affective domain.
(d) organising stage of affective domain.

574. A new teacher to start with, will have to
(a) enforce discipline in the class.
(b) establish rapport with the students.
(c) cut jokes with the students.
(d) All of the above.

575. Regional College of Education Mysore (RCEM), Mysore has sponsored the classification of Cognitive Domain as
(a) Knowledge - Comprehension - Application - Analysis - Synthesis and Evaluation
(b) Knowledge - Comprehension - Application - Creativity
(c) Knowledge-Comprehension-Application - Analysis - Creativity
(d) Knowledge - Comprehension - Application - Analysis - Synthesis - Creativity

576. Under the objective of Application, the mental abilities remain functional in
(a) Reasoning and formulation of hypothesis.
(b) Establishing a hypothesis and drawing conclusions.
(c) Predicting and analysing.
(d) All of the above.

577. An effective teacher will ensure
(a) cooperation among his students.
(b) laissez-faire role.
(c) involve their students in the teaching-learning process.
(d) All of the above.

578. Identify the Application objective on the basis of following Action-verbs.
(a) The students have the ability to verify the facts.
(b) The students have the ability to formulate a hypothesis.
(c) The students have the capacity to analyse the facts.
(d) The students have the ability of evaluations.

579. Suppose you are teaching in a class the topic 'Indian Freedom Movement'. What would you like to formulate application-oriented objectives on this topic?
(a) The students have the adequate ability to analyse the facts related to Indian Freedom Movement.

(b) The students have the ability to reasoned out the facts in favour of the success of Indian Freedom Movement.
(c) The students have the ability to explain the causes of Indian Freedom Movement.
(d) The students have the ability to recall the period and important dates related with Indian Freedom Movement.

580. On the top end of all the educational objectives have almost similar qualities which denote
(a) integration of all human faculties which is responsible for development of multi-facet personality of an individual.
(b) partial correlation of all mental faculties which enhances the attainment of basic goal of education.
(c) diversity of all mental faculties by which they all can maintain their uniqueness.
(d) None of the above.

581. Organised teaching is related with
(a) The selection of adequate teaching tactics.
(b) The adequate communication methods.
(c) The selection of appropriate audio-visual acids.
(d) All of the above.

582. A college teacher will really help the students when she/he
(a) dictates notes in the class.
(b) is objective in her evaluation.
(c) encourages students to ask questions.
(d) covers the syllabus completely in the class.

583. Teaching tactics are related to
(a) Learning structures
(b) Learning objectives
(c) Learning experiences
(d) Learning conditions

584. Which one of the following does not denote learning condition according to Davies?
(a) Signal learning
(b) Chain learning
(c) Concept learning
(d) Simulated learning

585. A teacher has to be
(a) a strict disciplinarian.
(b) well-versed in the subject.
(c) a continuous learner in the subject.
(d) sympathetic towards slow learners.

586. Signal learning explains that an organism should react with each stimuli in the following manner
(a) Uniform
(b) Separate
(c) Sometimes uniform sometimes in different forms
(d) Cannot say

587. Which one of the following phrase appears to be befitting in relation to signal learning?
(a) Prediction
(b) Vagueness in previous condition
(c) Impossibility of prediction
(d) Sudden occurrence of previous conditions

588. Our attitude towards knowledge should be
(a) to accept what is proved by science on the basis of empirical evidence.
(b) to accept believing in the scope for improvement.
(c) to accept as the final truth.
(d) not to accept anything that is not personally verified.

589. In Davies condition cycle the following five elements are included viz.

1. Signal 2. Chain
3. Discrimination 4. Concept
5. Principle

What will be the correct sequence of all these elements in a cyclic order?

(a) 1, 2, 3, 4, 5 (b) 1, 3, 5, 2, 4
(c) 1, 5, 3, 2, 4 (d) 5, 4, 3, 2, 1

590. Which one of the following teaching tactics one should use in a condition of Signal Learning?
(a) To give maximum intensity of stimuli to the students so that they are ready to respond.
(b) To reinforce the right responses of the students.
(c) To give such stimulation to the students that they gain mastery over the content.
(d) All the above teaching tactics should be used.

591. The best educational programme is one which is according to the
(a) need of the child.
(b) ability of the child.
(c) interest of child.
(d) All of these along with the need of the society.

592. Which one of the following is a good teaching tactics in relation to chain learning?
(a) To present exhaustively the complete chain of context in the classroom.
(b) To present stimulation as a progressive and retrogressive chain order.
(c) Both of the above.
(d) None of the above.

593. What are the learning measures for multiple discrimination type learning?
(a) To separate the stimuli and responses of the students upto certain limits.
(b) Again, present both stimuli and responses in paired form so that students differentiate between them.
(c) To give maximum freedom to the students so that they differentiate between stimuli and responses.
(d) All of the above.

594. In the final analysis, teaching must be thought of mainly as a process of
(a) directing the activities of the pupils.
(b) asking questions and evaluating the learning.
(c) Both (a) and (b).
(d) All of the above.

595. Which one of the following teaching tactics in not suitable in refrerence to 'Principle learning'?
(a) To do continuous exercise of the chain of concepts in order to make the difficult points more easier.
(b) To motivate the students for generalization.
(c) To give opportunities to students so that they make difference.
(d) None of the above.

596. Which one of the following learning objective is not achieved by a teacher through lecture method?
(a) Cognitive (b) Affective
(c) Psycho-motor (d) All of the above.

597. The functions of a teacher is in the order of
(a) guiding the child, helping him towards progress and evaluation.
(b) checking homework, guiding him and assigning further task.
(c) Both (a) and (b).
(d) None of the above.

598. The basic function of tutorials is the attainment of
(a) Cognitive goals
(b) Affective goals

(c) Psycho-motor goals
(d) Both (a) and (b).

599. A teacher can achieve the following learning objective through sensitive training?
(a) Cognitive objective
(b) Affective objective
(c) Psycho-motor objective
(d) Both (a) and (b).

600. Psycho-motor objective can be achieved through
(a) Lesson demonstration teaching strategy.
(b) Sensitive training teaching strategy.
(c) Both of the above.
(d) None of the above.

601. Which one of the following effect of audio-visual aids can be visualize on one's teaching?
(a) To improve the retention in students.
(b) To transfer the teaching in some other related contents.
(c) To acquire and reinforce the knowledge.
(d) All of the above.

602. Which one of the following learning objective can be realised through Tape recorder as an Audio-aid in a classroom?
(a) Cognitive (b) Affective
(c) Psycho-motor (d) All of the above.

603. The beneficial teaching aids pair in the following order to attain the learning objectives is
(a) Tape, Gramophone, TV
(b) Picture, Model, Cinema (Film)
(c) Excursion, Language lab and Radio
(d) Radio, TV and Tape

604. Which one of the following is adequate teaching Audio-visual aid for chain learning?
(a) Radio (b) Gramophone
(c) Film (d) Television

605. Which one of the following learning forms can be achieved through language laboratory?
(a) Signal, Chain, Multidiscriminatory learning.
(b) Direct, Principle and Multi-discriminatory learning.
(c) Signal, Direct and Principle learning.
(d) Chain, Principle and Multi-discriminatory learning.

606. Verbal guidance is least effective in teaching
(a) Attitude.
(b) Concept and facts.
(c) Relationship.
(d) Skills.

607. The advantage of Educational Excursions for the student is
(a) In direct learning
(b) In principle learning
(c) In chain learning
(d) In all the above

608. Which one of the following stands on the top in the hierarchy of needs-propounded by famous psychologist Maslow (1954)?
(a) Physical needs
(b) Needs for esteem
(c) Needs for self-realisation
(d) Needs for affection

609. A teacher meeting his students for the first time should
(a) start teaching without caring the students likes and dislikes.
(b) develop rapport with the class.
(c) give a broad outline of the whole subject
(d) All of the above.

610. Which one of the following elements of human behaviour can be regulated by motivation?
(a) Emergence of behaviour
(b) Stability of behaviour
(c) Directing the behaviour
(d) All of the above.

611. The motivational procedures can be classified as
(a) External procedures
(b) Internal procedures
(c) Both of the above.
(d) None of the above.

612. Teachers professionalism may be assessed in terms of all of the following commitments except
(a) commitment to the profession and students.
(b) commitment to the profession and students.
(c) commitment to the religion and castes.
(d) All of the above.

613. "Motivation is an internal mechanism which initiate or sustain the activity pertaining to human behaviour." This statement is given by
(a) R.S. Woodworth
(b) Gardner Murphy
(c) N.L. Munn
(d) None of the above.

614. Which one of the following is not included in motivation?
(a) Needs (b) Driver
(c) Goals (d) Reflex actions

615. Which one of the following characteristics one can witnessed in a motivational state of an individual?
(a) Chemical intensity
(b) Metabolic intensity
(c) Physical hyperactions
(d) All of the above.

616. What is the significance of motivation in practical classroom teaching?
(a) It strengthens the students' behaviour
(b) It helps in bringing desirable changes in students' behaviour
(c) It regulates the students' behaviour
(d) All of the above.

617. Praise and Blame both are the procedures applied for motivation. In which of the following case you would like to employ Blame as a motivational procedure in a actual classroom practices?
(a) Weak students
(b) Intelligent students
(c) Normal students
(d) None of the above.

618. The 'immediate knowledge of progress' can work as
(a) Satisfying behaviour
(b) Motivational behaviour
(c) Immediate reactionary behaviour
(d) None of the above.

619. In a psychological sense which one of the following motivation procedure is most suitable in routine classroom conditions?
(a) Competition
(b) Co-operation
(c) Appreciation
(d) Co-operation and appreciation

620. In selection of the motivational procedures, a teacher should follow the following criterion
(a) Needs of students
(b) Learning objectives
(c) Learning structures
(d) All of the above.

621. Reward and Punishment—the basic motivations are related to
(a) Bodily needs
(b) Social security
(c) Affection and belongingness
(d) None of the above.

622. Which one of the following can be categorised under the internal and external motivation?
(a) Novelty
(b) Knowledge of progress
(c) Competition and co-operation
(d) All of the above.

623. Generally the practical utility of 'Punishment' is to adopt it as a measure to maintain discipline in a class. This punishment can also employ as a procedure of motivation when it is used with
(a) Rewards
(b) Elimination of anti-social behaviour of the students
(c) (As) Immediate penalty for misbehaviour
(d) All of the above.

624. "The procedure which is related to specification of objectives and helping in problem-solving of concepts, principles, skills, language etc. is called instructional procedure." This definition is put forth by
(a) Davies (b) Glasgo
(c) Glaser (d) Robert Magor

625. Self-motivation is the highest category of motivation which is associated with
(a) Self-actualisation need
(b) Self-esteem need
(c) Both of the above.
(d) None of the above.

626. Which one of the following type of learning is not considered as learning in psychological sense?
(a) The learning generates from motivation.
(b) The learning originates from maturation.
(c) The learning causes through fatigue.
(d) The learning occurs through all the above.

627. The significant element of the instructional procedure is
(a) Formulation of objective - Content Analysis - Entry Behaviour - Teaching aid.
(b) Formulation of Objective - Content analysis - Entry Behaviour - Teaching procedure - Evaluation and Diagnosis.
(c) Formulation of objective - Content analysis - Evaluation.
(d) None of the above.

628. What is the basic utility of the teaching of concepts and principles?
(a) To familiarise the students with the objects present in the external environment.
(b) To educate the students about the mechanical activities.
(c) To give the instruction—a practical shape.
(d) All of the above.

629. Below are given the basic learning conditions in a jumbled form
1. Proximity 2. Reinforcement
3. Generalisation 4. Exercise
5. Discrimination

Search the correct order in the following alternatives.
(a) 1, 3, 5, 4, 2 (b) 1, 2, 3, 4, 5
(c) 2, 4, 5, 3, 1 (d) 5, 4, 3, 2, 1

630. According to Guilford creativity has the following four elements in it.
(a) OF2E (Originality, Fluency, Flexibility and Extension).
(b) OFE (Originality, Fluency, Flexibility and Emergence).
(c) O2FE (Originality, Origin, Fluency and Elasticity).
(d) OFE (Originality, Fluency, Flexibility and Enrichment).

631. Contiguity is associated with
(a) The presentation of two similar stimuli for an uniform response.
(b) The presentation of two similar responses in relation to a uniform stimulus.
(c) The collection of two stimuli as an unit.
(d) None of the above.

632. The chief characteristics of skilled teaching is
(a) Chaining of psycho motor activities.
(b) Co-ordination of physical and muscular activities.
(c) Chaining of complex psycho-motor activities.
(d) All of the above.

633. The basic assumption of interaction analysis is
(a) Teaching behaviour is a social interactional process.
(b) Teaching bahaviour is a teacher-centred process.
(c) Teaching behaviour is a motivated process.
(d) Teaching behaviour is a planned process.

634. The stages of skillful learning are
(a) Cognitive-Fixation-Autonomous
(b) Cognitive-Affective-Fixation
(c) Cognitive-Affective-Resistance
(d) None of the above.

635. In how many categories Flander has categories the Teacher's behaviour in a classroom condition?
(a) 3 (b) 2
(c) 4 (d) 5

636. Which one of the following is not appeared as criterion of indirect behaviour in Flander's Interactional Analysis?
(a) To accept the students' feelings.
(b) Praise and encouragement.
(c) Acceptance of students' ideas.
(d) To punish the students.

637. What is the basic assumption behind the ten categories procedure of Flander's Interactional Analysis?
(a) Emphasis on verbal behaviour in a class.
(b) Effectiveness of teacher's behaviour on the students.
(c) The interest of the students in democratic behaviour.
(d) All of the above.

638. Flander has determined the following criterion for the teacher's direct behaviours.
(a) To explain (b) To direct
(c) To criticise (d) All of the above

639. The teaching skill is a
(a) integrated form of teaching activities and behaviours.
(b) international condition of the class.
(c) conducive conditions for learning.
(d) All of the above.

640. The limitation of Flander's Interactional analysis is
(a) Only verbal communication can be observed.
(b) The classification of classroom activities in ten categories is inappropriate.
(c) The separate scoring system adopted for the teachers and students behaviours.
(d) All of the above.

641. The meaning of stimulus variation is
(a) Deliberate changes in the teacher's behaviour.
(b) Deliberate changes by the students in their behaviours.

(c) Deliberate changes in the class during the content delivery.
(d) None of the above.

642. Allen and Ryan has proclaimed the following numbers of skills
(a) 14 (b) 13
(c) 12 (d) 11

643. Induction is associated with
(a) Attention of the students.
(b) Motivation given by the teacher.
(c) Linking students' present knowledge with their previous knowledge.
(d) None of the above.

644. How does a teacher should begin with a new lesson?
(a) Through storytelling
(b) Through reciting a poetry
(c) Through displaying a picture
(d) Any two methods from above.

645. During Reinforcement Skill, the teacher deals with
(a) Students' praise
(b) Students' blame
(c) Students' rejection
(d) Tyranny on students'

646. Which one of the following is not associated with Micro-teaching?
(a) Knowledge acquiring
(b) Skill training
(c) Content transfer
(d) Atomic teaching procedure

647. Which one of the following is not the main characteristics of Task-analysis?
(a) The description of the students and their learning abilities.
(b) Identification of desirable behaviours.
(c) Identification of stimuli or situations by which one can expect student desirable behaviour.
(d) Identification of teaching objectives.

648. The adequacy of Blackboard work lies when a teacher will work on it
(a) In continuous manner and in a neat way.
(b) Through coloured chalks.
(c) In a brief and vivid manner.
(d) All of the above.

649. Generally job-analysis has been carried out by the
(a) Job-seekers
(b) Job-providers
(c) Both of the above.
(d) None of the above.

650. Benjamin S. Bloom is associated with
(a) Classification of Educational objectives.
(b) Classification of Educational theories of Learning.
(c) Classification of teaching models.
(d) None of the above.

651. Arrangement of content or topics elements in a sequence follows the maxim of
(a) From known to unknown.
(b) From simple to difficult.
(c) From concrete to abstract.
(d) All of the above.

652. Task-analysis can be carried out in relation to
(a) Content of the books
(b) Jobs for providing employment
(c) Skills to be learned
(d) All of the above.

653. Cognitive Domain is representing
(a) Neurological activities pertaining to human behaviour.
(b) Affective activities pertaining to human behaviour.
(c) Motor activities expressing human behaviour.
(d) None of the above.

654. The highest component of Affective Domain is
(a) Receiving (b) Characterisation
(c) Habit formation (d) Evaluation

655. Which one of the following is directly correspond to application?
(a) Comprehensions (b) Extrapolation
(c) Analysis (d) Articulation

656. Writing of learning objectives in behavioural term helps in
(a) Framing questions for examination papers in order to give every part an equal weightage.
(b) Making balance in teaching and learning process.
(c) Helping in objective-based evaluation.
(d) Preparing teaching strategies and all of the above.

657. Generally comprehension, Analysis and Application leads to
(a) Concept formation
(b) Generalisation
(c) Evaluation
(d) None of the above.

658. Evaluation as an objective denotes
(a) Judgement
(b) Estimation
(c) Critical evaluation
(d) All of the above.

659. The preliminary objective of cognitive do main i.e., knowledge can be expressed with the verbs
(a) Recall and Recognition
(b) Enlisting and Definition
(c) Stating and Measuring
(d) All of the above.

660. The important stages covered under organisation of teaching is
(a) Selection of appropriate teaching tactics.
(b) Selecting appropriate communication strategies.
(c) Selecting appropriate audio-visual aids.
(d) All of the above.

661. Gagne's Multiple Discrimination learning includes the teaching tactics of
(a) Reinforcement of correct responses.
(b) Presentation of stimuli in chain order.
(c) Promotion and separation of stimuli from responses.
(d) Discrimination between all the stimuli and responses.

662. Lecture as a teaching strategy is not having favourable implications on
(a) Cognitive domain
(b) Affective domain
(c) Psycho-motor domain
(d) All of the domains

663. Audio-visual aids such as TV is related with
(a) Chain learning
(b) Concept learning
(c) Principle learning
(d) All of the above.

664. Audio-visual aids are related to
(a) Perceptual apparatus
(b) Audible apparatus
(c) Both of the above
(d) None of the above.

665. Which one of the following role is not played by motivation in learning?
(a) Arousing human behaviour
(b) Persisting human behaviour
(c) Sustaining human behaviour
(d) Detecting human behaviour

666. Teaching of principles does not have the step of
(a) Describing the terminal behaviour.
(b) Analysis of the principle into its elements.
(c) Interpreting the principle involved.
(d) Drawing inferences from principles.

667. The meaning of the teaching skill 'Stimulus variation' is
   (a) A deliberate change in teaching activities by the teacher in order to focus the attention of the students.
   (b) A change in stimulus within the class by a teacher or by a student.
   (c) A sudden change in stimulus in a class.
   (d) A kind of state of the class where the stimuli are changing at a continuous interval.

668. Interaction Analysis techniques for verbal and non-verbal classroom behaviour have been developed by
   (a) Flander (b) Hurtz
   (c) Gagne (d) Brown

669. The essential elements of effective instructional procedures is
   (a) Writing of Educational objectives
   (b) Tast-Analysis
   (c) Entring Behaviour
   (d) All of the above.

670. The ten category of FIAS' observation matrics are jumbled and given as below
   1. Accepts feelings
   2. Accepts feelings and use ideas
   3. Lecturing
   4. Pupil-talk Response
   5. Pupil-Talk Initiation
   6. Praise and Encourage
   7. Ask Questions
   8. Giving directions
   9. Criticising
   10. Silence/Confusion

   The correct sequence is
   (a) 1,6,2,7,3,8,9,4,5,10
   (b) 1,2,3,4,5,6,7,8,9,10
   (c) 1,3,5,7,9,2,4,6,8,10
   (d) 1,2,3,8,9,4,5,6,7,10

671. Flander's Interaction Analysis category system measures Teacher's classroom Behaviour in the form of
   (a) Teacher-talk
   (b) Pupil-talk
   (c) Silence or confusion
   (d) All of the above.

672. "The teachers are born, they cannot be trained." What are the possibilities related with the above phrase?
   (a) Teaching method is innate in nature.
   (b) Teaching method can be learned.
   (c) Teaching method is empirical in nature.
   (d) Teaching method is the result of maturity.

673. The meaning of Teaching method is
   (a) Style of teaching
   (b) Way of teaching
   (c) Art of teaching
   (d) Substitution of the knowledge from outer world into child's intellect

674. A teaching method completes with the help of
   (a) Various techniques
   (b) Many tactics
   (c) Many postures
   (d) Many approaches

675. It is possible to teach without a teaching method but it is harmful because one can not
   (a) attain the objective.
   (b) develop perfection in learning situation.
   (c) deliver organised teaching.
   (d) All of the above.

676. Which of the following method is termed as an essential evil?
   (a) Lecture method
   (b) Lecture-cum-Demonstration method

(c) Assignment method
(d) Discussion method

677. What term has been used when the external knowledge of the environment is fused with a childs brain?
(a) Teaching method
(b) Teaching tactics
(c) Teaching skill
(d) Teaching process

678. The characteristics of Child-centred method is
(a) pile-up all the students in the centre of the class for teaching.
(b) to teach the students keeping in mind their needs and interests.
(c) to give full freedom to the students.
(d) to teach the students in a circular group.

679. The end product of Teacher-centred methods is
(a) to memorise the facts.
(b) to express belief in traditional agencies.
(c) to depend on teachers authority.
(d) All of the above.

680. Which one of the following characteristics is present in Teacher-centred method?
(a) Formality
(b) Teacher's authority
(c) Neglect of innovations
(d) All of the above.

681. Which of the following is not included in process dimension of Teacher-centred methods of teaching?
(a) Repetition
(b) Authority
(c) Memory
(d) Discovery approach

682. Which one of the following is not a characteristics of Child-centred method?
(a) To develop scientific attitude
(b) To establish democratic values
(c) To establish self-government
(d) To prepare formal and rigid classroom environment

683. The dimension of a teaching method is
(a) Factual (b) Process
(c) Environmental (d) All of these.

684. Generally in Child-centred methods of teaching, the role of teacher is
(a) to formulate the problematic situations.
(b) to collect the possible material and resources for the children.
(c) to help the children in formulation of their hypotheses.
(d) All of the above.

685. The main objective of Child-centred teaching method is
(a) to develop the learning abilities in children in free way.
(b) to develop the skills in children.
(c) to develop independence in students.
(d) All of the above.

686. The end product of Child-centred method is
(a) the development of high level inquiry methods in children.
(b) imparting full freedom to the children.
(c) enhancing the potentialities of the children.
(d) All of the above.

687. In which of the following the teacher emphasizes on democratic values?
(a) Child-centred methods
(b) Student-centred methods
(c) Both of the above.
(d) None of the above.

688. In which of the following the teacher is ready to follow the innovations?
(a) Child-centred methods
(b) Teacher-centred methods

(c) Both of the above.
(d) None of the above.

689. Which one of the following is not follow the teaching principle?
(a) Lecture method
(b) Heuristic method
(c) Assignment method
(d) Project method

690. The salient feature of lecture method is
(a) Economy
(b) Teacher leisure
(c) Communication of factual informations
(d) None of the above.

691. When a teacher is comparatively passive and the students are overtly active and sit as listeners only—this way of teaching method is called
(a) Lecture method
(b) Assignment method
(c) Project method
(d) None of the above.

692. In which of the following methods the teacher is taking least interest towards the attention of the students in a class room?
(a) Project method
(b) Assignment method
(c) Lecture method
(d) Discussion method

693. Which one of the following is required in Lecture method?
(a) Training (b) Exercise
(c) Maturity (d) Intellectual skills

694. Lecture method is most appropriate in the following condition.
(a) When a teacher starts a new and difficult topic.
(b) When a teacher explains a theoretical aspects.
(c) When a teacher explains about a demonstration.
(d) None of the above.

695. The defect of lecture method is
(a) lack in scientific attitude.
(b) devoid of the principle of learning by doing.
(c) a One-way teaching process.
(d) All of the above.

696. Which device would you like to adopt in order to make your lecture method more effective and interesting?
(a) You become humorous during lecturing process.
(b) You give liberty of asking questions to your students.
(c) You exploit the potentiality of Black-board to its maximum.
(d) All of the above.

697. The lecture should be
(a) Interesting
(b) Well-organised and systematic
(c) Medium level with proper modulations
(d) All of the above.

698. Generally Lecture method is assumed as the best method for
(a) High school students
(b) Intermediate students
(c) Graduates students
(d) All of the above.

699. In which of the following conditions would you like to term the lecture method as an effective method?
(a) When you speak—and the students follow you
(b) When you speak—and the students could not follow
(c) When you speak—and the students are trying to take sleep
(d) When you speak—and the students take it as a torture

700. Which one of the following is not a quality of a teacher?
(a) Economy (b) Fast pace
(c) Time saving (d) Free thinking

701. In modern classes how extent the authoritative behaviour of a teacher is suitable?
(a) To a great extent
(b) Not at all
(c) Can't say
(d) Depend on the teachers personality

702. Lecture and experimental demonstration when fused together which one of the following principle is followed in it?
(a) Concrete to abstract
(b) Difficult to easy
(c) Curiosity to neutrality
(d) Individuality to group ability

703. When a lecture method is fused with experimental demonstration, it enhances the advantage as
(a) Its extended form
(b) Its thinking
(c) Its psychological nature
(d) Its qualitative value

704. What is the correct point of identification of lecture-cum-demonstration methods excellence?
(a) Perfect testing in classroom conditions
(b) Rehearsal of the demonstration
(c) Judicious organisation
(d) All of the above.

705. If you are interested to eliminate lop-sidedness in lecture method what method would you like to adopt?
(a) You will instill humorous feelings in it.
(b) You will change it as highly motivational.
(c) You will add it with demonstration.
(d) You will make it more factual.

706. It is said about lecture-cum-demonstration method that 'Truth is that which works'. What is the real meaning of this phrase in the present context?
(a) The teacher is forced to conduct experiments in the class because the students realize only after witnessing the things to be happen in real sense.
(b) The teacher is forced to demonstrate some sort of magical tricks because this is the only way that the students follow him in the class.
(c) Teacher is a true person therefore everybody follow his teachings.
(d) The teacher should have such a magical band that the students become amazed of it.

707. What is the importance of rehearsal before actual demonstration carried out in the classroom?
(a) It creates self-confidence in a teacher.
(b) The teacher becomes familiar with the difficulties which many occur during experimentation in the classroom conditions.
(c) The teacher performs the experiment's demonstration in a perfect fashion.
(d) All of the above.

708. If you are a science teacher then how can you make your experiment most effective through lecture-cum-demonstration method?
(a) By arranging experiment in an excellent manner—for ex. students disciple maintenance by keeping a big and long table in the laboratory or in classroom.
(b) By making arrangement for sufficient natural light on the central table for conducting experiment.
(c) By arranging the demonstration equipment's and apparatus in a systematic and orderly manner.
(d) All of the above.

709. What precautions does a teacher should take to make lecture-cum-demonstration method a child-centred method?
   (a) To take active co-operation of students in arranging and organising the experiments, apparatus for demonstration purposes.
   (b) To impart freedom to the students to take readings independently.
   (c) To organise the demonstration in a step-by-step manner in order to satisfy students curiosities.
   (d) All of the above.

710. The teachers should do the following tasks in order to generate learning interest among the students
   (a) Entertainment during experimental presentation.
   (b) Suspense during experimentation.
   (c) To make experiment more interesting.
   (d) None of the above.

711. Which of the following should not be performed by a teacher during lecture-cum-demonstration method?
   (a) Use of inadequate and erroneous apparatuses.
   (b) Sudden starting of demonstration (without prior preparedness).
   (c) Under pressure on the students.
   (d) All of the above.

712. The single most important point for demonstration of a lesson is
   (a) Selection of content
   (b) Lesson pointers and selection of questions
   (c) Collection of essential apparatuses
   (d) All of the above.

713. Which of the following precaution should be taken by a teacher for presentation of content along with demonstration?
   (a) Use of examples
   (b) Presentation of right questions
   (c) Vivid pronunciation and proper language fluency
   (d) All of the above.

714. During demonstration the topic should be presented in4
   (a) Problematic manner
   (b) Debatable manner
   (c) Suspending manner
   (d) None of the above.

715. When a teacher conducts a demonstration in a poor fashion the behavioural outcomes in the students can be observed as
   (a) The students follow the poor skills of the teacher.
   (b) The students deprive from scientific method.
   (c) The students lack in scientific attitude.
   (d) All of the above.

716. Generally which one of the following errors can be committed by a teacher during demonstration?
   (a) The mistake of making poor coordination between the topic and objectives of the demonstration.
   (b) To commit mistake of loosing motivation in the students.
   (c) The mistake of long continuous verbalism during the demonstration.
   (d) All of the above.

717. Which one of the following should not be repeated by the teacher during experimental demonstration?
   (a) It's good ... it's good—it should be happened.
   (b) Bravo! Its correct.
   (c) Good! we want to witness it.
   (d) All of the above.

718. The demonstration method is treated as scientific method because
   (a) A psychologist has propounded this method.

(b) It is a device of 'Learning by Doing'.
(c) It satisfies the curiosities of the students.
(d) It is a child-oriented method.

719. The defect of lecture-cum-demonstration method is
(a) It is not child-centred
(b) It creates obstacles in the development of scientific attitude
(c) It neglects direct experiences
(d) All of the above.

720. The Pioneer of Heuristic method is
(a) Prof. H.E. Armstrong
(b) Prof. D.S. Kothari
(c) Prof. J.A. Stevenson
(d) Prof. Leopold Thorndike

721. The main characteristic of demonstration method is
(a) Economic
(b) Activity-oriented
(c) Eliminating lurking dangers as conducted by expert teachers
(d) All of the above.

722. The original idea of Armstrong is
(a) The realistic aim of science is discovery through pure researches.
(b) The student's participation is compulsory in pure researches.
(c) The pure researches should be conducted on the basis of traditional researches.
(d) The future of a country is safe in its pure researches.

723. "In discovery methods of teaching the students are generally forced to work as scientists." This statements is propounded by
(a) John Dewey (b) John Little
(c) Armstrong (d) Theodore Bit

724. The word 'Heuristic' is derived from
(a) Greek word heurisco
(b) Latin word heuriri
(c) English word humorous
(d) None of the above.

725. The exact meaning of the term Heurisco is
(a) To find out
(b) To discover
(c) To derive conclusions
(d) None of the above.

726. H.E. Armstrong was working as a Professor of
(a) Chemistry (b) Physics
(c) Education (d) Philosophy

727. The equivalent term of Heuristic is Euriskein which is meant
(a) To visualise science by doing
(b) To observe science
(c) To discover science
(d) None of the above.

728. A teacher-centred method is converted into child-centred method, if a teacher can do
(a) It partially in a deliberate manner.
(b) It perfectly through insight.
(c) It in a reversible fashion.
(d) It in the presence of large audience of the students.

729. Through which teaching method the following qualities can be accommodated
1. The method which is against the tradition
2. The method which is having excellent observational methods
3. The method which is observable
4. The method which focuses upon 'self-activity'

The method is
(a) Demonstration method
(b) Project method

(c) Heuristic method
(d) Assignment method

730. Westaway has presumed Heuristic method as
(a) Only a teaching method
(b) Only a training method
(c) Only a research method
(d) Only a method mend for acquiring knowledge

731. The central principle of Heuristic method is
(a) Learning by doing.
(b) Learning through personal working.
(c) Learning through labour.
(d) Learning through experiences.

732. Which of the following psychological principles have been followed by Heuristic method?
(a) Principle of freedom
(b) Principle of experience
(c) Principle of activity
(d) All of the above

733. What is the role of a teacher in Heuristic method?
(a) Teacher as a friend
(b) Teacher as a stage-setter
(c) Teacher as creator of inductive method of teaching
(d) All of the above.

734. Heuristic method put its faith in
(a) To train a child in scientific discovery and he will explore the knowledge spontaneously.
(b) To train a child in scientific methodology, he will become a little scientist.
(c) To develop the scientific attitude in children then he will not need to join a school.
(d) All of the above.

735. "Heuristic method is a formative not an informative". It means
(a) it generates observational potentialities in children.
(b) it creates excitement for free thinking.
(c) it approves experimental evidence as the basis of knowledge.
(d) All of the above.

736. The main characteristics of Heuristic method is
(a) Learning by doing
(b) Training in scientific method
(c) Independence
(d) All of the above.

737. Which one of the following is appeared to be a defect of Heuristic method?
(a) It assumes child as a little scientist.
(b) It treated child as a father of man.
(c) It teaches child through playway.
(d) None of the above.

738. Which of the following steps you consider first when employing Heuristic method?
(a) The selection of a problems which can be solved through scientific method.
(b) The collection of detailed evidence about the problems which can be solved.
(c) Explanation of collected data.
(d) All of the above.

739. The application of Heuristic method in Indian classrooms is
(a) Highly practical (b) Impractical
(c) Practical (d) Can not say

740. In order to implement the Heuristic method of teaching in a classroom, which one of the following is suitable condition for it?
(a) The classroom of gifted students.
(b) The classroom with a gifted teachers.
(c) The classroom with proper lab and library.
(d) All of the above.

741. "Science is for a laboratory or a laboratory is for a science." Which part of the above statements is correct according to your point of view?
(a) Second part of the statement
(b) First part of the statement
(c) The complete statement
(d) None part of the above statement.

742. Which of the following method do you think suitable in case you are interested in imparting of the training of hard work and deep study habits in your students?
(a) Lecture method
(b) Demonstration method
(c) Heuristic method
(d) Project method

743. Heuristic method is not suitable in the condition of
(a) Traditional curriculum
(b) Traditional classroom
(c) Traditional system of instruction
(d) All of the above.

744. The best use of Heuristic method takes place in
(a) Science club
(b) Classroom teaching
(c) Educational excursions
(d) None of the above.

745. The relationship between teacher and student in Heuristic method of teaching can be compared as of
(a) Guide and follower
(b) Friends in a cooperative venture
(c) Participants on a mutual venture
(d) All of the above.

746. The students get freedom from the Home-work while teaching through Heuristic method because
(a) The teachers escapes from checking the Homework of the students.
(b) All the activities are finished in the laboratory itself.
(c) The method requires heavy studies on the part of the students instead of taking notes.
(d) All of the above.

747. The 'Problem' is defined as
(a) An unanswered question
(b) A mental burden
(c) A continuous tension
(d) All of the above.

748. The fundamental basis of problem-solving resembles with
(a) Scientific method
(b) Heuristic method
(c) Project method
(d) None of the above.

749. The learning of abilities in a free manner gives birth to
(a) Self-development
(b) Spontaneity
(c) Self-expression
(d) All of the above.

750. 'Problem-solving' is a method which develop a problem in the minds of the students who find its judicious solution in a excited manner. The definition is putforth by
(a) Rusk (b) Woodworm
(c) Armstrong (d) None of these.

751. Problem-solving is defined as
(a) A Psychological concept
(b) A method of teaching
(c) A reflective thinking
(d) All of the above.

752. Generally problem-solving behaviour originates in the situation of
(a) Unexpected difficulties
(b) Normal classroom
(c) Classroom teaching
(d) Routine life

753. The important step of problem-solving method is

(a) Defining of a problem
(b) Collection of adequate data
(c) Observation of the events
(d) All of the above.

754. When you will be teaching through problem-solving method which one of the following you consider first?
(a) The problem should be concerned with education.
(b) The problem should be useful for students.
(c) The problem should be suitable to the students mental level.
(d) All of the above.

755. The main characteristic of problem-solving method is
(a) Learning by doing
(b) Development of scientific attitude
(c) Independence
(d) All of the above.

756. The problem-solving method cannot be implemented in an ordinary school because
(a) It does not concerned with its regular curriculum.
(b) It takes much more time in experimentation.
(c) It give emphasis on learning through experimentation.
(d) All of the above.

757. Which one of the following is the demerit of problem-solving method?
(a) Retarded speed
(b) Emphasis on experimental work
(c) Non availability of textbooks
(d) All of the above.

758. Generally there is a popular belief about the problem-solving method in the minds of the teachers. It is that
(a) This method can be employed by the gifted teachers only in the practical classroom conditions.
(b) This method can be employed only in the class of gifted students.
(c) This method can be employed under both the above conditions.
(d) None of the above conditions are feasible for it.

759. School assignment is associated with
(a) The assignment given to students in their classes.
(b) The experiments perform by the students in their school lab.
(c) Both of the above.
(d) None of the above.

760. The types of assignment are of
(a) 2 (b) 3
(c) 4 (d) 6

761. Assignment method is a mixed version of
(a) Lecture cum demonstration method and individual laboratory work.
(b) Project method and lecture method.
(c) Heuristic method and problem-solving method.
(d) None of the above.

762. Which one of the following evaluation procedure has been employed by the teacher during the assignment method of teaching?
(a) Preparation of Progress cards of the students.
(b) Daily checking of the students' notes.
(c) Noting down of the students daily performance in the lab.
(d) Any measure of the above.

763. The meaning of Home Assignment is
(a) To complete the teachers' work at home by the students.
(b) To complete the work at home with the help of tutor.
(c) To prepare the detailed account of class work at home by the students.
(d) None of the above.

764. The aim of the assignment is
  (a) The development of scientific attitude.
  (b) The training in scientific method.
  (c) The discovery of scientific facts and deviation of its principles.
  (d) All of the above.

765. What is the criterion of an excellent assignment?
  (a) The assignment should be related the given topic to the student.
  (b) The assignment should be brief and purposeful.
  (c) The assignment should be changed according to availability of resources and existing conditions.
  (d) All of the above.

766. Suppose a student's assignment is not upto the mark of satisfaction. What steps would you take against him?
  (a) Deprived the students from that school assignment.
  (b) Compelling the student to complete his Home Assignment again.
  (c) Expulsion of the student from the school.
  (d) Fail the student.

767. During the Preparation of Assignment of teacher should prepare in a following manner
  (a) The complete curriculum should be broke down into the separate assignments in the very beginning of the session.
  (b) To select the objectives for the assignment.
  (c) To consider the student's age, grade, intelligence level, etc. while distributing (allotting) the assignments.
  (d) All of the above.

768. Which one of the following is not a sequential step of assignment employed in a practical classroom conditions?
  (a) Advance preparedness for an assignment.
  (b) Selection of the problems coming in mind during the teaching.
  (c) Evaluation of students based on that unit of instruction.
  (d) Distribution of assignments completed by the students in the previous session in order to give detailed idea to the students.

769. Generally the practice in vogue in adopting assignment method is that the teacher suggests a list of books references to the students should be related to their assignments properly. In your opinion who among the following will be an excellent teacher employing assignment method in above context?
  (a) The teacher who is giving a list of references to the students along with assignments.
  (b) The teacher who is not only suggesting the list of references but quite aware of it in verbatim and advising the students accordingly.
  (c) The teacher who gives the hypothetical lists of non-available references to the students along with the assignment to maintain his false impression on the students.
  (d) None of the above.

770. The important defect of Assignment method is
  (a) Non-availability of the textbooks
  (b) Need of adequate library
  (c) Need of well-equipped laboratory
  (d) All of the above.

771. The pioneer of Project method is
  (a) John Dewey
  (b) W.A. Kilpatrick
  (c) Both of the above.
  (d) None of the above.

772. The central quality of Assignment method is
(a) students learning by doing taken place.
(b) the students develop the habit of hardwork.
(c) the method is economic.
(d) it saves teachers from exclusive evaluation.

773. Assignment method is suitable for
(a) High school and Intermediate students.
(b) Higher education students.
(c) University students.
(d) All of the above levels of students.

774. The basic philosophy of Project method is
(a) Progressivism (b) Idealism
(c) Pragmatism (d) Individualism

775. "Project is a problematic work which is completed under its natural situations in a spontaneous manner." This statements was put forth by
(a) J.A. Stevenson (b) Kilpatrick
(c) Ballard (d) None of these.

776. Which one of the following is not considered under the Project method?
(a) Considerations of curriculum according to child.
(b) Consideration of learning material according to child.
(c) Considerations on techniques according to child.
(d) All of the above.

777. The meaning of learning by living is
(a) The child learns through his own life because it is the collection of small projects.
(b) The child himself prepares the projects and completes them on the basis of his experiences.
(c) The child becomes trained through his experiences during his own life span.
(d) The training of life-oriented skills in imparted to the child.

778. Project method is based on the multi-disciplinarian approach in order to arrive at the conclusion. This important feature of project method is called
(a) Quality of Correlation
(b) Quality of Association
(c) Quality of mutual interdependence
(d) Quality of Abstract thinking

779. In project method emphasis is laid down on
(a) Learning by doing
(b) Learning by living
(c) Learning by cooperation and competition
(d) All of the above.

780. The steps of Project method are given here in a jumbled state as following
1. Construction of situations
2. Planning
3. Evaluation
4. Preparation of record
5. Implementation

Which of the following alternative state the correct sequence of Project method?
(a) 1, 2, 3, 4, 5 (b) 1, 2, 5, 3, 4
(c) 5, 4, 3, 2, 1 (d) 5, 3, 2, 1, 4

781. The most important characteristics of Project method is
(a) Child-centredness
(b) Training in scientific method
(c) Learning of science through playing
(d) Emphasis on democratic principle

782. The nature of the Project should be
(a) Most difficult (b) Most early
(c) Average level (d) Cann't say

783. The characteristics of an excellent Project is
(a) Purposiveness
(b) Favourable activities for focusing children's attention
(c) Freedom to work to children
(d) All of the above.

784. The role of a teacher in Project method is
(a) Like a friend
(b) Like a guide
(c) Like a co-worker
(d) All of the above.

785. Which one of the following Law of learning is fulfilled through project method?
(a) Law of readiness
(b) Law of exercise
(c) Law of effect
(d) All of the above.

786. The main objective of the Discussion method is
(a) To develop the method of self-reading and understanding in children.
(b) To inspire the children to make friendly relations with the teacher.
(c) To develop self-confidence in children.
(d) None of the above.

787. The greatest limitation of Project method is
(a) Wasting of time
(b) Extra work-load on a teacher
(c) High expectation from a teacher
(d) All of the above.

788. Project should be selected by
(a) The teachers only
(b) The students only
(c) Both of the above.
(d) None of the above.

789. The Discussion method is implemented
(a) First of all the teacher presents the background of the topic and its general explanation.
(b) Afterwards, the students are free for making group studies and discussions on the topic.
(c) The teacher provides the reference lists kept in school library.
(d) Then the teacher started discussions and thus all the above steps belong to this method.

790. Which one of the following consideration should be kept in mind by the teacher when employing discussion method?
(a) The topic should not be very easy or difficult.
(b) The students should be advised to read all the related references.
(c) The discussion should not be changed in a debate.
(d) All of the above.

791. The popular form of the Project method is
(a) Preparation of model by the students.
(b) To keep busy the children in their summer holidays.
(c) To distribute some projects among the students so that they can complete it in their summer vacations.
(d) All of the above.

792. In Inductive method one should move
(a) From specific example to generalisation.
(b) From general to specific.
(c) Both of the above.
(d) None of the above.

793. When principles, theories and generalisations are presented to the students and they verify them with the help of specific example, this method is called as
(a) Deductive method
(b) Inductive method
(c) Inductive-deductive method
(d) None of the above.

794. The Deductive method is applied in a reasoned manner in
   (a) a small group of children in lower grades who do not have the ability of exploration of scientific facts and unable to give reasons for them.
   (b) a group of adult students studying in higher grades who get the subject matter in a readily state.
   (c) a group of the children who follow short-cuts in their life and do not have the habit of hardworking.
   (d) All the classes where the possibilities of experimentations are negligible.

795. The advantage of Inductive method is
   (a) development of scientific attitude
   (b) development of reasoning
   (c) development of study habits
   (d) All of the above.

796. Which one of the following maxim is used in Deductive method of teaching?
   (a) From general to specific
   (b) From abstract to concrete
   (c) Both of the above.
   (d) None of the above.

797. The greatest limitation of the Deductive method is that
   (a) It is unpsychological method.
   (b) It gives emphasis on memory.
   (c) It is boring and difficult.
   (d) It does not evolve original thinking in children.

798. Inductive and deductive teaching methods are
   (a) Two separate methods.
   (b) Separate methods but dependent on each other.
   (c) Compensatory to each other.
   (d) Independent from each other.

799. Which one of the following precautions should be kept in mind by the teacher while selecting a teaching method?
   (a) The teaching method should be befitting with the teaching objectives in complete manner.
   (b) The teaching method should be interactive with external environment of the students.
   (c) The teaching method should impart adequate opportunities to the children from thinking, experimenting, and reasoning, etc.
   (d) All of the above.

800. Inductive and deductive methods are popularly used in
   (a) Maths teaching
   (b) Science teaching
   (c) Grammar teaching
   (d) All of the above.

801. The teacher should develop mastery over the teaching methods during their tenure of teaching profession in
   (a) Single method of teaching
   (b) More than one methods
   (c) All the methods
   (d) Cann't say

802. A teaching method must be compatible with the following quality.
   (a) To generate interest and motivation for learning in children.
   (b) To communicate informations in organised and systematic manner to the students.
   (c) To make teaching method more dynamic in nature.
   (d) All of the above.

803. In Indian scenario the position of child-centred innovative methods is
   (a) Pitiable...because there is least possibilities to implement them.
   (b) Psythetic...because there is no room for syllabus and laboratory according to them.

(c) Debatable...because the superficial works conducted by the students are generally rated as assignments, projects and exploratory excursions.
(d) All the above are correct statements.

804. A teaching method is a
(a) Ruling over the young mind by a mature mind.
(b) Exposure of young mind to external world in order to realize specific knowledge.
(c) Style of teaching adopted by a special teacher.
(d) Way of communicating to young mind.

805. Teacher-centred methods lay its emphasis on
(a) Central position of the teacher in the class.
(b) Teacher's table in the centre of the class.
(c) Teacher's highest dignity without caring for students.
(d) Teacher's attention focused on the class.

806. Teaching is an art presumes that
(a) No training is essential for teaching profession.
(b) Teaching profession is everybody's cup of tea.
(c) Teaching can be taught in artistic fashion.
(d) None of the above.

807. Teacher-centred method does not have the quality of
(a) Teacher dominance over the class.
(b) Rigorous discipline in the class.
(c) One-way teaching.
(d) Sympathetic attitude with the class.

808. Byron and Massialas has putforth the Dimensional approach as
(a) Substantive Dimension
(b) Procedural Dimension
(c) Environmental Dimension
(d) All of the above Dimension.

809. Pupil-centred method means
(a) Pupile-oriented teaching method
(b) Child-supportive method
(c) Liberal learning
(d) All of the above.

810. Procedural dimensions does not include the quality of
(a) Formal and Restrictive environment
(b) Teacher's dominance
(c) Memorization and Repetition
(d) Science of facts and information

811. The inherent Psychological principles of Heuristic method is
(a) Principle of freedom
(b) Principle of experience
(c) Principle of purposefulness
(d) All of the above.

812. The chief advantage of Heuristic method is
(a) Development of scientific and critical attitude.
(b) Development of learning by doing.
(c) Development of habits of hand work.
(d) All of the above.

813. During the application of Heuristic method it is desired from a teacher
(a) He must be well-prepared in advance.
(b) He must has the spirit and motivation.
(c) He should be adepted to the art of questionning.
(d) All of the above.

814. The main disadvantage of Heuristic method is
(a) High expectations from small students.
(b) Inadequate from curriculum point of view.

(c) The textbooks do not follow this method.
(d) All of the above.

815. Who is the chief exponent and modifier of the project method in recent time?
(a) W.H. Kilpatric and J.A. Stevenson
(b) W.H. Clarke and J.A. Stevenson
(c) Sir Percy Nunn and J.A. Stevenson
(d) John Dewey and Jean Sartre

816. Assignment method can be defined as
(a) The division of the prescribed course into a number of well connected units.
(b) The division of the prescribed course into a number of will programmed units.
(c) The division of the prescribed course in order of difficulty either in arcending form or discending form.
(d) The division of the prescribed course in all the as one bases in small units.

817. Assignment method of teaching is the mixture of
(a) Lecture-cum-demonstration method and individual has work.
(b) Lecture-cum-demonstration method and inductive-deductive method.
(c) Lecture-cum-demonstration and Heuristic method.
(d) None of the above.

818. The main advantage of Assignment method is
(a) It follows the principle of learning by doing.
(b) It is comparatively economical in nature.
(c) It develops scientific attitude.
(d) All of the above.

819. What is meant by the term project?
(a) A unit of activity in which pupils are made responsible for planning and purposing.
(b) A problematic art carried out for completion in its natural settings.
(c) A whole-hearted purposeful activity proceeding in a social environment.
(d) All of the above.

820. Which one of the following does not work as criteria of a good assignment?
(a) An assignment should be in relation to the topic under discussion and not in isolation from it.
(b) It should be clear in its purpose and should aim at realising those objectives.
(c) It should be presented in a way that promotes reflective thinking and giving freedom to students to discover things for themselves.
(d) All of the above.

821. Here below the steps of Project method have been jumbled down. Select the correct alternative which is representing precise arrangement of these steps
1. Providing a situation
2. Choosing and purposing
3. Evaluating
4. Recording
5. Executing

(a) 1, 2, 3, 4, 5 (b) 1, 2, 5, 3, 4
(c) 1, 3, 5, 2, 4 (d) 1, 5, 2, 4, 3

822. The project is based on the laws of
(a) Learning
(b) Teaching
(c) Thinking
(d) Interest and Attention

823. Which of the following alternative is representing a correct criterions of a good project?
(a) The project should import gainful learning.
(b) The project should be economical in time, money and labour.

(c) The project should be interesting and giving opportunities for recreation.
(d) The project should be realistic and challenging.

824. Which one of the following is the great disadvantage of project method?
(a) It promotes learning by self-ability
(b) It promotes quality of learn
(c) It is syllabus hampering method
(d) It gives importance to rote memory

825. Inductive and deductive methods are
(a) Independent methods
(b) Complementary to each other
(c) Dependent on each other
(d) None of the above.

826. What consideration on priority basis do you keep in mind about discussion method?
(a) Adequate class environment facilitating serious discussion among the students.
(b) A turn of debates to the normal discussion.
(c) Leave aside the unexpressive students in the class.
(d) Keep the discussion at the level of the students mental level.

827. Inductive method of teaching one should proceed from
(a) Rules or Laws to examples
(b) Examples to formulation of laws
(c) Assumptions to hypothesization
(d) Imagination to concretisation

828. The criterion point for evaluation is
(a) The extent to which specified educational objectives are being attained.
(b) The effectiveness of the learning experiences provided in the classroom.
(c) How will the goal of education have been accomplished.
(d) All of the above.

829. Summative evaluation is related to
(a) Decision-making process at the level of development of the learner.
(b) Judgement-making process about a finished product or process at the end of the year/session.
(c) Student's performances during continuous system of examination.
(d) None of the above.

830. Evaluation can be classified into
(a) 3 types (b) 2 types
(c) 4 types (d) 6 types

831. The steps of evaluation process are given in jumbled form as below. Select the correct alternative showing precise arrangement
1. Formulation of objectives
2. Clarifying and defining of objectives
3. Devising suitable assessment procedure
4. Evaluating the outcomes
5. Developing appropriate learning experiences

(a) 1, 2, 3, 4, 5 (b) 1, 2, 5, 3, 4
(c) 1, 2, 4, 5, 3 (d) 1, 2, 3, 5, 4

832. Which one of the following figure precisely represents the relationship among
1. Objectives of Teaching
2. Methods of Teaching
3. Curriculum
4. Tools and Techniques of Evaluation

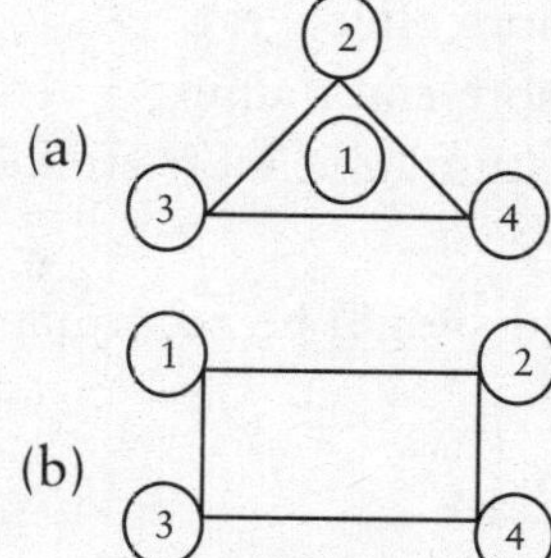

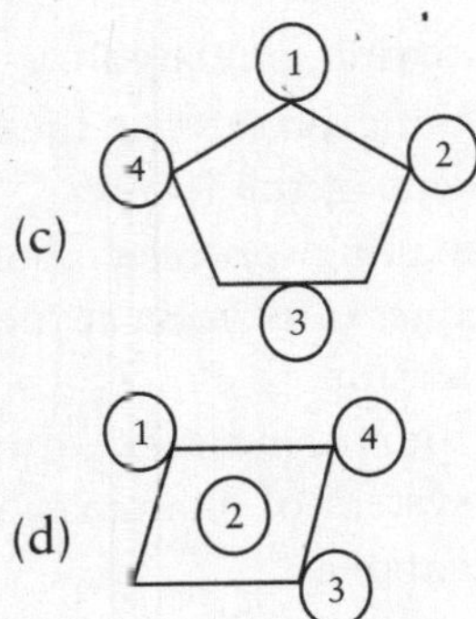

833. Which one of the following is not a projective technique?
   (a) Rorschach Ink Blot Test
   (b) Thematic Apperception Test
   (c) Word Association Test
   (d) Personals inventories

834. Which one of the following figure is representing paedocentric method?

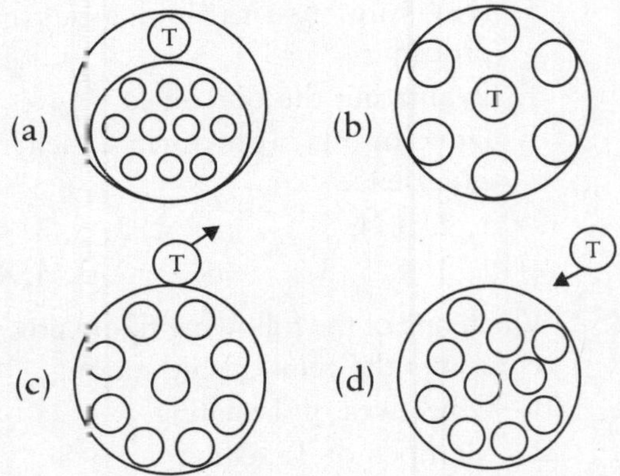

835. Teaching aids are used in teaching for making a
   (a) Teaching more effective
   (b) Teaching more entertaining
   (c) Teaching natural and more useful
   (d) All of the above.

836. The teaching aid should be according to
   (a) Students
   (b) Teachers
   (c) Class
   (d) Teaching objectives

837. Teacher himself works as an audio-visual material (aid) because
   (a) He/she makes himself/herself more beautiful in the class.
   (b) He/she takes help of postures and body language to make teaching more comprehensible.
   (c) He/she makes dramatising roles in the class.
   (d) He/she works as a picture on T.V. screen.

838. Which one of the following is not an application of teaching aid?
   (a) To make ornamental teaching
   (b) To enrich teaching
   (c) To promote teaching
   (d) To give freedom to teacher

839. Audio-visual aids are called as
   (a) Teaching aids
   (b) Toileteries (accessories)
   (c) Sensory aids
   (d) None of the above.

840. The audio-visual aid works as a
   (a) Catalyst (b) Medium
   (c) End (d) None of these

841. Audio-visual aids leave its effect because
   (a) It is based on direct experiences
   (b) It is attractive and creates excitement
   (c) It follows scientific principles
   (d) All of the above.

842. Which one of the following is the adequate definitions of audio-visual aids?
   (a) The aid which is assisting the oral or written delivery of a teacher in the class.
   (b) The aid which stimulates (catalyses) the teaching-learning process.
   (c) The aid which focuses the attention and interest of the students.
   (d) All of the above.

843. If teaching material is most effective and it is interwoven effectively with the lesson planning then it results into
(a) Replacement of a teacher in the class.
(b) Exit of students from the class.
(c) Exit of examiners out of Examination Hall.
(d) None of the above.

844. The audio-visual aid helps in
(a) Permanent learning
(b) Creating interest
(c) Making teaching more effective
(d) All of the above.

845. Audio-visual aids are
(a) Those in which the eyes and ears both sensory organs becomes more sensitive in order to participate in teaching process.
(b) Those where primary importance is laid down on eyes only.
(c) Those which influences all the sensory organs.
(d) None of the above.

846. Which one of the following objective does not associated with teaching aids?
(a) To determine the audio-visual aids by keeping in mind individual differences in the class.
(b) To make advertisements of attractive and miraculous events for students.
(c) To present difficult concepts in simpler forms for the students.
(d) To make the students comparatively more active and dynamic.

847. The fundamental objective of audio-visual aid is
(a) To create interest in students.
(b) To enhance retention of the learned material in the students.
(c) To impart innovative knowledge to students.
(d) All of the above.

848. The audio-visual aids make a content easier, comprehensible and clear because
(a) It changes abstract concepts into concrete ones.
(b) It expresses the difficult concepts in a easier form.
(c) It satisfies the students' curiosity according to their mental levels.
(d) All of the above.

849. The chief characteristic of the audio-visual aid is
(a) To minimise the teacher's verbalism.
(b) To impart empirical knowledge.
(c) To develop scientific attitude.
(d) All of the above.

850. Generally audio-visual aids enhance
(a) Retention of the students.
(b) Attention of the students.
(c) Recognition of the students.
(d) All of the above.

851. During teaching more benefits from audio-visual aids are fetched by
(a) The teachers only because they save themselves from verbal contradictions with the students.
(b) The students only because they learn through play-way method.
(c) Both of the above.
(d) None of the above.

852. We get the following amount of knowledge through our eyes
(a) 84 percent (b) 64 percent
(c) 16 percent (d) 14 percent

853. Which one of the following quality of the audio-visual aid, you prefer to leave during their application?
(a) Accuracy (b) Realism
(c) High cost (d) Interest

854. The significance of audio-visual aids is
(a) To stabilise motivation in learning process.

(b) To make teaching-learning more effective attractive and skillful.
(c) To pay attention on individual differences.
(d) All of the above.

855. The meaning of adaptability of the audio-visual aid is
(a) The audio-visual aid should be according to the students' mental level.
(b) The audio-visual aid should be according to teachers, capabilities.
(c) The audio-visual aid should be according to nature of content.
(d) All of the above.

856. The utility of audio-visual aid in your opinion is as following.
(a) It enhances the beauty of the classroom.
(b) It hides the weaknesses of the teacher.
(c) It makes teaching work more easier.
(d) It makes teaching-learning more attractive.

857. "Content should be taught instead of audiovisual aids."
The meaning of this phrase is
(a) The teacher should keep in mind his objective during the teaching.
(b) The teacher should furnish the general information about the teaching aid during his teaching.
(c) The teacher should make efforts in order to clarify the teaching objectives with the help of audio-visual aids.
(d) None of the above.

858. The audio-visual aid leaves important effect because these are
(a) Associated with our sensory organs.
(b) Associated with eyes which gives us detail information of our external would and these are associated with the audiovisual aids.
(c) Providing aesthetic value to the class.
(d) None of the above.

859. Which one of the following precautions must be observed by a teacher before entering into the class with audio-visual aids?
(a) Keep them confidential.
(b) Cover them properly before making a display.
(c) Open them only before their demonstration.
(d) All of the above.

860. The audio aids include
(a) Radio and tape recorder
(b) Television and VCR
(c) Film and slides
(d) None of the above.

861. The topmost point of a Experience cone has
(a) Abstract teaching aids
(b) Concrete teaching aids
(c) Exhibiting material (aids)
(d) None of the above.

862. The contribution of Edgar Dale is
(a) Cone of Experience
(b) Cycle of Experience
(c) Empirical learning curve
(d) Empirical teaching

863. Which one of the following you will get in Experience cone of Edgar Dale?
(a) Direct purposive experiences
(b) Dramatic co-operation
(c) Film
(d) Visual symbols

864. The teaching aids are categorised on the basis of projection as
(a) Projected and non-projected aids
(b) Visual, audio and audio-visual aids
(c) Software and Hardware
(d) None of the above.

865. Which one of the following important precautions would you like to take during the selection of audio-visual aids?
(a) It should be according to mental level of the student
(b) It must be helpful in completion of learning objectives
(c) It must be enrich students' interests
(d) All of the above.

866. The direct experiences of children are related to
(a) Excursions
(b) Environmental interactions
(c) Demonstrations of experiments
(d) All of the above.

867. When we compare all the three types of teaching aids viz., audio, video and audio-visual aids, then the most effective teaching aid is
(a) Audio aids
(b) Visual aids
(c) Audio-visual aids
(d) None of the above.

868. The arrangement in the Experience cone has been made of
(a) Audio-visual aids
(b) The increasing order of abstractness of audio-visual aids
(c) Both of the above.
(d) None of the above.

869. Suppose you have limited resources then which one of the following do you keep on top priority?
(a) Blackboard, Realistic objects, Model and Slide
(b) Museum, Radio, TV, and Slide Projector
(c) Teaching games, Film projectors and Tape recorder
(d) TV, VCR, Computer and Teaching Machine

870. The Blackboard is a
(a) Visual aid
(b) Audio aid
(c) Audio-visual aid
(d) None of the above.

871. Blackboard is required for
(a) The students (b) The teacher
(c) The principal (d) None of these

872. A teacher's personality is called a miror image of the class for
(a) Its Blackboard
(b) The work done on Blackboard
(c) His hand writing
(d) None of the above.

873. The blackboard can be used for
(a) Writing of the lesson's summary
(b) The brief explanation of the lesson taught
(c) Drawing of the different apparatus and equipments
(d) All of the above.

874. Who among the following scientists is associated with Blackboard?
(a) William James (b) James William
(c) James Watt (d) James Watson

875. Which of the following teaching aid is compulsorily recommended in operation Blackboard?
(a) Blackboard chalk
(b) Sitting rags and chalk
(c) Textbooks and note books
(d) All of the above.

876. The Roll-up Blackboard can be used
(a) By teacher trainees only
(b) By regular teachers only
(c) By special teachers only
(d) For doing class work in advance patiently

877. The main types of Blackboard are

(a) Wooden Blackboards
(b) Cement Blackboards
(c) Glass Blackboards
(d) All of the above.

878. When the teacher is doing writing work on the Blackboard it is not required that he
(a) Keeps vigil on the class
(b) Bothers about classroom discipline
(c) Supervises the class unnecessarily
(d) Does not keeping his own consciousness

879. The teacher himself function as a teaching material if he has the quality of
(a) Good hand
(b) Good speech
(c) Both of the above.
(d) None of the above.

880. If you have good hand in routine conditions then it can be assumed that your blackboard hand writing should be
(a) Good (b) Average
(c) Poor (d) Cann't say

881. The Polished Rexin Blackboard is called
(a) Roll-up Blackboard
(b) Mobile Blackboard
(c) Rexin Blackboard
(d) None of the above.

882. The teacher's opinion is that
(a) To write date, topic and subject, etc. on the Blackboard in the beginning is the sheer wastage of time.
(b) To write anything on the Black-board is harmful for ones fingers and clothes.
(c) If you are a teacher you are bounded to do maximum work on the Blackboard.
(d) The Blackboard teachers assumes themselves as excellent teachers.

883. Which one of the following precautions you will take during work on the Blackboard?
(a) Do not speak when facing towards Blackboard.
(b) Write the letter of 2-2½ cm. on Blackboard so that last student of the class can read it easily.
(c) Draw the figures with coloured chalk stick.
(d) All of the above.

884. "When you are moving out of the class leave your Blackboard as clear as you expect from your colleagues." The meaning of the above phrase is
(a) Always keep your Blackboard neat and clean.
(b) You must write on the Blackboard but clean it when the work is over.
(c) Don't think classroom Blackboard as your personal property.
(d) I think, after your class your colleague deserves a neat and clean Blackboard in the class.

885. The proportion angle between teacher's body posture and the Blackboard should be
(a) 45° approximately
(b) 30° approximately
(c) 120° approximately
(d) 90° approximately

886. Which one of the following is correct statement in the use of real objects as teaching aids?
(a) You will not demonstrate lively the living animals which can create nuisance or harm for the class viz., dog, monkey, cat, etc.
(b) You will demonstrate the plants which can be exhibited easily.
(c) You will like to demonstrate those real objects which are beyond the experiential limits of the students but can be demonstrated easily in the class.
(d) Both (b) and (c) are correct statements.

887. The participation of the students in the Blackboard work should be of
 (a) Minimum level (b) Maximum level
 (c) Ordinary level (d) Cannot say

888. The meaning of model is
 (a) Such a copy of the real object which can not be feasible to demonstrate in real way in the class.
 (b) Only a copy of a real object.
 (c) Only exhibiting object.
 (d) The persons associated with fashion advertisements.

889. Slides are prepared with the objective of the
 (a) study of the microbes in laboratory.
 (b) study of the viruses causing fatal diseases.
 (c) study of invisible real objects/animals in order to study them through microscope.
 (d) None of the above.

890. The advantages of a model in teaching is
 (a) Enhancing retention and comprehension of a real object in miniature form.
 (b) Enhancing aesthetic sense in a classroom.
 (c) Enhancing feelings of self-satisfaction.
 (d) None of the above.

891. On which types of films the photographic slides are prepared?
 (a) On simple photographic films available in market.
 (b) On photographic films especially mend for preparation of slides.
 (c) Through photographic cameras.
 (d) None of the above.

892. Which of the following you keep in mind for preparations a chart
 (a) It should be coloured and attractive.
 (b) It should be purposeful.
 (c) It should be demonstrable.
 (d) All the above characteristics should be there in it.

893. The preparedness of a classroom before exhibiting a film-strip should be in order of
 (a) Comprehensive discussions on the related subject-matter in advance.
 (b) Pre-teaching of the content to be exhibited through film-strip.
 (c) Detailed advance study of the content to be exhibited.
 (d) None of the above.

894. Film strip as a teaching aid is
 (a) Highly effective (b) Effective only
 (c) Non-effective (d) Can't say

895. Graph as a teaching aid has the quality which is related to
 (a) Vision
 (b) Audition
 (c) Audition and vision both
 (d) None of the above.

896. Documentary films are made in order to
 (a) Make a teaching-learning process more effective.
 (b) Give the knowledge about a core event or related phenomenon.
 (c) Describe the life achievements of a politician.
 (d) None of the above.

897. Graph should be prepared for
 (a) Effective teaching
 (b) Enhancing aesthetic sense
 (c) Focusing one's attention
 (d) None of the above.

898. The graph with multi angles is called
 (a) Polygon (b) Polyangle
 (c) Pie graph (d) Peripheral graph

899. If you are interested in displaying the constituents of air through experimental

demonstration, the suitable graphic display should be

(a) Pie graph (b) Bar diagram
(c) Polygon (d) None of these.

900. If you are interesting in developing a skill of drawing of a Beaker in your students then how would you like to impart training of this skill?

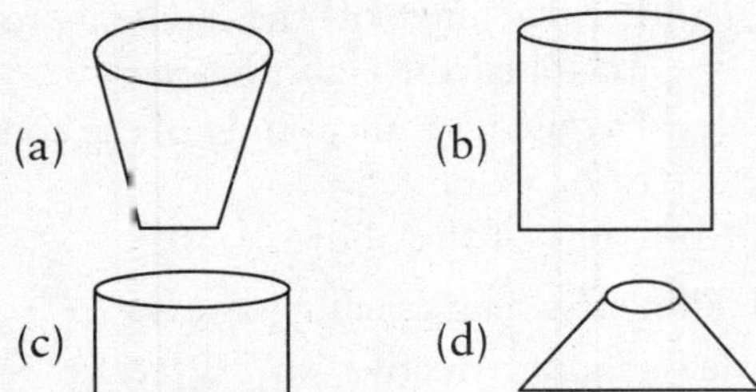

901. Bar Graphs are prepared for
(a) Classifying a variable in appropriate manner.
(b) Finding relationship between two variables.
(c) For completing the data with aesthetic sense.
(d) None of the above.

902. Which of the following precautions you would like to keep in mind while you are demonstrating a chart in the class?
(a) It should be related with your topic and having adequate relevance.
(b) It should be natural and realistic in appearance.
(c) It must be accurate and in precise proportion.
(d) All of the above.

903. The map is a rarest kind of visual aid because it tells about
(a) The exact distance between two places.
(b) The exact area of the specific place (country, region or state).
(c) The exact indication of physical climate of a particular place.
(d) All of the above.

904. Which one of the following aids has the long-lasting impact on teaching?
(a) When you will himself draw a diagram and also motivate the students to draw them.
(b) When you will bring a beautiful figure drawn on a roll-up Board.
(c) When you fetch some related diagram from the lab and use it as a teaching aid.
(d) When you will inform the students to draw the diagram from their home in advance.

905. A teacher should use the diagrams in the class
(a) On compulsorily basis in order to enhance of the attraction.
(b) Occasionally so that the motivation of the students may persist.
(c) Only whenever required and befitting the content.
(d) Whenever the teacher has his own will to teach through diagrams.

906. In a school museum we can collect
(a) All types of visual material.
(b) All types of audio-visual material.
(c) All subjects' visual material which has been organised and displayed properly.
(d) None of the above.

907. The diagrams should be used in the class according to
(a) Mental level of the students
(b) Mental abilities of the students
(c) Interests of the students
(d) All of the above.

908. Museums are built in order to satisfy students urges of first-hand experience and these make a teaching-learning process
(a) Easy and interesting
(b) Direct and experiential

(c) Motivating and skillful
(d) All of the above.

909. The academically advantageous museum is
(a) General public museum
(b) Local museum
(c) School museum
(d) All of the above.

910. Generally when more than two diagrams are drawn at once, the drawing sequence, kept in one's mind should be
(a) From right to left
(b) From left to right
(c) In any order without difficulty
(d) From above to below

911. The exhibition is advantageous to the school because
(a) It gives extra income to the school.
(b) It promote advertisement of the school without any cost.
(c) It entertains the school personnels free of cost.
(d) All of the above.

912. The focal point of arranging a museum is
(a) All the articles are arranged in an organised and sequential fashion.
(b) All the things have proper tag to give its detailed information.
(c) Every article should be kept in such a order so that it may remain away from unnecessary touches by the visitors.
(d) All of the above.

913. While you are organising an exhibition the central idea one should keep in mind is that
(a) It should be helpful to the students.
(b) It should keep the teacher's welfare.
(c) It should be helpful for a school principal.
(d) It should be in order to keep school personnel's welfare.

914. The Bulletin Board is used
(a) To exhibit school's programmes.
(b) To exhibit collection of information from different newspapers.
(c) To communicate educational, social and cultural informations.
(d) All of the above.

915. The size of a slide is
(a) 35 mm (b) 55 mm
(c) 45 mm (d) 50 mm

916. The teacher should seek the help of the students in order to organise a Bulletin Board by giving them responsibilities of
(a) Collection of the news on a given theme.
(b) Editing of the news on a given theme.
(c) Systematic organisation of the content.
(d) All of the above.

917. Generally Flannel Boards are prepared by
(a) Flannel
(b) Cotton (rugged) cloth
(c) Any sort of cloth
(d) Rubber sheets

918. The article's image projected through overhead projector is seen
(a) On the head of the speaker.
(b) On the head and backside of the speaker.
(c) On the head and backside of the speaker on a screen.
(d) None of the above.

919. Radio lessons should be broadcast
(a) After advance planning.
(b) After arranging radios in the classes.
(c) After giving advance information to the students.
(d) All of the above.

920. The machine which is being used for exhibiting slides is called
(a) Film projector (b) Slide projector
(c) Tape recorder (d) None of these.

921. The important point to be considered for organising an exhibition is
(a) It should be focused on a centralised theme.
(b) It should be organised with the help of the students.
(c) It should be implemented according to advance planning.
(d) All of the above.

922. Which one of the following is the most important audio-aid?
(a) Radio (b) Loudspeaker
(c) T.V. (d) Walky-Talky

923. The teacher makes an attempt along with the projection of the slide
(a) Adequate and relevant mixing of the exhibit in teaching.
(b) Entertainment of the students.
(c) Motivation of the students.
(d) None of the above.

924. Bulletin Board and Flannel Board are
(a) One and same things.
(b) Different in form and colour.
(c) Different from the point of view of the material to be displayed.
(d) Can't say.

925. OHP should be used when a teacher is interested in
(a) Explaining the drawings of some difficult diagrams.
(b) Explaining the difficult subject-matter.
(c) Enlarging the small things on a screen.
(d) All of the above.

926. Magic Lalterin is called
(a) Episcope (b) Diascope
(c) Overscope (d) Telescope

927. What is meant by an Epidiascope?
(a) An audio-visual apparatus.
(b) The projector which mend for projecting transparent and opaque things.
(c) A suitable fusion of Episcope and Diascope.
(d) The exhibition of the demonstrable articles in large size.

928. Magic Lalterin is mostly used in
(a) Rural regions
(b) Urban regions
(c) Metropolitan cities
(d) None of the above.

929. Which one of the following important precautions would you like to keep in mind on the basis of priority while you are using a OHP?
(a) Switch on the bulb while you use it and put off it immediately.
(b) To run the blower during you use it.
(c) Don't disturb the focal mirror frequently.
(d) Think properly and visualize your screen in order to satisfy the audience through adequate projection of the content.

930. Through OHP the subject-matter is prepared on
(a) Polythene sheets
(b) Standard transparencies
(c) Ordinary transparencies
(d) Rice paper

931. The film projectors generally used in schools are of
(a) 8 mm size (b) 16 mm size
(c) 24 mm size (d) Both (a) and (b)

932. The advantage of an Epidiascope is
(a) To enlarge the size of the diagrams printed in books or magazines.
(b) To prepare charts.
(c) Both of the above.
(d) None of the above.

933. 'Edusat' is a
(a) Educational satellite
(b) Instructional satellite

(c) Instructional technology
(d) Instructional device

934. The instrument generally used to write on a transparency is
(a) Permanent ink pen
(b) Ordinary sketch pen
(c) Ordinary ink pen
(d) None of the above.

935. The contribution of Television in teaching is
(a) Very high (b) Ordinary
(c) High (d) Zero

936. The Educational Television programme is related to
(a) Health
(b) Culture
(c) General awareness
(d) All of the above.

937. Which one of the following measures should be taken for employing TV network in the field of education?
(a) The transmission of TV content in all the schools under strict supervision of the teachers.
(b) The proper possibilities of the making advance arrangements of educational TV in rural areas.
(c) The proper utilisation of the time allotted to TV viewing by all the schools.
(d) All of the above.

938. The traditional Television has a great demerit of
(a) The lacking in interactions between the students and the teachers.
(b) Teacher's passive attitude towards teaching.
(c) Inability of teachers to teach through this media.
(d) Cannot say.

939. Television imparts teaching of
(a) Realistic nature
(b) Comprehensive nature
(c) Proper entertainment
(d) All of the above

940. Computer is a
(a) Boon for teaching
(b) Curse for teaching
(c) Revolution in teaching
(d) Ruining the teaching

941. The importance of Audio-visual aids in
(a) It develops scientific attitude in children.
(b) It works as attention compelling.
(c) It enhances effective learning.
(d) All of the above.

942. Who is called the father of Teaching machine?
(a) B.F. Skinner
(b) S.S. Pressey
(c) Carl Gustav Jung
(d) McDonald

943. The highest contribution of the sensory organ in effective learning belongs to
(a) Sense of Taste
(b) Sense of Hearing
(c) Sense of Seeing
(d) Sense of Touch

944. Through teaching aid the teaching can be done
(a) Very effectively
(b) Without teacher (teacher's substitution)
(c) In a amazing way
(d) In dishonouring manner

945. Which of the following principle would you like to follow in selection of the audio-visual aids?
(a) It should be well-integrated with learning.
(b) It should satisfy all the needs of the learners.

(c) It should be highly motivational in nature.
(d) All of the above.

946. The credit of sharing history of teaching aids goes to
(a) Rousseau, Froebel and Montessori
(b) Socrates, Plato and Aristotle
(c) Dewey, Nunn and Sartre
(d) Mahatma Gandhi, Gokhale, and Sarojini Naidu.

947. Which of the following principle should be followed by a teacher in the class during application of teaching aids?
(a) Active participation of the student desired.
(b) Enjoyment of the students should be kept in mind.
(c) Evaluation does not carried out during application.
(d) None of the above.

948. Under which condition the visual aid appears to be more suitable?
(a) When a subject is lying far too distant place.
(b) When the subject is having historical importance.
(c) When the subject is too small to visible the class.
(d) All of the above.

949. When you are employing Radio as an teaching aid, what precautionary measure do you like to adopt?
(a) Expert in formulating the Radio-programme.
(b) Radio programme must be well-integrated with the real content.
(c) Some other aids can be incorporated.
(d) All of the above.

950. Effective use of Blackboard exhibits
(a) Neat and bold writing
(b) Uniform and straight living
(c) Brief and continuous whole of the content
(d) All of the above.

951. Which one of the following is not classified under the Graphic aids?
(a) Photograph (b) Graphs
(c) Bulletin boards (d) Maps

952. The chief advantage of TV as an audio-visual aid is
(a) It gives live and real pictures.
(b) It sustains zeal and motivation in students.
(c) It helps in transmitting the content throughout country at a time.
(d) All of the above.

953. The central value point of using chart in the classroom is
(a) Elucidating the content
(b) Stimulating interest
(c) Attention-fetching
(d) All of the above.

954. Edgar Dale is famous for
(a) Experience come
(b) Salam Namste Movie
(c) Learning Syndrome
(d) None of the above.

955. The base of Edgar's Pyramid is
(a) Direct learning through first hand experiences.
(b) Vicarious learning through Audio-Visual aids.
(c) Vicarious learning through words and symbols.
(d) None of the above.

956. In Edgar Dale's cone of Experience the abstractive is highest at
(a) The point of upward angle
(b) The point of right-hand side angle
(c) The point of left-hand side angle
(d) None of the above.

957. The meaning of the word Evaluation is
(a) Quantitative description of individual/ students' achievement.
(b) Quantitative description of the one's abilities and achievement.
(c) Judgement of individual's ability and achievement.
(d) None of the above.

958. The evaluation tells about a trait
(a) How much of its quantity is present.
(b) What is the value of that trait.
(c) How can be expressed that trait.
(d) How can be measured that trait.

959. The relationship between measurement and evaluation is
(a) The measurement is the quantitative description of a trait or power but evaluation is its quantitative plus quantitative description.
(b) Evaluation is comprehensive and measurement is its constituent.
(c) The accuracy and significance of measurement influences its evaluation.
(d) All of the above.

960. Evaluation can be expressed as
(a) What is good and desirable from the point of view of individual and a society—Evaluation think over it.
(b) Evaluation determines the value of a thing or procedure.
(c) To what extent the Educational objectives have been attained—the judgement is called evaluation.
(d) All of the above.

961. In which constituent of the educational procedure does the evaluation present?
(a) In formulation of objectives.
(b) In content planning.
(c) In teaching-learning process.
(d) In all the above.

962. The basic principle of Evaluation is
(a) Value and judgement are essential in an evaluation procedure.
(b) Adequate efforts should be carried out in order to eliminate Evaluation errors.
(c) Evaluation procedure should improve the teaching process.
(d) All of the above.

963. "Evaluation is not an end in itself but a means." The meaning of this phrase is
(a) Evaluation is a means to attain the goals.
(b) Evaluation is the means of determining teaching-learning values.
(c) Evaluation is an objective means.
(d) All of the above.

964. According to NCERT (1960) the Evaluation means
(a) To know about the fact to what extent the predetermined objectives have been attained.
(b) To think on the fact that to what extent the learning experiences given in a class are affective.
(c) To explore the fact, to what extent the objectives of education are attained in a desirable manner.
(d) All of the above.

965. Evaluation aims at
(a) In refinement of content.
(b) In making effective of different teaching methods.
(c) It integrates the various aspects of teaching procedures.
(d) All of the above.

966. Evaluation in context of Kothari Commission is
(a) A continuous process
(b) A stagnant process
(c) A unipolar process
(d) A process with multi-applications

967. Education Evaluational is a complex process in reference to
(a) Teaching objectives
(b) Learning experiences
(c) Tools of evaluation
(d) All of the above.

968. Dr. Patel has expressed the maxims of Educational procedure as
(a) Educational objectives
(b) Content
(c) Learning process
(d) Evaluation process and all the above

969. Through Evaluation one can study
(a) The students (b) The teachers
(c) Both of these (d) None of these.

970. Which one of the following precautions should be observed in formulation of objectives?
(a) To think thoroughly on the content.
(b) To think properly on learning activities.
(c) To make adequate efforts to bring change in students' knowledge, understanding and skills.
(d) All of the above.

971. Evaluation is beneficial for
(a) Teachers
(b) Principal
(c) School management
(d) All of the above.

972. Which one of the following precautions should be taken by the teacher during the stage of providing learning experiences to the students?
(a) Teaching methods
(b) Age and mental level of students
(c) Self-personality
(d) Student's welfare

973. Teaching procedure of evaluation is
(a) Verbal examination
(b) Written examination
(c) Performance test
(d) All of the above.

974. Learning experiences are planned according to bring out
(a) Positive changes in the students' behaviour.
(b) Development in child's personality.
(c) Both of the above.
(d) None of the above.

975. The meaning of learning outcome is
(a) The change in student's behaviour.
(b) The change in teaching methods of a teacher.
(c) The refinement of content.
(d) None of the above.

976. Which one of the following is not included in observational methods?
(a) Anecdotal record
(b) Interview
(c) Check-list
(d) Rating scale

977. The important instruments of Evaluation are
(a) Teaching procedures
(b) Self-reporting techniques
(c) Observational methods
(d) All of the above.

978. The Projective techniques can be used
(a) To measure personal and social adjustments of the children.
(b) To explore the repressed desires of the children.
(c) To know the attitudes of the children.
(d) All of the above.

979. The criterion of adequate learning experience is
(a) Are the learning experiences directly associated with teaching objectives?
(b) Are the learning experiences meaningful and satisfying to the students?

(c) Are these learning experiences according to the maturity level of the students?
(d) All of the above.

980. Projection is not work as a criterion for
(a) Rorschach Ink Blot Test
(b) TAT
(c) Picture-Frustration Test
(d) None of the above.

981. In Evaluation the emergence of written tests takes place in
(a) 1900 (b) 1890
(c) 1800 (d) Cannot say

982. Evaluation is helpful in
(a) For improving the conditions of the school.
(b) For knowing content related activities.
(c) For collecting informations related to the different dimensions of teaching.
(d) All of the above.

983. The Achievement test measures
(a) The knowledge related to content.
(b) The interest level in content.
(c) The increment in the content.
(d) The power acquire with relation to content.

984. Historically the name of the person associated with the emergence of written examination is
(a) Horace Mann (b) Neyvelity
(c) Thorndike (d) Rice

985. Generally achievement tests are
(a) Power tests
(b) Speed tests
(c) Aptitude tests
(d) Students ability tests

986. The meaning of Educational Age of the child is
(a) The minimum age to get admission in a school.
(b) The minimum age required for appearing in competition.
(c) The average value of general achievement demonstrated by the students in different subjects.
(d) All of the above.

987. The meaning of the term achievement is
(a) The learned quality of the content by a student.
(b) The acquired amount of knowledge pertaining to curriculum by the student.
(c) Both of the above.
(d) None of the above.

988. The formula applied for calculating a student's Educational Quotient is
(a) Educational Age/Chronological Age × 100.
(b) Mental Age/Chronological Age × 100.
(c) Actual Age/Educational Age × 100.
(d) Educational Age/Mental Age × 100.

989. The teacher prepares Achievement test because
(a) It helps in students' classification.
(b) It directs the students.
(c) It promotes the students' learning.
(d) All of the above.

990. The relationship between an Achievement test and Diagnostic test is
(a) Diagnostic tests are the part and parcel of Achievement tests.
(b) Diagnostic tests are totally different from Achievement tests.
(c) Diagnostic tests are prepared under specific situations.
(d) None of the above.

991. The main limitation of an Achievement test is
(a) To make complicated teaching in order to improve students' learning.
(b) These tests cannot include a number of learning experiences.

(c) Its standardisation in all the educational areas is harmful.
(d) All of the above.

992. The Achievement Age of a child is
(a) The achievement level of the child in a particular subject in relation to his chronological age.
(b) The mental age of the child.
(c) The Educational age of the child.
(d) None of the above.

993. The highest quality of an excellent achievement test is
(a) Reliability (b) Validity
(c) Objectivity (d) All of these.

994. The accurate formula for calculation of Achievement Quotient is
(a) Educational Age/Mental Age × 100.
(b) Mental Age/Chronological Age × 100.
(c) Educational Age/Educational Quotient × 100.
(d) Mental Age/Intelligence Quotient × 100.

995. The Achievement tests which are generally formulated for the evaluation of routine classroom performances of the students are called
(a) Standardised Achievement Test
(b) Teacher-made Achievement Test
(c) Human Welfare Achievement Test
(d) Evaluation Test

996. Which of the following is the main characteristics of a standardised Achievement Test?
(a) Objectivity (b) Validity
(c) Reliability (d) All of these.

997. The main condition of an excellent Achievement test is
(a) The fulfillment of predetermined goals.
(b) In accordance to the mental level of the students.
(c) Having practical utility.
(d) All of the above.

998. Which one of the following is not a type of Teacher-made Achievement Test?
(a) Essay Type Test
(b) Objective Type Test
(c) Diagnostic Test
(d) Reading Test

ANSWERS

1. (a)	2. (d)	3. (c)	4. (a)	5. (a)	6. (c)
7. (a)	8. (b)	9. (a)	10. (b)	11. (b)	12. (a)
13. (b)	14. (a)	15. (c)	16. (a)	17. (c)	18. (c)
19. (c)	20. (a)	21. (d)	22. (d)	23. (d)	24. (a)
25. (d)	26. (a)	27. (c)	28. (c)	29. (d)	30. (d)
31. (c)	32. (b)	33. (b)	34. (a)	35. (a)	36. (d)
37. (d)	38. (a)	39. (d)	40. (d)	41. (d)	42. (a)
43. (b)	44. (d)	45. (d)	46. (a)	47. (b)	48. (a)
49. (b)	50. (c)	51. (c)	52. (a)	53. (c)	54. (d)
55. (d)	56. (b)	57. (a)	58. (b)	59. (d)	60. (c)
61. (a)	62. (d)	63. (b)	64. (c)	65. (a)	66. (b)

67. (b)	68. (d)	69. (d)	70. (a)	71. (a)	72. (c)
73. (a)	74. (b)	75. (b)	76. (a)	77. (d)	78. (d)
79. (a)	80. (c)	81. (a)	82. (a)	83. (a)	84. (b)
85. (c)	86. (a)	87. (a)	88. (a)	89. (c)	90. (b)
91. (b)	92. (c)	93. (c)	94. (b)	95. (b)	96. (d)
97. (b)	98. (a)	99. (b)	100. (d)	101. (d)	102. (c)
103. (d)	104. (a)	105. (a)	106. (a)	107. (b)	108. (a)
109. (a)	110. (b)	111. (d)	112. (d)	113. (b)	114. (d)
115. (a)	116. (a)	117. (a)	118. (b)	119. (b)	120. (b)
121. (a)	122. (d)	123. (a)	124. (b)	125. (c)	126. (d)
127. (d)	128. (d)	129. (c)	130. (a)	131. (a)	132. (d)
133. (a)	134. (c)	135. (a)	136. (d)	137. (a)	138. (a)
139. (d)	140. (d)	141. (b)	142. (d)	143. (b)	144. (d)
145. (a)	146. (d)	147. (a)	148. (d)	149. (d)	150. (c)
151. (c)	152. (a)	153. (d)	154. (a)	155. (b)	156. (c)
157. (a)	158. (d)	159. (d)	160. (c)	161. (d)	162. (d)
163. (b)	164. (c)	165. (d)	166. (d)	167. (b)	168. (d)
169. (a)	170. (a)	171. (a)	172. (a)	173. (c)	174. (c)
175. (d)	176. (c)	177. (c)	178. (d)	179. (a)	180. (c)
181. (b)	182. (b)	183. (d)	184. (c)	185. (c)	186. (c)
187. (a)	188. (c)	189. (d)	190. (b)	191. (d)	192. (b)
193. (b)	194. (c)	195. (d)	196. (b)	197. (a)	198. (a)
199. (d)	200. (c)	201. (b)	202. (d)	203. (b)	204. (a)
205. (b)	206. (b)	207. (b)	208. (d)	209. (c)	210. (a)
211. (c)	212. (d)	213. (b)	214. (c)	215. (c)	216. (d)
217. (a)	218. (c)	219. (a)	220. (a)	221. (a)	222. (c)
223. (d)	224. (c)	225. (c)	226. (d)	227. (a)	228. (c)
229. (a)	230. (c)	231. (d)	232. (d)	233. (b)	234. (d)
235. (d)	236. (a)	237. (b)	238. (d)	239. (d)	240. (b)
241. (d)	242. (d)	243. (a)	244. (d)	245. (b)	246. (a)
247. (d)	248. (c)	249. (d)	250. (a)	251. (a)	252. (b)
253. (b)	254. (d)	255. (c)	256. (d)	257. (d)	258. (a)
259. (d)	260. (d)	261. (a)	262. (b)	263. (b)	264. (c)
265. (c)	266. (a)	267. (c)	268. (b)	269. (a)	270. (b)

271. (a)	272. (a)	273. (a)	274. (a)	275. (a)	276. (d)
277. (a)	278. (a)	279. (b)	280. (a)	281. (c)	282. (a)
283. (a)	284. (b)	285. (c)	286. (a)	287. (b)	288. (a)
289. (c)	290. (a)	291. (c)	292. (d)	293. (d)	294. (d)
295. (a)	296. (a)	297. (d)	298. (c)	299. (d)	300. (c)
301. (d)	302. (d)	303. (a)	304. (b)	305. (c)	306. (a)
307. (c)	308. (a)	309. (b)	310. (a)	311. (c)	312. (b)
313. (c)	314. (a)	315. (c)	316. (d)	317. (a)	318. (b)
319. (a)	320. (b)	321. (b)	322. (a)	323. (c)	324. (d)
325. (a)	326. (c)	327. (d)	328. (a)	329. (c)	330. (a)
331. (c)	332. (d)	333. (c)	334. (d)	335. (d)	336. (d)
337. (a)	338. (d)	339. (d)	340. (d)	341. (a)	342. (b)
343. (c)	344. (b)	345. (d)	346. (b)	347. (c)	348. (d)
349. (c)	350. (d)	351. (c)	352. (d)	353. (b)	354. (a)
355. (a)	356. (c)	357. (d)	358. (a)	359. (c)	360. (a)
361. (a)	362. (a)	363. (a)	364. (c)	365. (b)	366. (c)
367. (c)	368. (d)	369. (a)	370. (c)	371. (d)	372. (b)
373. (c)	374. (a)	375. (a)	376. (a)	377. (c)	378. (d)
379. (b)	380. (d)	381. (b)	382. (a)	383. (a)	384. (d)
385. (b)	386. (b)	387. (b)	388. (d)	389. (d)	390. (d)
391. (b)	392. (a)	393. (b)	394. (c)	395. (a)	396. (c)
397. (a)	398. (a)	399. (d)	400. (a)	401. (c)	402. (b)
403. (c)	404. (c)	405. (d)	406. (c)	407. (d)	408. (a)
409. (b)	410. (b)	411. (a)	412. (d)	413. (b)	414. (a)
415. (d)	416. (b)	417. (c)	418. (a)	419. (d)	420. (c)
421. (b)	422. (d)	423. (a)	424. (b)	425. (a)	426. (b)
427. (d)	428. (d)	429. (a)	430. (a)	431. (d)	432. (b)
433. (b)	434. (a)	435. (a)	436. (a)	437. (a)	438. (a)
439. (a)	440. (a)	441. (b)	442. (d)	443. (a)	444. (a)
445. (d)	446. (a)	447. (a)	448. (a)	449. (a)	450. (b)
451. (b)	452. (b)	453. (a)	454. (a)	455. (b)	456. (b)
457. (d)	458. (b)	459. (c)	460. (b)	461. (b)	462. (d)
463. (a)	464. (a)	465. (b)	466. (b)	467. (d)	468. (c)
469. (a)	470. (c)	471. (b)	472. (d)	473. (b)	474. (b)

475. (a)	476. (a)	477. (d)	478. (d)	479. (a)	480. (c)
481. (d)	482. (d)	483. (a)	484. (a)	485. (d)	486. (c)
487. (d)	488. (d)	489. (c)	490. (c)	491. (d)	492. (a)
493. (a)	494. (c)	495. (d)	496. (d)	497. (a)	498. (a)
499. (a)	500. (a)	501. (d)	502. (d)	503. (b)	504. (a)
505. (a)	506. (d)	507. (d)	508. (d)	509. (a)	510. (d)
511. (a)	512. (d)	513. (d)	514. (d)	515. (a)	516. (d)
517. (b)	518. (a)	519. (b)	520. (a)	521. (a)	522. (d)
523. (d)	524. (d)	525. (d)	526. (d)	527. (c)	528. (d)
529. (d)	530. (d)	531. (d)	532. (c)	533. (a)	534. (d)
535. (a)	536. (b)	537. (c)	538. (a)	539. (d)	540. (a)
541. (a)	542. (c)	543. (a)	544. (a)	545. (d)	546. (d)
547. (d)	548. (a)	549. (d)	550. (d)	551. (a)	552. (a)
553. (b)	554. (a)	555. (d)	556. (a)	557. (a)	558. (d)
559. (d)	560. (d)	561. (d)	562. (b)	563. (a)	564. (a)
565. (d)	566. (a)	567. (a)	568. (a)	569. (d)	570. (b)
571. (a)	572. (a)	573. (a)	574. (d)	575. (b)	576. (d)
577. (d)	578. (b)	579. (b)	580. (a)	581. (d)	582. (a)
583. (a)	584. (d)	585. (c)	586. (b)	587. (c)	588. (b)
589. (a)	590. (d)	591. (a)	592. (c)	593. (d)	594. (d)
595. (a)	596. (c)	597. (d)	598. (d)	599. (d)	600. (c)
601. (d)	602. (d)	603. (a)	604. (a)	605. (a)	606. (a)
607. (d)	608. (d)	609. (d)	610. (c)	611. (c)	612. (d)
613. (b)	614. (d)	615. (d)	616. (d)	617. (c)	618. (b)
619. (d)	620. (d)	621. (a)	622. (d)	623. (d)	624. (d)
625. (a)	626. (d)	627. (b)	628. (d)	629. (a)	630. (a)
631. (a)	632. (d)	633. (a)	634. (a)	635. (a)	636. (d)
637. (d)	638. (d)	639. (d)	640. (d)	641. (a)	642. (a)
643. (a)	644. (d)	645. (a)	646. (d)	647. (d)	648. (d)
649. (c)	650. (a)	651. (d)	652. (d)	653. (a)	654. (b)
655. (b)	656. (d)	657. (a)	658. (d)	659. (d)	660. (d)
661. (c)	662. (c)	663. (d)	664. (c)	665. (d)	666. (d)
667. (c)	668. (a)	669. (d)	670. (a)	671. (b)	672. (a)
673. (d)	674. (a)	675. (d)	676. (a)	677. (a)	678. (b)

679. (c) 680. (d) 681. (d) 682. (d) 683. (d) 684. (d)
685. (c) 686. (d) 687. (a) 688. (a) 689. (a) 690. (a)
691. (a) 692. (c) 693. (b) 694. (d) 695. (d) 696. (d)
697. (d) 698. (c) 699. (a) 700. (d) 701. (a) 702. (a)
703. (c) 704. (d) 705. (c) 706. (a) 707. (d) 708. (a)
709. (d) 710. (b) 711. (d) 712. (d) 713. (d) 714. (a)
715. (d) 716. (d) 717. (d) 718. (a) 719. (d) 720. (a)
721. (d) 722. (a) 723. (c) 724. (a) 725. (a) 726. (a)
727. (c) 728. (a) 729. (c) 730. (b) 731. (a) 732. (d)
733. (d) 734. (a) 735. (d) 736. (d) 737. (a) 738. (d)
739. (c) 740. (d) 741. (a) 742. (c) 743. (d) 744. (a)
745. (d) 746. (b) 747. (d) 748. (a) 749. (d) 750. (a)
751. (d) 752. (a) 753. (d) 754. (d) 755. (d) 756. (d)
757. (d) 758. (c) 759. (b) 760. (a) 761. (a) 762. (a)
763. (a) 764. (d) 765. (d) 766. (a) 767. (d) 768. (d)
769. (b) 770. (d) 771. (c) 772. (a) 773. (a) 774. (c)
775. (a) 776. (d) 777. (a) 778. (a) 779. (d) 780. (b)
781. (b) 782. (c) 783. (d) 784. (d) 785. (d) 786. (a)
787. (d) 788. (c) 789. (d) 790. (d) 791. (d) 792. (a)
793. (a) 794. (a) 795. (d) 796. (c) 797. (a) 798. (c)
799. (d) 800. (d) 801. (c) 802. (d) 803. (d) 804. (b)
805. (a) 806. (a) 807. (d) 808. (d) 809. (d) 810. (a)
811. (c) 812. (d) 813. (d) 814. (d) 815. (a) 816. (a)
817. (a) 818. (d) 819. (d) 820. (b) 821. (b) 822. (a)
823. (a) 824. (c) 825. (d) 826. (a) 827. (a) 828. (d)
829. (b) 830. (a) 831. (b) 832. (a) 833. (d) 834. (a)
835. (a) 836. (d) 837. (b) 838. (d) 839. (a) 840. (a)
841. (d) 842. (d) 843. (d) 844. (d) 845. (a) 846. (b)
847. (d) 848. (d) 849. (d) 850. (d) 851. (c) 852. (a)
853. (d) 854. (d) 855. (c) 856. (d) 857. (c) 858. (b)
859. (d) 860. (a) 861. (a) 862. (a) 863. (a) 864. (a)
865. (d) 866. (d) 867. (c) 868. (b) 869. (a) 870. (a)
871. (b) 872. (b) 873. (d) 874. (b) 875. (a) 876. (a)
877. (d) 878. (c) 879. (c) 880. (d) 881. (a) 882. (c)

883. (d)	884. (b)	885. (a)	886. (d)	887. (b)	888. (a)
889. (c)	890. (a)	891. (b)	892. (d)	893. (a)	894. (a)
895. (a)	896. (b)	897. (d)	898. (a)	899. (a)	900. (c)
901. (a)	902. (d)	903. (d)	904. (a)	905. (c)	906. (c)
907. (d)	908. (d)	909. (d)	910. (a)	911. (c)	912. (d)
913. (a)	914. (d)	915. (a)	916. (d)	917. (a)	918. (c)
919. (c)	920. (b)	921. (d)	922. (a)	923. (a)	924. (c)
925. (d)	926. (b)	927. (b)	928. (a)	929. (a)	930. (b)
931. (d)	932. (c)	933. (a)	934. (a)	935. (a)	936. (d)
937. (d)	938. (a)	939. (d)	940. (a)	941. (d)	942. (b)
943. (c)	944. (a)	945. (d)	946. (a)	947. (a)	948. (d)
949. (d)	950. (d)	951. (c)	952. (d)	953. (d)	954. (a)
955. (a)	956. (a)	957. (c)	958. (b)	959. (d)	960. (d)
961. (d)	962. (d)	963. (d)	964. (d)	965. (d)	966. (a)
967. (d)	968. (d)	969. (c)	970. (d)	971. (d)	972. (b)
973. (d)	974. (c)	975. (a)	976. (b)	977. (d)	978. (d)
979. (d)	980. (c)	981. (b)	982. (d)	983. (d)	984. (a)
985. (a)	986. (c)	987. (c)	988. (a)	989. (d)	990. (a)
991. (d)	992. (a)	993. (d)	994. (a)	995. (b)	996. (d)
997. (d)	998. (d)				

2

Research Aptitude

1. Research Aptitude refers to
   (a) The potential or capacities to carried out research.
   (b) The latent to be used in a scientific way for desired purpose.
   (c) The cultivation of research skills in newcomers.
   (d) The developing of rationality in all academic pursuits.
2. How should a good hypothesis be?
   (a) Formulated in such a way that it can be tested by the data.
   (b) Of limited scope and should not have global significance.
   (c) Precise, specific and consistent with most known facts.
   (d) All of the above.
3. Bibliography given in a research report
   (a) helps those interested in further research and studying the problem from another angle.
   (b) shows the vast knowledge of the researcher.
   (c) makes the report authentic.
   (d) None of the above.
4. Who said that members of the same species are not alike?
   (a) Darwin (b) Herbert Spencer
   (c) Best (d) Good
5. Research basically is
   (a) A point of view
   (b) An attitude of inquiry
   (c) A step-wise-step exploration
   (d) All of the above.
6. A researcher selects only 20 members as a sample from the total population of 10000 and considers
   (a) he was guided by his supervisor.
   (b) he was a good researcher.
   (c) the population was homogeneous.
   (d) All of the above.
7. The research antagonistic to *ex-post facto* research is
   (a) experimental studies
   (b) library researches
   (c) normative researches
   (d) All of the above.
8. A statistical measure based upon the entire population is called parameter while measure based upon a sample is known as
   (a) Sample parameter
   (b) Inference
   (c) Statistic
   (d) None of the above.
9. According to George Mouly the research is
   (a) Systematic and scholarly effort.
   (b) Application of scientific method.
   (c) Providing solutions to educational problems.
   (d) All of the above.
10. How can the objectivity of the research be enhanced?

(a) Through its impartiality
(b) Through its reliability
(c) Through its validity
(d) All of the above.

11. An example of scientific knowledge is
(a) social traditions and customs.
(b) authority of the Prophet or great men.
(c) religious scriptures.
(d) laboratory and field experiments.

12. Generalised conclusion on the basis of a sample is technically known as
(a) statistical inference of external validity of the research.
(b) data analysis and interpretation.
(c) parameter inference.
(d) All of the above.

13. John W. Best formulates the definition of research as
(a) Systematic process
(b) Based on scientific method
(c) Systematic investigation
(d) All of the above.

14. Among the following, with which one the ethics in research is not related?
(a) Humanity (b) Reliability
(c) Self-interest (d) Scientific method

15. The process not needed in experimental researches is
(a) controlling
(b) observation
(c) manipulation and replication
(d) reference collection

16. A researcher selects a probability sample of 100 out of the total population. It is
(a) a cluster sample
(b) a random sample
(c) a stratified sample
(d) a systematic sample

17. Research's elements as
(i) Prolonged, purposeful and intensive search
(ii) Constitute a method of discovery
(iii) Comprises defining, redefining problem
(iv) Formulating hypothesis
(v) Correcting, organising and evaluating data

Proposed in the definition of
(a) Rusk (b) Clifford Woody
(c) P.M. Cook (d) W.S. Munroe

18. What is a Research?
(a) Self-contained process
(b) Discovery oriented process
(c) Value oriented process
(d) Passive process

19. Below are given some probable characteristics of an ineffective teacher, which of them is most likely to be characterised the ineffective teacher
(a) emphasis upon pupil discussion in the clarification of groups goals.
(b) emphasis upon standards.
(c) emphasis upon the control of the immediate situation.
(d) None of the above.

20. A researcher divides the populations into PG, graduates and 10 + 2 students and using the random digit table he selects some of them from each. This is technically called
(a) stratified sampling
(b) stratified random sampling
(c) representative sampling
(d) None of the above.

21. The priority to focus on research aptitude in NET examination is
(a) To trained as future scientists.
(b) To explore and screenedout the persons having scientific interests.

(c) To enable them in future to take training in research and transfer the skills in younger generation.
(d) To give arbitrarily a prestigious position in the society.

22. The research papers are generally made by
(a) the scientists.
(b) the research scholars.
(c) the research supervisors.
(d) All of the above.

23. The per capita income of India from 1950 to 1990 is four times. This study is
(a) Social (b) Factorial
(c) Longitudinal (d) Horizontal

24. The final result of a study will be more accurate if the sample drawn is
(a) taken randomly
(b) fixed by quota
(c) representative to the population
(d) purposive

25. Which one of the following is not representing the characteristics of research?
(a) Hypothesis-oriented.
(b) Employing reliable tools and techniques.
(c) Follow scientific method.
(d) Leading towards imaginary results.

26. Where the research papers generally presented in abundance?
(a) Symposium (b) Seminars
(c) Journals (d) None of these

27. Nine years old children are taller than 7 years old ones. It is an example of
(a) vertical studies
(b) cross-sectional studies
(c) experimental studies
(d) case studies

28. What educational research is?
(a) An activity which is directed towards the development of science of behaviour in educational conditions.
(b) Type of procedure employed in answering questions about education.
(c) Contributing towards finding solutions of educational problem.
(d) All of the above.

29. The reason for giving more importance to research papers than the research articles is
(a) research papers are incorporated with statistics.
(b) research papers are based on data.
(c) Both of the above.
(d) None of the above.

30. Attributes of objects, events or things which can be measured are called
(a) Data
(b) Qualitative measure
(c) Variables
(d) None of the above.

31. Area (cluster) sampling technique is used when
(a) population is scattered and large size of the sample is to be drawn.
(b) population is heterogeneous.
(c) long survey is needed.
(d) Both (a) and (c).

32. According to John W. Best the research can be divided into
(a) pure and applied research
(b) pure, applied and action research
(c) pure and basic research
(d) None of these.

33. What does the justification explains?
(a) The adequacy of the research.
(b) The inherent truth of a research.
(c) The logic of the research.
(d) The significance of the research.

34. In order to augment the accuracy of the study a researcher
   (a) should be honest and unbiased.
   (b) should increase the size of the sample.
   (c) should keep the variance high.
   (d) All of the above.

35. A researcher divides his population into certain groups and fixes the size of the sample from each group. It is called
   (a) stratified sample
   (b) quota sample
   (c) cluster sample
   (d) All of the above.

36. Research in education generally carried out for
   (a) Individual's professional growth.
   (b) Individual's personal prestige.
   (c) Individual's opportunities for getting job.
   (d) Enhancing the body of knowledge related to education.

37. The basis on which assumptions are formulated is
   (a) cultural background of a country.
   (b) universality.
   (c) specific characteristics of the castes.
   (d) All of the above.

38. Hypothesis cannot be stated in
   (a) declarative terms
   (b) null and question form terms
   (c) general terms
   (d) directional terms

39. Which one of the following is not the characteristics of education research?
   (a) Addition to the body of knowledge.
   (b) Exploration of new principles pertaining to education.
   (c) A logical and objective venture.
   (d) All of the above.

40. Symposium's characteristic is
   (a) to impart training for higher order of thinking.
   (b) to give freedom to express their ideas by the speakers as well as the audience.
   (c) to develop the comprehensive understanding of about the specific problems of research and its various dimensions.
   (d) All of the above.

41. All cause non-sampling errors except
   (a) faulty tools of measurement
   (b) inadequate sample
   (c) defect in data collection
   (d) non-response

42. Which technique is generally followed when the population is finite?
   (a) Area sampling technique
   (b) Purposive sampling technique
   (c) Systematic sampling technique
   (d) None of the above.

43. The objective of a research is
   (a) Theoretical (b) Factual
   (c) Practical (d) All of these.

44. How should be the method of Research reporting?
   (a) Personal
   (b) Scientific
   (c) Ethical and attractive
   (d) Favourite to globalisation.

45. Formulation of hypothesis may not be necessary in
   (a) survey studies
   (b) fact finding (historical) studies
   (c) experimental studies
   (d) normative studies

46. Validity of a research can be improved by
   (a) eliminating extraneous factors.
   (b) taking the true representative sample of the population.

(c) Both of the above measures.
(d) None of the above.

47. Action research is
(a) the research in action
(b) instant research
(c) research mend for quick implementation
(d) All of the above.

48. What is the significance of preface in a research thesis?
(a) To get freedom from gratitude of the supervisor.
(b) To become a little bit emotional at this occasion.
(c) To take blessings of the family members.
(d) To pay obeisance.

49. Who is regarded the father of scientific social surveys?
(a) Best (b) Booth
(c) Darwin (d) None of these.

50. Field study is related to
(a) real life situations
(b) experimental situations
(c) laboratory situations
(d) None of the above.

51. Experimental research deals with
(a) Variables
(b) Controls
(c) Scientific inferences
(d) All of the above.

52. What is the criteria of good case-study?
(a) Validity of the data
(b) Continuity
(c) Completeness of the data
(d) All of the above.

53. For doing external criticism (for establishing the authenticity of data) a researcher must verify
(a) the signature and handwriting of the author.
(b) the paper and ink used in that period which is under study.
(c) style of prose writing of that period.
(d) All of the above.

54. Independent variables are not manipulated in
(a) normative researches
(b) *ex-post facto* researches
(c) Both of the above.
(d) None of the above.

55. The levels of educational research are
(a) 4 in numbers (b) 3 in numbers
(c) 2 in numbers (d) Only one

56. What is the compulsion of publication of research paper?
(a) For all the teachers in higher educational institutions.
(b) Only for university teachers.
(c) Only for central university teachers.
(d) Can't say.

57. Survey study aims at
(i) knowing facts about the existing situation.
(ii) comparing the present status with the standard norms.
(iii) criticising the existing situation.
(iv) identifying the means of improving the existing situation.
(a) (i) and (ii)
(b) (i), (ii) and (iii)
(c) (i), (ii), (iii) and (iv)
(d) (ii) and (iii)

58. Level 1 is concerned with
(a) Data collection
(b) Internal validity
(c) External validity
(d) None of the above.

59. When the researcher lacks the quality of collection of the facts from social environment, such research will be called

(a) a malacious research.
(b) an irrelevant research.
(c) a pure research.
(d) not a pure research.

60. Which of the following is not the characteristic of a researcher?
(a) He is industrious and persistent on the trial of discovery.
(b) He is a specialist rather than a generalist.
(c) He is objective.
(d) He is not versatile in his interest and even in his native abilities.

61. The basic characteristic of Educational Research is
(a) It is based on sound philosophy of education.
(b) It is interdisciplinary in nature.
(c) It employs deductive reasoning processes.
(d) All of the above.

62. What is the basic requirement for preparing a research paper?
(a) The research skills in the person.
(b) The research attitudes in the person.
(c) The research orientation of the person.
(d) All of the above.

63. The validity and reliability of a research will be at stake when
(a) the incident was reported after a long period of time from that of its occurrence.
(b) the author who is the source of information is biased, incompetent or dishonest.
(c) the researcher himself is not competent enough to draw logical conclusions.
(d) All of the above.

64. "The process by which practitioners attempt to study their problems scientifically in order to guide, correct, and evaluate their decisions and actions is called action research." Who has given this Statement?
(a) John W. Best
(b) F.L. Whitney
(c) Stephen M. Corey
(d) W.S. Monroe

65. *Ex-Post Facto* method of research is associated with
(a) Control
(b) Sample
(c) Validity related with inference
(d) All of the above.

66. A researcher wants to study the future of the Congress I in India. For the study which tool is most appropriate for him?
(a) Questionnaire (b) Rating scale
(c) Interview (d) Schedule

67. In relation to aims the difference between fundamental research and action research is
(a) That fundamental research engages in discovery of new facts, theories and laws.
(b) That action reasearch brings immediate changes in any system or organisation.
(c) Both of the above are correct.
(d) Both of the above are incorrect.

68. The basis of classification of the survey method is
(a) the source of data collection.
(b) the nature of variable.
(c) the measurable class or group.
(d) All of the above.

69. Catharsis means discharge of emotions. A teacher can let off pent-up energy of his disciples through
(a) picnics/excursions
(b) mock-parliament
(c) celebration of festivals
(d) All of the above.

70. The experimental study is based on the law of
    (a) Single variable
    (b) Replication
    (c) Occupation
    (d) Interest of the subject
71. Generally Action researches are carried out its order to bring
    (a) Immediate changes in the system
    (b) Effectiveness in the system
    (c) Improvements in a system
    (d) All of the above.
72. The purposive sample is
    (a) based upon a specific objective of sampling procedure.
    (b) depending on the researcher's whims.
    (c) based on the excellent method of sampling.
    (d) None of the above.
73. Seeing a very big turnout, it was reported that JD will win the election, the conclusion was based on
    (a) random sampling.
    (b) cluster sampling.
    (c) purposive sampling.
    (d) systematic sampling.
74. All are example of qualitative variables except
    (a) Religion and castes
    (b) Sex
    (c) Observation
    (d) Interest of the subject
75. Action research hypothesis is
    (a) General in nature
    (b) Similar like in pure sciences
    (c) Written in two parts—one is goal part second is action part
    (d) A hypothesis in real sense
76. What is a systematic sampling?
    (a) An effective method of generalisation of data.
    (b) A comprehensive method of sample selection.
    (c) A simple method of sample selection.
    (d) All of the above.
77. A researcher divides his population into certain groups and fixes the size of the sample from each group. It is called
    (a) Stratified sample (b) Quota sample
    (c) Cluster sample (d) All of the above.
78. In order to study scientifically the historical background of the events to know its bearing on present conditions is called
    (a) Experimental research
    (b) Historical research
    (c) Philosophical research
    (d) Action research
79. A researcher should possess
    (a) scientific behaviour.
    (b) scientific attitude.
    (c) scientific thinking.
    (d) scientific feeling.
80. Which technique is generally followed when the population is finite?
    (a) Purposive sampling technique
    (b) Area sampling technique
    (c) Systematic sampling technique
    (d) None of the above.
81. A teacher encounters various problems during his professional experiences. He should
    (a) resign from his post in such situations.
    (b) do research on that problem and find a solution.
    (c) avoid the problematic situations.
    (d) take the help of head of the institution.
82. Generalisation can be made appropriately from
    (a) Fundamental researches.
    (b) Action researches.

(c) In both of the above.
(d) More intensively in fundamental research in comparison than the action researches.

83. How is the theoretical aims of the research?
(a) Inferential (b) Qualitative
(c) Explanatory (d) Quantitative

84. Which of the following is a non-probability sample?
(a) Quota sample
(b) Simple random sample
(c) Purposive sample
(d) Both (a) and (c).

85. A research problem is feasible only when
(a) it is researchable.
(b) it is new and adds something to knowledge.
(c) it has utility and relevance.
(d) All of the above.

86. Researches are generally treated as 'Identity symbols' of a nation because
(a) Researches reflect the progress of a nation.
(b) Researches focus on human development.
(c) Researches help in acquiring international prestige.
(d) All of the above.

87. The research is always
(a) verifying the old knowledge.
(b) exploring new knowledge.
(c) filling the gap between the knowledge.
(d) All of the above.

88. The analysis of the term *Anusandhan* gives two words
(a) A + nusandhan (b) An + usandhan
(c) Anu + sandhan (d) Au + nsandhan

89. Which among the following is not a characteristic of research
(a) Irrelevant conclusions
(b) Irrelevant data collection
(c) Irrelevant data analysis
(d) All of the above.

90. Service rules for college and university teachers should be in line with bureaucrats and executives. Do you support the statement?
(a) More or less with some modifications.
(b) Definitely not.
(c) Yes basically, but with major variation in many cases.
(d) All of the above.

91. Studying the social status of a population a researcher concluded that Mr. X is socially backward. His conclusion is
(a) Wrong (b) Right
(c) Inaccurate (d) Biased

Note: Such studies are conducted in relative terms.

92. In Hindi language the term *Anusandhan* refers to
(a) Follower of an aim
(b) Preying of an aim
(c) Attain the aim
(d) Become goal-oriented

93. Who gave the statement "Research is an honest effort carried out through insight"?
(a) Cook (b) Crick
(c) Watson (d) None of these.

94. The most important task in teaching is
(a) directing students in development of experiences.
(b) making assignments and hearing recitations.
(c) making monthly reports and maintaining records.
(d) None of the above.

95. A good hypothesis should be
(a) precise, specific and consistent with most known facts.

(b) formulated in such a way that it can be tested by the data.
(c) of limited scope and should not have global significance.
(d) All of the above.

96. The term *Anusandhan* in Hindi has been borrowed from
(a) The advantageous aims used in archery training in olden days.
(b) The objectives employed in modern Rifle Shooting competitions.
(c) Both of the above analogous and true in terminology's perspective.
(d) Both are the heterogenous and not related with the term in question.

97. What is an experimental method?
(a) A method deriving inferences.
(b) A variable controlling method.
(c) A method for verifying hypothesis.
(d) All of the above.

98. Hypothesis cannot be stated in
(a) null and question form terms.
(b) declarative terms.
(c) general terms.
(d) directional terms.

99. Which of the following statement matches with that of Mouly?
(a) Research is a process in which Exploratory procedure (method) has been employed.
(b) The application of Scientific method for experimentation and interpretation intellectually for solving the problems is called a research.
(c) Research is an intensive formal and organised procedure.
(d) Research can be defined in the form of study method of problem solving.

100. With which among the following is Descriptive Study associated?
(a) Case study method
(b) Experimental research method
(c) Survey research method
(d) All of the above.

101. While writing research report a researcher
(a) must arrange it in logical, topical and chronological order.
(b) must not use the numerical figures in numbers in the beginning of sentences.
(c) must compare his results with those of the other studies.
(d) All of the above.

102. Logic of induction is very close to
(a) the logic of sampling.
(b) the logic of observation.
(c) the logic of the controlled variable.
(d) None of the above.

103. Research is based, upon
(a) Scientific method
(b) Experiments
(c) Scientists
(d) General principles

104. What is the step of historical research method?
(a) To collect the data
(b) To criticise the data
(c) To identify the problem
(d) All of the above.

105. Which of the following is a primary source of data?
(a) Official records — governments' documents, information preserved by social religious organisations, etc.
(b) Personal records, letters, diaries, autobiographies, wills, etc.
(c) Oral testimony of traditions and customs
(d) All of the above.

106. In order to augment the accuracy of the study a researcher
(a) should increase the size of the sample.
(b) should be honest and unbiased.

(c) should keep the variance high.
(d) All of the above.

107. When a person deriving all the conclusions through observation and experimentation in his routine life. In this way the person can be treated as a
(a) Scientist
(b) Good citizen
(c) Intellectual person
(d) Normal person

108. What is a conference?
(a) Adequate solution of research problem.
(b) Wider manipulation of research inferences.
(c) Provision to discuss on serious matters.
(d) All of the above.

109. Field study is related to
(a) real life situations.
(b) laboratory situations.
(c) experimental situations.
(d) None of the above.

110. All causes non-sampling errors except
(a) faulty tools of measurement.
(b) inadequate sample.
(c) non-response.
(d) defect in data collection.

111. Generally a scientist's observations related to Experiment and Testing are based on
(a) Scientific principles
(b) Household rules
(c) Self-imagination
(d) Self-experiences

112. Who has the central role in a workshop?
(a) The expert
(b) The participants
(c) The director
(d) None of these.

113. A researcher divides the populations into PG, graduates and 10+2 students and using the random digit table he selects some of them from each. This is technically called
(a) stratified sampling
(b) stratified random sampling
(c) representative sampling
(d) None of these.

114. Total error in a research is equal to
(a) sampling error + non-sampling error
(b) $\sqrt{[(\text{samplinge error}) + (\text{non-sampling error})]^2}$
(c) only sampling error
(d) sampling error × 100

115. To become unscientific, it is sufficient
(a) Irrelevant arguments
(b) Prejudices
(c) Disagreement
(d) All of the above.

116. Where can a seminar be organised?
(a) In a school (b) In a class
(c) At district level (d) All of these.

117. A statistical measure based upon the entire population is called parameter while measure based upon a sample is known as
(a) Sample parameter
(b) Inference
(c) Statistic
(d) None of the above.

118. The probability of a head and a tail of tossing four coins simultaneously is
(a) 1/8 (b) 1/16
(c) 1/4 (d) 1/64

119. If you are repeating the mistake again and again then you are called a
(a) Excellent researcher
(b) Excellent forgetter
(c) Foolish person
(d) Normal person

120. What are the process involved in descriptive research?

(a) Investigation and generalisations of the events of the past.
(b) Description recording analysis and interpretation of the present conditions.
(c) Deliberate manipulation.
(d) None of the above.

121. Generalised conclusion on the basis of a sample is technically known as
(a) statistical inference of external validity of the research.
(b) parameter inference.
(c) data analysis and interpretation.
(d) All of the above.

122. If you are employing scientific method for solving a problem and interpretation of the results, then this process is called
(a) Scientific
(b) Self-satisfying
(c) Complementary to personal objectives
(d) None of the above.

123. The quality desired in a researcher in order to prepare a Research report is
(a) Scientific attitude.
(b) Mental balance.
(c) Skill oriented capabilities.
(d) All of the above.

124. For doing external criticism (for establishing the authenticity of data) a researcher must verify
(a) the signature and handwriting of the author.
(b) the paper and ink used in that period which is under study.
(c) style of prose writing of that period.
(d) All of the above.

125. McGrath and Watson have defined research as
(a) User of exploratory method
(b) A intellectual exploration
(c) Use of scientific method for analysis
(d) Problem-solving

126. Deliberate manipulation is always a part of
(a) Historical research.
(b) Fundamental research.
(c) Descriptive research.
(d) Experimental research.

127. Researches are generally treated as 'Identity symbols' of a nation because
(a) Researches reflect the progress of a nation
(b) Researches focus on human development
(c) Researches help in acquiring international prestige
(d) All of the above.

128. The validity and reliability of a research will be at stake when
(a) The author who is the source of information is biased, incompetent or dishonest
(b) The incident was reported after a long period of time from that of its occurrence
(c) The researcher himself is not competent enough to draw logical conclusions
(d) All of the above.

129. "Research in the method of study of the problems, where the solutions of the problems have been carried out through given facts." The statement is given by
(a) Munroe (b) Best
(c) Watson (d) Cook

130. The research that helps in developing theories by discovering broad generalisations and principles is
(a) Historical research.
(b) Fundamental research.

(c) Descriptive research.
(d) Experimental research.

131. The research that applies the laws at the time of field study to draw more and more clear ideas about the problem is
(a) Applied research.
(b) Action research.
(c) Experimental research.
(d) None of the above.

132. How can the beauty of the research thesis be enhanced?
(a) By keeping its excellent binding and title page.
(b) By keeping aesthetic sense in its topography.
(c) By giving good charts, flow diagrams and systematic graphs.
(d) All of the above.

133. The main condition which should be followed by research is
(a) Honest exploration
(b) Knowledge of facts and principles
(c) Standardized findings and conclusions
(d) All of the above.

134. The characteristic of a research is
(a) Serious and intensive study
(b) Wisdom
(c) Based on standardised conclusions
(d) All of the above.

135. "Action research is the process by which practitioner attempt to study their problems scientifically in order to guide correct and evaluate their decisions and actions." Who said this?
(a) Pestalozzy (b) Herbart
(c) Dr. Corey (d) None of these.

136. Seeing a very big rally it was reported that JD will win the election, the conclusion was based on
(a) random sampling
(b) cluster sampling
(c) systematic sampling
(d) purposive sampling

137. How should the title page of Research thesis be?
(a) Scientific and logical
(b) Aesthetic and attractive
(c) Brief and meaningful
(d) All of the above.

138. Reliability is the fundamental quality of a research which also reflects
(a) Validity (b) Verifiabihty
(c) Purity of data (d) Superiority

139. Which of the following is not a characteristic of a research?
(a) Irrelevant data collection
(b) Irrelevant data analysis
(c) Irrelevant conclusions
(d) All of the above.

140. Hypothesis can be classified into
(a) two broad divisions.
(b) three broad divisions.
(c) four broad divisions.
(d) five broad divisions.

141. The research is always
(a) Exploring new knowledge
(b) Verifying the old knowledge
(c) Filling the gap between the knowledge
(d) Including all the above

142. It is an example of negative correlation
(a) an increase in population will lead to a shortage of food grains.
(b) poor intelligence means poor achievement in school.
(c) corruption in India is increasing.
(d) poor working condition retards output.

143. In order to imbibe the quality of 'Prediction' in a research, it should be

(a) completed on the basis of solid data.
(b) based on one's own self-preferences.
(c) resultant of an astrologer.
(d) carried out in order to satisfy the public opinion.

144. Which of the following is the true statement regarding characteristics of an hypothesis?
(a) It should state relationship between variables.
(b) Hypothesis selected for research should be testable.
(c) It should be limited in scope.
(d) All of the above.

145. Generally the data of the research is
(a) quantitative only
(b) qualitative only
(c) Both of the above.
(d) None of the above.

146. The important sources of hypothesis according to Gooday Hatt are
(a) general culture, scientific theory, analysis and personal experience.
(b) competitive effort, investigation and logic.
(c) only scientific theory.
(d) None of the above.

147. The meaning of generalisation is
(a) to normalise a special quality.
(b) to implement the research conclusion at the larger level.
(c) to give advantages of research to normal person.
(d) None of the above.

148. Study the table which shows the income of five persons, and answer the question that follows?

Year	A	B	C	D	E
1960	55000	22000	43000	30000	40000
1965	75000	21900	47000	40000	60000
1970	76000	21880	42350	50000	65000
1975	83300	21750	72350	60000	90000
1980	93335	20000	54050	70000	75000
1985	102335	17000	84060	80000	105000
1990	103225	16500	85000	90000	120000

Which of the following conclusion is not correct?
(a) There has been an increase in the income of A but slight and steady decline in the income of B from 1960 to 1990.
(b) D and E have at least one property uncommon.
(c) Percentage increase of A is higher than E.
(d) C has fluctuating trend in his income.

149. If you are interested to perceive yourself as a 'Scientist' then what sort of changes will you prefer in yourself?
(a) Registration for PhD degree.
(b) Training under the guidance of a scientist.
(c) Full of scientific excitement.
(d) Development of scientific attitude.

150. The middle part of the Research Synopsis prepares
(a) the partial part of research.
(b) the middle most part of research.
(c) the complete part of research.
(d) the final part of research.

151. The aims of research is/are
(a) Factual (b) Verifiable
(c) Theoretical (d) All of these.

152. If you are doing experiment on a large group of sample which method of controlling will you adopt?
(a) Matching
(b) Randomisation
(c) Elimination and Matching
(d) Elimination

153. What is a Tippit table?
(a) A table used for sampling purposes
(b) A table used for verification of statistical inferences
(c) A statistical table
(d) All of the above.

154. Factual aims of research have the quality of
(a) descriptive nature
(b) foundation on human values
(c) cause-effect relatedness
(d) All of the above.

155. The other name of independent variable for an experimental research is/are
(a) treatment variable
(b) experimental variable
(c) manipulated variable
(d) All of the above.

156. When a research is repeated under the similar controlled conditions, such research is called as
(a) Reliable (b) Unreliable
(c) Changeable (d) Dynamic

157. What is the synopsis of research called?
(a) Base of a problem
(b) Blue print
(c) Mapping of problem
(d) All of the above.

158. The factual aims are most important in
(a) Historical researches
(b) Behavioural researches
(c) Theoretical researches
(d) Philosophical researches

159. The historical research is different from experimental research in the process of
(a) replication
(b) the formulation of the hypothesis
(c) the hypothesis testing
(d) All of the above.

160. The research reporting should be carried out
(a) in a scientific way.
(b) in an imaginary way.
(c) through copying.
(d) through discussion among the scientists.

161. What is a hypothesis?
(a) A temporary solution
(b) A forwarding statement
(c) A thoughtful statement
(d) All of the above.

162. Which of the following is classified in the category of the developmental research?
(a) Philosophical research
(b) Action-research
(c) Descriptive research
(d) All of the above.

163. The review of the related study is important while undertaking a research because
(a) it avoids repetition or duplication
(b) it helps in understanding the gaps
(c) it helps the researcher not to draw illogical conclusions
(d) All of the above.

164. According to Best, a hypothesis is a
(a) thoughtful statement.
(b) forward thinking.
(c) temporary solution.
(d) expected happening.

165. On the basis of contributions made, all the researches can be classified as
(a) Fundamental-Applied-Action Research
(b) Experimental-Historical-Philosophical
(c) Longitudinal and Cross-sectional
(d) None of the above.

166. Which of the following is not the characteristic of a researcher?

(a) He is a specialist rather than a generalist.
(b) He is industrious and persistent on the trial of discovery.
(c) He is not inspirational to his chosen field but accepts the reality.
(d) He is not versatile in his interest and even in his native abilities.

167. What is the meaning of a declarative hypothesis?
(a) The expression of the correlations among the variables.
(b) The declaration of the relationship among the variables.
(c) Both of these.
(d) None of these.

168. Research approaches are
(a) Longitudinal and cross-sectional
(b) Oblique and horizontal
(c) Long and short section
(d) None of the above.

169. Collective psychology of the whole period is a theory which
(a) can explain all phase of historical development.
(b) means the psychology of the whole society.
(c) means psychological approach of data collection.
(d) All of the above.

170. Among the following with whom the fundamental assumptions of experimental method is related to?
(a) Intermediary variables
(b) Law of single variable
(c) Law of two variable
(d) Controlled conditions

171. Generally the formulation and progress of new knowledge have been carried out through
(a) Fundamental researches
(b) Experimental researches
(c) Historical researches
(d) None of the above.

172. Bibliography given in a research report
(a) helps those interested in further research and studying the problem from another angle.
(b) makes the report authentic.
(c) shows the vast knowledge of the researcher.
(d) None of the above.

173. The need of objective observation is
(a) In performing experiment
(b) In research
(c) In normal behaviour
(d) In all the situations

174. If the sample drawn does not specify any condition about the parameter of the population, it is called
(a) Selected statistics
(b) Distribution free statistics
(c) Census
(d) None of the above.

175. Attributes of objects, events or things which can be measured are called
(a) Qualitative measure
(b) Data
(c) Variables
(d) None of the above.

176. The principles formulated by the Fundamental research are used in
(a) Applied researches
(b) Philosophical researches
(c) Action researches
(d) None of the above.

177. The research is (in reference to human nature)
(a) An attitude of inquiry
(b) A method of formulating principles

(c) A systematic and intellectual work
(d) A scientific method

178. Action-research is
(a) An applied research
(b) A research carried out to solve immediate problems
(c) A longitudinal research
(d) All of the above.

179. Which of the following is classified in the category of the developmental research?
(a) Philosophical research
(b) Action-research
(c) Descriptive research
(d) All of the above.

180. All are examples of qualitative variables except
(a) religion and castes
(b) sex
(c) observation
(d) interest of the subject

181. 'Ganga Action Plan' is an action research plan because it has
(a) to attain a definite goal
(b) to finish in a scheduled time
(c) a definite socio-economic order
(d) All of the above.

182. The single difference between Longitudinal and Cross-sectional researches is
(a) In Longitudinal researches, researcher works on single group of subjects for long-term duration while in cross-section, the immediate results have been derived after selecting a sample.
(b) In Longitudinal researches the researcher should have more patience to work than in cross-sectional researches.
(c) The Longitudinal researches have been generally carried out under the specific situation and with specific persons but it is not carried out in cross-sectional researches.
(d) All the above differences are correct.

183. The survey research are classified under the
(a) Fundamental researches
(b) Experimental researches
(c) Both of the above.
(d) None of the above.

184. Studying the social status of a population a researcher concluded that Mr. X is socially backward. His conclusion is
(a) wrong (b) right
(c) inaccurate (d) biased

185. The source of a problem is
(a) Historical records
(b) The virgin areas of research
(c) The conclusions whose verification is still to be carried out
(d) All of the above.

186. The research which is exploring new facts through the study of the part is called as
(a) Historical research
(b) Philosophical research
(c) Mythological research
(d) None of the above.

187. What is the objective of descriptive research?
(a) To collect the facts.
(b) To identify and focus on the present conditions.
(c) To study the subject on phenomenon in a speedy manner.
(d) All of the above.

188. The basis of selection of the problem is
(a) Two just opposite experiences
(b) The suggestions given after research
(c) The counselling with experts
(d) All of the above

189. Who is the profounder of the law of single variable?
(a) Dewey (b) James S. Will
(c) Best (d) Watson

190. Generally at present the following tradition has been observed for doing research.
(a) The supervisor putting the problem to student's mind without considering his ability, interest, etc.
(b) The researchers themselves work hard to search a good problem.
(c) By doing slight changes in the existing topics, variables, etc., new problems have been worked out easily.
(d) Both (a) and (c).

191. How many types of experimental designs are there according to linguistic?
(a) Five (b) Six
(c) Seven (d) Eight

192. The quality of a problem is
(a) Clarity
(b) Worth for solution
(c) Hypothesis oriented
(d) All of the above.

193. The basic need of a research is
(a) in preparation of a project
(b) in guidance
(c) in economic planning
(d) in sitting in library

194. The need of philosophical research method is desired in
(a) explorations of *Atma* and *Paramatma*.
(b) determining the role and extension of philosophy.
(c) philosophy related researches.
(d) all the researches involved in exploring the aims of social sciences.

195. Which one of the following is not a quality of a problem?
(a) Innate nature of the problem.
(b) Practicality of the problem.
(c) Problem according to the interests of the researcher.
(d) Measurability of problem.

196. The new values and principles establishes through
(a) Philosophical researches
(b) Natural researches
(c) Human motivation
(d) Social situations

197. The polluted facts can lead to the birth of
(a) errorless research
(b) human sorrows
(c) a good research
(d) polluted research

198. The basic principle of problem selection is
(a) Novelty of a problem
(b) Practicality of a problem
(c) Future-orientation of a problem
(d) All of the above.

199. Which one of the following is treated as basis of evaluation for the proposed problem of research?
(a) Novelty of a problem.
(b) Presence of problem-solving potentiality.
(c) Possibilities of data collection from the sample.
(d) All of the above.

200. Which one of the following generally does not participate in conference?
(a) Intelligent and curious person.
(b) Ignorant and dull persons.
(c) Experts.
(d) Research scholars.

201. The background of the Historical researches is

(a) In the form of chronological sequence.
(b) In the form of historical data and facts.
(c) Both of the above.
(d) None of the above.

202. How should the words of preface be?
(a) Balanced, alert and humble
(b) In ornamental words
(c) Full of emotions
(d) Multi meaningful.

203. Longitudinal Approach is related with
(a) Long-term researches
(b) Transverse researches
(c) Horizontal researches
(d) All of the above.

204. The justifiable scientific list of all references is called
(a) Book reference (b) Reference
(c) Index (d) Bibliography

205. The advantages of synopsis is/are
(a) It clearly shows the way of research.
(b) It visualizes the various difficulties related with different steps of research.
(c) It helps in planning various steps of the research.
(d) All of the above.

206. On the basis of the approach the classification of researches has taken birth (emerged from)
(a) Biological sciences
(b) Pure sciences
(c) Psychology
(d) None of the above

207. In longitudinal approaches, primarily the researches are related with
(a) Temporal sequence
(b) Eugenics
(c) Sample
(d) None of the above

208. A Year Book has the detailed contents of
(a) a single year only.
(b) a specific year only.
(c) details of the last two years only.
(d) details of specific issues on annual basis.

209. The type of hypothesis is
(a) Interrogative form
(b) Declarative form
(c) Directional form
(d) All of the above

210. Cross-sectional researches are fundamentally related with
(a) Sample (b) Statistics
(c) Tendencies (d) Eugenics

211. What is the advantage of the survey of related literature?
(a) It helps in preparation of research design.
(b) It helps in formulating objectives and hypothesis of the research.
(c) It is like a backbone of the research.
(d) All of the above.

212. The research carried out by a person who has some prejudices in relation to some problem is called
(a) polluted research.
(b) inadequate research.
(c) prejudiced research.
(d) value oriented research.

213. When a possible solution to the problem has been written in desired direction, this type of hypothesis is called
(a) Directional hypothesis
(b) Non-directional hypothesis
(c) Declarative hypothesis
(d) None of the above.

214. Below are given the steps of Educational research in jumbled form.

(1) Statement of the problem
(2) Title of Research
(3) Formulation of the problem
(4) Defining of the problem
(5) Selection of the problem

Tick on the right arrangement of these

(a) 5, 3, 2, 1, 4 (b) 1, 2, 3, 4, 5
(c) 2, 3, 4, 5, 1 (d) 5, 4, 3, 2, 1

215. Considering the research, which of the both is the wrong statement among the following?
(a) The research has been carried out for ornamental degrees.
(b) The research has been carried out for name and fame.
(c) The research has been carried out for invention.
(d) None of the above.

216. Which of the following precaution should be kept in mind by the researcher during the selection of a representative sample?
(a) Deep knowledge of the target population.
(b) The adequate knowledge of the sampling techniques.
(c) Accurate implementation of the sampling design.
(d) All of the above.

217. The novica researchers generally committed the following errors.
(a) Refers broad area of study.
(b) Narrowing a topic to such an extent that it becomes insignificant for research purposes.
(c) Employing unscientific terms of argumentative and biased nature.
(d) All of the above.

218. Research becomes valueless when
(a) a researcher becomes prey of hallucinations.
(b) a researcher feels agreement with imaginary assumptions.
(c) a researcher's behaviour become prejudiced.
(d) All of the above.

219. The meaning of the probability sampling is
(a) where lies the uniform probability of inclusion of all the elements of the population in a sample.
(b) where the complete representativeness of the population is considered.
(c) where no prejudices exist with any element of the sample.
(d) All of the above.

220. The problem can be stated as
(a) Posing a question
(b) Making a declarative statement
(c) Both of the above.
(d) None of the above.

221. Intention of the research should be
(a) in the interest of all the living creatures.
(b) in self-interest.
(c) in the interest of human beings.
(d) in the interest of religion.

222. In Non-probability sampling the probabality exists of
(a) Insufficient population
(b) Limitations of data
(c) Both of the above.
(d) None of the above.

223. Defining a problem means
(a) Raising a boundry wall around the problem.
(b) Fencing of the problem.
(c) Drawing a perimeter around the problem.
(d) All of the above.

224. What is the importance of graphs and figures in research thesis?
(a) They enhance the spontaneity to researched faith.

(b) They produce the perceptual quality in a research.
(c) They enhance the aesthetic sense in a research.
(d) All of the above.

225. The meaning of Randomisation is
(a) Each element of population has equal chances to be included in the sample.
(b) The selection of an individual from population does not pose threat to the selection of other individuals in the sample.
(c) The method does not include the personal basis.
(d) All of the above.

226. Synopsis of a research is
(a) Blue print of research
(b) Summary of research
(c) Extract of research
(d) A plan of research

227. The function of the president of a specific session in a seminar is
(a) to maintain discipline.
(b) to control the debates between speakers and audience.
(c) to co-ordinate the activities in that session.
(d) All of the above.

228. The method of Randomisation is
(a) Lottery or coin method
(b) Blind folded on dice method
(c) Tippit's table of irregular members
(d) All of the above.

229. Etymological meaning of the term hypothesis is
(a) The statement tentative to verification.
(b) The statement leads to prediction.
(c) The statement giving tentative solutions.
(d) None of the above.

230. Research conferences can be conducted at
(a) international level.
(b) national level.
(c) regional level.
(d) All of the above.

231. The advantage of random sampling is
(a) It is the excellent method of sample selection.
(b) It is an economic method in terms of money, time, and energy.
(c) It produces accurate results.
(d) All of the above.

232. Which one of the following is not the definition of a hypothesis?
(a) Any supposition which we make in order to endeavour to deduce conclusion.
(b) A tentative supposition which seems to explain the situation under observation.
(c) A tentative generalisation the validity of which remains to be tested.
(d) All of the above.

233. The constituents of a seminar are
(a) president - chairman - workers.
(b) chairman - participants only.
(c) organiser - chairman - speakers - participants.
(d) None of the above.

234. The quality of probable sample is
(a) It represents the population in excellent manner.
(b) It has normal distribution of the data gathered from the sample.
(c) The data is analysed through normal statistical techniques.
(d) All of the above.

235. What assumption is?
(a) Taking things for granted so that the situation is simplified for logical procedure.

(b) It facilitates the progress of an agreement through a partial simplification.
(c) It means restrictive condition before the argument can become valid.
(d) All of the above.

236. Benefits of a conference is
(a) guidance of new researchers.
(b) mutual exchange of ideals.
(c) development of democratic value.
(d) All of the above.

237. The limitation of the probability sample is
(a) It does not guarantee representativeness of the sample from a population.
(b) The data do not fulfil the standards of the normal probability curve.
(c) It has great risk of generalisation of the results.
(d) All the above statements are correct.

238. How a researcher can define a postulate?
(a) As a working beliefs of most scientific activity.
(b) An unproved state and accepted due to their face-validity.
(c) Assisting in discovery of other facts of nature.
(d) All of the above.

239. Field of research borrowed the term 'workshop' from
(a) Medical (b) Engineering
(c) Management (d) Theatres

240. The quality of Non-probability sampling is
(a) Easy and convenient selection of the sample.
(b) It has no question of probability of selection of an element.
(c) It can be analysed through simple statistical method.
(d) All the above are correct.

241. Which one of the following represent the actual nature of hypothesis?
(a) Present of specific conceptual element.
(b) Verbal statement of a specific concept.
(c) An empirical referent.
(d) All of the above.

242. The human resources of a workshop is
(a) Organisers - coordinator - expert - researcher.
(b) Organisers - coordinator - expert.
(c) Organisers - coordinator - expert - participant.
(d) None of the above.

243. In Stratified sampling the units are selected
(a) after dividing the population in different groups on the basis of specific standard and then taking an equal proportion of units from each group.
(b) after dissociating the population in different groups on the basis of specific standard and then the units are selected from these groups.
(c) after dividing the population in different 'strata' and then selecting any one strata out of them.
(d) None of the above.

244. Which one of the following is not exactly the function of a Hypothesis?
(a) It provides a tentative solution to a problem.
(b) It leads to formulation of another hypothesis.
(c) It is the basic requisite of all excellent researches.
(d) It sensitizes the researcher to work selectively.

245. What opportunities does a seminar provide to the researcher?
(a) Exchange of ideas
(b) Expressions of feelings
(c) Spontaneous learning
(d) All of the above.

246. Suppose the population is quite comprehensive and distributed in a large geographical area. In such a situation what kind of sampling procedure would you like to prefer?
(a) Multi level sampling
(b) Systematic sampling
(c) Cluster sampling
(d) None of the above.

247. Which of the following statement reflect the basic advantage of hypothesis in educational research?
(a) Hypothesis have focus over the research.
(b) Hypothesis leads towards formulation of specific goals.
(c) Hypothesis avoids blank look towards research.
(d) All of the above.

248. Which among the following cannot be considered as a type of seminar?
(a) National seminar
(b) International seminar
(c) House-committee
(d) Focal seminar

249. The Purposive sample will be
(a) Depending on the researcher's whims
(b) Based upon a specific objective of sampling procedure
(c) Based on the excellent method of sampling
(d) None of the above.

250. Generally the hypotheses can be classified into
(a) Question form Hypothesis and Declarative Hypothesis
(b) Directional Hypothesis and Non-directional Hypothesis
(c) Both (a) and (b).
(d) None of the above.

251. Which of the following studies is the related to research?
(a) Experimental situations
(b) Laboratory situations
(c) Real life situations
(d) None of the above.

252. The types of Historical method are
(a) Descriptive and Analytical.
(b) Historical-Constitutional and Reporting.
(c) School survey and social surveys.
(d) Survey Examination-Questionnaire survey.

253. When a hypothesis is stated in interrogative form and it has the lowest level of empirical observation, it is termed as
(a) Question-form hypothesis
(b) Declarative hypothesis
(c) Directional hypothesis
(d) Non-directional hypothesis

254. The process by which historical research differs from the experimental research is
(a) the hypothesis testing.
(b) replication.
(c) the formulation of the hypothesis.
(d) All of the above.

255. The position of sample in Survey method is
(a) Essential (b) Partial
(c) Constant (d) None of these.

256. When a hypothesis expresses anticipated relationship or differences among the variables, it is called as
(a) Question-form hypothesis
(b) Declarative hypothesis
(c) Directional hypothesis
(d) Non-directional hypothesis

257. When a person undertakes a research work then the review of the related study is important because

(a) it helps in understanding the gap.
(b) it avoids repetition or duplication.
(c) it helps the researcher not to draw illogical conclusions.
(d) All of the above.

258. Non-directional hypothesis is also called as
(a) Statistical hypothesis
(b) Null hypothesis
(c) Ho Hypothesis
(d) All of the above.

259. Which of the following method is free from the difficulties related with sampling, control and validity of inferences?
(a) Historical method
(b) Philosophical method
(c) Experimental method
(d) Survey method

260. Most of the researchers conducting survey researches are interested in the formulation of the hypothesis which are
(a) Objective in nature
(b) Null-oriented in nature
(c) Question-oriented in nature
(d) Empirical in nature

261. By seeing the huge crowd in the rally of certain party, it was concluded that will win the election. The conclusion was based on
(a) systematic sampling.
(b) purposive sampling.
(c) random sampling.
(d) cluster sampling.

262. The internal validity related with inferences is associated to
(a) *Ex post facto* method of research
(b) Experimental method of research
(c) Both of the above.
(d) None of the above.

263. If a researcher rejects a null hypothesis it shows
(a) The difference is existed between two variables under consideration.
(b) The difference is not existed between two variables under consideration.
(c) The difference may exist or not exist between two variables under consideration.
(d) None of the above.

264. Which one of the following research methods have the similarity in nature when compared in relation to sample, control and validity of inferences?
(a) Experimental and *Ex post facto* method.
(b) Historical and philosophical method.
(c) Survey and Experimental method.
(d) None of the above.

265. Which one of the following is the important quality of a Null hypothesis?
(a) It is self-explanatory and statistical in nature.
(b) It shows no difference and no relationship on the basis of evidences which have been tested.
(c) It does not influence the researcher by convincing the desired results.
(d) All of the above.

266. The one among the following which is not an example of qualitative variables is
(a) interest of the subject.
(b) observation.
(c) religion and castes.
(d) sex.

267. Survey method is associated with
(a) Those exercises which are continued regularly
(b) Those processes which are continued regularly
(c) The experiences which have been already realised
(d) All of the above.

268. $H_0(\mu_1 - \mu_2 = 0)$. This formula represents
(a) Zero difference exists between the two population means or the treatments.
(b) Two populations are almost similar in all respect.
(c) Population-1 (μ_1) can be reduced from population-2 (μ_2).
(d) None of the above.

269. A University teacher should normally
(a) publish annually at least two scholarly research articles.
(b) be preoccupied with sensitive research areas.
(c) concentrate on writing textbooks.
(d) strike a balance between teaching, research and guidance.

270. Which one of the characteristics is not related to survey method of research?
(a) It organises scientific principles.
(b) It is comparatively more difficult and changeable.
(c) It requires imaginary planning.
(d) It is not related with person's qualities.

271. Type 1 Error or Alpha Error (α) occurs when
(a) an alternative hypothesis H_1, may be accepted and null hypothesis (H_0) is rejected.
(b) null hypothesis (H_0) as accepted and alternative hypothesis (H_1) is rejected.
(c) null hypothesis as well as alternative hypothesis are rejected.
(d) None of the above.

272. Review of research reports should be done in the light of
(a) cultural context.
(b) methodological facts.
(c) cultural context.
(d) All of the above.

273. The characteristic of survey method is
(a) To solve the problems at local level.
(b) To enhance the body of knowledge.
(c) To solve the present problems.
(d) All of the above.

274. The basic difference between Type 1 and Type 2 errors is that
(a) In Type 1 Error, the difference does not exists due to chance errors or sampling errors.
(b) In Type 2 the existing difference is not realistic in nature.
(c) Both of the above are correct.
(d) None of the above.

275. Among the following statements, which one of them is not correct?
(a) One research gives birth to another research.
(b) A good researcher is a nice person.
(c) A researcher is expected to be a well-read person.
(d) All researchers contribute to the existing knowledge.

276. On the basis of the nature of variable, the types of survey method are
(a) Stratified survey and survey researches.
(b) Sample and population related researches.
(c) Surveys through Questionnaire and interviews.
(d) All of the above.

277. The basis of the formulation of Hypothesis is
(a) Observation (b) Reflection
(c) Deduction (d) All of these.

278. A person's reaction to the statement "a good teacher is essentially a good researcher" is that
(a) it is something he finds difficult to agree.
(b) it is only a hypothesis.

(c) it is his firm belief.
(d) it is something which he accepts only as an option.

279. Descriptive study is related with
(a) Survey research method
(b) Experimental research method
(c) Case study method
(d) All of the above.

280. The hypothesis originals from
(a) The method of agreement.
(b) The method of analogy.
(c) The method of concomitant variation.
(d) All of the above.

281. Generalised conclusion made on the basis of a sample is technically called
(a) data analysis and interpretation.
(b) parameter inference.
(c) statistical inference of external validity of the research.
(d) All of the above.

282. The objective of Descriptive Research is
(a) To identify and focus on the present conditions.
(b) To study the subject on phenomenon in a speedy manner.
(c) To collect the facts.
(d) All of the above.

283. Fundamental basis of hypothesis is
(a) The operational level
(b) The conceptual level
(c) Both of the above.
(d) None of the above.

284. The final result of a study will be more accurate
(a) if the sample drawn is fixed by quota.
(b) if the sample drawn is representative to the population.
(c) if the sample drawn is purposive.
(d) if the sample drawn is taken randomly.

285. The meaning of the Historical method of research is
(a) To employ scientific method in order to study the historical problems.
(b) To establish relationship between historical facts and current events.
(c) To make specific investigation of the past events.
(d) All of the above.

286. Independent variable is the variable which can be manipulated by the
(a) Researcher (b) Subject
(c) Supervisor (d) All of the above.

287. In which of the following independent variables are not manipulated?
(a) In *ex-post facto* researches
(b) In normative researches
(c) Both (a) and (b).
(d) None of these.

288. The steps of the Historical method of research are given in a jumbled state. Select them in a scientific order from the following options
1. Identification of the problem
2. Criticism of data
3. Interpretation of data
4. Collection of data

(a) 1, 4, 3 and 2 (b) 1, 2, 3 and 4
(c) 1, 3, 2 and 4 (d) 4, 3, 2 and 1

289. The difference between control and intervening variables lies in the statement
(a) All are intervening except independent variable and dependent variables but out of these a few variables can be controlled which are called control variable.
(b) Conceptually no difference between two.
(c) Intervening variables are causing interference but control variable does not do so.
(d) Cannot say.

290. Which one of the following procedure should be adopted in order to list the hypothesis?
(a) It should be stated in such a manner that deductions can be made from it and that decisions can be reached as to whether or not it explains the facts being considered.
(b) It should be worded clearly and unequivocally in operational terms leaving no doubt as to what action, what predictions, what quality or quantity, or who is involved.
(c) It must have simplicity. A complex hypothesis should be divided into sub-hypothesis.
(d) All of the above.

291. If a researcher divides his population into certain groups and fixes the size of the sample from each group it is called
(a) cluster sample.
(b) stratified sample.
(c) quota sample.
(d) All of the above.

292. The experimental method is
(a) A method for verifying a hypothesis.
(b) A method deriving inferences.
(c) A variable controlling method.
(d) None of the above.

293. Which of the following alternatives specifically denote the criteria for evaluating a hypothesis in researches?
(a) Plausibility of explanation
(b) Testability of explanation
(c) Levels of explanation
(d) All of the above.

294. The first question that a researcher interested in the application for statistical techniques to his research has to ask, is
(a) whether appropriate statistical techniques are available.
(b) whether wroth while inferences could be drawn.
(c) whether the data could be quantified.
(d) whether analysis of data would be possible.

295. The wrong statement in relation to experimental method is
(a) Observation under controlled condition is experiment.
(b) It is the method of effective control of variables.
(c) Careful observation of a phenomenon under controlled conditions.
(d) It is a useful method in laboratories.

296. Which of the following uses of Hypothesis is denoting its adequacy in reference to various types of the researches?
(a) It is indispensable in experimental researches and make their crucial parts.
(b) Hypotheses are essential in Normative survey type researches.
(c) In Historical researches there is no scope of hypothesis.
(d) All of the above.

297. What is the main difference between an administrator and a researcher?
(a) The administrator takes a global view of things while the researcher penetrates deep into specific issues.
(b) The administrator is more interested in social outcomes while the researcher in finding out as to why things happen as they do.
(c) The administrator is more concerned only with the what of things while the researcher is interested both in the why and what of things.
(d) The administrator approaches problems in a practical manner while the researcher is purely theoretical.

298. Generally variables are of

(a) Two types — Independent and dependent variables.
(b) Three types — Independent, dependent and intervening variables.
(c) Four types — Independent, dependent, Intervening and control variables.
(d) None of the above.

299. Steps involved in research design are
(a) Selection and defining the problem
(b) Sources of information
(c) Nature of study
(d) All of the above.

300. Why a person undertakes research?
(a) To refute what has already been accepted as a fact.
(b) To verify what has already been established.
(c) To describe and explain a new phenomenon.
(d) All of the above.

301. The characteristic(s) of experimental method is/are
(a) It follows the law of single variable.
(b) It is the laboratory method of research and has borrowed from pure sciences.
(c) It follows the scientific method.
(d) All the above statements are correct.

302. The chief characteristic of a good research design is
(a) Unbiased in nature
(b) Free from confounding effect
(c) Statistical precision
(d) All of the above.

303. For establishing a fact, which of the following will be acceptable?
(a) Availability of observable evidence.
(b) Opinion of a large number of people.
(c) Reference in the ancient literature.
(d) Traditionally in practice over a long period of time.

304. The meaning of *ex post racto* Research is
(a) The research carried out after the incident
(b) The research carried out prior to the incident
(c) The research carried out along with the happening of an incident
(d) The research carried out keeping in mind the possibilities of an incident

305. What a sampling is?
(a) A fragment of a phenomenon that might advance our knowledge.
(b) A fractional part of the respondent.
(c) Both of the above.
(d) None of the above.

306. Which of the following processes is not needed in experimental researches?
(a) Manipulation and replication
(b) Reference collection
(c) Observation
(d) Controlling

307. In correlation design of *ex post facto* Research we study
(a) The variable which has been measured in advance and will work as a causative factor for second variable.
(b) The second variable which is going to be measured and will work as a causative factor for antecedent variable.
(c) The third variable which cannot be measured but works as a causative factor for first and second variable.
(d) All the above three situations and occurrence of variables.

308. The chief characteristics of sampling is
(a) Economy (b) Reliability
(c) Feasibility (d) All of these.

309. A researcher while studying the social status of a population concluded that Mr. Y is socially backward. His conclusion is

(a) Biased (b) Inaccurate
(c) Wrong (d) Right

310. The contribution of case-study is
(a) In study and data collection of a case related to caste, age, sex, religion, problems, intellectual level, socio-economic status, etc.
(b) In evaluation of historical facts related with persons or case.
(c) In study of institutionalised groups and families.
(d) All the above studies.

311. Which one of the following is not called a demerit of a sample?
(a) Less accuracy
(b) High reliability
(c) Misleading conclusions
(d) Requires specialised training

312. Among the following formulation of hypothesis may not be necessary in
(a) experimental studies.
(b) survey studies.
(c) historical studies.
(d) normative studies.

313. The objective of case-study is
(a) Remedial (b) Diagnostic
(c) Educational (d) All of these.

314. When a researcher requires the sampling?
(a) When a vast population is under study.
(b) When utmost accuracy is not the aim of study.
(c) When the nature of data is unlimited.
(d) All of the above.

315. Case-study collects the data from the following sources
(a) From individual
(b) From anecdotal records
(c) From government documents
(d) From all the above.

316. A Good sample has the quality of
(a) Representativeness
(b) Adequacy
(c) Homogeneity
(d) All of the above.

317. The sequence of the steps in scientific method is
(a) Hypothesis - Theory - Observation - Experiments - Establishment of law or principle.
(b) Experiments - Observation - Theory - Hypothesis - Establishment of law or principle.
(c) Observation - Experiments - Theory- Hypothesis - Establishment of law or principle.
(d) Observation - Hypothesis - Experiments - Theory - Establishment of law or principle.

318. The criteria of a good case-study is
(a) Continuity
(b) Completeness of the data
(c) Validity of the data
(d) All of the above.

319. A salient feature of randomisation is
(a) Each element has equal chance of being selected
(b) Free from personal biases
(c) Ensure representative sample
(d) All of the above.

320. Applied research is called
(a) a fundamental research.
(b) an experimental research.
(c) a field research.
(d) None of the above.

321. The following steps of case-study have been jumbled with each other:
1. Focus of study
2. Identification of cause-effect symptoms
3. Remedy for adjustment

4. Follow-up programme
5. Data collection

The correct sequence in above steps is:

(a) 1,5,2,3 and 4 (b) 1,4,5,2 and 3
(c) 1,2,3,4 and 5 (d) 5,4,3,2 and 1

322. Generally the method employed for generalisation is
(a) Lottery method
(b) Tossing of a coin
(c) Throwing a dice
(d) All of the above.

323. Steps for the solution of a problem follows the following sequence.
(a) Constructing hypothesis - Identifying the problem - Discussion - Collection of data - Presentation of data - Analysis of data - Result.
(b) Identifying the problem - Discussion-constructing hypothesis - Collection of data - Presentation of data - Analysis of data - Result.
(c) Collection of data - Presentation of data - Analysis of data - Identifying the problem - Discussion - Constructing hypothesis - Result.
(d) None of the above.

324. The limitation of case-study is
(a) It has subjectivity
(b) It is difficult to formulate assumptions
(c) It is difficult to employ complex statistical methods
(d) All the above are correct.

325. Blind-folded method is used in case of
(a) Cluster sampling
(b) Random sampling
(c) Systematic sampling
(d) All of the above.

326. According to J.C. Aggrawal, tools of research have been classified into
(a) five broad divisions.
(b) six broad divisions.
(c) four broad divisions.
(d) three broad divisions.

327. Research is a
(a) Value oriented process
(b) Passive process
(c) Self-contained process
(d) Discovery oriented process

328. According to Gooday and Hatte, interviews are divided into
(a) four divisions (b) six divisions
(c) nine divisions (d) seven divisions

329. The research should be value oriented
(a) in the interest of mankind.
(b) in the interest of all the living creatures.
(c) in the self-interest.
(d) in the interest of religion.

330. Which one of the following is a disadvantage of Randomisation?
(a) Unrepresentativeness
(b) Economy
(c) Convenience
(d) Statistical in nature

331. A direct interview is
(a) Structured (b) Not structured,
(c) Elaborate (d) None of these

332. The research is an 'ethical process'. Here the meaning of ethics is
(a) The external beauty of the research.
(b) The quality of the research content.
(c) The fulfillment of research values in an investigation.
(d) None of the above.

333. Probability sampling has the quality of
(a) Each element of population has equal probability of the selection in a sample.
(b) Employing parametric statistics.
(c) Representativeness.
(d) All of the above.

334. Focused interview aims on

(a) responses from the respondents on a wide variety of subjects.
(b) responses from the respondents on a specific event.
(c) responses from the respondents on the events which had recently occurred.
(d) None of the above.

335. The Ethics in research is not related to
(a) Self-interest
(b) Scientific method
(c) Reliability
(d) Humanity

336. The statement "Rating is in essence, directed observation" was given by
(a) Ruth Strong (b) A.S. Bars
(c) Best (d) J.C. Aggarwal

337. Suppose a researcher has some prejudices in relation to some problem, then the research carried out by him, is called as
(a) Value oriented research
(b) Polluted research
(c) Inadequate research
(d) Prejudiced research

338. Which of the following statements regarding the hypothesis is correct?
(a) It should have unlimited scope.
(b) It should not have state relationship between variables.
(c) It should be limited in scope.
(d) None of the above.

339. What will you do to make your research value oriented?
(a) You pay the cost of its writing to a ghost writer.
(b) You will charge the market rate for the work, you have conducted so far.
(c) You will ensure honesty and faith in the research work.
(d) You will undertake a plagiarism.

340. Problem is
(a) Obstacle in the way of needs
(b) Suggested question for a problem
(c) An interrogative question
(d) All of the above.

341. Steps for preparation of report is as follows:
(a) Reference section - Main body of the report - Preliminary section.
(b) Main body of the report - Preliminary section - Reference section.
(c) Preliminary section - Main body of the report - Reference section.
(d) Reference section - Preliminary section - Main body of the report.

342. When a researcher is engaged in research in a subjective manner, the result will be
(a) inadequate formulation of objectives.
(b) inadequate selection of apparatus.
(c) inadequate collection of data.
(d) All of the above.

343. Kerlinger has written about a problem
(a) It is description of an interrogative question.
(b) It is a posed question for problem-solving.
(c) It is an unanswered question
(d) None of the above.

344. Footnote is
(a) very essential in report writing.
(b) somewhat essential in report writing.
(c) not at all essential in report writing.
(d) never used in report writing.

345. "The research should not be carried out with blind-folded eyes"—the meaning of this phrase is
(a) The research should be free from all personal biases.
(b) The research should be free from personal limitations.

(c) The research should be separated from personal ideology.
(d) All of the above.

346. The sources of a problem is
(a) Historical records.
(b) The virgin areas of research.
(c) The conclusions whose testing of verifiability is still to be carried out.
(d) All of the above.

347. Council of Scientific and Industrial Research was constituted as an autonomous society in
(a) 1940 (b) 1942
(c) 1952 (d) 1950

348. Central Road Research Institute is located in
(a) Delhi (b) Mumbai
(c) Kolkata (d) Chennai

349. In order to inculcate the ethical values in the researches, it is essential that it should be
(a) In accordance with the researcher's abilities.
(b) Providing opportunities to the researcher to work freely.
(c) Inculcate maturity in the researcher.
(d) All of the above.

350. Nation Aeronautical Laboratory is located in
(a) Delhi (b) Kolkata
(c) Jamshedpur (d) Bangalore

351. Each word of a research should be
(a) Justifiable (b) Full of wisdom
(c) Enjoyable (d) Entertaining

352. How one can select a new problem of research from the researches which have been already completed?
(a) By collecting comprehensive informations from the research worker who have completed the research.
(b) By collecting informations from the research supervisor.
(c) By searching the literature in the library.
(d) None of the above is correct.

353. National Chemical Laboratory is located in
(a) Bangalore (b) Pune
(c) Jamshedpur (d) Ranchi

354. If a researcher has the quality of exploration and has the fine skills in his field of research, the research will be
(a) Value oriented
(b) Comprehension oriented
(c) Anxiety oriented
(d) Thinking oriented

355. The problem arises from two opposite experiences when
(a) They generate conflicts
(b) They generate struggles
(c) They come in compromise with each other
(d) None of the above conditions exist

356. Bose Institute, Kolkata is devoted to
(a) fundamental and applied research in physical and life sciences.
(b) research on atomic energy.
(c) research on solar energy.
(d) None of the above.

357. The research papers are written in order to
(a) Gain name and fame
(b) Communicate the research
(c) Get promotions
(d) None of the above.

358. The gaps in explanation is meant by
(a) When there is disagreement in the expression of an explanation.
(b) When there appears difference in explanation.

(c) When there is a vagueness in an explanation.
(d) All of the above.

359. Which of the following is not essential for communicating a research work?
(a) Statement of objectives
(b) Command over language
(c) Procedure followed
(d) Conclusions drawn

360. According to Good, Ban and Scates one of the following is not the source of a problem
(a) Specific studies
(b) Analysis of the field of knowledge
(c) Suggestions of an intelligent person
(d) Different areas under the study

361. A researcher divided his population into certain group and fixes the size of the sample from each group. It is called
(a) cluster sample
(b) quota sample
(c) stratified sample
(d) All of the above.

362. When do we use "Depth Studies" in educational research?
(a) A thorough investigation is required through instance.
(b) We are required to trace back the previous research in a chosen area.
(c) The data collected allow through statistical analysis.
(d) We want to prove into the unconscious causes and elements of a behaviour.

363. The research papers writing methodology has slight variations in reference to
(a) The standards maintained by research journals.
(b) The interests of the researchers.
(c) The research traditions.
(d) All of the above statements are correct with slight variations.

364. Which one of the following is not a quality of a problem?
(a) Innate nature of the problem.
(b) Practicality of the problem.
(c) Problem according to the interests of the researcher.
(d) Measurability of problem.

365. Attributes of objects, events or things which can be measured are called
(a) Data
(b) Variables
(c) Qualitative measure
(d) All of the above.

366. Generally the format of research resembles with
(a) A long essay
(b) A synopsis
(c) A writing technique
(d) A report preparing method

367. Generally in all researches, an abstract of each article has been prepared which focuses upon
(a) the central theme of the research paper
(b) the research-innovation employed in research paper
(c) the effective conclusions of the research paper
(d) All of the above.

368. If a problem is very expensive and the possibility of data collection is also appears to be very difficult then what would you like to do?
(a) Accepting challenge of selection of such problem.
(b) Forging such problem.
(c) Trying to solve such problem.
(d) Escaping from such problem.

369. The primary source of data is
(a) oral testimony of traditions and customs

(b) personal records, letters, diaries, autobiographies, wills, etc.
(c) official records - government documents, information preserved by social-religious organisations, etc.
(d) All of the above.

370. The background of the research paper may be
(a) Philosophical (b) Historical
(c) Contemporary (d) None of these

371. The meaning of the definition of a problem is
(a) To define the complex words in the problem and suggest their meaning in the light of the problem.
(b) To limit the problem in words.
(c) To present the definition of different authors related to problem.
(d) None of the above.

372. The review of the related study is important while understanding a research because
(a) it helps in understanding the gaps.
(b) it helps the researcher not to draw illogical conclusion.
(c) it avoids repetition or duplication.
(d) All of the above.

373. Generally research papers have been given more weightage instead of research articles because these will be
(a) Based on data
(b) Incorporated with statistics
(c) Both of the above.
(d) None of the above.

374. The researcher should keep a precaution while he is defining a problem
(a) He should not have used the words having more than one meaning.
(b) He should forecast the results on its basis.
(c) He should precise its nature.
(d) All of the above.

375. The first step for making a statistical investigation is
(a) Collection of data.
(b) Samples.
(c) Organisation.
(d) None of the above.

376. Generally research papers are presented abundantly in
(a) Seminars (b) Journals
(c) Symposiums (d) All the above.

377. Constitution of direct personal interviews include
(a) Secondary data.
(b) Primary data.
(c) Both of the above.
(d) None of the above.

378. Conference is a
(a) Provision to discuss on serious matters
(b) Adequate solution of research problems
(c) Wider manipulation of research inferences
(d) All of the above.

379. The research problems available in the field of philosophy are called as
(a) Philosophical problems
(b) Historical problems
(c) Presentable problems
(d) Invisible problems

380. What are indirect oral interviews called?
(a) Secondary data
(b) Primary data
(c) Both (a) and (b).
(d) None of the above.

381. The main objective of organising a work shop is
(a) To improve the skills of the researchers in order to solve the specific problem.
(b) To impart practical training to the researchers.

(c) To make perfect the researchers in an area of research.
(d) All of the above.

382. What do we call if the variables are varying in the opposite directions?
(a) Linear correlation
(b) Negative correlation
(c) Positive correlation
(d) None of the above.

383. Generally the objective of organising a workshop is
(a) To develop the research attitude in the researchers
(b) To tell about the research methodology to the neo-researchers
(c) To impart practical training of conducting research
(d) None of the above.

384. Which one of the following is not a type of a problem?
(a) Philosophical problem
(b) Correlational problems
(c) Survey Problems
(d) Longitudinal Problems

385. Among the following statements, which one is incorrect?
(a) A good researcher is a nice person.
(b) One research gives birth to another research.
(c) A researcher is expected to be a well read person.
(d) All researches contribute to the existing knowledge.

386. Among the following which one is acceptable for establishing a fact?
(a) Reference in the ancient literature.
(b) Opinion of a large number of people.
(c) Availability of observable evidence.
(d) Traditionally in practice over a long period of time.

387. The characteristic feature of a workshop is
(a) To attain the higher cognitive and psycho-motor objectives of the research.
(b) To comprehend the theoretical and practical aspects of the research.
(c) To explore the possibilities of applied aspects of the research.
(d) All of the above.

388. The advantage of synopsis is
(a) It clearly shows the way of research.
(b) It visualizes the various difficulties related with different steps of research.
(c) It helps in planning various steps of the research.
(d) All of the above.

389. The standard of research is judged by
(a) depth of the research.
(b) experience of the researcher.
(c) methodology followed in conducting the research.
(d) relevance of research.

390. Seminar is
(a) The process of promoting the reflective level.
(b) The process of nurturing the higher cognition.
(c) The interactional process of thinking.
(d) All of the above.

391. A good synopsis is considered as
(a) A half-way research
(b) A complete research
(c) A partial research
(d) A beginning of research

392. In which form the objectives of a research can be written?
(a) Only in statement form
(b) In hypothetical form
(c) Both question and statement form
(d) Only in question form.

393. The main cognitive objective of seminar is
(a) To develop critical and analytical capacities in a researcher.
(b) To develop observational and experiential presenting capabilities in a researcher.
(c) To develop synthetic and evaluation-related abilities in a researcher.
(d) All of the above are correct statements.

394. The preparation of a synopsis is
(a) An art
(b) A science
(c) Both of the above.
(d) None of the above.

395. What is the Latin root term of the word 'Curriculum'?
(a) Collection of contents fixed for education.
(b) The subjects taught through school alone.
(c) A path or course to be run.
(d) Collection of contents fixed for education.

396. The constituents of a seminar are
(a) Organiser - Chairman - Speakers - Participants
(b) President - Chairman - Workers
(c) Chairman - Participants only
(d) None of the above.

397. Generally the steps of scientific method are also the steps of
(a) Research
(b) Human life
(c) Literary collection
(d) None of the above.

398. The state of the psyche designated as super ego by the psycho-analysts, is found
(a) among human beings alone.
(b) among men and animals as well.
(c) among men practicing yogic exercise.
(d) in higher animal also.

399. Which one of the following is not a type of Seminar?
(a) House-committee
(b) International Seminar
(c) National Seminar
(d) Focal Seminar

400. Hypothesis is
(a) A thoughtful statement
(b) A forwarding statement
(c) A temporary solution
(d) All of the above.

401. What should be the number of questions in a questionnaire?
(a) 5
(b) 7
(c) 8
(d) As small as possible keeping in view the purpose of the survey.

402. Seminar provides the following opportunity to a researcher
(a) Expression of feelings
(b) Exchange of ideas
(c) Spontaneous learning
(d) All of the above.

403. Best has defined hypothesis as
(a) It is a thoughtful statement
(b) It is a forward thinking
(c) It is an expected happening
(d) It is a temporary solution

404. Prior to using secondary data the only thing to be seen so that they are
(a) adequate for the purpose in hand.
(b) representative.
(c) reliable.
(d) All of the above.

405. The primary aim of organising the Seminar is

(a) Attaining knowledge
(b) Communication of research inferences
(c) The exhibition of research creativity
(d) None of the above.

406. The nature of a hypothesis is
(a) Conceptual (b) Declarative
(c) Action-oriented (d) All the above.

407. The most suitable method of collecting the data when the informants are literate and are spread over a vast area is
(a) interview by investigator.
(b) mailed questionnaire method.
(c) direct personal interview.
(d) None of these.

408. According to Von Dalen the main importance of hypothesis in research is
(a) It is the strong chain between the problem and its solution.
(b) It reflects the whole working design of the research.
(c) It delimits the research to be carried out.
(d) All the above statements are correct.

409. Herber Specer favoured Pestalozzi's learning theory as a process of
(a) self-activity.
(b) serving the cause of nation.
(c) internal self-instruction.
(d) programmed instructional material.

410. Symposium is
(a) Intellectual entertainment
(b) Hearty entertainment
(c) TV related entertainment
(d) Research with entertainment

411. Primary data are
(a) less reliable compared to secondary data.
(b) depends on the agency collecting the data.
(c) always more reliable compared to secondary data.
(d) depends on the care with which data have been collected.

412. Symposium is a
(a) A well organised group of a few speakers with large audience.
(b) Arrival at the certain goal through mutual exchange of ideas.
(c) Process of taking decisions in a group.
(d) All of the above.

413. Reliance of most of the investigations depend on
(a) Primary data (b) Secondary data
(c) Both (a) and (b) (d) None of these.

414. The aim of symposium is
(a) To develop the knowledge about current problems and the capacity to identify them.
(b) To take decision about the problems related to research topics.
(c) To seek advice of the experts in the area.
(d) All of the above.

415. While editing primary data we have just to notice the information contained in the questionnaire is
(a) Homogeneous (b) Consistent
(c) Complete (d) All of these.

416. The method of research reporting should be
(a) Scientific
(b) Ethical and attractive
(c) Personal
(d) Favourable to globalisation

417. Which of the following precaution should be kept in mind by the researcher during the selection of a representative sample?
(a) Deep knowledge of the target population.

(b) The adequate knowledge of the sampling techniques.
(c) Accurate implementation of the sampling design.
(d) All of the above.

418. Among the following which of the following is not a characteristic of research?
(a) Research is not a process.
(b) Research is not inactive.
(c) Research is problem-oriented.
(d) Research is systematic.

419. The advantage of research report writing in a scientific manner is
(a) Global Standardisation
(b) Global Communication
(c) Global Awakening
(d) Global Welfare

420. Reference serves the purpose
(a) the authenticity of the given content.
(b) of insightful decision-making by the researcher.
(c) of giving ornamental value to the research.
(d) it exhibits the great achievements of the piece of research.

421. In Non-probability sampling the probability exists of
(a) Insufficient population
(b) Limitations of data
(c) Both of the above
(d) None of the above

422. In primary source, we include
(a) hand written manuscripts only.
(b) the original writings of the authors.
(c) direct collection from the thesis.
(d) All of the above.

423. Generally the synopsis of the research is compared with human body. In spite of the differences existing in its different parts, it must have
(a) Uniformity
(b) Equality
(c) Functional continuity
(d) None of the above.

424. The advantage of the sample is
(a) Time-saving (b) Money-saving
(c) Energy-saving (d) All of the above.

425. In evidence sources we include
(a) primary and secondary sources.
(b) pure and applied sources.
(c) active and passive sources.
(d) None of the above.

426. When a thesis has been submitted in order to attain a degree or related contain objective, the supervisor's certificate has been produced because
(a) It ensures the quality of research.
(b) It gives name and fame to the worker.
(c) It gives clearance from all boundations.
(d) It ensures authenticity of the research work.

427. The delimitations of a sample are
(a) Possibilities of biases
(b) Needs of trained persons
(c) Inconsistency of sample units
(d) All of the above.

428. What will you put on top priority while giving the suggestions in your research?
(a) The difficulties you have faced during your research work.
(b) The limitations of your research work.
(c) The futuristic improvements to be carried out by other researchers.
(d) All of the above.

429. In Research thesis the importance of introduction is
(a) It imbibes the importance of problem in it.
(b) It determines the direction of survey related to problem.

(c) It explains the objectives of the problem.
(d) All of the above.

430. When a thesis has been submitted in order to attain a degree or related contain objective, the supervisor's certificate has been produced because
(a) it ensures the quality of research.
(b) it gives clearance from all boundations.
(c) it gives name and fame to the worker.
(d) it ensures authenticity of the research work.

431. In order to ensure maximum acceptability of data analysis and its interpretation, the help should be taken from
(a) Statistics
(b) Graphs and diagrams
(c) Computer
(d) Appreciable typing

432. The quality of probable sample is
(a) It represents the population in excellent manner.
(b) It has normal distribution of the data gathered from the sample.
(c) The data is analysed through normal statistical techniques.
(d) All of the above.

433. What will you put on top priority while giving the suggestions in your research?
(a) The difficulties you have faced during your research work.
(b) The limitations of your research work.
(c) The futuristic improvements to be carried out by other researchers.
(d) All of the above.

434. The limit of the probability sample is
(a) It is not giving guarantee of representativeness of the sample from a population.
(b) The data do not fulfil the standards of the normal probability curve.
(c) It has great risk of generalisation of the results.
(d) All the above statements are correct.

435. Metaphysics is concerned with
(a) Knowledge of reality
(b) Methods of teaching
(c) The validity of human knowledge
(d) None of the above.

436. Epistemology is related to
(a) Naturalism (b) Idealism
(c) Pragmatism (d) Existentialism

437. Experiment is
(a) It consists an event in making which occurs in known conditions.
(b) A question framed on the basis of what is known and addressed to nature to elicit further knowledge.
(c) It is a proof of hypothesis.
(d) All of the above.

438. Experimental method is based on
(a) J.S. Mill's Cannon of Sigle Variable
(b) Scientific method
(c) Researcher's point of view
(d) Formulation of hypothesis

439. The salient feature of experimental method is
(a) Indispensable method of educational research.
(b) Implemented in education with the limitation of human material.
(c) Ethical issues are raised in education.
(d) None of the above.

440. What will you do to make your research value oriented?
(a) You pay the cost of its writing to a ghost writer.
(b) You will charge the market rate for the work, you have conducted so far.
(c) You will ensure honesty and faith in the research work.
(d) You will make a Paligarism.

441. Below are given the steps of experimental method in jumbled form
1. Selecting the problem
2. Preparing the experimental design
3. Carrying out the experiment
4. Analyzing the outcomes
5. Drawing conclusions
6. Reviewing the literature
7. Defining the population
8. Measuring the outcomes

The correct arrangement of these steps is
(a) 1,2,3,4,5,6,7,8 (b) 1,2,7,3,8,4,5,6
(c) 1,3,5,7,2,4,6,8 (d) 1,5,7,8,6,4,2,3

442. In the three dimensions of the Philosophy the study of value has been carried out under
(a) Metaphysics (b) Epistemology
(c) Ethics (d) None of these

443. The important characteristics of the survey method is
(a) It is capable for collecting data from a large group (population) simultaneously
(b) Here the work is being carried out on predetermined problem
(c) The aims of this method are fixed and specific
(d) All of the above statements are correct

444. The control in Survey method is required
(a) to a great extent.
(b) to a less extent.
(c) to a normal extent.
(d) not at all.

445. Which one of the characteristic is not related to survey method of research?
(a) It organises scientific principles
(b) It is comparatively more difficult and changeable
(c) It requires imaginary planning
(d) It is not related with person's qualities

446. The informations to be collected in survey method are related to
(a) Present position
(b) Aims of the research
(c) The attainment of the aim of the research
(d) All of the above.

447. The position of sample in Survey method is
(a) essential (b) partial
(c) constant (d) None of these.

448. According to Mouly, the type of research methods is
(a) Historical method.
(b) Survey method.
(c) Experimental method.
(d) All of the above.

449. The survey method is classified on the basis of
(a) the nature of variable.
(b) the measurable class or group.
(c) the source of data collection.
(d) All of the above.

450. The Historical method is related with
(a) the history oriented researches only.
(b) the researches of history and Archaeology.
(c) the historical researches conducted in all the disciplines.
(d) None of the above is correct.

451. The steps of historical research method are
(a) To identify the problem
(b) To collect the data
(c) To criticise the data
(d) All of the above.

452. The problem for the research related to metaphysics can be
(a) What is meant by existence?
(b) What are the qualities of the existence of the objects?

(c) How knowledge of individuality of the objects can be realised?
(d) All of the above.

453. The basic principles of problem selection is
(a) novelty of a problem.
(b) practicality of a problem.
(c) future-orientation of a problem.
(d) All of the above.

454. In Epistemology, the following problem can be solved
(a) What is known to the brain beyond the knowledge of its own ideas?
(b) How do the knowwldege becomes objective as well as subjective simultaneously?
(c) What is the criteria of judgement of Truth and False?
(d) All of the above are correct.

455. Ethics is related with
(a) Beliefs of the person
(b) Nature of Law
(c) Civic principles and rights
(d) All of the above.

456. According to Good, Barr and Scates which one of the following is not the source of a problem?
(a) Specific studies.
(b) Analysis of the field of knowledge.
(c) Suggestions of an intelligent person.
(d) Different areas under the study.

457. How can one select a new problem of research from the researches which have been already completed?
(a) By collecting comprehensive informations from the research worker who have completed the research.
(b) By collecting informations from the research supervisor.
(c) By searching the literature in the library.
(d) None of the above.

458. The fundamental assumption of experimental method is related with
(a) Law of single variable
(b) Law of two variable
(c) Controlled conditions
(d) Intermediary variables

459. The propounder of the law of single variable is
(a) James S. Will (b) Thomas Hobbes
(c) William Kant (d) Dewey

460. The meaning of variable is
(a) The quality having different values
(b) The nature of happening which influences other happenings through its presence
(c) Both of the above.
(d) None of the above.

461. Generally variable are of
(a) Two types—Independent and dependent variable
(b) Three types—Independent, dependent and Intervening variables
(c) Four types—Independent, dependent, Intervening and control variables
(d) None of the above.

462. The step of experimental method is
(a) Selection and definition of a problem
(b) Survey of the related literature
(c) Experimental design
(d) All of the above.

463. According to Lindquist the types of experimental design are
(a) Six (b) Four
(c) Two (d) None of these.

464. Case-study method denotes
(a) The study of a case in its vicinity
(b) The extensive study of a case
(c) The cumulative study of a case
(d) All of the above.

465. The main types of case study are
(a) Four (b) Five
(c) Six (d) Not at all

466. The meaning of Crossed Reaction Experimental Design is
(a) Such an experimental design where all the reactions are carried out with the subjects in a sequential fashion.
(b) Such an experimental design where the subject related errors are eliminated.
(c) Both of the above are correct.
(d) None of the above are correct.

467. Research Ethics shows
(a) Moral values in the research
(b) Utilisation values in the research
(c) Egalitarian values in the research
(d) All of the above.

468. Research ethics represents
(a) Humanitarian venture in research
(b) Researches for human welfare
(c) Researches as the accumulated human efforts of the centuries
(d) All of the above.

469. Ethics in researches can be develop vices due to the presence of
(a) Prejudices
(b) Fallacies
(c) Contaminated facts
(d) All of the above.

470. Fallacies are caused due to
(a) The researcher's take notions about research
(b) The ornamental criterion of research in the mind of the researcher
(c) The researcher's poor skills and incompetencies
(d) All of the above.

471. The researches, generally lost its basic ethical qualities when a researcher
(a) imposes his personalized sentiments in it
(b) has poor skills as well as abilities
(c) has malice intention in deriving results
(d) All of the above.

472. Along with Ethics the other philosophical elements involved in a research are
(a) Metaphysics and Epistemology
(b) Naturalism and Idealism
(c) Pragmatism and Existentialism
(d) None of the above.

473. Prejudices in researches caused due to the reason that the researcher has his own
(a) Priorities (b) Interests
(c) Thinking (d) All the above.

474. Which one of the following take notion is leading the researches towards the fallacy?
(a) Lack of knowledge about research designs.
(b) The poor grit over statistical operations.
(c) The research is merely reduced to an ornamental degree.
(d) All of the above.

475. Rationality in researches refer to the quality of
(a) Objectivity (b) Reliability
(c) Validity (d) All of these.

476. Most of the PhD thesis have committed such errors which are leading to fallacies which ultimately leading in loosing
(a) Research ethics
(b) Research quality
(c) Research practice
(d) Both (a) and (b)

477. A poor rationalisation on the part of the researcher leads to
(a) Poor quality of research
(b) Poor consistency of facts
(c) Poor explanation of findings
(d) All of the above.

478. Reliability and validity of a research can be maintained by
(a) Contaminated facts
(b) Real facts
(c) Invariable facts
(d) Uninviting facts

479. The transfer of the values and qualities of the researcher takes place
(a) In the research works carried out by him
(b) In all the works performed by him
(c) In the vocational works carried out by him
(d) None of the above.

480. The wrong statement related with research is
(a) The research has been carried out for invention
(b) The research has been carried out for name and fame
(c) The research has been carried out for ornamental degrees
(d) All the above items are incorrect in relation to research

481. The value of a research has been lost when
(a) A researcher behaviour become prejudiced
(b) A researcher becomes prey of hallucinations
(c) A researcher feels agreement with imaginary assumptions
(d) All of the above.

482. Suppose a researcher has some prejudices in relation to some problem, then the research carried out by him, is called as
(a) Value oriented research
(b) Polluted research
(c) Inadequate research
(d) Prejudiced research

483. The polluted facts can give birth to
(a) A good research
(b) Errorless research
(c) Polluted research
(d) Human sorrows

484. Some research scholars thinks that when a little extension will be made in dissertation, it will be equivalent to the degree of PhD. This idea denotes
(a) The illusions on the part of researcher
(b) The truth on the part of researcher
(c) The miserable behaviour of the researcher
(d) The pitiable behaviour of the researcher

485. When a researcher do not possess the quality of collection of the facts from social environment, such research will
(a) not be a pure research
(b) be a mallacious research
(c) be a irrelevant research
(d) pure research

486. The research work is not influenced by
(a) The researcher himself
(b) His pre-established assumptions
(c) The curse of some other researchers
(d) The wrong calculations

487. The organisational structure of conference consists
(a) A post of President
(b) A post of Secretary
(c) A post of Treasurer
(d) All of the above.

488. The difference lying in research paper and research article is
(a) Research articles are theoretical content which have been interwoven scientifically on the basis of inductive-deductive reasoning
(b) Research papers are Empirical propositions which have been

interwoven scientifically with the testing of hypothesis
(c) Both (a) and (b) are correct.
(d) None of the above.

489. Which one of the following is the chief aim of organising a conference?
(a) To communicate the research findings for open discussions and criticism from a plateform.
(b) To provide a common plateform to discuss the current issues from different dimensions.
(c) To accomplish a task within timebound schedule in a joint manner.
(d) All of the above.

490. Which one of the following is not reflecting the advantage of conference?
(a) Democratic sharing of ideas pertaining to scientific issues.
(b) A break from monotonous routine of teaching.
(c) Promoting long association among the workers working in specific field and benefited from them.
(d) Exploration of new and innovative fields of research.

491. Which one of the following phrase is conveying the correct meaning of workshop?
(a) The term in Engineering perspective has meaning the job done by one's hand.
(b) The conative behaviour of an individual.
(c) The skill-oriented training.
(d) All of the above.

492. The affective aspects of a workshop one should be interested to promote is
(a) awareness of the problem in present context.
(b) readiness towards immediate problem.
(c) proficiency in research methods.
(d) All of the above.

493. The limitation of a research workshop is
(a) required too much time on the part of the researcher.
(b) develops disinterestedness and monotony in the researchers.
(c) requirement of skilful expertise.
(d) All of the above.

494. The organisation of a workshop has the following active personnels
1. Convenor
2. Experts/Resource person
3. Participants
4. Organiser

The hierarch of these personnel in ascending order is
(a) 3, 2, 4, 1 (b) 1, 2, 3, 4
(c) 2, 3, 1, 4 (d) 3, 4, 2, 1

495. The cognitive objective of a seminar is
(a) To facilitate critical and analytical capacities in research workers
(b) To promote synthetic and analytical reasoning in researches
(c) To develop the potentialities of observational and experiential presentation
(d) All of the above.

496. The advantage of a seminar is
(a) The attainment of higher cognitive and affective objectives
(b) The promotion of democratic ideology
(c) The development of skills of discussion
(d) All of the above.

497. Affective objectives of a seminar focuses upon
(a) To develop tolerance for contrasting ideas and even results
(b) To appreciate the research results of others and sharing of ideas with them

(c) To promote emotional stability and motivation in the young researchers
(d) All of the above.

498. Symposium's literal meaning is
(a) Intellectual entertainment
(b) Mental recreation
(c) Urges for creativity
(d) Motivational urges

499. The chief characteristics of a symposium is
(a) It gives clear picture about the specific problem and helps in comprehension of its different dimensions
(b) It gives freedom to the listner and the speaker for expressing their views
(c) It imparts training in higher level of thinking
(d) All of the above

500. The compulsion of publication of research-paper is
(a) Only for University Teachers
(b) Only for Central University Teachers
(c) For all the teachers in higher education institutions
(d) Cannot say

501. The advantages of preparing the research paper is
(a) The exchange of ideas related to research
(b) The familiarity with the research approaches
(c) The awareness about present researches
(d) All of the above

502. The research paper does not has its advantage when it does not
(a) Improve the goal-oriented researches
(b) Present for wider criticism of its inferences
(c) Nourish the wider causes of the society
(d) Imparts fame at regional and national levels

503. The research paper and the research article are
(a) Two separate name of one and same thing
(b) First is factual and later a theoretical in nature
(c) First is having survey background the later is experiment in nature
(d) (b) and (c) are the correct statements

504. In colleges, universities the promotion on the post of Reader under the Personal Promotion Scheme, the required minimum number of published papers is
(a) 3 to 5 (b) Only one
(c) Only two (d) None of these

505. The basic requirement for preparing a research paper is
(a) The research orientation of the person
(b) The research skills in the person
(c) The research attitudes in the person
(d) All of the above.

506. Generally in a research conference the following person is not present
(a) Permanent member
(b) Common person
(c) Expert
(d) Chairman of Conference

507. The main Psycho-motor objective of the workshop is
(a) The expertise of formulating research design
(b) The ability of selection and determining of the problems
(c) The skills of construction of research apparatus
(d) All of the above.

508. The step of research workshop is
(a) The presentation and explanation of the topic
(b) The practice of following an approach

(c) Follow-up and evaluation of a topic
(d) All of the above.

509. The advantage of Seminar is
(a) The attainment of higher Cognitive and Affective objectives of the research
(b) The development of democratic values
(c) The formation of good learning habits
(d) All of the above.

510. The characteristic of symposium is
(a) To develop the comprehensive understanding about the specific problems of research and its various dimensions
(b) To give freedom to express their ideas by the speakers as well as the audience
(c) To impart training for higher order of thinking
(d) All of the above.

511. In present time the Seminars are organised
(a) for promoting the teachers.
(b) for revamping teachers with research potentialities.
(c) for converting low grade teachers into higher grades.
(d) None of the above.

512. The basic need of thesis writing refers to
(a) Enhancing communicability of the research report to the general public
(b) Suggestions for new problems and areas of research
(c) Clarifying research designs and allied aspects of research
(d) All of the above.

513. The importance of thesis writing lies in
(a) Expansion of knowledge
(b) Presentation of conclusion for information
(c) Verification of validity
(d) All of the above.

514. In a seminar the main function of the president of a specific session is
(a) To coordinate the activities in that session
(b) To exercise his power to control the debatable discussions between Speakers and Audience
(c) To maintain as disciplining agency
(d) All of the above statements are correct

515. The Doctoral Dissertation can be divided into
(a) Preliminaries (b) Textual Body
(c) References (d) All of the above.

516. Besides preface the preliminary section of a thesis includes
(a) Tables of contents
(b) List of tables
(c) List of figures
(d) All of the above.

517. The mechanics of a report writing includes
(a) Foot-notes (b) Headings
(c) Figures (d) All of the above.

518. Textual body of a thesis consist of
(a) Theoretical framework
(b) Review of related literature
(c) Design of the research
(d) All of the above.

519. 'Acknowledgement' in a research thesis is written because
(a) It is the effort on the part of researcher to repay the academic debts.
(b) It is the custom to recognize the other's contribution in your work.
(c) It is just obligatory in nature in order to forget the bad taste in mouth during its completion.
(d) All of the above.

520. In general case, an appendix include
(a) Tools and Techniques of the research employed.
(b) Raw Data and Statistical tests.

(c) Blank tools and Manuals, letters of significance, etc.
(d) All of the above.

521. *Ibid.* page means
(a) Same page as in earlier footnotes.
(b) Same book as in earlier footnotes.
(c) Same content as in earlier footnotes.
(d) None of the above.

522. Which of the following considerations should be kept in mind by the researcher during writing a report?
(a) Report should be written as using third person.
(b) Report should be prepared in Past Tense.
(c) Report should consisted of scientific language instead of literary or local dialects.
(d) All of the above.

523. The advantage of Research report writing in a scientific manner is
(a) Global Standardisation
(b) Global Communication
(c) Global Awakening
(d) Global Welfare

524. What is the importance of an abstract of research?
(a) It gives complete glimpse of the research work.
(b) It serves the purpose of wider communication.
(c) It circulates area, aims and objectives of research.
(d) All of the above.

525. The basic need of writing an abstract is
(a) High comprehensibility
(b) Sample testing opportunities on the part of examiner
(c) Quoting facility by the other researchers
(d) All of the above.

526. The quality of a good abstract is
(a) An economical device
(b) Lucid linguistic presentation
(c) Dissemination of new knowledge
(d) All of the above.

527. Before preparing your Research report you consult with
(a) Your supervisor
(b) Your elder collegues
(c) Your predecessor's works
(d) All of the above.

528. The main parts of the Body of Research Synopsis are
(a) Title Page—Trunk—Posterior Part
(b) Title Page and Main Body
(c) Title Page and Posterior Part
(d) None of the above.

529. In priorities of the Research synopsis, one can include
(a) Title Page, Table of Content, and Index of Tables
(b) Title Page and List of Graph only
(c) Title Page and Supervisor's Certificate only
(d) None of the above.

530. The title page of Research thesis should be
(a) Brief and meaningful
(b) Scientific and logical
(c) Aesthetic and attractive
(d) All the above and 'Catchy'.

531. When a Research worker do not has the desired ability of reporting of research, then the work carried out by him, will be of
(a) Low grade quality
(b) Good grade quality
(c) Excellent grade quality
(d) Cann't say

532. The devaluation of Research proposal will take place when

(a) You will try to give extra importance to certain person
(b) You will become unbiased for all the persons who have directly or indirectly contributed in your work
(c) You will be giving thanks to persons in the light of your personal relations
(d) You will make a justice with all the persons

533. There is a need for the qualities of labelling, page-numbering and refinement in the graphical figures in a researcher
(a) Specific qualities
(b) Artistic qualities
(c) Appreciative qualities
(d) Painter's qualities

534. In which of the following objective's achievement, the related literature is not useful?
(a) In defining the problem
(b) In formulating the problem
(c) In selection of the tool
(d) In exploration of the inferences

535. What will you put on top priority while giving the suggestions in your research?
(a) The difficulties you have faced during your research work.
(b) The limitations of your research work.
(c) The futuristic improvements to be carried out by other researchers.
(d) All of the above.

536. The Research design is related to
(a) Sample selection
(b) Formulation of Experimental design
(c) Selection and construction of the tool
(d) All of the above.

537. Evidences in research collect from
(a) Primary and secondary sources
(b) Pure and applied sources
(c) Active and passive sources
(d) None of the above.

538. Year Books contains the detailed content of
(a) A specific year only
(b) A year only
(c) Details of specific issues on annual basis
(d) Cann't say

539. Generally in the last pages of each thesis there is a provision of writing suggestions and recommendations, because
(a) It enhances your repute as a great scholar
(b) It communicates the best researcher's qualities in your
(c) It gives authencity to your research work
(d) It is mere a tradition

540. Foot-notes in a thesis serve as a
(a) To substantiate the quotations or citation
(b) To give credit to the source of material
(c) To verify the authencity and accuracy of material quoted
(d) All of the Above.

541. In primary sources we include
(a) Hand written manuscripts only
(b) The original writings of the authors
(c) Direct collection from the thesis
(d) All of the above.

542. There exists a single most important difference between the reference and bibliography
(a) The references have the actual page numbers
(b) The references have the last name of the person (Surname) on its first priority
(c) The references have the minute details in order to verify them
(d) All of the above are correct

543. The content edited in Encyclopaedia is

(a) Primary source
(b) Secondary source
(c) Continuous source
(d) Infinite source

ANSWERS

1. (a)	2. (a)	3. (a)	4. (a)	5. (d)	6. (c)
7. (a)	8. (c)	9. (d)	10. (d)	11. (d)	12. (a)
13. (c)	14. (c)	15. (d)	16. (b)	17. (b)	18. (c)
19. (c)	20. (b)	21. (c)	22. (d)	23. (c)	24. (c)
25. (d)	26. (d)	27. (b)	28. (b)	29. (c)	30. (c)
31. (d)	32. (b)	33. (a)	34. (d)	35. (b)	36. (d)
37. (a)	38. (c)	39. (d)	40. (d)	41. (b)	42. (c)
43. (d)	44. (b)	45. (b)	46. (c)	47. (d)	48. (d)
49. (b)	50. (a)	51. (d)	52. (d)	53. (d)	54. (c)
55. (a)	56. (a)	57. (b)	58. (a)	59. (d)	60. (d)
61. (d)	62. (d)	63. (d)	64. (c)	65. (d)	66. (a)
67. (c)	68. (d)	69. (d)	70. (a)	71. (c)	72. (a)
73. (b)	74. (d)	75. (c)	76. (d)	77. (b)	78. (b)
79. (b)	80. (c)	81. (b)	82. (d)	83. (c)	84. (d)
85. (d)	86. (d)	87. (d)	88. (c)	89. (d)	90. (c)
91. (c)	92. (a)	93. (d)	94. (a)	95. (d)	96. (c)
97. (c)	98. (c)	99. (b)	100. (d)	101. (d)	102. (a)
103. (a)	104. (d)	105. (d)	106. (d)	107. (d)	108. (d)
109. (a)	110. (b)	111. (a)	112. (a)	113. (b)	114. (b)
115. (d)	116. (d)	117. (c)	118. (b)	119. (c)	120. (b)
121. (a)	122. (a)	123. (d)	124. (d)	125. (a)	126. (d)
127. (d)	128. (d)	129. (b)	130. (b)	131. (a)	132. (d)
133. (d)	134. (d)	135. (c)	136. (b)	137. (d)	138. (a)
139. (d)	140. (a)	141. (d)	142. (a)	143. (a)	144. (d)
145. (c)	146. (a)	147. (b)	148. (c)	149. (d)	150. (b)
151. (d)	152. (b)	153. (d)	154. (a)	155. (d)	156. (b)
157. (d)	158. (a)	159. (d)	160. (a)	161. (d)	162. (b)
163. (d)	164. (a)	165. (a)	166. (d)	167. (c)	168. (a)
169. (a)	170. (b)	171. (a)	172. (a)	173. (d)	174. (b)

175. (c 176. (a) 177. (a) 178. (b) 179. (b) 180. (d)
181. (d 182. (d) 183. (a) 184. (c) 185. (d) 186. (a)
187. (d 188. (d) 189. (b) 190. (d) 191. (b) 192. (d)
193. (a 194. (d) 195. (a) 196. (a) 197. (d) 198. (d)
199. (d 200. (b) 201. (c) 202. (a) 203. (a) 204. (b)
205. (d 206. (a) 207. (a) 208. (d) 209. (d) 210. (a)
211. (d 212. (a) 213. (a) 214. (a) 215. (d) 216. (d)
217. (d 218. (d) 219. (d) 220. (c) 221. (a) 222. (c)
223. (d 224. (d) 225. (d) 226. (a) 227. (d) 228. (d)
229. (a 230. (d) 231. (d) 232. (d) 233. (c) 234. (d)
235. (d 236. (d) 237. (d) 238. (d) 239. (b) 240. (d)
241. (d 242. (c) 243. (a) 244. (c) 245. (d) 246. (c)
247. (d 248. (c) 249. (b) 250. (c) 251. (c) 252. (b)
253. (a 254. (d) 255. (a) 256. (b) 257. (d) 258. (d)
259. (a 260. (b) 261. (d) 262. (b) 263. (a) 264. (b)
265. (d 266. (a) 267. (d) 268. (a) 269. (d) 270. (a)
271. (a 272. (b) 273. (d) 274. (c) 275. (d) 276. (a)
277. (d 278. (c) 279. (d) 280. (d) 281. (c) 282. (d)
283. (c 284. (b) 285. (d) 286. (a) 287. (c) 288. (a)
289. (a 290. (d) 291. (b) 292. (a) 293. (d) 294. (c)
295. (d 296. (d) 297. (b) 298. (c) 299. (d) 300. (b)
301. (d 302. (d) 303. (a) 304. (a) 305. (c) 306. (b)
307. (d 308. (d) 309. (b) 310. (d) 311. (b) 312. (b)
313. (d 314. (d) 315. (d) 316. (d) 317. (d) 318. (d)
319. (d 320. (c) 321. (a) 322. (d) 323. (b) 324. (d)
325. (d 326. (a) 327. (a) 328. (d) 329. (a) 330. (a)
331. (a 332. (c) 333. (d) 334. (b) 335. (a) 336. (a)
337. (b 338. (c) 339. (c) 340. (d) 341. (c) 342. (d)
343. (a 344. (a) 345. (d) 346. (d) 347. (b) 348. (c)
349. (a 350. (d) 351. (a) 352. (c) 353. (a) 354. (a)
355. (a 356. (a) 357. (b) 358. (d) 359. (a) 360. (c)
361. (b 362. (c) 363. (d) 364. (a) 365. (b) 366. (b)
367. (d 368. (b) 369. (d) 370. (d) 371. (a) 372. (d)
373. (c 374. (d) 375. (a) 376. (d) 377. (b) 378. (d)

379. (a)	380. (b)	381. (d)	382. (b)	383. (c)	384. (d)
385. (d)	386. (c)	387. (d)	388. (d)	389. (d)	390. (d)
391. (a)	392. (c)	393. (d)	394. (c)	395. (c)	396. (a)
397. (a)	398. (a)	399. (b)	400. (d)	401. (d)	402. (d)
403. (a)	404. (d)	405. (a)	406. (d)	407. (a)	408. (d)
409. (a)	410. (a)	411. (d)	412. (d)	413. (b)	414. (d)
415. (d)	416. (a)	417. (d)	418. (b)	419. (b)	420. (a)
421. (c)	422. (d)	423. (c)	424. (d)	425. (a)	426. (c)
427. (d)	428. (a)	429. (d)	430. (d)	431. (b)	432. (d)
433. (c)	434. (d)	435. (a)	436. (b)	437. (d)	438. (a)
439. (a)	440. (d)	441. (b)	442. (d)	443. (d)	444. (b)
445. (a)	446. (d)	447. (a)	448. (d)	449. (d)	450. (c)
451. (d)	452. (d)	453. (d)	454. (d)	455. (d)	456. (c)
457. (c)	458. (a)	459. (a)	460. (c)	461. (c)	462. (d)
463. (a)	464. (d)	465. (c)	466. (c)	467. (a)	468. (d)
469. (d)	470. (d)	471. (d)	472. (a)	473. (d)	474. (d)
475. (d)	476. (d)	477. (d)	478. (b)	479. (b)	480. (d)
481. (d)	482. (b)	483. (c)	484. (a)	485. (a)	486. (c)
487. (d)	488. (c)	489. (d)	490. (b)	491. (d)	492. (d)
493. (d)	494. (a)	495. (d)	496. (d)	497. (d)	498. (a)
499. (d)	500. (c)	501. (d)	502. (c)	503. (d)	504. (a)
505. (d)	506. (b)	507. (d)	508. (d)	509. (d)	510. (d)
511. (b)	512. (d)	513. (d)	514. (d)	515. (d)	516. (d)
517. (d)	518. (d)	519. (a)	520. (d)	521. (a)	522. (d)
523. (b)	524. (d)	525. (d)	526. (d)	527. (d)	528. (a)
529. (a)	530. (d)	531. (a)	532. (a)	533. (b)	534. (d)
535. (d)	536. (d)	537. (a)	538. (c)	539. (d)	540. (d)
541. (d)	542. (d)	543. (b)			

3

Reading Comprehension

Read the following passages carefully and answer the questions given below each passage.

PASSAGE-1

Observe your mind. Can you hear the noise of thought currents within? Scientists say 30 to 31 brain waves are constantly in flow. These waves belong to the neuro-linguistic system of our mind. Research indicates that whenever we are engaged in intense mental work, arguments and counter-arguments, the waves are in Beta range. When we take a break from the heavy load of responsibilities and try to relax for a while, the brain emits Alpha waves. During vacation, when we experience the mood of fun, the mind is sending Theta range waves. Even when we are fast asleep, the brain remains active and emanates waves—sometimes Theta and occasionally Delta.

In the mind, the tussle of thought currents continues unabated. The mind remains busy at all times. We could say, the function of the mind is to think and it is acting as per its nature! So let it go.... Why mind it?

There is definitely something wrong in it. Think about a machine whose parts are made of metals. If the machine remains functioning without a break, day and night, what will be the result? It will get all heated up. Similarly, the brain, too gets stressed; when thoughts are generated on a continuous basis, it also gets heated up. Anger, tension, agitation—all these are the result of increase in the level of 'temperature' of the brain. Increase in the level of noise pollution is one of the reasons for hypertension, stress and depression. If the noise outside can create such a disastrous situation, think of the impact of internal noise—the dissonance produced by a multitude of thoughts.

If we do not think, how would we work and function? Thinking is not at all wrong. Just avoid unnecessary thinking that is similar to noise pollution. When a scientist creates an electric circuit, he is always cautious of the 'noise factor', which indicates the 'undesirable electrical disturbance' or the avoidable obstruction. In the presence of such disturbances, the circuit doesn't accept the signals of current properly; it doesn't allow it to pass through in the right measure, nor gives the desired output. Likewise, within the circuit of mind, due to the disturbance of useless thoughts, we are unable to take proper decisions. It hampers our sense of discrimination and a reasonable understanding of the issues.

1. Brain waves belong to
   (a) neuro-linguistic system
   (b) neuro-anatomic system
   (c) congnitive psychology
   (d) None of these

2. In case of arguments and counter-arguments, the waves are
   (a) in Alpha range (b) in Beta range
   (c) in Theta range (d) in Delta range

3. When we relax, the brain emits
   (a) X-rays (b) Gamma rays
   (c) Alpha waves (d) Beta waves
4. When the mind is in the mood of fun, it sends
   (a) Gamma waves (b) Alpha waves
   (c) Delta waves (d) Theta waves
5. Unnecessary thinking results in
   (a) increase in noise pollution.
   (b) increase in temperature of brain.
   (c) decrease in temperature of brain.
   (d) None of the above.
6. Due to useless thoughts
   (a) we are unable to take proper decisions.
   (b) we are able to relax our mind.
   (c) our sense of discrimination and reasonable understanding of issues get hamper.
   (d) Both (a) and (c).

PASSAGE-2

The enlightenment of Gautama at Bodh Gaya made a great impact on human consciousness and changed our future course. In Rabindranath Tagore's novel *Ghaire-Baire* (Home and World), the author-protagonist declares: 'It was Buddha who conquered the world, not Alexander'—for Buddha threw light on something of eternal value.

The doctrine of the middle path, which emphasises moderation in all things, accommodation of antithetical points of view, and primacy of a common-sense approach, is not without its possible misuses. To arrive at the middle path is not to compromise but to hold a harmonious view among conflicting interpretations. This is a difficult task. At a deeper level, it denotes unity of mind and thought.

In Buddha's conception of dharma, there was no place for priest-craft and ritualism. Love and kindness are the very basis of society. Hatred, he said, is never appeased by more hatred—it could only be defused by friendship and sympathy.

Our ordinary sense of love and compassion is involved with attachment. The deep feeling of compassion and love for one's own family is related to attachment, and so is confined to a limited circle. It is centred on familial relationship. In contrast to this is a clear recognition of the importance and rights of others. Developed from that viewpoint, compassion will reach even your enemy.

Buddha believed that every individual must find the truth in his own way and should question everything, even his own words and sayings. In this new rationality there was no place for blind faith.

Buddha is today seen as a rationalist, an empiricist, and a social prophet, and his dharma based on non-violence and compassion presents a practical ideology for a new age. In his teachings he never deviated from human nature and natural surroundings. He would emphasise that enlightenment was natural to human experience and so was not the preserve of a select few.

The approach of rational self-enquiry also enables a person to achieve a higher state of discipline and harmony beyond narrow sectarian and national prejudices. All these become axiomatic when seen in the light of the well-known Buddhist maxim: 'Be a lamp unto yourself.'

7. Buddha got enlightenment at
   (a) Bodh Gaya (b) Kushinagar
   (c) Lumbani (d) Sarnath
8. According to Tagore's novel *Ghaire-Baire*, ...conquered the world.
   (a) Alexander
   (b) Buddha
   (c) Ashoka
   (d) Chandragupta Maurya

9. Hatred could be defused by
   (a) more hatred
   (b) friendship
   (c) sympathy
   (d) Both (b) and (c)
10. In Buddha's conception of dharma, there is no place for
   (a) love (b) kindness
   (c) ritualism (d) sympathy
11. Buddha is today seen as
   (a) secularist (b) non-secularist
   (c) rationalist (d) None of these
12. Rational self-enquiry enables a person to achieve
   (a) a higher state of discipline and harmony.
   (b) a narrow sectarian and national prejudices.
   (c) Both (a) and (b).
   (d) None of the above.
13. Find the word in the passage which means 'nirvana'.
   (a) consciousness (b) empiricist
   (c) enlightenment (d) self-enquiry

PASSAGE-3

The path of evolutionary enlightenment, like all enlightenment teachings, is one of ego-transcendence that's a means to a higher end, to open up some space within the self-space for evolution to occur.

Being inspired by the idea of conscious evolution is one thing, while actually engaging in the process of evolution is something else altogether. Many people are moved by the notion of evolutionary becoming. But within themselves they are not free. They are trapped in psychological hang-ups and attachments, with little or no space for that which is new. Their souls are not liberated, and their choices and actions are still being shaped by unconscious adherence to values and perspectives that have nothing to do with being a liberated vessel for the evolution of consciousness and culture.

Merely being inspired by the potential for conscious revolution does not automatically give us access to the fearless inner freedom to actualise that potential. In order to find that freedom, to open up that space for the new, it is essential that you liberate yourself to a significant degree from your personal fears and desires and your culturally conditioned values.

This inner freedom is not different from the goal of traditional enlightenment where feedom is an end in itself. Ideally, freedom becomes the foundation from which to engage in conscious evolution. You must disentangle yourself, free yourself from your karma, your history, culture and personal ego.

How does one discover enlightened awareness? There are two ways that you can gain access to the intoxicating joy and ecstatic wakefulness of that timeless spiritual attainment: spontaneously, or through making noble effort.

14. Being inspired by the potential for conscious revolution does not give access to
   (a) fearless inner freedom
   (b) fearful inner freedom
   (c) personal fears and desires
   (d) None of these
15. The path of evolutionary enlightenment is
   (a) easy to achieve
   (b) ego-transcendence
   (c) Both (a) and (b)
   (d) None of these
16. Within themselves people are not free. They are trapped in
   (a) psychological hang-ups
   (b) attachments

(c) conscious evolution
(d) Both (a) and (b)

17. In order to find fearless inner freedom, you should liberate yourself from
(a) personal fears
(b) personal desires
(c) culturally conditioned values
(d) All of the above

18. One can discover enlightened awareness
(a) through making noble effort
(b) spontaneously
(c) Both (a) and (b)
(d) None of these

PASSAGE-4

Scientists in the US claim to have developed the world's first 'biological computer' that is made from biomolecules and can decipher images encrypted on DNA chips.

A team from the Scripps Research Institute in California and the Technion-Israel Institute of Technology claims it has created the computing system using biomolecules, Angewandte Chemie journal reported.

In the research, when suitable software was applied to the biological computer, the scientists found that it could decrypt, separately, fluorescent images of Scripps Research Institute and Technion logos. And, although DNA has been used for encryption in the past, this is the first experimental demonstration of a molecular cryptosystem of images based on DNA computing, say the scientists led by professor Ehud Keinan.

"In contrast to electronic computers, there are computing machines in which all four components are nothing but molecules," Keinan said.

"For example, all biological systems and even entire living organisms are such computers. Every one of us is a biomolecular computer, a machine in which all four components are molecules that 'talk' to one another logically," he said.

The hardware and software in these devices, Keinan notes, are complex biological molecules that activate one another to carry out some predetermined chemical work.

The input is a molecule that undergoes specific, predetermined changes, following a specific set of rules (software), and the output of this chemical computation process is another well-defined molecule.

But, what a biological computer looks like?

"This computer is built by combining chemical components into a solution in a tube. Various small DNA molecules are mixed in solution with selected DNA enzymes and ATE. The latter is used as the energy source of the device."

It's a clear solution—you don't really see anything.

Molecules start interacting upon one another, and we watch what happens.

19. The world's first biological computer is made from
(a) biochemicals (b) biomolecules
(c) RNA molecules (d) None of these

20. Biological computer uses...for encryption.
(a) DNA
(b) RNA
(c) RNA and DNA both
(d) None of these

21. The hardware and software of biological computers are
(a) made of nano-particles
(b) made of semi-conducting materials
(c) complex biological molecules
(d) All of the above

22. The energy source of the biological computer is

(a) DNA enzymes (b) ATE
(c) solar energy (d) alkaline battery

PASSAGE-5

The tip of a girl's 40,000-year-old pinky finger found in a cold Siberian cave, paired with faster and cheaper genetic sequencing technology, is helping scientists draw a surprisingly complex new picture of human origins. The new view is fast supplanting the traditional idea that modern humans triumphantly marched out of Africa about 50,000 years ago, replacing all other types that had gone before.

Instead, the genetic analysis shows, modern humans encountered and bred with at least two groups of ancient humans in relatively recent times: the Neanderthals, who lived in Europe and Asia, dying out roughly 30,000 years ago, and a mysterious group known as the Denisovans, who lived in Asia and most likely vanished around the same time. Their DNA lives on in us even though they are extinct. "In a sense, we are a hybrid species," Chris Stringer, a paleoanthropologist who is the research leader in human origins at the Natural History Museum in London, said in an interview.

The Denisovans were first described a year ago in a groundbreaking paper in the journal Nature made possible by genetic sequencing of the girl's pinky bone and of an oddly shaped molar from a young adult. Those findings have unleashed a spate of new analyses. Scientists are trying to envision the ancient couplings and their consequences: when and where they took place, how they happened, how many produced offspring and what effect the archaic genes have on humans today. Other scientists are trying to learn more about Denisovans: who they were, where they lived and how they became extinct.

A revolutionary increase in the speed and a decline in the cost of gene-sequencing technology have enabled scientists at the Max Planck Institute for Evolutionary Anthropology in Leipzig, Germany, to map the genomes of both the Neanderthals and the Denisovans. Comparing genomes, scientists concluded that today s humans outside Africa carry an average of 2.5% Neanderthal DNA, and that people from parts of Oceania also carry about 5% Denisovan DNA. A study published in November found that Southeast Asians carry about 1% Denisovan DNA in addition to their Neanderthal genes. It is unclear whether Denisovans and Neanderthals also interbred.

A third group of extinct humans, Homo fioresiensis, nicknamed "hobbits" because they were so small, also walked the earth until about 17,000 years ago. It is not known whether modern humans bred with them because the hot, humid climate of the Indonesian island of Plores impairs the preservation of DNA. This means that our modern era, since Homo fioresiensis died out, is the only time in the four-million-year human history that just one type of human has been alive, said David Reich, a geneticist at Harvard Medical School.

For scientists, the epicenter of the story on human origins is the Denisova cave in Altai Mountains of Siberia, where the girl's finger bone was found. It is the only known place where three types of humans—Denisovan, Neanderthal, modern—lived.

23. A girl's 40,000-year-old pinky finger was found in
    (a) Siberian cave (b) Africa
    (c) London (d) Neatherland
24. Neanderthals were lived in
    (a) Europe (b) Asia
    (c) Africa (d) Both (a) and (b)
25. Denisovans were lived in
    (a) Europe (b) Asia
    (c) Africa (d) Both (a) and (b)

26. Neanderthals and Denisovans died
    (a) nearly 30,000 years ago
    (b) nearly 40,000 years ago
    (c) nearly 50,000 years ago
    (d) cannot be said
27. The nick name of homo fioresiensis is
    (a) Hobbits (b) Robotis
    (c) Genotis (d) None of these
28. The place where three types of humans—Denisovan, Neanderthal, modern—lived is
    (a) Plores (b) Ajanta cave
    (c) Denisova cave (d) Not known

PASSAGE-6

International astronomers have found the fourth potentially habitable planet outside our solar system with temperatures that could support water and life about 22 light-years from Earth.

The team analyzed data from the European Southern Observatory about a star known as GJ 667C, which is known as an M-class dwarf star and puts out much less heat than our Sun.

However, at least three planets are orbiting close to the star, and one of them appears to be close enough that it likely absorbs about as much incoming light and energy as Earth, has similar surface temperatures and perhaps water.

The new rocky planet, GJ 667Cc, orbits its star every 28.15 days—meaning its year equals about one Earth month—and has a mass at least 4.5 times that of Earth, according to the research published in Astrophysical Journal Letters.

"This planet is the new best candidate to support liquid water and, perhaps, life as we know it," said Guillem Anglada-Escude who has conducted the research. The theory about water, however, cannot be confirmed until astronomers learn more about the planet's atmosphere. Other planets circling the same star—which is part of a three-star system could include a gas-giant and an additional super-Earth with an orbital period of 75 days, but more observations are needed to confirm that.

29. The fourth potentially habitable planet outside our solar system is at the distance of ----- from the earth.
    (a) 21 thousand kilometer
    (b) 22 light-years
    (c) 22 thousand light-years
    (d) None of the above
30. GJ 667C is known as
    (a) N-class dwarf star
    (b) M-class dwarf planet
    (c) N-class dwarf planet
    (d) M-class dwarf star
31. How many planets are orbiting close to GJ 667C?
    (a) Three (b) Four
    (c) Six (d) One
32. The planet which orbits its star every 28.15 days is
    (a) GJ 667C (b) GJ 667Cc
    (c) CJ 667C (d) None of these
33. A year on planet GJ 667Cc will be equal to
    (a) 28.15 days on earth
    (b) 30 days on earth
    (c) 45 days on earth
    (d) 60 days on earth

PASSAGE-7

Candidates for election pay close attention to statements and actions that will make the voters see them favourably. In ancient Rome candidates wore pure white togas (the Latin word candidatus means "clothed in white") to indicate that they were pure, clean, and above any "dirty work". However, it is interesting to note that such a toga was not worn after election.

In more modern history, candidates have allied themselves with political parties. Once a voter knows and favours the views of a certain political party, he may vote for anyone with that party's label. Nevertheless, divisions of opinion develop, so that today there is a wide range of candidate views in any major party.

34. The best conclusion to be drawn from the first paragraph is that after an election
    (a) all candidates are dishonest.
    (b) candidates are less concerned with symbols of integrity.
    (c) candidates do not change their ideas.
    (d) officials are always honest.
    (e) policies always change.
35. A fair statement is that most candidates from the same political party today are likely to
    (a) have the same views.
    (b) be different in every view.
    (c) agree on almost all points.
    (d) agree on some points and disagree on others.
    (e) agree only by accident.

PASSAGE-8

In 1812 Napoleon had to withdraw his forces from Russia. The armies had invaded successfully and reached the city of Moscow. There was no question of French army disloyalty or unwillingness to fight. As winter came, the Russian army moved out of the way, leaving a wasted land and burned buildings. Other conquered European nations seized upon Napoleon's problems in Russia as their chance to rearm and to break loose from French control.

36. According to the passage, it may be inferred that the main reason for Napoleon's withdrawal from Russia was the
    (a) disloyalty of the French troops
    (b) Russian winter
    (c) burned buildings
    (d) revolts in other countries
    (e) Russian army

PASSAGE-9

By 1915 events of World War I were already involving the United States and threatening its neutrality. The sinking of the British liner Lusitania in that year by a German submarine caused great resentment among Americans. Over a hundred United States citizens were killed in the incident. President Wilson had frequently deplored the use of submarines by Germany against the United States. Since the United States was neutral, it was not liable to acts of war by another nation.

However, Wilson resolved to represent the strong feeling in the country (notably in the Midwest) and in the Democratic Party that United States neutrality should be maintained. He felt that the United States should have "peace with honor," if possible.

There were also people, mostly in the East, who wanted to wage a preventive war against Germany. Such leaders as Theodore Roosevelt bitterly attacked Wilson as one who talked a great deal but did nothing.

By 1917 Germany again used unrestricted submarine warfare and Wilson broke off relations with Germany. In February British agents uncovered the Zimmerman Telegram. This was an attempt by the German ambassador to Mexico to involve that nation in a war against the United States. And in March several American merchant ships were sunk by German submarines. His patience at an end, Wilson at last took the position of a growing majority of Americans and asked Congress to declare war on Germany. Thus, the United States entered World War I.

37. This passage tries to explain that
    (a) Wilson wanted the United States to go to war against Germany.
    (b) Wilson tried to avoid war with Germany.
    (c) Germany wanted the United States to enter the war.
    (d) Other nations were pressuring the United States to enter the war.
    (e) Mexico was our main enemy.
38. We can conclude from the passage that most citizens of the United States in 1917 were
    (a) totally opposed to war with Germany.
    (b) in favour of war before Wilson was.
    (c) willing to accept war after Wilson persuaded them.
    (d) neutral.
    (e) trying to avoid war.
39. The last event in the series of happenings that led to a declaration of war against Germany was
    (a) the Zimmerman Telegram
    (b) attacks on U.S. merchant ships
    (c) Wilson's war message to Congress
    (d) a change in public opinion
    (e) the sinking of the Lusitania

PASSAGE-10

Slowly but surely the great passenger trains of the United States have been fading from the rails. Short-run commuter trains still rattle in and out of the cities. Between major cities you can still find a train, but the schedules are becoming less frequent. The Twentieth Century Limited, The Broadway Limited, and other luxury trains that sang along the rails at 60 to 80 miles an hour are no longer running. Passengers on other long runs complain of poor service, old equipment, and costs in time and money. The long-distance traveler today accepts the noise of jets, the congestion at airports, and the traffic between airport and city. A more elegant and graceful way is becoming only a memory.

40. With respect to the reduction of long-run passenger trains, this writer expresses
    (a) regret (b) pleasure
    (c) grief (d) elation
    (e) anger
41. The author seems to feel that air travel is
    (a) costly (b) slow
    (c) streamlined (d) elegant
    (e) uncomfortable

PASSAGE-11

When the United States was founded at the end of the eighteenth century, it was a small and weak country, made up mostly of poor farmers. Foreign policy, reflecting this domestic condition, stressed "no entangling alliances". The State Department then had a staff of less than half a dozen persons, whose total salary was $6600 (of which $3500 went to the Secretary of State), and a diplomatic service budget (July, 1790) of $40,000. Militarily, too, the country was insignificant. The first United States army, soon after the American Revolution, was made up of one captain (John Doughty) and 80 men. Clearly, the United States did not consider itself a real power and was not taken seriously by the rest of the world. It was not until immense changes took place inside the United States that the country began to play an important role in foreign affairs. By the beginning of the twentieth century, the United States had ceased to be a predominantly agricultural nation and had become an industrial one. Its population had grown to more than 30 times its original number. George Washington was president of 3,000,000 Americans; Theodore Roosevelt, of 100,000,000.

42. A country today cannot expect to play an important part in world affairs unless it

I. has wealth
II. has a large population
III. is strong internally
(a) I only (b) III only
(c) I and II only (d) II and III only
(e) I, II, and III

43. The writer seems to think that a major factor in making the United States a world power was
(a) industrialisation
(b) the passing of time
(c) a change in government policies
(d) the presidency of Theodore Roosevelt
(e) the avoidance of entangling alliances

PASSAGE-12

Writer I: No nation should tolerate the slacker who will not defend his country in time of war. The so-called conscientious objector is a coward who accepts the benefits of his country but will not accept the responsibility. By shirking his fair share, he forces another person to assume an unfair burden.

Writer II: A democratic nation should have room for freedom of conscience. Religious training and belief may make a man conscientiously opposed to participation in war. The conscientious objector should be permitted to give labour service or some form of noncombat military duty. His beliefs should be respected.

Writer III: The rights of the conscientious objector should be decided by each individual. No government should dictate to any person or require him to endanger his life if the person, in conscience, objects. There need be no religious basis. It is enough for a free individual to think as he pleases and to reject laws or rules to which he conscientiously objects.

44. A balanced opinion on this subject is presented by
(a) Writer I
(b) Writer II
(c) Writer III
(d) All of the writers
(e) None of the writers

45. We can conclude that the writer most likely to support a person who refuses any military service is
(a) Writer I
(b) Writer II
(c) Writer III
(d) All of the writers
(e) None of the writers

46. An authoritarian person is most likely to agree with
(a) Writer I
(b) Writer II
(c) Writer III
(d) All of the writers
(e) None of the writers

PASSAGE-13

Above all, colonialism was hated for its explicit assumption that the civilisations of colonized peoples were inferior. Using slogans like The White Man's Burden and La Mission Civilicatrice, Europeans asserted their moral obligation to impose their way of life on those endowed with inferior cultures. This orientation was particularly blatant among the French. In the colonies, business was conducted in French. Schools used that language and employed curricula designed for children in France. One scholar suggests that Muslim children probably learned no more about the Maghreb than they did about Australia. In the Metropole, intellectuals discoursed on the weakness of Arabo-Islamic culture. A noted historian accused Islam of being hostile to science. An academician wrote that Arabic—the holy language of religion, art and the Muslim sciences—is "more of an encumbrance than an aid to the mind. It is absolutely devoid of precision". There was of course an element of truth in the criticisms. After all, Arab reformists had been engaging in self-criticism for decades. Also, at least some Frenchmen honestly believed they were helping the colonized. A Resident General in Tunisia, for example, told an assemblage of Muslims with sincerity, "We shall distribute to you all that we have of learning; we shall make you a party to everything that makes for the strength of our intelligence." But none of this could change or justify the cultural racism in colonial ideologies. To the French, North Africans were only partly civilized and could be saved only by becoming Frenchmen. The reaction of the colonized was of course to defend their identity and to label colonial policy, in the words of Algerian writer Malek Hadad, "cultural asphyxia." Throughout North Africa, nationalists made the defense of Arabo-Islamic civilisation a major objective, a value in whose name they demanded independence. Yet the crisis of identity, provoked by colonial experiences, has not been readily assured and lingers into the post-colonial period. A French scholar describes the devasting impact of colonialism by likening it to "the role played for us (in Europe) by the doctrine of original sin." Frantz Fanon, especially in his Studies in a Dying Colonialism, well expresses the North African perspective. Factors producing militant and romantic cultural nationalism are anchored in time. Memories of colonialism are already beginning to fade and, when the Maghreb has had a few decades in which to grow, dislocations associated with social change can also be expected to be fewer. Whether this means that the cultural nationalism characteristic of the Maghreb today will disappear in the future cannot be known. But a preoccupation with identity and culture and an affirmation of Arabism and Islam have characterised the Maghreb since independence and these still remain today important elements in North African life.

A second great preoccupation in independent North Africa is the promotion of a modernist social revolution. The countries of the Maghreb do not pursue development in the same way and there have been variations in policies within each country. But all three spend heavily on development. In Tunisia, for example, the government devotes 20-25% of its annual budget to education, and literacy has climbed from 15% in 1956 to about 50% today. A problem, however, is that such advances are not always compatible with objectives flowing from North African nationalism. In Morocco, for instance, when the government decided to give children an "Arab" education, it was forced to limit enrollments because, among other things, most Moroccans had been educated in French and the country consequently had few teachers qualified to teach in Arabic. Two years later, with literacy rates declining, this part of the Arabisation program was postponed. The director of Arabisation declared, "We are not fanatics; we want to enter the modern world."

47. Which of the following titles best describes the content of the passage?
    - (a) Education in the Levant
    - (b) Nationalism in North Africa
    - (c) Civilisation in the Middle East
    - (d) Muslim Science
    - (e) Culture and Language
48. Which of the following is not used to present the author's arguments?
    - (a) Colonialism demoralised the local inhabitants.
    - (b) Colonialism produced an identity crisis.
    - (c) Cultural nationalism will soon disappear.

(d) Decolonization does not always run smoothly.
(e) Colonialists assumed that local cultures were inferior.

49. The author's attitude toward colonialism is best described as one of
(a) sympathy (b) bewilderment
(c) support (d) hostility
(e) ambivalence

50. Which of the following does the author mention as evidence of cultural colonialism?
(a) Native children in North Africa learned little about local culture.
(b) Science was not taught in the Arabic language.
(c) Colonial policy was determined in France.
(d) Colonialists spent little on development.
(e) Native teachers were not employed in public schools.

51. The author provides information that would answer which of the following questions?
(a) What was the difference between French and German attitudes toward their colonies?
(b) Why did Europeans impose their way of life on their colonies?
(c) Why was colonialism bad?
(d) Why was colonialism disliked?
(e) When did colonialism end in North Africa?

PASSAGE-14

Man and nature were the culprits as Venice sank hopelessly—or so it seemed—into the 177 canals on which the city is built. While nature's work took ages, man's work was much quicker and more brutal. But now man is using his ingenuity to save what he had almost destroyed. The sinking has been arrested and Venice should start rising again, like an oceanic phoenix from the canals.

The saving of Venice is the problem of the Italian Government, of course, but Venice is also a concern for Europe. And it happened that in the second half of 1975 Italy was in the chair of the European Council of Ministers. But the EC as such has no program for the salvation of Venice. "The Community is not a cultural community," explained one Commission official. "There are some areas where it just does not have competence, the preservation of historical landmarks being one of them." So the efforts to save Venice have taken on a wotldwide, rather than a Community-wide dimension.

Industrialisation of the Potto Marghera area brought economic benefits to Venice, but it also raped the city as growing air and water pollution began to take their toll on the priceless works of art and architecture. The danger of the imminent disappearance of Venice's cultural heritage was first brought to public attention in November 1966 when tides rose over six feet to flood Venice's canals and squates. Since then, various national and international organisations have sought ways and means to halt the destruction of the "queen of the Adriatic," though no one program has proved wholly satisfactory.

The US "Save Venice" group and the Btitish "Venice in Peril" committee were formed to raise money for the resroration of priceless works of art and monuments. In 1967 the United Nations Educational, Scientific and Cultural Organisation (UNESCO) took on the task of helping to save Venice by setting up a joint international advisory committee with the Italian Government. Such distant lands as Pakistan, no sttanger to aid programs itself joined in the effort, giving UNESCO a gift of 10,000 postage stamps for "Venice in

Peril". Even a group of famous cartoonists felt moved to draw attention to the fact that "Venice must be saved" and organised an exhibit in 1973, with the Council of Europe in Strasbourg, France, and this year a ballet festival drew people and funds to Venice.

Though Venice, the city of bridge-linked islands, was built in the fifth century, the land on which it was built has been sinking "naturally" for a billion years. Movements of the earth's crust have caused the very slow and gradual descent of the Po Valley. And nature's forces aren't easily countered. Each year, Venice has been sinking about one millimeter into the lagoon which holds this Adriatic jewel. To add to Venice's peril, the slow melting of the polar cap causes the level of the sea to rise another millimeter. If nothing is done to reverse nature's work, Venice is doomed to be another Atlantis, lost for ever beneath the murky sea.

Man's part in the sink-Venice movement has been for reasons mainly economic. For the last 400 years, the population of Venice has been drifting toward the mainland to escape the isolation and inconvenience of living on a series of islets. Between 1951 and 1971, Venice lost 63,000 inhabitants. To curtail this migration, new, artificial land areas, on the Dutch model, were added to the old Venice. Venice's original builders had not been far-sighted enough and set the ground level at only a few inches above what they expected to be the maximum tides. The combination of reclaimed land and Porto Marghera industrialization have "squeezed" the lagoon until its waters have no place to go but...up.

As Porto Marghera grows as an industrial port, and more and deeper channels are added for larger ships, currents become faster and dikes make the ravaging tides even more violent. The "acqua alta" has always been a problem for Venice, but with increased industrialization, flooding has become more frequent, sometimes occurring 50 times a year. Added to the violent "scirocco" that blows up to 60 miles an hour, Venice is rendered all the more vulnerable.

Yet Venice is not crumbling. Despite the visible decay caused by repeated floods and despite pollution that peels the stucco off the palazzi and eats away at their bottom-most steps, the structures are solid. The Rialto Bridge still stands safely on its ancient foundations supported by 6,000 piles. And something has been done to stop the damage done by water. Indeed, one simple measure has proved to work miracles. The ban on pumping from the thousands of artesian wells in and around the city—an easy source of water, but also a folly that caused a further descent of 5 millimeters a year—has been so effective that Venice should rise an inch in the next 20 years.

52. According to the passage, between 1951 and 1971, Venice lost approximately how many residents annually?
    (a) 475
    (b) 3,150
    (c) 6,300
    (d) 15,500
    (e) 63,000

53. The author's point of view is that Venice
    (a) cannot be saved from destruction.
    (b) is in danger of imminent disappearance.
    (c) is doomed to become another "Atlantis".
    (d) can be saved, but much work is necessary.
    (e) must become a member of the EC.

54. Which of the following conditions has not contributed to Venice's peril?
    (a) Movement of the earth's crust
    (b) Natural causes
    (c) Melting of the polar cap
    (d) Industrialisation
    (e) Shipping on the canals

55. According to the passage, which of the following figures indicates the approximate year when Venice first began sinking?
    (a) 400 B.C. (b) A.D. 1400
    (c) A.D. 1966 (d) A.D. 1970
    (e) None of the above

56. The author feels that Venice is an example of
    (a) a doomed city like Atlantis.
    (b) uncontrolled conditions.
    (c) a combination of natural and human destruction.
    (d) international neglect.
    (e) benign concern by international agencies.

PASSAGE-15

India has two national languages for central administrative purposes: Hindi and English. Hindi is the national, official, and main link language of India. English is an associate official language. The Indian Constitution also officially approves twenty-two regional languages for official purposes.

Dozens of distinctly different regional languages are spoken in India, which share many characteristics such as grammatical structure and vocabulary. Apart from these languages, Hindi is used for communication in India. The homeland of Hindi is mainly in the north of India, but it is spoken and widely understood in all urban centers of India. In the southern states of India, where people speak many different languages that are not much related to Hindi, there is more resistance to Hindi, which has allowed English to remain a lingua franca to a greater degree.

Since the early 1600s, the English language has had a toehold on the Indian subcontinent, when the East India Company established settlements in Chennai, Kolkata, and Mumbai, formerly Madras, Calcutta, and Bombay respectively. The historical background of India is never far away from everyday usage of English. India has had a longer exposure to English than any other country which uses it as a second language, its distinctive words, idioms, grammar and rhetoric spreading gradually to affect all places, habits and culture.

In India, English serves two purposes. First, it provides a linguistic tool for the administrative cohesiveness of the country, causing people who speak different languages to become united. Secondly, it serves as a language of wider communication, including a large variety of different people covering a vast area. It overlaps with local languages in certain spheres of influence and in public domains.

Generally, English is used among Indians as a 'link' language and it is the first language for many well-educated Indians. It is also the second language for many who speak more than one language in India. The English language is a tie that helps bind the many segments of our society together. Also, it is a linguistic bridge between the major countries of the world and India.

English has special national status in India. It has a special place in the parliament, judiciary, broadcasting, journalism, and in the education system. One can see a Hindi-speaking teacher giving their students instructions during an educational tour about where to meet and when their bus would leave, but all in English. It means that the language permeates daily life. It is unavoidable and is always expected, especially in the cities.

The importance of the ability to speak or write English has recently increased significantly because English has become the *de facto* standard. Learning English language has become popular for business, commerce and cultural reasons and especially for internet communications throughout the world. English is a language that has become a standard not because it has been approved by any 'standards' organization but because it is widely used by many information and technology industries and recognised as being standard. The call centre phenomenon has stimulated a huge expansion of internet-related activity, establishing the future of India as a cyber-technological super-power. Modern communications, videos, journals and newspapers on the internet use English and have made 'knowing English' indispensable.

The prevailing view seems to be that unless students learn English, they can only work in limited jobs. Those who do not have basic knowledge of English cannot obtain good quality jobs. They cannot communicate efficiently with others, and cannot have the benefit of India's rich social and cultural life. Men and women who cannot comprehend and interpret instructions in English, even if educated, are unemployable. They cannot help with their children's school homework everyday or decide their revenue options of the future.

A positive attitude to English as a national language is essential to the integration of people into Indian society. There would appear to be virtually no disagreement in the community about the importance of English language skills. Using English you will become a citizen of the world almost naturally. English plays a dominant role in the media. It has been used as a medium for inter-state communication and broadcasting both before and since India's independence. India is, without a doubt, committed to English as a national language. The impact of English is not only continuing but increasing.

57. According to the writer, the Indian constitution recognizes
   (a) 22 official languages
   (b) Hindi as the national language
   (c) 2 national, official languages
   (d) 2 national languages

58. English's status as a lingua franca is helped by
   (a) its status in northern India.
   (b) the fact that it is widely understood in urban centres.
   (c) the fact that people from the south speak languages not much related to Hindi.
   (d) it shares many grammatical similarities with Hindi.

59. In paragraph 3, 'toehold' means that English
   (a) dominated India.
   (b) changed the names of some cities in India.
   (c) has had a presence in India.
   (d) has been in India longer than any other language.

60. Hindi-speaking teachers
   (a) might well be heard using English.
   (b) only use English.
   (c) only use English for instructions.
   (d) do not use English.

61. In paragraph eight, it says 'the prevailing view', which suggests that
   (a) the view is correct.
   (b) the view is held by the majority.
   (c) the view is incorrect.
   (d) the view is held by the minority.

62. English in India
   (a) is going to decrease.
   (b) has decreased since independence.
   (c) causes disagreement.
   (d) is going to have a greater importance.

PASSAGE-16

Quinn: Our state is considering raising the age at which a person can get a driver's license to eighteen. This is unfair because the age has been sixteen for many years and sixteen-year-olds today are no less responsible than their parents and grandparents were at sixteen. Many young people today who are fourteen and fifteen years old are preparing to receive their licenses by driving with a learner's permit and a licensed driver, usually one of their parents. It would not be fair to suddenly say they have to wait two more years.

Dakota: It is true that people have been allowed to receive a driver's license at sixteen for generations. However, in recent years, the increase in traffic means drivers face more dangers than ever and must be ready to respond to a variety of situations. The fact that schools can no longer afford to teach drivers education results in too many young drivers who are not prepared to face the traffic conditions of today.

63. What is the point at issue between Quinn and Dakota?
    (a) Whether sixteen-year-olds should be required to take driver's education before being issued a license.
    (b) Whether schools ought to provide driver's education to fourteen- and fifteen-year-old students.
    (c) Whether the standards for issuing driver's licenses should become more stringent.
    (d) Whether sixteen-year-olds are prepared to drive in today's traffic conditions.
    (e) Whether parents are able to do a good job teaching their children to drive.

64. On what does Quinn rely in making her argument?
    (a) Statistics (b) Emotion
    (c) Fairness (d) Anecdotes
    (e) Actualities

65. On what does Dakota rely in making her argument?
    (a) Statistics (b) Emotion
    (c) Fairness (d) Anecdotes
    (e) Actualities

PASSAGE-17

Keshava, the washerman had a donkey. They worked together all day, and Keshava would pour out his heart to the donkey. One day, Keshava was walking home with the donkey when he felt tired. He tied the donkey to a tree and sat down to rest for a while, near a school. A window was open, and through it, a teacher could be heard scolding the students. 'Here I am trying to turn you donkeys into human beings, but you just won't study!' As soon as Keshava heard these words, his ears pricked up. Aman who could actually turn donkeys into humans! This was the answer to his prayers. Impatiently, he waited for school to be over that day when everyone had gone home, and only the teacher remained behind to check some papers, Keshava entered the classroom.

'How can I help you?' asked the teacher. Keshava scratched his head and said, I heard what you said to the children. This donkey is my companion. If you made it human, we could have such good times together.' The teacher decided to trick Keshava. He pretended to think for a while and then said, 'Give me six months and it will cost you a thousand rupees.' The washerman agreed and rushed home to get the money. He then left the donkey in the teacher's care.

After the six months were up, Keshava went to the teacher. The teacher had been using the donkey for his own work. Not wanting to give it up, he said, "Oh, your donkey became so clever that it ran away. He is the headman of the next village." When

Keshava reached the next village he found the village elders sitting under a tree, discussing serious problems. How surprised they were when Keshava marched up to the headman, grabbed his arm and said, 'How dare you? You think you are so clever that you ran away? Come home at once!'

The headman understood someone had played a trick on Keshava. I am not your donkey!' he said. 'Go find the sage in the forest.' Keshava found the sage sitting under a tree with his eyes closed, deep in meditation. He crept up and grabbed the sage's beard. 'Come back home now!' he shouted. The startled sage somehow calmed Keshava. When he heard what had happened, he had a good laugh. Then he told the washerman kindly, "The teacher made a fool of you. Your donkey must be still with him. Go and take it back from him. Try to make some real friends, who will talk with you and share your troubles. A donkey will never be able to do that!" Keshava returned home later that day with his donkey, sadder and wiser.

66. Which of the following can be said about the teacher?
   (a) He had the ability to transform animals into human beings.
   (b) He took advantage of Keshava's simple nature.
   (c) He had plotted with the village headman to cheat Keshava.
   (d) He was honest and used Keshava's money to care for the donkey.

67. Why did Keshava talk to his donkey while working?
   (a) He wanted to practise his communication skills because he wanted to make friends.
   (b) To entertain himself because he found his work monotonous.
   (c) The donkey helped him to find answers to Ids problems.
   (d) He regarded the donkey as his friend and confided in him.

68. How did Keshava get his donkey back?
   (a) He threatened to take the teacher to the village elders.
   (b) The sage forced the teacher to release the donkey.
   (c) The teacher returned it on learning that Keshava had learnt his lesson.
   (d) None of the above.

69. Which of the following is not true in the context of the passage?
   (i) The donkey was overburdened by the teacher.
   (ii) The teacher was cunning by nature.
   (iii) The sage laughed at Keshava and treated him unkindly.
   (a) Both (i) and (iii)
   (b) Both (ii) and (iii)
   (c) All (i), (ii) and (iii)
   (d) None of the above

70. What made Keshava pull the sage's beard?
   (a) He wanted to wake up the sage who was a sleep under the tree.
   (b) The headman requested him to move the sage from under the tree.
   (c) He misunderstood the village headman and took the sage to be his donkey.
   (d) He wanted the sage to explain what had happened to the donkey.

71. Why did the teacher ask Keshava to leave the donkey with him for six months?
   (i) He realised that the donkey would require a lot of training.
   (ii) To reduce Keshava's dependence on the donkey.
   (iii) He wanted to rescue the donkey from Keshava who did not know to treat the donkey properly.

(a) Only (iii) (b) Only (ii)
(c) Both (i) and (ii) (d) None of these

PASSAGE-18

The news that the Union Cabinet has considered the draft of a bill to prohibit the denigration of women in photographs, advertisements and films, is welcome. There has been for sometime growing criticism of the projection of women in these three media. Advertisements in print media as well as in films and television, frequently rely on female sex appeal to attract attention to products or to suggest that these products make Casanova of old mortals. Things are even worse in films. Some of them unabashedly rely on sex for box office success, showing scantily attired women in provocative postures. In these, as well as in many advertisements, women clearly appear as objects of erotic stimulation. By showing heroes misbehaving with heroines and easily getting away with it, films invite emulation in real life, resulting in the molestation of women in public places.

72. The passage says that the bill to prohibit media exploitation of women
    (a) has been made a Law.
    (b) has been discussed in Union Cabinet.
    (c) is being drafted.
    (d) is going to create a lot of controversy.
73. 'Denigration' in the phrase 'denigration of women' means
    (a) abuse
    (b) ill-treatment
    (c) scandalizing
    (d) tarnishing a good image
74. Feminine sex appeal is used in advertisements to
    (a) entertain the customers.
    (b) distract the customers' attraction.
    (c) get the attention of prospective customers.
    (d) show how women at home would like the product.
75. 'Unabashedly' means
    (a) with great shyness
    (b) openly
    (c) indifferently
    (d) with no sign of being ashamed
76. Which of the following media can be labeled as the worst in the denigration of women?
    (a) Print media
    (b) Television
    (c) Films
    (d) All are equally bad
77. Based on the passage, which of the following is responsible for provoking molestation of women in public places?
    (a) Poor ethics from childhood
    (b) Scantily attired women
    (c) Emulation of films in real life
    (d) Confidence that the offender can go scot-free

PASSAGE-19

India is dedicated to free institutions and principles of democracy. We are striving to give everyone an opportunity and raise the standard of living for all. A democracy is one where people have the right to live their own lives and develop themselves in their own way under the guidance of their chosen representatives. If our political democracy is to succeed, it is essential that it be buttressed by steps towards economic equality or what has been referred to as the 'socialistic pattern of society'. Poverty and unemployment hold the biggest threat to the successful working of our democratic system.

78. In a democratic system
    (a) government serves the people.
    (b) the government is run by the people themselves.

(c) people do not have political freedom.
(d) commodities are freely bought and sold.

79. One may infer from the paragraph that in a socialistic pattern of society
(a) the socialist party dominates.
(b) all the inhabitants are treated equal.
(c) to provide employment to all is the greatest problem.
(d) None of the above.

80. Democracy can fail if there is
(a) a weak government
(b) economic inequality
(c) unemployment
(d) opportunity for development

81. The word buttressed in the paragraph means
(a) dictating (b) declared
(c) guided (d) supported

82. The successful working of Indian democratic system is under a threat of
(a) poverty
(b) unemployment
(c) economic inequality
(d) All of the above

83. According to the passage the socialistic pattern of society is required in India to
(a) reduce economic inequality.
(b) to ensure thriving of free institutions.
(c) to improve the quality of chosen representatives.
(d) All of the above.

PASSAGE-20

India's role on the international stage was moulded by history rather than by the pomp and circumstances of war. As a separate entity of the British empire, India became a founder member of the League of Nations in the same way as Australia and Canada, and thus acquired a somewhat unique international status long before independence. During the days of the League when India's interests were affected, such as in matters of trade or the position of Indians overseas, the Indian delegation did not hesitate to make known its independent position, for what it was worth. Some Indian delegates were in demand for chairing meetings riddled with contention and controversy, because of their reputation for impartiality and talent for mediation.

These were the small beginnings of India's later entry into the United Nations in 1945, again as a founder member before independence. The drafting of Chapter IX and X of the UN Charter, which deal with international social and economic cooperation, was entrusted to a group that was presided over by an Indian. It is important, however, to bear in mind that fact that the Government of independent India had no part in the drafting of the UN Charter, although in accepted the obligations contained therein. The UN was primarily the creation of three powers—The USA, UK and Russia.

The size, population, resources and potential of India lent it the weight of a medium power in the functioning of the United Nations. The fact that India was among the first nations to liberate itself from the imperialist domination through non-violent means endowed it with a moral obligation to work in and outside the UN for the independence of nations still under colonial rule. India has served on the Security Council for 10 years or 5 terms, on the Trusteeship Council for 12 years or 4 terms and on the Economic and Social Council for 21 years or 7 terms.

84. The title below that best expresses the ideas of the passage is
(a) India's role at the United Nations
(b) India and Her Neighbours

(c) India's International Prestige
(d) British Colonial Expansion

85. Through a part of the British Empire, India enjoyed great prestige at the League in as much as Indian delegates were in demand for chairing meeting to consider controversial issues. It was because:
(I) Indian delegates were well known for their impartiality
(II) Indian delegates had talent for mediation
(III) India was considered a power to reckon with.
(a) I and III are correct
(b) I and II are correct
(c) II and III are correct
(d) Only I is correct

86. Which articles of the UN Charter deal with International, Social and Economic Co-operation?
(a) Articles IX and X
(b) Articles XI and XII
(c) Articles VIII and XIII
(d) Articles VI and VII

87. Which of the following countries does not find any coverage in the passage?
(a) The USA (b) Britain
(c) The Russia (d) Sri Lanka

PASSAGE-21

The genesis of service tax emanates from the ongoing structural transformation of the Indian economy, whereby presently more than one-half of GDP originates from the services sector. Despite the growing presence of the services sector in the Indian economy it remained out of the tax net prior to 1994-95, leading to a steady deterioration in tax-GDP ratio. The service tax was introduced in 1994-95 on a select category of services at a low rate of five per cent. While the service tax rate and the coverage of services being taxed have increased ever since, the combined tax-GDP ratio of the Centre and States, nevertheless, deteriorated from 16.4 per cent in 1985-86 to 14.1 per cent in 1999-2000. It may be noted that between 1990-91 and 1998-99, the share of industrial sector in GDP dropped by 6.4 percentage points whereas almost 64 per cent of the tax revenue was generated by indirect taxes for which industrial sector continues to be the principal tax base. On the other hand, during the same period, the share of services sector in GDP has increased by 10 percentage points and this sector has still remained poorly taxed.

The rationale for service tax, therefore, lies not only in arresting the falling tax-GDP ratio but also in *ipso facto* improving allocative efficiency in the economy as well as promoting equity. Against this backdrop, the service tax needs to be designed taking into account the fact that (i) the share of services in GDP is expanding; (ii) failure to tax services distorts consumer choices and encourages spending on services at the expense of goods; (iii) untaxed service traders are unable to claim value added tax (VAT) on service inputs, which encourages businesses to develop in-house services, creating further distortions; and (iv) most services that are likely to become taxable are positively correlated with expenditure of high-income households and, therefore, service tax improves equity.

In the Indian context, taxation of services assumes importance in the wake of the need for improving the revenue system, ensuring a measure of neutrality in taxation between goods and services and eventually helping to evolve an efficient system of domestic trade taxes, both at the Central and the State levels.

88. What, according to the passage, was the impact of exclusion of service tax till the

first half of the last decade of the past century?

(a) There was no impact as there was no service tax.
(b) There was a steady deterioration in the GDP.
(c) Tax-GDP ratio had steadily and gradually aggravated.
(d) Service sector used to flourish exorbitantly.

89. The origin of service tax is attributed to
(a) increase in Gross Domestic Product (GDP).
(b) existence of service sector.
(c) tax of the future.
(d) metamorphosis of our country's economy.

90. Which of the following is most likely to provide neutrality to various economic activities?
(a) Increase in revenue buoyancy.
(b) fairness in tax administration.
(c) Equity and efficiency in various activities.
(d) Consistency in tax structure and revenue buoyancy.

91. Levying service tax is most likely to achieve which of the following?
(i) Check on reducing tax-GDP ratio.
(ii) Enhancement in allocative efficiency.
(iii) Promoting equity.
(a) Both (i) and (ii) (b) Both (ii) and (iii)
(c) Both (i) and (iii) (d) All the three

92. Which of the following factors helps service tax improve fairness across different economic strata of society?
(a) Taxable services are mostly those that are utilised by the rich.
(b) Untaxed service traders are prevented from claiming value-added tax.
(c) Encouragement to in-house services is effected.
(d) It improves revenue system.

93. Which of the following is likely to happen if services are not brought under the tax net?
(i) Misrepresentation of customers' choices.
(ii) Stimulating enhancement in spending on services at the cost of goods.
(iii) Inability of taxpayers to reclaim their taxes already paid by them.
(a) Both (i) and (ii) (b) Both (ii) and (iii)
(c) Both (i) and (iii) (d) All the three

PASSAGE-22

It was during one of the most dreadful smallpox epidemics in England that Edward Jenner, a country doctor, made a discovery which was to alter the course of history. Jenner noticed that the disease seldom struck those who lived in rural areas and worked around cattle. Most farmers and dairy workers had contracted cowpox and had recovered with nothing more serious than a putsule which left a scar. This observation led Dr. Jenner to think: Why not vaccinate people with cowpox to protect them from smallpox? On May 14, 1876, Dr. Jenner took a healthy boy, James Phillips, to a dairy maid, Sarah Nelmes, who had a cowpox putsule on her hand resulting from an infection from her master's cow. Dr. Jenner made two shallow cuts on James Phillips' arm and inoculated them with matter taken from the cowpox sore. A putsule developed on the boy's arm formed a scab and healed. In July of the same year, Dr. Jenner inoculated James with matter from a smallpox putsule. During the next two weeks, the doctor watched for signs of smallpox. They did not develop. The vaccination was successful. Dr. Jenner wrote a paper explaining his method of vaccination.

At first the doctors were hostile and would not listen to a ridiculous procedure. Many towns people organised anti vaccination campaigns. Gradually, however, the doctors and their patients accepted vaccination.

94. The fact that Edward Jenner was a country doctor, was important in the discovery of smallpox vaccine, because
   (a) he had enough time to pursue his research in the rural areas.
   (b) he noticed that the disease was prevalent where people worked around cattle.
   (c) he noticed that the disease seldom struck people who worked around the cattle.
   (d) he found that he could convince rural people more easily than city people.

95. Dr. Jenner was successful as cowpox virus produces
   (a) severe infection in humans resulting in deaths.
   (b) a mild infection in humans which is not enough to produce active immunity.
   (c) a mild infection in humans which is enough to produce active immunity.
   (d) no infection in humans.

96. Dr. Jenner made his experiment on a healthy boy who
   (a) died after experimentation.
   (b) could not be relieved of his mark of putsule.
   (c) developed the signs of putsule on his body when he was injected the matter of cowpox.
   (d) was paid for it.

97. Passage here is having a/an
   (a) narrative style
   (b) analytic style
   (c) provocative style
   (d) idiomatic style

PASSAGE-23

Children are the part of social and political philosophy of a country. Any attitude shown towards them is the important factor which decides whether their needs will be fulfilled or not or they will get their rights or not. Any society which is looking towards the future will give attention to the caring of children during disasters. At present, there are several parts of the world where there is no opportunity to bring up children with the feeling of peace and brotherhood. The most horrifying record of wars and terrorism we get in journalism always shows pictures of the ruins of the houses and bodies of dead family members of the children and babies, who are left behind to cry over it (or pictures of children who are so afraid that they can't even cry). In such countries where the wars are continuing or in such societies where such actions are presented in their own ways, there the children playing without any hurdle will show the acceptance of such incidents in today's society, which will compel us to think whether there lies any opportunity for the crores of children who are affected by such philosophy of countries to gain their rights to grow up in peace. And definitely the discriminations laid by one or a group of people formed on the basis of caste, creed, sex or religion of a nation or society despite of universal acceptance of the needs of children on which the rights are based, abstain the children from their rights.

98. Which among the following statements is not helpful in developing the feeling of peace and brotherhood in children?
   (a) When the aged people leave their children to experience war.
   (b) When mature people do the discrimination based on caste.
   (c) When the society presents the war stories in an attractive way.

(d) When political philosophy of a country advocates for universal brotherhood.

99. War related works are
   (a) avoided by the society
   (b) followed by the society
   (c) criticised by the society
   (d) accepted by the society

100. Elders have duty towards children. How much care is being taken of children by any particular society is reflected by
   (a) what is done for them during disasters.
   (b) how much care of the elders is being taken.
   (c) how alert the elders are for their rights.
   (d) how developed the society is.

101. The view of the writer is that
   (a) children have right to grow in peace.
   (b) philosophy of the countries supports the rights of the children.
   (c) despite of the wars children gain their rights to live peacefully.
   (d) children rights should depend on the conditions of the society.

PASSAGE-24

Till some time ago, this fact was widely accepted that environment always provides support to us for life and livelihood. It will continue to give this shelter and air for breathing, water for drinking, food for eating and raw materials for most of our industries.

This is our biological wealth. These are the fundamental materials on that our total productivity depends. If we destroy this, then our most progressive technique will come to nought and any economy unstable. But still there is danger of the extinction of our biological property through using techniques, for the expansion of the most things in the modern world the credit goes to technique. The property obtained by human labour is widely made and enriched by the technique. Technique has increased our lifespan and made living more comfortable. All this strengthens the belief that technique is truly profitable.

To put a question mark against this belief, the main reason which has drawn the attention of the masses is environmental pollution. Slowly it has become clear that this is the cost that we have paid for taking many advantages of technique. For playing our motor vehicles we are paying in the form of disease; for getting the great benefits of modern pesticides we are paying in form of our dwindling wildlife; for nuclear energy we are paying in the form of putting human life in danger ways, and for increased agricultural land we are paying in the form of water pollution.

102. The abstract is mainly about
   (a) our means of life and livelihood.
   (b) the dangers created by environmental pollution.
   (c) comparative advantages and disadvantages of technique.
   (d) technique which has contributed a lot for our life and our beliefs.

103. "After that the danger of the integrity of biological property is technique itself." What is the meaning of integrity?
   (a) Quality of being true to your character.
   (b) Universal and undiminished values.
   (c) Continued progress.
   (d) Preservation of environment.

104. In the last paragraph, the author
   (a) expresses doubts about the complete usefulness of technique.
   (b) criticises nuclear energy.
   (c) shows sympathy for human beings and wildlife.
   (d) recommendation of the abolishment of the pesticides and fertilisers.

PASSAGE-25

Political education may be defined as the preparation of a citizen to take well informed, responsible and sustained action for participation in the national struggle for the realization of the socio-economic objectives of the country. The over-riding socio-economic objectives in India are the abolition of poverty and the creation of a modern democratic, secular and socialist society in place of the present traditional, feudal, hierarchical and inegalitarian one.

Under the British rule, the Congress leaders argued that political education was an important part of education and refused to accept the official view that education and politics should not be mixed with one another. But when they came to power in 1947 they almost adopted the British policy and began to talk of education being defiled by politics. 'Hands off education' was the call to political parties. But in spite of it, political infiltration into the educational system has greatly increased in the sense that different political parties vie with each other to capture the minds of teachers and students. The wise academicians wanted political support, without political interference. What we have actually received is infinite political interference with little genuine political support. This interference with the educational system by political parties for their own ulterior motives is no political education at all; and with the all-round growth of elitism, it is hardly a matter for surprise that real political education within the school system (which really means the creation of a commitment to social transformation) has been even weaker than in the pre-independence period.

At the same time, the freedom struggle came to an end and the major non-formal agency of political education disappeared. The press could and did provide some political education. But it did not utilize the opportunity to the full and the stronghold of vested interests continued to dominate it. The same can be said of political parties as well as of other institutions and agencies outside the school system which can be expected to provide political education.

105. According to the passage political education in the real sense should prepare
   (a) citizens for social change.
   (b) well-informed politicians.
   (c) responsible students of political science.
   (d) devoted social workers.

106. The theme of the passage could be
   (a) British rule in India and Education.
   (b) Education and Politics.
   (c) Education for Freedom.
   (d) Leadership and Education.

107. The author emphasizes in the passage that
   (a) non-formal agencies of political education do not exist in India.
   (b) vested interests dominate politics.
   (c) real political education is lacking in India.
   (d) the Britishers were opposed to real political education.

108. The author condemns the
   (a) role of the Britishers in organizing education in India.
   (b) role of the Congress in politics after independence.
   (c) political interference in education in India.
   (d) role of the Press in political education.

PASSAGE-26

It is necessary to be clear about the definition and scope if the word science, as also its distinction from technology. Among the few powerful forces that hold the key to the future of mankind, science is perhaps the only important one that enjoys the unique position of being accepted by all, practically without exception. Even in the case of those rare individuals who seem to entertain an antipathy to science, a casual conversation with them will bring out the fact that they are actually opposed not to science, but to technology which is concerned with the applications of the findings of science to satisfy diverse human needs.

By science we mean today the fundamental knowledge of our world and its environment, the controlled and steady pursuit of that knowledge in all its aspects, without necessarily any desire to use it for public ends. And by technology we refer to the numerous ways of pressing science into human service, the concentrated study of the ways in which things may be made or changed for human ends. To make a concrete differentiation between the two one can cite examples from the presently highly popular fields of nuclear science and technology. It is science here when measurements are made of the number and nature of particles emitted in the break-up or fission of the nucleus of the heavy metallic element uranium. It is, however, technology when this scientific knowledge is used either to design and build an atomic power station for generating electricity or to design and make an atomic bomb. As such, it is technology which acquires ethical overtones and can be labelled as moral or immoral. Science is neutral or amoral and can never be opposed to ethics or human welfare, although a scientist as a human being technologist can be.

109. The writer is trying to
   (a) plead for a better attitude to science.
   (b) suggest we apply science for public good.
   (c) study ethical science rather than physical science.
   (d) distinguish between science and technology.

110. According to the writer, science
   (a) is the only force which determines the future of mankind.
   (b) is one of the few determining forces of human destiny.
   (c) will be the only concern of human beings in the future.
   (d) is one of the many obstacles that block the progress of man.

111. This passage is
   (a) rhetorical (b) descriptive
   (c) narrative (d) expository

112. The study of fission of the nucleus of uranium can be
   (a) thought of as an example of modern technology.
   (b) thought of as an application of principles of electricity.
   (c) thought of as having no moral implication.
   (d) thought of as important to the welfare of all human beings.

PASSAGE-27

The most important fact, which a leader who wishes to motivate others should bear in mind, is that an individual has an incessant and gnawing craving for importance. There is no exception to this psychological need. Barring his biological needs, practically all his actions are directed at satisfying his continuing need to feel important. According to William James, the deepest principle in human nature is the craving to be appreciated. The individual who can honestly satisfy this burning hunger for importance on the part of his fellow human beings can literally rule the world. He can motivate and influence any person, big or small, high or low, educated or uneducated, rich or poor, man or woman, provided he is capable of making the other person feel truly important. By discovering the special and particular gifts of an individual, by giving due recognition and sincere appreciation to that singular gift or talent, you can win him or her over to your side easily.

You have to create an eager want on the part of the other individual if you wish to motivate him. In other words, you have to make the horse feel thirsty if your aim is to make it drink. Fortunately for you, there is an inborn, ever-present, gnawing hunger on the part of every human being to gain recognition and appreciation. This want is already there and you don't have to create it. All you have to do is to satisfy this hunger. If you objectively analyse your own motives and needs, you will find that this need for recognition is the strong driving factor behind your aspiration to become a leader. It was this urge for importance which made Alexander the Great embark on a world conquest, and made many emperors wage inumerable battles and wars. This urge has driven artists, authors, scientists, inventors and others to attain great heights in their chosen fields and produce the best results.

113. Which one of the following statements is correct?
 (a) Many scientists and inventors have excelled because of the availability of research facilities.
 (b) Artists and authors have made contribution to society because of their innate genius.
 (c) Many athletes have won gold medals in the Olympics because of their coaches.
 (d) People in different areas have been successful because of the need of recognition.

114. Which one of the following statements is not correct?
 (a) Hunger for recognition has to be developed over the years in one's personality.
 (b) Need to gain recognition is an inborn trait.
 (c) Many wars have been waged to satisfy the need to get importance.
 (d) Craving for importance is a natural psychological need of every human being.

115. Which one of the following statements is correct?
 (a) A successful leader must be able to identify the need of importance of others.
 (b) Need for recognition is a trait only of high professionals.
 (c) To motivate a person, an increase of his salary is the best strategy.
 (d) Monetary success is the driving force for a leader.

ANSWERS

1. (a)	2. (b)	3. (c)	4. (d)	5. (b)	6. (d)
7. (a)	8. (b)	9. (d)	10. (c)	11. (c)	12. (a)
13. (c)	14. (a)	15. (b)	16. (d)	17. (d)	18. (c)
19. (b)	20. (a)	21. (c)	22. (b)	23. (a)	24. (d)
25. (b)	26. (a)	27. (a)	28. (c)	20. (b)	30. (d)
31. (a)	32. (b)	33. (a)	34. (b)	35. (c)	36. (d)

37. (b) 38. (b) 30. (b) 40. (a) 41. (e) 42. (e)
43. (a) 44. (b) 45. (c) 46. (a) 47. (b) 48. (c)
49. (d) 50. (a) 51. (e) 52. (b) 53. (d) 54. (e)
55. (e) 56. (c) 57. (b) 58. (b) 59. (c) 60. (a)
61. (b) 62. (d) 63. (d) 64. (c) 65. (c) 66. (c)
67. (a) 68. (b) 69. (c) 70. (d) 71. (b) 72. (b)
73. (b) 74. (c) 75. (b) 76. (c) 77. (c) 78. (a)
79. (b) 80. (b) 81. (d) 82. (d) 83. (a) 84. (a)
85. (b) 86. (a) 87. (d) 88. (c) 89. (d) 90. (d)
91. (d) 92. (a) 93. (d) 94. (c) 95. (c) 96. (c)
97. (a) 98. (b) 99. (b) 100. (c) 101. (a) 102. (d)
103. (d) 104. (a) 105. (a) 106. (b) 107. (c) 108. (c)
109. (a) 110. (a) 111. (d) 112. (a) 113. (d) 114. (a)
115. (a)

4

Communication

1. Which one of the following was the newspaper published by Annie Besant?
   (a) *The Hindu*
   (b) *The Indian Express*
   (c) *The Times of India*
   (d) *The New India*
2. Which one of the following statements is true for Journals?
   (a) They are not a part of the print media.
   (b) They concentrate an industry-specific, stream-specific or trade-specific issues, which are defined before hand.
   (c) They given all types of news, views, and entertaining events.
   (d) They are not prepared under the guidance of expert editors, writers and researchers but by journalists and freelance writers from the open market.
3. Following are the experimental learning activities adopted by a teacher. Arrange them in cyclic order.
   (i) Accommodation (ii) Converging
   (iii) Assimilation (iv) Diverging
   (a) (i), (ii), (iii), (iv) (b) (iv), (iii), (ii), (i)
   (c) (ii), (iii), (iv), (i) (d) (iii), (i), (ii), (iv)
4. The nature of communication can be expressed as a process of
   (a) Establishing mutual relationship
   (b) Exchange of ideas between two persons
   (c) Discussion
   (d) All of the above.
5. *Bombay Samachar* a/an ________ daily published from Mumbai, is the oldest existing newspaper in India.
   (a) Hindi (b) Marathi
   (c) Gujarati (d) English
6. Cinema is a/an
   (a) visual media
   (b) audio-visual media
   (c) audio media
   (d) print media
7. Which of the following methods of communication is the most effective?
   (a) Presenting written materials
   (b) Presenting written material alongwith film projector
   (c) Multi-media method
   (d) Cannot be determined
8. Communication can be defined as
   (a) A process by which an idea is transferred from a source to receiver with the intention of changing his behaviour.
   (b) A process of mutual exchange of facts, thoughts or perceptions leading to a common understanding of all parties.
   (c) As a transfer of information from the sender to receiver with the information being understood by the receiver.
   (d) All of the above.
9. In present network Akashvani comprises of how many broadcasting centres?

(a) 197 (b) 137
(c) 127 (d) 130

10. The MMS is a/an
    (a) visual media
    (b) audio media
    (c) audio-visual media
    (d) None of the above.

11. Better classroom management means
    (a) per group work and better interaction among pupils.
    (b) prior preparation of teacher in the making of suitable aids.
    (c) punctuality of the teachers in coming in the class and finishing the course in time.
    (d) All of the above.

12. In the process of communication the task performed by the sender is
    (a) Formulation (b) Encoding
    (c) Transmitting (d) All of these.

13. How many relay centres does Akashvani has?
    (a) 10 (b) 12
    (c) 14 (d) 15

14. The Conditional Access System (CAS) allows the viewers to
    (a) select TV channels of their choice.
    (b) interact with TV channels through the set-up boxes.
    (c) cut down the costs of television viewing.
    (d) None of the above.

15. Arrange the following activities of interaction in logical order
    (i) Analysis of the work done.
    (ii) Planning and preparation.
    (iii) Presentation of material.
    (iv) Modification and improvement.
    (a) (i), (ii), (iii), (iv) (b) (ii), (iii), (i), (iv)
    (c) (iv), (i), (ii), (iii) (d) (i), (iii), (iv), (ii)

16. Elements of communication consist of
    (a) Source and message
    (b) Channel and symbol
    (c) Encoding and decoding
    (d) Feedback and all of the above

17. When did Radio Broadcasting started in India?
    (a) 1987 (b) 1957
    (c) 1927 (d) 1937

18. Communication needs a
    (a) Sender (b) Receiver
    (c) Channel (d) All of these.

19. Which of the following skills has the largest share in communication time in schools/college?
    (a) Listening (b) Reading
    (c) Writing (d) Speaking

20. When an individual becomes a 'source' in the process of communication he is called
    (a) A messenger (b) A living source
    (c) A receiver (d) A translator

21. Which were the two privately owned transmitters when AIR started?
    (a) Mumbai and Kolkata
    (b) Delhi and Mumbai
    (c) Kolkata and Chennai
    (d) None of the above

22. Communication helps in
    (a) Persuasion
    (b) Entertainment
    (c) Integration
    (d) Cultural Promotion

23. All are the components of listening except
    (a) hearing
    (b) attending—being attentive
    (c) answering
    (d) understanding and remembering

24. 'Channel' in communication is

(a) The way or medium by which a message travels.
(b) The linking process between sender and receiver.
(c) A functional state of communication.
(d) None of the above.

25. How many short wave transmitters are there?
(a) 45 (b) 35
(c) 55 (d) None

26. Intrapersonal communication is
(a) Person-to-person contact.
(b) Talking to oneself.
(c) When more than two persons are involved.
(d) None of the above.

27. Which one of the following does not work as a barrier in communication?
(a) Physical Barriers
(b) Psychological Barriers
(c) Background Barriers
(d) Feedback related Barriers

28. When did Vividh Bharati start?
(a) 1987 (b) 1967
(c) 1957 (d) 1937

29. Which of the communication has an emotional appeal?
(a) Intrapersonal communication
(b) Interpersonal communication
(c) Group communication
(d) Mass communication

30. The most important aspect of communication-listening, can be improved by
(a) making the attention fully paid.
(b) making the communicated material novel—interesting and need based.
(c) making voice effective and impressive.
(d) All of these.

31. Barriers in the process of communication can be eliminated through
(a) Enhancing comprehension of the content
(b) Focusing by the listner
(c) Proper attention
(d) All of the above.

32. When was the FM privatised?
(a) July 6, 1999 (b) July 6, 1998
(c) July 6, 1997 (d) July 6, 1996

33. Audience and feedback are the two main components of
(a) Intrapersonal communication
(b) Interpersonal communication
(c) Mass communication
(d) None of the above.

34. Listening to a lecture is
(a) informational listening
(b) evaluative listening
(c) emphatic listening
(d) None of the above.

35. 'Chronemics' is related to
(a) Time-related communication
(b) Muscular-related communication
(c) Signal-related communication
(d) Expression-related communication

36. When was commercial broadcasting started in Akashvani?
(a) Nov. 1, 1967 (b) Nov. 2, 1957
(c) Nov. 6, 1987 (d) Nov. 1, 1937

37. "The reach of mass media is quite strong in India, but comparatively, the access to them is very weak." This statement is
(a) Definitely true (b) Probably true
(c) Definitely false (d) Probably false

38. The main purpose of evaluative listening is
(a) to accept or reject an idea given to the listener.
(b) to evaluate the speaker's credibility and personality.
(c) Both of the above.
(d) None of the above.

39. Which one of the following is not a function of communication?
   (a) Promotes healthy interactions between teacher and students.
   (b) Eliminate mutual biases and prejudices.
   (c) Promotes career prospects.
   (d) Promotes mental readiness.

40. When was, the national channel started to broadcast quality music, features and plays?
   (a) 18 May, 1988 (b) 18 May, 1958
   (c) 18 May, 1987 (d) 18 May, 1986

41. Speaker-Speech-Audience are the elements of whose model of communication?
   (a) Claud Shannon
   (b) Aristotle
   (c) Harold Lasswell
   (d) Wilbur Schramm

42. A student helps a teacher to solve the problem while the teacher was delivering the lecture. He was
   (a) an emphatic listener.
   (b) an evaluative listener.
   (c) a realistic listener.
   (d) an informational listener.

43. Principle of better communication is
   (a) Clarity of the meassage
   (b) Adequacy of information
   (c) Transmission of information
   (d) All of the above.

44. When was television started in India?
   (a) 1959 (b) 1969
   (c) 1979 (d) 1989

45. Who introduced the concept of noise in his model of communication?
   (a) Wilbur Schramm
   (b) George Gerbner
   (c) Charles E. Osgood
   (d) Claud Shannon and Warren Weaves

46. The process of communication enhances through
   (a) belongingness.
   (b) security and freedom to make choices.
   (c) informality of meeting and avoidance of pressure.
   (d) All of the above.

47. The word communication is derived from
   (a) Communis (b) Communique
   (c) Communil (d) Commune

48. In 1976
   (a) Doordarshan was separated from AIR.
   (b) TV was introduced in India.
   (c) AIR started Vividh Bharati.
   (d) Autonomous Broadcasting Corporation started.

49. Which model refers to 'Gatekeeper' concept?
   (a) Theodore Newcomb's
   (b) Shannon and Weaver's
   (c) Bruce Westley and Maclean's
   (d) None of the above.

50. Software computer cannot be used
   (a) for demonstration.
   (b) for reading and writing.
   (c) as a systematic programmed learning techniques.
   (d) as a machine for evaluating students progress.

51. The term communis is taken from
   (a) Latin language
   (b) Greek language
   (c) Hebrew language
   (d) English language

52. Prasar Bharati is a
   (a) Television channel
   (b) Newspaper
   (c) Magazine
   (d) Autonomous Broadcasting Corporation

53. When was the television service at the Delhi Kendra inaugurated?
(a) Sept. 20, 1958 (b) Sep. 15, 1959
(c) Aug. 15, 1959 (d) Nov. 15, 1958

54. Which of the following cannot be a good way of communication in promoting literacy among villagers?
(a) Demonstration
(b) Reading and writing
(c) Providing material on TV and film projector
(d) Large group discussion

55. The meaning of communis is
(a) Differences (b) Normal
(c) Sensation (d) Etiquettes

56. The first newspaper in India started in
(a) Delhi (b) Mumbai
(c) Kolkata (d) Madras

57. In how many states was the SITE (Satellite Instructional Television Experiment) programmes launched?
(a) 3 (b) 4
(c) 5 (d) 6

58. All are the examples of the media of two-way communication except
(a) Public meeting
(b) Padyatra
(c) Streetplays
(d) Procession and rallies

59. Communication is possible
(a) Between two animals of the same species.
(b) Between a living organism and machines.
(c) Between an individual and a group.
(d) In all the above situations.

60. The oldest existing newspaper is
(a) *The Times of India*
(b) *The Hindu*
(c) *Mumbai Samachar*
(d) *Calcutta Review*

61. When was the first English newspaper, *Bengal Gazette* published?
(a) 1770 A.D. (b) 1780 A.D.
(c) 1790 A.D. (d) 1795 A.D.

62. The latest development in the hardware technology is the introduction of
(a) FM channels (b) Z channels
(c) M channels (d) Star channel

63. Anderson quoted
(a) Communication—A dynamic process
(b) Communication—A process of exchange of ideas
(c) Communication—A process of association of ideas
(d) None of the above.

64. *Mumbai Samachar* is a magazine in
(a) Hindi (b) Gujarati
(c) Sindhi (d) Marathi

65. Who is known as the father of Indian language journalism in India?
(a) Raja Ram Mohan Roy
(b) Bhupendra Nath Dutta
(c) Vivekananda
(d) V.D. Savarkar

66. CHEER stand for
(a) Children Enrichment Education Through Radio.
(b) Child Health Education Electronic Recording.
(c) Children for Engineers and Energy Requirement.
(d) None of the above.

67. According to Legons, the meaning of communication is
(a) exchange of ideas between two or more than two individuals.
(b) dialogue between two persons.
(c) interaction between two persons.
(d) All of the above.

68. The oldest existing English daily of India is

(a) *The Times of India*
(b) *The Hindustan Times*
(c) *The Hindu*
(d) *The Telegraph*

69. Microphone is a hi-fi instrument. Here 'fi' means
(a) Finish (b) Final
(c) Fidelity (d) Finical

70. Educational TV was first introduced in India in
(a) 1961 (b) 1959
(c) 1968 (d) 1961

71. Communication is a
(a) Process—which is going on between the Source and the Receiver.
(b) A condition of exchange of ideas.
(c) A method of transfer of informations.
(d) All of the above.

72. The oldest magazine published from Calcutta since 1944 is
(a) *The Calcutta Review*
(b) *The Anand Bazar Patrika*
(c) *The India Today*
(d) None of the above.

73. Which of these is a characteristic of radio?
(a) A medium of sound
(b) A mass medium
(c) An intimate medium
(d) All of the above.

74. SITE stands for
(a) System for International Technology and Engineering.
(b) Satellite Instructional Television Experiment.
(c) South Indian Trade Estate.
(d) None of the above.

75. The nature of communication is
(a) Process of exchange of ideas
(b) A purposive process
(c) A psycho-social process
(d) All of the above.

76. The largest single edition regional Newspaper is
(a) *Anand Bazar Patrika*
(b) *Dainik Janamabhumi*
(c) *Janasatta*
(d) *Nai Dunia*

77. Which of these is not a characteristic of TV?
(a) A democratic medium
(b) A mobile medium
(c) A living room medium
(d) A medium of immediacy

78. Visualisation in the instructional process cannot increase
(a) interest and motivation
(b) retention and adaptation
(c) stress and boredom
(d) curiosity and concentration

79. Which of the following is not matched with the nature of communication?
(a) A directional process
(b) A feedback process
(c) A dynamic process
(d) A passive process

80. In which language the highest newspapers are published?
(a) English (b) Hindi
(c) Assamese (d) Bengali

81. _____ is the supreme medium to express yesterday, today, and tomorrow with its own unique language. What should be filled in the blank?
(a) Cinema (b) Radio
(c) Newspaper (d) Television

82. Which of the following teachers will you like most?
(a) One who uses board occasionally.
(b) One who uses chart and maps.

(c) One who uses film projector along with the proper use of the board.
(d) One who uses motion picture as a last resort.

83. The basic elements of communication are
(a) The Source and the Receiver
(b) The Messenger and the Receiver
(c) The Source and the Channel
(d) All of the above.

84. *Reader's Digest* is a
(a) Monthly periodical
(b) Newspaper
(c) Weekly periodical
(d) Fortnightly periodical

85. Large and highly diverse groups that represent the broad cross-section of the society form the audience.
(a) Elite (b) General
(c) Specialised (d) None of these.

86. Overhead projector is superior to short circuit TV in a classroom teaching.
(a) It is cheap and self devised.
(b) Pictures in it may be shown in a desired sequence and with a minimum of lost motion (material).
(c) Information presented though it is easily retained.
(d) It is easy to use.

87. The simple process of communication consists of the following elements
(a) Message source—Medium—Message Receiver
(b) Message Source—Encoding—Decoding—Message Receiver
(c) Message Source—Message Receiver
(d) Message Source—Feedback

88. Press Trust of India is
(a) News agency
(b) Staff reporter
(c) Newspaper
(d) None of the above.

89. Dyadic communication is the transfer of messages from a person
(a) to another person and *vice versa*
(b) to a group of persons
(c) to a mass audience
(d) None of these.

90. Which of the following groups of students can be most benefited computer based education programme?
(a) Small group of low IQ
(b) Large group of moderate intelligence
(c) Heterogeneous groups in IQ
(d) All of the above.

91. The work of Messenger is
(a) to develop a message
(b) to encode the message
(c) to transmit the message
(d) All of the above.

92. Full form of UNI is
(a) United Nations Information
(b) United New of India
(c) Union News of India
(d) All of the above.

93. The promoter of a product cannot deliver the following to a mass audience through currently used media vehicles.
(a) Information
(b) Music
(c) Products
(d) He can deliver literally anything through such vehicles

94. Closed circuit television is useful
(a) only for a restricted audience residing at a particular place.
(b) for large group communication.
(c) only for poor students of the class.
(d) None of the above.

95. The way through which message passes, is called
(a) Channel
(b) Transmission medium

(c) Transmission channel
(d) Transmission system

96. When did modern postal service started in India?
(a) 1867 (b) 1877
(c) 1837 (d) 1827

97. In downward communication, messages
(a) flow from the bottom to the top of the organization structure.
(b) flow from the top to the bottom of the organization structure.
(c) are meant to be exchanged between the members of the top brass.
(d) None of the above.

98. Televised educational programme is useful because
(a) it can present the natural phenomenon of the world in natural form.
(b) it can magnify the microscopic forms of life and can be presented on TV.
(c) it affords the opportunity for large audience in the same auditorium or in different locations to view it clearly.
(d) All of the above.

99. The Receiver should follow the inevitable condition in order to receive the messages
(a) He has the ability to transmit a message.
(b) He has the ability to decoding the message.
(c) He has the ability to interpret the message.
(d) He has all the above abilities.

100. In 1854
(a) IU postal system was introduced.
(b) post office savings bank started.
(c) the first postage stamp introduced.
(d) pin code started.

101. Who developed the first paper for the mankind?
(a) The Chinese (b) The Sumerians
(c) The Aryans (d) The Mayans

102. Teaching on TV is superior to classroom instruction because
(a) very large classes are made possible and thus it is economically advantageous.
(b) experts for teaching a difficult topic can be arranged and others can be benefited from them.
(c) teaching materials can be filmed for reuse.
(d) All of the above.

103. The messages are changed into symbols through the process of
(a) Encoding (b) Decoding
(c) Sign language (d) None of these.

104. The CEO can deal with the resistance through
(a) Education and Communication
(b) Participation and Involvement
(c) Negotiation and Agreement
(d) All of the above.

105. Who was not a part of the team that developed the transistor?
(a) John Bardeen
(b) Walter Brattain
(c) JE Lilienfield
(d) William Shockley

106. All of the following are the limitations of televised instruction except
(a) televised lesson moves at a fixed speed and thus cannot take the individual differences of students into account.
(b) it does not permit the exchange of ideas between the teachers and taught.
(c) it does not properly help the students in making the materials clearly understood.
(d) experts consume much time in planning and preparation of the programme.

107. Decoding is associated with
   (a) Message Sender
   (b) Message Receiver
   (c) Both of the above.
   (d) None of the above.

108. PIN code means
   (a) Postal Index Number
   (b) Postal Identity Number
   (c) Posting Index Number
   (d) None of the above.

109. Who invented the TV?
   (a) Alexander Graham Bell
   (b) John Logie Baird
   (c) C. Francis Jenkins
   (d) Chester Carlson

110. Which of the following is not a successful communicator?
   (a) One who presents material in a precise and clear way.
   (b) One who is able to adapt himself according to the language of the communicatee.
   (c) One who knows a lot but is somewhat reserve in his attitude.
   (d) One who sometimes becomes informal before the receiver and develops rapport.

111. Which of the following process has been incorporated for the decoding of the messages?
   (a) The messages are changed into signs.
   (b) The interpretation of the secret messages has been carried out.
   (c) The obstacles are created in messaging service.
   (d) The messages are changed through encoding.

112. The air mail service started in
   (a) 1854 (b) 1952
   (c) 1862 (d) 1864

113. Which one of the following is not a traditional media?
   (a) Literature (b) Painting
   (c) TV (d) Music

114. Which of the following teachers will you like most?
   (a) A loving teacher.
   (b) A teacher of highly idealist philosophy.
   (c) A teacher who often amuses his students.
   (d) A disciplined teacher.

115. The types of communication are
   (a) Two (b) Four
   (c) Six (d) Eight

116. Postal department was set up in
   (a) 1854 (b) 2001
   (c) 1811 (d) 1912

117. Which one of the following is not a modern media?
   (a) The Press (b) Radio
   (c) Cinema (d) Sculpture

118. As a chairman of UPSC while selecting a teacher you should be
   (a) fair and impartial.
   (b) able to judge the personality of candidates.
   (c) encouraging to those appearing for interview.
   (d) All of the above.

119. The verbal communication completes through
   (a) Verbal medium
   (b) Symbolic medium
   (c) Lips medium
   (d) Bodily organs medium

120. Where was the first telegraph line in the country opened for traffic?
   (a) Between Delhi and Kolkata
   (b) Between Mumbai and Chennai

(c) Between Kolkata and Diamond Harbour
(d) Between Delhi and Mumbai

121. According to who mass media are primarily moulders of society as well as reflectors of it?
(a) Denis McQuail
(b) Harold Lasswell
(c) Wilbur Schramm
(d) George Gerbner

122. When you are unable to follow the foreigner's language, the communication of message will be carried out through
(a) Speaking loudly or screaming
(b) Symbolic language
(c) Learning his language
(d) Cann't say

123. In 1881-82 the first telephone service was started in
(a) Kolkata (b) Shimla
(c) Delhi (d) Mumbai

124. Selective exposure and selective perception are two concepts of which theory?
(a) Bullet Theory
(b) Individual Difference Theory
(c) Personal Influence Theory
(d) None of the above.

125. The non-verbal communication is possible through
(a) Speech symbols (b) Eyes
(c) Sense of touch (d) All of the above

126. The first automatic telephone exchange was commissioned at
(a) Delhi (b) Mumbai
(c) Chennai (d) Shimla

127. Who called his mass communication theory as "cultivation of dominant image patterns"?
(a) Donald L. Shaw
(b) Maxwell McCombs
(c) Davidson
(d) George Gerbner

128. The barrier of the communication can be categorised as
(a) Physical barriers
(b) Language barriers
(c) Psychological barriers
(d) All of the above.

129. Communication technology NSD means
(a) National System of Dialling
(b) National School of Drama
(c) National Subscriber Dialling
(d) None of the above.

130. Who classified his theories on the basis of world's national media systems?
(a) Siebertetal
(b) Sandra Ball
(c) Nelvin De Pleur
(d) Geogre Gerbner

131. The biggest barrier of the communication is
(a) Noise
(b) Person
(c) Language
(d) Previous Experiences

132. When was VSNL formed?
(a) 1986 (b) 1996
(c) 1936 (d) 1976

133. 'Liberation Theory' is also called as
(a) Authoritarian Theory
(b) Social Responsibility Theory
(c) Free Press Theory
(d) Communist Media Theory

134. The barriers of communication can be eliminated when it is
(a) simple and comprehensible.
(b) associated with feedback.
(c) following the rules for excellent listening.
(d) All of the above.

135. ISP means
(a) Internet Service Provider
(b) Internet Subscribing Provider
(c) Internet System Provider
(d) None of the above.

136. Soviet Media Theory is another name for
(a) Social Responsibility Theory
(b) Communist Media Theory
(c) Development Communication Theory
(d) Democratic-Participant Media Theory

137. The barriers in communication can be overcome if
(a) The listener has all the desirable competencies of best listening.
(b) The listener is in a state of motivator.
(c) The listener has some extra incentives.
(d) All of the above.

138. India's largest Internet Service Provider is
(a) BSNL (b) MTNL
(c) HTML (d) VSNL

139. When was censorship introduced on Indian Press?
(a) 1790 (b) 1792
(c) 1795 (d) 1797

140. Which one of the following does not work as a barrier in communication?
(a) Physical Barriers
(b) Psychological Barriers
(c) Background Barriers
(d) Feedback related Barriers

141. The term communis is taken from
(a) Latin language
(b) Greek language
(c) Hebrew language
(d) English language

142. When was the first press ordinance issued?
(a) 1820 (b) 1823
(c) 1826 (d) 1829

143. Which of the following teacher's quality is associated with his best teaching?
(a) The abilities of the teacher
(b) Teacher's abstinence
(c) The oral expression of the teacher
(d) The vocational commitment and love for the profession

144. The nature of communication is
(a) process of exchange of ideas
(b) a purposive process
(c) a psycho-social process
(d) All of the above.

145. In which language was *Amrita Bazer Patrika* first published before changing over to English language?
(a) Hindi (b) Urdu
(c) Bengali (d) Punjabi

146. An efficient teacher ensures
(a) feelings of co-operation in his students.
(b) full freedom on his own part without any restriction.
(c) competition among his students.
(d) feelings of either co-operation or competition as the conditions permit in his students.

147. Generally in a communication the position of perception, retention and recall will be
(a) like source variables
(b) like messages variables
(c) like message deceivers
(d) like channel variables

148. *The Times of India* came into being with the amalgamation of which of these papers?
(a) *The Standard* and *The Telegraph*
(b) *The Bombay Times* and *The Courier*
(c) *The Standard* and *The Courier*
(d) Both (a) and (b)

149. When your friend point out at your gross mistake which you have committed in the class during teaching, then your reaction will be
(a) resisting him and tell him confidently that it does not come under the purview of a mistake.

(b) discussing on the mistake, try to put your stand, if he does not agree then accepting your mistake.
(c) warning him that he should not behave in such a manner in future.
(d) requesting him politely that he should not tell it to any other person.

150. The work of a messenger is
(a) to encode message
(b) to decline message
(c) to develop message
(d) All of the above.

151. Who is known as the 'father of Indian Cinema'.
(a) Torney
(b) J.F. Madan
(c) Dada Saheb Phalke
(d) Natraj Mudaliar

152. If your students remain unsatisfied even after your teaching a particular lesson or content, what would you like to do under these conditions?
(a) You will leave aside all fruitful efforts of teaching in order to enhance their understanding.
(b) You will be doing your best efforts again and again till they will not understand the content.
(c) You will think that again and again repetition of the same content is mere a destroying the time.
(d) You will be keeping sympathetic behaviour with the students.

153. Decoding is associated with
(a) message sender
(b) message receiver
(c) Both (a) and (b)
(d) Only (a)

154. Which media would be ideal to attract the attention of children to sell chocolates to them?
(a) Radio
(b) Newspapers
(c) TV (advertisements)
(d) Leaflets

155. What is the essential step for an effective communicator?
(a) Selection of the channel for communication.
(b) Think about the evaluation procedure.
(c) Determining the objectives of communication.
(d) Identifying various mediums of communication.

156. What is the meaning of circulation in the parlance of the print media?
(a) Number of copies printed
(b) Number of copies sold
(c) Number of editions
(d) None of the above

157. If you get appointment in a college as a teacher, how could you behave with your students?
(a) Autocratic manner
(b) Democratic manner
(c) Laissez-faire manner
(d) Intellectual manner

158. In an excellent communication, it is not desired
(a) to change in voice
(b) involvement of students
(c) communication of adequate feelings
(d) physical beauty

159. An interview is a type of
(a) dyadic communication
(b) multiadic communication
(c) mass communication
(d) None of the above.

160. Which special train was running in order to disseminate scientific awareness in the country?

(a) Science and Technology rail
(b) The Great Indian rail
(c) Science rail
(d) None of the above.

161. Eyes helps in
(a) nonverbal communication
(b) written communication
(c) verbal communication
(d) None of the above.

162. A journalist need not be _____ while covering an event.
(a) impartial (b) meticulous
(c) domineering (d) inquisitive

163. If you are interested in communicating democratic tendencies among your students, which of the following system will enabled them with this objective?
(a) You discuss and debate on the issue of advantages of Democratic system with students and indoctrinate them about it by changing their beliefs.
(b) You conduct the election for students' Assembly and give them responsibilities to share.
(c) You give priority to democratic values in your day-to-day practice of working and engage whole class in its adequate management and give them suitable duties.
(d) You call excellent speakers and dignitaries in school and divert the attention of students towards their speech about the great persons of the world.

164. The messages are changed into symbols by a process of
(a) Decoding
(b) Symbolic expression
(c) Encoding
(d) All of the above.

165. Which ones of the following do not provide entertainment to the targeted audience?
(a) TV Programmers
(b) Magazines
(c) Leaflets
(d) Newspaper features

166. In order to a teacher should have effective communication, it is essential that
(a) The teacher should become master of his own subject.
(b) The teacher should prepare a good teaching aid.
(c) The teacher should discuss the questions asked in previous year's examination.
(d) The teacher should start at that point from where students are ready to learn.

167. The main element of communication is
(a) the source and the channel.
(b) the source and the receiver.
(c) the messenger only.
(d) None of the above.

168. What is average frequency?
(a) Total Exposures/Audience Reach.
(b) Audience Reach/Total Exposures.
(c) Total Exposures in a given time period.
(d) None of the above.

169. In a process of communication, the final objective of Feedback is
(a) To bring desirable change in the process of communication.
(b) To understand about the content.
(c) To identify the defects of the communicator.
(d) To diagnose the limits of the message sender.

170. An efficient teacher ensure

(a) competition among his students.
(b) feelings of either co-operation or competition as the conditions permit in students.
(c) only co-operation.
(d) None of the above.

171. What do you understand by GRPs?
(a) The number of readers reading an advertisement.
(b) The number of advertising insertions in one campaign.
(c) The number of points earned by an advertising campaign.
(d) Any one of these.

172. What is the fundamental principle of Educational Psychology?
(a) To teach the tricks of teaching profession.
(b) To develop insight about the different aspects of modern education.
(c) To develop insights about the needs, problems and styles of behaviours of the students.
(d) To develop the research designs for modern teaching processes.

173. The limit of Mass Communication is
(a) it is in a very poor state.
(b) the feedback system is not well developed.
(c) it is costly.
(d) None of the above.

174. What is Print Run?
(a) Print Run – Complementary Copies.
(b) Print Run – Wapasi.
(c) Print Run + Complementary Copies.
(d) The number of books sold by one particular retailer.

175. If a teacher is unable to communicate his ideas to the students in adequate manner, the result of it will be
(a) the end of discipline in the class.
(b) the end of students' interest in the topic.
(c) the maximum absence of students from the class.
(d) All of the above.

176. For a teacher to become effective communicator it is essential that
(a) the teacher should start from the point from where the children are eager to learn.
(b) the teacher should use good teaching aid.
(c) the teacher should be master in his subject.
(d) All of the above.

177. What are net sales in the parlance of book publishing?
(a) The number of books or magazines sold by one retailer or bookshop.
(b) The number of books or magazines printed by a publisher at one time.
(c) The number of books or magazines available for sales.
(d) None of the above.

178. If you are a teacher, how should you behave with the children?
(a) Intellectually (b) Democratically
(c) Autocratically (d) Morally

179. Which sampling involves picking up of cases that are judged to be 'typical' of the population?
(a) Cluster sampling
(b) Accidental sampling
(c) Quota sampling
(d) Purposive sampling

180. In which of the following situations the students can interact to one another in more liberal (free) environment?
(a) In discussions within the small group
(b) By using Film Projector

(c) By TV viewing
(d) In Expert's lectures

181. When you are unable to follow the foreigner's language, the communication of messages will be carried out through
(a) speaking loudly
(b) screaming
(c) body language
(d) symbolic language

182. Closed-ended type of question are questions calling for
(a) simple 'yes-no'
(b) agree-disagree answers
(c) multiple choice type of responses
(d) All of these.

183. In which of the following condition the class appears to be most effective?
(a) When the teacher imparts experiences according to the levels of students.
(b) When the teacher keeps students in a state of relaxation during teaching.
(c) When teacher teaches the subject-matter in a clear and loud voice.
(d) When teacher establishes strict discipline in the class.

184. The way through which message passes, is called
(a) trannsmission wire
(b) channel
(c) system
(d) medium of transmission

185. In open-ended question, the respondent is provided with
(a) No answers
(b) Multiple type answers
(c) Objective type answers
(d) None of the above.

186. If you are interested in maintaining effective communication in your class, what will you do?
(a) Teaching of the subject-matter with clarity and students' pace.
(b) To use appropriate media for teaching.
(c) To capture the sender's message in toto and decode it appropriately by the students.
(d) To receive the messages immediately.

187. Hegons gives the meaning of communication as
(a) dialogue between two persons
(b) interaction among two groups
(c) Both (a) and (b).
(d) None of the above.

188. Who enforced the Vernacular Press Act?
(a) Lord Canning
(b) Lord Lytton
(c) Queen Victoria
(d) East India Company

189. Which one of the following is not treated as an obstacle in the way of effective communication?
(a) A long statement
(b) An inadequate statement
(c) A brief statement
(d) A statement which permits the listener to derive the conclusions

190. The barrier of the communication can be classified as
(a) language barrier
(b) physical barrier
(c) psychological barrier
(d) All of the above.

191. The name given to the first radio programme was
(a) India Radio Times
(b) The Indian listener
(c) Akashvani
(d) None of the above.

192. Which of the following element is essential for communicating a research work?

(a) Process
(b) Mastery over the language
(c) Statement of aim
(d) Both (b) and (c).

193. In the way of effective communication a long statement is
(a) Barrier (b) Not a barrier
(c) Only (b) (d) None of these.

194. When were the Bombay and Calcutta stations inaugurated by the Indian Broadcasting Company?
(a) 1925 (b) 1926
(c) 1927 (d) 1928

195. When a teacher is being treated as an effective communicator, the teacher's duty should be
(a) That he will be communicating thinking ability in students.
(b) That he will be imparting knowledge through lesson-teaching and healthy discussions.
(c) That he will be discussing the content with students.
(d) All the above are correct.

196. When was the name All India Radio adopted?
(a) June 10, 1935 (b) April 8, 1936
(c) January 8, 1935 (d) June 8, 1936

197. In all formal and informal communications the following quality is comprised of
(a) Structuredness
(b) Unstructuredness
(c) Discrimination
(d) Similarity

198. The essential step for an effective communicator is
(a) thinking about the revaluation procedure.
(b) determining the objective of communication.
(c) Only (a).
(d) None of the above.

199. When was the first National Orchestra set up, with Pandit Ravi Shankar?
(a) 1950 (b) 1951
(c) 1952 (d) 1954

200. Generally in a communication the position of perception, retention and recall will be
(a) Like source variables
(b) Like message variables
(c) Like message receivers
(d) Like channel variables

201. In the process of communication, the final objective of feedback is
(a) to understand about the content.
(b) to diagnose the demerits of the communicators.
(c) to bring some desirable changes in the process of communication.
(d) None of the above.

202. Independent variable and dependent variable are variables of which method available to communications researcher?
(a) Historical Method
(b) Experimental Method
(c) Survey Method
(d) Content Analysis Method

203. Which of the following step you keep in priority for a effective communication?
(a) To select a channel for communication.
(b) To plan a evaluation procedure.
(c) To specify the objectives of communication.
(d) To select various types of media for communication.

204. In formulating a research work which of the following elements is essential?
(a) Statement of aim
(b) Process
(c) No fixed plan
(d) None of the above.

205. Which is the probability technique used in survey research?
(a) Simple random sample
(b) Stratified random sample
(c) Cluster sample
(d) All of the above.

206. In an effective communication there is no need of
(a) Modulations in voice and speech
(b) Adequate gestures
(c) Mastery over the content
(d) Handsome personality

207. In discussions within small group, the students can interact with one another in
(a) restricted environment
(b) a more liberal environment
(c) a less liberal environment
(d) fully restricted environment

208. The non-probability technique used in Survey research is
(a) Accidental sample
(b) Quota sample
(c) Purposive sample
(d) All of the above.

209. Which of the following is not a true statement?
(a) A good communicator cannot be judged as a good teacher
(b) A good communicator has the satirical (Humerous) expressions
(c) A good communicator is an exhaustive reader
(d) A good communicator has the mastery over language

210. The most essential step for an effective communicator is
(a) identifying mediums of communication.
(b) selection of channel.
(c) determining objectives for communication.
(d) Only (b).

211. Using of all elements in the population and taking a lottery to select the desired number of elements from the totality is
(a) Simple Random Sampling
(b) Stratified Random Sampling
(c) Cluster Sampling
(d) None of the above.

212. The biggest obstacle in the way of communication in a class is
(a) excess of noise in a class.
(b) vagueness about the content of a teacher.
(c) the noise out of class and other related obstacles.
(d) lack in teaching aid material.

213. A teacher can be effective in teaching if
(a) he is knowledgeable
(b) he gives rich learning experience to students
(c) he clarifies all doubts of children
(d) None of the above.

214. Multi-stage sampling is also called as
(a) Quota sampling
(b) Cluster sampling
(c) Purposive sampling
(d) Stratified sampling

215. An effective communication produces in receiver
(a) Happiness
(b) Acceptance
(c) Its access to other people
(d) Thinking

216. Effective communication will be possible only when
(a) the receiver is active.
(b) the message is designed according to the listeners.
(c) the latest communication technology is applied.
(d) None of the above.

217. "They have high status in the society. Their number is small but their influence is strong." This is with reference to what kind of audience?
   (a) Elite (b) General
   (c) Specialised (d) None of these.

218. Which of the following measure should be adopted by a teacher in order to adjust himself as an effective communicator?
   (a) He uses more and more teaching aids
   (b) Whatever he teaches, it should be adequate to all the levels of students
   (c) He should ask questions to the students' during teaching
   (d) He should extend help in searching the best answers of the questions

219. An effective communication produces in receiver's
   (a) Thinking (b) Discussing
   (c) Acceptance (d) Happiness

220. Which is the method used for receiving information in market based feedback system?
   (a) Audience Decision-making
   (b) Direct Feedback
   (c) Media Review
   (d) All of the above.

221. Generally it has been witnessed that the communication in the class disrupted, because
   (a) The students' attention is not focused on it.
   (b) The teacher delivers a monotonous lecture.
   (c) The students are not taking proper interest in the lesson taught by the teacher.
   (d) The loud noise is continued within and outside the classroom.

222. In an effective communication there is no need of
   (a) adequate language
   (b) handsome personality
   (c) mastery over content
   (d) All of the above.

223. Who differentiated between 'hot and cold' messages?
   (a) Marshall McLuhan
   (b) Wilbur Schramm
   (c) Raymond Williams
   (d) Val Geilgud

224. The effective communication will be taking place if
   (a) The source is attractive and autocratic
   (b) The message is designed according to the listeners
   (c) The latest communication technology has been employed
   (d) The receiver is passive to receive the messages

225. Who called our society as a 'dramatised' society?
   (a) Marshall McLuhan
   (b) Raymond Williams
   (c) James Augustus
   (d) Gutenberg

226. Which of the following is not a biggest barrier of the communication?
   (a) Person (b) Personality
   (c) Language (d) None of these

227. When was the first printing press established in India?
   (a) 1670 (b) 1672
   (c) 1674 (d) 1676

228. Which of the following group is not making a communication process defective in a classroom?
   (a) Reversing—Evaluating—Focusing
   (b) Evaluating—Focusing—Eliciting
   (c) Evaluating—Focusing—Exaggerating
   (d) Evaluating—Eliciting—Exaggerating

229. The communication of teacher's ideas to the student is meant
(a) inculcating ideas in the student's brain.
(b) to impart lectures.
(c) to impart ideas.
(d) to continue teaching process.

230. What is the other name of Hicky's Bengal Gazette?
(a) The Bengal News
(b) Calcutta General Advertiser
(c) Bengal Journal
(d) Bengal Harkarv

231. Which of the following is a best method to control noise in the classroom situation?
(a) To give warning to the students that they must keep silence.
(b) To speak loudly by the teacher to keep pace with the noise in the class.
(c) To watch the class silently and minutely scan the class.
(d) To ignore the student's noise, stand confidently and start teaching.

232. IIMC is situated in
(a) Delhi (b) Mumbai
(c) Chennai (d) Kolkata

233. Which theory is derived from the studies of Saussure and Peirce?
(a) Mass Society Theory
(b) Hegemony Theory
(c) Culture and Semiotic Theory
(d) Political Economic Media Theory

234. Below are given some traits of a good teacher
1. Mastery over the content.
2. Effective verbal communication.
3. Handsome personality.
4. Potentiality to seek respect from students.
5. Potentiality to seek respect from community leaders.

Which of the above qualities you should prefer in an effective teacher?
(a) 1, 2 and 3 (b) 1, 2 and 4
(c) 1, 2 and 5 (d) 1, 3 and 5

235. The types of communication can be classified in
(a) one group (b) four group
(c) two group (d) Only (b)

236. Which theories derived strength from Marxist ideology?
(a) Mass Society Theory
(b) Political Economic Media Theory
(c) Social Responsibility Theory
(d) None of the above.

237. The obstacles of communication can be eliminated when it is
(a) associated with feed-basis
(b) follows the rules for excellent listening
(c) simple and comprehensible
(d) All of the above.

238. When was the channel 'Yuva Vani' started in Delhi?
(a) 1965 (b) 1966
(c) 1967 (d) 1969

239. The advantage of Feedback in the process of communication is
(a) It clarifies the communication.
(b) It is beneficial in understanding of the subject-matter.
(c) It diagnose the defects in message sender or communicator.
(d) It explores the defects in receiver.

240. Find which of the following is not matched with the nature of communication?
(a) A dynamic process
(b) A feedback process
(c) A directional process
(d) A passive process

241. Where was the highest AIR station set-up in 1971?

(a) Mumbai (b) Leh
(c) Himachal (d) Nainital

242. Which of the following alternative is representing the effective communication?
(a) The teacher should crack the jokes during teaching in the class.
(b) The teacher should impart multidimension sensory influence on the students through his teaching.
(c) The teacher should speak authoritatively.
(d) The teacher should teach whatever is beneficial to the students.

243. When was the Bombay TV centre inaugurated?
(a) 1970 (b) 1971
(c) 1972 (d) 1974

244. When were educational programmes by UGC started on TV?
(a) 1980 (b) 1982
(c) 1983 (d) 1984

245. When you are delivering a lecture in a class, it is better if you
1. Know the ideas of other persons
2. Know that all the students in the class are not Homogeneous in nature
3. Give due respect to other's ideas
Which one of the following pair is correct in the above context?
(a) 1 and 2 (b) 3 only
(c) 1 and 3 (d) 1, 2 and 3

246. The verbal communication completes through
(a) Lips
(b) Body language
(c) Symbolic language
(d) Verbal medium

247. When was the moving transmission of TV started?
(a) 1980 (b) 1985
(c) 1987 (d) 1989

248. A teacher will be having effective teaching if
(a) He explains adequately the expected content to his students in a class.
(b) He repeats the explanations in order to grasp by all the students.
(c) He gives rich learning experiences to the students.
(d) He gives right answers to all the queries of the students.

249. Which of the following step would you give priority for a effective communication?
(a) To select a channel for communication.
(b) To specify the objectives of communication.
(c) To select media for communication.
(d) None of the above.

250. In which year did Doordarshan started its 5 metro channels?
(a) 1990 (b) 1993
(c) 1994 (d) 1992

251. Sometimes it has been witnessed that in a large class, students are trying to ditch their teacher in disciplinarian art. In your opinion the problem lies with
(a) The students
(b) The process
(c) The content to be taught
(d) The time taken for teaching

252. Which committee criticised the Doordarshan for concentrating on the North for its programme contents?
(a) Verghese Committee
(b) Joshi Committee
(c) Chandra Committee
(d) None of the above.

253. In order to adjust as an effective communicator the following measures are to be adopted by a teacher.

(a) use more teaching techniques.
(b) use more aids.
(c) ask questions to students.
(d) should extend help in searching the best answer to questions.

254. Which committee recommended separation of AIR and Television?
(a) Chanda Committee
(b) Verghese Committee
(c) Joshi Committee
(d) None of the above.

255. Good communicator
(a) cannot be judged as a good teacher
(b) has the satirical expression
(c) is an exhaustive teacher
(d) All of these.

256. Effective communication does not require
(a) Voice modulation
(b) Handsome appearance
(c) Appropriate gestures
(d) Students involvement

257. Excess of noise in a class is
(a) the biggest obstacle in the way of communication in a class.
(b) the least obstacle in the way.
(c) does not effect in the way of communication in a class.
(d) None of the above.

258. Effective teaching is, by and large, a function of the teacher.
(a) Scholarship
(b) Punctuality
(c) Ability for verbal expression
(d) Liking for the profession

259. To control noise in the class which of the following is a best methods?
(a) Ignore the student's noise, stand confidently and start teaching.
(b) Watch the class silently and minutely scan the class.
(c) Give warning to the student that they must keep silence.
(d) None of the above.

260. Which of the following is an ambitious computerisation programme aimed at connecting 60,000 government and aided schools through internet?
(a) Vidya Vahini
(b) Vidya Vani
(c) Gyan Vani
(d) None of the above

261. Which of the following statements is true?
(a) An effective communication produces in receivers — Thinking
(b) An effective communication does not require — Handsome personality
(c) The meaning of communis is — Sensation
(d) None of the above.

262. An effective teacher will ensure
(a) Cooperation among his students
(b) Laissez-faire role on his part
(c) Competition among his students
(d) Competition or cooperation as the situation demands

263. Which of the following is the fastest way of communicating messages?
(a) E-mails (b) Telegrams
(c) Letters (d) Postcards

264. Which of the following statement is true?
(a) Communis means - sensation
(b) The work of messenger - to encode the message
(c) Acceptance - non-effective communication produced by the reciever
(d) All of the above.

265. World's first sky bus station was inaugurated recently at

(a) Tees Hazari, Delhi
(b) Madgaon, Goa
(c) Tollygunj, Kolkata
(d) None of the above.

266. *India Today* belongs to
(a) Times of India Group
(b) Living Media India Ltd.
(c) Indian Express
(d) NDTV Group

267. Name the project which will connect all police stations in the country in one network
(a) POLNET (b) TOLNET
(c) POL.COM (d) IPOL.COM

268. Communication — "A dynamic Process" is quoted by
(a) Jawaharlal Nehru
(b) Lincoln
(c) Anderson
(d) None of the above.

269. A colleague who overhears you committing a mistake while teaching in your class points out this to you. How will you react?
(a) Tell him that you have never committed any mistake.
(b) Discuss with him and if convinced thank him and correct it in the next class.
(c) Warn him against interfering in such matters.
(d) Request him not to tell it to anybody else.

270. Which of the following could be classified under the software of educational technology?
(a) Tape recorder
(b) TV
(c) Programmed instructed material
(d) None of the above.

271. Which of the following styles of action regarding instruction is preferred by you?
(a) Enrich the textual material by gathering relevant aspects from other books and experts.
(b) Limit learning experiences to what is required by the textual material.
(c) Discuss probable questions so that the students can fare well in the examination.
(d) Ask pupils to read the textbook in advance and hold discussions on its basis.

272. Characteristics of all formal and informal communication is
(a) same structure
(b) different structure
(c) Both (a) and (b).
(d) None of the above.

273. The students do not understand what is taught in the classroom, the teacher may
(a) give up the attempt.
(b) explain in a different way.
(c) think that it is mere waste of time to continue.
(d) sympathise with the students.

274. The interaction between teacher and students or between buyer and seller is classified by the socialist as a social interaction of
(a) secondary type (b) primary type
(c) multiple type (d) None of these.

275. Which of the following steps would you consider first as an effective communicator?
(a) Select the channels of communication.
(b) Plan the evaluation procedure.
(c) Determine the objectives of communication.
(d) Identify various means for communication.

276. When you are delivering a lecture in a class, it is better if you
   (a) know the ideas of the other persons
   (b) give due respect to other's ideas
   (c) know that all the students in the class are not Homogeneous in nature
   (d) All of the above.

277. The facial expression of students relate to which element of the communication process?
   (a) Message (b) Receiver
   (c) Channel (d) Sender

278. While planning education for development which of the following characteristics will you stress?
   (a) All round development of the individual.
   (b) Development sustainable throughout life.
   (c) Transferable to all walks of life.
   (d) All the three above.

279. Communication is possible
   (a) between two animals of the same species.
   (b) between a living organism and machines.
   (c) between an individual and a group.
   (d) All of the above.

280. The initial step to be taken by a teacher while introducing a new topic of study
   (a) Assessing their previous knowledge.
   (b) Beginning with group discussions.
   (c) Giving a broad outline of the topic to be learnt.
   (d) Showing some audio-visual aids.

281. Which of the following consists simple process of communication?
   (a) Message source - feedback
   (b) Message source - message receiver
   (c) Message source - medium - message receiver
   (d) None of the above.

282. The test effectiveness of instruction is
   (a) Effectiveness of learning
   (b) Sufficient use of audio-visual aids
   (c) Maintenance of discipline in the class
   (d) Regular attendance of students

283. Which of the following statements is true?
   (a) Decoding is associated with message sender.
   (b) The type of communication are eight.
   (c) The non-verbal communication is possible through eyes.
   (d) None of the above.

284. Which of the following steps do you prefer while transacting the curriculum?
   (a) Present the learning materials in the question answer form and thus ensure good performance in the examination.
   (b) Frequently conduct test papers in which question papers resemble those used in public examination.
   (c) Explain the concepts and principles clearly and ensure understanding, by all.
   (d) Present learning activities suited for the realisation of predetermined instructional objectives.

285. The advantage of feedback in the process of communication is that
   (a) it explores the defects in receiver.
   (b) it classifies the communication.
   (c) it is beneficial in understanding of the subject-matter.
   (d) None of the above.

286. You want to instil in the pupils of your class the spirit of democracy. Which of

the following strategy do you think, is most efficient for the purpose.

(a) Organise a discussion on the advantages of democracy over other systems and convince the pupils of its superiority.
(b) Conduct election for a class assembly and give the representatives certain responsibilities.
(c) Maintain a democratic atmosphere in your dealings and make the pupils unitedly responsible for class management, sharing duties among themselves.
(d) Invite speakers to the school and make them deliver speeches about world leaders who worked for democracy.

287. Which of the following step would you keep in priority for an effective communication?
(a) To plan evaluation procedure.
(b) To specify the objectives of communication.
(c) To select various types of mediator communication.
(d) None of the above.

288. Discussion in the class will be most effective if the topic of discussion is
(a) not introduced by the teacher.
(b) stated immediately before the start of discussion.
(c) written in the Blackboard without introducing it.
(d) informed to the students well in advance.

289. If a teacher is unable to communicate his ideas to students in adequate manner, the result of it will be
(a) the end of students' interest from the class.
(b) the maximum absence of students.
(c) the end of discipline in the class.
(d) All of the above.

290. Teacher's communication will be more effective if
(a) the teacher is a master in his subject
(b) he prepares a good number of instructional aids
(c) he discusses previous question papers
(d) he starts from what students already know

291. The receiver should follow the inevitable condition in order to receive the messages
(a) he has the ability to interpret
(b) he has the ability to interpret the message
(c) he has the ability decoding the message
(d) All of the above.

292. The recently launched "Vidya Vahini" is a project related to
(a) School computerisation programme
(b) TV programme related to mass literacy
(c) Establishment of libraries in rural areas
(d) None of the above.

293. The psychological aspects of the classroom are best managed by
(a) the class teacher
(b) the subject teacher
(c) the principal
(d) the student

294. The most critical factor that determines the professional status of a teacher is
(a) Unity among teachers
(b) High salary
(c) Character
(d) Instructional competency

295. Books can be a powerful source of communication provided

(a) content is abstract
(b) English medium
(c) content is illustration
(d) Hindi medium

296. The final goal of feedback in a communication system is to
(a) make necessary modifications in the communication process.
(b) understand more about the content.
(c) identify the defects of the communicator.
(d) detect the limitations of the receiver.

297. Who among the following has been awarded the first Pearl Journalism Award?
(a) Mark Tully
(b) Jean Raffari
(c) Mohammad Bazzi
(d) Daniel Michael

298. The main function of educational Psychology is to provide prospective teachers with
(a) rules of thumb to deal with every day classroom situation.
(b) insight into the various aspects of modern education.
(c) insight into the needs, problems and styles of behaviour of learners.
(d) research procedures for evaluating current teaching procedures.

299. Name the first of its kind computer generated comic strip created by the times of India group
(a) Strange Man
(b) Dubyaman's Duniya
(c) Word of Alice
(d) Meri-Teri-Unki-Bat

300. Failure of the teacher to communicate his ideas well to the students may result into
(a) Classroom indiscipline
(b) Loss of students' interest in the topic being taught
(c) Increased number of absentees in the class
(d) All of the above.

301. The film, "Monority Report" was directed by
(a) Piers Brosnann
(b) Michael Doughlas
(c) Tom Cruez
(d) Steran Speilberg

302. What will be your ultimate goal while planning instructional procedures?
(a) To enable all pupils secure high scores in the public examination.
(b) To make classes interesting and meaningful to students.
(c) To ensure that pupils master the learning materials.
(d) To realise all the developmental goals anticipated.

303. The first commercial film made by Film Division is
(a) Devdas (b) Dukhi Ram
(c) Dekha (d) Barat

304. India's first 100 per cent computer literate village is
(a) Chamravattam village (Kerala)
(b) Sasamosa (Bihar)
(c) Guru Nagar (Punjab)
(d) None of the above.

305. Who is the director of film Devdas, in which Shahrukh Khan played the title role and and being nominated for 'Oscar' by Indian Motions Picture Producers Association?
(a) Sanjay Leela Bhansali
(b) Deepa Mehta
(c) Mahesh Bhatt
(d) Shabana Azmi

306. Which of the following, in your opinion, is a clear evidence for positive attitude towards the National Anthem?

(a) Ability to recite it melodiously.
(b) Feeling proud as an Indian when it is heard.
(c) Standing silently whenever it is sung in function.
(d) Studying its historical and national background and significance.

307. In which State the maximum number of periodicals are brought out for public information?
(a) Punjab (b) Kerala
(c) UP (d) Tamil Nadu

308. What role would you take up in the developmental programmes of the society?
(a) Attend discussions and present views.
(b) Closely watch the programmes and print out lapses in time.
(c) Actively participate in their planning and execution.
(d) Encourage social audit and evaluation.

309. Which of the following is the oldest newspaper in Asia?
(a) *The Blitz*
(b) *The Times of India*
(c) *Mumbai Samachar*
(d) *Amrit Bazar Patrika*

310. The technique adopted to find out the level of acceptability of an individual by members of a group is
(a) Personality testing
(b) Projective techniques
(c) Psychometry
(d) Sociometry

311. Where is the Satyajit Ray Film and Television intitute being set up?
(a) Kolkata (b) Mumbai
(c) Pune (d) Noida

312. Major limitation of mass communication is that
(a) It is very costly for the receiver.
(b) More time is required to produce the message.
(c) The success of the programme mainly depends upon the producers.
(d) The feedback system is weak.

313. What is Tehlka?
(a) A Newspaper
(b) A TV Channel
(c) A Radio Channel
(d) A Website

314. For problematic situations are given below:
(i) A student is abnormally withdrawing in nature.
(ii) A considerable number of students always score low in your subject.
(iii) Students of your class are found to create disturbances in the class of a particular teacher.
(iv) In spite of warning most of the students of a class are irregular with assignments.

Which of these warrant action research?
(a) (ii) and (iv) (b) (i), (ii) and (iv)
(c) (ii) and (iii) (d) All the four

315. TV channel launched for covering only Engineering and Technology subjects is known as
(a) Kisan (b) Eklavya
(c) Gyan Darshan (d) Vyas

316. Which of the following provides more freedom for the learners to interact actively?
(a) Small group discussions
(b) Use of film projector
(c) Viewing of the television
(d) Lecture by experts

317. Sometimes it has been witnessed that in a large class, students are trying to ditch their teacher in disciplinarian art. In your opinion the problem lies with
(a) the time taken for teaching
(b) the students

(c) the content to be taught
(d) the process

318. Programmed instruction is a direct application of which of the following?
(a) Cognitive Development theory
(b) Reinforcement theory
(c) Humanistic Psychology
(d) Classical Conditioning theory

319. The advantage of Feedback in the process of communication is
(a) it explores the defects in receiver.
(b) it clarifies the communication.
(c) it is beneficial in understanding of the subject matter.
(d) it diagnose the defects in message sender or communicator.

320. Which of the following can make a class most effective?
(a) Making the learning experiences learner centred.
(b) Keeping the students relaxed while teaching.
(c) Explaining the subject matter clearly and loudly.
(d) Keeping strict discipline in the class.

321. Which of the following groups is not making a communication process defective in a classroom?
(a) Reversing - Evaluating - Focusing
(b) Evaluating - Eliciting - Exaggerating
(c) Evaluating - Focusing - Exaggerating
(d) Evaluating - Focusing - Eliciting

322. After attending an inservice course you are offered one book from among the four listed below. Which one will be your first preference?
(a) A novel written by a famous author.
(b) A book on innovative instructional strategies.
(c) The autobiography of your favourite political leader.
(d) A book on the philosophy of Rousseau.

323. Generally it has been witnessed that the communication in the class is disturbed, because
(a) the students attention is not focused on it.
(b) the teacher delivers a monotonous lecture.
(c) the students are not taking proper interest in the lesson taught by the teacher.
(d) the loud noise is continued within and outside the classroom.

324. The Education Department invites projects or action research on instructional problems related to your subject of specialisation. How will you react to this?
(a) Prepare a project in case you have experienced a genuine complex problem.
(b) Prepare a project on any problem that might be faced by teachers.
(c) Do not act to the invitation at all.
(d) Prepare a project in case an award is declared.

325. The biggest obstacle in the way of communication in a class is the
(a) excess of noise in a class.
(b) vagueness about the content of a teacher.
(c) the noise out of a class and other related obstacles.
(d) lack in teaching aid material.

326. There is a suggestion to a group of students according to their ability. In that case which group will you prefer?
(a) The brilliant group
(b) The average group

(c) The backward group
(d) No special preference

327. Which of the following steps you keep in the priority for a effective communication?
(a) To select a channel for communication.
(b) To plan a evaluation procedure.
(c) To specify the objectives of communication.
(d) To select various types of media for communication.

328. Communication will be effective if it is
(a) delivered slowly and clearly.
(b) delivered using appropriate media.
(c) received as intended by the sender.
(d) received immediately.

329. In all formal and informal communications the following quality is comprised of
(a) Structuredness (b) Similarity
(c) Unstructuredness (d) Discrimination

330. Which of the following helps a learner best to consolidate knowledge in the cognitive structure?
(a) Explaining the subject matter to others.
(b) Reading more and more library books.
(c) Depending on a number of guide books.
(d) Closely attending to what the teacher tells.

331. When a teacher is being treated as effective communicator, the teacher's duty should be
(a) that he will be communicating thinking ability in students.
(b) that he will be discussing the content with students.
(c) that he will be imparting knowledge through lesson-teaching and healthy discussions.
(d) All of the above.

332. The most important reason why the present education system has to be modified is
(a) It does not provide for harmonious development of a student.
(b) It is very old.
(c) It is too theoretical.
(d) It cannot cope up with modern developments.

333. The Library and information Science Department of Mysore University has taken up an ambitious project which aims to create an online database of all doctoral theses and dissertations published by Indian Universities. The project sponsored by the Union Science and Technology Ministry is known as
(a) Vidya Bharti (b) Vidya Bahini
(c) March Ahead (d) Vidya Nidhi

334. In which of the following conditions the class appears to be most effective?
(a) When teacher establishes strict discipline in the class.
(b) When a teacher teaches the subject matter in a clear and loud voice.
(c) When the teacher imparts experiences according to the levels of students.
(d) When the teacher keeps students in a state of relaxation during teaching.

335. Which special train will be spreading awareness about various scientific and technological achievements of the country
(a) Rail Vigyan
(b) Vigyan Rail
(c) Science Rail
(d) Science and Technology Rail

336. If a teacher is unable to communicate his ideas to the students in adequate manner, the result of it will be
(a) the end of students interest in the topic.

(b) the maximum absence of students from the class.
(c) the end of discipline in the class.
(d) All of the above.

337. The teacher should provide an opportunity for cooperative learning (peer learning) as it
(a) encourages self-study habits among the students.
(b) prepares the students to learn by sharing experiences and expertise.
(c) helps students in decision-making.
(d) helps students in collecting authentic information.

338. The teachers of "Philosophy of Life" affect the pupils because
(a) The teacher teaches them
(b) It affects the method of teaching
(c) The teachers model will be imitated
(d) It reflects the philosophy of the society

339. If your students remain unsatisfied even after your teaching a particular lesson or content, what would you like to do under these conditions?
(a) You will think that again and again repetition of the same content is mere a destroying the time.
(b) You will be doing your best efforts again and again till they will not understand the content.
(c) You will be keeping sympathetic behaviour with the students.
(d) You will leave aside all fruitful efforts of teaching in order to enhance their understanding.

340. 'Projection' is a defence mechanism in which the individual
(a) Finds justification of one's own action.
(b) Goes back to the previous stage of development.
(c) Channelises energy to the 'id' to acceptable channels.
(d) Attributes the reason for one's behaviour to some other source.

341. When your friend points out at your gross mistake which you have committed in the class during teaching, then your reaction will be
(a) discussing on the mistake, try to put your stand, if he does not agree then accepting your mistake.
(b) requesting him politely that he should not tell it to any other person.
(c) warning him that he should not behave in such a manner in future.
(d) resisting him and tell him confidently that it does not come under the purview of a mistake.

342. Which of the following teacher's quality is associated with his best teaching?
(a) The abilities of the teacher.
(b) The vocational commitment and love for the profession.
(c) Teacher's abstinence.
(d) The oral expression of the teacher.

343. The barriers in communication can be overcome if
(a) the listener is in a state of motivator
(b) the listener has some extra incentives
(c) the listener has all desirable competencies of best listening
(d) All of the above.

344. Which of the following will not hamper effective communication in the class?
(a) A lengthy statement.
(b) An ambiguous statement.
(c) A precise statement.
(d) A statement which allows the listener to draw his own conclusion.

345. The receiver should follow the inevitable condition in order to receive the message

(a) he has the ability to decoding the message.
(b) he has ability to transmit a message.
(c) he has the ability to interpret the message.
(d) he has all the above abilities.

346. Recitation is beneficial in which one of the following case?
(a) At the beginning of learning.
(b) As a preparation during the period of the test.
(c) All the time of the learning.
(d) At the end of learning.

347. Which of the following processes has been incorporated for the decoding of the message?
(a) The messages are changed into signs.
(b) The messages are changed through encoding.
(c) The interpretation of the secret messages has been carried out.
(d) The obstacles are created in messaging services.

348. "A lamp can never light another lamp unless it continues to burn its own flame." This statement implies that
(a) The teacher preparation programme should be continuously evaluated.
(b) The teacher should attend continuously education programmes.
(c) The teacher should go on learning continuously.
(d) The teacher should teach continuously.

349. The meaning of communis is
(a) Normal (b) Etiquettes
(c) Differences (d) Sensation

350. National Film Archive of India (NFAI) has regional centres at Bangalore, Kolkata and
(a) Mumbai
(b) Chennai
(c) Rajkot
(d) Thiruvananthapuram

351. The effective means in educational instrument is
(a) Visible means
(b) Audio means
(c) Audio-visible means
(d) Blackboard writing

352. Lubrizol India Limited a Public-Sector Undertaking, was incorporated in 1966 in collaboration with Lubrizol Corporation of
(a) U.K. (b) U.S.A.
(c) Sweden (d) Germany

353. The steam locomotives for railways is manufactured by
(a) Chittranjan Locomotives Works
(b) Tata
(c) Mahindra Ltd.
(d) Maruti Udyog

354. Which of the Ports handles the iron-ore export?
(a) Chennai (b) Mumbai
(c) Kandla (d) Mormugao

355. The National Highway No. 1 covers a total length of
(a) 456 km. (b) 126 km.
(c) 346 km. (d) 540 km.

356. Mike Moore the head of World Trade Organisation belongs to
(a) U.K. (b) U.S.A.
(c) New Zealand (d) Australia

357. Which one is a natural port?
(a) Cochin (b) Kandla
(c) Kolkata (d) Nhava Sheva

358. Which of the following Ports lies in the west coast?
(a) Paradip (b) Tuticorin
(c) Mangalore (d) Visakhapatnam

359. The first cinema advertisement appeared in
(a) *The Hindu*
(b) *The Hindustan Times*
(c) *The Times of India*
(d) *Amrit Bazar Patrika*

360. The diamond mining giant De Beers is a cartel belonging to which country?
(a) U.S.A. (b) South Africa
(c) Britain (d) Brazil

361. The term GOMBAS is applied to
(a) currency market players
(b) overpaid MBAs
(c) the stock market
(d) how paid unintelligent MBA's

362. Fox base is a software package for
(a) Data entry (b) Database
(c) Only (a) (d) None of these.

363. Which of the companies uses 'Challenge is the limit' in its advertising?
(a) Samsung (b) Aiwa
(c) LG (d) Sony

364. "Now make the ice, in half the time" is the punchline of the refrigerator
(a) Daewoo (b) Whirlpool
(c) Kelvinator (d) None of these.

365. A leading newspaper published from Cairo (Eqypt) is
(a) Nishat (b) Al-Sadiq
(c) Al-Ahram (d) Le Monde

366. Param Padama is the most powerful in India
(a) Super Computer
(b) First generation computer
(c) Second generation computer
(d) None of the above.

367. Who is referred to as the Pope of Modern Advertising?
(a) Rise and Trout
(b) David Oglivy
(c) Alber Saatchi
(d) None of the above.

368. Pressman Advertising and Marketing Ltd. has its headquarters in
(a) Chennai (b) Ahmedabad
(c) New Delhi (d) Kolkata

369. A new service in Hindi was launched by Press Trust of India under the credit line
(a) PTI Bhasha (b) Prasar Bharati
(c) Vividh Bharati (d) None of these.

370. In September 2000, The General Conference of Non-Aligned News Agencies pool was held in, hosted by Yogoslav News Agency Tanjug
(a) Tehran (b) Moscow
(c) Belgrade (d) Jakarta

371. Indian Herald the first nationalist paper in English was published by Pandit Ayodhyanath in
(a) Madhya Pradesh (b) Uttar Pradesh
(c) Maharashtra (d) Delhi

372. The national english daily which became the first newspaper in Asia to be awarded the ISO-9002 Certification is
(a) *The Times of India*
(b) *The Hindustan Times*
(c) *The Hindu*
(d) *The Indian Express*

373. *New Statesman* is a leading newspaper published from
(a) New York (b) Delhi
(c) Mumbai (d) None of these.

374. Which of the following newspapers is printed from USA?
(a) *Daily News*
(b) *The Daily Mirror*
(c) *The Times*
(d) *People's Daily*

375. *Merdeka* is a leading newspaper published from

(a) Indonesia (b) America
(c) Delhi (d) None of these.

376. Who began publishing the paper Indian Sociologist with the aim to secure "home to India"?
(a) V.P. Savarkar
(b) Lala Hardayal
(c) Madam Bhikaji Cama
(d) Shyamji Krishna Varma

377. *Bengal Gazette*, the first newspaper (weekly) is also known as
(a) *Hicky's Gazette* (b) *James Gazette*
(c) *Delhi Gazette* (d) *Bengali News*

378. Which of the following States does not share the line constructed by the Konkan Railway Corporation Limited?
(a) Maharashtra (b) Tamil Nadu
(c) Kerala (d) Karnataka

379. Broadcasting started in India in 1927 with two privately owned transmitters one is Mumbai and the other is in
(a) Chennai (b) Delhi
(c) Kolkata (d) Jaipur

380. The Indian Railways are the largest electrified system in the world _____
(a) first (b) second
(c) third (d) fourth

381. Commercial Broadcasting on AIR started in
(a) 1976 (b) 1970
(c) 1967 (d) 1980

382. The news service of PTI in Hindi is called
(a) Bhasha (b) Varta
(c) Khabar (d) PTI Varta

383. AIR has its broadcast in which language
(a) Chinese (b) Italian
(c) Mexican (d) Brazilian

384. The regular service by Doordarshan with a news bulletin was started in
(a) 1969 (b) 1975
(c) 1959 (d) 1965

385. The Bi-monthly published by transduction and programme exchange of AIR
(a) Awaz (b) Vinimaya
(c) Bharat (d) Voice

386. Which of the following is the longest rail route?
(a) Amritsar - Puri
(b) Delhi - Mumbai
(c) Delhi - Kolkata
(d) Guwahati - Thiruvananthapuram

387. The first television school of India was commissioned at
(a) Delhi (b) Mumbai
(c) Kolkata (d) Chennai

388. Lassa Kaul awards are given by
(a) Doordarshan (b) NSD
(c) PTI (d) AIR

389. Bhartendu Harishchandra is an award given for Creative writing in Hindi by
(a) AIR
(b) Doordarshan
(c) Publication division
(d) None of the above.

390. Gyandeep is the Doordarshan programme in which broadcasts
(a) Programmes of DU
(b) IGNOU programme
(c) ABVSP programme
(d) None of the above.

391. Which of the following was reconstituted in 1980 after amalgamation of the Indian Motion Picture Export Corporation and Film Finance Corporation?
(a) FITI (b) NFDC
(c) NSP (d) IFFI

392. The Song and Drama division of AIR started in

(a) 1964 (b) 1965
(c) 1970 (d) None of these.

393. Which of the following is not a publication of Publication Division of India?
(a) Swagat (b) Jagaran
(c) Yojana (d) Kurukshetra

394. The first child artist on Indian screen was
(a) Raja (b) Balachandra
(c) Manju (d) Ravi

395. MTNL started Internet Telephone to 1968 countries under the brand name
(a) Talky (b) Talk Time
(c) Bol Anmol (d) Batein Anmol

396. The Konkan Railway project covers a route length of
(a) 760 km. (b) 840 km.
(c) 1960 km. (d) 1000 km.

397. Iridium is a
(a) Satellite-based Mobile Service
(b) Mobile Company
(c) Telephone line
(d) None of the above.

398. The Konkan Railway project covers four states—Maharashtra, Kerala, Karnataka and
(a) Tamil Nadu
(b) Andhra Pradesh
(c) Goa
(d) Gujarat

399. The first Indian IT company to be listed on NASDAQ was
(a) Satyam Infoway (b) IBM
(c) HCL (d) Infosys

400. Visakhapatnam is the deepest landlocked port
(a) Visakhapatnam is not a port
(b) True
(c) False
(d) None of the above.

401. The four news agencies PTI, United News of India, Samachar Bharati and Hindustan Samachar were merged and operated from 1976 to 1978 as
(a) Varta (b) News of India
(c) Voice of India (d) Samachar

402. Airport is the first to be built by private sector at
(a) Nedumbassery
(b) Mumbai
(c) Thiruvananthapuram
(d) Chennai

403. Computers and Telephone lines are lined in
(a) E-mail (b) Telex
(c) Telegram (d) Pager

404. The first daily electronic news and information service in India is
(a) India World (b) Wek World
(c) Satyam (d) None of these.

405. Rajasansi Airport is in
(a) Amritsar (b) Goa
(c) Bangalore (d) Chennai

406. Among the Interpublic group of companies the one of the largest communication service conglomerate has its headquarters in
(a) New York (b) Paris
(c) Los Angeles (d) London

407. *Pravda* is a leading newspaper published from
(a) China (b) Indonesia
(c) France (d) Russia

408. *Dawn* is a newspaper of
(a) Pakistan (b) Britain
(c) China (d) USA

409. *Izvestia* is a leading newspaper published from
(a) Germany (b) India
(c) Netherlands (d) None of these.

410. Satellite communication works through
   (a) Transported (b) Tansmitter
   (c) Receptor (d) Radar

411. Antara is a
   (a) Newspaper (b) Television
   (c) News agency (d) None of these.

412. Mega terminals to be built at _____ in Delhi and at _____ in Kolkata.
   (a) Sangam Vihar, Silchan
   (b) Shahdara, Purulia
   (c) Anand Vihar, Chitpur
   (d) Tis-Hazari, Siligudi

413. Associated Press is a
   (a) TV Brand (b) News agency
   (c) Both (a) and (b) (d) None of these

414. In which of the following types of communication methods can 'Audio Conferencing' be classified?
   (a) One-sided verbal
   (b) Two-sided verbal
   (c) One-sided non-verbal
   (d) Two-sided non-verbal

415. Antara is a news agency of
   (a) Pakistan (b) Iran
   (c) Indonesia (d) Thailand

416. Which one of the following is less important in effective communication method?
   (a) Full control on language
   (b) Good vocabulary
   (c) Attractive personality of messenger
   (d) Full control over communicable subject material

417. Reuters is the news agency of
   (a) Australia (b) U.K.
   (c) U.S.A. (d) None of these.

418. The Indian Railways entered in the metro age with the opening of Metro rail in
   (a) Delhi (b) Kolkata
   (c) Madras (d) Mumbai

419. The Indian Railways started Metro service from
   (a) 1984-85 (b) 1994-95
   (c) 1996-97 (d) 1986-87

420. The press can be an important opinion builder if
   (a) it is owned by government.
   (b) subject to censorship regulations.
   (c) subject to control of political parties.
   (d) free from interference of government and big business houses.

421. A pilot project for demonstration of satellite-based developmental communication and training has been taken up in _____ in Madhya Pradesh
   (a) Jabalpur (b) Jabhua
   (c) Balaghat (d) Bastar

422. Jhelum Express runs between Jammu Tawi and
   (a) Pune (b) Lucknow
   (c) Hawrah (d) Amritsar

423. The airport situated at the highest attitude in India is in
   (a) Leh
   (b) Amausi
   (c) Indira Gandhi
   (d) Meenambakam

424. Distant vision orbital programme on Doordarshan is arranged by
   (a) I.I.M.C. (b) I.P.N.O.
   (c) C.I.C. (d) D.P.T.

425. Which is the correct ascending order of newspapers published in the year 2001?
   I. Delhi II. UP
   III. Maharashtra IV. MP

   Codes:
   (a) III, II, I, IV (b) IV, I, III, II
   (c) II, I, III, IV (d) I, II, III, IV

426. Match List I and List II finding the correct answers from the given codes:

List I

I. Satellite Money order
II. Co-operative money order Services
III. Speed Post Service
IV. Rural Postal Life Insurance

List II

A. May 1995
B. August 1986
C. December 1994
D. March 1995

Codes:	**I**	**II**	**III**	**IV**
(a)	C	D	B	A
(b)	C	A	B	D
(c)	A	B	C	D
(d)	C	D	A	C

ANSWERS

1. (d)	2. (b)	3. (b)	4. (d)	5. (c)	6. (b)
7. (c)	8. (d)	9. (a)	10. (c)	11. (d)	12. (d)
13. (a)	14. (a)	15. (b)	16. (d)	17. (c)	18. (d)
19. (a)	20. (a)	21. (a)	22. (c)	23. (c)	24. (a)
25. (c)	26. (b)	27. (d)	28. (c)	29. (b)	30. (d)
31. (d)	32. (a)	33. (c)	34. (a)	35. (a)	36. (a)
37. (a)	38. (c)	39. (c)	40. (a)	41. (b)	42. (a)
43. (d)	44. (a)	45. (d)	46. (d)	47. (a)	48. (a)
49. (c)	50. (a)	51. (a)	52. (d)	53. (b)	54. (b)
55. (b)	56. (c)	57. (d)	58. (c)	59. (d)	60. (c)
61. (b)	62. (a)	63. (a)	64. (b)	65. (a)	66. (a)
67. (d)	68. (a)	69. (c)	70. (b)	71. (d)	72. (a)
73. (d)	74. (b)	75. (d)	76. (a)	77. (b)	78. (c)
79. (d)	80. (b)	81. (a)	82. (c)	83. (a)	84. (a)
85. (b)	86. (b)	87. (a)	88. (a)	89. (a)	90. (d)
91. (d)	92. (a)	93. (c)	94. (a)	95. (a)	96. (c)
97. (b)	98. (d)	99. (d)	100. (c)	101. (a)	102. (d)
103. (a)	104. (d)	105. (c)	106. (c)	107. (b)	108. (a)
109. (b)	110. (c)	111. (b)	112. (a)	113. (c)	114. (a)
115. (a)	116. (a)	117. (d)	118. (d)	119. (a)	120. (c)
121. (a)	122. (b)	123. (a)	124. (b)	125. (b)	126. (d)
127. (d)	128. (d)	129. (c)	130. (a)	131. (a)	132. (a)
133. (c)	134. (d)	135. (a)	136. (b)	137. (d)	138. (d)
139. (c)	140. (d)	141. (a)	142. (b)	143. (d)	144. (d)
145. (c)	146. (d)	147. (d)	148. (d)	149. (b)	150. (d)

151. (c)	152. (b)	153. (b)	154. (c)	155. (c)	156. (b)
157. (b)	158. (b)	159. (a)	160. (a)	161. (a)	162. (c)
163. (c)	164. (c)	165. (c)	166. (d)	167. (b)	168. (a)
169. (a)	170. (b)	171. (b)	172. (c)	173. (b)	174. (b)
175. (d)	176. (a)	177. (b)	178. (b)	179. (d)	180. (a)
181. (d)	182. (d)	183. (b)	184. (b)	185. (a)	186. (c)
187. (c)	188. (b)	189. (c)	190. (d)	191. (a)	192. (d)
193. (a)	194. (c)	195. (a)	196. (d)	197. (d)	198. (b)
199. (c)	200. (d)	201. (c)	202. (b)	203. (c)	204. (a)
205. (d)	206. (d)	207. (b)	208. (d)	209. (d)	210. (c)
211. (a)	212. (a)	213. (b)	214. (b)	215. (b)	216. (b)
217. (a)	218. (d)	219. (c)	220. (d)	221. (d)	222. (b)
223. (a)	224. (b)	225. (b)	226. (d)	227. (c)	228. (d)
229. (a)	230. (b)	231. (c)	232. (a)	233. (c)	234. (b)
235. (c)	236. (d)	237. (d)	238. (d)	239. (a)	240. (c)
241. (b)	242. (d)	243. (c)	244. (d)	245. (d)	246. (d)
247. (c)	248. (c)	249. (b)	250. (c)	251. (b)	252. (b)
253. (d)	254. (a)	255. (d)	256. (b)	257. (a)	258. (d)
259. (b)	260. (a)	261. (d)	262. (d)	263. (a)	264. (b)
265. (b)	266. (b)	267. (a)	268. (c)	269. (b)	270. (c)
271. (a)	272. (b)	273. (b)	274. (a)	275. (c)	276. (d)
277. (a)	278. (d)	279. (d)	280. (c)	281. (c)	282. (a)
283. (c)	284. (d)	285. (b)	286. (c)	287. (b)	288. (d)
289. (d)	290. (b)	291. (d)	292. (d)	293. (a)	294. (a)
295. (c)	296. (d)	297. (c)	298. (a)	299. (b)	300. (c)
301. (d)	302. (d)	303. (b)	304. (d)	305. (a)	306. (a)
307. (b)	308. (b)	309. (c)	310. (c)	311. (c)	312. (d)
313. (b)	314. (a)	315. (b)	316. (d)	317. (d)	318. (a)
319. (b)	320. (b)	321. (b)	322. (a)	323. (d)	324. (b)
325. (a)	326. (a)	327. (c)	328. (d)	329. (b)	330. (c)
331. (a)	332. (a)	333. (d)	334. (d)	335. (d)	336. (d)
337. (b)	338. (d)	339. (b)	340. (c)	341. (a)	342. (b)
343. (d)	344. (d)	345. (d)	346. (a)	347. (c)	348. (c)
349. (a)	350. (d)	351. (c)	352. (b)	353. (a)	354. (d)

355. (a)	356. (c)	357. (a)	358. (c)	359. (c)	360. (b)
361. (b)	362. (b)	363. (a)	364. (c)	365. (c)	366. (a)
367. (b)	368. (d)	369. (a)	370. (c)	371. (b)	372. (d)
373. (d)	374. (a)	375. (d)	376. (d)	377. (a)	378. (b)
379. (c)	380. (d)	381. (c)	382. (a)	383. (a)	384. (d)
385. (b)	386. (d)	387. (a)	388. (d)	389. (c)	390. (d)
391. (d)	392. (d)	393. (a)	394. (b)	395. (c)	396. (b)
397. (a)	398. (d)	399. (d)	400. (a)	401. (d)	402. (a)
403. (a)	404. (a)	405. (a)	406. (a)	407. (d)	408. (a)
409. (d)	410. (b)	411. (c)	412. (c)	413. (b)	414. (c)
415. (c)	416. (c)	417. (d)	418. (b)	419. (a)	420. (d)
421. (b)	422. (a)	423. (a)	424. (b)	425. (c)	426. (b)

5

Mathematical Reasoning

1. The sum of a number and its reciprocal is $2\frac{1}{20}$. The number is
   (a) $\frac{5}{4}$ (b) $\frac{3}{4}$
   (c) $\frac{4}{3}$ (d) $\frac{1}{6}$
2. If all the prime numbers from 1 to 49 are removed, then how many numbers will remain?
   (a) 33 (b) 34
   (c) 32 (d) 36
3. Ravi has an annual income of ₹ 2500. He spends 10% on education. 20% of the remaining income is spent on housing. The remaining 15% is deposited in saving schemes and the rest income is spend on food and clothes. How much percentage of income does he spend on food and cloth?
   (a) 65% (b) 61.2%
   (c) 60% (d) 55%
4. A two digit number is such that the product of the digits is 8. When 18 is added to the number, the digits are reversed. The number is
   (a) 18 (b) 24
   (c) 81 (d) 42
5. If all the odd numbers from 3 to 36 are removed, then how many numbers will remain?
   (a) 16 (b) 20
   (c) 15 (d) 17
6. A car goes 35 km in 1 hour, next 270 km in 3 hrs. and next 80 km in 2½ hrs. Find the average speed of the car?
   (a) 59.23 km/h (b) 61.5 km/h
   (c) 80 km/h (d) None of these.
7. The perimeter of a rectangle is 82 m and its area is 400 m^2. The breadth of the rectangle is
   (a) 25 m (b) 16 m
   (c) 9 m (d) 20 m
8. If all the squared numbers, and those numbers, the sum of whose digits is 9 from 4 to 65 are removed, then how many numbers will remain?
   (a) 49 (b) 55
   (c) 51 (d) 45
9. Mohan is younger than his father by 20 years, 5 years ago his father was 3 times than him. Find the age of his father at present?
   (a) 30 yrs (b) 25 yrs
   (c) 35 yrs (d) None of these.
10. Out of a group of swans, $\left(\frac{7}{2}\right)$ times the square root of the number are swimming in water while two remaining are playing on the shore. The total number of swans is

(a) 4 (b) 8
(c) 12 (d) 16

11. If all the numbers from 7 to 59, which are divisible by 3 are arranged in descending order then which number will be at 10th place from the bottom?
(a) 35 (b) 39
(c) 30 (d) 27

12. If $\sqrt[3]{32} = 2^x$ then x is equal to
(a) 5 (b) 3
(c) 3.5 (d) 5/3

13. Among all the numbers from 3 to 87, which are divisible by 4 and also whose sum of digits is 9, which will have the least digit?
(a) 7 (b) 3
(c) 2 (d) 6

14. Toffees are distributed among A, B, C, D and E in such a way that A gets one less than B, C gets 5 more than D and E gets 3 more than B. If B and D's share are equal who got the maximum number of toffees?
(a) A (b) B
(c) D (d) C

15. If $3^{4x-2} = 729$, then the value of x is
(a) 1 (b) 1.5
(c) 2 (d) 2.5

16. If from 8 to 80 all the squared numbers and those numbers the sum of whose digits is 9 are arranged in descending order, then which number will be at 12th place?
(a) 36 (b) 49
(c) 45 (d) 30

17. If the number of two digits are reversed it becomes 18 greater than the number. Find the number if the sum of the digits is equal to 4?
(a) 31 (b) 13
(c) 22 (d) 40

18. If $\left(\frac{a}{b}\right)^{x-1} = \left(\frac{b}{a}\right)^{x-3}$, then x is equal to
(a) 1 (b) 1/2
(c) 7/2 (d) 2

19. From 6 to 39, how many numbers are such which are divisible by 3 or 5?
(a) 17 (b) 10
(c) 12 (d) 15

20. Raja said to Kabir, "If you give me ₹ 2.10 shall be double to you and you will become tripple to Aisha. How much money does Aisha have?
(a) ₹ 5 (b) ₹ 8
(c) ₹ 2 (d) ₹ 3

21. If $2^x - 2^{x-1} = 4$, then the value of x^x is
(a) 27 (b) 4
(c) 1 (d) 256

22. From 9 to 79, how many numbers are such which are divisible by 4 as well as by 6?
(a) 5 (b) 6
(c) 7 (d) 4

23. A number which when divided by 4, 8, 16 leaves a remainder 3. If that number is divisible by 7 find the number?
(a) 49 (b) 77
(c) 147 (d) 99

24. The value of x for which $2^{x+4} - 2^{x+2} = 3$, is
(a) 0 (b) −2
(c) 2 (d) −1

25. What will be the middle digit of that number which will be exactly in the middle when the following numbers are arranged in descending order?

465, 352, 698, 245, 875, 529, 812

(a) 4 (b) 7
(c) 5 (d) 2

26. Mohan purchased a bike for ₹ 800 including sales tax of 20%. Find the selling price of the bike

(a) ₹ 666.66 (b) ₹ 600
(c) ₹ 1000 (d) ₹ 900

27. If $x = y^a$, $y = z^b$ and $z = x^c$, then the value of abc is

(a) 4 (b) 3
(c) 2 (d) 1

28. If the following numbers are arranged in descending order, what will be the middle digit of the number which will be exactly in the middle?

729, 215, 575, 882, 661, 796, 631

(a) 6 (b) 2
(c) 1 (d) 8

29. My father distributed ₹ 280 in such a way that each girl received ₹ 20 and each boy ₹ 10. If the number of boys is less than that of girls by 2 find the number of boys?

(a) 8 (b) 15
(c) 10 (d) 7

30. If $2^X = 3^y = 6^{-z}$, then $\left(\frac{1}{x}+\frac{1}{y}+\frac{1}{z}\right)$ is equal to

(a) 0 (b) 1
(c) 3/2 (d) −1/2

31. If the digits of the following numbers are reversed and then the numbers are arranged in descending order, then what will be the middle digit of the middle term?

329, 215, 175, 295, 539, 486, 765

(a) 1 (b) 9
(c) 7 (d) 6

32. A student was asked to add 16 and subtract 10 from a number. He by mistake subtracted 16 and added 10 and found the answer 14. What is the right answer.

(a) 20 (b) 26
(c) 30 (d) 32

33. If $a^x = b$, $b^y = c$ and $c^z = a$, then the value of xyz is

(a) 0 (b) 1
(c) 1/3 (d) 1/2

34. If the following numbers are written in ascending order then what will be the middle digit of the middle term?

745, 657, 825, 475, 692, 612, 735

(a) 2 (b) 9
(c) 4 (d) 7

35. A student attempted 108 questions in an examination. In this examination every wrong answer was given 1/3 minus mark and right answer was given 1 mark. If the student scored zero marks how many wrong questions were done by him?

(a) 85 (b) 81
(c) 89 (d) None of these.

36. The denominator of a rational number is 3 more than its numerator. If the numerator is increased by 7 and the denominator is decreased by 2, we obtain 2. The rational number is

(a) 1/4 (b) 5/8
(c) 7/10 (d) 8/11

37. If the following numbers are written in ascending order then what will be the middle digit of the middle term?

815, 686, 795, 835, 765, 822, 719

(a) 8 (b) 1
(c) 3 (d) 9

38. If the area of a given square ABCD is 3. Find the total area of the entire figure?

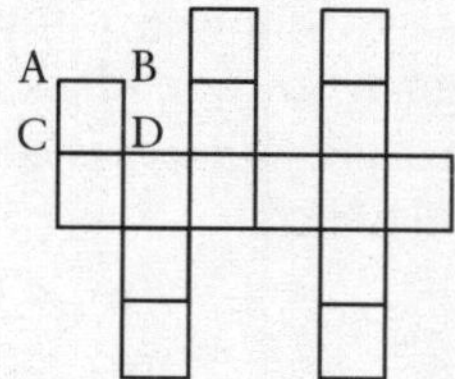

(a) 452 (b) 45
(c) 48 (d) 31

39. If 1 is added to the denominator of a fraction, it becomes (1/2) and if 1 is added to the numerator, the fraction becomes 1. The fraction is
(a) 4/7 (b) 5/9
(c) 2/3 (d) 10/11

40. If the digits of the following numbers are reversed and then the numbers are arranged in ascending order then what will be the middle digit of the middle term?
375, 682, 315, 792, 865, 129, 875
(a) 3 (b) 6
(c) 7 (d) 8

41. A spider climbs 10 metres of a pole in 20 minutes and slips down 2 metres at the very moment. If it takes 3 hrs to climb on its top find the length of the pole?
(a) 74 metres (b) 72 metres
(c) 80 metres (d) 90 metres

42. Four-fifth of a number is more than three-fourth of the number by 4. The number is
(a) 64 (b) 72
(c) 80 (d) 84

43. If the numbers from 1 to 24, which are divisible by 2 are arranged in descending order, then which number will be at 8th place from the bottom?
(a) 10 (b) 12
(c) 16 (d) 18

44. A class started at 1.00 p.m. and lasted till 3.52 p.m. In this duration 4 regular periods are held and 4 minutes were also given to go from one class to another to attend the class. What is the exact duration of each period?
(a) 41 min (b) 43 min
(c) 62 min (d) 40 min

45. On dividing 50 into two parts such that the sum of their reciprocals is 1/12, we get the parts as
(a) 20, 30 (b) 24, 26
(c) 28, 22 (d) 36, 14

46. If the numbers which are divisible by 3 from 1 to 61 are arranged in descending order, then which numbers will be at 5th place and at 15th place from above?
(a) 45, 18 (b) 48, 18
(c) 48, 21 (d) 45, 15

47. If 15 apples and 20 oranges cost as much as 20 apples and 15 oranges which of the following conclusions is correct?
(a) Orange and apple have identical prices
(b) Orange's price is double that of apple
(c) No conclusion can be drawn
(d) Apple is cheaper than orange

48. There are two numbers such that the sum of twice the first and thrice the second is 18, while the sum of thrice the first and twice the second is 17. The larger of the two is
(a) 4 (b) 6
(c) 8 (d) 12

49. How many numbers there from 6 to 90, which are divisible by 5 and either unit digit or tenth digit or both include 5?
(a) 7 (b) 8
(c) 10 (d) 9

50. Anil sold a commodity in ₹ 450 at the loss of 10%. At what price did he purchase it?
(a) ₹ 495 (b) ₹ 500
(c) ₹ 405 (d) None of these.

51. The sum of three numbers is 102. If the ratio between first and second be 2:3 and that between second and third be 5:3, then the second number is
(a) 30 (b) 45
(c) 27 (d) 48

52. There are 23 steps to reach a temple. On descending from the temple Ram takes two steps in the same time. Shyam ascends one step. If they start to work simultaneously, at which step will they meet each other?
(a) 8th (b) 9th
(c) 10th (d) 11th

53. A wagon has the capacity of 12 adults or 20 children. How many adults can be boarded with 15 children?
(a) 3 adults (b) 5 adults
(c) 6 adults (d) None of these

54. Of the three numbers, the first is twice the second and is half of the third. If the average of these numbers be 56, the numbers in order are
(a) 48, 96, 24 (b) 48, 24, 96
(c) 96, 24, 48 (d) 96, 48, 24

55. There are 35 steps to reach a temple. On descending from the temple Soni takes two steps in the same time Gunjan ascends four steps. If they start to work simultaneously, at which step will they meet each other?
(a) 18th (b) 10th
(c) 24th (d) 17th

56. If the following series of numbers is written in the reverse order which number will be the seventh to the right of the fourth number from the left.
1, 8, 3, 9, 7, 4, 10, 6, 2, 11, 13, 5, 14, 16
(a) 3 (b) 9
(c) 13 (d) 2

57. Three numbers are in the ratio 3:4:5. The sum of the largest and the smallest equals the sum of the third and 52. The smallest number is
(a) 20 (b) 27
(c) 39 (d) 52

58. How many numbers are there from 4 to 53 which are either divisible by 3 or of which any digit contains zero?
(a) 20 (b) 15
(c) 16 (d) 19

59. In a row of children Perveen is 7th from the left, Babloo is fourth from the right. When each of them exchanges their positions Perveen will be 15th from the left. Find the total number of children.
(a) 18 girls (b) 20 girls
(c) 21 girls (d) 19 girls

60. Of the three numbers, the sum of the first two is 45, the sum of the second and third is 55 and the sum of the third and thrice the first is 90. The third number is
(a) 20 (b) 25
(c) 30 (d) 35

61. Supply the missing figure in the matrix?

4	8	20
9	3	13
6	6	?

(a) 29 (b) 13
(c) 18 (d) 20

62. A boy was asked to multiply a certain number by 25. He multiplied it by 52 and got his answer more than the correct one by 324. The number to be multiplied was
(a) 12 (b) 15
(c) 25 (d) 52

63. Find the value of M in the following figure.

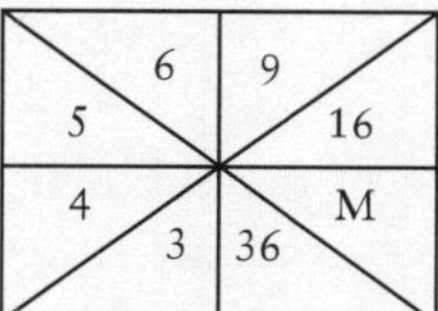

(a) 25 (b) 36
(c) 49 (d) 42

64. Three pieces of timber 42 m, 49 m and 63 m long have to be divided into planks of the same length. What is the greatest possible length of each plank?
(a) 7 m (b) 14 m
(c) 42 m (d) 63 m

Direction: Each of the questions (65 to 69) is based on the following diagram. In the diagram small triangle stands Traders, big triangle for post graduates, rectangle for ladies and circle for workers. Find out the correct answer for each question.

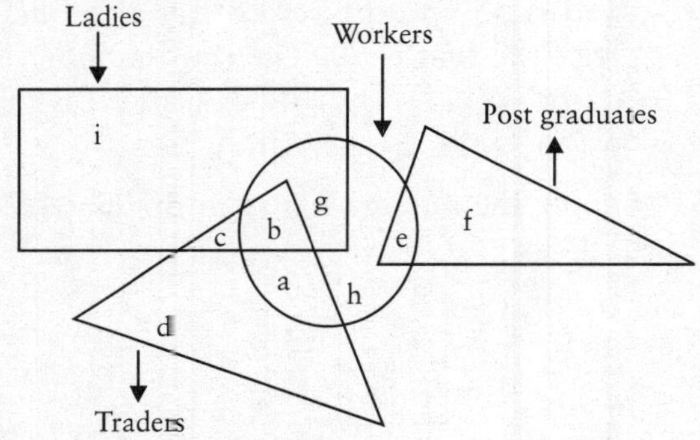

65. Which one of the following worker is not trader?
(a) e, g, h (b) a, g, h
(c) b, g, e (d) a, e, g, h

66. Which one of the following is worker or trader but not lady?
(a) a, b, d (b) a, e, h
(c) a, g, h (d) a, d, e, h

67 Which one of the following is lady, trader and worker?
(a) a, h (b) b, g
(c) b (d) b, h

68. Which one of the following is trader but neither post graduate nor worker?
(a) b, d, g (b) a, d, h
(c) c, d (d) b, e

69 Which one of the following is lady but neither trader nor worker?
(a) i, g (b) b, c, i, g
(c) b, i, e (d) i

70. A garden has as many flower bearing trees as fruit bearing trees. 3/4 trees are old and 1/2 are grafted. Which of the following interferences are definitely true?
(a) All flower bearing trees are grafted
(b) Only fruit bearing trees are grafted
(c) At least one half of the flower bearing trees are old
(d) All of the above.

71. L.C.M. of two numbers is 14 times of their H.C.F. The sum of L.C.M. and H.C.F. is 600. If one number is 280, then the other is
(a) 40 (b) 60
(c) 80 (d) 100

72. On a six point scale if a student get grade E in English, grade O in Maths, grade B in Science, grade C in Social Science and grade B in PT. Find out his over all grade.
(a) A (b) O
(c) C (d) B

Direction: In the figure given below (Qs. No. 73 and 74), triangle represents girls, square represents sports persons and circle represents coaches.

73. Which portion of the figure represents girls who are sportspersons but not coaches?

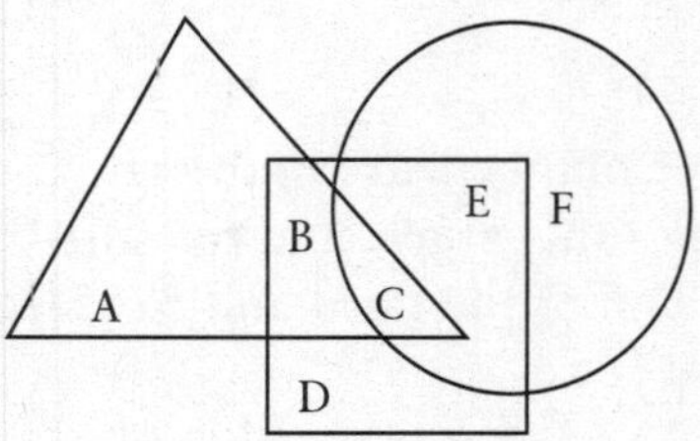

(a) A (b) B
(c) C (d) D

74. In the above figure which portion represents girls who are also sportsperson and coaches?
(a) D (b) C
(c) B (d) E

75. The least number which when divided by 5, 6, 7 and 8 leaves a remainder 3, but when divided by 9 leaves no remainder, is
(a) 1683 (b) 1677
(c) 2523 (d) 3363

76. In a group of students 600 of them passed in all five subjects. 200 failed in all the subjects, 100 in English only and 150 in Science only. Find the percentage of results of the school.
(a) 57.1% (b) 61%
(c) 80% (d) None of these

Direction: Each of the questions (77 to 81) is based on the following diagram. In the diagram square represents Physicists, rectangle represents Mathematicians, triangle represents Geography specialists while circle represents Historians.

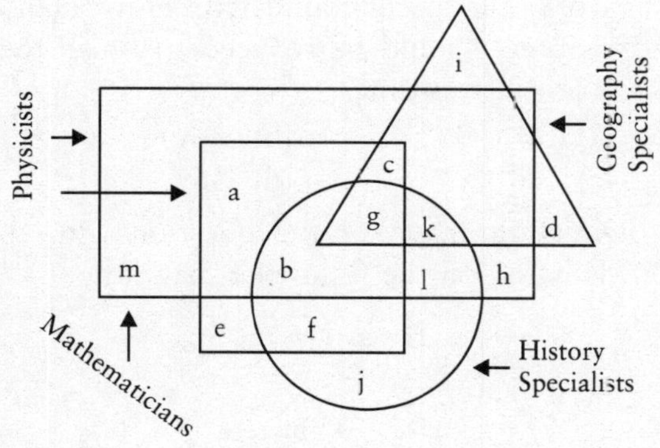

77. Which of the following Mathematicians are not History specialist?
(a) a, m, h (b) a, m, c, h
(c) l, k, h (d) a, i, d

78 Which of the following are Geography or History specialists but not physicists?
(a) c, g, k (b) k
(c) d, h (d) l, h, d

79. Which of the following are Mathematicians, Physicists as well as Geography specialists?
(a) c, g (b) b, k, c
(c) a, k, h (d) l, h

80. Which of the following are Geography specialists. History specialist and Mathematicians?
(a) c, i (b) g, c
(c) m, h (d) g, k

81. Which one of the following are Physicists but neither Mathematicians nor Geography specialists?
(a) j, k (b) e, f
(c) m, l (d) f, j

82. The greatest number of four digits which is divisible by each one of the numbers 12, 18, 21 and 28 is
(a) 9848 (b) 9864
(c) 9828 (d) 9636

83. In a class, Ravi's rank is 15th from the top and 21st from the bottom. How many students are there in the class?
(a) 31 (b) 36
(c) 35 (d) None of these

84. Which number indicates good speakers who are neither post graduates nor doctors?

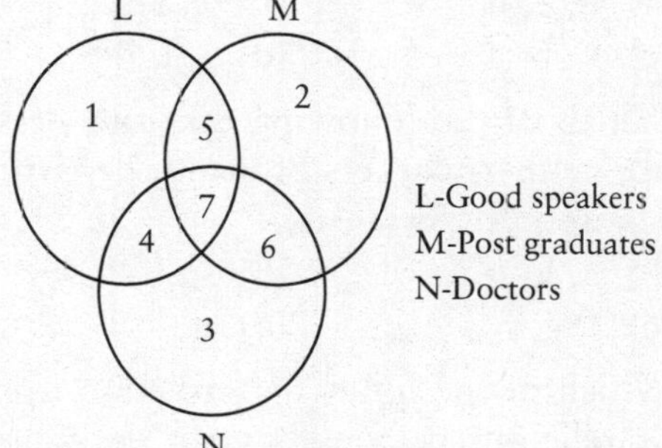

(a) 6 (b) 2
(c) 5 (d) 1

85. The least perfect square which is divisible by 3, 4, 5, 6, 8 is
(a) 900 (b) 1200
(c) 2500 (d) 3600

86. The ratio of boys and girls in a school is 4 : 3. If there are 480 boys in the school, find the number of girls?
(a) 360 (b) 320
(c) 315 (d) None of these

87. The product of two numbers is 1600 and their H.C.F. is 5. The L.C.M. of the numbers is
(a) 8000 (b) 1600
(c) 320 (d) 1605

Direction: Each of the questions (88 to 92) is based on the following diagram:

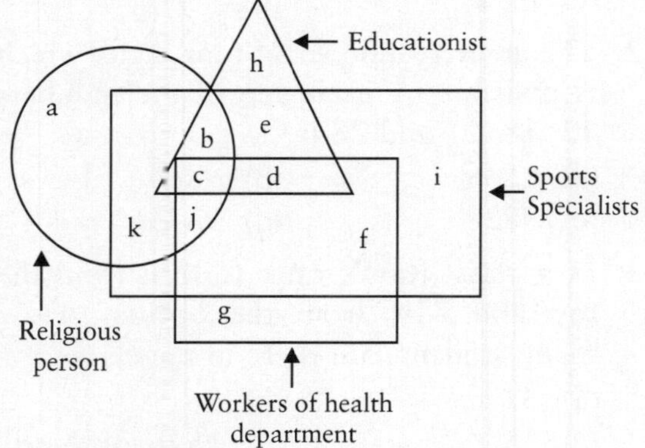

88. Which of the following educationists are not the workers of health department?
(a) b, e, h (b) e, i
(c) k, b, e (d) j, i, d

89. Which of the following religious persons are neither workers of health department nor sports specialists?
(a) a, k, g (b) a, b, j
(c) f, g, i (d) a

90. Which of the following are educationists or religious persons but not the workers of health department?
(a) h, e (b) a, k
(c) b (d) c, d, j

91. Which of the following are/is the workers of health department sportsman specialists and religious persons?
(a) a, h, c (b) c
(c) b, c, d (d) f, i, j, e

92. Which one of the following is/are sportsman specialists but neither educationists nor religious persons?
(a) f (b) f, g
(c) d, f, j (d) b, e, i

93. A car needs 12 litre of petrol to cover a distance of 153 kms. How much petrol is needed to cover a distance of 204 kms?
(a) 15.3 litre (b) 16 litre
(c) 18 litre (d) 11 litre

94. The product of two two-digit numbers is 2160 and their G.C.M. is 12. The numbers are
(a) 72, 30 (b) 36, 60
(c) 96, 25 (d) 34, 58

95. A contractor undertook to finish a work in 62. He employed 60 men for this. After 32 days he found that 2/3 of the work has been completed. How many workers should be reduced to finish the work just in time?
(a) 30 (b) 20
(c) 28 (d) 36

Direction: Each of the questions (96 to 100) is based on the following diagram:

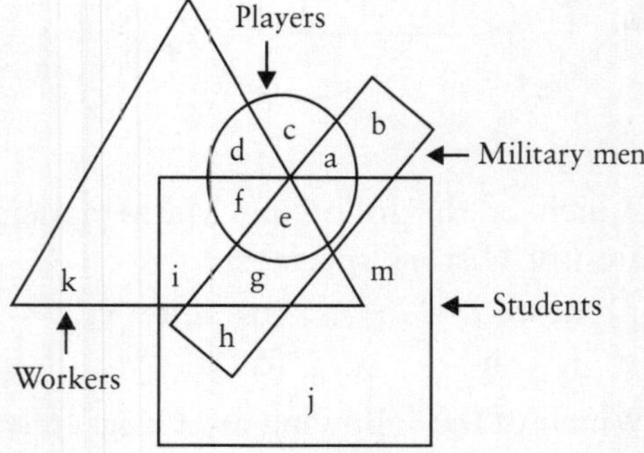

96. Which one of the following are students but not workers?
(a) g, j, m (b) h, l, f
(c) h, j (d) h, b

97. Which of the following are military men but neither players nor workers?
(a) a, b, m (b) e, g
(c) c, a, e (d) b, h

98. Which of the following are students, players and workers?
(a) e, f (b) e, d, g
(c) a, c, e (d) g, h

99. Which of the following is/are players, or students but not military men?
(a) a, f (b) a, c, d
(c) d, e, f (d) f

100. Which one of the following is/are students but neither military men nor workers?
(a) b, h (b) j
(c) d, e (d) j, l, m

101. What percentage of 180.50 is 36.1?
(a) 20% (b) 25%
(c) 22-50% (d) None of these

102. 21 mango trees, 42 apple trees and 56 orange trees have to be planted in rows such that each row contains the same number of trees of one variety only. Minimum number of rows in which the above trees may be planted is
(a) 3 (b) 15
(c) 17 (d) 20

103. A number is as much greater than 17 as it is less than 57. Find the number.
(a) 36 (b) 37
(c) 40 (d) 44

104. The value of $\left[\dfrac{(2.3)^3 - .027}{(2.3)^2 + .69 + .027}\right]$ is
(a) 2.6 (b) 2
(c) 2.33 (d) 2.27

105. A dealer sold a mixer for ₹ 540 lossing 10%. At what price should he have sold to earn a 10% profit?
(a) ₹ 660 (b) ₹ 650
(c) ₹ 600 (d) None of these.

Direction: In each of the questions (106 to 120) the numbers are arranged in a certain order. In one place a question mark is given. Find out which one of the answers will replace the question mark?

106.

10	12	14	16
12	14	16	18
8	10	12	14
14	?	18	20
6	8	10	12

(a) 10 (b) 16
(c) 12 (d) 18

107.

6	7	4	15
7	15	25	28
8	13	?	20
3	5	7	9

(a) 14 (b) 22
(c) 18 (d) 20

108.

5	7	6	10
8	11	13	18
14	19	27	?
26	35	55	66

(a) 34 (b) 36
(c) 30 (d) 38

109.

1	7	6
3	3	?
5	4	8
35	74	104

(a) 1 (b) 2
(c) 3 (d) 4

110.

7	11	14
8	?	10
9	10	16
6	10	8

(a) 8 (b) 10
(c) 9 (d) 11

111.

2	5	15
6	7	27
5	7	?
2	5	17

(a) 12 (b) 32
(c) 54 (d) 25

112.

6	8	6	9
5	3	9	6
3	4	7	?
33	44	105	60

(a) 4 (b) 3
(c) 2 (d) 5

113.

6	9	11	27
2	4	5	12
13	7	4	25
20	25	7	?

(a) 42 (b) 52
(c) 53 (d) 64

114.

2	7	10	26
4	8	15	7
5	6	12	?
12	22	38	34

(a) 1 (b) 0
(c) 6 (d) 5

115.

2	1	6
3	7	?
4	8	2
24	56	48

(a) 4 (b) 3
(c) 2 (d) 5

116. 4 7 / 53   6 9 / 87   1 7 / ?

(a) 49 (b) 50
(c) 48 (d) 55

117.

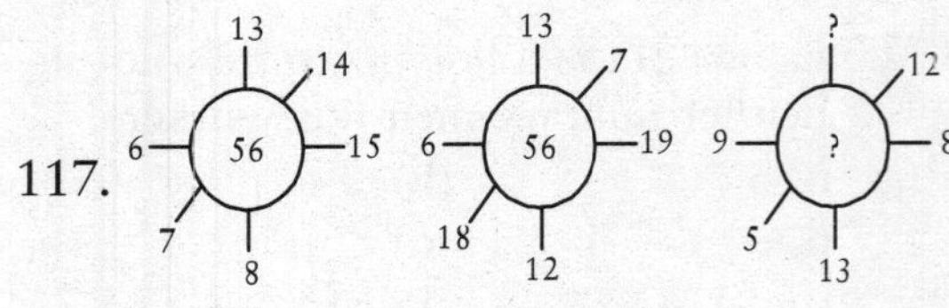

(a) 5 (b) 7
(c) 4 (d) 6

118.

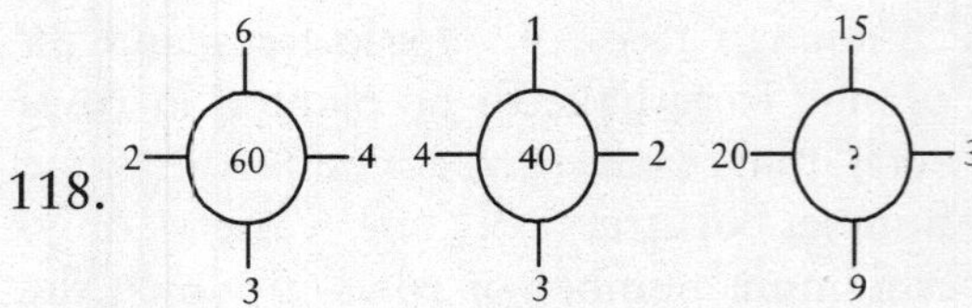

(a) 235 (b) 141
(c) 144 (d) 188

119.

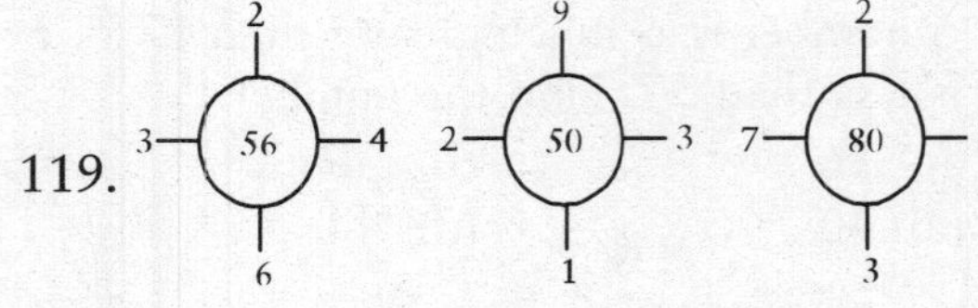

(a) 9 (b) 11
(c) 10 (d) 12

120. 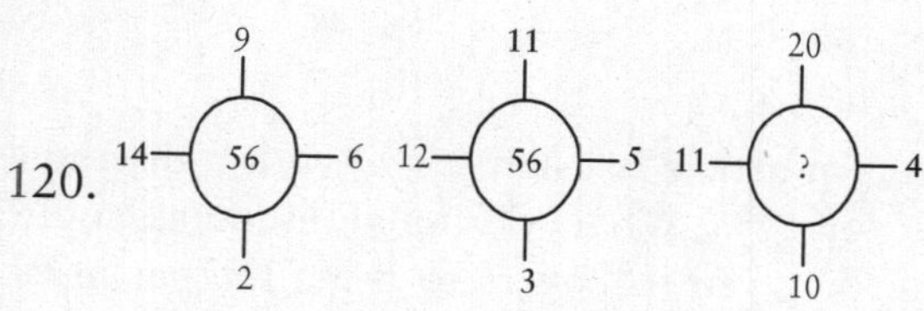

(a) 210 (b) 450
(c) 70 (d) 150

121. Mohan's salary is 25% above Raja. Then how much percentage Raja's salary is less than Mohan.
(a) 20% (b) 25
(c) 24 (1/6%) (d) None of these.

122. The H.C.F. of 0.54, 1.8 and 7.2 is
(a) 1.8 (b) .18
(c) .018 (d) 18

123. A reduction of 20% in the price of apples enables a buyer to get one dozen more for ₹ 50. Find the reduced price per dozen of apples?
(a) ₹ 8 (b) ₹ 12
(c) ₹ 10 (d) None of these.

124. The G.C.D. of 1.08, .36 and .9 is
(a) .03 (b) .9
(c) .18 (d) .108

125. A cube of side 3 cm is coloured pinkish on all sides. It is then cut into smaller cubes of 1 cm side. How many cubes will have two faced coloured?
(a) 9 (b) 8
(c) 16 (d) 12

126. The value of $.53\overline{6}$ is
(a) $\frac{536}{1000}$ (b) $\frac{536}{999}$
(c) $\frac{536}{990}$ (d) $\frac{161}{300}$

127. A cube is painted blue on all sides. It is then cut into 125 smaller equal cubes. How many cubes will be there whose no face is coloured?
(a) 27 (b) 8
(c) 16 (d) 24

128. The difference in selling price of a radio at gains of 10% and 15% is ₹ 30. Find the price of the radio?
(a) 660 (b) 670
(c) 680 (d) 600

129. The value of $0.\overline{63}+0.\overline{37}$ is
(a) 1 (b) $\frac{100}{99}$
(c) $\frac{100}{90}$ (d) $\frac{100}{98}$

130. Twenty-seven cubes are arranged in a block as shown below. How many cubes will be surrounded by other cubes on all sides?

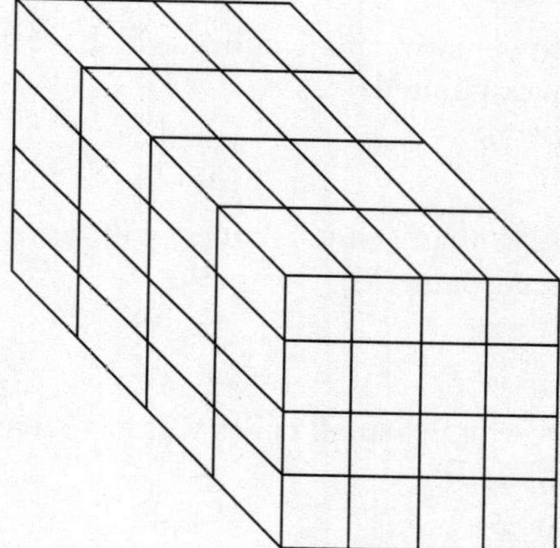

(a) 9 (b) 1
(c) 1 (d) 6

131. A sum of money becomes 7/5 of itself in 8 years at certain rate of interest. Find the rate.
(a) 5% (b) 6%
(c) 8% (d) 12%

132. Which part contains the fractions in ascending order?

(a) $\frac{11}{14}, \frac{16}{19}, \frac{16}{21}$ (b) $\frac{16}{19}, \frac{11}{14}, \frac{16}{21}$

(c) $\frac{16}{21}, \frac{11}{14}, \frac{16}{19}$ (d) $\frac{16}{19}, \frac{16}{21}, \frac{14}{14}$

Direction: Answer the following questions (133 to 137) based on the given statement.

A cube of size 4 cm is coloured black on all sides. It is then cut into smaller cubes of size 1 cm.

133. How many small cubes will have no coloured faces?
(a) 5 (b) 8
(c) 10 (d) 20

134. How many small cubes will have four faces black?
(a) 10 (b) 8
(c) 12 (d) None of these

135. How many small cubes will have three faces painted?
(a) 16 (b) 12
(c) 8 (d) 24

136. How many small cubes will have two faced painted?
(a) 36 (b) 48
(c) 12 (d) 24

137. How many small cubes will have one face painted?
(a) 24 (b) 48
(c) 12 (d) 96

138. The difference between simple and compound rate of interest on a certain sum of money for 2 years at 5% rate of interest is ₹ 25. Find the sum.
(a) ₹ 15000 (b) ₹ 12000
(c) ₹ 10000 (d) ₹ 1500

139. If $\sqrt{1+\frac{27}{169}} = \left(1+\frac{x}{13}\right)$, then the value of x is
(a) 1 (b) 3
(c) 5 (d) 7

140. An article is listed ₹ 150 with a discount of 20%. What additional discount should be given to buyers to bring the net price to ₹ 108.
(a) 10% (b) 12%
(c) 9% (d) None of these.

141. The smallest perfect square number which is divisible by 15, 18 and 25 is
(a) 625 (b) 900
(c) 450 (d) 225

Direction: Answer the following questions (142 to 147) based on the given statement.

A cube is coloured red on one face, green on the opposite face, yellow on another face and blue on a face adjacent to the yellow face. The other two faces are left uncoloured. It is then cut into 125 smaller cubes of equal size.

142. How many cubes are uncoloured on all faces?
(a) 27 (b) 36
(c) 48 (d) 64

143. How many cubes are coloured blue on one face, red or green on another face and have four uncoloured faces?
(a) 8 (b) 12
(c) 16 (d) 23

144. How many cubes are coloured red on one face and have the remaining faces uncoloured?
(a) 8 (b) 10
(c) 12 (d) 16

145. How many cubes have at least one green face?
(a) 4 (b) 5
(c) 16 (d) 25

146. How many cubes have at least two coloured faces?

(a) 23 (b) 21
(c) 20 (d) 19

147. A solid cube of size 6 cm, whose opposite faces are painted red, green and pinkish respectively, is cut into smaller cubes of size 1 cm each, then how many small cubes will be there with no face painted?
(a) 9 (b) 8
(c) 32 (d) 24

148. What will be the speed of the water if a boat going at 9 km/hr in still water and 12 km/hr in downstream and comes back in total three hours?
(a) 4 km/h (b) 5 km/h
(c) 4.5 km/h (d) 3 km/h

149. A gardener plants 17956 trees in such a way that there are as many rows as there are trees in a row. The number of trees in a row are
(a) 136 (b) 134
(c) 144 (d) 154

150. A man saves 25% of his salary. If due to price rise he increase his monthly expenses by 25% and he is able to save only ₹ 25 per month. Find his monthly salary.
(a) ₹ 400 (b) ₹ 500
(c) ₹ 600 (d) ₹ 650

151. A group of students decided to collect as many rupees from each member of the group as is the number of members. If the total collection amounts to ₹ 2209, the number of members in the group is
(a) 37 (b) 47
(c) 43 (d) 107

152. The volume of a wall is 16128 cubic metre. Its height is 6 times to its breadth and length is 7 times to its height. Find the breadth.
(a) 4.0 m (b) 4.5 m
(c) 3.5 m (d) None of these.

153. In a class of 100 students, the mean marks obtained in a subject is 30 and in another class of 50 students the mean marks obtained in the same subject is 60. The mean marks obtained by the students of two classes taken together is
(a) 40 (b) 45
(c) 48 (d) 50

154. A vessel contains 100 litres of milk 50% of it is taken out every day and equal amount of water is added to. How much quantity of milk will remain after 3 days?
(a) 12 litre (b) 15 litre
(c) 12¼ litre (d) 12½ litre

155. Average monthly income of a family of four earning members was ₹ 2940. One of the earning members died and therefore the average income came down to ₹ 2600. The income of the deceased was
(a) ₹ 3280 (b) ₹ 3960
(c) ₹ 2770 (d) ₹ 5540

156. One fifth of a number exceeds its one seventh by 154. Find the number.
(a) 2695 (b) 2606
(c) 2700 (d) 350

157. The average age of a committee of 8 members is 40 years. A member aged 55 years retired and his place was taken by another member aged 39 years. The average age of the present committee is
(a) 35 years (b) 36 years
(c) 38 years (d) 39 years

158. If 20/X = X/45 then X = ?
(a) 25 (b) 27
(c) 45 (d) 30

159. 5 years ago, the average age of A, B, C and D was 45. With E joining them now, the average age of all the five is 49 years. How old is E?
(a) 25 years (b) 40 years
(c) 45 years (d) 64 years

160. A man sold 10 eggs for one rupee and thus gained 20% profit. How many eggs did he buys for ₹ 1?
(a) 12 (b) 14
(c) 10 (d) 15

161. The average age of a husband and wife was 23 years when they were married 5 years ago. The average age of the husband, the wife and a child who was born during the interval, is 20 years now. How old is the child now?
(a) 9 months (b) 1 year
(c) 3 yerars (d) 4 years

162. A and B invested ₹ 3000 and ₹ 2000 respectively in a partnership business in which A was sleeping partner. At the end of one month both received ₹ 150 each as profit. Find B's remuneration for his work?
(a) ₹ 50 (b) ₹ 30
(c) ₹ 60 (d) None of these.

163. The average age of a family of 6 members is 22 years. If the age of the youngest member be 7 years, the average age of the family at the birth of the youngest member, was
(a) 15 years (b) 17 years
(c) 17.5 years (d) 18 years

164. In an examination 40% students fail in Maths, 30% in English and 15% in both. Find the pass percentage?
(a) 50% (b) 65%
(c) 30% (d) 45%

165. The mean temperature of Monday to Wednesday was 37°C and that of Tuesday to Thursday was 34°C. If the temperature on Thursday was 4/5th that of Monday. What was the temperature on Thursday?
(a) 34°C (b) 35.5°C
(c) 36°C (d) 36.5°C

166. Out of three given numbers, the first one is twice the second and three times the third. If the average of these numbers is 88, then the difference between first and third is
(a) 48 (b) 72
(c) 96 (d) 32

Direction: Answer the following questions (167 to 171) based on the given statement.

A cube is coloured red on two opposite faces, blue on two adjacent and yellow on the two remaining faces. It is then cut into two halves parallel to the red faces. One piece is then cut into four equal cubes and the other one into 32 equal cubes.

167. How many cubes do not have any coloured face?
(a) 0 (b) 2
(c) 4 (d) 8

168. How many cubes do not have any red face?
(a) 8 (b) 16
(c) 20 (d) 24

169. How many cubes have atleast two coloured faced?
(a) 20 (b) 24
(c) 28 (d) 32

170. How many cubes have each a yellow face with other faces blank?
(a) 4 (b) 14
(c) 16 (d) 17

171. How many cubes have atleast one blue face?
(a) 4 (b) 14
(c) 16 (d) 17

172. The average of marks obtained by 120 candidates was 35. If the average of passed candidates was 39 and that of failed candidates was 15, the number of candidates who passed the examination, is

(a) 100 (b) 110
(c) 120 (d) 150

173. The sum of age of a man and his son is 100 years. 30 years ago the man was three times as old as his son. Find the age of his son at present.
(a) 35 (b) 40
(c) 50 (d) None of these.

174. What least number must be subtracted from each of the numbers 14, 17, 34, 42 so that the remainders may be proportional?
(a) 0 (b) 1
(c) 2 (d) 7

175. If 3 apples and 4 oranges cost 40 paisa and 4 apples and 3 oranges cost 37 paisa. Find the cost of an orange?
(a) 3.5 paisa (b) 3 paisa
(c) 6 paisa (d) 7 paisa

176. ₹ 4850 have been divided among A, B, C such that if their shares be diminished by ₹ 15, ₹ 10 and ₹ 25 respectively, the remainders are in the ratio 3:4:5. Then, B's share is
(a) ₹ 1595 (b) ₹ 1610
(c) ₹ 1626.66 (d) ₹ 1600

177. Average age of 24 students is 15. If teacher's age is included the average age increases by 1. Find the age of the teacher?
(a) 40 yrs (b) 45 yrs
(c) 24 yrs (d) 18 yrs

178. A bag contains ₹ 600 in the form of one-rupee, 50 paise and 25 paise coins in the ratio 3:4:12. The number of 25 paise coins is
(a) 600 (b) 900
(c) 1200 (d) 1376

179. 20 litres of a mixture contains milk and water in the ratio 5:3. If 4 litres of this mixture are replaced by 4 litres of milk, the ratio of milk to water in the new mixture will become
(a) 2:1 (b) 1:2
(c) 7:3 (d) 8:3

180. A and B entered into partnership investing ₹ 12000 and ₹ 16000 respectively. After 3 months, B withdrew ₹ 5000 while A invested ₹ 5000 more. Out of a total annual profit of ₹ 16000, the share of A exceeds that of B by
(a) ₹ 1000 (b) ₹ 1500
(c) ₹ 2000 (d) ₹ 2500

181. ₹ 5625 are divided among A, B, C so that A may receive one-half as much as B and C together receive and B receives one-fourth of what A and C together receive. The share of A is more than that of B by
(a) ₹ 750 (b) ₹ 775
(c) ₹ 1500 (d) ₹ 1600

182. Arun, Maya and Satya started a shop by investing ₹ 27000, ₹ 81000 and ₹ 72000 respectively. At the end of the year the profit was distributed in the ratio of their investments. If Maya's share of profit be ₹ 36000, the total profit was
(a) ₹ 63000 (b) ₹ 80000
(c) ₹ 108000 (d) ₹ 116000

183. The prices of a scooter and a moped are in the ratio 9:5. If a scooter costs ₹ 6800 more than a moped, the price of a scooter is
(a) ₹ 17000 (b) ₹ 13600
(c) ₹ 15300 (d) ₹ 16200

184. A and B invest in a business in the ratio 3:2. If 5% of the total profit goes to charity and A's share is ₹ 85500, the total profit (in rupees) is
(a) 142500 (b) 150000
(c) 153750 (d) 157600

185. The cost of making an article is divided between materials, labour and overheads

in the ratio of 5:3:1. If the materials cost ₹ 6.90, the cost of the article is

(a) ₹ 13.80 (b) ₹ 12.42
(c) ₹ 11.56 (d) ₹ 9.83

186. In a mixture of 60 litres, the ratio of milk and water is 2:1. If the ratio of milk and water is to be 1:2, then the amount of water (in litres) to be further added is

(a) 20 (b) 30
(c) 40 (d) 60

187. A, B, C subscribe ₹ 47000 for a business. If A subscribes ₹ 7000 more than B and B ₹ 5000 more than C, then out of a total profit of ₹ 9400, B receives

(a) ₹ 1737.90 (b) ₹ 2000
(c) ₹ 3000 (d) ₹ 4400

188. An agent buys a TV set listed at ₹ 10000 and gets 10% and 20% successive discounts. He spends 10% of his C.P. on transport. At what price (in rupees) should he sell the TV set to earn a profit of 10%?

(a) 8692 (b) 8702
(c) 8712 (d) 8722

189. A, B, C enter into partnership. A invests some money at the beginning. B invests double the amount after 6 months and C invests thrice the amount after 8 months. If the annual profit be ₹ 9000, then C's share is

(a) ₹ 3000 (b) ₹ 2875
(c) ₹ 3600 (d) ₹ 3750

190. Tarun bought a TV with 20% discount on the labelled price. Had he bought it with 25% discount, he would have saved ₹ 500. At what price did he buy the TV?

(a) ₹ 5000 (b) ₹ 10000
(c) ₹ 12000 (d) None of these.

191. The manufacturer of a certain item can sell all he can produce at the selling price of ₹ 60 each. It costs him ₹ 40 in materials and labour to produce each item and he has overhead expenses of ₹ 3000 per week in order to operate the plant. The number of units he should produce and sell in order to make a profit of at least ₹ 1000 per week, is

(a) 400 (b) 300
(c) 250 (d) 200

192. A dishonest dealer sells his goods at the cost price and still earns a profit of 25% by underweighing. What weight does he use for a kg?

(a) 750 gm (b) 800 gm
(c) 825 gm (d) 850 gm

193. If 4 examiners can examine a certain number of answer books in 8 days by working 5 hours a day, for how many hours a day would 2 examiners have to work in order to examine twice the number of answer books in 20 days?

(a) 6 hours (b) 7½ hours
(c) 8 hours (d) 9 hours

194. A retailer buys a sewing machine at a discount of 15% and sells it for ₹ 1955. Thus, he makes a profit of 15%. The discount is

(a) ₹ 270 (b) ₹ 290
(c) ₹ 300 (d) ₹ 280

195. A, B and C together can finish a piece of work in 4 days; A alone can do it in 12 days and B alone in 18 days. How many days will be taken by C to do it alone?

(a) 21 (b) 16
(c) 14 (d) 9

196. If a commission of 10% is given on the marked price of a book, the publisher gains 20%. If the commission is increased to 15%, the gain is

(a) $16\frac{2}{3}\%$ (b) $13\frac{1}{3}\%$
(c) $15\frac{1}{6}\%$ (d) 15%

197. While selling a watch, a shopkeeper gives a discount of 5%. If he gives a discount of 7%, he earns ₹ 15 less as profit. The marked price of the watch is

(a) ₹ 697.50 (b) ₹ 712.50
(c) ₹ 787.50 (d) ₹ 750

198. If 20 men working 7 hours a day can do a piece of work in 10 days, in how many days will 15 men working for 8 hours a day to the same piece of work?

(a) $15\frac{5}{21}$ days (b) $11\frac{2}{3}$ days
(c) $6\frac{9}{16}$ days (d) $4\frac{1}{5}$ days

199. If 5 engines consume 6 metric tonnes of coal when each is running 9 hours a day. How much coal (in metric tonnes) will be needed for 8 engines, each running 10 hours a day, it being given that 3 engines of the former type consume as much as 4 engines of latter type?

(a) 8 (b) $3\frac{1}{8}$
(c) 6.48 (d) $8\frac{5}{9}$

200. A and B can do a given piece of work in 8 days; B and C can do the same work in 12 days and A, B, C complete it in 6 days. In how many days can A and C finish it?

(a) 8 (b) 12
(c) 16 (d) 24

201. A is thrice as good a workman as B and takes 10 days less to do a piece of work than B takes. The number of days taken by B to finish the work is

(a) 12 (b) 15
(c) 20 (d) 30

202. A can do a piece of work in 24 days while B alone can do it in 16 days. With the help of C, they finish the work in 8 days. In how many days can C alone do the work?

(a) 32 (b) 36
(c) 40 (d) 48

203. A can finish a work in 12 days and B can do it in 15 days. After A had worked for 3 days, B also joined A to finish the remaining work. In how many days, the remaining work will be finished?

(a) $5\frac{1}{2}$ (b) $4\frac{1}{2}$
(c) 5 (d) 6

204. 4 men and 6 women finish a job in 8 days, while 3 men and 7 women finish it in 10 days. In how many days will 10 women finish it?

(a) 24 (b) 32
(c) 36 (d) 40

205. A can do a piece of work in 14 days which B can do in 21 days. They begin together but 3 days before the completion of the work, A leaves off. The total number of days to complete the work is

(a) $6\frac{3}{5}$ (b) $8\frac{1}{2}$
(c) $10\frac{1}{5}$ (d) $13\frac{1}{2}$

206. The ratio of Laxmi's age to the age of her mother is 3:11. The difference of their ages is 24 years. The ratio of their ages after 3 years will be

(a) 1:3 (b) 2:3
(c) 3:5 (d) 2:5

207. If 9 men working 7½ hours a day can finish a work in 20 days, then how many days will be taken by 12 men working 6 hours a day to finish the work, it being given that 3 men of latter type work as much as 2 men of the former type in the same time?

(a) $12\frac{1}{2}$ (b) 13

(c) $9\frac{1}{2}$ (d) 11

208. A and B can complete a task in 30 days when working together. After A and B have been working together for 11 days, B is called away and A, all by himself completes the task in the next 28 days. Had A been working alone, the number of days taken by him to complete the task would have been

(a) $42\frac{1}{9}$ (b) $44\frac{4}{9}$

(c) $47\frac{3}{11}$ (d) None of these

209. If 3 men or 5 women or 8 boys can finish a work in 38 days, then the number of days taken by 6 men, 10 women and 6 boys to finish the work is

(a) 4 (b) 6

(c) 8 (d) 10

210. 8 children and 12 men complete a certain piece of work in 9 days. Each child takes twice the time taken by a man to finish the work. In how many days will 12 men finish the same work?

(a) 8 (b) 9

(c) 12 (d) 15

211. A tank can be filled by one tap in 20 min. and by another in 25 min. Both the taps are kept open for 5 min. and then the second is turned off. In how many minutes more is the tank completely filled?

(a) 6 (b) 11

(c) 12 (d) $17\frac{1}{2}$

212. The age of a man is 4 times that of his son. Five years ago, the man was nine times as old as his son was at that time. The presentage of the man is

(a) 28 years (b) 32 years

(c) 40 years (d) 44 years

213. 10 years ago, Mona's mother was 4 times older than her daughter. After 10 years, the mother will be twice older than the daughter. Mona's present age is

(a) 5 years (b) 10 years

(c) 20 years (d) 30 years

214. The ratio of Meena's age and Kamla's age is 3:5 and the sum of their ages is 80 years. The ratio of their ages after 10 years will be

(a) 2:3 (b) 1:2

(c) 3:2 (d) 3:5

215. A person takes a loan of ₹ 200 at 5% simple interest. He returns ₹ 100 at the end of 1 year. In order to clear his dues at the end of 2 years, he would pay

(a) ₹ 100 (b) ₹ 105

(c) ₹ 110 (d) ₹ 115.50

216. The age of a father 10 years ago was thrice the age of his son. Ten years hence, the father's age will be twice that of his son. The ratio of their present ages is

(a) 5:2 (b) 9:2

(c) 7:3 (d) 13:4

217. The simple interest on a sum of money will be ₹ 600 after 10 years. If the principal is trebled after 5 years, what will be the total interest at the end of the tenth year?

(a) ₹ 600 (b) ₹ 900

(c) ₹ 1200 (d) Data inadequate

218. The sum of the ages of a son and his father is 56 years. After 4 years, the age of the father will be three times that of his son. Their ages respectively are

(a) 12 years, 44 years

(b) 16 years, 42 years

(c) 16 years, 48 years
(d) 18 years, 36 years

219. The simple interest on a sum of money is $\frac{1}{9}$ of the principal and the number of years is equal to the rate percent per annum. The rate percent per annum is

(a) 3 (b) $\frac{1}{3}$
(c) $3\frac{1}{3}$ (d) $\frac{3}{10}$

220. A man lends ₹ 10000 in four parts. If he gets 8% on ₹ 2000; $7\frac{1}{2}\%$ on ₹ 4000 and $8\frac{1}{2}\%$ on ₹ 1400, what percent must he for the remainder part, if the average interest is 8.13%?

(a) 7% (b) 9%
(c) $9\frac{1}{4}\%$ (d) $10\frac{1}{2}\%$

221. Satish borrowed ₹ 830 from Nitin at 12% rate of interest for 3 years. He then added some more money to the borrowed sum and lent it to Deepak for the same time at 14% simple interest. If Satish gains ₹ 93.90 in the whole transaction, then the sum lent by him to Deepak is

(a) ₹ 865 (b) ₹ 885
(c) ₹ 910 (d) ₹ 935

222. The rates of simple interest in two banks A and B are in the ratio 5:4. A person wants to deposit his total savings in two banks in such a way that he received equal half yearly interest from both. He should deposit the savings in banks A and B in the ratio

(a) 5:2 (b) 2:5
(c) 4:5 (d) 5:4

223. A lent ₹ 1200 to B for 3 years at certain rate of simple interest and ₹ 1000 to C for the same time at the same rate. If he gets ₹ 50 more from B than from C, then the rate per cent is

(a) $10\frac{1}{3}\%$ (b) $6\frac{2}{3}\%$
(c) $8\frac{1}{3}\%$ (d) $9\frac{2}{3}\%$

224. How much should a person lend at simple rate of interest of 15% in order to have ₹ 784 at the end of the year?

(a) ₹ 640 (b) ₹ 620
(c) ₹ 610 (d) ₹ 680

225. Two equal amounts of money are deposited in two banks, each at 15% per annum, for $3\frac{1}{2}$ years and 5 years. If the difference between their interests is ₹ 144, each sum is

(a) ₹ 460 (b) ₹ 500
(c) ₹ 640 (d) ₹ 720

226. The rate of interest on a sum of money is 4% per annum for the first 2 years, 6% per annum for the next 4 years and 8% per annum for the period beyond 6 years. If the simple interest accrued by the sum for a total period of 9 years is ₹ 1120. What is the sum?

(a) ₹ 1500 (b) ₹ 2000
(c) ₹ 2500 (d) ₹ 4000

227. If A lends ₹ 3500 to B at 10% p.a. and B lends the same sum to C at 11.5% p.a., then the gain of B (in ₹) in a period of 3 years is

(a) 107.50 (b) 115.50
(c) 157.50 (d) 177.50

228. A sum of ₹ 2500 is lent out in two parts, 1 one at 12% and another one at $12\frac{1}{2}\%$.

If the 2 total annual income is ₹ 306, the money lent at 12% is

(a) ₹ 1200 (b) ₹ 1300
(c) ₹ 1240 (d) ₹ 1340

229. Out of a sum of ₹ 625, a part was lent at 5% and the other at 10% simple interest. If the interest on the first part after 2 years is equal to the interest on the second part after 4 years, then the second sum (in ₹) is

(a) 125 (b) 200
(c) 250 (d) 300

230. A sum was put at simple interest at a certain rate for 2 years. Had it been put at 3% higher rate, it would have fetched ₹ 72 more. The sum is

(a) ₹ 1600 (b) ₹ 1500
(c) ₹ 1200 (d) ₹ 1800

231. The compound interest on ₹ 5000 for 3 years at 8% for first year, 10% for second year and 12% for third year, will be

(a) ₹ 1652.80 (b) ₹ 1560.40
(c) ₹ 1565.60 (d) ₹ 1500

232. The difference between the simple interest and compound interest for 2 years at 4% per annum is ₹ 20. The principal amount (in rupees) will be

(a) 12000 (b) 12500
(c) 13000 (d) 13500

233. The compound interest on a certain sum of money for 2 years at 10% per annum is ₹ 420. The simple interest on the same sum at the same rate and for the same time will be

(a) ₹ 350 (b) ₹ 375
(c) ₹ 380 (d) ₹ 400

234. The difference between the compound in terest and the simple interest on a sum of money lent for 2 years at 10% is ₹ 40. The sum is

(a) ₹ 8000 (b) ₹ 6000
(c) ₹ 5000 (d) ₹ 4000

235. The simple interest on ₹ 10 for 4 months at the rate of 3 paise per rupee per month is

(a) ₹ 1.20 (b) ₹ 12
(c) ₹ 120 (d) ₹ 1200

236. A saving bank gives interest which compounds annually. Mr. X deposited ₹ 1000 and received ₹ 121 as cumulative interest at the end of second year. Rate of compound interest per annum is

(a) 10% (b) 20%
(c) 10.5% (d) 20.5%

237. A sum of money amounts to ₹ 6690 after 3 years and to ₹ 10035 after 6 years on compound interest. The sum is

(a) ₹ 4400 (b) ₹ 4460
(c) ₹ 4520 (d) ₹ 4445

238. A sum of money trebles itself in 15 years 6 months. In how many years it would double itself?

(a) 6 years 3 months
(b) 7 years 9 months
(c) 8 years 3 months
(d) 9 years 6 months

239. The difference between compound interest and simple interest at the same rate for ₹ 5000 for 2 years is ₹ 72. The rate of interest per annum is

(a) 6% (b) 8%
(c) 10% (d) 12%

240. A sum of ₹ 550 was taken as a loan. This is to be paid back in two equal annual instalments. If the rate of interest be 20% compounded annually, then the value of each instalment is

(a) ₹ 421 (b) ₹ 396
(c) ₹ 360 (d) ₹ 350

241. The difference between the simple interest and the compound interest on ₹ 600 for

1 year at 10% per annum, reckoned half-yearly is
(a) Nil (b) ₹ 6.50
(c) ₹ 4.40 (d) ₹ 1.50

242. If ₹ 64 amount to ₹ 83.20 in 2 years, what will ₹ 86 amount in 4 years at the same rate per cent per annum?
(a) ₹ 127.40 (b) ₹ 124.70
(c) ₹ 114.80 (d) ₹ 137.60

243. A boy borrowed ₹ 500 at the rate of 5% per annum S.I. What amount will he pay to clear the debt after 4 years?
(a) ₹ 200 (b) ₹ 550
(c) ₹ 600 (d) ₹ 700

244. Poonam finds that an increase in the rate of interest from $4\frac{7}{8}$ to $5\frac{1}{8}$ % per annum increases her yearly income by ₹ 25. Her investment is
(a) ₹ 10000 (b) ₹ 12000
(c) ₹ 15000 (d) ₹ 20000

245. Manjit borrows ₹ 300 at 5% and ₹ 450 at 6% at the same time and on the condition that the whole loan will be repaid when the total interest amounts to ₹ 126. The loan will have to be repaid after how many years?
(a) 2 (b) 3
(c) 4 (d) 5

246. The difference between the interests received from two different banks on ₹ 500 for 2 years is ₹ 2.50. The difference between their rates is
(a) 1% (b) 0.5%
(c) 0.25% (d) 2.5%

247. The rate of interest on a sum of money is 4% p.a. for the first 2 years, 6% p.a. for the next 3 years and 8% p.a. for the period beyond 3 years. If the simple interest accrued by the sum for a total period of 8 years is ₹ 1280. What is the sum?
(a) ₹ 1523 (b) ₹ 1680
(c) ₹ 2560 (d) ₹ 2840

248. Manju invested ₹ 1600 for 3 years and ₹ 1100 for 4 years at the same rate of simple interest. If the total interest from these investments is ₹ 506, the rate of interest was
(a) $2\frac{3}{4}$% (b) $5\frac{1}{3}$%
(c) $5\frac{1}{2}$% (d) 6%

249. A certain sum of money lent out at S.I. amounts to ₹ 690 in 3 years and ₹ 750 in 5 years. The sum lent is
(a) ₹ 400 (b) ₹ 450
(c) ₹ 500 (d) ₹ 600

250. A monthly instalment of ₹ 180 is required to be paid for repayment of an interest free loan in 40 months. If it is decided to pay it in 30 months. How much will be the monthly instalment in rupees?
(a) 60 (b) 198
(c) 240 (d) 330

251. The simple interest on a sum of money is $\frac{1}{9}$ of the sum. The number of years is numerically equal to the rate per cent per annum. The rate per cent per annum is
(a) $3\frac{1}{3}$ (b) 5
(c) $6\frac{2}{3}$ (d) 10

252. The interest on a certain deposit at 4.5% p.a. is ₹ 202.50 in one year. How much will the additional interest in one year be on the same deposit at 5% p.a.?
(a) ₹ 22.5 (b) ₹ 20.25
(c) ₹ 225 (d) ₹ 427.50

253. A sum of ₹ 1550 was lent partly at 5% and partly at 8% p.a. simple interest. The total interest received after 3 years was ₹ 300. The ratio of the money lent at 5% to that lent at 8% is

(a) 8:5 (b) 5:8
(c) 31:6 (d) 16:15

254. A vessel is filled with liquid, 3 parts of which are water and 5 parts syrup. How much of the mixture must be drawn off and replaced with water so that the mixture may be half water and half syrup?

(a) 1/3 (b) 1/4
(c) 1/5 (d) 1/7

255. A lady invests an amount of ₹ 15860 in the names of her three sons A, B and C in such a way that they get the same amount after 2, 3 and 4 years respectively. If the rate of simple interest is 5%, then the ratio of amounts invested among A, B and C will be

(a) 10:15:20 (b) 22:23:24
(c) 6:4:3 (d) 2:3:4

256. Tea worth ₹ 126 per kg and ₹ 135 per kg are mixed with a third variety in the ratio 1:1:2. If the mixture is worth ₹ 153 per kg, the price of the third variety per kg will be

(a) ₹ 169.50 (b) ₹ 170
(c) ₹ 175.50 (d) ₹ 180

257. A milk vendor has 2 cans of milk. The first contains 25% water and the rest milk. The second contains 50% water. How much milk should he mix from each of the containers so as to get 12 litres of milk such that the ratio of water to milk is 3:5?

(a) 4 litres, 8 litres
(b) 6 litres, 6 litres
(c) 5 litres, 7 litres
(d) 7 litres, 5 litres

258. Consider the following statements:
If a sum of money is lent at simple interest, then the

1. money gets doubled in 5 years if the rate 2 of interest is $16\frac{2}{3}\%$.
2. money gets doubled in 5 years if the rate of interest is 20%.
3. money becomes four times in 10 years if it gets doubled in 5 years.

(a) 1 and 3 are correct
(b) 3 alone is correct
(c) 2 alone is correct
(d) 2 and 3 are correct

259. In what ratio must a grocer mix two varieties of tea worth ₹ 60 a kg and ₹ 65 a kg so that by selling the mixture at ₹ 68.20 a kg he may gain 10%?

(a) 3:2 (b) 3:4
(c) 3:5 (d) 4:5

260. The simple interest on ₹ 1820 from March 9, 2010 to May 21, 2010 at $7\frac{1}{2}\%$ rate will be

(a) ₹ 29 (b) ₹ 28.80
(c) ₹ 27.30 (d) ₹ 22.50

261. Find the ratio in which rice at ₹ 7.20 a kg be mixed with rice at ₹ 5.70 a kg to produce a mixture worth ₹ 6.30 a kg.

(a) 1:3 (b) 2:3
(c) 3:4 (d) 4:5

262. The difference between compound interest and simple interest on a sum for 2 years at 10% per annum, when the interest is compounded annually is ₹ 16. If the interest were compounded half yearly, the difference in two interest would be

(a) ₹ 24.81 (b) ₹ 31.61
(c) ₹ 32.40 (d) ₹ 26.90

263. An error 2% in excess is made while measuring the side of a square. The percentage of error in the calculated area of the square is

(a) 2% (b) 2.02%
(c) 4% (d) 4.04%

264. Vikas borrows ₹ 12500 from a bank at 20% compound interest. At the end of every year he pays ₹ 2000 as part repayment. How much does he till owe to the bank after three such instalments?

(a) ₹ 15600 (b) ₹ 12864
(c) ₹ 12000 (d) ₹ 14320

265. A towel, when bleached, was found to have lost 20% of its length and 10% of its breadth. The percentage of decrease in area is

(a) 10% (b) 10.08%
(c) 20% (d) 28%

266. The difference between compound interest and simple interest earned on a sum of money at the end of 4 years is ₹ 256.40. To find out the sum, which of the following informations given in the statements P and Q is/are necessary?

P : Amount of simple interest accrued after 4 years.

Q : Rate of interest per annum

(a) Only P is necessary
(b) Only Q is necessary
(c) Either P or Q is necessary
(d) Neither P nor Q is necessary

267. What is the least number of squares tiles required to pave the floor of a room 15 m 17 cm long and 9 m 2 cm broad?

(a) 814 (b) 820
(c) 840 (d) 844

268. At what rate of compound interest per annum will a sum of ₹ 1200 become ₹ 1348.32 in 2 years?

(a) 7% (b) 6%
(c) 7.5% (d) 6.5%

269. A tank is 25 m long, 12 m wide and 6 m deep. The cost of plastering its walls and bottom at 75 paise per sq. m, is

(a) ₹ 456 (b) ₹ 458
(c) ₹ 558 (d) ₹ 568

270. To find out the total compound interest accrued on a sum of money after 5 years, which of the following informations given in the statements P and Q will be sufficient?

P : The sum was ₹ 20000

Q : The total amount of simple interest on the sum after 5 years was ₹ 4000

(a) Only P is sufficient
(b) Only Q is sufficient
(c) Either P or Q is sufficient
(d) Both P and Q are sufficient

271. In the first 10 overs of a cricket game, the run rate was only 3.2. What should be the run rate in the remaining 40 overs to reach the target of 282 runs?

(a) 6.25 (b) 6.5
(c) 6.75 (d) 7

272. A sum of ₹ 12000 deposited at compound interest becomes double after 5 years. After 20 years it will become

(a) ₹ 1200000 (b) ₹ 192000
(c) ₹ 124000 (d) ₹ 96000

273. The average of 20 numbers is zero. Of them, at the most, how many may be greater than zero?

(a) 0 (b) 1
(c) 10 (d) 19

274. A sum of money becomes ₹ 13380 after 3 years and ₹ 20070 after 6 years on compound interest. The sum is

(a) ₹ 8800 (b) ₹ 8890
(c) ₹ 8920 (d) ₹ 9040

275. The captain of a cricket team of 11 members is 26 years old and the wicket keeper is 3 years older. If the ages of these two are excluded, the average age of the remaining players is one year less than the average age of the whole team. What is the average age of the team?
   (a) 23 years (b) 24 years
   (c) 25 years (d) None of these

276. A sum of money amounts to ₹ 4624 in 2 years and to ₹ 4913 in 3 years at compound interest. The sum is
   (a) ₹ 4096 (b) ₹ 4330
   (c) ₹ 4338 (d) ₹ 4365

277. If the average marks of three batches of 55, 60 and 45 students respectively is 50, 55, 60 then the average marks of all the students is
   (a) 53.33 (b) 54.68
   (c) 55 (d) None of these

278. A sum of ₹ 1100 was taken as a loan. This is to be repaid in two equal instalments. If the rate of interest be 20% compounded annually, then the value of each instalment is
   (a) ₹ 842 (b) ₹ 792
   (c) ₹ 720 (d) ₹ 700

279. The true discount on a bill of ₹ 540 is ₹ 90. The banker's discount is
   (a) ₹ 60 (b) ₹ 108
   (c) ₹ 110 (d) ₹ 112

280. A tree increases annually by $\frac{1}{8}$th of its height. What will be its height after 2 years, if it stands today 64 cm high?
   (a) 72 cm (b) 74 cm
   (c) 75 cm (d) 81 cm

281. The present worth of ₹ 169 due in 2 years at 4% per annum compound interest is
   (a) ₹ 150.50 (b) ₹ 154.75
   (c) ₹ 156.25 (d) ₹ 158

282. The banker's discount on ₹ 1600 at 15% per annum is the same as true discount on ₹ 1680 for the same time and at the same rate. The time is
   (a) 3 months (b) 4 months
   (c) 6 months (d) 8 months

283. The compound interest on ₹ 30000 at 7% per annum for a certain period is ₹ 4347. The period is
   (a) 2 years (b) $2\frac{1}{2}$ years
   (c) 3 years (d) 4 years

284. The certain worth of a certain sum due sometime hence is ₹ 1600 and the true discount is ₹ 160. The banker's gain is
   (a) ₹ 20 (b) ₹ 24
   (c) ₹ 16 (d) ₹ 12

285. The difference between the compound in terest on ₹ 1600 for one year at 20% per annum, when compounded half yearly and quarterly is
   (a) ₹ 8.81 (b) ₹ 9.41
   (c) ₹ 10.36 (d) ₹ 8.50

286. The banker's discount of a certain sum of money is ₹ 72 and the true discount on the same sum for the same time is ₹ 60. The sum due is
   (a) ₹ 360 (b) ₹ 432
   (c) ₹ 540 (d) ₹ 1080

287. A sum of money becomes 8 times of itself in 3 years at compound interest. The rate of interest is
   (a) 100% (b) 8%
   (c) 1% (d) Data inadequate

288. A man takes twice as long to row a distance against the stream as to row the same distance in favour of the stream. The ratio of the speed of the boat (in still water) and the stream is
   (a) 2:1 (b) 3:1
   (c) 3:2 (d) 4:3

289. Three unbiased coins are tossed. What is the probability of getting exactly two heads?

(a) $\frac{1}{3}$ (b) $\frac{3}{8}$

(c) $\frac{2}{3}$ (d) $\frac{1}{2}$

290. A man's speed with the current is 15 km/hr and the speed of the current is 2.5 km/hr. The man's speed against the current is

(a) 8.5 km/hr (b) 9 km/hr

(c) 10 km/hr (d) 12.5 km/hr

291. Tickets numbered 1 to 20 are mixed up and then a ticket is drawn at random. What is the probability that the ticket drawn bears a number which is a multiple of 3?

(a) $\frac{3}{20}$ (b) $\frac{3}{10}$

(c) $\frac{2}{5}$ (d) $\frac{1}{2}$

292. In one hour, a boat goes 11 km/hr along the stream and 5 km/hr against the stream. The speed of the boat in still water (in km/hr) is

(a) 3 km/hr (b) 5 km/hr

(c) 8 km/hr (d) 9 km/hr

293. Speed of a boat in standing water is 9 kmph and the speed of the stream is 1.5 kmph. A man rows to a place at a distance of 105 km and comes back to the starting point. The total time taken by him is

(a) 16 hours (b) 18 hours

(c) 20 hours (d) 24 hours

294. January 1, 2007 was Monday. What day of the week lies on January 1, 2008?

(a) Monday (b) Tuesday

(c) Wednesday (d) Sunday

295. One card is drawn at random from a pack of 52 cards. What is the probability that the card drawn is a face card?

(a) $\frac{4}{13}$ (b) $\frac{1}{4}$

(c) $\frac{9}{52}$ (d) $\frac{1}{13}$

296. What was the day of the week on 17th June, 1998?

(a) Monday (b) Tuesday

(c) Wednesday (d) Thursday

297. One card is drawn of random from a pack of 52 cards. What is the probability that the card drawn is a king?

(a) $\frac{1}{13}$ (b) $\frac{1}{52}$

(c) $\frac{3}{13}$ (d) $\frac{1}{4}$

298. On what dates of April, 2001 did Wednesday fall?

(a) 1st, 8th, 15th, 22nd, 29th

(b) 2nd, 9th, 16th, 23rd, 30th

(c) 3rd, 10th, 17th, 24th

(d) 4th, 11th, 18th, 25th

299. In a simultaneous throw of two dice, what is the probability of getting a doublet?

(a) $\frac{1}{6}$ (b) $\frac{1}{4}$

(c) $\frac{3}{4}$ (d) $\frac{2}{3}$

300. The calendar for the year 2007 will be the same for the year

(a) 2014 (b) 2016

(c) 2017 (d) 2018

301. In a simultaneous throw of two dice, what is the probability of getting a total of 10 or 11?

(a) $\frac{7}{12}$ (b) $\frac{5}{36}$
(c) $\frac{1}{6}$ (d) $\frac{1}{4}$

302. 3 pumps, working 8 hours a day, can empty a tank in 2 days. How many hours a day must 4 pumps work to empty the tank in 1 day?
(a) 9 (b) 10
(c) 11 (d) 12

303. Tickets numbered from 1 to 20 are mixed up and a ticket is drawn at random. What is the probability that the ticket drawn has a number which is a multiple of 3 or 7?
(a) $\frac{1}{15}$ (b) $\frac{1}{2}$
(c) $\frac{2}{5}$ (d) $\frac{7}{20}$

304. A fort had provision of food for 150 men for 45 days. After 10 days, 25 men left the fort. The number of days for which the remaining food will last, is
(a) $29\frac{1}{5}$ (b) $37\frac{1}{4}$
(c) 42 (d) 54

305. A bag contains 6 black balls and 8 white balls. One ball is drawn at random. What is the probability that the ball drawn is white?
(a) $\frac{4}{7}$ (b) $\frac{3}{4}$
(c) $\frac{4}{3}$ (d) $\frac{1}{8}$

306. If a quarter kg of potato costs 60 paise, how many paise will 200 gm cost?
(a) 48 paise (b) 54 paise
(c) 56 paise (d) 72 paise

307. A bag contains 8 red and 5 white balls. 2 balls are drawn at random. What is the probability that both are white?
(a) $\frac{5}{16}$ (b) $\frac{2}{13}$
(c) $\frac{3}{26}$ (d) $\frac{5}{39}$

308. An industrial loom weaves 0.128 metres of cloth every second. Approximately, how many seconds will it take for the loom to weave 25 metres of cloth?
(a) 178 (b) 195
(c) 204 (d) 488

309. Two cards are drawn at random from a pack of 52 cards. What is the probability that the drawn cards are both aces?
(a) $\frac{1}{221}$ (b) $\frac{2}{13}$
(c) $\frac{3}{26}$ (d) $\frac{1}{24}$

310. The reflex angle between the hands of a clock at 10.25 is
(a) 180° (b) 192½°
(c) 195° (d) 197½°

311. The odds against the occurrence of an event are 5:4. The probability of its occurrence is
(a) $\frac{4}{5}$ (b) $\frac{4}{9}$
(c) $\frac{1}{5}$ (d) $\frac{1}{4}$

312. At what time between 7 and 8 o'clock will the hands of a clock be in the same straight line but, not together?
(a) 5 min. past 7
(b) $5\frac{2}{7}$ min. past 7

(c) $5\frac{3}{11}$ min. past 7

(d) $5\frac{5}{11}$ min. past 7

313. An urn contains 9 red, 7 white and 4 black balls. A ball is drawn at random. What is the probability that the ball drawn is not red?

(a) $\frac{1}{11}$ (b) $\frac{9}{11}$

(c) $\frac{2}{11}$ (d) $\frac{11}{20}$

314. At 3.40, the hour hand and the minute hand of a clock form an angle of

(a) 120° (b) 125°

(c) 130° (d) 135°

315. 4.036 divided by 0.04 gives

(a) 1.009 (b) 10.09

(c) 100.9 (d) None of these

316. A card is drawn from a pack of 52 cards. A card is drawn at random. What is the probability that it is neither a heart nor a king?

(a) $\frac{4}{13}$ (b) $\frac{9}{13}$

(c) $\frac{2}{13}$ (d) $\frac{4}{11}$

317. The compound interest on a certain sum for 2 years at 10% per annum is ₹ 525. The simple interest on the same sum for double the time at half the rate per cent per annum is

(a) ₹ 400 (b) ₹ 500

(c) ₹ 600 (d) ₹ 800

318. The probability of occurrence of two events E and F are 0.25 and 0.30 respectively. The probability of their simultaneous occurrence is 0.14. The probability that either E occurs or F occurs is

(a) 0.31 (b) 0.61

(c) 0.69 (d) 0.89

319. A bank offers 5% compound interest calculated on half-yearly basis. A customer deposits ₹ 1600 each on 1st January and 1st July of a year. At the end of the year, the amount he would have gained by way of interest is

(a) ₹ 120 (b) ₹ 121

(c) ₹ 122 (d) ₹ 123

320. In how many different ways can the letters of the word 'CORPORATION' be arranged so that the vowels always come together?

(a) 810 (b) 1440

(c) 2880 (d) 50400

321. At what rate of compound interest per annum will a sum of ₹ 1200 become ₹ 1348.32 in 2 years?

(a) 6% (b) 6.5%

(c) 7% (d) 7.5%

322. In how many different ways can the letters of the word 'MATHEMATICS' be arranged so that the vowels always come together?

(a) 10080 (b) 4989600

(c) 120960 (d) 12800

323. 3.87 – 2.59 = ?

(a) 1.20 (b) 1.2

(c) 1.27 (d) 1.28

324. If the simple interest on a sum of money for 2 years at 5% per annum is ₹ 50, what is the compound interest on the same at the same rate and for the same time?

(a) ₹ 51.25 (b) ₹ 52

(c) ₹ 54.25 (d) ₹ 60

325. In how many different ways can the letters of the word 'DETAIL' be arranged in such a way that the vowels occupy only the odd positions?
(a) 32 (b) 48
(c) 36 (d) 60

326. What decimal of an hour is a second?
(a) .0025 (b) .0256
(c) .00027 (d) .000126

327. In how many different ways can the letters of the word 'MACHINE' be arranged so that the vowels may occupy only the odd positions?
(a) 210 (b) 576
(c) 144 (d) 1728

328. The value of $\frac{(0.96)^3 \times (0.1)^3}{(0.96)^2 + 0.096 + (0.1)^2}$ is
(a) 0.86 (b) 0.95
(c) 0.97 (d) 1.06

329. In how many ways can a group of 5 men and 2 women be made out of a total of 7 men and 3 women?
(a) 63 (b) 90
(c) 126 (d) 45

330. If $\log_x (9) = -1$, then x is equal to
(a) –3/4 (b) 3/4
(c) 81/256 (d) 256/81

331. The expression (11.98 × 11.98 + 11.98 × x + 0.02 × 0.02) will be a perfect square for x equal to
(a) 0.02 (b) 0.2
(c) 0.04 (d) 0.4

332. 34.95 + 240.016 + 23.98 = ?
(a) 298.0946 (b) 298.111
(c) 298.946 (d) 299.09

333. In how many ways a committee, consisting of 5 men and 6 women can be formed from 8 men and 10 women?
(a) 266 (b) 5040
(c) 11760 (d) 86400

334. If $\log_{10} 5 + \log_{10} (5x + 1) = \log_{10} (x + 5) + 1$, then x is equal to
(a) 1 (b) 3
(c) 5 (d) 10

335. Two ships are sailing in the sea on the two sides of a lighthouse. The angle of elevation of the top of the lighthouse is observed from the ships are 30° and 45° respectively. If the lighthouse is 100 m high, the distance between the two ships is
(a) 173 m (b) 200 m
(c) 273 m (d) 300 m

336. If log 27 = 1.431, then the value of log 9 is
(a) 0.934 (b) 0.945
(c) 0.954 (d) 0.958

337. In a group of 6 boys and 4 girls, four children are to be selected. In how many different ways can they be selected such that at least one boy should be there?
(a) 159 (b) 194
(c) 205 (d) 209

338. From a point P on a level ground, the angle of elevation of the top tower is 30°. If the tower is 100 m high, the distance of point P from the foot of the tower is
(a) 149 m (b) 156 m
(c) 173 m (d) 200 m

339. A box contains 2 white balls, 3 black balls and 4 red balls. In how many ways can 3 balls be drawn from the box, if at least one black ball is to be included in the draw?
(a) 32 (b) 48
(c) 64 (d) 96

340. If log 2 = 0.3010 and log 3 = 0.4771, the value of $\log_5 512$ is
(a) 2.870 (b) 2.967
(c) 3.876 (d) 3.912

341. 15 litres of a mixture contains 20% alcohol and the rest water. If 3 litres of water be mixed in it, the percentage of alcohol in the new mixture will be

(a) 17 (b) $16\frac{2}{3}$

(c) $18\frac{1}{2}$ (d) 15

342. If $\log_{10} 2 = 0.3010$, the value of $\log_{10} 80$ is

(a) 1.6020 (b) 1.9030

(c) 3.9030 (d) None of these.

343. Kantilal mixes 80 kg. of sugar worth of ₹ 6.75 per kg. with 120 kg. worth of ₹ 8 per kg. At what rate shall he sell the mixture to gain 20%?

(a) ₹ 7.50 (b) ₹ 9

(c) ₹ 8.20 (d) ₹ 8.85

344. Which one of the following is not a prime number?

(a) 31 (b) 61

(c) 71 (d) 91

345. A jar full of whisky contains 40% of alcohol. A part of this whisky is replaced by another containing 19% alcohol and now the percentage of alcohol was found to be 26. The quantity of whisky replaced is

(a) $\frac{2}{5}$ (b) $\frac{1}{3}$

(c) $\frac{2}{3}$ (d) $\frac{3}{5}$

346. (935421 × 625) = ?

(a) 575648125 (b) 584638125

(c) 584649125 (d) 585628125

347. 729 ml. of a mixture contains milk and water in ratio 7:2. How much more water is to be added to get a new mixture containing milk and water in the ratio 7:3?

(a) 600 ml. (b) 710 ml.

(c) 520 ml. (d) None of these

348. In a mixture of 60 litres, the ratio of milk and water is 2:1. If the ratio of the milk and water is to be 1:2, then the amount of water to be further added is

(a) 20 litres (b) 30 litres

(c) 40 litres (d) 60 litres

349. The difference of two numbers is 1365. On dividing the larger number by the smaller, we get 6 as quotient and the 15 as remainder. What is the smaller number?

(a) 240 (b) 270

(c) 295 (d) 360

350. A train covers a certain distance in 50 minutes, if it runs at a speed of 48 kmph on an average. The speed at which the train must run to reduce the time of journey to 40 minutes, will be

(a) 50 km/hr (b) 55 km/hr

(c) 60 km/hr (d) 70 km/hr

351. The sum of first 45 natural numbers is

(a) 1035 (b) 1280

(c) 2070 (d) 2140

352. 9 + 3/4 + 7/17 + 2/15 – (9 + 1) = ?

(a) 7 + 719/1020 (b) 9 + 817/1020

(c) 9 + 719/1020 (d) 7 + 817/1020

353. The ratio between the rates of walking of A and B is 3:4. If the time taken by B to cover a certain distance is 36 minutes, the time taken by A to cover that much distance is

(a) 27 min (b) 48 min

(c) $15\frac{3}{7}$ min (d) None of these

354. What will be remainder when $(67^{67} + 67)$ is divided by 68?

(a) 1 (b) 63

(c) 66 (d) 67

355. A car takes 6 hours to cover a journey at a speed of 45 kmph. At what speed must

it travel in order to complete the journey in 5 hours?

(a) 55 km/hr (b) 54 km/hr
(c) 53 km/hr (d) 52 km/hr

356. A number when divided by 296 leaves 75 as remainder. When the same number is divided by 37, the remainder will be

(a) 1 (b) 2
(c) 8 (d) 11

357. An aeroplane travels different distances 2500 km, 1200 km and 500 km at the rate of 500 km/hr, 400 km/hr and 250 km/hr respectively. The average speed (in kmph) is

(a) 405 (b) 410
(c) 420 (d) 575

358. How many of the following numbers are divisible by 3 but not by 9? 2133, 2343, 3474, 4131, 5286, 5340, 6336, 7347, 8115, 9276

(a) 5 (b) 6
(c) 7 (d) None of these

359. A girl goes to school from her village at 3 kmph and returns back at 2 kmph. If she takes 5 hours in all, the distance between the village and the school is

(a) 6 km (b) 7 km
(c) 3 km (d) 10 km

360. A and B travel the same distance at 9 kmph and 10 kmph respectively. If A takes 36 minutes longer than B, the distance travelled by each is

(a) 48 km (b) 54 km
(c) 60 km (d) 125 km

361. A and B invest in a business in the ratio 3:2. If 5% of the total profit goes to charity and A's share is ₹ 855, the total profit is

(a) ₹ 1425 (b) ₹ 1500
(c) ₹ 1537.50 (d) ₹ 1576

362. Walking at $\frac{7}{6}$ of his usual speed, a man is 25 min. too late. His usual time is

(a) $1\frac{1}{2}$ hrs (b) $2\frac{1}{2}$ hrs
(c) $1\frac{6}{7}$ hrs (d) $2\frac{4}{5}$ hrs

363. Three partners shared the profit in a business in the ratio 5:7:8. They had partnered for 14 months, 8 months and 7 months respectively. What was the ratio of their investments?

(a) 5:7:8 (b) 20:49:64
(c) 38:28:21 (d) None of these

364. In covering a certain distance, the speed of A and B are in the ratio of 3:4. If A takes 20 minutes more than B to reach the destination, the time taken by A to reach the destination is

(a) $1\frac{1}{4}$ hrs (b) $1\frac{1}{3}$ hrs
(c) 2 hrs (d) $2\frac{1}{2}$ hrs

365. Aman started a business investing ₹ 70,000. Rakhi joined him after six months with an amount of ₹ 1,05,000 and Sagar joined them with ₹ 1.4 lakhs after another six months. The amount of profit earned should be distributed in what ratio among Aman, Rakhi and Sagar respectively, 3 years after Aman started the business?

(a) 7:6:10
(b) 12:15:16
(c) 42:45:56
(d) Cannot be determined

366. Two students appeared at an examination. One of them secured 9 marks more than the other and his marks was 56% of the sum of their marks. The marks obtained by them are

(a) 39, 30 (b) 41, 32
(c) 42, 33 (d) 43, 34

367. A is twice as fast as B and B is thrice as fast as C. The journey covered by C in 54 minutes will be covered by B in
(a) 18 min (b) 27 min
(c) 38 min (d) 9 min

368. In a certain school, 20% of students are below 8 years of age. The number of students above 8 years of age is 2/3 of the number of students of 8 years of age which is 48. What is the total number of students in the school?
(a) 72 (b) 80
(c) 120 (d) 100

369. A van can finish a certain journey in 10 hours at a speed of 48 kmph. In order to cover the same distance in 8 hours, the speed of the van must be increased by
(a) 6 km/hr (b) 7.5 km/hr
(c) 12 km/hr (d) 15 km/hr

370. Two tailers X and Y are paid a total of ₹ 550 per week by their employer. If X is paid 120 per cent of the sum paid to Y. How much is Y paid per week?
(a) ₹ 200 (b) ₹ 250
(c) ₹ 300 (d) None of these

371. Train K leaves Meerut at 5 a.m. and reaches Delhi at 9 a.m. Another train S leaves Delhi at 7 a.m. and reaches Meerut at 10.30. At what time do the two trains cross one an other?
(a) 8.26 a.m. (b) 8 a.m.
(c) 7.36 a.m. (d) 7.56 a.m.

372. In how many different ways can the letters of the word 'LEADING' be arranged in such a way that the vowels always come together?
(a) 360 (b) 480
(c) 720 (d) 5040

373. If Raju walks from his house to school at the rate of 4 kmph, he reaches the school 10 minutes earlier than the scheduled time. However, if he walks at the rate of 3 kmph, he reaches 10 minutes late. The distance of the school from his house is
(a) 6 km (b) 4.5 km
(c) 4 km (d) 3 km

374. In how many ways can a group of 5 men and 2 women be made out of a total of 7 men and 3 women?
(a) 63 (b) 90
(c) 126 (d) 45

375. A boy takes 5 hours 45 min. in walking to a certain place and riding back. He would have gained 2 hours by riding both ways. The time he would take to walk both ways, is
(a) 3 hrs 45 min (b) 7 hrs 30 min
(c) 7 hrs 45 min (d) 11 hrs 45 min

376. A box contains 2 white balls, 3 black balls and 4 red balls. In how many ways can 3 balls be drawn from the box, if at least one black ball is to be included in the draw?
(a) 32 (b) 48
(c) 64 (d) 96

377. Two women start together to walk to a certain destination, one at 3 kmph and another at 3.75 kmph. The latter arrives half an hour before the former. The distance is
(a) 6 km (b) 7.5 km
(c) 8 km (d) 9.5 km

378. Two pipes A and B can fill a cistern in 37½ minutes and 45 minutes respectively. Both pipes are opened. The cistern will be filled in just half an hour, if the B is turned off after
(a) 5 min (b) 9 min
(c) 10 min (d) 15 min

379. A rickshaw has to cover a distance of 80 km in 10 hours. If it covers half of the journey in 3/5 the time, what should be its speed to cover the remaining distance in the time left?
(a) 8 km/hr (b) 6.4 km/hr
(c) 10 km/hr (d) 20 km/hr

380. A tank is filled in 5 hours by three pipes A, B and C. The pipe C is twice as fast as B and B is twice as fast as A. How much time will pipe A alone take to fill the tank?
(a) 20 hours
(b) 25 hours
(c) 35 hours
(d) Cannot be determined

381. Arvind can cover a certain distance in 1 hr 24 min by covering two-third of the distance at 4 kmph and the rest at 5 kmph. The total distance is
(a) 5 km (b) 6 km
(c) 8 km (d) 9.2 km

382. A large tanker can be filled by two pipes A and B in 60 minutes and 40 minutes respectively. How many minutes will it take to fill the tanker from empty state if B is used for half the time and A and B fill it together for the other half?
(a) 15 min (b) 20 min
(c) 27.5 min (d) 30 min

383. The ratio between the rates of walking of A and B is 3:4. If the time taken by B to cover a distance is 24 minutes, the time taken by A to cover that much distance is
(a) 18 min (b) 32 min
(c) $10\frac{6}{7}$ min (d) $13\frac{5}{7}$ min

384. A bag contains 2 red, 3 green and 2 blue balls. Two balls are drawn at random. What is the probability that none of the balls drawn is blue?
(a) 10/21 (b) 11/21
(c) 2/7 (d) 5/7

385. A tourist travels for 14 hours 40 minutes. He covers half of the journey by train at the rate of 60 kmph and the rest half by road at the rate of 50 kmph. The distance travelled by him is
(a) 720 km (b) 800 km
(c) 960 km (d) 1000 km

386. Three unbiased coins are tossed. What is the probability of getting at most two heads?
(a) 3/4 (b) 1/4
(c) 3/8 (d) 7/8

387. A boy runs at 15.6 kmph. How many metres does he run in 2 minutes?
(a) 260 m (b) 312 m
(c) 520 m (d) 1040 m

388. Two dice are tossed. The probability that the total score is a prime number is
(a) 1/6 (b) 5/12
(c) 1/2 (d) 7/9

389. A boy riding a cycle at 12 kmph can reach a town in 4 hours 30 min. If he is delayed by 1 hour 30 min at the start, then in order to reach his destination in time, he should ride with a speed of
(a) 15 kmph (b) 16 kmph
(c) 18 kmph (d) 20 kmph

390. A father said to his son, "I was as old as you are at the present at the time of your birth." If the father's age is 38 years now, the son's age five years back was
(a) 14 years (b) 19 years
(c) 33 years (d) 38 years

391. The ratio between the speeds of A and B is 2:3 and therefore A takes 10 minutes more than the time taken by B to reach a destination. If A had walked at double the speed, he would have covered the distance in

(a) 30 min (b) 25 min
(c) 20 min (d) 15 min

392. A, B and C start at the same time in the same direction to run around a circular stadium. A completes a round in 252 seconds, B in 308 seconds and C in 198 seconds, all starting at the same point. After what time will they again at the starting point?
(a) 26 minutes and 18 seconds
(b) 42 minutes and 36 seconds
(c) 45 minutes
(d) 46 minutes and 12 seconds

393. Six years ago, the ratio of the ages of Kunal and Sagar was 6:5. Four years hence, the ratio of their ages will be 11:10. What is Sagar's age at present?
(a) 16 years
(b) 18 years
(c) 20 years
(d) Cannot be determined

394. Walking at $\frac{3}{4}$ of his usual speed, a boy is late by $2\frac{1}{2}$ hrs. The usual time would have been
(a) $7\frac{1}{2}$ hrs (b) $3\frac{1}{2}$ hrs
(c) $3\frac{1}{4}$ hrs (d) $\frac{7}{8}$ hrs

395. Find the greatest number that will divide 43, 91 and 183 so as to leave the same remainder in each case.
(a) 4 (b) 7
(c) 9 (d) 13

396. Two cars travel to a place at 45 kmph and 60 kmph respectively. If the second car takes $5\frac{1}{2}$ hours less than the first for the same journey, the length of journey is
(a) 900 km (b) 945 km
(c) 990 km (d) 1350 km

397. The product of two numbers is 4107. If the H.C.F. of these numbers is 37, then the greater number is
(a) 101 (b) 107
(c) 111 (d) 185

398. Walking at the rate of 4 kmph a boy covers a certain distance in 2 hours 45 min. Running at a speed of 16.5 kmph, he will cover the same distance in
(a) 40 min (b) 45 min
(c) 100 min (d) 41 min 15 sec

399. If one-third of one-fourth of a number is 15, then three-tenth of that number is
(a) 35 (b) 36
(c) 45 (d) 54

400. Sreyas travelled 1200 km by air which formed 2/5 of his trip. One-third of the whole trip, he travelled by car and the rest of the journey he performed by train. The distance travelled by train was
(a) 480 km (b) 800 km
(c) 1600 km (d) 1800 km

401. A two-digit number is such that the product of the digits is 8. When 18 is added to the number, then the digits are reversed. The number is
(a) 18 (b) 24
(c) 42 (d) 81

402. If the selling price of an article is $\frac{4}{3}$ times its cost price, the profit per cent is
(a) $33\frac{1}{3}$ (b) $25\frac{1}{4}$
(c) $20\frac{1}{2}$ (d) $20\frac{1}{3}$

403. The product of two numbers is 120 and the sum of their squares is 289. The sum of the number is

(a) 20 (b) 23
(c) 169 (d) None of these

404. Tomin purchased 35 kg of rice at the rate of ₹ 9.50 per kg and 30 kg at the rate of ₹ 10.50 per kg. He mixed the two. Approximately, at what price per kg should he sell the mixture to make 35% profit in the transaction?
(a) ₹ 12 (b) ₹ 12.50
(c) ₹ 13 (d) ₹ 13.50

405. The length of sthe bridge, which a train 130 metres long and travelling at 45 km/hr can cross in 30 seconds, is
(a) 200 m (b) 225 m
(c) 245 m (d) 250 m

406. By selling an article, Suresh earned a profit equal to $\frac{1}{4}$th of the price he bought it. If he sold it for ₹ 375, what was the cost price?
(a) ₹ 281.75 (b) ₹ 300
(c) ₹ 312.50 (d) ₹ 350

407. Two trains are moving in opposite directions @ 60 km/hr and 90 km/hr. Their lengths are 1.10 km and 0.9 km respectively. The time taken by the slower train to cross the faster train in seconds is
(a) 36 (b) 45
(c) 48 (d) 49

408. A reduction of 25% in the price of bananas will enable one to buy 4 dozen more bananas for ₹ 96. What is the price per dozen?
(a) 8 (b) 6
(c) 10 (d) 2

409. A 300 metre long train crosses a platform in 39 seconds while it crosses a signal pole in 18 seconds. What is the length of the platform?
(a) 320 m (b) 350 m
(c) 650 m (d) Data inadequate

410. Vinod purchased 120 reams of paper at ₹ 80 per ream. He spent ₹ 280 on transportation, paid octroi at the rate of 40 paise per ream and paid ₹ 72 to the coolie. If he wants to have a gain of 8%, what must be the selling price per ream?
(a) ₹ 90 (b) ₹ 87.48
(c) ₹ 89 (d) ₹ 86

411. In a 100 m race, A can give B 10 m and C 28 m. In the same race B can give C
(a) 18 m (b) 20 m
(c) 27 m (d) 9 m

412. Anish purchased 120 tables at a price of ₹ 110 per table. He sold 30 tables at a profit of ₹ 12 per table and 75 tables at a profit of ₹ 14 per table. The remaining tables were sold at a loss of ₹ 7 per table. What is the average profit per table?
(a) ₹ 12.875 (b) ₹ 10.04
(c) ₹ 10.875 (d) ₹ 12.80

413. At a game of billiards, A can give B 15 points in 60 and A can give C to 20 points in 60. How many points can B give C in a game of 90?
(a) 30 points (b) 20 points
(c) 10 points (d) 12 points

414. Gopi bought an article and sold it at a loss of 10%. If he had bought it for 20% less and sold it for ₹ 55 more, he would have had a profit of 40%. The C.P. of the article is
(a) ₹ 200 (b) ₹ 225
(c) ₹ 250 (d) ₹ 150

415. In a 300 m race A beats B by 22.5 m or 6 seconds. B's time over the course is
(a) 86 sec (b) 80 sec
(c) 76 sec (d) None of these

416. A shopkeeper sold three-fourth of his articles at a gain of 20% and the remaining at C.P. The gain earned by him in the whole transaction is

(a) 25% (b) 20%
(c) 15% (d) 10%

417. Two numbers are respectively 20% and 50% more than a third number. The ratio of the two numbers is
(a) 2:5 (b) 3:5
(c) 4:5 (d) 6:7

418. The percent profit made when an article is sold for ₹ 78 is twice as much as when it is sold for ₹ 69. What is the cost price of the article?
(a) ₹ 51 (b) ₹ 55.50
(c) ₹ 60 (d) ₹ 55

419. The salaries A, B, C are in the ratio 2:3:5. If the increments of 15%, 10% and 20% are allowed respectively in their salaries, then what will be new ratio of their salaries?
(a) 3:3:10
(b) 10:11:20
(c) 23:33:60
(d) Cannot be determined

420. Profit earned by selling an article for ₹ 1060 is 20% more than the loss incurred by selling the article for ₹ 950. At what price should the article be sold to earn 20% profit?
(a) ₹ 980 (b) ₹ 1080
(c) ₹ 1800 (d) ₹ 1200

421. Mr. Thomas invested an amount of ₹ 13,900 divided in two different schemes A and B at the simple interest rate of 14% p.a. and 11% p.a. respectively. If the total amount of simple interest earned in 2 years be ₹ 3508. What was the amount invested in Scheme B?
(a) ₹ 6400 (b) ₹ 6500
(c) ₹ 7200 (d) ₹ 7500

422. Sachin buys mangoes at the rate of 3 kg for ₹ 21 and sells them at 5 kg for ₹ 50. To earn ₹ 102 as profit, he must sell
(a) 26 kg (b) 32 kg
(c) 34 kg (d) 56 kg

423. A person takes a loan of ₹ 200 at 5% simple interest. He returns ₹ 100 at the end of 1 year. In order to clear his dues at the end of 2 years, he would pay
(a) ₹ 105 (b) ₹ 110
(c) ₹ 115 (d) ₹ 115.50

424. A vendor loses the S.P. of 4 oranges on selling 36 oranges. His loss per cent is
(a) $12\frac{1}{2}\%$ (b) $11\frac{1}{9}\%$
(c) 10% (d) 11%

425. If $a - b = 3$ and $a^2 + b^2 = 29$, find the value of ab.
(a) 10 (b) 12
(c) 15 (d) 18

426. Two mixers and one TV cost ₹ 7000, while two TVs and a mixer cost ₹ 9800. The value of one TV is
(a) ₹ 2800 (b) ₹ 2100
(c) ₹ 4200 (d) ₹ 8400

427. One-third of Rahul's savings in National Savings Certificate is equal to one-half of his savings in Public Provident Fund. If he has ₹ 1,50,000 as total savings. How much has he saved in Public Provident Fund?
(a) ₹ 30,000 (b) ₹ 50,000
(c) ₹ 60,000 (d) ₹ 90,000

428. A machine is sold at a profit of 10%. Had it been sold for ₹ 80 less, there would have been a loss of 10%. The C.P. of the machine is
(a) ₹ 350 (b) ₹ 400
(c) ₹ 450 (d) ₹ 520

429. Eight people are planning to share equally the cost of a rental car. If one person withdraws from the arrangement and the others share equally the entire cost of the

car, then the share of each of the remaining persons increased by

(a) 1/7 (b) 1/8
(c) 1/9 (d) 7/8

430. The marked price of a machine is ₹ 620. Due to off season, a 15% discount is allowed. The S.P. of the machine is

(a) ₹ 427 (b) ₹ 527
(c) ₹ 537 (d) ₹ 547

431. A man has some hens and cows. If the number of heads be 48 and the number of feet equals 140, then the number of hens will be

(a) 22 (b) 23
(c) 24 (d) 26

432. A shopkeeper sold an article at a loss of 2%. Had he sold it for ₹ 100 more, he would have gained 7½%. To gain 12½%, he should sell it for

(a) ₹ 850 (b) ₹ 925
(c) ₹ 1080 (d) ₹ 1125

433. The least perfect square, which is divisible by each of 21, 36 and 66 is

(a) 213444 (b) 214344
(c) 214434 (d) 231444

434. A fruit seller purchases oranges at the rate of 3 for ₹ 5 and sells them at 2 for ₹ 4. His profit in the transaction is

(a) 10% (b) 15%
(c) 20% (d) 25%

435. If $x = 3 + 1$ and $y = 3 - 1$, then the value of $(x^2 + y^2)$ is

(a) 10 (b) 13
(c) 14 (d) 15

436. A sells a bicycle to B at a profit of 20% and B sells it to C at a profit of 25%. If C pays ₹ 1500, what did A pay for it?

(a) ₹ 825 (b) ₹ 1000
(c) ₹ 1100 (d) ₹ 1125

437. The square root of 64009 is

(a) 253 (b) 347
(c) 363 (d) 803

438. What price should a shopkeeper mark on an article, costing him ₹ 153, to gain 20% after allowing a discount of 15%?

(a) ₹ 224 (b) ₹ 216
(c) ₹ 184 (d) ₹ 162

439. If a person walks at 14 km/hr instead of 10 km/hr, he would have walked 20 km more. The actual distance travelled by him is

(a) 50 km (b) 56 km
(c) 70 km (d) 80 km

440. If A:B = 8:15, B:C = 5:8 and C:D = 4:5, then A:D is equal to

(a) 2:7 (b) 4:15
(c) 8:15 (d) 15:4

441. If 0.4:1.4::1.4:x, the value of x is

(a) 49 (b) 4.9
(c) 0.49 (d) 0.4

442. In a flight of 600 km, an aircraft was slowed down due to bad weather. Its average speed for the trip was reduced by 200 km/hr and the time of flight increased by 30 minutes. The duration of the flight is

(a) 1 hour (b) 2 hours
(c) 3 hours (d) 4 hours

443. If $A = \frac{1}{3}$ B and $B = \frac{1}{2}$ C, then A:B:C is

(a) 1:3:6 (b) 3:1:2
(c) 2:3:6 (d) 3:2:6

444. A, B and C can do a piece of work in 20, 30 and 60 days respectively. In how many days can A do the work if he is assisted by B and C on every third day?

(a) 12 days (b) 15 days
(c) 16 days (d) 18 days

445. In a ratio which is equal to 3:4, if the antecedent is 12, then consequent is

(a) 9 (b) 16
(c) 20 (d) 24

446. A can do a piece of work in 4 hours; B and C together can do it in 3 hours, while A and C together can do it in 2 hours. How long will B alone take to do it?
(a) 8 hours (b) 10 hours
(c) 12 hours (d) 24 hours

447. If the ratio of A to B is 9 times the ratio of B to A, then $\frac{A}{B}$ could be
(a) 9 (b) 3
(c) $\frac{1}{3}$ (d) $\frac{1}{9}$

448. P can complete a work in 12 days working 8 hours a day. Q can complete the same work in 8 days working 10 hours a day. If both P and Q work together, working 8 hours a day. In how many days can they complete the work?
(a) $5\frac{5}{11}$ (b) $5\frac{6}{11}$
(c) $6\frac{5}{11}$ (d) $6\frac{6}{11}$

449. If $\frac{a}{3}=\frac{b}{4}=\frac{c}{7}$, then $\frac{a+b+c}{c}$ is equal to
(a) 7 (b) 2
(c) $\frac{1}{2}$ (d) $\frac{1}{7}$

450. A, B and C can complete a piece of work in 24, 6 and 12 days respectively. Working together, they will complete the same work in
(a) $\frac{1}{24}$ day (b) $\frac{7}{24}$ day
(c) $3\frac{3}{7}$ days (d) 4 days

451. What same number must be added to each term of the ratio 7:13 so that the ratio becomes 2:3?
(a) 1 (b) 2
(c) 3 (d) 5

452. What number should be added to each of the numbers 8, 21, 13 and 31 so that the resulting numbers, in this order form a proportion?
(a) 2 (b) 3
(c) 5 (d) 7

453. Twenty women can do a work in sixteen days. Sixteen men can complete the same work in fifteen days. What is the ratio between the capacity of a man and a woman?
(a) 3:4 (b) 4:3
(c) 5:3 (d) Data inadequate

454. A and B together have ₹ 1210 with them. If $\frac{4}{15}$ of A's amount is equal to $\frac{2}{5}$ of B's amount. How much amount does B have?
(a) ₹ 466 (b) ₹ 484
(c) ₹ 550 (d) ₹ 664

455. The true discount on ₹ 2562 due 4 months hence is ₹ 122. The rate per cent is
(a) 12% (b) 13¼%
(c) 15% (d) 14%

456. An amount of ₹ 735 was divided between A, B and C. If each of them had received ₹ 25 less, their shares would have been in the ratio of 1:3:2. The money received by C was
(a) ₹ 195 (b) ₹ 200
(c) ₹ 225 (d) ₹ 245

457. A man buys a watch for ₹ 1950 in cash and sells it for ₹ 2200 at a credit of 1 year. If the rate of interest is 10% per annum, the man
(a) gains ₹ 55 (b) gains ₹ 50
(c) loses ₹ 30 (d) gains ₹ 30

458. ₹ 407 are to be divided among A, B and C so that their shares are in ratio $\frac{1}{4}:\frac{1}{5}:\frac{1}{6}$. The respective shares of A, B, C are
(a) ₹ 165, ₹ 132, ₹ 110
(b) ₹ 165, ₹ 110, ₹ 132
(c) ₹ 132, ₹ 110, ₹ 165
(d) ₹ 110, ₹ 132, ₹ 165

459. In a shower, 5 cm of rain falls. The volume of water that falls on 1.5 hectares of ground is
(a) 75 cu. m (b) 750 cu. m
(c) 7500 cu. m (d) 75000 cu. m

460. The ratio of the ages of father and son is 7:3. If the sum of their ages is 60 years, what is the difference in their ages?
(a) 42 years (b) 24 years
(c) 18 years (d) 4 years

461. The slant height of a right circular cone is 10 m and its height is 8 m. Find the area of its curved surface.
(a) 30π m^2 (b) 40π m^2
(c) 60π m^2 (d) 80π m^2

462. The sides of a triangle are in ratio $\frac{1}{2}:\frac{1}{3}:\frac{1}{4}$ and its perimeter is 104 cm. The length of longest side is
(a) 52 cm (b) 48 cm
(c) 32 cm (d) 26 cm

463. A large cube is formed from the material obtained by melting three smaller cubes of 3, 4 and 5 cm side. What is the ratio of the total surface areas of the smaller cubes and the large cubes?
(a) 2:1 (b) 3:2
(c) 25:18 (d) 27:20

464. 60 kg of an alloy A is mixed with 100 kg of alloy B. If alloy A has lead and tin in the ratio 3:2 and alloy B has tin and copper in the ratio 1:4, then the amount of tin in the new alloy is
(a) 36 kg (b) 44 kg
(c) 53 kg (d) 80 kg

465. A cistern of capacity 8000 litres measures externally 3.3 m by 2.6 m by 1.1 m and its walls are 5 cm thick. The thickness of the bottom is
(a) 90 cm (b) 1 dm
(c) 1 m (d) 1.1 cm

466. If three numbers in the ratio 3:2:5 be such that the sum of their squares is 1862, the middle number will be
(a) 7 (b) 14
(c) 21 (d) 35

467. A sum of money is divided among A, B, C such that to each rupee A gets, E gets 65 paise and C gets 35 paise. If C's share is ₹ 28, the sum is
(a) ₹ 120 (b) ₹ 140
(c) ₹ 160 (d) ₹ 180

468. How many bricks, each measuring 25 cm × 11.25 cm × 6 cm, will be needed to build a wall of 8 m × 6 m × 22.5 cm?
(a) 5600 (b) 6000
(c) 6400 (d) 7200

469. ₹ 120 are divided among A, B, C such that A's share is ₹ 20 more than B's and ₹ 20 less than C's. What is B's share?
(a) ₹ 10 (b) ₹ 15
(c) ₹ 20 (d) ₹ 25

470. The present worth of ₹ 1404 due in two equal half-yearly instalments at 8% per annum simple interest is
(a) ₹ 1325 (b) ₹ 1300
(c) ₹ 1350 (d) ₹ 1500

471. A 5 cubic centimeter cube is painted on all its side. If it is sliced into 1 cubic centimeter cubes, how many 1 cubic

centimeter cubes will have exactly one of their sides painted?

(a) 9 (b) 61
(c) 98 (d) 54

472. A hollow iron pipe is 21 cm long and its external diameter is 8 cm. If the thickness of the pipe is 1 cm and iron weighs 8 g/cm^3, then the weight of the pipe is

(a) 3.6 kg (b) 3.696 kg
(c) 36 kg (d) 36.9 kg

473. The area of a square field is 24200 sq m. How long will a lady take to cross the field diagonally at the rate of 6.6 km/hr?

(a) 3 minutes
(b) 2 minutes
(c) 2.4 minutes
(d) 2 minutes 40 seconds

474. The circumference of the front wheel of a cart is 30 ft long and that of the back wheel is 36 ft long. What is the distance travelled by the cart, when the front wheel has done five more revolutions than the rear wheel?

(a) 20 ft (b) 25 ft
(c) 750 ft (d) 900 ft

475. A 5 cm cube is cut into as many 1 cm cubes as possible. What is the ratio of the surface area of the larger cube to that of the sum of the surface areas of the smaller cubes?

(a) 1:6 (b) 1:5
(c) 1:25 (d) 1:125

476. If the sides of a triangle measure 72, 75 and 21, what is the measure of its in radius?

(a) 37.5 (b) 24
(c) 9 (d) 15

477. If each interior angle of a regular polygon is 150 degrees, then it is

(a) Octagon (b) Decagon
(c) Dodecagon (d) Tetrahedron

478. The surface area of the three coterminous faces of a cuboid are 6, 15, 10 sq. cm respectively. Find the volume of the cuboid

(a) 30 (b) 20
(c) 40 (d) 35

479. Four horses are tethered at 4 corners of a square field of side 70 metres so that they just cannot reach one another. The area left ungrazed by the horses is

(a) 1050 sq. m (b) 3850 sq. m
(c) 950 sq. m (d) 1075 sq. m

480. If the diagonal and the area of a rectangle are 25 m and 168 m^2, what is the length of the rectangle?

(a) 17 m (b) 31 m
(c) 12 m (d) 24 m

481. A 4 cm cube is cut into 1 cm cubes. What is the percentage increase in the surface area after such cutting?

(a) 4% (b) 300%
(c) 75% (d) 400%

482. 252 can be expressed as a product of primes as

(a) $2 \times 2 \times 3 \times 3 \times 7$
(b) $2 \times 2 \times 2 \times 3 \times 7$
(c) $3 \times 3 \times 3 \times 3 \times 7$
(d) $2 \times 3 \times 3 \times 3 \times 7$

483. A tank is fitted with 8 pipes, some of them that fill the tank and others that are waste pipe meant to empty the tank. Each of the pipes that fill the tank can fill it in 8 hours, while each of those that empty the tank can empty it in 6 hours. If all the pipes are kept open when the tank is full, it will take exactly 6 hours for the tank to empty. How many of these are fill pipes?

(a) 2 (b) 4
(c) 6 (d) 5

484. A and B together have ₹ 1210. If $\frac{4}{15}$ of A's amount is equal to $\frac{2}{5}$ of B's amount, how much amount does B have?
(a) ₹ 460 (b) ₹ 484
(c) ₹ 550 (d) ₹ 664

485. Pipe A fills a tank of 700 litres capacity at the rate of 40 litres a minute. Another pipe B fills the same tank at the rate of 30 litres a minute. A pipe at the bottom of the tank drains the tank at the rate of 20 litres a minute. If pipe A is kept open for a minute and then closed and pipe B is kept open for a minute and then closed and then pipe C is kept open for a minute and then closed and the cycle repeated, how long will it take for the empty tank to overflow?
(a) 42 minutes (b) 14 minutes
(c) 39 minutes (d) None of these

486. If ₹ 782 be divided into three parts, proportional to $\frac{1}{2}:\frac{2}{3}:\frac{3}{4}$, then the first part is
(a) ₹ 182 (b) ₹ 190
(c) ₹ 196 (d) ₹ 204

487. There are 12 pipes that are connected to a tank. Some of them are fill pipes and the others are drain pipes. Each of the fill pipes can fill the tank in 8 hours and each of the drain pipes can drain the tank completely in 6 hours. If all the fill pipes and drain pipes are kept open, an empty tank gets filled in 24 hours. How many of the 12 pipes are fill pipes?
(a) 6 (b) 8
(c) 7 (d) 5

488. A car travelling with $\frac{5}{7}$ of its actual speed covers 42 km in 1 hr 40 min 48 sec. Find the actual speed of the car.
(a) 18 km/hr (b) 25 km/hr
(c) 30 km/hr (d) 35 km/hr

489. Pipe A usually fills a tank in 2 hours. On account of a leak at the bottom of the tank, it takes pipe A 30 more minutes to fill the tank. How long will the leak take to empty a full tank if pipe A is shut?
(a) 2 hours 30 minutes
(b) 5 hours
(c) 4 hours
(d) 10 hours

490. A can lay railway track between two given stations in 16 days and B can do the same job in 12 days. With help of C, they did the job in 4 days only. Then, C alone can do the job in
(a) $9\frac{1}{3}$ days (b) $9\frac{1}{2}$ days
(c) $9\frac{5}{7}$ days (d) 10 days

491. There are 12 pipes attached to a tank. Some of them are fill pipes and some are drain pipes. Each of the fill pipes can fill the tank in 12 hours, while each of the drain pipes will take 24 hours to drain a full tank completely. If all the pipes are kept open when the tank was empty, it takes 2 hours for the tank to overflow. How many of these pipes are drain pipes?
(a) 6 (b) 11
(c) 4 (d) 7

492. The interest on ₹ 750 for 2 years is the same as the true discount on ₹ 960 due

2 years hence. If the rate of interest is the same in both cases, it is

(a) 12% (b) 14%
(c) 15% (d) 16¼%

493. When 26854 and 27584 are divided by a certain two digit prime number, the remainder obtained is 47. Which of the following choices is a possible value of the divisor?

(a) 61 (b) 71
(c) 73 (d) 89

494. Goods were bought for ₹ 600 and sold the same for ₹ 688.50 at a credit of 9 months and thus gaining 2%. The rate of interest per annum is

(a) $16\frac{2}{3}\%$ (b) $14\frac{1}{2}\%$
(c) $13\frac{1}{4}\%$ (d) 15%

495. How many times will the digit '0' appear between 1 and 10,000?

(a) 4000 (b) 4003
(c) 2893 (d) 3892

496. A does 80% of a work in 20 days. He then calls in B and they together finish the remaining work in 3 days. How long B alone would take to do the whole work?

(a) 23 days (b) 37 days
(c) 37½ days (d) 40 days

497. The sum of the first 100 numbers, 1 to 100 is divisible by

(a) 2, 4 and 8 (b) 2 and 4
(c) 2 only (d) All of these

498. The sum of five numbers is 290. The average of the first two numbers is 48.5 and the average of the last two numbers is 53.5. What is the third number?

(a) 72 (b) 84
(c) 96 (d) None of these

499. In a mixture of milk and water the proportion of water by weight was 75%. If in 60 gm of mixture 15 gm water was added, what would be the percentage of water? (Weight in gm)

(a) 75% (b) 88%
(c) 90% (d) None of these

500. In how many different ways can the letters of the word 'SMART' be arranged?

(a) 25 (b) 60
(c) 180 (d) None of these

501. What is the minimum number of square marbles required to tile a floor of length 5 metres 78 cm and width 3 metres 74 cm?

(a) 176 (b) 187
(c) 54043 (d) 748

502. If + means –, – means ×, × means ÷ and ÷ means +, then which of the following equations is not correct?

(a) $10 \times 5 - 2 \div 4 + 6 = 2$
(b) $7 - 15 \times 3 + 6 \div 4 = 33$
(c) $12 \times 4 + 5 \div 9 - 2 = 16$
(d) $14 \div 7 - 5 + 10 \times 2 = 45$

503. If A stands for +, B stands for –, C stands for ×, then what is the value of (10 C 4) A (4 C 4) B6 ?

(a) 60 (b) 56
(c) 50 (d) 46

504. On a School's Annual Day sweets were to be equally distributed amongst 112 children. But on that particular day, 32 children were absent. Thus the remaining children got 6 extra sweets. How many sweets was each child originally supposed to get?

(a) 24
(b) 18

(c) 15
(d) Cannot be determined

505. If + means +, × means −, ÷ means × and − means +, then 8 + 6 × 4 + 3 ÷ 4 = ?

(a) −12 (b) $\frac{-20}{3}$
(c) 12 (d) None of these

506. An order was placed for supply of carpet of breadth 3 metres, and the length of the carpet was 1.44 times of breadth. Subsequently the breadth and length were increased by 35 and 40 percent respectively. At the rate of ₹ 45 per square metre, what would be the increase in the cost of the carpet?

(a) ₹ 1020.60 (b) ₹ 398.80
(c) ₹ 437.40 (d) ₹ 583.20

507. If the numerator of a fraction is increased by 200% and the denominator is increased by 350%, the resultant fraction is $\frac{5}{12}$. What was the original fraction?

(a) $\frac{5}{9}$ (b) $\frac{5}{8}$
(c) $\frac{7}{12}$ (d) $\frac{11}{12}$

508. If × means ÷, − means x, ÷ means + and + means −, then (3 − 15 ÷ 19) × 8 + 6 = ?

(a) 8 (b) 4
(c) 2 (d) −1

509. The difference between $\frac{3}{4}$ of $\frac{4}{5}$ of a number and $\frac{1}{6}$ of $\frac{2}{5}$ of the same number is 648. What is the number?

(a) 1110 (b) 1215
(c) 1325 (d) 1440

510. If − means ÷, + means ×, ÷ means − and × means +, then which of the following equations is correct?

(a) 52 ÷ 4 + 5 × 8 − 2 = 36
(b) 43 × 7 ÷ 5 + 4 − 8 = 25
(c) 36 × 4 − 12 + 5 ÷ 3 = 420
(d) 36 − 12 × 6 ÷ 3 + 4 = 60

511. If + means ÷, × means +, ÷ means − and − means ×, then 16 + 4 × 8 ÷ 15 − 2 = ?

(a) 18 (b) 6
(c) 12 (d) None of these

512. Which one of the four interchanges in signs and numbers would make the given equation correct?

3 × 15 ÷ 7 = 35

(a) × and ÷, 3 and 7
(b) × and ÷, 15 and 7
(c) × and ÷, 3 and 15
(d) None of the above

513. If × means −, − means +, + means ÷ and ÷ means ×, then 15 − 4 × 10 + 2 ÷ 3 = ?

(a) 4 (b) 42
(c) 10 (d) None of these

514. Which one of the four interchanges in signs and numbers would make the given equation correct?

3 + 5 − 2 = 4

(a) + and −, 2 and 3
(b) + and −, 2 and 5
(c) + and −, 3 and 5
(d) None of the above

515. If A stands for ÷, B stands for ×, C stands for + and D stands for −, then

15 A 3 C 9 B 3 D 5 = ?

(a) 25 (b) 22
(c) 27 (d) None of these

ANSWERS

1. (a)	2. (b)	3. (b)	4. (b)	5. (d)	6. (a)
7. (b)	8. (c)	9. (c)	10. (d)	11. (a)	12. (d)
13. (c)	14. (d)	15. (c)	16. (a)	17. (b)	18. (d)
19. (d)	20. (c)	21. (a)	22. (b)	23. (c)	24. (b)
25. (d)	26. (a)	27. (d)	28. (a)	29. (a)	30. (a)
31. (b)	32. (b)	33. (b)	34. (b)	35. (b)	36. (b)
37. (c)	38. (b)	39. (c)	40. (b)	41. (a)	42. (c)
43. (c)	44. (d)	45. (a)	46. (b)	47. (a)	48. (a)
49. (d)	50. (b)	51. (b)	52. (a)	53. (a)	54. (b)
55. (c)	56. (b)	57. (c)	58. (a)	59. (a)	60. (c)
61. (c)	62. (a)	63. (a)	64. (a)	65. (a)	66. (d)
67. (c)	68. (c)	69. (d)	70. (c)	71. (c)	72. (d)
73. (b)	74. (b)	75. (a)	76. (a)	77. (b)	78. (b)
79. (a)	80. (d)	81. (b)	82. (c)	83. (c)	84. (d)
85. (d)	86. (a)	87. (c)	88. (a)	89. (d)	90. (c)
91. (b)	92. (a)	93. (b)	94. (b)	95. (c)	96. (c)
97. (d)	98. (a)	99. (d)	100. (b)	101. (a)	102. (c)
103. (b)	104. (b)	105. (a)	106. (b)	107. (d)	108. (a)
109. (b)	110. (c)	111. (d)	112. (a)	113. (c)	114. (b)
115. (a)	116. (b)	117. (c)	118. (d)	119. (a)	120. (c)
121. (a)	122. (b)	123. (c)	124. (c)	125. (d)	126. (d)
127. (a)	128. (d)	129. (b)	130. (b)	131. (a)	132. (c)
133. (b)	134. (d)	135. (c)	136. (d)	137. (a)	138. (c)
139. (a)	140. (a)	141. (b)	142. (a)	143. (a)	144. (d)
145. (d)	146. (b)	147. (c)	148. (c)	149. (b)	150. (a)
151. (b)	152. (a)	153. (a)	154. (d)	155. (b)	156. (a)
157. (c)	158. (d)	159. (c)	160. (a)	161. (d)	162. (a)
163. (d)	164. (d)	165. (c)	166. (c)	167. (c)	168. (b)
169. (a)	170. (a)	171. (d)	172. (a)	173. (b)	174. (c)
175. (d)	176. (b)	177. (a)	178. (b)	179. (c)	180. (c)
181. (a)	182. (b)	183. (c)	184. (b)	185. (b)	186. (d)
187. (a)	188. (c)	189. (a)	190. (d)	191. (d)	192. (b)
193. (c)	194. (c)	195. (d)	196. (b)	197. (d)	198. (b)

199. (a) 200. (a) 201. (b) 202. (d) 203. (c) 204. (d)
205. (c) 206. (a) 207. (a) 208. (d) 209. (c) 210. (c)
211. (b) 212. (b) 213. (c) 214. (a) 215. (d) 216. (c)
217. (c) 218. (a) 219. (c) 220. (b) 221. (d) 222. (c)
223. (c) 224. (a) 225. (c) 226. (b) 227. (c) 228. (b)
229. (a) 230. (c) 231. (a) 232. (b) 233. (d) 234. (d)
235. (a) 236. (a) 237. (b) 238. (b) 239. (d) 240. (c)
241. (d) 242. (d) 243. (c) 244. (a) 245. (b) 246. (c)
247. (c) 248. (c) 249. (d) 250. (c) 251. (a) 252. (a)
253. (d) 254. (c) 255. (c) 256. (c) 257. (b) 258. (c)
259. (a) 260. (c) 261. (b) 262. (a) 263. (d) 264. (d)
265. (d) 266. (b) 267. (a) 268. (b) 269. (c) 270. (d)
271. (a) 272. (b) 273. (d) 274. (c) 275. (a) 276. (a)
277. (b) 278. (c) 279. (b) 280. (d) 281. (c) 282. (b)
283. (a) 284. (c) 285. (a) 286. (a) 287. (a) 288. (b)
289. (b) 290. (c) 291. (b) 292. (c) 293. (d) 294. (b)
295. (a) 296. (c) 297. (a) 298. (d) 299. (a) 300. (d)
301. (b) 302. (d) 303. (c) 304. (c) 305. (a) 306. (a)
307. (d) 308. (b) 309. (a) 310. (d) 311. (b) 312. (b)
313. (d) 314. (c) 315. (c) 316. (b) 317. (b) 318. (b)
319. (b) 320. (d) 321. (a) 322. (c) 323. (d) 324. (a)
325. (c) 326. (c) 327. (b) 328. (a) 329. (a) 330. (d)
331. (c) 332. (c) 333. (c) 334. (b) 335. (c) 336. (c)
337. (d) 338. (c) 339. (c) 340. (c) 341. (b) 342. (b)
343. (b) 344. (d) 345. (c) 346. (b) 347. (d) 348. (d)
349. (b) 350. (c) 351. (a) 352. (d) 353. (b) 354. (c)
355. (b) 356. (a) 357. (c) 358. (b) 359. (a) 360. (b)
361. (b) 362. (b) 363. (b) 364. (b) 365. (b) 366. (c)
367. (a) 368. (d) 369. (c) 370. (d) 371. (d) 372. (c)
373. (c) 374. (a) 375. (c) 376. (c) 377. (b) 378. (b)
379. (c) 380. (c) 381. (b) 382. (d) 383. (b) 384. (a)
385. (b) 386. (d) 387. (c) 388. (b) 389. (c) 390. (a)
391. (c) 392. (d) 393. (a) 394. (a) 395. (a) 396. (c)
397. (c) 398. (a) 399. (d) 400. (b) 401. (b) 402. (a)

403. (b)	404. (d)	405. (c)	406. (b)	407. (c)	408. (a)
409. (b)	410. (a)	411. (b)	412. (c)	413. (c)	414. (c)
415. (b)	416. (c)	417. (c)	418. (c)	419. (c)	420. (d)
421. (a)	422. (c)	423. (c)	424. (c)	425. (a)	426. (c)
427. (c)	428. (b)	429. (a)	430. (b)	431. (d)	432. (d)
433. (a)	434. (c)	435. (c)	436. (b)	437. (a)	438. (b)
439. (a)	440. (b)	441. (b)	442. (a)	443. (a)	444. (b)
445. (b)	446. (c)	447. (b)	448. (a)	449. (b)	450. (c)
451. (d)	452. (c)	453. (b)	454. (b)	455. (c)	456. (d)
457. (b)	458. (a)	459. (b)	460. (b)	461. (c)	462. (c)
463. (c)	464. (b)	465. (b)	466. (b)	467. (c)	468. (c)
469. (c)	470. (a)	471. (d)	472. (b)	473. (b)	474. (d)
475. (b)	476. (c)	477. (c)	478. (a)	479. (a)	480. (d)
481. (b)	482. (a)	483. (b)	484. (b)	485. (d)	486. (d)
487. (c)	488. (d)	489. (d)	490. (c)	491. (c)	492. (b)
493. (c)	494. (a)	495. (c)	496. (c)	497. (c)	498. (d)
499. (d)	500. (d)	501. (b)	502. (d)	503. (c)	504. (c)
505. (b)	506. (c)	507. (b)	508. (c)	509. (b)	510. (a)
511. (d)	512. (c)	513. (a)	514. (c)	515. (c)	

6

Logical Reasoning

1. Which of the following figures correctly represents the relation between Languages, English and Hindi?

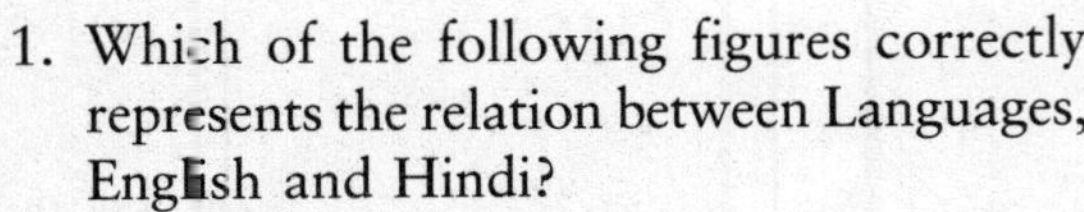

2. Which of the following diagrams indicates the best relation between Judges, Thieves and Criminals?

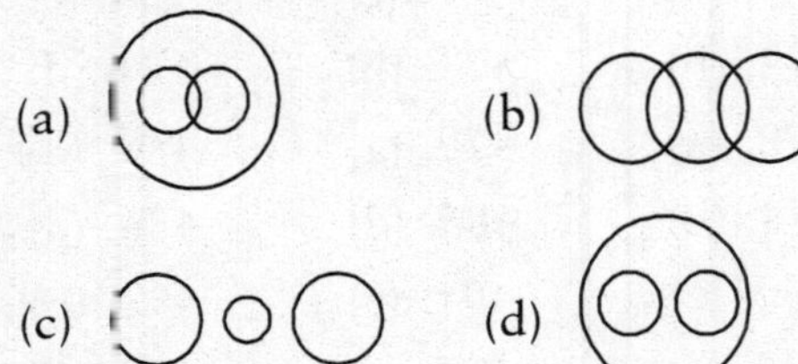

3. Which one of the following Venn diagrams correctly illustrates the relationship among the classes?

   Carrot, Food, Vegetables

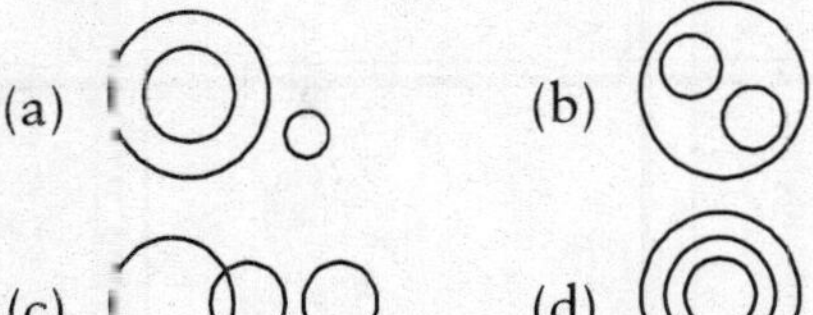

Direction: (4-7) Read the following statements and identify the letters of the region asked in each question.

There are three interlocking circles, I, S and P where circle I stands for Indians, circles S for Scientists and circle P for Politicians. Different regions of the figure are lettered from a to g.

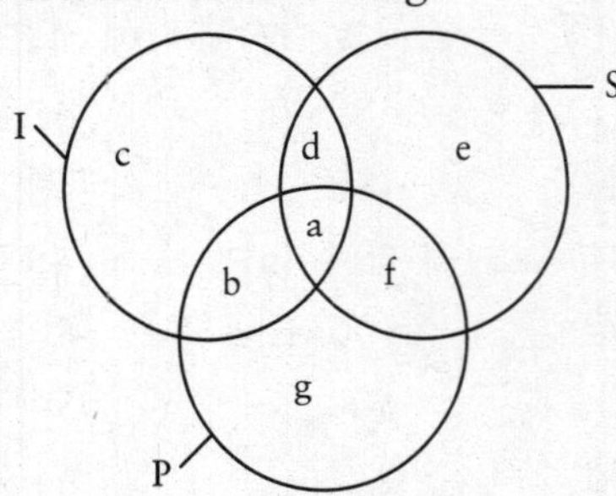

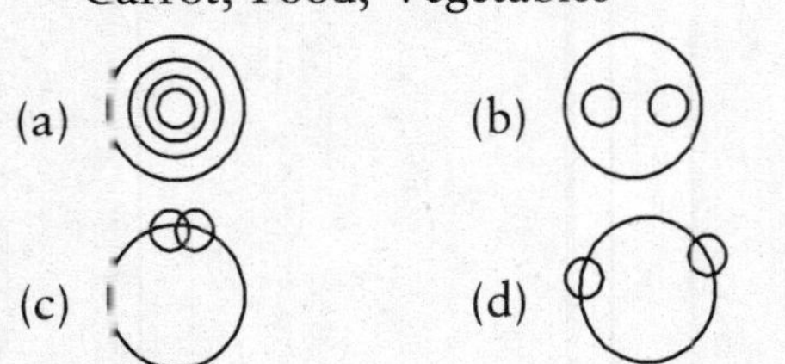

4. The region which represents the Indians who are politicians but not scientists.
   (a) a (b) g
   (c) f (d) b
5. The region which represents the scientists who are Indians but not politicians.
   (a) d (b) f
   (c) a (d) b
6. The region which represents Non-Indian scientists who are politicians.
   (a) b (b) f
   (c) d (d) a
7. The region which represents Indians who are neither scientists nor politicians.
   (a) c (b) g
   (c) e (d) a

Direction: (8-12) Each question below contains three groups of things. You are to choose from the following four numbered diagrams, the diagram that depicts the correct relationship among the three groups of things in each question.

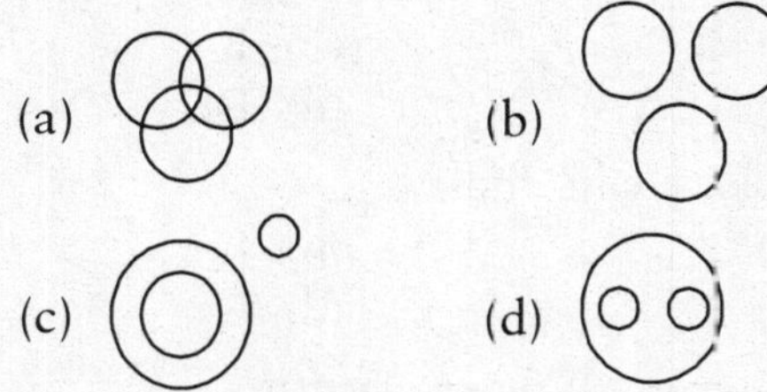

8. Vegetable, Fruit, Brinjal
9. Door, Window, House
10. Honest, Intelligent, Poor
11. Car, Train, Automobile
12. Zinc, Copper, Iron

13. The circles represent girls who wear different types of clothes indicated against them. Identify the girls who wear frock, jeans as well as the churidar pyjama.

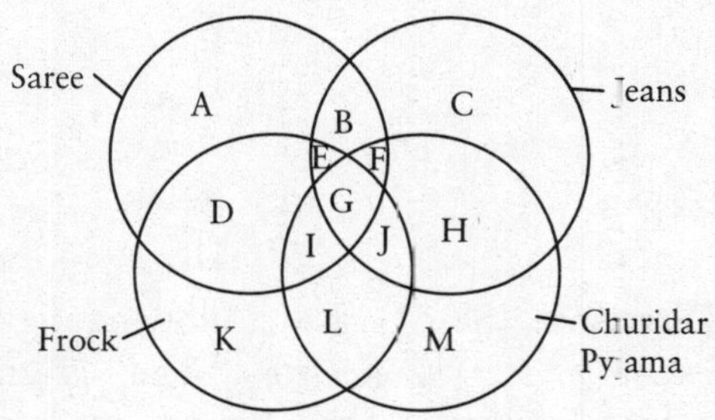

(a) L (b) J
(c) F (d) H

Direction: (14-22) Out of the four alternatives in each of the following questions, three alternatives are such that the three words in each are related among themselves in one of the five ways represented by (a), (b), (c), (d) and (e) below. And one of the alternatives represents a relationship which is not represented by any of the figures given below. Identify that alternative.

(a)  (b) 

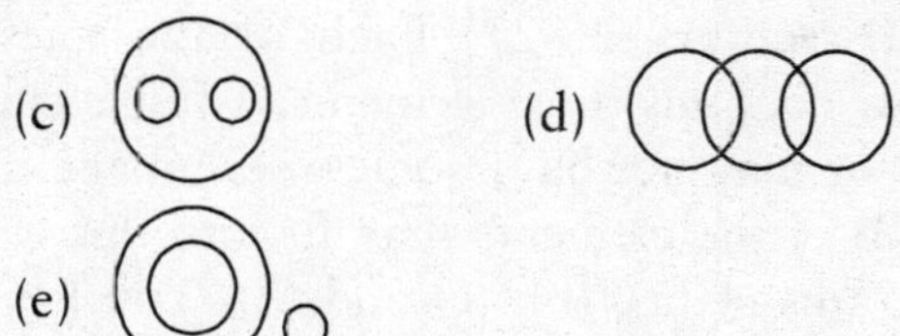

14. (a) Army, General, Colonel
(b) Boy, Student, Player
(c) Painter, Scholar, Table
(d) Man, Typist, Peon
15. (a) Hen, Dog, Cat
(b) Body, Ear, Mouth
(c) Bed, Ward, Nurse
(d) Tiger, Animal, Carnivorous
16. (a) Mineral, Iron, Copper
(b) Dean, Painter, Singer
(c) Seed, Leaf, Root
(d) Piston, Engine, Wheel
17. (a) Director, Engineer, Musician
(b) Apple, Orange, Mango
(c) Fruit, Mango, Grass
(d) Oxygen, Air, Water
18. (a) Bed, Ward, Hospital
(b) Boy, Girl, Player
(c) Copper, Zinc, Iron
(d) Book, Page, Paragraph
19. (a) Atmosphere, Air, Oxygen
(b) Boy, Girl, Student
(c) Man, Worker, Garden
(d) Animal, Dog, Cat
20. (a) Body, Hand, Finger
(b) Mammal, Nurse, Woman
(c) Cereal, Wheat, Rice
(d) Males, Cousins, Nephews
21. (a) Star, Sun, Mars
(b) Professor, Scholar, Politician
(c) Nurse, Doctor, Compounder
(d) Swimmer, Carpenter, Singer
22. (a) Animal, Mammal, Cow
(b) Colour, Cloth, Merchant
(c) Colour, Red, Blue
(d) Male, Horse, Mare

Direction: (23-27) Each of the question below contains three elements. These elements may or may not have some interlinkage. Each group of the elements may fit into one of the diagrams at (a), (b), (c) and (d). You have to indicate groups of elements in each of the questions correctly fit into which of the diagrams.

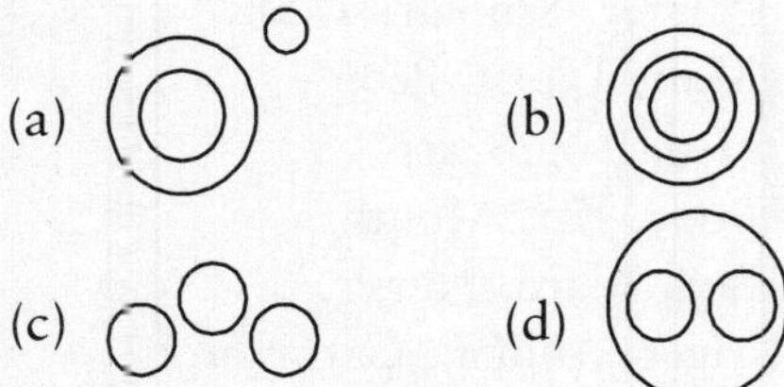

23. Pencil, Stationery, Jeep
24. Factory, Machinery, Product
25. Vegetable, Brinjal, Cauliflower
26. Honesty, Intelligence, Aptitude
27. Truck, Ship, Rail

Direction: (28-37) Each of the questions given below contains three groups of things. You have to choose from the following five numbered diagrams, the diagram that depicts the correct relationship among the three groups of things in each question.

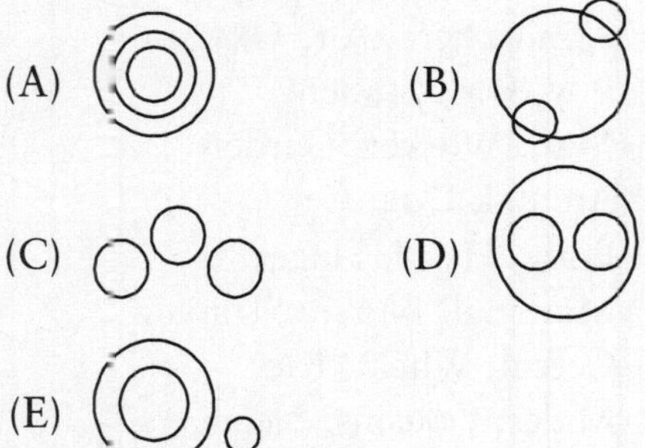

28. Pop, Songs, Classical
    (a) C (b) E
    (c) D (d) B
29. Maize, Sugarcane, Crops
    (a) A (b) B
    (c) C (d) D
30. Birds, Owls, Elephants
    (a) A (b) B
    (c) C (d) E
31. Apples, Mangoes, Oranges
    (a) A (b) B
    (c) C (d) D
32. Asia, Delhi, India
    (a) A (b) B
    (c) C (d) D
33. Lawyers, Women, Doctors
    (a) A (b) B
    (c) C (d) D
34. Brinjal, Glass, Spoon
    (a) A (b) B
    (c) C (d) D
35. Pen, Stationery, Powder
    (a) A (b) B
    (c) C (d) E
36. Vehicle, Car, Jeep
    (a) A (b) B
    (c) C (d) D
37. Year, Month, Day
    (a) A (b) B
    (c) C (d) D

Direction: (38-41) The following figures represent a set of persons. The Triangle represents Sportsmen, the Square represents Students, the Circle represents Professors and the Ellipse represents Artists.

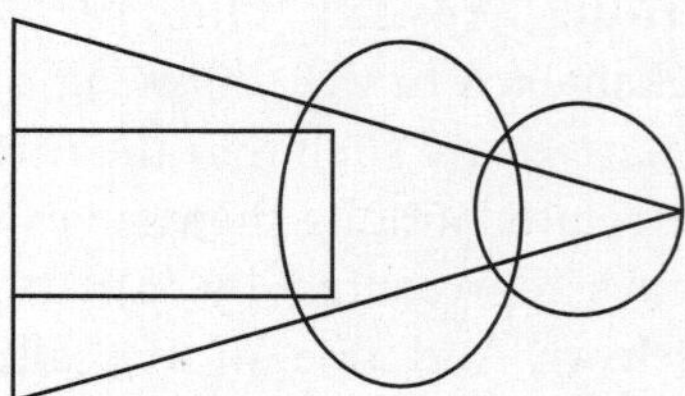

38. Looking at the figure we can conclude that
    (a) All Sports Students are Professors
    (b) All Sportsmen are Professors

(c) All Professor Artists are Sportsmen
(d) Some Professor Artists are Sportsmen

39. According to the Figure we can say that
(a) Artists are not Professors
(b) Students are not Professors
(c) Some Students are Artists
(d) Some Artists are Sportsmen.

40. On the basis of this figure it can be concluded that
(a) Some of the Sportsmen Artists are Professors
(b) None of the Sportsmen Artists is a Student
(c) None of the Sportsmen Artists is a Professor
(d) None of the above statements is correct.

41. According to the given figure we can say that
(a) Some of the Professors are Artists too
(b) Some of the Sportsmen are Professors
(c) Some of the Sportsmen are not Professors
(d) Some of the Professor Artists are Students too

Direction: (42-45) Study the following diagram in which the rectangle stands for illiterate, the square stands for employed, the triangle stands for farmers and the circle stands for backward.

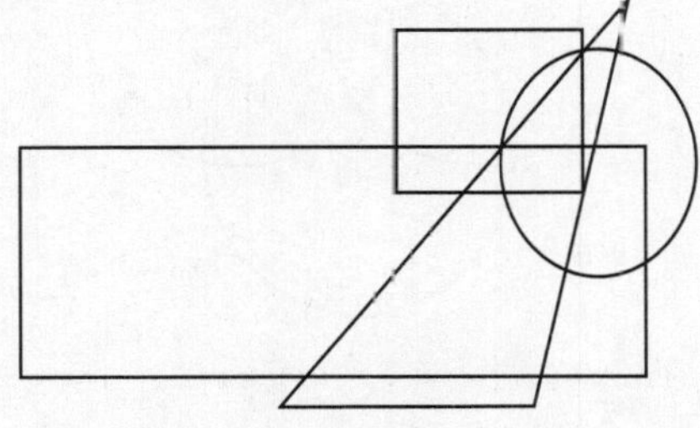

42. In the above diagram which of the following statements is true?
(a) All illiterate farmers who are employed are backward.
(b) All illiterate non-farmers are backward.
(c) Some farmers who are backward are unemployed.
(d) All non-farmers who are literate are employed or backward but not both.

43. In the above diagram which of the following statements is not true?
(a) Some unemployed farmers are backward and illiterate.
(b) All farmers who are employed are either backward or illiterate or both.
(c) All backward persons who are not illiterate are farmers or employed or both.
(d) All backward persons who are not illiterate are neither farmers nor employed.

44. In the above diagram which of the following statements is true?
(a) All unemployed non-farmers are either backward or literate.
(b) All employed farmers are not illiterate.
(c) All farmers who are unemployed are either backward or illiterate.
(d) Some non-farmers who are employed are either illiterate or backward or both.

45. In the above diagram, which one of the following statements is true?
(a) All illiterate persons who are employed are not backward.
(b) All farmers who are illiterate are either unemployed or backward.
(c) All backward persons who are farmers are employed.
(d) Some unemployed farmers are illiterate.

Direction: (46-50) The following figure represents a set of persons: the triangle represents educated persons, the rectangle represents policemen, the circle represents road tax-payers and ellipse represents shopkeepers.

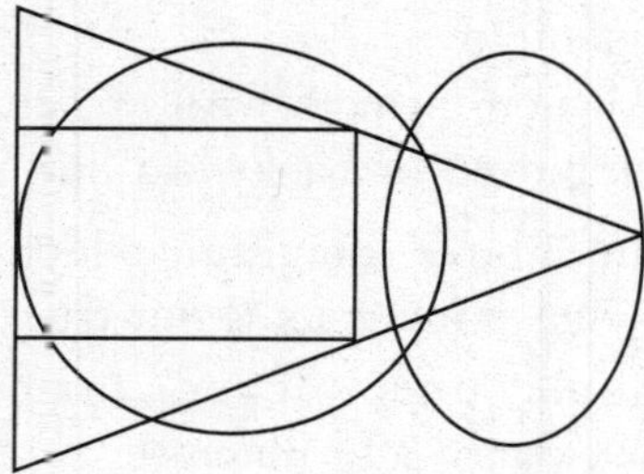

46. Looking at the figure we can conclude that
    (a) All educated shopkeepers pay road tax.
    (b) All road tax paying policemen are educated.
    (c) All educated policemen pay road tax.
    (d) All road tax paying shopkeepers are educated.
47. On the basis of this figure, it can be concluded that
    (a) None of the educated shopkeepers is a policeman though an uneducated policeman is a shopkeeper.
    (b) Some of the educated shopkeepers are road taxpayers even though they discharge duties of a policeman.
    (c) Some of the educated policemen who pay road tax are sharing profits with uneducated shopkeepers.
    (d) None of the educated shopkeepers is a policeman nor an educated policeman is a shopkeeper.
48. According to this figure, we can say that
    (a) Policemen do not pay road tax.
    (b) Shopkeepers do not pay road tax.
    (c) Some shopkeepers are educated.
    (d) Some policemen are shopkeepers.
49. According to the given figure, we can say that
    (a) Some of the road tax payee policemen are shopkeepers too.
    (b) Some of the educated shopkeepers pay road tax.
    (c) Some of the road taxpayee shop-keepers are policemen too.
    (d) Some of the uneducated policemen pay road tax.
50. Looking at the given figure we can say that
    (a) Some persons who are neither shopkeepers nor policemen are educated.
    (b) Some persons who are either shopkeepers or policemen pay road tax, though uneducated.
    (c) Some persons who are either shopkeepers or policemen pay road tax and are also educated.
    (d) All the above statements are correct.
51. A survey was conducted on a sample of 1000 persons with reference to their knowledge of English, French and German. The result is presented in the Venn diagram. The ratio of the number of persons who do not know the three languages to those who know all the three languages is

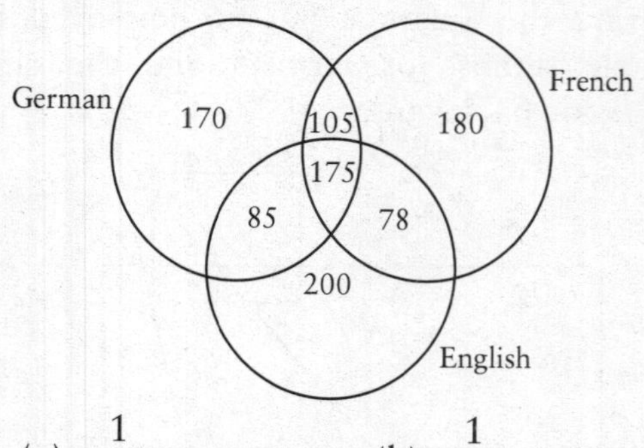

(a) $\frac{1}{27}$ (b) $\frac{1}{25}$

(c) $\frac{7}{550}$ (d) $\frac{175}{1000}$

Direction: (52-56) In the following diagram, numbers are given in the different sections of the diagram. On the basis of these, answer the questions given below.

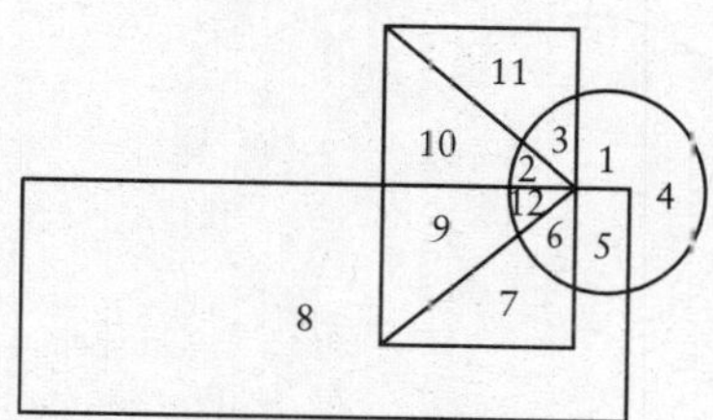

Rectangle - males

Circle - urban

Square - educated

Triangle - civil servants

52. Urban, educated, male, civil servants are represented by
    (a) 3 (b) 2
    (c) 12 (d) 8
53. Non-urban, non-civil servants, educated males are represented by
    (a) 6 (b) 7
    (c) 8 (d) 1
54. Rural, educated, non-male, civil servants are represented by
    (a) 9 (b) 8
    (c) 7 (d) 10
55. Urban, educated, female, civil servants are represented by
    (a) 1 (b) 5
    (c) 2 (d) 9
56. Non-civil servants, non-educated, urban males are represented by
    (a) 1 (b) 5
    (c) 2 (d) 4

Direction: (57-62) These questions are based on the following diagram in which the triangle represents female graduates, small circle represents self-employed females and the big circle represents self-employed females with bank loan facility. Numbers are shown in the different sections of the diagram. On the basis of these numbers, answer the following questions.

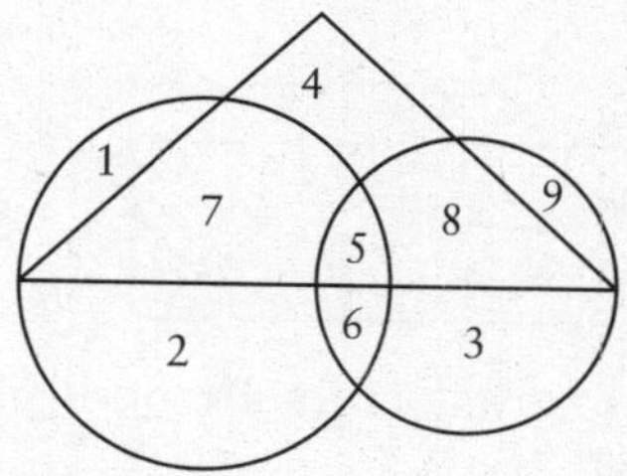

57. How many self-employed female graduates are with bank loan facility?
    (a) 20 (b) 12
    (c) 5 (d) 7
58. How many non-graduate self-employed females are with bank loan facility?
    (a) 3 (b) 8
    (c) 9 (d) 12
59. How many female graduates are not self-employed?
    (a) 4 (b) 15
    (c) 12 (d) 10
60. How many female graduates are self-employed?
    (a) 12 (b) 15
    (c) 20 (d) 13
61. How many non-graduate females are self-employed?
    (a) 12 (b) 9
    (c) 11 (d) 21
62. In a survey, 30% of the people surveyed owned a cellular telephone and 75% owned a personal computer. If 25% owned both a cellular telephone and a personal computer, the percentage of people who owned a cellular telephone or a personal computer or both is
    (a) 70% (b) 80%
    (c) 60% (d) 75%

Direction: (63-67) Study the following figure carefully and answer following questions. The triangle represents doctors. The circle represents players and the rectangle represents artists.

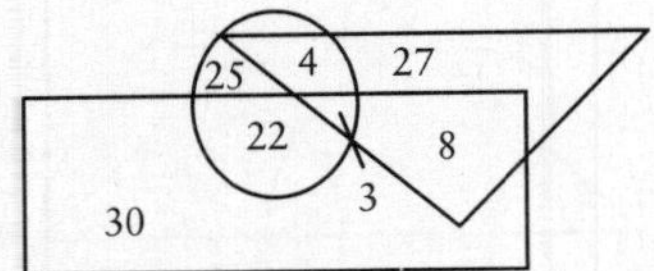

63. How many doctors are both players and artists?
(a) 4 (b) 11
(c) 3 (d) 8

64. How many artists are players?
(a) 30 (b) 25
(c) 22 (d) 29

65. How many artists are neither players nor doctors?
(a) 25 (b) 29
(c) 22 (d) None of these

66. How many doctors are neither players nor artists?
(a) 30 (b) 8
(c) 27 (d) None of these

67. How many players are neither artists nor doctors?
(a) 4 (b) 8
(c) 22 (d) None of these

68. In the given diagram circle represents strong men, square represents tall men, triangle represents army officers. Which region represents army officers who are tall but not strong?

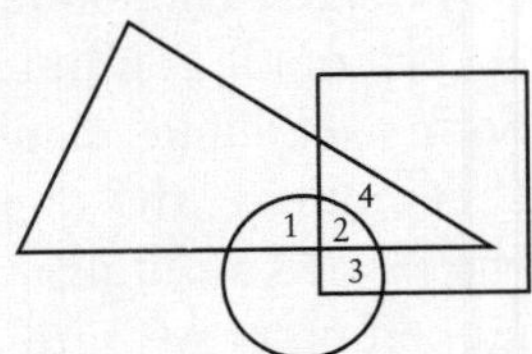

(a) 1 (b) 3
(c) 4 (d) 2

69. Which number indicates good speakers who are neither postgraduates nor doctors?

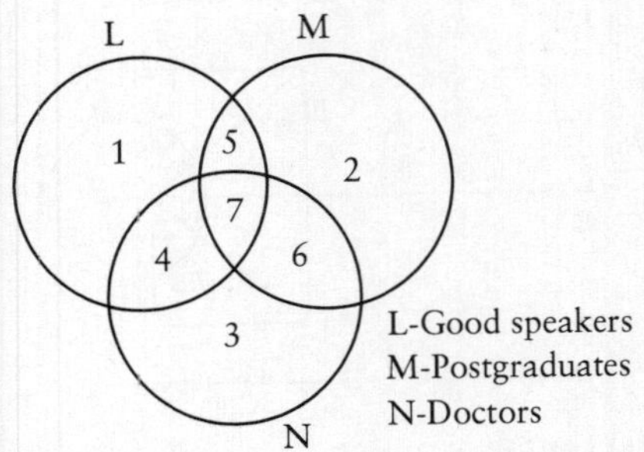

(a) 6 (b) 2
(c) 5 (d) 1

70. Find the urban, corrupt politicians in the following diagram.

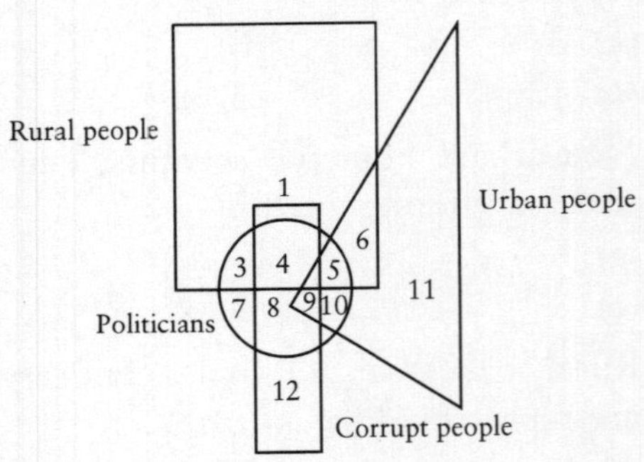

(a) 4 (b) 10
(c) 9 (d) 5

71. In the following diagram, R represents businessmen, S represents rich men, T represents honest men. Which number will represent honest rich men?

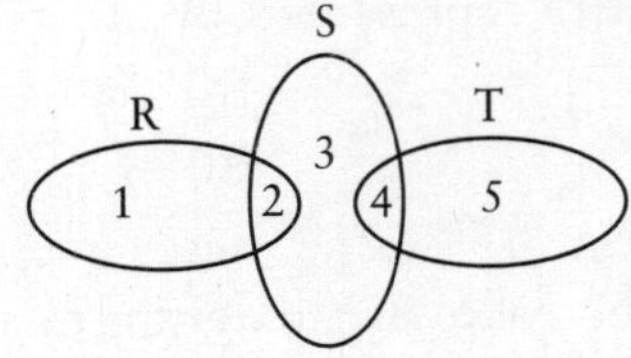

(a) 3 (b) 2
(c) 5 (d) 4

Direction: (72-75) These questions are based on the diagram given below. In the diagram, the triangle stands for graduates, square for membership of professional organisations and the circle for membership of social organisations. Read each statement and find out the appropriate number(s) to represent the people covered by statement.

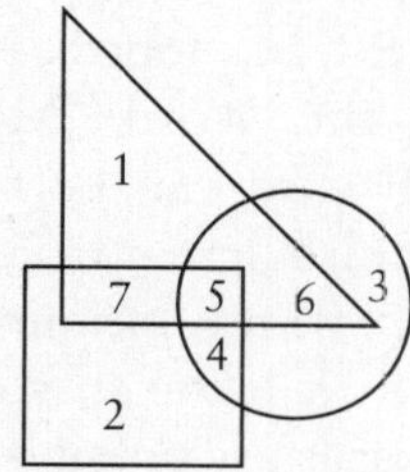

72. Number of graduates in social organisations is represented by
(a) 1 (b) 5
(c) 6 (d) 5 and 6

73. Number of graduates in social organisations only, is represented by
(a) 3 (b) 4
(c) 5 (d) 6

74. Number of graduates in professional organisations is represented by
(a) 5 and 7 (b) 4, 5 and 6
(c) 6 and 7 (d) 5, 6 and 7

75. Number of non-graduates in social and professional organisations is represented by
(a) 2 (b) 3
(c) 4 (d) 6

76. If the first and sixth letters of the word 'CREDENTIALS' were interchanged, also the second and seventh letters and so on, which of the following would be 8th letter from your right?
(a) A (b) T
(c) D (d) None of these

77. If the first and 11th letters of the word 'DISTURBANCE' were interchanged, also the second and 10th letters and so on, which would be the 7th letter from your right?
(a) R (b) B
(c) A (d) None of these

78. If the following series is written in reverse order, then which will be 12th letter to the right of 10th letter from your right?
ABCDEFGHIJKLMNOPQRSTUVW XYZ
(a) X (b) U
(c) V (d) None of these

79. If the first and fifth letters of the word 'BILINGUAL' were interchanged, also the second and sixth letters, and so on, which of the following would be 7th letter from your right?
(a) A (b) I
(c) G (d) None of these

80. If the first and second letters of the word 'DEHYDRATION' were interchanged, also the third and fourth letters and so on, which of the following would be the 3rd letter to the right of 7th letter from your left?
(a) N (b) H
(c) I (d) None of these

81. If in the following series the letters at the even places are denoted by lower letters as b for B, d for D and so on then how will the next month of November be written?
ABCDEFGHIJKLMNOPQRSTUVW XYZ
(a) DECEMbEr (b) deCeMber
(c) dEcEMbER (d) dECEMbEr

82. If the first and 7th letters of the word 'GRAPHOLOGIST' were interchanged,

also the second and 9th letters, third and 11th letters, fourth and 6th letters and fifth and 12th letters, which would be 6th letter to the right of the 10th letter from your left?

(a) S (b) T
(c) G (d) None of these

83. If in the following series all the letters at the even places are deleted and the order of deleting begins from B, then which will be the third letter to the left of 5th letter from your right?

ABCDEFGHIJKLMNOPQRSTUVW XYZ

(a) I (b) W
(c) M (d) None of these

84. If with the first, third, fifth and 9th letters of the word 'IGNORANCE' a meaningful word can be formed, which would be the third letter of that word ? If no meaningful word is possible then X is the answer and if more than one, words are possible then M is the answer.

(a) I (b) E
(c) M (d) None of these

85. If the following series is written in reverse order and then all the vowels are deleted, which will be the 8th letter from the right in the new series?

ABCDEFGHIJKLMNOPQRSTUVW XYZ

(a) L (b) H
(c) K (d) J

86. If with the first, fourth, fifth and eighth letters of the word "LAUREATE" a meaningful word can be formed, which would be the first letter of that word? If no meaningful word is possible then X is the answer and if more than one, words are possible then M is the answer.

(a) X (b) E
(c) M (d) None of these

87. If in the following series all the letters at the odd places are deleted then which will be the 8th letter to the right of 7th letter from your right in the new series?

ABCDEFGHIJKLMNOPQRSTUVW XYZ

(a) X (b) D
(c) A (d) None of these

88. If with the first, fourth, fifth and 8th letters of the word 'MIGRAINE' a meaningful word can be formed, which would be third letter from the right of that word? If no meaningful word is possible then X is the answer and if more than one words are possible than M is the answer.

(a) X (b) A
(c) R (d) M

89. If the following series is written in reverse order then which will be 17th letter to the right of 10th letter from your left?

ABCDEFGHIJKLMNOPQRSTUVW XYZ

(a) Z (b) Y
(c) H (d) None of these

90. If with the second, fourth, sixth and 10th letters of the word 'SHOPKEEPER' a meaningful word can be formed, which would be the last letter of that word? If no meaningful word is possible then 'X' is the answer and if more than one words can be formed then the answer is 'M'.

(a) M (b) X
(c) P (d) None of these

91. Which is the 3rd letter to the right of 5th letter from your left in the following series?

ABCDEFGHIJKLMNOPQRSTUVW XYZ

(a) B (b) H
(c) A (d) None of these

92. If with the first, fifth, eighth and 10th letters of the word 'HOMOGENEOUS' a meaningful word can be formed, which would be the first letter of that word? If no meaningful word can be formed then the answer is 'X' and if more than one words can be formed then 'M' is the answer.

(a) H (b) X
(c) M (d) None of these

93. In the following series which is the 9th letter to the left of 7th letter from your left?

ABCDEFGHIJKLMNOPQRSTUVW XYZ

(a) K (b) O
(c) P (d) None of these

94. If with the first, sixth, seventh, eighth and 10th letters of the word 'SYMPATHETIC a meaningful word can be formed which would be the middle letter of that word? If no meaningful word can be formed then 'X' is the answer and if more than one words are possible, then the answer is 'M'.

(a) X (b) M
(c) I (d) None of these

95. Two letters of the word 'SYNDROME' have as many letters between them in the word as in the alphabet. The letter which comes earlier in the alphabet is your answer. If no such pair is there, then your answer is 'X'.

(a) M (b) X
(c) N (d) None of these

96. Which is the 10th letter to the left of 15th letter from your right in the following series?

ABCDEFGHIJKLMNOPQRSTUVW XYZ

(a) U (b) B
(c) V (d) None of these

97. Which is the 7th letter to the right of 9th letter from your right in the following series?

ABCDEFGHIJKLMNOPQRSTUVW XYZ

(a) Y (b) L
(c) J (d) None of these

98. Two letters of the word 'YESTERDAY' have as many letters between them in the word as in the alphabet. The letter which comes earlier in the alphabet is your answer. If no such pair is there, then your answer will be 'X'.

(a) R (b) S
(c) X (d) M

99. Which is the 8th letter to the right of 6th letter from your right in the following series?

ABCDEFGHIJKLMNOPQRSTUVW XYZ

(a) O (b) D
(c) C (d) None of these

100. Which is the 17th letter to the left of 10th letter from your left in the following series?

ABCDEFGHIJKLMNOPQRSTUVW XYZ

(a) A (b) S
(c) B (d) None of these

Direction: Each of the following questions (101-115) consists of two sets of figures. Figures a, b, c and d constitute the Problem Set while figures 1, 2, 3, 4 and 5 constitute the Answer Set. There is a definite relationship between figures a and b. Establish a similar relationship between figures c and d by selecting a suitable figure from the Answer Set that would replace the question mark (?) in fig. (d).

101. Select a suitable figure from the Answer Figures that would replace the question mark (?).

Problem Figures: Answer Figures:

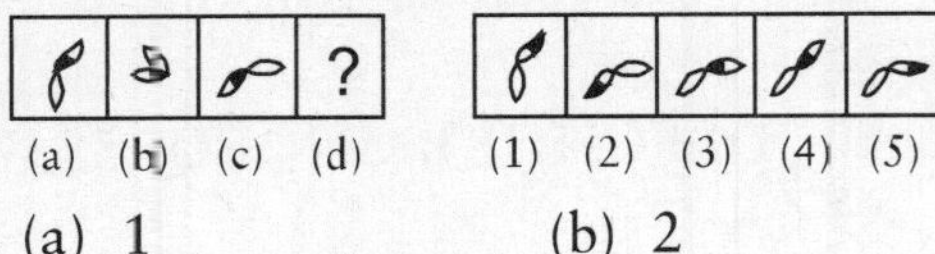

(a) 1
(b) 2
(c) 3
(d) 4
(e) 5

102. Select a suitable figure from the Answer Figures that would replace the question mark (?).

Problem Figures: Answer Figures:

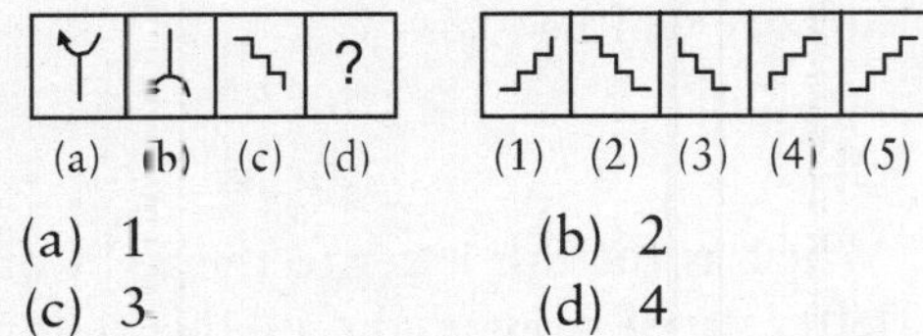

(a) 1
(b) 2
(c) 3
(d) 4
(e) 5

103. Select a suitable figure from the Answer Figures that would replace the question mark (?).

Problem Figures: Answer Figures:

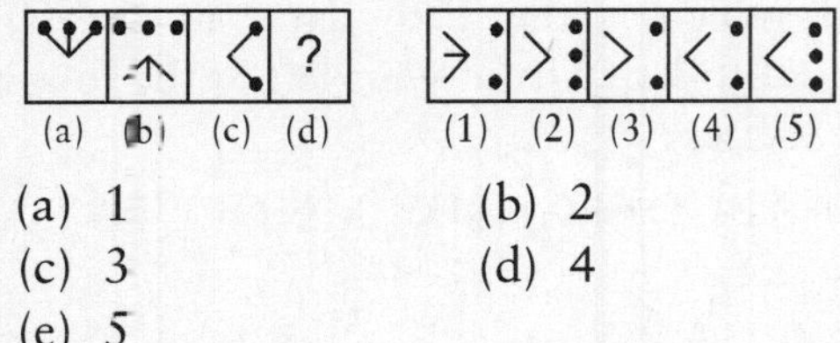

(a) 1
(b) 2
(c) 3
(d) 4
(e) 5

104. Select a suitable figure from the Answer Figures that would replace the question mark (?).

Problem Figures: Answer Figures:

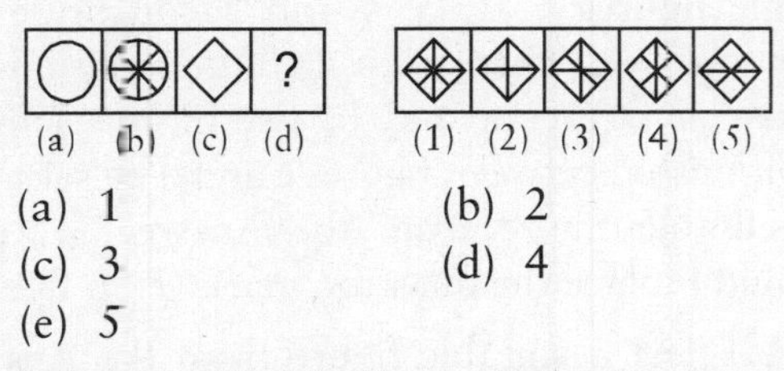

(a) 1
(b) 2
(c) 3
(d) 4
(e) 5

105. Select a suitable figure from the Answer Figures that would replace the question mark (?).

Problem Figures: Answer Figures:

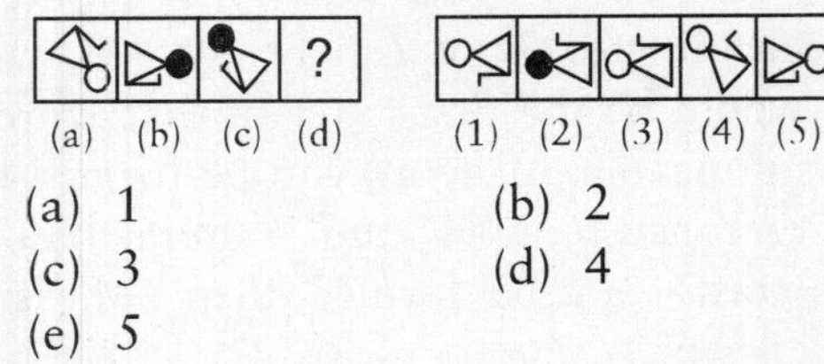

(a) 1
(b) 2
(c) 3
(d) 4
(e) 5

106. Select a suitable figure from the Answer Figures that would replace the question mark (?).

Problem Figures: Answer Figures:

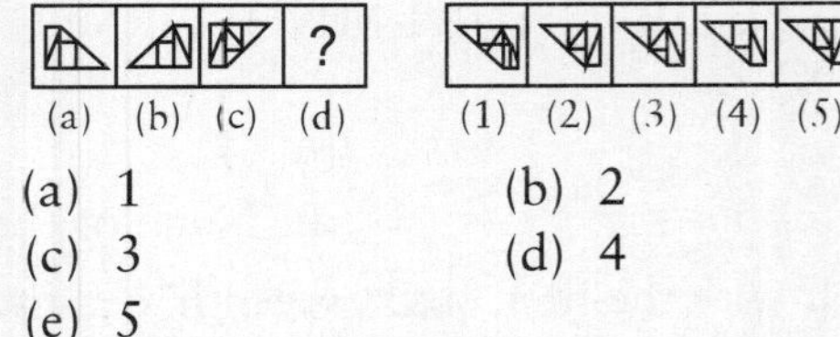

(a) 1
(b) 2
(c) 3
(d) 4
(e) 5

107. Select a suitable figure from the Answer Figures that would replace the question mark (?).

Problem Figures: Answer Figures:

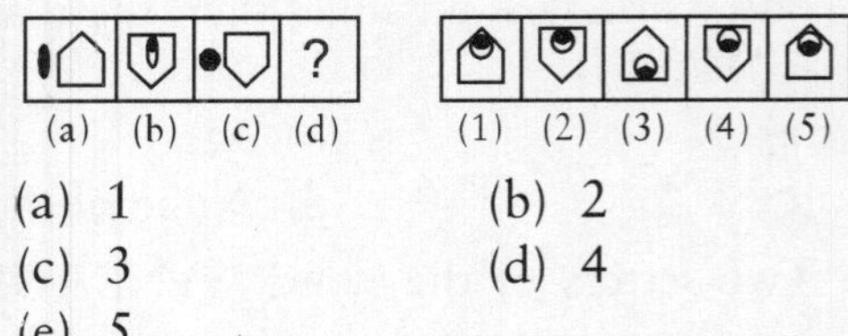

(a) 1
(b) 2
(c) 3
(d) 4
(e) 5

108. Select a suitable figure from the Answer Figures that would replace the question mark (?).

Problem Figures: Answer Figures:

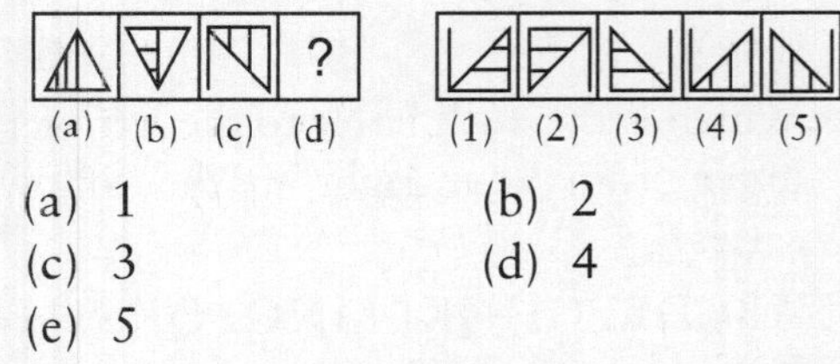

(a) 1
(b) 2
(c) 3
(d) 4
(e) 5

109. Select a suitable figure from the Answer Figures that would replace the question mark (?).

Problem Figures: Answer Figures:

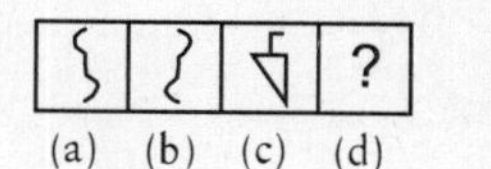

(a) (b) (c) (d) (1) (2) (3) (4) (5)

(a) 1 (b) 2
(c) 3 (d) 4
(e) 5

110. Select a suitable figure from the Answer Figures that would replace the question mark (?).

Problem Figures: Answer Figures:

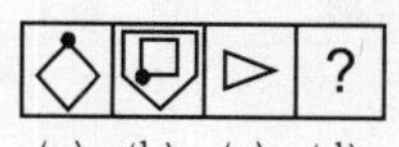

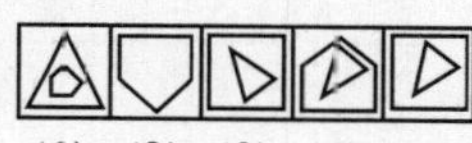

(a) (b) (c) (d) (1) (2) (3) (4) (5)

(a) 1 (b) 2
(c) 3 (d) 4
(e) 5

111. Select a suitable figure from the Answer Figures that would replace the question mark (?).

Problem Figures: Answer Figures:

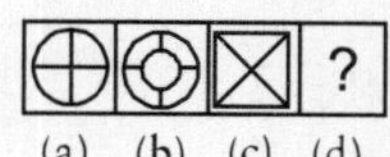

(a) (b) (c) (d) (1) (2) (3) (4) (5)

(a) 1 (b) 2
(c) 3 (d) 4
(e) 5

112. Select a suitable figure from the Answer Figures that would replace the question mark (?).

Problem Figures: Answer Figures:

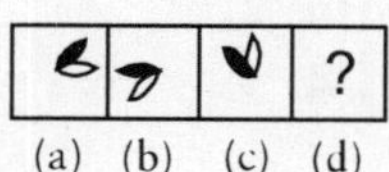

(a) (b) (c) (d) (1) (2) (3) (4) (5)

(a) 1 (b) 2
(c) 3 (d) 4
(e) 5

113. Select a suitable figure from the Answer Figures that would replace the question mark (?).

Problem Figures: Answer Figures:

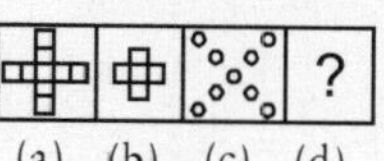

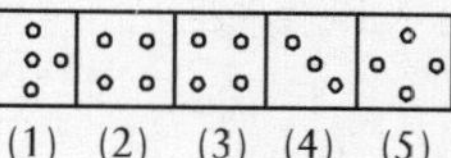

(a) (b) (c) (d) (1) (2) (3) (4) (5)

(a) 1 (b) 2
(c) 3 (d) 4
(e) 5

114. Select a suitable figure from the Answer Figures that would replace the question mark (?).

Problem Figures: Answer Figures:

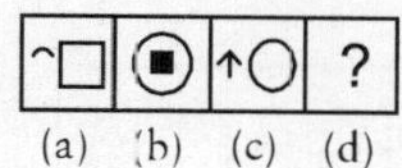

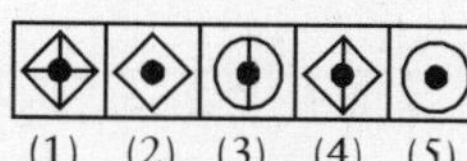

(a) (b) (c) (d) (1) (2) (3) (4) (5)

(a) 1 (b) 2
(c) 3 (d) 4
(e) 5

115. Select a suitable figure from the Answer Figures that would replace the question mark (?).

Problem Figures: Answer Figures:

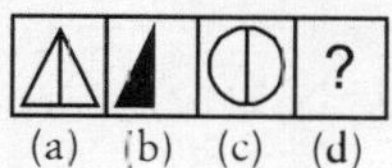

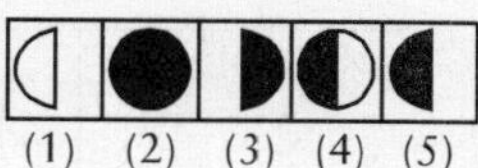

(a) (b) (c) (d) (1) (2) (3) (4) (5)

(a) 1 (b) 2
(c) 3 (d) 4
(e) 5

Direction: (116-129) in each problem, out of the five figures marked (1), (2), (3), (4) and (5), four are similar in a certain manner. However, one figure is not like the other four. Choose the figure which is different from the rest.

116. Choose the figure which is different from the rest.

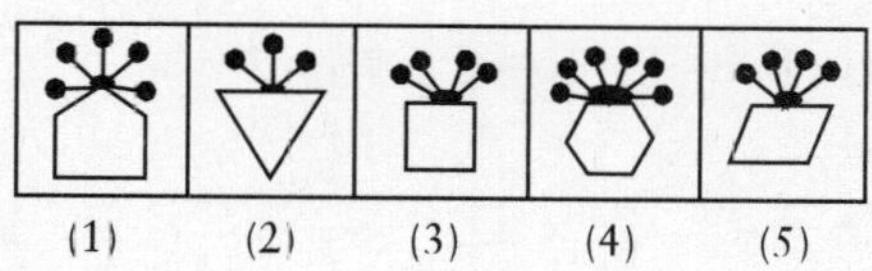

(1) (2) (3) (4) (5)

(a) 1 (b) 2
(c) 3 (d) 4
(e) 5

117. Choose the figure which is different from the rest.

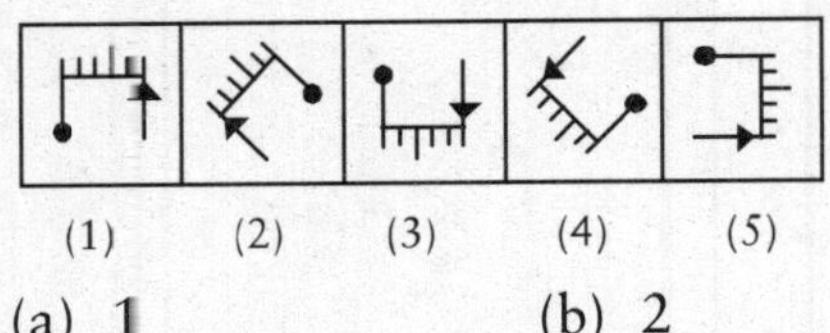

(1) (2) (3) (4) (5)

(a) 1 (b) 2
(c) 3 (d) 4
(e) 5

118. Choose the figure which is different from the rest.

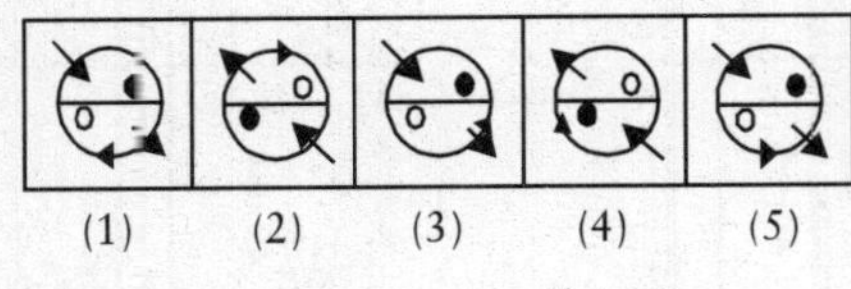

(1) (2) (3) (4) (5)

(a) 1 (b) 2
(c) 3 (d) 4
(e) 5

119. Choose the figure which is different from the rest.

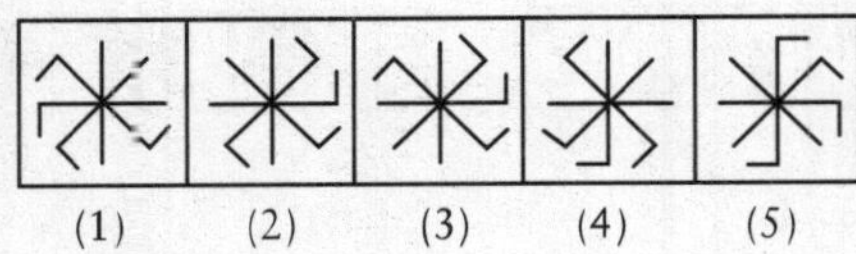

(1) (2) (3) (4) (5)

(a) 1 (b) 2
(c) 3 (d) 4
(e) 5

120. Choose the figure which is different from the rest.

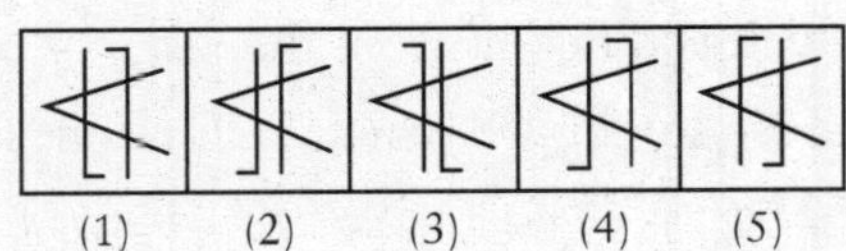

(1) (2) (3) (4) (5)

(a) 1 (b) 2
(c) 3 (d) 4
(e) 5

121. Choose the figure which is different from the rest.

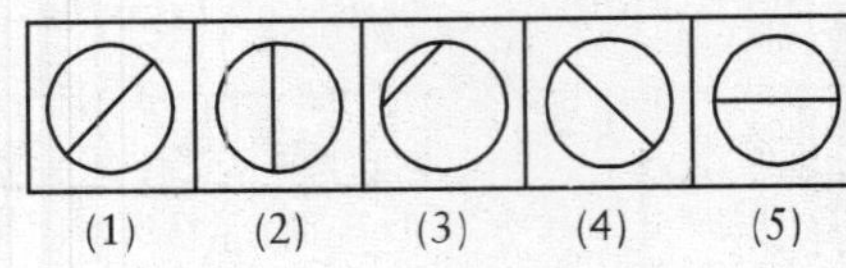

(1) (2) (3) (4) (5)

(a) 1 (b) 2
(c) 3 (d) 4
(e) 5

122. Choose the figure which is different from the rest.

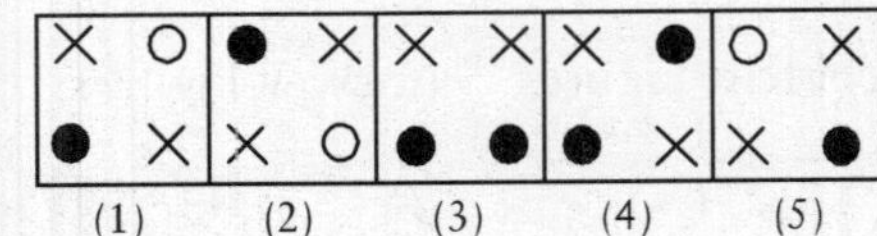

(1) (2) (3) (4) (5)

(a) 1 (b) 2
(c) 3 (d) 4
(e) 5

123. Choose the figure which is different from the rest.

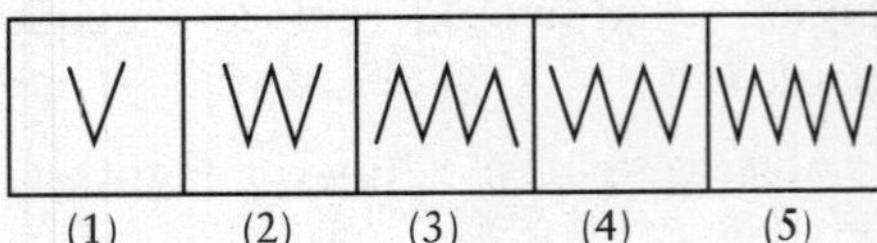

(1) (2) (3) (4) (5)

(a) 1 (b) 2
(c) 3 (d) 4
(e) 5

124. Choose the figure which is different from the rest.

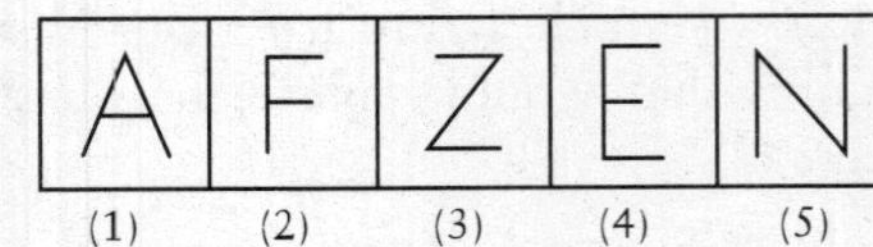

(1) (2) (3) (4) (5)

(a) 1 (b) 2
(c) 3 (d) 4
(e) 5

125. Choose the figure which is different from the rest.

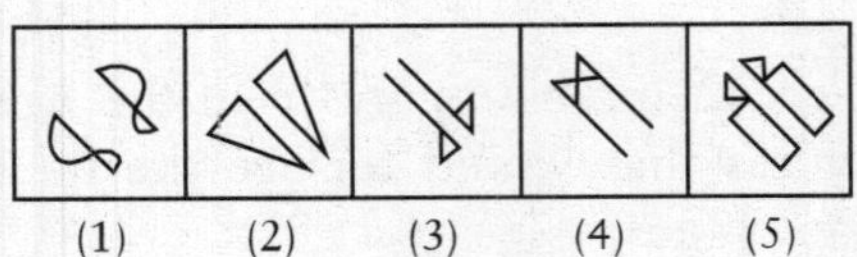

(1) (2) (3) (4) (5)

(a) 1 (b) 2
(c) 3 (d) 4
(e) 5

126. Choose the figure which is different from the rest.

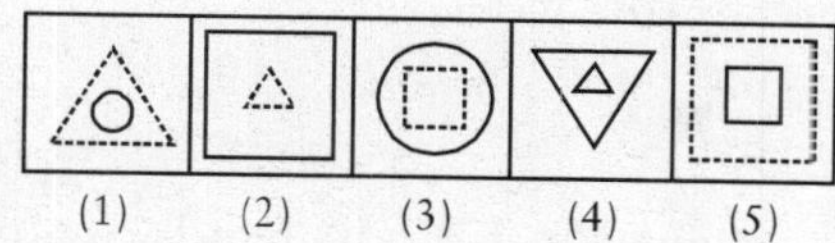

(a) 1 (b) 2
(c) 3 (d) 4
(e) 5

127. Choose the figure which is different from the rest.

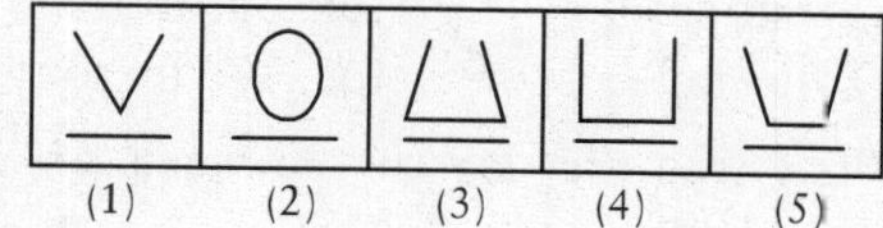

(a) 1 (b) 2
(c) 3 (d) 4
(e) 5

128. Choose the figure which is different from the rest.

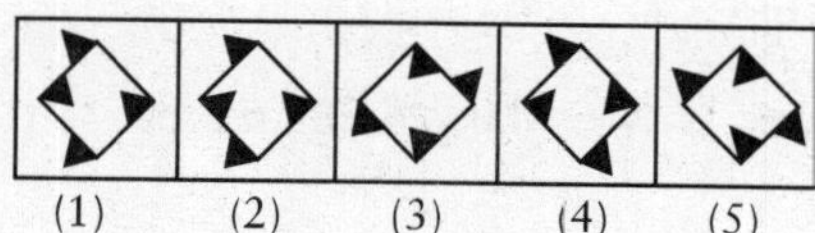

(a) 1 (b) 2
(c) 3 (d) 4
(e) 5

129. Choose the figure which is different from the rest.

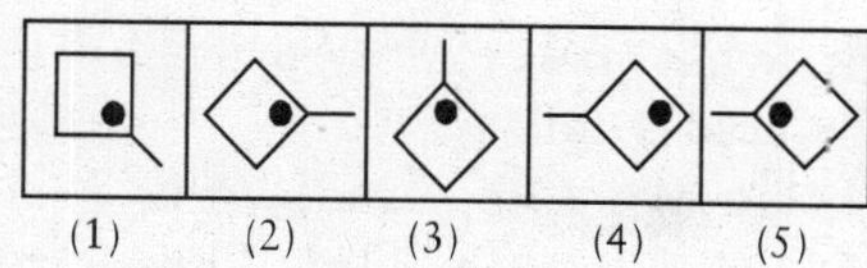

(a) 1 (b) 2
(c) 3 (d) 4
(e) 5

130. A watch which gains 5 seconds in 3 minutes was set right at 7 a.m. In the afternoon of the same day, when the watch indicated quarter past 4 o'clock, the true time is

(a) 59/7 min. past 3/12
(b) 4 p.m.
(c) 58/7 min. past 3/11
(d) 2/3 min. past 4/11

131. The angle between the minute hand and the hour hand of a clock when the time is 4.20, is

(a) 0° (b) 10°
(c) 5° (d) 20°

132. An accurate clock shows 8 o'clock in the morning. Through how may degrees will the hour hand rotate when the clock shows 2 o'clock in the afternoon?

(a) 144° (b) 150°
(c) 168° (d) 180°

133. How much does a watch lose per day, if its hands coincide ever 64 minutes?

(a) $32\frac{8}{11}$ min. (b) $36\frac{5}{11}$ min.
(c) 90 min. (d) 96 min.

134. A clock is started at noon. By 10 minutes past 5, the hour hand has turned through

(a) 145° (b) 150°
(c) 155° (d) 160°

135. At what time between 5.30 and 6 will the hands of a clock be at right angles?

(a) $43\frac{5}{11}$ min. past 5

(b) $43\frac{7}{11}$ min. past 5

(c) $\frac{40}{5}$ min. past 5

(d) 45 min. past 5

136. A watch which gains uniformly is 2 minutes low at noon on Monday and is 4 min 48 sec fast at 2 p.m. on the following Monday. When was it correct?
(a) 2 p.m. on Tuesday
(b) 2 p.m. on Wednesday
(c) 3 p.m. on Thursday
(d) 1 p.m. on Friday

137. At what angle the hands of a clock are inclined at 15 minutes past 5?
(a) 58½° (b) 64°
(c) 67½° (d) 72½°

138. The angle between the minute hand and the hour hand of a clock when the time is 8.30, is
(a) 30° (b) 75°
(c) 60° (d) 105°

139. At 3.40, the hour hand and the minute hand of a clock form an angle of
(a) 120° (b) 125°
(c) 130° (d) 135°

140. At what time between 4 and 5 o'clock will the hands of a watch point in opposite directions?
(a) $\frac{45}{4}$ min. past 4
(b) 40 min. past 4
(c) $50\frac{4}{11}$ min. past 4
(d) $54\frac{6}{11}$ min. past 4

141. How many times in a day, are the hands of a clock in straight line but opposite in direction?
(a) 20 (b) 22
(c) 24 (d) 48

142. How many times in a day, the hands of a clock are straight?
(a) 22 (b) 24
(c) 44 (d) 48

143. How many times are the hands of a clock at right angle in a day?
(a) 22 (b) 24
(c) 44 (d) 48

144. The reflex angle between the hands of a clock at 10.25 is
(a) 180° (b) 192½°
(c) 195° (d) 197½°

145. How many times do the hands of a clock coincide in a day?
(a) 20 (b) 21
(c) 22 (d) 24

146. It was Sunday on Jan. 1, 2006. What was the day of the week Jan. 1, 2010?
(a) Sunday (b) Saturday
(c) Friday (d) Wednesday

147. What was the day of the week on 17th June, 1998?
(a) Monday (b) Tuesday
(c) Wednesday (d) Thursday

148. If 6th March, 2005 is Monday, what was the day of the week on 6th March, 2004?
(a) Sunday (b) Saturday
(c) Tuesday (d) Wednesday

149. Today is Monday. After 61 days, it will be
(a) Wednesday (b) Saturday
(c) Tuesday (d) Thursday

150. What was the day of the week on 28th May, 2006?
(a) Thursday (b) Friday
(c) Saturday (d) Sunday

151. On what dates of April, 2001 did Wednesday fall?
(a) 1st, 8th, 15th, 22nd, 29th
(b) 2nd, 9th, 16th, 23rd, 30th
(c) 3rd, 10th, 17th, 24th
(d) 4th, 11th, 18th, 25th

152. How many days are there in x weeks x days?

(a) $7x^2$ (b) $8x$
(c) $14x$ (d) 7

153. What will be the day of the week 15th August, 2010?
(a) Sunday (b) Monday
(c) Tuesday (d) Friday

154. The last day of a century cannot be
(a) Monday (b) Wednesday
(c) Tuesday (d) Friday

155. January 1, 2007 was Monday. What day of the week lies on Jan. 1, 2008?
(a) Monday (b) Tuesday
(c) Wednesday (d) Sunday

156. The calendar for the year 2007 will be the same for the year
(a) 2014 (b) 2016
(c) 2017 (d) 2018

157. On 8th Dec. 2007 Saturday falls. What day of the week was it on 8th Dec. 2006?
(a) Sunday (b) Thursday
(c) Tuesday (d) Friday

158. January 1, 2008 is Tuesday. What day of the week lies on Jan. 1, 2009?
(a) Monday (b) Wednesday
(c) Thursday (d) Sunday

159. Which of the following is not a leap year?
(a) 700 (b) 800
(c) 1200 (d) 2000

160. On 8th Feb. 2005 it was Tuesday. What was the day of the week on 8th Feb. 2004?
(a) Tuesday (b) Monday
(c) Sunday (d) Wednesday

Direction: (161-170) in each of the following questions has a group. Find out which one of the given alternatives will be another member of the group or of that class.

161. Apple, Grape, Orange
(a) Vegetable (b) Fruits
(c) Stems (d) Oats

162. Lucknow, Patna, Bhopal, Jaipur
(a) Shimla (b) Mysore
(c) Pune (d) Indore

163. Lock, Shut, Fasten
(a) Window (b) Door
(c) Iron (d) Block

164. Wheat, Barley, Rice
(a) Food (b) Agriculture
(c) Farm (d) Gram

165. Pathology, Cardiology, Radiology, Ophthalmology
(a) Biology (b) Hematology
(c) Zoology (d) Geology

166. Mars, Earth, Jupiter
(a) Planets (b) Cosmos
(c) Orbits (d) Astronauts

167. Lungs, Liver, Kidney
(a) Neck (b) Testis
(c) Heart (d) Nose

168. Basic, Pascal, Fortran
(a) Cobol (b) Bhopal
(c) Calculator (d) Cyclotron

169. Root, Stem, Branch
(a) Fertilizer (b) Leaf
(c) Tree (d) Wood

170. Volleyball, Hockey, Football
(a) Aquatics (b) Baseball
(c) Athletes (d) Sports

Direction: In each of the questions from (171-195), which one of the alternatives is different from the rest?

171. (a) 24-42 (b) 36-63
(c) 37-73 (d) 35-51

172. (a) 4-7 (b) 7-16
(c) 17-36 (d) 16-32

173. (a) 27-57 (b) 63-18
(c) 28-81 (d) 36-96

174. (a) 51-28 (b) 37-62
(c) 81-104 (d) 99-76

175. (a) 111-11 (b) 15-105
(c) 7-91 (d) 3-81

176. (a) 2-4 (b) 6-36
(c) 7-35 (d) 9-81

177. (a) 7654 (b) 4567
(c) 9876 (d) 4321

178. (a) 5876 (b) 1435
(c) 2543 (d) 8576

179. (a) 63, 18 (b) 29, 46
(c) 47, 34 (d) 28, 41

180. (a) 1365 (b) 5713
(c) 3175 (d) 7513

181. (a) 3-27 (b) 4-64
(c) 7-353 (d) 6-216

182. (a) 9-27 (b) 15-45
(c) 10-30 (d) 20-60

183. (a) 10-45 (b) 20-85
(c) 40-180 (d) 60-270

184. (a) 2437 (b) 2419
(c) 5407 (d) 1459

185. (a) 2547 (b) 3456
(c) 3715 (d) 5678

186. (a) 2731 (b) 1357
(c) 2571 (d) 2357

187. (a) 15-40 (b) 18-56
(c) 24-76 (d) 12-58

188. (a) 6-36 (b) 5-25
(c) 7-49 (d) 3-9

189. (a) 7224 (b) 7525
(c) 4214 (d) 3612

190. (a) 9-40 (b) 20-95
(c) 17-80 (d) 16-78

191. (a) 133 (b) 326
(c) 515 (d) 429

192. (a) 2355 (b) 2753
(c) 7159 (d) 7359

193. (a) 111 (b) 37
(c) 148 (d) 63

194. (a) 13 (b) 61
(c) 97 (d) 117

195. (a) 200 (b) 500
(c) 700 (d) 600

Direction: (196-220) in each of the questions which letters group is different from the rest?

196. (a) MNW (b) OPY
(c) JKT (d) GHO

197. (a) PRW (b) CDJ
(c) EFG (d) LMH

198. (a) ACCUSE (b) OPAQUE
(c) ASSUME (d) ANIMAL

199. (a) ERY (b) HAN
(c) CUT (d) DOT

200. (a) UNITE (b) UNDER
(c) UNTIL (d) UPPER

201. (a) TEAM (b) THAN
(c) TATA (d) TILE

202. (a) BANISH (b) OPTION
(c) ATOMIC (d) EDIBLE

203. (a) MADE (b) SHED
(c) CEDE (d) DOLT

204. (a) KMPTZ (b) DFIMR
(c) HJMQV (d) ACFJO

205. (a) PLH (b) DFH
(c) EKO (d) MKI

206. (a) QRY (b) IPQ
(c) BCJ (d) RXY

207. (a) CROTON (b) CRUSH
(c) CRIMP (d) CRINGE

208. (a) CRIET (b) CRIME
(c) COPIER (d) CONVENIENT

209. (a) CORDIAL (b) CORIANDER
(c) CORDATE (d) CORNEA

210. (a) CONVOKE (b) CONVOLUTE
(c) CONVOLVE (d) CONVIVIAL

211. (a) CRY (b) JOY
(c) FRY (d) TRY

212. (a) EMBOLISM (b) EMBOLDEN
(c) EMIGRATE (d) EMIGRANT

213. (a) FAMOUS (b) FRUCTUOUS
(c) FANCIED (d) FAVOUR

214. (a) FRUGAL (b) FULGENT
(c) FURBISH (d) FRETFUL

215. (a) GLARY (b) GLAZE
(c) GLARE (d) GLADE

216. (a) GILD (b) GIFT
(c) GIMP (d) GIBE

217. (a) GAUD (b) GEAR
(c) GOAL (d) GIVE

218. (a) NOM (b) BCA
(c) JIH (d) RSQ

219. (a) ACE (b) MOQ
(c) HJL (d) VTR

220. (a) MQT (b) ADG
(c) HKN (d) RUX

Direction: (221-232) in each of the following questions find out the odd one.

221. (a) Lawyer (b) Judge
(c) Council (d) Advocate

222. (a) Flower (b) Stem
(c) Branch (d) Roots

223. (a) Science (b) Physics
(c) Chemistry (d) Biology

224. (a) Day (b) Week
(c) Time (d) Month

225. (a) Liver (b) Nails
(c) Lungs (d) Heart

226. (a) College-Students
(b) Hospital-Patient
(c) Bus stand-Driver
(d) Stadium-Viewer

227. (a) Cotton (b) Terene
(c) Silk (d) Wool

228. (a) Carrot (b) Potato
(c) Ginger (d) Beet
(e) Cabbage

229. (a) Cloth (b) Weaver
(c) Thread (d) Cotton
(e) Garments

230. (a) Ruby (b) Sapphire
(c) Graphite (d) Bauxite

231. (a) Television (b) Record-player
(c) Refrigerator (d) Radio
(e) Cassette-player

232. (a) Sparrow (b) Chicken
(c) Pigeon (d) Owl

Direction: (233-245) in each of the following questions find the word or pair of words which is different from the other three words or pairs of words.

233. (a) Hypothesis (b) Assumption
(c) Observation (d) Experiment

234. (a) Disperse (b) Congregate
(c) Accumulate (d) Aggregate

235. (a) Tame (b) Wild
(c) Domesticated (d) Docile

236. (a) Shirt-Dress
(b) Boy-Girl
(c) Book-Library
(d) Table-Furniture

237. (a) Mango-Fruit (b) Rice-Corn
(c) Student-Class (d) Tomato-Potato

238. (a) Sweet-Sour (b) Unhappy-Sad
(c) In-Out (d) Up-Down

239. (a) Lake (b) Brook
(c) Stream (d) River

240. (a) Equity (b) Fairness
(c) Partiality (d) Justice

241. (a) Light-Heavy (b) Broad-Wide
(c) Big-Large (d) Tiny-Small

242. (a) Unique (b) Peerless
(c) Common place (d) Unequalled

243. (a) Foggy (b) Transparent
(c) Turbid (d) Cloudy

244. (a) Skirmish (b) Fray
(c) Fight (d) Detente

245. (a) Cover-Page (b) Circle-Radius
(c) Chair-Leg (d) Flower-Petal

Direction: (246-282) in each of the following questions find the alternatives which will replace the question mark (?)

246. BEGK : ADFJ :: PSVY :?
(a) ROUX (b) ORUX
(c) LQUT (d) LOQT

247. MAD : JXA :: RUN :?
(a) OSQ (b) PRJ
(c) UXQ (d) ORK

248. AZEY : CXDW :: EVFU :?
(a) GTHS (b) GHTS
(c) GSTH (d) TGSH

249. NOTE : RSXI :: RISK :?
(a) VMXP (b) VMWO
(c) VJMP (d) VMWP

250. ACEG : IKMO :: QSUW :?
(a) YZCE (b) YACD
(c) YACE (d) YBCE

251. TAME : OVHZ :: LUDO :?
(a) QZIT (b) GQAM
(c) GPYJ (d) GOYJ

252. BCFG : HILM :: NORQ :?
(a) TXWU (b) TXUW
(c) TUXW (d) TVWX

253. LOVE : KMSA :: HATE :?
(a) GXQA (b) DRXD
(c) ECWI (d) GYQA

254. ZRYQ : KCJB :: PWOV :?
(a) GBHA (b) ISJT
(c) ELDK (d) EOFP

255. DIG : CFB :: JOT :?
(a) KRY (b) ILM
(c) ILO (d) KLO

256. KeaC : CaeK :: XgmF :?
(a) GmcF (b) FmgX
(c) EgmX (d) EmgF

257. DCBA : ZCBE :: HNNS :?
(a) ROMI (b) RMOG
(c) RIMA (d) TMOI

258. Corden : zrogbq :: ? : pxivro
(a) mulmul (b) Sulsul
(c) munmun (d) srspql

259. TGIR : QJLO :: PKMN :?
(a) NMKP (b) MNPK
(c) OLNM (d) QJKP

260. LKJ : pon ::? : hgf
(a) dcle (b) DBC
(c) dcd (d) DCB

261. BYVE : GTQJ :: CXUF :?
(a) HSQJ (b) IROL
(c) HSPK (d) GTRI

262. Computer : fqprxvht :: Language :?
(a) oxpixdig (b) ocqicyig
(c) Ocqixcjg (d) ocqixcig

263. MNOP : KLMN :: CRAV :?
(a) APYT (b) XIZE
(c) QRST (d) ABCD

264. AEFJ : KOPT :: ? : QUVZ
(a) GKLP (b) GLKP
(c) HKLP (d) HKQL

265. JOCK : QLXP :: HEAT :?
(a) OBTX (b) SVZG
(c) PHWY (d) SVYF

266. PASS : QBTT :: FAIL :?
(a) GJBM (b) GBJM
(c) MBJG (d) MJBG

267. RIDE : LNBE :: HELP :?
(a) NINP (b) BAJP
(c) JPCH (d) BJJP

268. QIOK : MMKO :: YAWC :?
(a) UESG (b) USGA
(c) VUES (d) SUEG

269. BLOCKED : YOLXPVW :: ? : OZFMXS
(a) DEBATE (b) RESULT
(c) LABOR (d) LAUNCH

270. SONG : GONT :: FELT :?
(a) TELE (b) TMDG
(c) TLEG (d) ELTG

271. CEDH : HDEC :: ? : PNRV
(a) VRNP (b) RNPV
(c) NRVP (d) VNRP

272. ? : QEHMDF :: WIDELY : HVCDXK
(a) FRINGE (b) STRING
(c) FRANCE (d) DEMAND

273. GERM : MERG :: STAR :?
(a) TSRA (b) RTSA
(c) RTAS (d) TARS

274. DFHJ : LNPR :: TVXZ :?
(a) DBFH (b) DBHF
(c) BDFH (d) FDBH

275. ACEG : ? :: BDFH : KMOQ
(a) NLPR (b) LMNO
(c) JLNP (d) JNLO

276. PSQR : CFED :: JMKL :?
(a) UVXZ (b) YVZX
(c) YXZW (d) WZYX

277. ACFJ : ZXUQ :: EGIN :?
(a) VUSQ (b) UTRP
(c) VRPM (d) VTRM

278. CFDG : LOMP :: HKIL :?
(a) QTRU (b) QRTU
(c) PSQT (d) RUSV

279. REASON : SFBTPO :: THINK :?
(a) SGHMJ (b) UIJOL
(c) UHNKI (d) UJKPM

280. ZINC : AFSV :: SONI :?
(a) TPOJ (b) TRSP
(c) TLSB (d) RLIB

281. ABCD : WXYZ :: EFGH :?
(a) STUV (b) ZYXW
(c) VUTS (d) WXZY

282. FIELD : GJFME :: SICKLE :?
(a) RHBJKD (b) RHJBKD
(c) TJLDMF (d) TJDLMF

Direction: (283-312) in each of the following questions find out the alternative which will replace the question mark (?)

283. CUP : LIP :: BIRD :?
(a) BUSH (b) GRASS
(c) FOREST (d) BEAK

284. Flow : River :: Stagnant :?
(a) Rain (b) Stream
(c) Pool (d) Canal

285. Paw : Cat :: Hoof :?
(a) Lamb (b) Elephant
(c) Lion (d) Horse

286. Ornithologist : Bird :: Archealogist :?
(a) Islands (b) Mediators
(c) Archealogy (d) Aquatic

287. Peacock : India :: Bear :?
(a) Australia (b) America
(c) Russia (d) England

288. Shade : Tree :: Warmth :?
(a) Self-respect (b) Mother
(c) Wealth (d) Ease

289. REASON : SFBTPO :: THINK :?
(a) SGHMJ (b) UIJOL
(c) UHNKI (d) UJKPM

290. Carbon : Diamond :: Corundum :?
(a) Garnet (b) Ruby
(c) Pukhraj (d) Pearl

291. NATION : ANTINO :: HUNGRY :?
(a) HNUGRY (b) UHNGYR
(c) YRNGUH (d) UNHGYR

292. Architect : Building :: Sculptor :?
(a) Museum (b) Stone
(c) Chisel (d) Statue

293. Eye : Myopia :: Teeth :?
(a) Pyrrhoea (b) Cataract
(c) Trachoma (d) Eczema

294. Conference : Chairman :: Newspaper :?
(a) Reporter (b) Distributor
(c) Printer (d) Editor

295. Safe : Secure :: Protect :?
(a) Lock (b) Sure
(c) Guard (d) Conserve

296. MASTER : OCUVGT :: LABOUR :?
(a) NCDQWT (b) NDERWT
(c) NBERWT (d) NEDRWT

297. Microphone : Loud :: Microscope :?
(a) Elongate (b) Investigate
(c) Magnify (d) Examine

298. Melt : Liquid :: Freeze :?
(a) Ice (b) Condense
(c) Solid (d) Force

299. College : Student :: Hospital :?
(a) Nurse (b) Doctor
(c) Treatment (d) Patient

300. Tree : Forest :: Grass :?
(a) Lawn (b) Garden
(c) Park (d) Field

301. Video : Cassette :: Computer :?
(a) Files (b) Floppy
(c) Bits (d) Adit

302. South : North-West :: West :?
(a) North (b) South-West
(c) North-East (d) East

303. Cloth : Mill :: Newspaper :?
(a) Editor (b) Reader
(c) Paper (d) Press

304. Country : President :: State :?
(a) Governor (b) M.P.
(c) Legislator (d) Minister

305. Race : Fatigue :: Fast :?
(a) Food (b) Laziness
(c) Hunger (d) Race

306. Peace : Chaos :: Creation :?
(a) Build (b) Construction
(c) Destruction (d) Manufacture

307. Tiger : Forest :: Otter :?
(a) Cage (b) Sky
(c) Nest (d) Water

308. Poles : Magnet ::? : Battery
(a) Cells (b) Power
(c) Terminals (d) Energy

309. Cassock : Priest ::? : Graduate
(a) Cap (b) Tie
(c) Coat (d) Gown

310. Ice : Coldness :: Earth :?
(a) Weight (b) Jungle
(c) Gravitatism (d) Sea

311. Parts : Strap :: Wolf :?
(a) Fox (b) Animal
(c) Wood (d) Flow

312. Physician : Treatment :: Judge :?
(a) Punishment (b) Judgement
(c) Lawyer (d) Court

Direction: (313-327) in each of the following questions find the alternative which will replace the question mark (?)

313. Violet—Yellow; Blue—Red; Indigo—?
(a) White (b) Black
(c) Yellow (d) Orange

314. Pen—Cap; Bottle—Cork; Body—?
(a) Cloth (b) Cot
(c) Food (d) Water

315. Pen—Write; Brush—Teeth; Spade—?
(a) Cut (b) Dig
(c) Wood (d) Iron

316. Draw—Board; Write—Paper; Walk—?
(a) Ground (b) Foot
(c) Stick (d) Food

317. Blue—Moon; White—Hot; Black—?
(a) Cloud (b) Sky
(c) Sheep (d) Star

318. Tight—Loose; Love—Hate; Earth—?
(a) Sun (b) Cloud
(c) Sky (d) Height

319. Cat—Kitten; Goat—Kid; Sheep—?
(a) Raven (b) Colt
(c) Lamb (d) Filly

320. Man—House; Bird—Nest; Fish—?
(a) River (b) Hole
(c) Water (d) Rain

321. Bathroom—Sink; House—Kitchen; Cloister—?
(a) Monk (b) Statue
(c) Gatekeeper (d) Pray

322. Temple—Ear; Shoulder—Hand; Gum—?
(a) Lip (b) Tongue
(c) Vein (d) Tooth

323. Examiner—Examinee; Pleader—Client; Preceptor—?
(a) Disciple (b) Customer
(c) Guest (d) Host

324. Cataract—Eye; Jaundice—Liver; Pyorrhoea—?
(a) Breath (b) Nausea
(c) Tongue (d) Ooth

325. Dumb—Speak; Deaf—Hear; Bald—?
(a) Hand (b) Eye
(c) Hair (d) Nose

326. Blind—Sight; Paralysis—Motion; Anaemia—?
(a) Sleep (b) Blood
(c) Health (d) Loss of appetite

327. Tuberculosis—Lung; Piles—Buttock; Hernia—?
(a) Intestine (b) Abdomen
(c) Kidney (d) Stomach

Direction: (328-341) in each of the questions from 1 to 15 find out the alternative which will replace the question mark (?)

328. but, tub; yap, pay; dial, ?
(a) liad (b) laid
(c) dali (d) ladi

329. diaphragm—hra; enunciate—cia; feudalism—?
(a) dal (b) eud
(c) lis (d) ali

330. jar, raj; net, ten; emir, ?
(a) remi (b) reim
(c) rime (d) mire

331. tip, pit; gum, mug; emit, ?
(a) time (b) mite
(c) teim (d) tiem

332. ward, draw; stop, pots; tame, ?
(a) team (b) etam
(c) mate (d) emat

333. dog, gid; net, tan; tub, ?
(a) bit (b) but
(c) bot (d) bib

334. wed, wid; met, mit; set, ?
(a) sut (b) tes
(c) sit (d) sat

335. Water, Wutar; Bihar, Behur; Tempo, ?
(a) Tempa (b) Tampi
(c) Tampu (d) Tempi

336. dial, laid; liar, rail; yard, ?
(a) dray (b) rayd
(c) yrad (d) dyar

337. most, notu; tone, uooe; patna, ?
(a) quuou (b) qauma
(c) qauoa (d) qeuoe

338. plug, qmah, evil, iwom; made, ?
(a) neeo (b) nuea
(c) nbef (d) neei

339. leg, gel; dog, god; wed, ?
(a) ewd (b) wde
(c) dew (d) dwe

340. sanjay, ajy; mita, ia; dhirendra, ?
(a) hrnr (b) hrnra
(c) hinr (d) hedr

341. sanju, snu, nivedita, nvdt; snehal, ?
(a) snh (b) sea
(c) sha (d) seh

Direction: (342-357) in each word of the following questions consists of pair of words bearing a relationship among these, from amongst the alternatives, pick up the pair that best illustrate a similar relationship.

342. Glove : Hand
(a) Neck : Collar (b) Tie : Shirt
(c) Socks : Feet (d) Coat : Pocket

343. Lawyer : Court
(a) Chemist : Laboratory
(b) Businessman : Office
(c) Labour : Factory
(d) Athlete : Olympics

344. Letter : Word
(a) Page : Book
(b) Product : Factory
(c) Club : People
(d) Homework : School

345. Lively : Dull
(a) Employed : Jobless
(b) Flower : Bud
(c) Factory : Labour
(d) Happy : Gay

346. Silence : Noise
(a) Quiet : Peace
(b) Baldness : Hair
(c) Talk : Whisper
(d) Sing : Dance

347. Kick : Football
(a) Wash : Dishes (b) Dust : Rage
(c) Mop : Sweep (d) Throw : Ring

348. Scales : Fish
(a) Bear : Fur (b) Woman : Dress
(c) Skin : Man (d) Tree : Leaves

349. Numismatist : Coins
(a) Jeweller : Jewels
(b) Cartographer : Maps
(c) Philatelist : Stamps
(d) Geneticist : Chromosomes

350. Sunrise : Sunset
(a) Dawn : Twilight
(b) Noon : Midnight
(c) Morning : Night
(d) Energetic : Lazy

351. Stove : Kitchen
(a) Window : Bedroom
(b) Sink : Bathroom
(c) Pot : Pan
(d) Television : Living room

352. Candle : Wick
(a) Hammer : Nail
(b) Light : Bulb
(c) Oven : Fire
(d) Bicycle : Wheel

353. Sound : Muffled
(a) Moisture : Humid
(b) Colour : Faded
(c) Despair : Anger
(d) Odour : Pungent

354. Platform : Train
(a) Aeroplane : Aerodrome
(b) Hotel : Tourist
(c) Quay : Ship
(d) Footpath : Traveller

355. Train : Track
(a) Water : Boat
(b) Bullet : Barrel
(c) Idea : Brain
(d) Fame : Television

356. Chalk : Blackboard
(a) Type : Point (b) Table : Chair
(c) Door : Handle (d) Ink : Paper

357. Rectangle : Pentagon
(a) Side : Angle
(b) Diagonal : Perimeter
(c) Triangle : Rectangle
(d) Circle : Square

358. Find a group similar to 3, 7, 11.
(a) 2, 9, 21 (b) 2, 17, 23
(c) 4, 6, 14 (d) 7, 9, 16

359. A number of friends decided to go on a picnic and planned to spend ₹ 96 on eatables. Four of them, however, did not turn up. As a consequence, the remaining ones had to contribute ₹ 4 each extra. The number of those who attended the picnic was
(a) 8 (b) 12
(c) 16 (d) 24

360. Find a group similar to 77, 55, 33.
(a) 45, 30, 20 (b) 70, 60, 45
(c) 60, 40, 35 (d) 5, 75, 65

361. A tailor had a number of shirt pieces to cut from a roll of fabric. He cut each roll of equal length into 10 pieces. He cut at the rate of 45 cuts a minute. How many rolls would be cut in 24 minutes?
(a) 32 rolls (b) 54 rolls
(c) 108 rolls (d) 120 rolls

362. An institute organised a fete and 1/5 of the girls and 1/8 of the boys participated in the same. What fraction of the total number of students took part in the fete?
(a) 2/13 (b) 13/40
(c) Data inadequate (d) None of these

363. In a garden, there are 10 rows and 12 columns of mango trees. The distance between the two trees is 2 metres and a distance of one metre is left from all sides of the boundary of the garden. The length of the garden is
(a) 20 m (b) 22 m
(c) 24 m (d) 26 m

364. As 675 is related to 929 in the same way 123 is related to
(a) 242 (b) 246
(c) 248 (d) 423

365. 36, 35, 34 are related to 15, 20, 25 in the same way 42, 43, 44 are related to
(a) 17 22 27 (b) 28 13 18
(c) 27 22 17 (d) 18 23 28

366. Two bus tickets from city A to B and three tickets from city A to C cost ₹ 77 but three tickets from city A to B and two tickets from city A to C cost ₹ 73. What are the fares for cities B and C from A?
(a) ₹ 4, ₹ 23 (b) ₹ 13, ₹ 17
(c) ₹ 15, ₹ 14 (d) ₹ 17, ₹ 13

367. In a class, there are 18 boys who are over 160 cm tall. If these constitute three-fourths of the boys and the total number of boys is two-thirds of the total number of students in the class. What is the number of girls in the class?
(a) 6 (b) 12
(c) 18 (d) 24

368. As 125 is related to 17, 18, 21 in the same way 458 is related to
(a) 27 28 31 (b) 29 32 33
(c) 30 31 35 (d) 28 29 32

369. A, B, C, D and E play a game of cards. A says to B, "If you give me three cards, you will have as many as E has and if I give you three cards, you will have as many as D has." A and B together have 10 cards more than what D and E together have. If B has two cards more than what C has and the total number of cards be 133. How many cards does B have?
(a) 22 (b) 23
(c) 25 (d) 35

370. 12-year-old Manick is three times as old as his brother Rahul. How old will Manick be when he is twice as old as Rahul?
(a) 14 years (b) 16 years
(c) 18 years (d) 20 years

371. As 425 is related to 2, in the same way 613 is related to

(a) 1 (b) 2
(c) 3 (d) 4

372. Mac has ₹ 3 more than Ken, but then Ken wins on the horses and trebles his money, so that he now has ₹ 2 more than the original amount of money that the two boys had between them. How much money did Mac and Ken have between them before Ken's win?
(a) ₹ 9 (b) ₹ 11
(c) ₹ 13 (d) ₹ 15

373. The total of the ages of Amar, Akbar and Anthony is 80 years. What was the total of their ages three years ago?
(a) 71 years (b) 72 years
(c) 74 years (d) 77 years

374. A father is now three times as old as his son. Five years back, he was four times as old as his son. The age of the son (in years) is
(a) 12 (b) 15
(c) 18 (d) 20

375. As 246 is related to 36, 16, 04 in the same way 357 is related to
(a) 09 49 25 (b) 49 16 04
(c) 49 25 09 (d) 36 16 04

376. 3 : 24 :: 5 :?
(a) 61 (b) 122
(c) 34 (d) 128

377. 11 : 17 :: 19 :?
(a) 23 (b) 27
(c) 33 (d) 21

378. Fraud : Money :: Exercise :?
(a) Education (b) Read
(c) Sleep (d) Health

379. Money : Poverty :?
(a) Knowledge (b) Illiteracy
(c) Greediness (d) Unsuccess

380. Magazine : Editor : Drama :?
(a) Director (b) Hero
(c) Heroine (d) Painter

381. Pole : Magnet ::? : Battery
(a) Cell (b) Power
(c) Terminal (d) Energy

382. Video : Cassettee :: Computer :?
(a) Reels (b) Floppy
(c) Recordings (d) Files

383. Museum : Curator :: Prison :?
(a) Warden (b) Monitor
(c) Manager (d) Jailor

384. A student got twice as many sums wrong as he got right. If he attempted 48 sums in all, how many did he solve correctly?
(a) 12 (b) 16
(c) 18 (d) 24

385. If 'DEAR' is coded as 'FGCT', then how will 'READ' be coded as
(a) TGCF (b) FGCF
(c) TSFC (d) TCGF

386. David gets on the elevator at the 11th floor of a building and rides up at the rate of 57 floors per minute. At the same time, Albert gets on an elevator at the 51st floor of the same building and rides down at the rate of 63 floors per minute. If they continue travelling at these rates, then at which floor will their paths cross?
(a) 19 (b) 28
(c) 30 (d) 37

387. If 'THRASH' is coded as 'UGSZTG', then how will 'HEAD' be coded?
(a) IECD (b) GDZC
(c) IDBC (d) GDBC

388. If 'SWAMINATHAN' is coded as 'NAHTANIMAWS', then how will 'SIRNAME' be coded?
(a) EMAMSIR (b) EMARNIS
(c) EMNARIS (d) EMANRIS

389. I have a few sweets to be distributed. If I keep 2, 3 or 4 in a pack, I am left with one sweet. If I keep 5 in a pack, I am left with none. What is the minimum number of sweets I have to pack and distribute?
(a) 25 (b) 37
(c) 54 (d) 65

390. If a clock takes seven seconds to strike seven. How long will it take to strike ten?
(a) 7 seconds (b) 9 seconds
(c) 10 seconds (d) None of these

391. In a group of cows and hens, the number of legs are 14 more than twice the number of heads. The number of cows is
(a) 5 (b) 7
(c) 10 (d) 12

392. A father tells his son, "I was of your present age when you were born." If the father is 36 now. How old was the boy five years back?
(a) 13 (b) 15
(c) 17 (d) 25

393. If 'TOMB' is coded as 'MBOR', then how will 'GOAL' be coded?
(a) ALOG (b) ALOE
(c) LOAG (d) EALO

394. If 'CAMERA' is coded as 'CMRCMR' then hows will 'CHAPRA' be coded?
(a) CARCAR (b) CARHPA
(c) HPACAR (d) RACRAC

395. If 'DAILY' is coded as 'XKHZC' then how will 'FERTILE' be coded?
(a) DKHSEDQS (b) DMHUQFE
(c) DKHSQDE (d) DJHRQCE

396. If 'MANAGER' is coded as 'QPLPTOB' then how will 'RANGE' be coded?
(a) BPLTO (b) BPQTO
(c) BPTQO (d) BLTPO

397. If 'GOAL' is coded as 'HPBM' and 'FROCK' is coded as 'GSPlJL' then how will 'LOFAR' be coded?
(a) MPGZO (b) MNEBS
(c) MPGBS (d) MPEBR

398. If 'CHAMBER' is coded as 'XSZNYVI' then how will 'WLFYOV' be coded?
(a) DOVBLE (b) DOUCLF
(c) DLUBOE (d) DOUBLE

399. IF 'TORCH' is codded as 'SXILG' then how will 'MANUAL' be coded?
(a) OBFMZN (b) OZEOZN
(c) OZFMZN (d) NZFMZK

400. If the code of 'PARK' is '5394' code for 'SHIRT' is '17698' and code for 'PANDIT' is '532068' then what will be the code for 'NISHAR'?
(a) 266734 (b) 231954
(c) 201739 (d) 261739

401. If 'INSURE' is coded as 951395, then how 'PATRIOT' be coded?
(a) 7129962 (b) 7129962
(c) 7129962 (d) 7129962

402. If 'SLAUTER' is coded as 1313259 then how will 'POVERTY' be coded?
(a) 7645927 (b) 7645927
(c) 7645927 (d) 7645927

403. If 'MARE' is coded as 'NESI' and 'LOVER' as 'MUWIS' then how will 'ABOVE' be coded?
(a) BCPWF (b) ECUWI
(c) EZUTI (d) ZCNWD

404. If 'TAME' is coded as 'SULA' and 'NIDUS' as 'MACOR' then how will 'EMOTIONS' be coded?
(a) ALISEIMR (b) DLNSHNMR
(c) ALISEIOR (d) ANIUEIOT

405. If code for 'FUNTASTIC' is 635211293, and for 'JUNGLE' is 135735, then how will 'CONJUGATE' be coded?
(a) 365137125 (b) 365137125
(c) 365137125 (d) 365137125

406. If 'PEN' is coded as 'TREE', 'TREE' as 'ROAD-ROUTE', 'ROAD-ROUTE' as 'SKY', 'SKY' as 'RAIL-ROUTE' and 'RAIL-ROUTE' as 'POLLUTION' then where does 'AEROPLANE' fly?
(a) POLLUTION (b) ROAD-ROUTE
(c) RAIL-ROUTE (d) SKY

407. If 'MAULVI' is coded as 'PUJARI', 'PUJARI' as 'SENIK', 'SENIK' as 'BEGGAR', 'BEGGAR' as 'RANGKARMI, 'RANGKARMI' as 'SCIENTIST' and 'SCIENTIST' as 'THIEF' then safety of the country should be given to whom?
(a) SENIK (b) BEGGAR
(c) RANGKARMI (d) SCIENTIST

408. If 'BEAR' is coded as 'FISH', 'FISH' as CROW, 'CROW' as 'DOG', 'DOG' as 'ELEPHANT' and 'ELEPHANT' as 'ASS', then who cannot remain alive in other place than water?
(a) FISH (b) ELEPHANT
(c) DOG (d) CROW

409. If 'Library' is coded as 'Court', 'Court' as 'College', 'College' as 'Gymnasium', 'Gym nasium' as 'Chamber', 'Chamber as 'Cinema hall' and 'Cinema hall' as 'Hospital', then where will the cases of the people be decided?
(a) College (b) Court
(c) Gymnasium (d) Chamber

410. 'Vehicle' is coded as 'Book', 'Book' as 'Flower', 'Flower' as 'Sweet' 'Sweet' as 'House', 'House' as 'Mental Hospital', and 'Mental Hospital' as 'Temple', then where is treasure of huge amount of knowledge hidden?
(a) Book (b) Sweet
(c) Vehicle (d) Rower

411. If in a certain code '123' means I am servant', '279' means 'Servant always merciful' and '684' means 'Poverty a curse', then which digit is used for 'Merciful'?
(a) 2 (b) 7
(c) 9 (d) Data inadequate

412. If in a certain code '493' means 'Friendship difficult challenge', '961', means, 'Struggle difficult Exam.' and '178' means 'Exam believable subject', then which digit is used for 'believable'?
(a) 7 or 8 (b) 7 or 9
(c) 8 (d) 8 or 1

413. If in a certain code '157' means 'Mother always affectionate', '619' means 'Always fortunate future' and '952' means 'Mother very fortunate' then which digit is used for 'future'?
(a) 9 (b) 6
(c) Data inadequate (d) 1

414. If in a certain code '268' means 'Equality and prosperity', '839' means 'prosperity nasty position' and '361' means 'Equality respected position', then for which word the digit '2' is used?
(a) Respected (b) And
(c) Prosperity (d) Equality

415. How many such 7's are there in the following number series which are not followed by 4 but preceded by 5?

6 5 7 2 3 5 7 1 2 5 7 3 4 3 5 6 5 4 5 7 6 5 7 4 5 7

(a) 2 (b) 3
(c) 4 (d) None of these

416. How many such 3's are there in the following number series which are preceded by 4 but not followed by 8?

4 2 8 4 3 2 3 4 3 8 7 5 4 3 8 2 5 4 3 2 4 3 2 7

(a) 4 (b) 3
(c) 5 (d) 2

417. In the following number series how many times have 2, 3 and 8 come together in

such a way that 2 is in the middle and 3 and 8 are at extreme positions?

2 4 5 2 3 8 2 3 4 6 7 3 2 8 8 2 3 4 5 6 8 2 3 6 2 8 3 2 8

(a) 3 (b) 2
(c) More than 4 (d) 4

418. In the following series how many times the sum of two consecutive digits is even?

1 2 3 4 6 3 4 2 5 9 3 6 7 4 1 2 3 6 7 6 5 4 3

(a) 3 (b) 4
(c) 5 (d) 2

419. In the following series how many times an odd number is followed by two consecutive even numbers?

4 2 3 2 5 4 2 5 3 2 6 4 3 5 7 2 8 6 7 9 4 5 4 2 9 6 1 3 2

(a) 4 (b) More than 4
(c) 2 (d) 3

420. In the following number series, how many such 6's are there which are divisible by its just preceding and following numbers?

4 6 3 2 5 6 3 7 5 3 6 2 7 5 3 6 4 5 2 6 7 1 2 6 4 3 2 6

(a) 2 (b) 1
(c) 3 (d) 4

421. In the following number series, how many such 8's are there which are divisible by its just preceding number but not divisible by its just following number?

2 8 4 3 2 8 5 4 8 2 6 7 8 5 8 2 4 8 2 6 8 2 4 8 6 7 8 2

(a) 2 (b) 3
(c) 1 (d) None of these

422. In the following number series how many such 5's are there which are neither preceded by 3 nor followed by 7?

2 7 5 3 4 5 7 6 3 5 2 1 2 5 4 6 5 9 3 5 7 5

(a) 4 (b) 5
(c) 3 (d) 2

423. In the following number series how many such 7's are there which are preceded by an odd number and followed by an even number?

2 4 5 3 7 6 3 2 5 7 3 5 4 2 3 4 5 3 6 7 3 5 7 3 9 3

(a) 2 (b) 3
(c) 1 (d) None of these

424. How many such odd digits are there in the given series which are followed by an odd digit?

7 3 2 9 5 7 4 1 3 6 4 9 5 4 6 5 2 7 2 4 1 6 7 2 1 3

(a) 4 (b) 6
(c) More than 6 (d) 3

425. In the following number series how many 4's are there which are preceded by a prime number but not followed by a prime number?

3 4 9 5 4 2 6 3 8 4 5 3 2 4 3 6 5 4 8 3 5 4 3 9 2 3 7 4 3

(a) 3 (b) 1
(c) 2 (d) None of these

426. How many such groups of 3 digits are there in the following number series in which middle digit is an even number while atleast one of the two remaining digits is an odd number?

3 4 3 2 4 2 3 5 1 7 2 5 9 6 4 3 5 8 2 1 4 6 5 6 7 4

(a) 6 (b) 5
(c) 4 (d) More than 6

427. In the following series how many such 1's are there which are preceded by an odd number and this odd number is preceded by a prime number?

4 3 5 1 6 3 1 2 7 1 4 9 3 1 7 8 9 3 1 5 4 1 3 2 5 1

(a) 3 (b) 2
(c) 4 (d) None of these

428. In the following number series how many such groups of 4, 5 and 9 are there in which prime number of these three digits must be in the middle?

4 5 9 6 9 4 5 7 4 9 5 6 7 4 9 5 4 3 5 9 4 4 9 5 5 4 9

(a) 3 (b) 4
(c) 2 (d) More than 4

429. In the following series how many such even digits are there which are preceded by any prime number but not followed by an even number?

4 6 3 6 4 9 5 7 5 6 4 6 8 2 4 7 5 6 7 6 9 5 3 2

(a) 2 (b) 3
(c) 4 (d) 1

430. In the following letter series how many such groups of L, S and W are there in which W should be the middle of the group?

M L W S A L S W N B Q W S L W P L S N O L W T R W S L

(a) 2 (b) 3
(c) 4 (d) None of these

431. How many such N's are there in the following series which are preceded by M and thus M is not preceded by R?

P N R R M N S T N M R R M N Q L N M R M N Q P L N M R M N R

(a) None (b) 3
(c) 2 (d) 1

432. How many such H's are in the series, which are preceded by P and followed by E?

P H C R Q P H E T P H L H C P E H P S R Q E H P H C P H

(a) 2 (b) 3
(c) 1 (d) 4

433. How many such R's are there in the series, which are followed by H?

L R M Q R H P R H J R T V R I U R H W R H X R H

(a) 4 (b) 5
(c) 6 (d) 3

434. How many such K's are there in the series, which are preceded by P and followed by T?

R K L P U K L G T K P K L T V K P R S Q K B E R K P T K

(a) 1 (b) 2
(c) 3 (d) None of these

435. How many X's are in the following series which are preceded by E and followed by N?

P E X R T N E X L R E N X U P E X T A X F E X L N E X

(a) 2 (b) 3
(c) 1 (d) None of these

436. Pointing to a photograph of a boy Suresh said, "He is the son of the only son of my mother." How is Suresh related to that boy?

(a) Brother (b) Uncle
(c) Cousin (d) Father

437. Q's mother is sister of P and daughter of M. S is daughter of P and sister of T. How is M related to T?

(a) Father
(b) Grandfather
(c) Grandmother
d) Maternal grandfather or grandmother

438. If A + B means A is the mother of B; A – B means A is the brother B; A ÷ B means A is the father of B and A × B means A is the sister of B, which of the following shows that P is the maternal uncle of Q?

(a) Q – N + M × P (b) P + S × N – Q
(c) P – M + N × Q (d) Q – S ÷ P

439. If 'P + Q' means 'P is the husband of Q', 'P ÷ Q' means 'P is the sister of Q' and

'P × Q' means 'P is son of Q, which of the following shows 'A is daughter of B'?

(a) A + D × B
(b) D × B + C ÷ A
(c) B + C × A
(d) C × B ÷ A

Direction: The following questions (440-441) based on given statements.

(a) 'P + Q' means 'P is the sister of Q'
(b) 'P – Q' means 'P is the mother of Q'
(c) 'P × Q' means 'P is the brother of Q'
(d) 'P ÷ Q' means 'P is the father of Q'

440. Which of the following means 'M is the maternal uncle of R'?

(a) M × T – R (b) M ÷ T – R
(c) M + T ÷ K – R (d) M ÷ N + J – R

441. To arrive at the answer to the above question which of the following statements can be dispensed with?

(a) (b) only (b) (c) only
(c) (d) only (d) (a) and (d)

442. If A is the brother of B; B is the sister of C; and C is the father of D, how D is related to A?

(a) Brother
(b) Sister
(c) Nephew
(d) Cannot be determined

443. If D is the brother of B, how B is related to C? To answer this question which of the statements is/are necessary?

1. The son of D is the grandson of C.
2. B is the sister of D.

(a) Only 1
(b) Only 2
(c) Either 1 or 2
(d) 1 and 2 both are required

444. Pointing to a photograph a man said, "I have no brother or sister but that man's father is my father's son." Whose photograph was it?

(a) His son's (b) His own
(c) His father's (d) His nephew's

445. Deepak said to Nitin, "That boy playing with the football is the younger of the two brothers of the daughter of my father's wife." How is the boy playing football related to Deepak?

(a) Son (b) Brother
(c) Cousin (d) Brother-in-law

446. A is father of C and D is son of B. E is brother of A. If C is sister of D, how is B related to E?

(a) Brother-in-law (b) Sister-in-law
(c) Husband (d) Daughter

447. Pointing to a photograph. Bajpai said, "He is the son of the only daughter of the father of my brother." How Bajpai is related to the man in the photograph?

(a) Nephew
(b) Brother
(c) Father
(d) Maternal Uncle

448. A man pointing to a photograph says, "The lady in the photograph is my nephew's maternal grandmother and her son is my sister's brother-in-law." How is the lady in the photograph related to his sister who has no other sister?

(a) Mother (b) Mother-in-law
(c) Cousin (d) Sister-in-law

449. Pointing to a photograph Lata says, "He is the son of the only son of my grandfather." How is the man in the photograph related to Lata?

(a) Brother
(b) Uncle
(c) Cousin
(d) Data is inadequate

450. If P + Q means P is the father of Q. P – Q means P is the brother of Q. P + Q means P is the mother of Q and P × Q means P is

the sister of Q, then which of the following doesn't show the relation A is the aunt of B?

(a) A × C – D + B (b) A × C – D ÷ B
(c) A × C ÷ D + B (d) A × C ÷ D – B

451. Veena who is the sister-in-law of Ashok, is the daughter-in-law of Kalyani. Dheeraj is the father of Sudeep who is the only brother of Ashok. How Kalyani is related to Ashok?
(a) Mother-in-law (b) Aunt
(c) Wife (d) None of these

452. X tells Y, Z is my mother's brother and Z tells Y, your mother is my sister. How is X related to Y?
(a) Brother
(b) Sister
(c) Nephew
(d) Data inadequate

453. Introducing a boy, a girl said, "He is the son of the daughter of the father of my uncle." How is the boy related to the girl?
(a) Brother (b) Nephew
(c) Uncle (d) Son-in-law

454. Pointing to a photograph a lady tells Mohan, "I am the only daughter of this lady and her son is your maternal uncle." How is the speaker related to Mohan's father?
(a) Wife
(b) Sister-in-law
(c) Either of the two
(d) Neither of the two

455. Amit said, "This girl is the wife of the grandson of my mother." How is Amit related to the girl?
(a) Father (b) Grandfather
(c) Husband (d) Father-in-law

456. Prema has a son named Anand. Rajiv is Prema's brother. Neha too has a daughter named Rashmi. Neha is Rajiv's sister. What is Anand's relationship to Rashmi?
(a) Uncle (b) Brother-in-law
(c) Cousin (d) No relationship

457. A and B are children of D. Who is the father of A? To answer this question which of the statements (1) and (2) is necessary?
1. C is the brother of A and the son of E.
2. F is the mother B.
(a) Only (1)
(b) Only (2)
(c) Either (1) or (2)
(d) Both (1) and (2)

458. P is brother of Q. R is sister of Q. S is sister of R. How is Q related to S?
(a) Brother
(b) Sister
(c) Brother or sister
(d) Data inadequate

459. Introducing Suchendra, Naman says, "She is the wife of only nephew of only brother of my mother." How Suchendra is related to Naman?
(a) Wife
(b) Sister
(c) Sister-in-law
(d) Data is inadequate

460. 'P + Q' implies that P is the brother of Q, 'P – Q' implies that P is the mother of Q, whereas, 'P × Q' implies that P is the sister of Q. Which of the following implies. 'M is the maternal uncle of R'?
(a) M – R + K
(b) M + K – R
(c) M + K × Q
(d) There is no such a sign

461. Pointing to a gentleman, Deepak said, "His only brother is the father of my daughter's father." How is the gentleman related to Deepak?

(a) Father (b) Grandfather
(c) Uncle (d) Brother-in-law

462. Introducing a woman, Shashank said, "She is the mother of the only daughter of my son." How that woman is related to Shashank?
(a) Daughter
(b) Sister-in-law
(c) Wife
(d) Daughter-in-law

463. P is Q's brother. R is Q's mother. S is R's father. T is S's mother. How is P related to Q?
(a) Granddaughter (b) Great grandson
(c) Grandson (d) Grandmother

464. P is the mother of K; K is the sister of D; D is the father of J. How is P related to J?
(a) Mother
(b) Grandmother
(c) Aunt
(d) Data inadequate

465. Kalyani is the mother-in-law of Veena who is sister-in-law of Ashok. Dheeraj is father of Sudeep the only brother of Ashok. How is Kalyani related to Ashok?
(a) Mother-in-law (b) Aunt
(c) Wife (d) None of these

466. Introducing a man, a woman said, "He is the only son of the mother of my mother." How is the woman related to the man?
(a) Mother (b) Sister
(c) Niece (d) Maternal aunt

467. If A is B's brother, B is C's sister and C is D's father then D is A's...
(a) Brother (b) Sister
(c) Nephew (d) Data inadequate

468. Pointing to a lady a person said, "The son of her only brother is the brother of my wife." How is the lady related to the person?
(a) Maternal aunt
(b) Grandmother
(c) Sister of father-in-law
(d) None of these

469. If A + B means A is the father of B, A – B means A is the brother of B, A + B means A is the wife B and A × B means A is the mother of B, then which of the following represents M is the maternal grand mother of T?
(a) M × N ÷ S ÷ T
(b) M × N – S ÷ T
(c) M × S – N ÷ T
(d) M × N × S ÷ T

470. 1. B5D means B is the father of D.
2. B9D means B is the sister of D.
3. B4D means B is the brother of D.
4. B3D means B is the wife of D.

Which of the following means F is the mother of K?
(a) F3M5K (b) F5M3K
(c) F9M4N3K (d) F3M5N3K

471. A family consists of six members P, Q, R, X, Y and Z. Q is the son of R, but R is not the mother of Q. P and R are the married couple. Y is the brother of R. X is the daughter of P. Z is the brother of P. Who is the brother-in-law of R?
(a) P (b) Z
(c) Y (d) X

472. If A $ B means A is the brother of B; B C means B is the son of C; C @ D means C is the wife of D and A # D means A is the son of D. How C is related to A?
(a) Maternal grandmother
(b) Maternal aunt
(c) Aunt
(d) Mother

Direction: Read the following information carefully and answer the questions (473-477) given below.

(a) P, Q, R, S, T and U are six students procuring their masters degree in six different subjects—English, History, Philosophy, Physics, Statistics and Mathematics.
(b) Two of them stay in Hostel, two stay as paying guest (PG) and studies Philosophy.
(c) R does not stay as PG and studies Philosophy.
(d) The student studying Statistics and History does not stay as paying guest.
(e) T studies Mathematics and S studies Physics.
(f) U and S stay in hostel. T stays as PG and Q stays at home.

473. Which of the following pairs of students stays one each at hostel and at home?
(a) US (b) SR
(c) QR (d) Data inadequate

474. Who studies English?
(a) S (b) T
(c) U (d) None of these

475. Which of the following pairs of students stay at home?
(a) PQ (b) QR
(c) RS (d) ST

476. Which of the following combinations of subject and place of stay is not correct?
(a) Physics—Hostel
(b) English—Hostel
(c) Philosophy—Home
(d) Mathematics—Paying Guest

477. Which subject(s) does Q study?
(a) History
(b) Statistics
(c) History or Statistics
(d) Data inadequate

Read the following information and answer the given questions (478-479).

1. A + B means A is the mother of B.
2. A – B means A is the sister of B.
3. A B means A is the father of B.
4. A ? B means A is the brother of B.

478 Which of the following means Q is the grandfather of P?
(a) P + N M Q
(b) Q N M + P
(c) Q ? M ? N P
(d) None of these

479 Which of the following means that N is the maternal uncle of M?
(a) N ? P – L + E – M
(b) N – Y + A? M
(c) M – Y P – N
(d) N ? C + F M

Direction: Study the following information to answer the given questions (480-486).

(a) A, B, C, D, E, F and G are seven members of a family.
(b) There are two doctors, two teachers, two professors and one lawyer.
(c) No lady is either teacher or lawyer.
(d) Teacher's wife is a professor and lawyer's wife is also a professor.
(e) C is daughter-in-law of F and mother E.
(f) B a doctor, is son of G and E who is not a professor, is the daughter of lawyer.
(g) A's husband is a teacher and A is mother-in-law of C and grandmother of B.
(h) F is grandfather of B and D.

480. Which of the following is the profession of G?
(a) Teacher (b) Lawyer
(c) Professor (d) None of these

481. Which of the following is one of the married couples?

(a) GC (b) FC
(c) GA (d) None of these

482. How many female members are there in the family?

(a) One (b) Two
(c) Three (d) None of these

483. These family members belong to how many generations?

(a) Four
(b) Two
(c) Either two or three
(d) None of these

484. What is D to C?

(a) Daughter-in-law
(b) Son-in-law
(c) Daughter
(d) None of these

485. Which of the following is the profession of D?

(a) Doctor (b) Professor
(c) Lawyer (d) None of these

486. How D is related to A?

(a) Granddaughter (b) Son
(c) Grandson (d) None of these

Direction: Each of these questions (487-488) is based on the following information.

1. M % N means M is the son of N.
2. M @ N means M is the sister of N.
3. M $ N means M is the father of N.

487. Which of the following shows the relation that C is the granddaughter of E?

(a) C % B $ F $ E
(b) B $ F $ E % C
(c) C @ B % F % E
(d) E % B $ F $ C

488. Which of the following shows the relation that S is the father of Q?

(a) S @ P $ Q (b) Q @ P % S
(c) Q $ S @ P (d) None of these

Direction: Read the following informations carefully and answer the questions (489-492) given below:

(a) P, Q, R, S, T and U are six members of a family, each of them are engaged in a different profession—Doctor, Lawyer, Teacher, Engineer, Nurse, Manager.
(b) Each of them remains at home on a different day of the week from Monday to Saturday.
(c) The Lawyer in the family remains at home on Thursday.
(d) R remains at home on Tuesday.
(e) P, the Doctor does not remain at home either on Saturday or on Wednesday, S is neither the Doctor nor the Teacher and remains at home on Friday.
(f) Q is the Engineer and T is the Manager.

489. Who among them remains at home on the following day of the Nurse?

(a) Q (b) Q or T
(c) R (d) S
(e) None of these

490. Which of the following combinations is not correct?

(a) R—Teacher (b) Q—Engineer
(c) T—Manager (d) S—Nurse
(e) All are correct

491. Which of the following combinations is correct?

(a) Lawyer—Tuesday
(b) Teacher—Wednesday
(c) Manager—Friday
(d) Engineer—Thursday
(e) Nurse—Friday

492. Who remains at home on Saturday?

(a) S (b) T
(c) R (d) Q or T
(e) None of these

Direction: Study the following informations and answer the questions (493-496) given below.

(a) Jayant, Kunal, Namrata, Anjali and Tanmay are five members of a family.
(b) They have their birth dates from January to May each member in one of these months.
(c) Each one likes one particular item for his/her birthday out of Bengali Sweets, Chocolate, Pastries, Ice Cream, Dry Fruits.
(d) The one who likes Pastries is bom in the month which is exactly middle in the months given.
(e) Anjali does not like Ice Cream but brings Chocolates for Jayant in February.
(f) Tanmay who is fond of Bengali Sweets is born in the next month immediately after Namrata.
(g) Namrata does not like Dry Fruits or Ice Cream.

493. What is the choice of Kunal?

(a) Bengali Sweets
(b) Dry Fruits
(c) Ice Cream
(d) Cannot be determined

494. In which month was Kunal born?

(a) January (b) May
(c) January or May (d) Data inadequate

495. Which combination of month and item is 'TRUE' for Jayant?

(a) February—Ice Cream
(b) February—Pastry
(c) March—Pastry
(d) Cannot be determined
(e) None of these

496. What is the choice of Anjali?

(a) Dry Fruits
(b) Pastries
(c) Bengali Sweets
(d) Cannot be determined

Direction: (497-513) in the following questions find out the group of letters in place of question in the letter series.

497. BFJ, IMQ, PTX, ?

(a) XBF (b) XAE
(c) WAE (d) WBF

498. CHM, MRW, WBG, ?

(a) FLP (b) FLQ
(c) GLQ (d) GLP

499. PNR, QKQ, SHO, VEL, ZBH, ?

(a) EZC (b) EYC
(c) DYB (d) FZB

500. DG, GJ, JM, ?

(a) NP (b) MQ
(c) MO (d) MP

501. EIO, IOU, OUA, ?

(a) UAI (b) UAE
(c) AEI (d) EIO

502. EFI, FGJ, GHK, ?, UM

(a) HIL (b) HIM
(c) HIK (d) GHL

503. H3M, 150, L9S, Q17A, ?

(a) X33Q (b) Z33P
(c) X33P (d) W33R

504. BDO, CFR, DHN, EJS, ?

(a) FLM (b) FKM
(c) FNM (d) FLN

505. $\frac{1}{R}, \frac{3}{O}, \frac{5}{K}, \frac{9}{F}, \frac{13}{Z}, ?$

(a) $\frac{19}{S}$ (b) $\frac{20}{T}$
(c) $\frac{19}{T}$ (d) $\frac{21}{R}$

506. A2E, B7D, D17B, G37Y, ?
(a) K87V (b) K67U
(c) R57U (d) K77U

507. B0M, D1L, G1J, K2G, ?
(a) Q4C (b) P5C
(c) P3C (d) P3B

508. $\frac{4}{Z}, \frac{11}{W}, \frac{25}{Q}, \frac{46}{H}$, ?
(a) $\frac{67}{W}$ (b) $\frac{74}{V}$
(c) $\frac{60}{U}$ (d) $\frac{81}{V}$

509. UV3, VU8, XS15, AP24, ?
(a) DL35 (b) EL37
(c) DK37 (d) EL35

510. ISR, 2UO, 5WL, 16YI, ?
(a) 49AF (b) 33BG
(c) 65AF (d) 65AG

511. $\frac{1}{C}, \frac{3}{E}, \frac{5}{G}, \frac{7}{I}$, ?
(a) $\frac{9}{L}$ (b) $\frac{9}{I}$
(c) $\frac{9}{K}$ (d) $\frac{11}{K}$

512. 1BR, 2E0, 6HL, 15KI, ?
(a) 22NF (b) 3INF
(c) 26NE (d) 28NF

513. $\frac{1}{AB}, \frac{6}{EF}, \frac{15}{JK}, \frac{32}{PQ}$, ?
(a) $\frac{64}{WX}$ (b) $\frac{65}{XY}$
(c) $\frac{66}{YZ}$ (d) $\frac{65}{WX}$

Direction: (514-528) in the following series find the number in place of question mark?

514. 8, 13, 18, 11, 16, 21, 16, 21, 26, ?
(a) 28, 88, 38 (b) 23, 28, 33
(c) 22, 27, 32 (d) 21, 26, 31

515. 23, 19, ?, 12, 9.
(a) 14 (b) 15
(c) 16 (d) 17

516. 25, 22, 30, ?, 35.
(a) 27 (b) 26
(c) 28 (d) 29

517. 2, 8, 14, 26, 38, 56, ?
(a) 78 (b) 80
(c) 74 (d) 75

518. $8\frac{4}{7}, 9\frac{3}{3}, 11\frac{5}{5}, 13\frac{8}{4}$, ?
(a) $\frac{80}{3}$ (b) $\frac{70}{3}$
(c) $\frac{50}{3}$ (d) 20

519. 29, 24, 26, 21, 23, ?
(a) 20 (b) 19
(c) 17 (d) 18

520. 2, 6, 8, 10, 10, 16, 20, 22, 24, 24, 30, ?
(a) 34 (b) 36
(c) 32 (d) 30

521. 2, 4, 12, 6, 12, 36, 18, 36, 108, ?
(a) 72 (b) 54
(c) 90 (d) 108

522. 2, 7, 15, 26, 40, 57, ?
(a) 80 (b) 81
(c) 75 (d) 77

523. 3, 5, 6, 8, 11, 13, ?
(a) 17 (b) 18
(c) 15 (d) 20

524. 5, 13, ?, 109, 325, 973.
(a) 39 (b) 36
(c) 37 (d) 35

525. 2, 5, 11, ?, 47.
(a) 17 (b) 18
(c) 21 (d) 26

526. 324, 289, 256, 225, 196, ?
(a) 196 (b) 121
(c) 144 (d) 169

527. 11, 5, 20, 12, ?, 26, 74, 54.
(a) 30 (b) 38
(c) 43 (d) 28

528. 1, 4, 7, 10, ?, 16, 19, ?
(a) 13, 22 (b) 11, 22
(c) 13, 21 (d) 13, 23

Direction: (529-543) in each question below is given statements followed by conclusions. You have to assume everything in the statement to be true, then consider the conclusions together and decide which of them logically follows beyond a reasonable doubt from the information given in the statements.

529. **Statements**
(i) All microprocessors are computers.
(ii) All computers are modems.

Conclusions
I. All microprocessors are modems.
II. All modems are microprocessors.
III. All modems are computers.
IV. Some computers are microprocessors.
(a) Only I follow
(b) Both I and IV follow
(c) Both I and II follow
(d) None of these.

530. **Statements**
(i) Some roots are ships.
(ii) Some roots are apples.

Conclusions
I. Some apples are ships.
II. Some ships are apples.
III. No root is a ship.
IV. Some apples are not roots.
(a) Both I and II follow
(b) Both III and IV follow
(c) All follow
(d) None of these.

531. **Statements**
(i) All the express trains stop here.
(ii) Rajdhani does not stop here.

Conclusions
I. Rajdhani is a passenger train.
II. Rajdhani is a superfast train.
III. Rajdhani is not an express train.
IV. Rajdhani is a special train.
(a) Only II follow
(b) Both I and III follow
(c) Both II and IV follow
(d) None of these.

532. **Statements**
(i) All chairs are stars.
(ii) Some chairs are round.

Conclusions
I. Some rounds are stars.
II. Some stars are round.
III. No star is round.
IV. Some stars are not round.
(a) Both I and II follow
(b) Both III and IV follow
(c) Either II or III follow
(d) None of these.

533. **Statements**
(i) All worms are mosquitoes.
(ii) All mosquitoes are birds.

Conclusions
I. All mosquitoes are worms.
II. All worms are birds.
III. All birds are worms.
IV. Some mosquitoes are birds.
(a) Both I and II follow
(b) Only I follow
(c) Both II and IV follow
(d) None of these.

534. **Statements**
(i) Some actors are doctors.
(ii) All architects are doctors.

Conclusions

I. All actors are doctors.
II. Some architects are doctors.
III. All doctors are actors.
IV. Some actors are architects.

(a) Only II follow
(b) Both II and IV follow
(c) Both III and IV follow
(d) None of these.

535. **Statements**

(i) All lawyers are uncles.
(ii) All girls are lawyers.

Conclusions

I. All girls are uncles.
II. All uncles are girls.
III. Some girls are not uncles.
IV. Some uncles are lawyers.

(a) Both I, II and IV follow
(b) Both I and IV follow
(c) Both II and IV follow
(d) None of these.

536. **Statements**

(i) The cabinet passed the bill.
(ii) He is a member of the cabinet.

Conclusions

I. He passed the bill.
II. The bill was passed by him.
III. A member of the cabinet can pass the bill.
IV. No minister could pass the bill.

(a) Only I follow
(b) Only II follow
(c) Only III follow
(d) None of these.

537. **Statements**

(i) Water is a liquid.
(ii) Ice is water.

Conclusions

I. Ice is liquid.
II. Ice is not liquid.
III. No ice is liquid.
IV. Some ice is not liquid.

(a) Only I follow
(b) Only II follow
(c) Either I or II follow
(d) None of these.

538. **Statements**

(i) Some triangles are figures.
(ii) Some triangles are pentagons.

Conclusions

I. No pentagons are figures.
II. Some figures are pentagons.
III. No triangle is a figure.
IV. No triangle is pentagon.

(a) Both III and IV follow
(b) Both I and II follow
(c) Either I or II follow
(d) None of these.

539. **Statements**

(i) All sauces are pickles.
(ii) Some sauces are ketchup.

Conclusions

I. All ketchup are sauces.
II. All pickles are ketchup.
III. All sauces are ketchup.
IV. Some pickles are ketchup.

(a) Both I and II follow
(b) Both II and III follow
(c) Both I and III follow
(d) None of these.

540. **Statements**

(i) If it is cloudy, lion will roar.
(ii) Lions don't roar.

Conclusions

I. It is not cloudy.
II. It is cloudy.
III. Lions roar only in cloudy night.
IV. Lion will roar only in cloudy day.

(a) Either I or II follow
(b) Only I follow

(c) Only II follow
(d) None of these.

541. **Statements**
(i) Gold is ductile.
(ii) This substance is not ductile.

Conclusions
I. This substance is not gold.
II. Gold is not ductile.
III. Ductiles are not gold.
IV. No substance is ductile.
(a) Only IV follow
(b) Only I follow
(c) Both I and IV follow
(d) None of these.

542. **Statements**
(i) India includes Bengal.
(ii) Bengal does not include UP.

Conclusions
I. India does not include UP.
II. UP is also a part of India.
III. Bengal includes UP.
IV. UP is not a part of India.
(a) Either II or IV follow
(b) Only I follow
(c) Only II follow
(d) None of these.

543. **Statements**
(i) All tigers have four legs
(ii) No cat is tiger.

Conclusions
I. No cat has four legs.
II. No four leggers are cats.
III. Tigers are cats.
IV. Cats have four legs.
(a) Both I and II follow
(b) Only III follow
(c) Only IV follow
(d) None of these.

Direction: (544-553) in the following questions, two statements are followed by two conclusions. Read the conclusions carefully and then decide which of the given conclusions logically follows from the above given two statements in each question. Mark (a) if only conclusion (I) follow, (b) if only conclusion (II) follow, (c) if neither (I) nor (II) follow and (d) if both (I) and (II) follow.

544. **Statements**
(i) Some crows are dogs.
(ii) All dogs are faithful.

Conclusions
(I) All faithful animals are dogs.
(II) Some crows are faithful.

545. **Statements**
(i) Some essayists are poets.
(ii) All poets are dramatists.

Conclusion
I. Some poets are essayists.
II. Some essayists are dramatists.

546. **Statements**
(i) All books are chairs.
(ii) All chairs are pens.

Conclusions
I. All books are pens.
II. Some pens are books.

547. **Statements**
(i) All pencils are bricks.
(ii) All bricks are bottles.

Conclusions
I. Some bottles are pencils.
II. Some bottles are bricks.

548. **Statements**
(i) Some trees are horses.
(ii) Biscuit is a tree.

Conclusions
I. Biscuit is not a horse.
II. Some horses are trees.

549. **Statements**
(i) Some poets are fools.
(ii) All fools are goats.

Conclusion

(I) Some poets are goats.

(II) Some fools are poets.

550. **Statements**

(i) All poets are authors.

(ii) All singers are authors.

Conclusions

I. All singers are poets.

II. Some authors are not singers.

551. **Statements**

(i) All tables are ants.

(ii) Some ants are chairs.

Conclusions

I. Some tables are chairs.

II. Some chairs are tables.

552. **Statements**

(i) All tables are horses.

(ii) All horses are rivers.

Conclusions

I. All tables are rivers.

II. Some rivers are tables.

553. **Statements**

(i) All cats are dogs.

(ii) Some dogs are black.

Conclusions

I. Some cats are blacky

II. Black dogs are not cats.

Direction: (554-582) in each of the following questions, a statement is followed by two conclusions numbered I and II. The candidates have to assume everything in the statement to be true and consider both the conclusions together, then decide which of the two given conclusions logically follow beyond a reasonable doubt from the information given in the statement. Give answer:

(a) If only conclusion I follow

(b) If only conclusion II follow

(c) If either I or II follow

(d) If neither I nor II follow

(e) If both I and II follow.

554. **Statement:** The oceans are a storehouse of practically every mineral, including uranium. But like most other minerals it is found in extremely low concentrations about three grams for 1000 tons of water.

Conclusions

I. Sea water contains gold.

II. The oceans harbour radiation hazards.

555. **Statement:** In a one day cricket match, the total runs made by a team were 200. Out of these 160 runs were made by spinners.

Conclusions

I. 80% of the team consists of spinners.

II. The opening batsmen were spinners.

556. **Statement:** Devil is an enemy because he deceives the people.

Conclusions

I. Those who deceive the people are enemies.

II. All those who deceive the men are devils.

557. **Statement:** Government has spoiled many top ranking financial institutions by appointing bureaucrats as Directors of these institutions.

Conclusions

I. Government should appoint Directors of the financial institutes taking into consideration the expertise of the person in the area of finance.

II. The Director of the financial institute should have expertise commensurate with the financial work carried out by the institute.

558. **Statement:** Some students are disturbing.

Conclusions

I. Some who are disturbing are students.

II. Some students are not disturbing.

559. **Statement:** Prime age school-going children in urban India have now become

avid as well as more regular viewers of television, even in households without a TV. As a result there has been an alarming decline in the extent of readership of newspapers.

Conclusions

I. Method of increasing the readership of newspapers should be devised.

II. A team of experts should be sent to other countries to study the impact of TV on the readership of newspapers.

560. **Statement:** This man can't succeed because he is not truthful.

Conclusions

I. Those who can get success are truthful.

II. All truthful persons succeed.

561. **Statement:** Monitoring has become an integral part in the planning of social development programmes. It is recommended that Management Information System be developed for all programmes. This is likely to give a feedback on the performance of the functionaries and the efficacy with which services are being delivered.

Conclusions

I. All the social development programmes should be evaluated.

II. There is a need to monitor the performance of workers.

562. **Statement:** All students are not genius.

Conclusions

I. Many students are not genius.

II. All genius are students.

563. **Statement:** The manager humiliated Sachin in the presence of his colleagues.

Conclusions

I. The manager did not like Sachin.

II. Sachin was not popular with his colleagues.

564. **Statement:** In a certain community only widows do not apply Kumkum to their foreheads. Ratna, who belongs to that community applies Kumkum to her forehead.

Conclusions

I. Ratna is an unmarried girl.

II. Ratna is a married woman.

565. **Statement:** Reading makes a full man, conference a ready man and writing an exact man.

Conclusions

I. Pointed and precise expression comes only through extensive writing.

II. Extensive reading makes a complete man.

566. **Statement:** He is a historian, so he cannot write novels.

Conclusions

I. No historian can write novels.

II. Some historians can write novels.

567. **Statement:** Use 'Kraft' colours. They add colour to our life.—An advertisement.

Conclusions

I. Catchy slogans do not attract people.

II. People like dark colours.

568. **Statement:** From all available cultural records, it is evident that even in ancient India, both the masters and disciples valued not the quantity but the quality of knowledge.

Conclusions

I. Giving importance to quantity of knowledge is meaningless.

II. There was an identity of educational values between teachers and students in ancient India.

569. **Statement:** Modern man influences his destiny by the choice he makes unlike in the past.

Conclusions

I. Earlier there were fewer options available to man.

II. There was no desire in the past to influence the destiny.

570. **Statement:** He does not go to the mosque so he is not a true Muslim.

Conclusions

I. Only true Muslims go to the mosque.

II. All true Muslims must go to the mosque.

571. **Statement:** People who speak too much against dowry are those who had taken it themselves.

Conclusions

I. It is easier said than done.

II. People have double standards.

572. **Statement:** About 50 percent of animal by-products hair, skin, horn, etc. is edible protein. Indian chemists have developed a method of isolating 45 percent of this protein. They used an enzyme developed in Japan to break down Soya protein.

Conclusions

I. Indians have not been able to develop enzymes.

II. If an economically feasible process is developed, there would be plenty of edible protein available.

573. **Statement:** The national norm is 100 beds per thousand populations but in this state, 150 beds per thousand are available in the hospitals.

Conclusions

I. Our national norm is appropriate.

II. The state's health system is taking adequate care in this regard.

574. **Statement:** In spite of the claim of the Government of terrorism being under check, killing continues.

Conclusions

I. The terrorists have not come to an understanding with the government.

II. The government has been constantly telling a lie.

575. **Statement:** The serious accident in which a person was run down by a car yesterday had again focused attention on the most unsatisfactory state of roads.

Conclusions

I. The accident that occurred was fatal.

II. Several accidents have so far taken place because of unsatisfactory state of roads.

576. **Statement:** A bird in hand is worth two in the bush.

Conclusions

I. We should be content with what we have.

II. We should not crave for what is not.

577. **Statement:** Any student who does not behave properly while in the school brings bad name to himself and also for the school.

Conclusions

I. Such student should be removed from the school.

II. Stricter discipline does not improve behaviour of the students.

578. **Statement:** A Corporate General Manager asked four managers to either submit their resignations by the next day or face termination orders from service. Three of them had submitted their resignations by that evening.

Conclusions

I. The next day, the remaining manager would also resign.

II. The General Manager would terminate his services the next day.

579. **Statement:** To cultivate interest in reading, the school has made it compulsory from June this year for each student to read two books per week and submit a weekly report on the books.

Conclusions

I. Interest in reading can be created by force.

II. Some students will eventually develop interest in reading.

580. **Statement:** Company X has marketed the product. Go ahead; purchase it if price and quality are your considerations.

Conclusions

I. The product must be good in quality.

II. The price of the product must be reasonable.

581. **Statement:** The standard of education in private schools is much better than Municipal and Zila Parishad-run schools.

Conclusions

I. The Municipal and Zila Parishad should make serious efforts to improve standard of their schools.

II. All Municipal and Zila Parishad schools should be closed immediately.

582. **Statement:** Fashion is a form of ugliness so intolerable that we have to alter it every six months.

Conclusions

I. Fashion designers do not understand the public mind very well.

II. The public by and large is highly susceptible to novelty.

Direction: (583-611) in the following questions, a statement is followed by two assumptions I and II. The candidate has to consider each statement and assumptions that follow and decide which of the assumption(s) is/are implicit in the statement.

Marked answer

(a) If only assumption I is implicit
(b) If only assumption II is implicit
(c) If either I or II is implicit
(d) If neither I nor II is implicit
(e) If both I and II are implicit.

583. **Statement:** A few people demanded one-man-one-post in the case of the Minister for strengthening the party and for efficient administration.

Assumptions

I. No human being can be efficient in two spheres.

II. A person attending to only administration or party work will be able to do much.

584. **Statement:** "You are hereby appointed as a programmer with a probation period of one year and your performance will be reviewed at the end of the period for confirmation."—A line in an appointment letter.

Assumptions

I. The performance of an individual generally is not known at the time of appointment offer.

II. Generally an individual tries to prove his worth in the probation period.

585. **Statement:** Happiness is to be shared. Unhappy people suffer.

Assumptions

I. Unhappy nation shares sufferings.

II. Happy people do not suffer.

586. **Statement:** "In order to bring punctuality in our office, we must provide conveyance allowance to our employees."—In charge of a company tells Personnel Manager.

Assumptions

I. Conveyance allowance will not help in bringing punctuality.

II. Discipline and reward should always go hand in hand.

587. **Statement:** Each nation must maintain an army.

Assumptions

I. It makes nation strong.

II. It is indispensable for the defence of the nation.

588. **Statement:** "If you trouble me, I will slap you."—A mother warns her child.

Assumptions

I. With the warning, the child may stop troubling her.

II. All children are basically naughty.

589. **Statement:** Spicy food damages the liver. The patient is advised to take a liver-tonic.

Assumptions

I. The patient takes spicy food.

II. A healthy liver is necessary to digest fat.

590. **Statement:** A warning in a train compartment—"To stop train, pull chain. Penalty for improper use ₹ 500."

Assumptions

I. Some people misuse the alarm chain.

II. On certain occasions, people may want to stop a running train.

591. **Statement:** The Railway authorities have decided to increase the freight charges by 10 percent in view of the possibility of incurring losses in the current financial year.

Assumptions

I. The volume of freight during the remaining period may remain same.

II. The amount so obtained may set off a part or total of the estimated deficit.

592. **Statement:** If it is easy to become an engineer, I don't want to be an engineer.

Assumptions

I. An individual aspires to be professional.

II. One desires to achieve a thing which is hard earned.

593. **Statement:** India's economy is depending mainly on forests.

Assumptions

I. Trees should be preserved to improve Indian economy.

II. India wants only maintenance of forests to improve economic conditions.

594. **Statement:** "The bridge was built at the cost of ₹ 128 crores and even civil bus service is not utilizing it, what a pity to see it grossly underutilized."—A citizen's view on a new flyover linking east and west sides of a suburb.

Assumptions

I. The building of such bridges does not serve any public objective.

II. There has to be some accountability and utility of money spent on public projects.

595. **Statement:** USA re-emerged as India's largest import source in the early nineties.

Assumptions

I. With swift political developments in the Soviet Union, India began to rely on USA.

II. The USA was the only country which wanted to meet the requirements of India.

596. **Statement:** Detergents should be used to clean clothes.

Assumptions

I. Detergents form more lather.

II. Detergents help to dislodge grease and dirt.

597. **Statement:** Go by aeroplane from Delhi to Chennai to reach quickly.

Assumptions

I. Delhi and Chennai are connected by air services.

II. There is no other means of going from Delhi to Chennai.

598. **Statement:** Never before such a lucid book was available on the topic.

Assumptions

I. Some other books were available on this topic.

II. You can write lucid books on very few topics.

599. **Statement:** Let the government increase the present rate of taxation to recover the deficit in the budget.

Assumptions

I. Present rate of taxes is very low.

II. If government wants to get away with the budgetary deficit, it should increase tax rate.

600. **Statement:** "I have not received telephone bills for nine months inspite of several complaints."—A telephone customer's letter to the editor of a daily.

Assumptions

I. Every customer has a right to get bills regularly from the telephone company.

II. The customer's complaints point to defect in the services which are expected to be corrected.

601. **Statement:** Successful man has the ability to judge himself correctly.

Assumptions

I. Successful man cannot make a wrong judgement.

II. To judge others is of no use for successful man.

602. **Statement:** The government has decided to pay compensation to the tune of ₹ 1 lakh to the family members of those who are killed in railway accidents.

Assumptions

I. The government has enough funds to meet the expenses due to compensation.

II. There may be reduction in incidents of railway accidents in near future.

603. **Statement:** The new education policy envisages major modification in the educational system.

Assumptions

I. The present education system needs improvement.

II. The present education system is inconsistent with the national needs.

604. **Statement:** Apart from the entertainment value of television, its educational value cannot be ignored.

Assumptions

I. People take television to be a means of entertainment only.

II. The educational value of television is not realised properly.

605. **Statement:** Ghosts haunt deserted places only.

Assumptions

I. They do not want the interference of human being.

II. Every deserted residence is haunted.

606. **Statement:** 'Double your money in five months.'—An advertisement.

Assumptions

I. The assurance is not genuine.

II. People want their money to grow.

607. **Statement:** Of all the newspapers published in India, 'The Hindu' has the largest number of readers.

Assumptions

I. The volume of readership of all newspapers in India is known.

II. No newspaper in India other than 'The Hindu' has a large readership.

608. **Statement:** The campaign of 'Keep your city clean' started by the Civil Council did not evoke any response from the citizens.

Assumptions

I. People do not desire to keep their city clean.

II. The Civil Council has failed in its campaign.

609. **Statement:** An Indian beautician is opening a beauty parlour in New York.

Assumptions

I. New York lacks beauty parlours.

II. There are better business prospects in New York.

610. **Statement:** Of all the radio sets manufactured in India, the 'X' brand has the largest sale.

Assumptions

I. The sale of all the radio sets manufactured in India is known.

II. The manufacturing of no other radio set in India is as large as 'X' brand radio.

611. **Statement:** Consult me before taking any decision on investment.

Assumptions

I. You may take a wrong decision if you don't consult me.

II. It is important to take right decision on investment.

Direction: (612-664) Each question given below consists of a statement, followed by two arguments numbered I and II. You have to decide which of the arguments is a 'strong' argument and which is a 'weak' argument.

Marked answer

(a) If only argument I is strong

(b) If only argument II is strong

(c) If either I or II is strong

(d) If neither I nor II is strong

(e) If both I and II are strong.

612. **Statement:** Should India encourage exports, when most things are insufficient for internal use itself?

Arguments

I. Yes. We have to earn foreign exchange to pay for our imports.

II. No. Even selective encouragement would lead to shortages.

613. **Statement:** Should education be given by the government to the people free of charge?

Arguments

I. Yes, it will help in universalisation of education in the country.

II. No, there will be budgetary pressure creating some new problems.

614. **Statement:** Should there be students union in college/university?

Arguments

I. No. This will create a political atmosphere in the campus.

II. Yes, it is very necessary. Students are future political leaders.

615. **Statement:** Should students study in early hours of morning?

Arguments

I. Yes, mind is fresh and alert at that time

II. No, early risers feel sleepy throughout the day.

616. **Statement:** Should cottage industries be encouraged in rural areas?

Arguments

I. Yes. Rural people are creative.

II. Yes. This would help to solve the problem of unemployment to some extent.

617. **Statement:** Should sex education be given in schools?

Arguments

I: Yes, it is given in western countries.

II: No, it is naturally gained when children grow into adolescence.

618. **Statement:** Should all the annual examinations up to Std. V be abolished?

Arguments

I. Yes. The young students should not be burdened with such examinations which hampers their natural growth.

II. No. The students will not study seriously as they will get automatic promotion to the next class and this will affect them in future.

619. **Statement:** Should India support economic liberalisation?

Arguments

I. Yes, it will boost up industrial development leading to more supply of the commodities and low price.

II. No, it is against the Nehru's dream of democratic socialism.

620. **Statement:** Should we scrap the system of formal education beyond graduation?

Arguments

I. Yes. It will mean taking employment at an early date.

II. No. It will mean lack of depth of knowledge.

621. **Statement:** Should the private companies be allowed to operate passenger train services in India?

Arguments

I. Yes. This will improve the quality of service in Indian Railways and it will be faced with severe competition.

II. No. The private companies may not agree to operate in the non-profitable sectors.

622. **Statement:** Should new big industries be started in Mumbai?

Arguments

II. Yes. It will create job opportunities.

II. No. It will further add to the pollution of the city.

623. **Statement:** Should there be an upper age limit of 65 years for contesting Parliamentary/Legislative Assembly elections?

Arguments

I. Yes. Generally, people above the age of 65 lose their dynamism and will power.

II. No. The lifespan is so increased that people remain physically and mentally active even up to the age of 80.

624. **Statement:** Does India need so many plans for development?

Arguments

I. Yes. Nothing can be achieved without proper planning.

II. No. Too much time, money and energy is wasted on planning.

625. **Statement:** Should the prestigious people who have committed crime unknowingly, be met with special treatment?

Arguments

I. Yes. The prestigious people do not commit crime intentionally.

II. No. It is our policy that everybody is equal before the law.

626. **Statement:** Should internal assessment in colleges be abolished?

Arguments

I. Yes. This will help in reducing the possibility of favouritism.

II. No, teaching faculty will lose control over students.

627. **Statement:** Should all the unauthorised structures in the city be demolished?

Arguments

I. No. Where will the people residing in such houses live?

II. Yes. This will give a clear message to general public and they will refrain from constructing unauthorised buildings.

628. **Statement:** Should so much money be spent on advertisements?

Arguments

I. Yes. It is an essential concomitant in a capitalist economy.

II. No. It leads to wastage of resources.

629. **Statement:** Should there be reservation in Government jobs for candidates from single child family?

Arguments

I. No. This is not advisable as the jobs should be offered to only deserving candidates without any reservation for a particular group.

II. Yes. This will help reduce the growing population in India as the parents will be encouraged to adopt single child norm.

630. **Statement:** Are nuclear families better than joint families?

Arguments

I. No. Joint families ensure security and also reduce the burden of work.

II. Yes. Nuclear families ensure greater freedom.

631. **Statement:** Should the railways immediately stop issuing free passes to all its employees?

Arguments

I. No. The employees have the right to travel free.

II. Yes. This will help railways to provide better facility.

632. **Statement:** Should school education be made free in India?

Arguments

I. Yes. This is the only way to improve the level of literacy.

II. No. It will add to the already heavy burden on the exchequer.

633. **Statement:** Should luxury hotels be banned in India?

Arguments:

I. Yes. They are places from where international criminals operate.

II. No. Affluent foreign tourists will have no place to stay.

634. **Statement:** Should there be a complete ban on manufacture of fire-crackers in India?

Arguments

I. No. This will render thousands of workers jobless.

II. Yes. The fire-cracker manufacturers use child labour to a large extent.

635. **Statement:** Should the sex determination test during pregnancy be completely banned?

Arguments

I. Yes. This leads to indiscriminate female foeticide and eventually will lead to social imbalance.

II. No. People have a right to know about their unborn child.

636. **Statement:** Should the tuition fees in all postgraduate courses be hiked considerably?

Arguments

I. Yes. This will bring in some sense of seriousness among the students and will improve the quality.

II. No. This will force the meritorious poor students to stay away from postgraduate courses.

637. **Statement:** Should officers accepting bribe be punished?

Arguments

I. No. Certain circumstances may have compelled them to take bribe.

II. Yes. They should do the job they are entrusted with, honestly.

638. **Statement:** Should India allow the multinationals to explore the resources available under sea in its vast economic zone?

Arguments

I. Yes. India does not have enough technical and financial resources to conduct such explorations.

II. No. This will endanger the sovereign status of the country.

639. **Statement:** Should there be a restriction on the migration of people from one state to another state in India?

Arguments

I. No. Any Indian citizen has a basic right to stay at any place of his/her choice and hence they cannot be stopped.

II. Yes. This is the way to effect an equitable distribution of resources across the states in India.

640. **Statement:** Should articles of only deserving authors be allowed to be published?

Arguments

I. Yes, it will save a lot of paper which falls short of supply.

II. No, it is not possible to draw a demarcation between the deserving and the undeserving authors.

641. **Statement:** Should there be more than one High Court in each state in India?

Arguments

I. No. This will be a sheer wastage of taxpayers' money.

II. Yes. This will help reduce the backlog of cases pending for a very long time.

642. **Statement:** Has the medical science really lengthened the span of life?

Arguments

I. Yes, the new drugs have been able to combat the diseases and increase the span of life.

II. No, the eternal truth that every person's days are numbered cannot be denied.

643. **Statement:** Should students take part in politics?

Arguments

I. Yes. It inculcates in them qualities of leadership.

II. No. They should study and build up their career.

644. **Statement:** Should sales tax be abolished?

Arguments

I. Yes, it will eliminate an important source of corruption.

II. Yes, it will bring the prices of commodities down and hence consumers will be benefited.

645. **Statement:** Should mass media be fully controlled by the government?

Arguments

I. Yes, the contradictory news only confuses the people.

II. No, its credibility will be doubtful if it confuses people.

646. **Statement:** Should there be women chief ministers in states?

Arguments

I. Yes, only then the plight of women will be removed and their conditions will improve.

II. No, a woman is not capable of ruling a state.

647. **Statement:** Computer based technology is very fruitful for industrial development in India.

Arguments

I. Yes, accuracy, fast production and fineness are possible through computer technology.

II. No, it will increase unemployment in the country.

648. **Statement:** Should the opinion polls predicting outcome of elections before the elections be banned in India?

Arguments

I. Yes. This may affect the voters' mind and may affect the outcome.

II. No. Such polls are conducted all over the world.

649. **Statement:** Should India have nuclear weapons?

Arguments

I. Yes, it is necessary to protect the sovereignty and integrity of the country.

II. No, this will disturb the balance of power in the region.

650. **Statement:** Should agriculture in rural India be mechanised?

Arguments

I. Yes. It would lead to higher production.

II. No. Many villagers would be left unemployed.

651. **Statement:** Should public meeting and conferences be banned in the country.

Arguments

I. Yes, it is the place where opponents are abused.

II. No, it is against fundamental rights given to citizens of India.

652. **Statement:** Should there be concentration of foreign investment in only few states?

Arguments

I. No. It is against the policy of overall development of the country.

II. Yes. A large number of states lack infrastructure to attract foreign investment.

653. **Statement:** Should higher education be restricted to the most deserving students.

Arguments

I. Yes, only deserving people are entitled to this luxury.

II. No, it is against the principles of equality of educational opportunity.

654. **Statement:** Should religion be banned?

Arguments

I. Yes, it develops fanaticism among people.

II. No, religion binds people together.

655. **Statement:** Should guides published by private agencies be banned?

Arguments

I. Yes, only then students will start reading textbooks.

II. No, they are of immense help for weak students at the eleventh hour.

656. **Statement:** Should workers be allowed to participate in the management of factories in India?

Arguments

I. Yes, it is the present management theory.

II. No, many workers are illiterate and their contribution will not be of value.

657. **Statement:** Do good quality products need wide publicity?

Arguments

I. Yes, in the present day world of competition, customers cannot know about a new product without proper publicity.

II. No, good quality products automatically attract customers and thus speak for themselves.

658. **Statement:** Should the political parties be banned?

Arguments

I. Yes, it is necessary to teach a lesson to the politicians.

II. No, it will lead to an end of democracy.

659. **Statement:** Should smoking be prohibited?

Arguments

I. Yes, it damages the liver and the lung.

II. No, it will drive millions of tobacco workers out.

660. **Statement:** Should the duration of the parliamentary government be increased?

Arguments

I. Yes, it will reduce the expenses on elections and also reduce inflation.

II. No, it will take longer time to change a ruling party even if it is corrupt.

661. **Statement:** Should the educated people be given necessary work in villages?

Arguments

I. Yes, they can revolutionise agriculture and revamp the rural atmosphere.

II. No, their education might be wasted there in villages.

662. **Statement:** Is the youngest child happy when a new baby takes birth in the family?

Arguments

I. Yes, it is exciting for him to have a new member in the family.

II. No, he becomes jealous of the new born.

663. **Statement:** Should the agriculture in India be mechanised?

Arguments

I. Yes, it would lead to higher production.

II. No, many villagers would be left unemployed.

664. **Statement:** Should the government stop aiding to minority institutions of education?

Arguments:

I. Yes, their poor quality as well as quantity of education is wasting the fund.

II. No, ruling party will lose its vote bank in the coming elections.

665. Which symbol will be on the face opposite to the face with symbol?

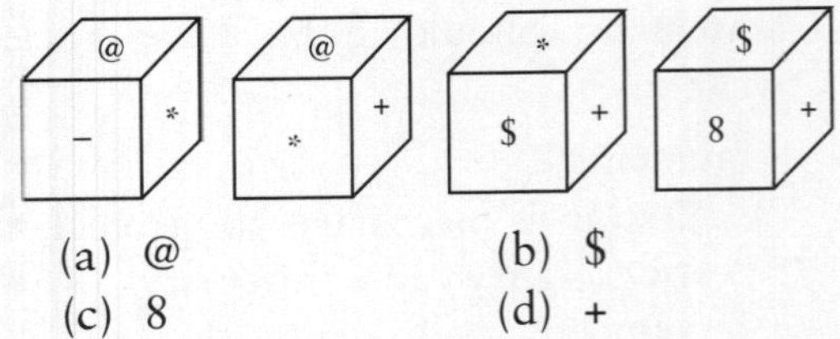

(a) @ (b) $
(c) 8 (d) +

666. Here two positions of dice are shown. If there are two dots in the bottom, then how many dots will be on the top?

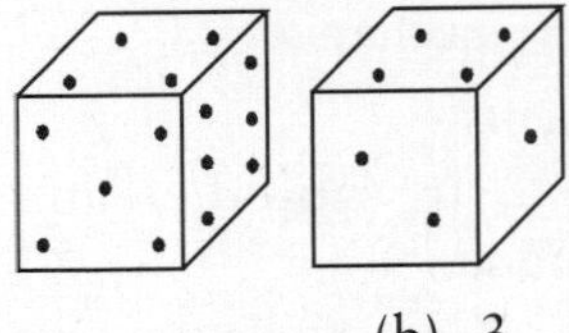

(a) 2 (b) 3
(c) 5 (d) 6

667. Two positions of dice are shown below. How many points will appear on the opposite to the face containing 5 points?

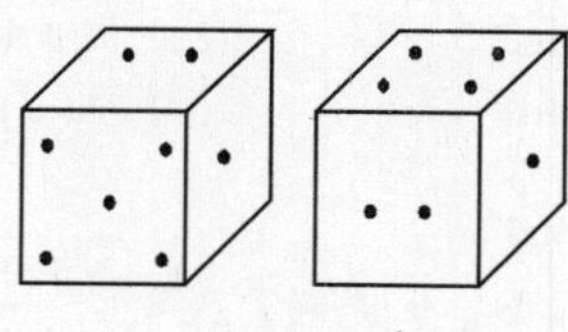

(a) 3 (b) 1
(c) 2 (d) 4

668. From the four positions of a dice given below, find the colour which is opposite to yellow?

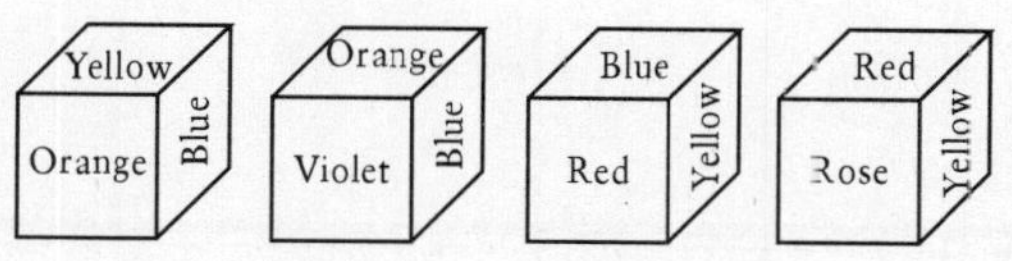

(a) Violet (b) Red
(c) Rose (d) Blue

669. Which digit will appear on the face opposite to the face with number 4?

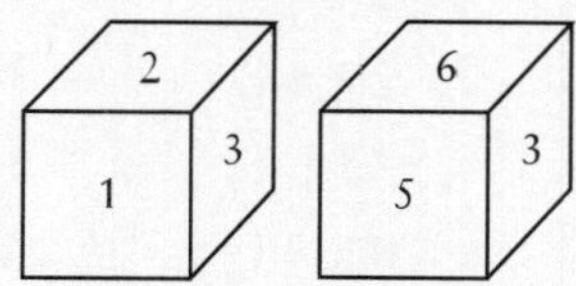

(a) 3 (b) 5
(c) 6 (d) 2/3

670. Two positions of a dice are shown below. When number '1' is on the top, what number will be at the bottom?

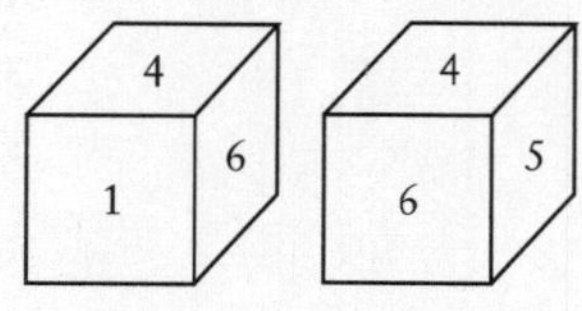

(a) 3 (b) 5
(c) 2 (d) 6

671. Two positions of a dice are shown below. Which number will appear on the face opposite to the face with the number 5?

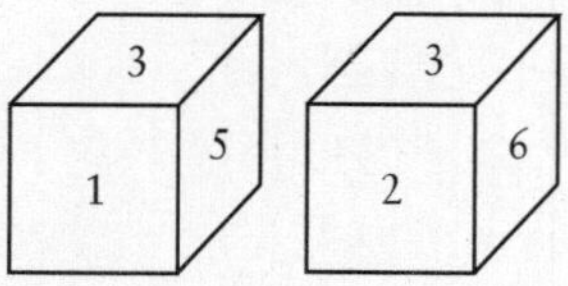

(a) 2/6 (b) 2
(c) 6 (d) 4

672. Four positions of a dice are shown below. Which number of the face will be opposite to the face with number 3?

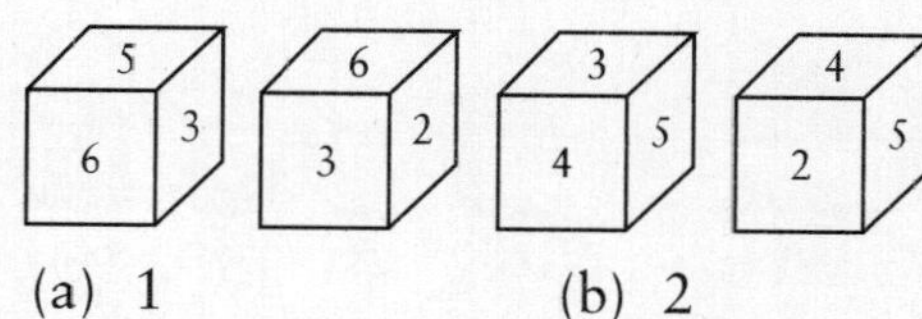

(a) 1 (b) 2
(c) 4 (d) 5

673. Observe the dots on the dice (one to six dots) in the following figures. How many dots are contained on the face opposite to the containing four dots?

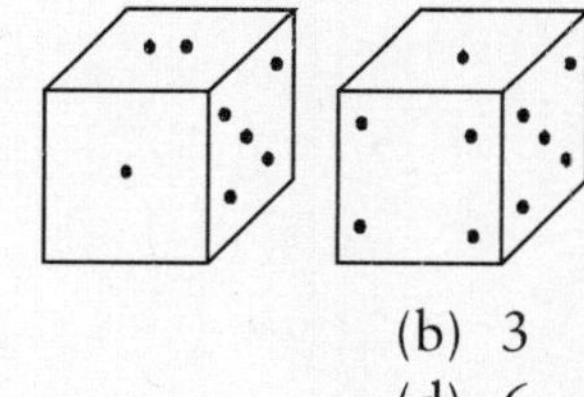

(a) 2 (b) 3
(c) 5 (d) 6

674. From the positions of a cube are shown below, which letter will be on the face opposite to face with 'A'?

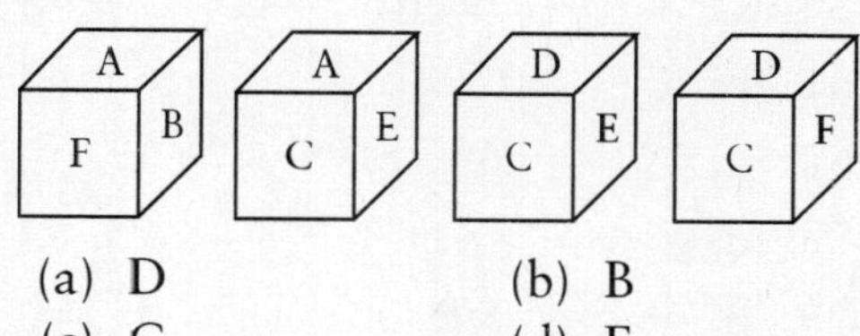

(a) D (b) B
(c) C (d) F

675.

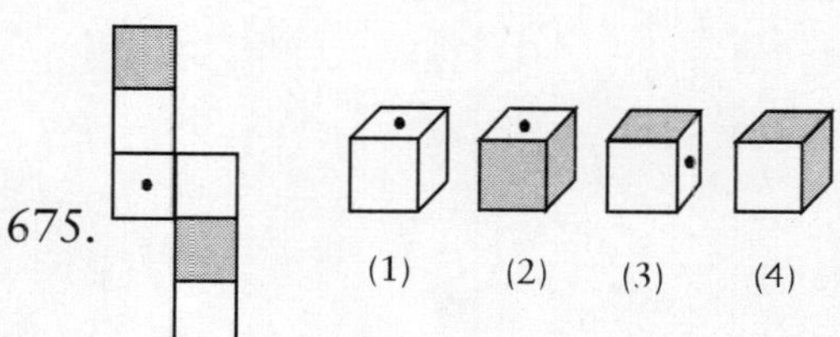

(a) 2 and 3 (b) 1, 3 and 4
(c) 2 and 4 (d) 1 and 4

676. 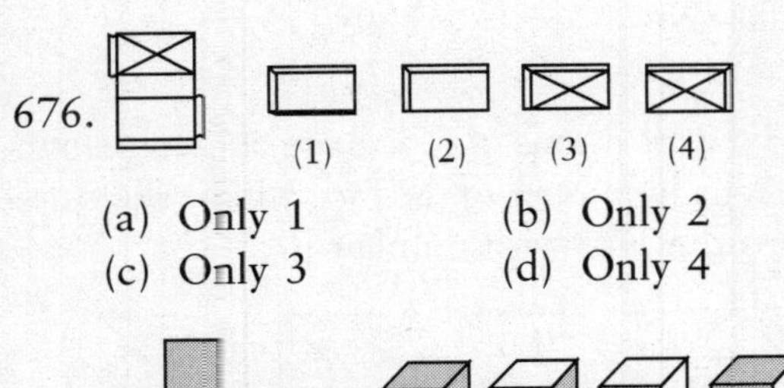

(a) Only 1 (b) Only 2
(c) Only 3 (d) Only 4

677. 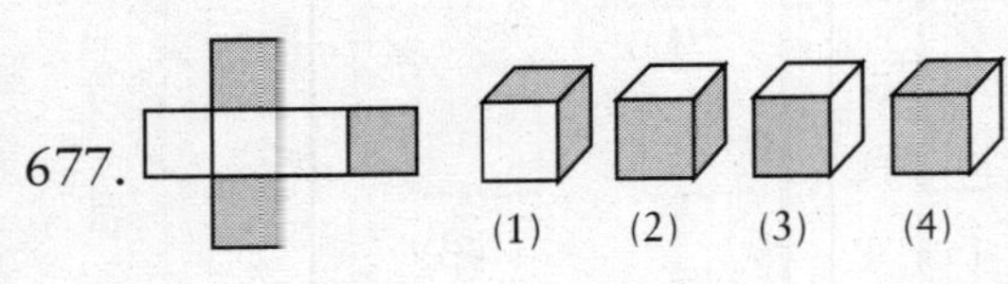

(a) 1 and 3 (b) 2 and 4
(c) 2 and 3 (d) 1, 2, 3 and 4

678. 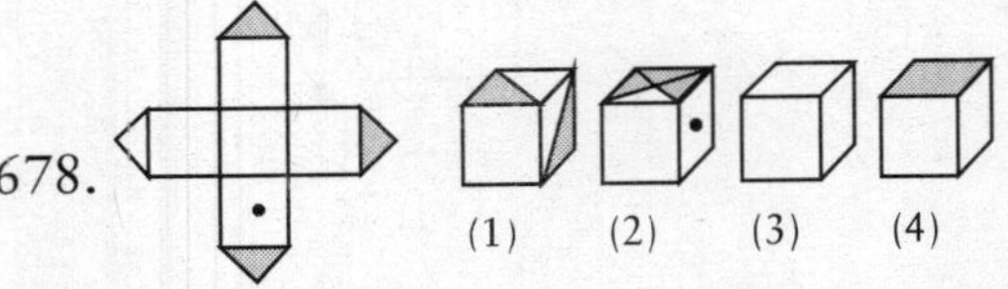

(a) 1 and 2 (b) 2 and 4
(c) 2 and 3 (d) 1 and 4

ANSWERS

1. (d)	2. (a)	3. (a)	4. (d)	5. (a)	6. (b)
7. (a)	8. (c)	9. (d)	10. (a)	11. (c)	12. (b)
13. (b)	14. (c)	15. (a)	16. (c)	17. (b)	18. (c)
19. (c)	20. (d)	21. (c)	22. (a)	23. (a)	24. (b)
25. (d)	26. (c)	27. (c)	28. (d)	29. (d)	30. (d)
31. (c)	32. (a)	33. (d)	34. (c)	35. (d)	36. (d)
37. (a)	38. (d)	39. (b)	40. (b)	41. (d)	42. (c)
43. (a)	44. (d)	45. (d)	46. (b)	47. (d)	48. (c)
49. (b)	50. (d)	51. (b)	52. (c)	53. (b)	54. (d)
55. (c)	56. (b)	57. (b)	58. (c)	59. (a)	60. (c)
61. (b)	62. (b)	63. (c)	64. (b)	65. (d)	66. (c)
67. (d)	68. (c)	69. (d)	70. (c)	71. (d)	72. (d)
73. (d)	74. (a)	75. (c)	76. (a)	77. (b)	78. (a)
79. (d)	80. (c)	81. (d)	82. (d)	83. (d)	84. (a)
85. (c)	86. (c)	87. (b)	88. (d)	89. (a)	90. (b)
91. (a)	92. (a)	93. (c)	94. (c)	95. (a)	96. (b)
97. (d)	98. (a)	99. (c)	100. (b)	101. (c)	102. (a)
103. (c)	104. (a)	105. (c)	106. (c)	107. (a)	108. (a)
109. (b)	110. (c)	111. (a)	112. (e)	113. (b)	114. (a)
115. (e)	116. (a)	117. (a)	118. (e)	119. (b)	120. (d)
121. (c)	122. (c)	123. (c)	124. (d)	125. (c)	126. (d)
127. (b)	128. (d)	129. (d)	130. (b)	131. (b)	132. (d)
133. (a)	134. (c)	135. (b)	136. (b)	137. (c)	138. (b)

139. (c)	140. (d)	141. (b)	142. (c)	143. (c)	144. (d)
145. (c)	146. (c)	147. (c)	148. (b)	149. (b)	150. (d)
151. (d)	152. (b)	153. (a)	154. (a)	155. (b)	156. (a)
157. (d)	158. (c)	159. (a)	160. (d)	161. (b)	162. (a)
163. (d)	164. (d)	165. (b)	166. (a)	167. (c)	168. (a)
169. (b)	170. (b)	171. (d)	172. (d)	173. (c)	174. (b)
175. (a)	176. (c)	177. (b)	178. (b)	179. (c)	180. (a)
181. (c)	182. (a)	183. (b)	184. (d)	185. (c)	186. (b)
187. (b)	188. (a)	189. (b)	190. (b)	191. (d)	192. (a)
193. (b)	194. (d)	195. (a)	196. (d)	197. (c)	198. (d)
199. (a)	200. (d)	201. (c)	202. (d)	203. (c)	204. (a)
205. (a)	206. (d)	207. (a)	208. (b)	209. (c)	210. (d)
211. (b)	212. (c)	213. (b)	214. (a)	215. (a)	216. (d)
217. (d)	218. (c)	219. (d)	220. (a)	221. (c)	222. (d)
223. (a)	224. (c)	225. (b)	226. (c)	227. (b)	228. (e)
229. (b)	230. (c)	231. (c)	232. (b)	233. (d)	234. (a)
235. (b)	236. (b)	237. (d)	238. (b)	239. (a)	240. (c)
241. (a)	242. (c)	243. (b)	244. (d)	245. (a)	246. (b)
247. (d)	248. (a)	249. (b)	250. (c)	251. (c)	252. (c)
253. (d)	254. (c)	255. (c)	256. (b)	257. (a)	258. (b)
259. (b)	260. (d)	261. (c)	262. (c)	263. (a)	264. (a)
265. (b)	266. (b)	267. (d)	268. (a)	269. (d)	270. (b)
271. (a)	272. (a)	273. (c)	274. (c)	275. (c)	276. (d)
277. (d)	278. (d)	279. (b)	280. (c)	281. (a)	282. (d)
283. (d)	284. (c)	285. (d)	286. (c)	287. (c)	288. (a)
289. (b)	290. (b)	291. (b)	292. (d)	293. (a)	294. (d)
295. (c)	296. (a)	297. (c)	298. (c)	299. (d)	300. (a)
301. (b)	302. (c)	303. (d)	304. (a)	305. (c)	306. (c)
307. (d)	308. (c)	309. (d)	310. (c)	311. (d)	312. (b)
313. (d)	314. (a)	315. (d)	316. (a)	317. (c)	318. (c)
319. (c)	320. (c)	321. (b)	322. (d)	323. (a)	324. (d)
325. (c)	326. (b)	327. (a)	328. (b)	329. (d)	330. (c)
331. (a)	332. (d)	333. (c)	334. (c)	335. (b)	336. (a)
337. (c)	338. (d)	339. (c)	340. (a)	341. (b)	342. (c)

343. (a) 344. (a) 345. (a) 346. (b) 347. (d) 348. (c)
349. (c) 350. (c) 351. (d) 352. (d) 353. (b) 354. (c)
355. (b) 356. (d) 357. (c) 358. (b) 359. (a) 360. (d)
361. (d) 362. (a) 363. (b) 364. (c) 365. (a) 366. (b)
367. (b) 368. (d) 369. (c) 370. (b) 371. (a) 372. (c)
373. (a) 374. (b) 375. (c) 376. (b) 377. (a) 378. (d)
379. (b) 380. (a) 381. (c) 382. (b) 383. (d) 384. (b)
385. (a) 386. (c) 387. (c) 388. (d) 389. (a) 390. (d)
391. (b) 392. (a) 393. (b) 394. (a) 395. (c) 396. (a)
397. (c) 398. (d) 399. (c) 400. (d) 401. (c) 402. (d)
403. (b) 404. (a) 405. (d) 406. (c) 407. (b) 408. (d)
409. (a) 410. (d) 411. (d) 412. (a) 413. (b) 414. (b)
415. (c) 416. (b) 417. (c) 418. (b) 419. (a) 420. (b)
421. (a) 422. (c) 423. (c) 424. (b) 425. (c) 426. (d)
427. (a) 428. (c) 429. (b) 430. (d) 431. (a) 432. (c)
433. (b) 434. (d) 435. (d) 436. (d) 437. (b) 438. (c)
439. (a) 440. (c) 441. (d) 442. (d) 443. (d) 444. (a)
445. (b) 446. (b) 447. (d) 448. (b) 449. (a) 450. (c)
451. (d) 452. (d) 453. (a) 454. (a) 455. (d) 456. (c)
457. (b) 458. (c) 459. (a) 460. (b) 461. (c) 462. (d)
463. (b) 464. (b) 465. (d) 466. (c) 467. (d) 468. (c)
469. (a) 470. (a) 471. (b) 472. (d) 473. (b) 474. (d)
475. (b) 476. (b) 477. (c) 478. (d) 479. (a) 480. (b)
481. (a) 482. (c) 483. (d) 484. (d) 485. (d) 486. (c)
487. (c) 488. (d) 489. (b) 490. (e) 491. (e) 492. (d)
493. (c) 494. (c) 495. (e) 496. (a) 497. (c) 498. (c)
499. (b) 500. (d) 501. (b) 502. (a) 503. (a) 504. (a)
505. (a) 506. (d) 507. (c) 508. (b) 509. (d) 510. (c)
511. (c) 512. (b) 513. (d) 514. (b) 515. (c) 516. (a)
517. (c) 518. (d) 519. (d) 520. (a) 521. (b) 522. (d)
523. (b) 524. (c) 525. (a) 526. (d) 527. (b) 528. (a)
529. (b) 530. (d) 531. (d) 532. (a) 533. (c) 534. (a)
535. (b) 536. (d) 537. (a) 538. (c) 539. (d) 540. (b)
541. (b) 542. (a) 543. (d) 544. (b) 545. (d) 546. (d)

547. (d)	548. (b)	549. (d)	550. (c)	551. (c)	552. (d)
553. (c)	554. (a)	555. (d)	556. (a)	557. (e)	558. (a)
559. (d)	560. (a)	561. (e)	562. (d)	563. (d)	564. (d)
565. (e)	566. (a)	567. (d)	568. (b)	569. (a)	570. (b)
571. (e)	572. (d)	573. (b)	574. (a)	575. (e)	576. (e)
577. (d)	578. (c)	579. (b)	580. (e)	581. (a)	582. (b)
583. (b)	584. (e)	585. (a)	586. (b)	587. (c)	588. (a)
589. (c)	590. (e)	591. (b)	592. (b)	593. (a)	594. (b)
595. (b)	596. (b)	597. (a)	598. (a)	599. (b)	600. (e)
601. (d)	602. (a)	603. (c)	604. (e)	605. (a)	606. (b)
607. (a)	608. (e)	609. (b)	610. (a)	611. (c)	612. (a)
613. (e)	614. (e)	615. (a)	616. (b)	617. (d)	618. (e)
619. (e)	620. (b)	621. (a)	622. (c)	623. (d)	624. (a)
625. (b)	626. (a)	627. (b)	628. (a)	629. (d)	630. (e)
631. (d)	632. (a)	633. (b)	634. (a)	635. (a)	636. (a)
637. (b)	638. (e)	639. (a)	640. (d)	641. (b)	642. (a)
643. (c)	644. (a)	645. (b)	646. (d)	647. (e)	648. (a)
649. (a)	650. (a)	651. (b)	652. (a)	653. (d)	654. (b)
655. (b)	656. (b)	657. (e)	658. (b)	659. (a)	660. (b)
661. (a)	662. (d)	663. (a)	664. (a)	665. (c)	666. (c)
667. (d)	668. (a)	669. (a)	670. (b)	671. (c)	672. (a)
673. (a)	674. (a)	675. (b)	676. (a)	677. (d)	678. (c)

7

Data Interpretation

Direction: Study the table and answer the question regarding opinion polling.

	Voting for	Voting against	Indifferent	Total
Men	350	750	250	1350
Women	450	1250	50	1750
Total	300	2000	300	3100

1. Which of the following conclusions drawn is most correct?
   (a) 10% people did not take part in the polling.
   (b) Women are less interested in polling as compared to men.
   (c) Polling have become unpopular in India.
   (d) 64.5% people voted not in favour of the party.

Direction: Study the table and answer the question.

Year	Firm's outlay	Proceeds
1960	3400	4000
1970	3800	4500
1980	4500	5400
1990	7400	8000

2. Which of the following conclusion is not true?
   (a) There has been a steady growth in percentage profit of the firm.
   (b) Income of the firm becomes double in 30 years.
   (c) Percentage profit in 1980 was 17.6%.
   (d) There is 117.65% increase in the expenses of the firm from 1960 to 1990.

Direction: The following bar diagram shows the registration of cars and total vehicles during first six months of the year 1998 in Delhi.

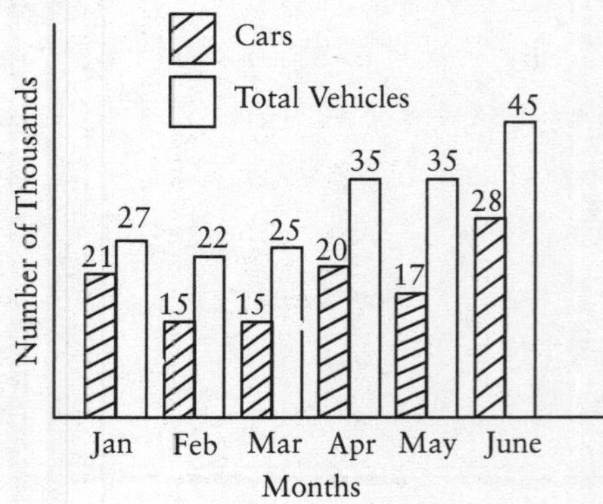

Study the above diagram and answer the questions (3 to 5) given below.

3. What was the increase in registration of vehicles other than cars from January to April 1998?
   (a) 5000 (b) 10000
   (c) 15000 (d) 9000

4. What was the percentage increase in registration of cars from May to June 1998?
   (a) 11% (b) 39.28%
   (c) 64.7% (d) None

5. What was the number of vehicles other than cars registered in March 1998?
   (a) 5000 (b) 10000
   (c) 40000 (d) 37000

Direction: (Q. 6-13) Read the following charts and figures and choose the appropriate answers.

Car sales in 2003	Average cost
Sub-Compact	₹ 2.5 lakhs
Compact	₹ 3.5 lakhs
Mid-Premium	₹ 5.25 lakhs
Premium	₹ 8 lakhs
Super Premium	₹ 12.5 lakhs

No. of Cars sold in various segments

Sub-Compact		Compact		Mid-Premium	
Maruti 800	112,000	Maruti Zen	49,000	Opel Corsa	5,300
Maruti Omni	63,000	Maruti Wagon R	16,250	Fiat Sienna	2,550
Premier/Amby	53,000	Fiat Palio	24,850	Hyundai Accent	10,150
Fiat Uno	12,500	Tata Indica	72,250	Honda City 1.3	4,700
Hyundai Santro	55,750	Ford Ikon 1.3	7,250		
Others	17,250	Others	7,950	Others	1,350

Premium		Super Premium	
Maruti Baleno	2,600	Honda Accord	1,250
Opel Astra	2,450	Ford Monded	750
Honda City 1.5	8,750	Hyundai Sonata	1,300
Ford Ikon 1.6	6,650		
Others	450	Others	450

Average Cost

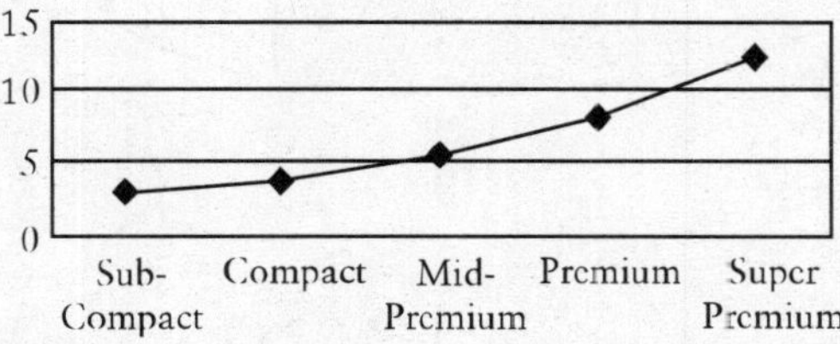

6. How many Palio's should Fiat have sold to have its current volume market share (of the compact segment) higher by 20 points?
   (a) 24850 (b) 45210
   (c) 70060 (d) 56820

7. The sub-compact segment grew by 1% over last year and Maruti 800 increased its share by 1%. What were the approximate sales of Maruti 800 last year?
   (a) 108000
   (b) 107000
   (c) 110000
   (d) Inappropriate Data

8. In what segment do the others models than Maruti have the largest share?
   (a) Sub-Compact (b) Premium
   (c) Compact (d) Super Premium

9. What is the share of premium segment to the total car market (in volume terms)?
   (a) 3.9%
   (b) 38.7%
   (c) 4.0%
   (d) None of the above

10. If Accent was classified in the premium segment what would be its share of the premium segment?
    (a) 10% (b) 19%
    (c) 32% (d) 33%

11. What is the volume share of the Ford Ikon (1-3 and 1-6 Ltrs.) across the mid and the premium segment?
    (a) 21.6% (b) 23.2%
    (c) 26.6% (d) 31.8%

12. In value terms, what is the share of cars from the Maruti stable to the total car market?
    (a) 37.9% (b) 45%
    (c) 44.7% (d) 44.8%

13. In case of buyers of super premium cars decided to purchase compact cars instead of super premium cars. In the same money how many compact cars would they have purchased?
    (a) 3750 (b) 13393
    (c) 9643 (d) 22605

Direction: Study the following pie chart and attempt the following questions.

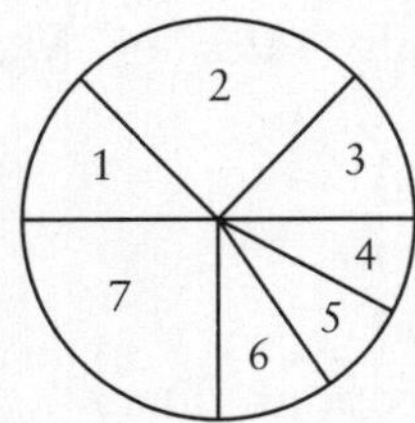

Expenses of a family.

1. Clothes
2. Vegetables
3. Meat
4. Rent
5. Petrol
6. Others
7. Foodgrains

14. Which conclusion based on the diagram is true here?
   (a) Expenses on foodgrains is less than those on rent and petrol.
   (b) Expenses on clothes and vegetables is greater than on rent, petrol and others.
   (c) 2/3 of the family's income is spent on all except foodgrains.
   (d) Equal amount of money is spent on vegetables and meat.

Direction: Study the pie chart given below and answer the questions (15-17).

Percentage of money spent on household items

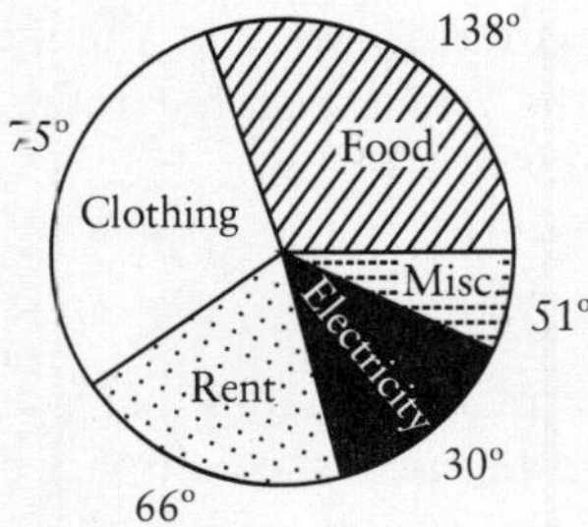

15. The ratio between the money spent on electricity and other fuels and clothing is
   (a) 1 : 3 (b) 3 : 1
   (c) 4 : 1 (d) None of these

16. If the income of a family is ₹ 14000 per month, ratio of the expenditure on food and rent is
   (a) 2 : 1 (b) 3 : 1
   (c) 4 : 1 (d) 1 : 2

17. If the income of a family is ₹ 21,240 the difference between the expenditure on clothing, electricity and fuels is nearly
   (a) 3000 (b) 2600
   (c) 2650 (d) None of these

Direction: (18-19) Answer these questions based on the pie charts given below.

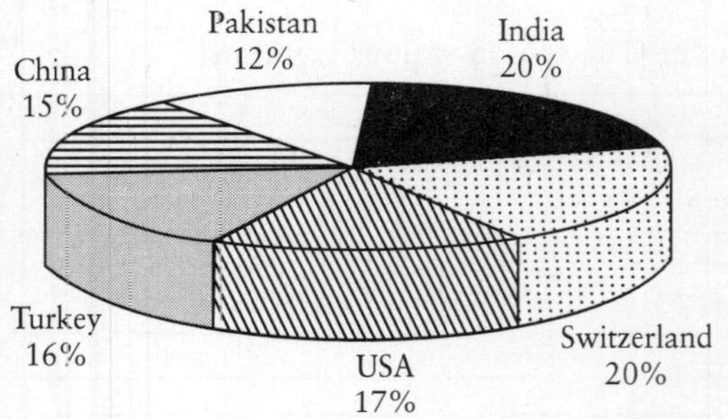

Chart 1

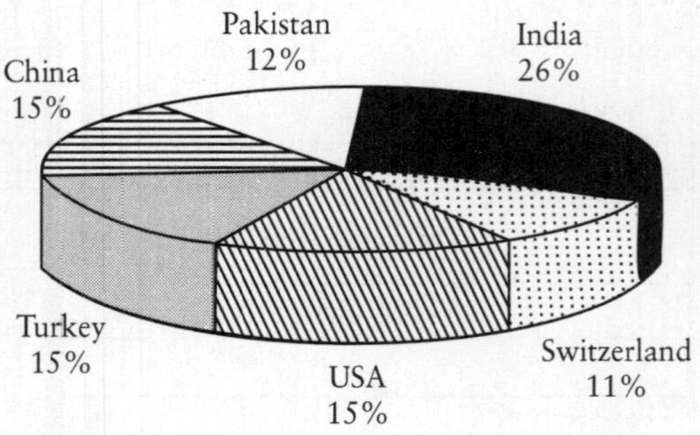

Chart 2

Chart 1 shows the distribution by value of top 6 suppliers of MFA Textiles in 1995. Chart 2 shows pie distribution by quantity of top 6 suppliers of MFA Textiles in 1995. The total value is 5760 million Euro (European currency). The total quantity is 1055 million tonnes.

18. The country, which has the highest average price, is
(a) USA (b) Switzerland
(c) Turkey (d) India

19. The average price in Euro/Kg for Turkey is roughly
(a) 6.20 (b) 5.60
(c) 4.20 (d) 4.80

Direction: Study the following graph and answer the questions (20-23).

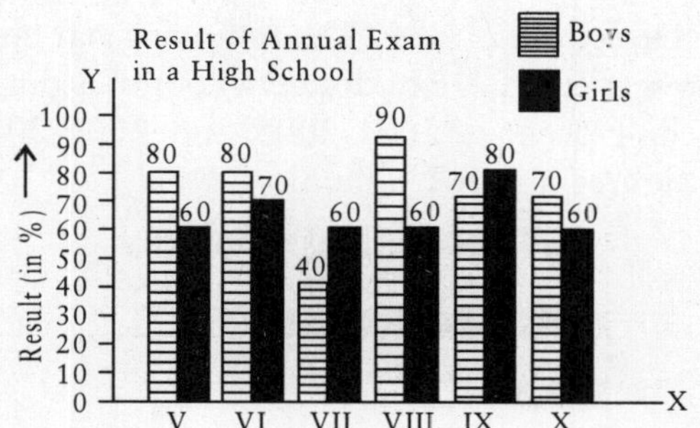

20. In which standard is the difference between the results of girls and boys maximum?
(a) V (b) VII
(c) X (d) VIII

21. In which standard is the result of boys less than the average result of the girls?
(a) VII (b) IX
(c) VI (d) VIII

22. In which pair of standards are the results of girls and boys in inverse proportion?
(a) V and X (b) VI and VIII
(c) V and IX (d) VI and IX

23. In which standard is the result of the girls more than the average result of the boys for the school?
(a) IX (b) VI
(c) VIII (d) X

24. For the purpose of preparing a pie-chart the Government's expenditures on different heads in angles are given below. Study them and answer the given questions.

Industries	90°
Transport	60°
Social Services	60°
Agriculture	45°
Power	45°
Inventories	30°
Small scale industries	15°
Irrigation	15°

The statement which is not true is
(a) Expenditure on transport and social service combined is 1/3 of the total expenditure
(b) Expenditure on industries is triple that of agriculture
(c) Expenditure on irrigation is 25.6% of the total expenditure
(d) 25% of budget is spent on industries

Direction: The following Pie diagrams shows the amounts that a family spends on food, clothing, rent, miscellaneous expenditure and savings.

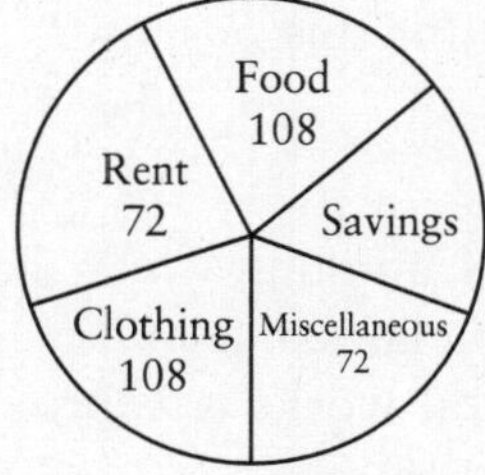

25. If the annual income of the family is ₹ 60000, then the savings are
(a) ₹ 3000 (b) ₹ 6000
(c) ₹ 7500 (d) ₹ 9000

Direction: (26-30) The diagram below depicts the sources and uses of funds in a Public Sector Enterprise. The total outlay is ₹ 4000 crores.

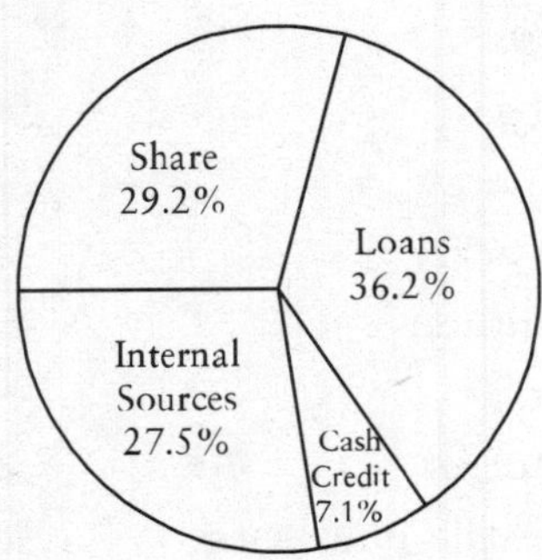

Sources

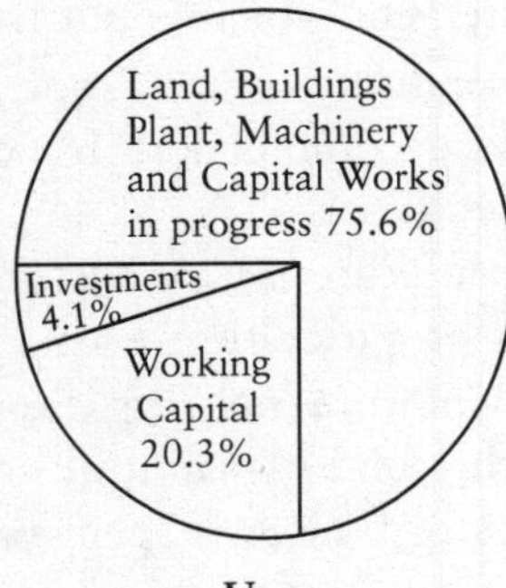

Uses

26. If working capital has to be managed out of loan funds, what percentage (approximately) of loan funds should be set apart for this purpose?
(a) 25% (b) 40%
(c) 55% (d) 70%

27. The total amount which has been used for buying land, machinery, setting plants and capital works is approximately
(a) 2000 crores (b) 3000 crores
(c) 3500 crores (d) 3800 crores

28. The total cash credits acquired by the company are approximately
(a) 200 crores (b) 240 crores
(c) 270 crores (d) 285 crores

29. The company is in need of more working capital. How much capital it can acquire by redeeming its investments?
(a) 144 crores (b) 152 crores
(c) 164 crores (d) 184 crores

30. If the company were to manage its total working capital from internal resources alone. How much fund from this resource will still be left for other use?
(a) 288 crores (b) 312 crores
(c) 344 crores (d) 422 crores

Direction: (31-34) The following bar chart represents the GDP of different countries during the half decades 2001-2005 and 2006-2010. All figures are in ₹ billion.

GDP of Various Countries

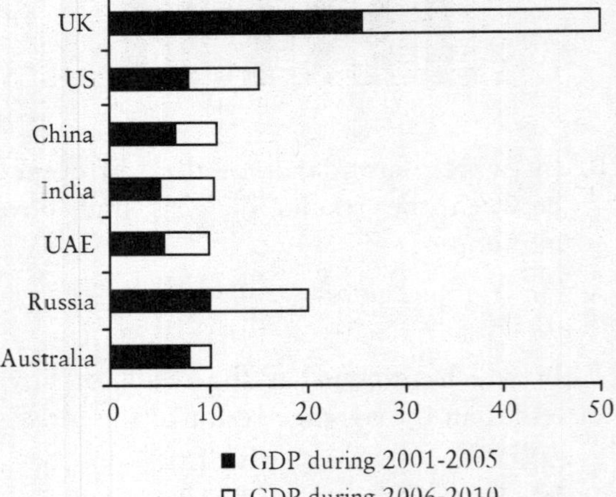

31. Which of the countries listed below accounts for the maximum GDP during the half decade 2006 to 2010?
(a) UAE (b) US
(c) India (d) China

32. The GDP of UAE is what fraction of GDP of the UK for the decade (approximately)?
(a) (1/4)th (b) (1/5)th
(c) (1/6)th (d) Data inadequate

33. Which of the countries listed below accounts for the highest GDP during the half decade 2001 to 2005?
(a) Russia (b) China
(c) India (d) UAE

34. Out of every ₹ 10,000 spent during the decade 2001-2010 approximately how much was the GDP of Russia during the half decade 2001-2005?
(a) ₹ 700 (b) ₹ 1400
(c) ₹ 2800 (d) None of these

Direction: The following pie chart shows the annual agricultural yield of a certain place.

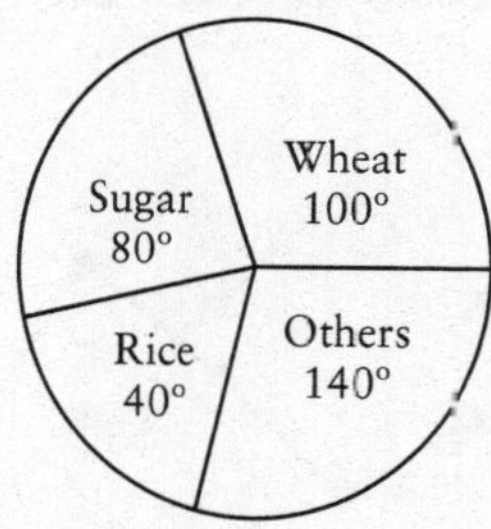

Study the above chart and answer the questions (35 to 37) given below.

35. If the total production is 8100 tons, then the yield of rice (in tons) is
(a) 3240 (b) 900
(c) 4860 (d) None

36. If the yield of sugar is 2400 tons, then the yield of wheat (in tons) is
(a) 3000 (b) 1920
(c) $666\frac{2}{3}$ (d) None

37. The production of wheat exceeds that of rice by
(a) 50% (b) 150%
(c) 100% (d) 250%

Direction: Study the graph and answer the questions (38-42) given below. In the following pie graph is marks obtained by a candidate in five subjects—Math, English, Hindi, Science, Social Science are given. Full marks of the examination is 540.

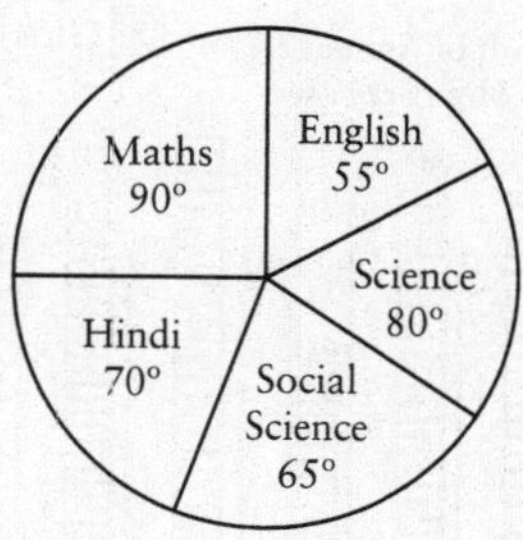

38. What is the percentage marks in Math of the full marks?
(a) 20% (b) 30%
(c) 35% (d) 25%

39. What is percentage marks of the total marks in English, Science and Social Science of the Full marks?
(a) 45% (b) $44\frac{4}{9}$%
(c) 55% (d) $55\frac{5}{9}$%

40. In which subject student get 22.2% marks?
(a) Hindi (b) Science
(c) Social Science (d) English

41. In which subject student got 105 marks?
(a) Math (b) Science
(c) Hindi (d) English

42. What percentage mark is more than the marks obtain in three subject—English, Science and Social Science from the marks obtain in Hindi and Math?
(a) 10% (b) 11%
(c) $11\frac{1}{9}$% (d) $10\frac{1}{9}$%

Direction: Study the following graph carefully and answer the question (43-46) which follow the graph.

Results of annual examination in a high school.

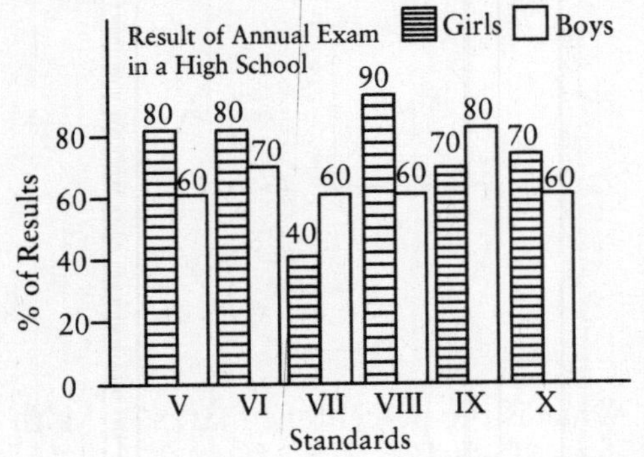

43. In which standard is the failure of girls lowest?
    (a) IX (b) X
    (c) VII (d) VII
44. The percentage difference between the results of girls and the boys is maximum in which standard?
    (a) VII (b) VIII
    (c) V (d) None of these
45. In which standard the result of the boys is more than the average result of the girls?
    (a) V (b) VI
    (c) VII (d) IX
46. In which standard is the result of the girls less than the average result of school?
    (a) V (b) VI
    (c) VII (d) VIII

Direction: Study the graph and attempt question.

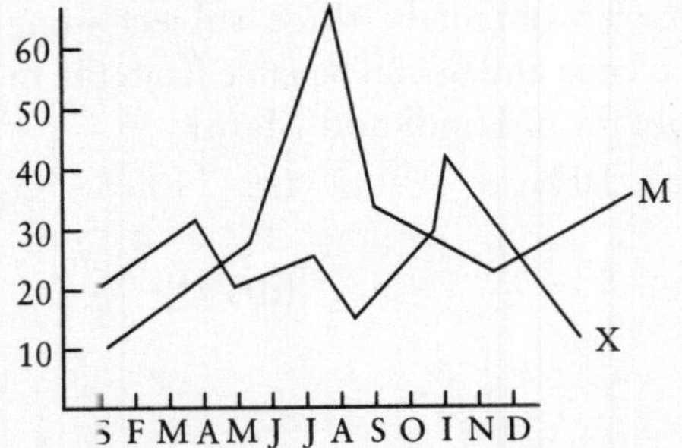

47. Which conclusions cannot be drawn from the graph?
    (a) Import and export both have favourable prospects
    (b) Import was maximum in July but minimum in January
    (c) In July export was minimum but import was maximum
    (d) Export and import both were equal in April and December

Direction: Study the following line graph and answer the questions (48-53).

Exports from Three Companies Over the Years (in ₹ crores)

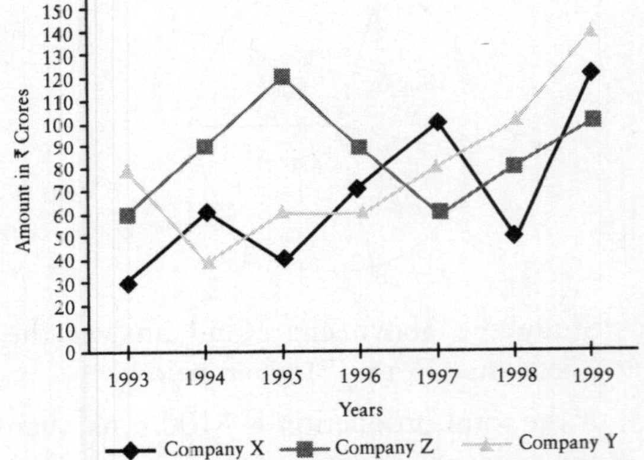

48. For which of the following pairs of years the total exports from the three Companies together are equal?
    (a) 1995 and 1998
    (b) 1996 and 1998
    (c) 1997 and 1998
    (d) 1995 and 1996
49. Average annual exports during the given period for Company Y is approximately what percent of the average annual exports for Company Z?
    (a) 87.12% (b) 89.64%
    (c) 91.21% (d) 93.33%
50. In which year was the difference between the exports from Companies X and Y the minimum?

(a) 1994 (b) 1995
(c) 1996 (d) 1997

51. What was the difference between the average exports of the three Companies in 1993 and the average exports in 1998?
(a) ₹ 15.33 crores
(b) ₹ 18.67 crores
(c) ₹ 20 crores
(d) ₹ 22.17 crores

52. In how many of the given years, were the exports from Company Z more than the average annual exports over the given years?
(a) 2 (b) 3
(c) 4 (d) 5

53. In how many of the given years, were the exports from Company Z more than the average annual exports over the given years?
(a) 2 (b) 3
(c) 4 (d) 5

Direction: Study the following table carefully and answer the questions (54-58) given below it.

Number of Toys in Five Types Manufactured by Company over years (in '000)

Years	Toys				
	A	B	C	D	E
1982	200	150	78	90	65
1983	150	180	100	105	70
1984	180	175	92	110	85
1985	195	160	120	125	75
1986	220	185	130	135	80

54. What was the percentage (approximately) increase in production of D type toys from 1983 to 1985?
(a) 10 (b) 20
(c) 19 (d) 25

55. In the case of which type of toys was the total production of the given five years the maximum?
(a) C (b) B
(c) A (d) D

56. What was the percentage drop on production of A type toys from 1982 to 1984?
(a) 30 (b) 10
(c) 20 (d) 50

57. In the case of which type of toys was there a continuous increase in production over the years?
(a) B (b) A
(c) C (d) D

58. The production of E type toys in 1986 was what percent of production of B type toys in 1985?
(a) 80 (b) 50
(c) 100 (d) 200

Direction: Population growth in India is shown through a bar diagram. Study it and answer the question No. 59.

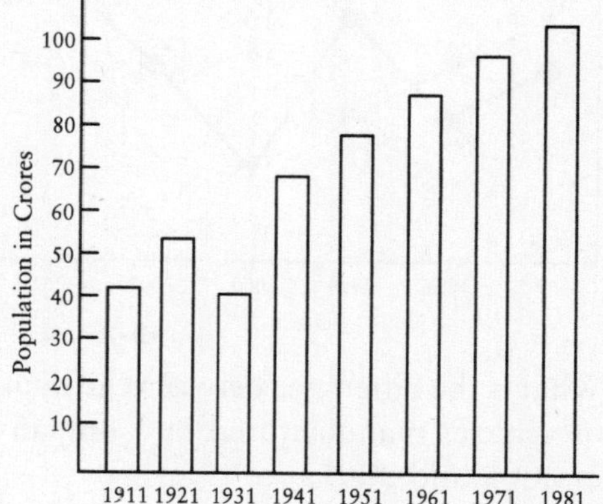

59. Which of the following conclusions is not true?
(a) Average annual increase of India's population is about one crore.
(b) Population of India in 1990 is expected to rise by 10% or more.

(c) Population in India in 1901 must have been less than 25 crores.
(d) Growth rate of population from 1951 to 1961 is maximum.

60. Runs scored by three players in 6 matches are given below, which player you would like to select as a captain of the team?

Players	I	II	III	IV	V	VI
A	20	15	85	80	5	35
B	40	50	50	45	55	30
C	10	130	20	10	100	30

(a) C, because of his average
(b) B, because of his average and consistency
(c) Both C and B
(d) Both A and B

Direction: Study the following line graph and answer the questions (61-65) based on it.

Number of Vehicles Manufactured by Two companies over the years (Number in Thousands)

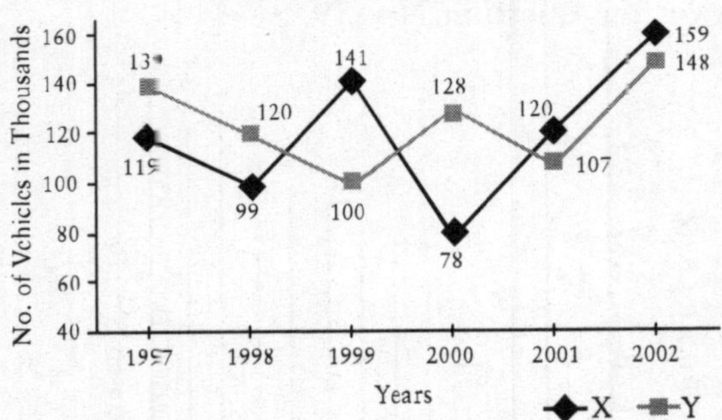

61. What is the difference between the number of vehicles manufactured by Company Y in 2000 and 2001?
(a) 50000 (b) 42000
(c) 33000 (d) 21000

62. What is the difference between the total productions of the two Companies in the given years?
(a) 19000 (b) 22000
(c) 26000 (d) 28000

63. What is the average numbers of vehicles manufactured by Company X over the given period? (rounded off to nearest integer)
(a) 119333 (b) 113666
(c) 112778 (d) 111223

64. In which of the following years, the difference between the productions of Companies X and Y was the maximum among the given years?
(a) 1997 (b) 1998
(c) 1999 (d) 2000

65. The production of Company Y in 2000 was approximately what percent of the production of Company X in the same year?
(a) 173 (b) 164
(c) 132 (d) 97

Direction: Study the following graph carefully and answer the question (66-70) given below.

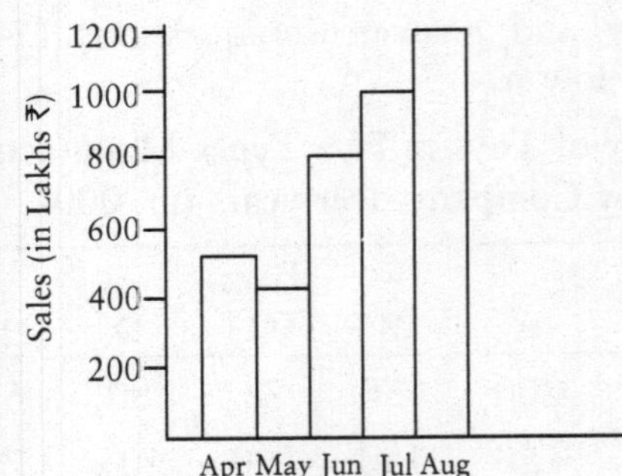

66. In which of the following duration, there is steady increase in sales?
(a) May to July (b) May to August
(c) June to August (d) None of these

67. During which of the following months, the proportion of the sales to that of the previous month is the largest?
(a) April (b) May
(c) June (d) July

68. The sales in August is _____ times the sales in May
(a) 2.5 (b) 3.00
(c) 3 (d) None of these

69. How much did the total sales (in lakhs of rupees) increase from April to August?
(a) 800 (b) 700
(c) 1200 (d) 400

70. Average monthly sales is (in lakhs of rupees)
(a) 600 (b) 650
(c) 780 (d) 620

Direction: Study the graph and answer the question No. 71.

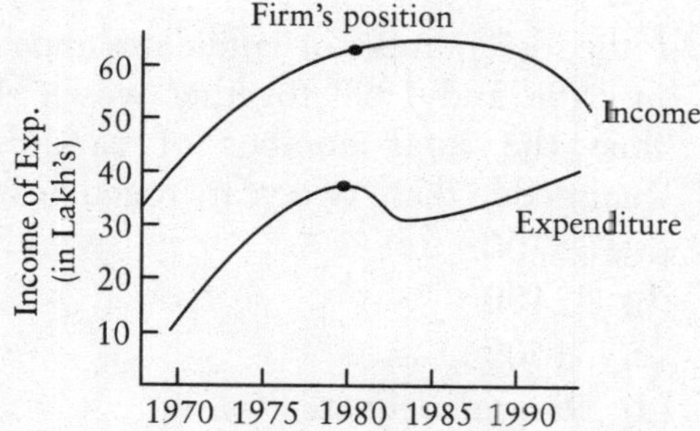

71. Which conclusion is not true?
(a) Profit of the firm was minimum in 1980 and maximum in 1985.
(b) Rate of increase in income is less than that of increase in expenditure upto 1980.
(c) There is a direct relation between income and expenditure after 1980.
(d) All of the above.

Direction: The following table shows the value of exports from India, study the table and answer the question No. 72.

	Export in ₹ crores		
Country	1960-61	1970-71	1980-81
UK	13983	17040	51012
USA	11588	20734	54953
Russia	1038	20985	44039
Japan	1027	20348	54034
Germany	—	3231	23434
Malaysia	550	1173	2984
Pakistan	42	410	6066
Total including other countries	60064	153516	514332

72. Which of the following conclusions is correct?
(a) Total export between 1970-80 increased by about 200%
(b) The relative share of the UK and USA went down considerably to the total export
(c) Japan became the major importing country from India in 1980
(d) The share of these seven countries was more than half to the total export during the whole period

Direction: (73-77) The bar graph given below shows the sales of books (in thousand number) from six branches of a publishing company during two consecutive years 2000 and 2001.

Sales of books (in thousand numbers) from six branches - B1, B2, B3, B4, B5 and B6 of a publishing company in 2000 and 2001.

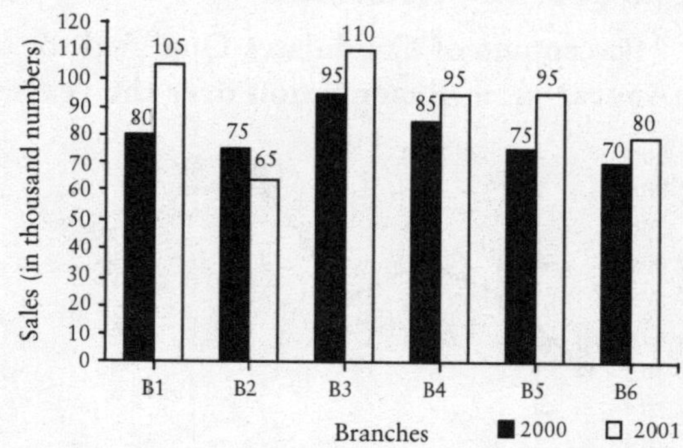

73. What is the ratio of the total sales of branch B2 for both years to the total sales of branch B4 for both years?
(a) 2:3 (b) 3:5
(c) 4:5 (d) 7:9

74. Total sales of branch B6 for both the years is what percent of the total sales of branches B3 for both the years?
(a) 68.54% (b) 71.11%
(c) 73.17% (d) 75.55%

75. What percent of the average sales of branches B1, B2 and B3 in 2001 is the average sales of branches B1, B3 and B6 in 2000?
(a) 75% (b) 77.5%
(c) 82.5% (d) 87.5%

76. What is the average sales of all the branches (in thousand numbers) for the year 2000?
(a) 73 (b) 80
(c) 83 (d) 88

77. Total sales of branches B1, B3 and B5 together for both the years (in thousand numbers) is?
(a) 250 (b) 310
(c) 435 (d) 560

Direction: (Q. 78-82) The following line graph gives the percentage of the number of candidates who qualified an examination out of the total number of candidates who appeared for the examination over a period of seven years from 1994 to 2000.

Percentage of Candidates Qualified to Appear in an Examination over the years

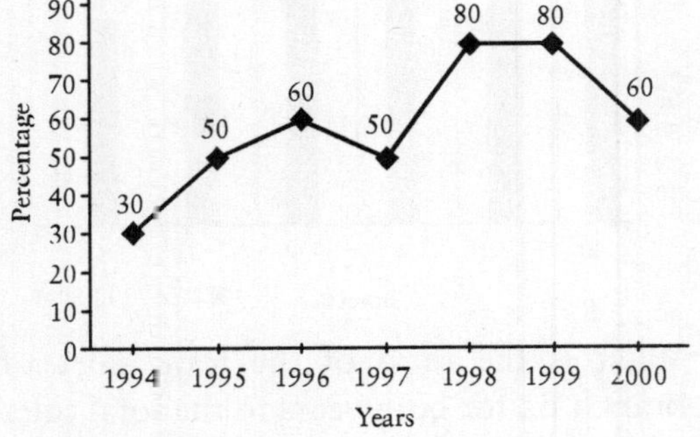

78. The difference between the percentage of candidates qualified to appeared was maximum in which of the following pairs of years?
(a) 1994 and 1995 (b) 1997 and 1998
(c) 1998 and 1999 (d) 1999 and 2000

79. In which pair of years was the number of candidates qualified, the same?
(a) 1995 and 1997
(b) 1995 and 2000
(c) 1998 and 1999
(d) Data inadequate

80. If the number of candidates qualified in 1998 was 21200, what was the number of candidates appeared in 1998?
(a) 32000 (b) 28500
(c) 26500 (d) 25000

81. If the total number of candidates appeared in 1996 and 1997 together was 47400, then the total number of candidates qualified in these two years together was?
(a) 34700
(b) 32100
(c) 31500
(d) Data inadequate

82. The total number of candidates qualified in 1999 and 2000 together was 33500 and the number of candidates appeared in 1999 was 26500. What was the number of candidates in 2000?
(a) 24500 (b) 22000
(c) 20500 (d) 19000

Direction: Study the following graph and answer the questions (83-86) which follow the graph.

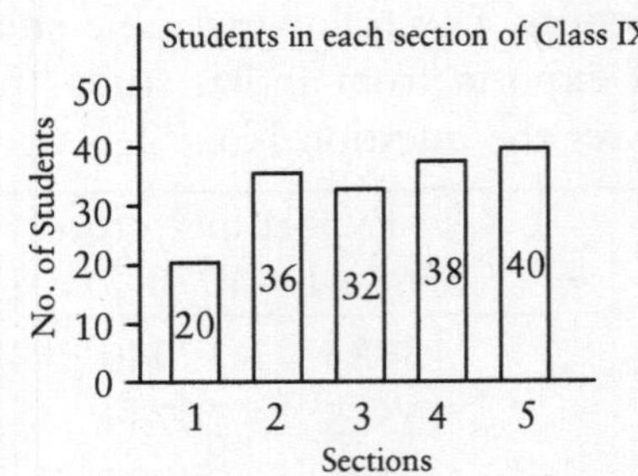

83. Which section has the maximum number of students?
(a) 5 (b) 4
(c) 3 (d) 2

84. Which section has the minimum number of students?
(a) 1 (b) 2
(c) 3 (d) 4

85. Which section has double the number of the students as compared to another section?
(a) 4 (b) 3
(c) 5 (d) 1

86. Which section has half the number of students of one of the sections?
(a) 1 (b) 2
(c) 3 (d) 4

Direction: Study the data given in the following table carefully and answer the questions (87-91) given below it.

Wheat Production (in lakh tonnes)

States	1986	1987	1988	1989	1990
A	9.0	10-7	8.9	11.6	8.4
B	14.5	16.3	16.2	16.4	16.8
C	14.9	15.7	16.8	16.9	17.8
D	7.6	8.4	7.4	7.9	8.6
E	21.0	22.6	23.2	22.2	23.9

87. In 1988, which states contributed close to one-eighth of the total production of all the five states?
(a) A (b) B
(c) C (d) D

88. In which year did the production of state D fall for the first time?
(a) 1986 (b) 1987
(c) 1988 (d) 1989

89. In which state, the production in 1989 showed the highest increase over that in 1986?
(a) A (b) B
(c) C (d) D

90. In which year does the production in state E show the higher percentage of increase over that in the previous year?
(a) 1986 (b) 1987
(c) 1988 (d) 1990

91. In which state did the production of wheat increase continuously from 1986 to 1990?
(a) A (b) B
(c) C (d) D

Direction: (Q. 92-98) Study the following line graph which gives the number of students who joined and left the school in the beginning of year for six years, from 1996 to 2001.

Initial Strength of School in 1995 = 3000.

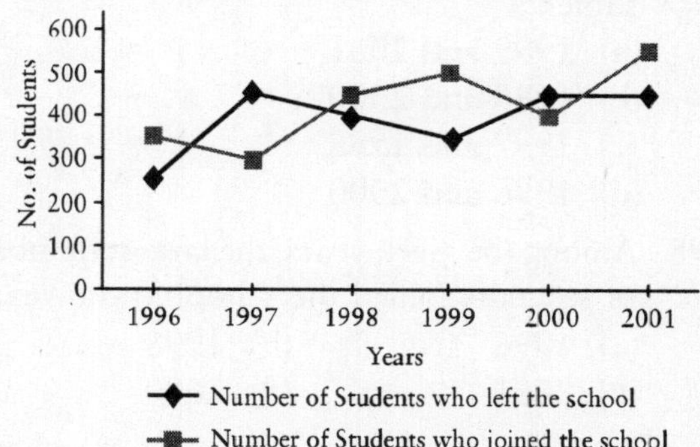

92. The number of students studying in the school during 1999 was
(a) 2950 (b) 3000
(c) 3100 (d) 3150

93. For which year, the percentage rise/fall in the number of students who left the school compared to the previous year is maximum?
(a) 1997 (b) 1998
(c) 1999 (d) 2000

94. The strength of school increased/decreased from 1997 to 1998 by approximately what percent?

(a) 1.2% (b) 1.7%
(c) 2.1% (d) 2.4%

95. The number of students studying in the school in 1998 was what percent of the number of students studying in the school in 2001?
(a) 92.13% (b) 93.75%
(c) 96.88% (d) 97.25%

96. The ratio of the least number of students who joined the school to the maximum number of students who left the school in any of the years during the given period is
(a) 7:9 (b) 4:5
(c) 3:4 (d) 2:3

97. During which of the following pairs of years, the strength of the school was same?
(a) 1999 and 2001
(b) 1998 and 2000
(c) 1997 and 1998
(d) 1996 and 2000

98. Among the given years, the largest number of students joined the school in the year
(a) 1996 (b) 1998
(c) 2001 (d) 2000

Direction: Study the following pie-chart and the table and answer the questions (99-102) based on them.

Proportion of Population of Seven Villages in 1997

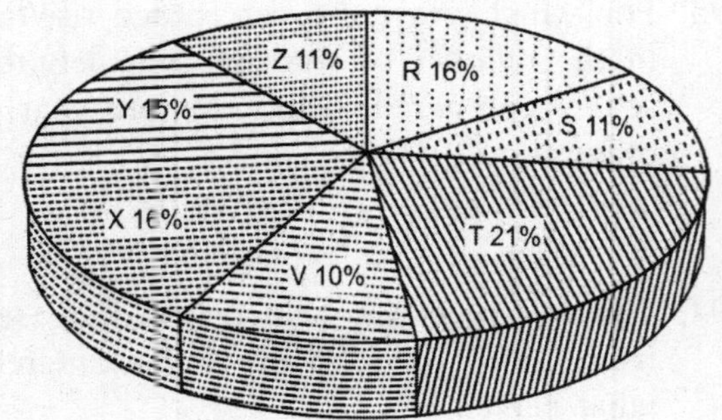

Village	% Population Below Poverty Line
X	38
Y	52
Z	42
R	51
S	49
T	46
V	58

99. If the population of village R in 1997 is 32000, then what will be the population of village Y below poverty line in that year?
(a) 14100 (b) 15600
(c) 16500 (d) 17000

100. The ratio of population of village T below poverty line to that of village Z below poverty line in 1997 is
(a) 11 : 23 (b) 13 : 11
(c) 23 : 11 (d) 11 : 13

101. Find the population of village S if the population of village X below poverty line in 1997 is 12160.
(a) 18500 (b) 20500
(c) 22000 (d) 26000

102. If in 1998, the population of villages Y and V increase by 10% each and the percentage of population below poverty line remains unchanged for all the villages, then find the population of village V below poverty line in 1998, given that the population of village in 1997 was 30000.
(a) 11250 (b) 12760
(c) 13140 (d) 13780

Direction: The following table shows the number of working hours and the number of employees in a small scale industrial unit.

No. of working hours	No. of employees
3-5 hours	7
5-7 hours	10
7-9 hours	18
9-11 hours	57
11-13 hours	14
13-15 hours	8

103. What is the average working hours of an employee?
(a) 9.5 (b) 10.22
(c) 11 (d) 12

Direction: The following pie-chart shows the sources of funds to be collected by the National Highways Authority of India (NHAI) for its Phase II projects. Study the pie-chart and answers the question that follow.

Sources of funds to be arranged by NHAI for Phase II projects (in ₹ crores)

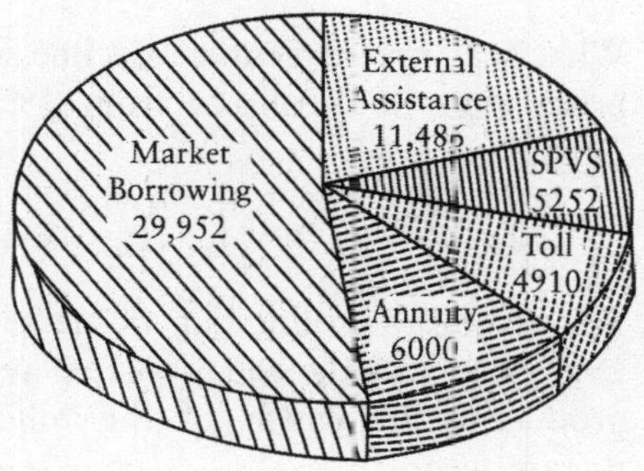

104. Near about 20% of the funds are to be arranged through
(a) SPVS
(b) External Assistance
(c) Annuity
(d) Market Borrowing

105. If NHAI could receive a total of ₹ 9695 crores as External Assistance, by what percent (approximately) should it increase the Market Borrowing to arrange for the shortage of funds?
(a) 4.5% (b) 7.5%
(c) 6% (d) 8%

106. If the toll is to be collected through an outsourced agency by allowing a maximum 10% commission, how much amount should be permitted to be collected by the outsourced agency, so that the project is supported with ₹ 4910 crores?
(a) ₹ 6213 crores (b) ₹ 5827 crores
(c) ₹ 5401 crores (d) ₹ 5316 crores

107. The central angle corresponding to Market Borrowing is
(a) 52° (b) 137.8°
(c) 187.2° (d) 192.4°

108. The approximate ratio of the funds to be arranged through Toll and that through Market Borrowing is
(a) 2:9 (b) 1:6
(c) 3:11 (d) 2:5

Direction: Study the following table and answer the questions (109-113) given below.

Year-wise and discipline-wise number of candidates selected in an Industry

Years → Disciplines ↓	1981	1982	1983	1984	1985	1986
Science	16	20	25	15	14	16
Commerce	08	12	12	11	15	13
Arts	04	08	8.5	10	11	13
Agriculture	01	03	3.0	2.5	1.0	2.0
Engineering	0.5	01	1.0	1.0	0.5	0.5
Others	0.5	01	0.5	0.5	0.5	0.5
Total	30	45	50	40	42	45

109. The number of selected candidates of which discipline is increasing every year?
(a) Science (b) Engineering
(c) Agriculture (d) Arts

110. Approximately what percent of candidates of science discipline were selected for the given period?

(a) 38 (b) 42
(c) 45 (d) None of these

111. If all the class graduates were eligible to apply, which of the following inferences is probably true?
(a) Among the applicants the number of science discipline candidates is the largest.
(b) If written test was given for selection the test was biased towards science discipline.
(c) The industry required science discipline graduates more in its personnel.
(d) None of the above.

112. In which year is the percentage of Agriculture discipline candidates the highest?
(a) 1982 (b) 1983
(c) 1984 (d) 1985

113. In which year for the first time did the Arts discipline candidates constitute more than 25 percent of selected candidates?
(a) 1982 (b) 1983
(c) 1984 (d) 1985

Direction: Refer to the following pie chart and answer the questions (114-115) given below.

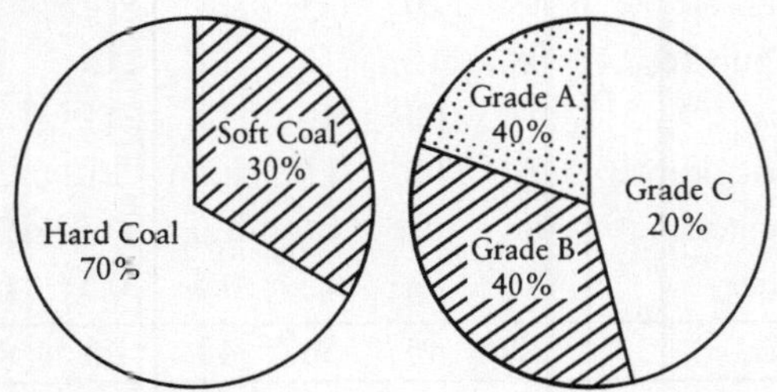

114. The chart above shows the distribution of coal production in a certain country. The chart on the left shows the percentage of hard and soft coal, and that on the right shows the distribution of grades of hard coal. What percent of the total production was grade B hard coal?
(a) 14% (b) 21%
(c) 28% (d) 34%

115. In the pie chart on the left how many degrees are there in the central angle of the sector for soft coal?
(a) 108 (b) 102
(c) 144 (d) 160

Direction: Study the bar chart and answer the question based on it.

Production of Fertilizers by a Company (in 1000 tonnes) over the years

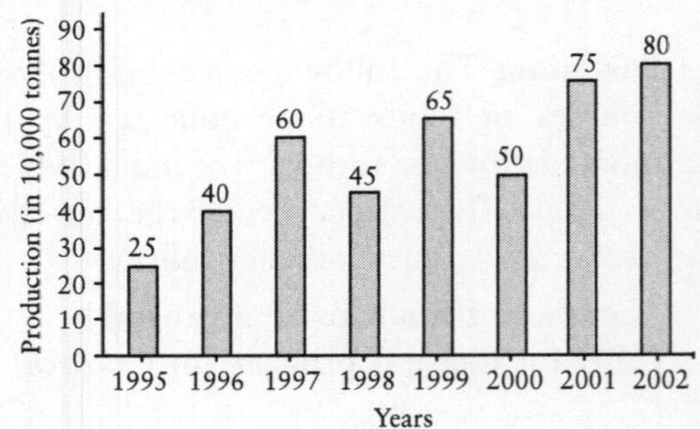

116. What was the percentage decline in the production of fertilizers from 1997 to 1998?
(a) 33(1/3)% (b) 20%
(c) 25% (d) 21%

117. The average production of 1996 and 1997 was exactly equal to the average production of which of the following pairs of years?
(a) 2000 and 2001
(b) 1999 and 2000
(c) 1998 and 2000
(d) 1995 and 2001

118. What was the percentage increase in production of fertilizers in 2002 compared to that in 1995?
(a) 320% (b) 300%
(c) 220% (d) 200%

119. In which year was the percentage increase in production as compared to the precious year the maximum?

(a) 2002 (b) 2001
(c) 1997 (d) 1996

120. In how many of the given years was the production of fertilizers more than the average production of the given years?
(a) 1 (b) 2
(c) 3 (d) 4

Direction: Study the following table carefully and answer the questions (121-124) given below it.

Production in Million Tonnes

Crops	1976	1977	1978	1979	1980	1981
Rice	44.0	39.6	48.7	41.9	52.7	52.1
Wheat	21.8	24.1	28.8	29.9	31.8	37.0
Other Cereals	28.8	26.1	30.4	28.9	30.0	30.2
Pulses	10.0	10.5	13.0	11.4	12.0	12.2
Potatoes	4.8	6.3	7.3	8.1	8.3	10.2

121. In the case of which crop the production increase is by more than 10 lakh tonnes any year?
(a) Wheat (b) Pulses
(c) Rice (d) None of these

122. In which year the production of rice and wheat together was the least?
(a) 1979 (b) 1978
(c) 1977 (d) None of these

123. In the case of which crop the production is having ups and downs every alternate year?
(a) Rice (b) Wheat
(c) Pulses (d) None of these

124. In the case of which crop, the production in 1981 show the highest increase over that in 1976?
(a) Wheat (b) Other cereals
(c) Potatoes (d) None of these

Direction: The bar graph given below shows the percentage distribution of the total expenditures of a company under various expense heads during 2003.

Percentage Distribution of Total Expenditure of a Company

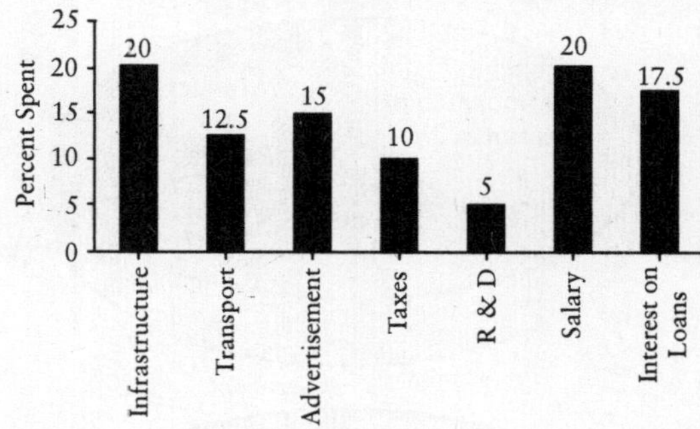

125. The total amount of expenditures of the company is how many times of expenditure on research and development?
(a) 27 (b) 20
(c) 18 (d) 8

126. If the expenditure on advertisement is ₹ 2.10 crores then the difference between the expenditure on transport and taxes is?
(a) ₹ 1.25 crores (b) ₹ 95 lakhs
(c) ₹ 65 lakhs (d) ₹ 35 lakhs

127. What is the ratio of the total expenditure on infrastructure and transport to the total expenditure on taxes and interest on loans?
(a) 5:4 (b) 8:7
(c) 9:7 (d) 13:11

128. If the interest on loans amounted to ₹ 2.45 crores then the total amount of expenditure on advertisement, taxes and research and development is?
(a) ₹ 7 crores (b) ₹ 5.4 crores
(c) ₹ 4.2 crores (d) ₹ 3 crores

129. The expenditure on the interest on loans is by what percent more than the expenditure on transport?
(a) 5% (b) 10%
(c) 20% (d) 40%

Direction: Study the following pie-diagrams carefully and answer the questions given below it.

Percentage Composition of Human Body

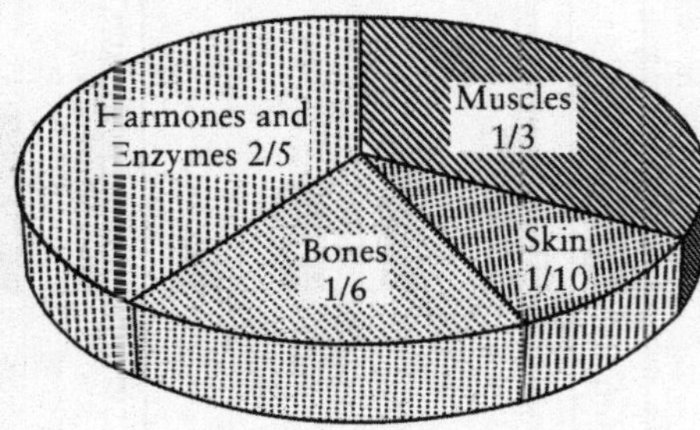

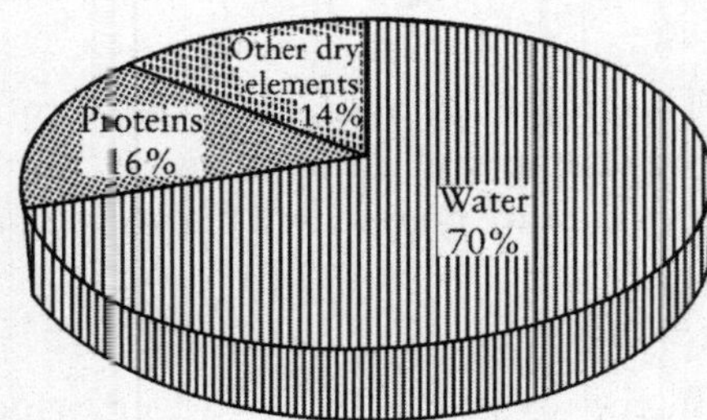

130. What percent of the total weight of human body is equivalent to the weight of the proteins in skin in human body?
(a) 0.016 (b) 1.6
(c) 0.16 (d) Data inadequate

131. What will be the quantity of water in the body of a person weighing 50 kg?
(a) 20 kg (b) 35 kg
(c) 41 kg (d) 42.5 kg

132. What is the ratio of the distribution of proteins in the muscles to that of the distribution of proteins in the bones?
(a) 1:18 (b) 1:2
(c) 2:1 (d) 18:1

133. To show the distribution of proteins and other dry elements in the human body, the arc of the circle should subtend at the centre an angle of
(a) 54° (b) 126°
(c) 108° (d) 252°

134. In the human body, what part is made of neither bones nor skin?
(a) 1/40 (b) 3/80
(c) 2/5 (d) None of these

Direction: Study the table carefully and answer the questions (135-139) given below.

Loans disbursed by five banks over the years (in crores of rupees)

Banks	Years				
	1982	1983	1984	1985	1986
I	18	23	45	30	70
II	27	33	18	41	37
III	29	29	22	17	11
IV	31	16	28	32	43
V	13	19	27	34	42
Total	118	120	140	154	203

135. In which bank was the disbursement of loans more, than 25 percent of all banks in 1986?
(a) I (b) II
(c) III (d) IV

136. In which of the following banks did disbursement of loans continuously increase over the years?
(a) I (b) II
(c) V (d) IV

137. In which year the disbursement of loans was least as compared to the average disbursement of loans over the years?
(a) 1982 (b) 1983
(c) 1984 (d) 1985

138. If 20% of the total disbursement of loans in the preceding year was the minimum target, how many banks did achieve the largest in 1983?
(a) 2 (b) 4
(c) 3 (d) None of these

139. What was the percentage increase of disbursement of loans of all banks taken together in 1984 and 1985?

(a) 4 (b) 6
(c) 8 (d) 10

Direction: The following pie chart shows the marks obtained by a student in an examination, who scored 540 marks in all. Study the graph and answer the questions (140-142) given below.

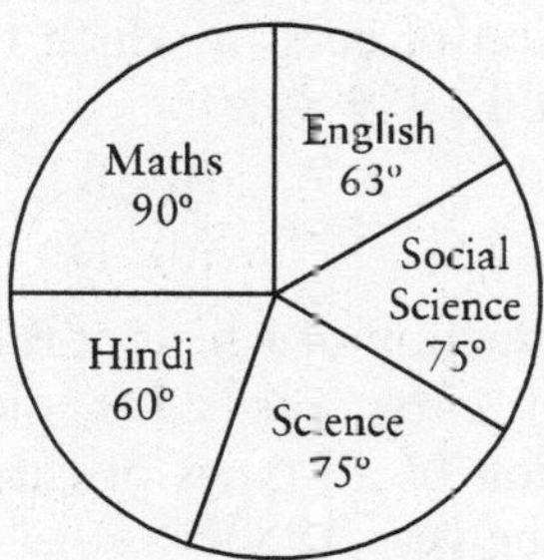

140. The subject in which the student scored 108 marks is
(a) Science (b) Hindi
(c) English (d) Social Science

141. The subject in which the student scored $16\frac{2}{3}\%$ is
(a) Social Science (b) Hindi
(c) English (d) Science

142. The marks scored in Hindi and Mathematics differ from the marks scored in English, Science and Social Science by
(a) 90 (b) 72
(c) 85 (d) 61

Direction: The circle graph given below shows the spending of a family on various items and its savings a year. Study the graph and answer the following questions (143-146).

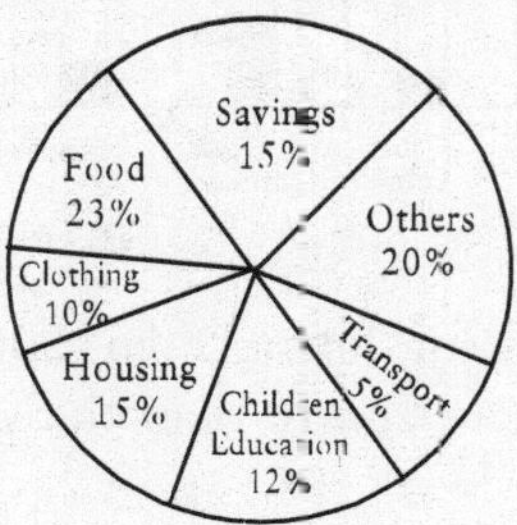

143. If the total income of the family is ₹ 75000, the expenditure on children's education is
(a) ₹ 9000 (b) ₹ 900
(c) ₹ 7500 (d) ₹ 750

144. What percentage of the income was spent on transport and other items?
(a) 25% (b) 20%
(c) 30% (d) 32%

145. Out of the total of ₹ 75000, the difference of the expenses on housing and transport was
(a) ₹ 8500 (b) ₹ 7500
(c) ₹ 8200 (d) ₹ 6350

146. Out of the total of ₹ 75000, the expenditure on food was more than that on clothing by
(a) ₹ 8250 (b) ₹ 6750
(c) ₹ 9750 (d) ₹ 7350

Directions: The following graph shows the quarterly price index of a textile company during 1984-85. Examine it carefully and answer questions (147-151).

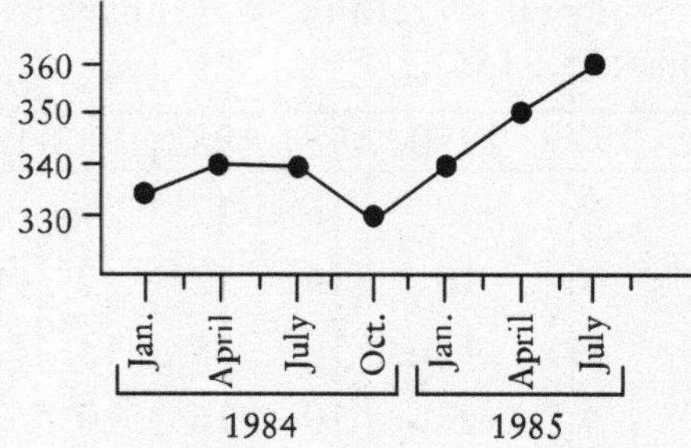

147. During which quarter was the rate of increase of price index the maximum?
(a) October 1984 - January 1985
(b) January 1984 - April 1984
(c) April 1985 - July 1985
(d) January 1985 - April 1985

148. In which of the following months, was the price index maximum?
(a) April 1984 (b) July 1984
(c) April 1985 (d) July 1985

149. During which of the following quarters, did the price index remain the same throughout
(a) April 1984 - July 1985
(b) April 1984 - October 1984
(c) July 1984 - January 1985
(d) None of these

150. The increase in price index was approximately the same during the periods
(a) October-December, 1984 and April-June, 1985
(b) January-March, 1984 and October-December, 1984
(c) January-March, 1985 and April-June, 1985
(d) None of these

151. Approximately, what is the percentage of increase in price index during the period January 1984-July 1985?
(a) 7% (b) 8%
(c) 10% (d) 7.5%

Directions: The following table shows production of cars in a company from 1979 to 1984. Study it carefully and answer the questions (152-156).

Years	1979	1980	1981	1982	1983	1984
A	8	20	16	17	21	6
B	16	10	14	12	12	14
C	21	17	16	15	13	8
D	4	6	10	16	20	31
E	25	18	19	30	14	27
Total	74	71	75	90	80	86

152. In which year, the production of all types of cars taken together was approximately equal to the average of the total production during the period?
(a) 1979 (b) 1981
(c) 1983 (d) 1984

153. In which year, the total production of cars of types A and B together was equal to the total production of cars of types C and D together?
(a) 1980 (b) 1981
(c) 1984 (d) 1983

154. There was a continuous increase in production of cars of which type during the period 1979-84?
(a) A (b) B
(c) C (d) D

155. The production of which of the following types of cars was 25% of the total production of all types of cars produced during the year 1983?
(a) A (b) B
(c) C (d) D

156. The percent increase in total production of all types of cars in 1982 to that in 1981 was
(a) 15 (b) 20
(c) 25 (d) 30

Direction: A cosmetic company provides five different products. The sales of these five products (in lakh number of packs) during 1995 and 2000 are shown in the following bar graph.

Sales (in lakh number of packs) of five different products of Cosmetic Company during 1995 and 2000

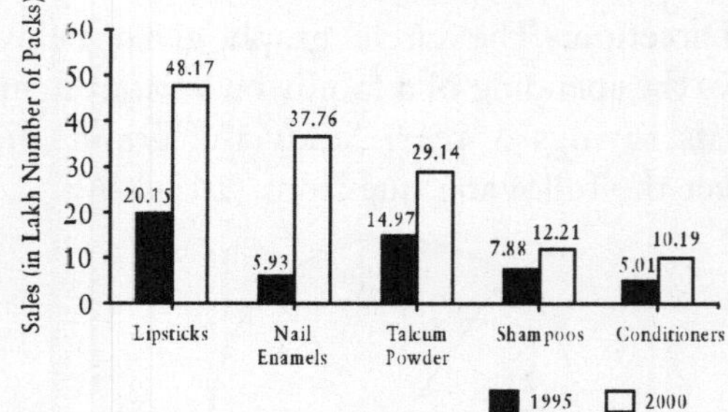

157. The sales of lipsticks in 2000 was by what percent more than the sales of nail

enamels in 2000? (rounded off to nearest integer)

(a) 33% (b) 31%
(c) 28% (d) 22%

158. During the period 1995-2000, the minimum rate of increase in sales is in the case of?

(a) Shampoos (b) Nail enamels
(c) talcum powders (d) Lipsticks

159. What is the approximate ratio of the sales of nail enamels in 2000 to the sales of talcum powders in 1995?

(a) 7:2 (b) 5:2
(c) 4:3 (d) 2:1

160. The sales have increase by nearly 55% from 1995 to 2000 in the case of?

(a) Lipsticks (b) Nail enamels
(c) Talcum powders (d) Shampoos

161. The sales of conditioners in 1995 was by what percent less than the sales of shampoos in 1995? (rounded off to nearest integer)

(a) 57% (b) 36%
(c) 29% (d) 25%

Direction: The names of the various political parties and the seats won by them in 1996 general elections are given in the following table. After a careful study of the information select the correct answer for questions (162-165).

Sr.No.	Name of the Party	Southern India	Eastern India	West India	North India
1.	Congress (I)	40	37	35	27
2.	BJP	06	26	76	86
3.	National front/ Left parties	83	71	04	21
4.	Others	01	07	03	11
	Total	130	141	118	145

162. BJP won the largest number of seats from

(a) Eastern India (b) Southern India
(c) Western India (d) Northern India

163. In Southern India the % of seats won by Congress (I) is

(a) 40% (b) 30.8%
(c) 20.7% (d) 40.7%

164. The total number of candidates elected is

(a) 543 (b) 535
(c) 534 (d) 524

165. The party which won highest number of seats is

(a) National front/Left parties
(b) Congress (I)
(c) BJP
(d) Others

Direction: The bar graph given below shows the percentage distribution of the total production of a car manufacturing company into various models over two years.

Percentage of Six different types of Cars manufactured by a Company over Two years

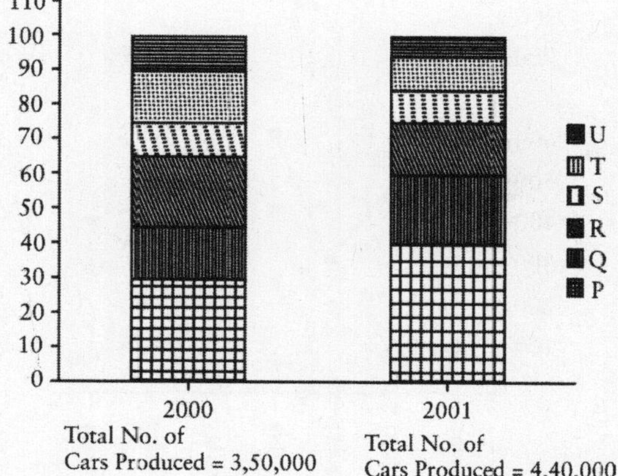

166. What was the difference in the number of Q type cars produced in 2000 and that produced in 2001?

(a) 35,500 (b) 27,000
(c) 22,500 (d) 17,500

167. Total number of cars of models P, Q and T manufactured in 2000 is?

(a) 2,45,000 (b) 2,27,500
(c) 2,10,000 (d) 1,92,500

168. If the percentage production of P type cars in 2001 was the same as that in 2000, then the number of P type cars produced in 2001 would have been
(a) 1,40,000 (b) 1,32,000
(c) 1,17,000 (d) 1,05,000

169. If 85% of the S type cars produced in each year were sold by the company. How many S type cars remain unsold?
(a) 7650 (b) 9350
(c) 11,850 (d) 12,250

170. For which model the percentage rise/fall in production from 2000 to 2001 was minimum?
(a) Q (b) R
(c) S (d) T

Directions: The graph given below represents the variations in earnings in rupees over a week. Study the graph and answer questions (171-175).

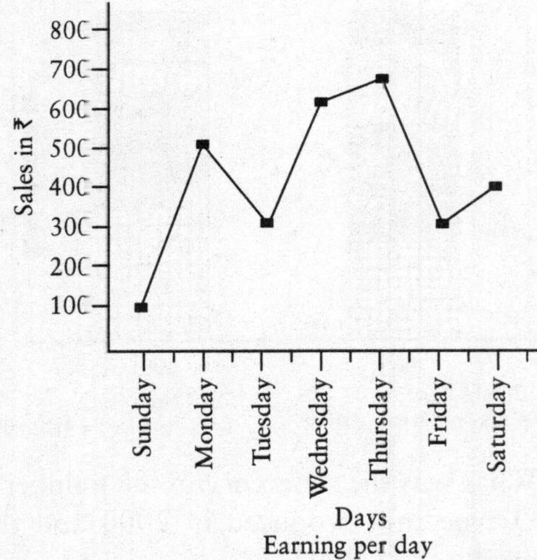

Earning per day

171. The difference in earnings was large between
(a) Sunday-Monday
(b) Tuesday-Wednesday
(c) Thursday-Friday
(d) None of these

172. Highest earnings were on
(a) Monday (b) Wednesday
(c) Thursday (d) Saturday

173. The average earnings per day during the week was
(a) ₹ 325 (b) ₹ 400
(c) ₹ 270 (d) ₹ 375

174. The earnings were least on
(a) Saturday
(b) Sunday
(c) Wednesday-Thursday
(d) None of these

175. The money transactions between Sunday-Monday and Tuesday-Wednesday were
(a) Unequal (b) Equal
(c) More (d) Less

Direction: Given below is a bar diagram and percentage of Hindus, Sikhs and Muslims in a state during the years from 1991-1994. Study the above diagram and answer the following questions (176-183).

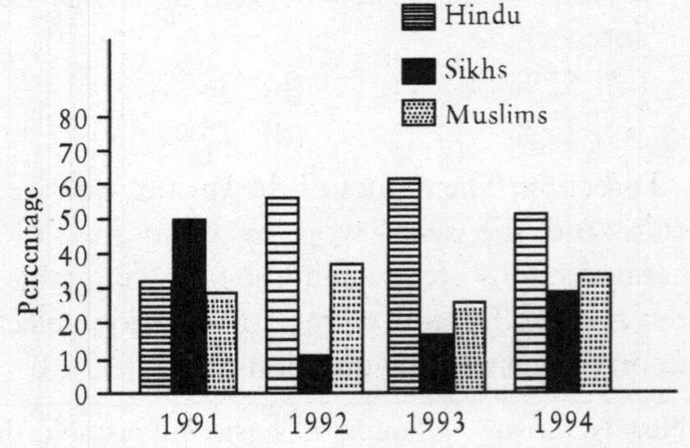

176. The ratio between Hindus and Sikhs in 1991 was
(a) 3:2
(b) 2:3
(c) cannot be calculated
(d) None of these

177. If the total population of state in 1992 is 1 million then the Hindu population was
(a) 5500000 (b) 55000
(c) 550000 (d) 5500

178. What was the percentage of Sikhs over Hindus in 1993?
(a) 25% (b) 40%
(c) 140% (d) 240%

179. What percentage was the increase in Hindus population from 1991 to 1994?
(a) 15% (b) 45%
(c) 50% (d) 25%

180. If the population of the state in 1991 is 6 lakhs, then what is total population of Hindus and Muslims in that year?
(a) 270000 (b) 3300000
(c) 330000 (d) 33000

181. During which year was the Hindu percentage maximum?
(a) 1991 (b) 1992
(c) 1993 (d) 1994

182. What percentage was the decrease in Muslim population from 1992 to 1994?
(a) 14.29% (b) 100%
(c) 200% (d) 20%

183. If the total population in 1994 is 2 millions, then the Sikh population is
(a) 1300000 (b) 130000
(c) 500000 (d) 13000000

ANSWERS

1. (d)	2. (c)	3. (d)	4. (c)	5. (b)	6. (b)
7. (c)	8. (d)	9. (a)	10. (d)	11. (c)	12. (a)
13. (b)	14. (b)	15. (b)	16. (a)	17. (c)	18. (b)
19. (b)	20. (d)	21. (a)	22. (d)	23. (a)	24. (b)
25. (b)	26. (c)	27. (b)	28. (d)	29. (c)	30. (a)
31. (b)	32. (b)	33. (a)	34. (d)	35. (b)	36. (c)
37. (c)	38. (d)	39. (d)	40. (b)	41. (c)	42. (c)
43. (c)	44. (b)	45. (d)	46. (c)	47. (a)	48. (d)
49. (d)	50. (c)	51. (c)	52. (c)	53. (c)	54. (c)
55. (c)	56. (b)	57. (d)	58. (b)	59. (b)	60. (b)
61. (d)	62. (c)	63. (a)	64. (d)	65. (b)	66. (c)
67. (c)	68. (c)	69. (b)	70. (c)	71. (c)	72. (b)
73. (d)	74. (c)	75. (d)	76. (b)	77. (d)	78. (b)
79. (d)	80. (c)	81. (d)	82. (c)	83. (a)	84. (a)
85. (c)	86. (a)	87. (a)	88. (c)	89. (a)	90. (d)
91. (c)	92. (d)	93. (a)	94. (b)	95. (b)	96. (d)
97. (d)	98. (c)	99. (b)	100. (c)	101. (c)	102. (d)
103. (a)	104. (b)	105. (c)	106. (c)	107. (c)	108. (b)
109. (d)	110. (b)	111. (c)	112. (a)	113. (d)	114. (c)
115. (a)	116. (c)	117. (d)	118. (c)	119. (d)	120. (d)

121. (c)	122. (c)	123. (a)	124. (a)	125. (b)	126. (d)
127. (d)	128. (c)	129. (d)	130. (b)	131. (b)	132. (c)
133. (c)	134. (d)	135. (a)	136. (c)	137. (a)	138. (c)
139. (d)	140. (d)	141. (b)	142. (a)	143. (a)	144. (a)
145. (b)	146. (c)	147. (c)	148. (d)	149. (d)	150. (d)
151. (d)	152. (c)	153. (d)	154. (d)	155. (d)	156. (b)
157. (c)	158. (a)	159. (b)	160. (d)	161. (b)	162. (d)
163. (b)	164. (c)	165. (c)	166. (a)	167. (c)	168. (b)
169. (c)	170. (b)	171. (a)	172. (c)	173. (b)	174. (b)
175. (a)	176. (b)	177. (c)	178. (a)	179. (c)	180. (c)
181. (c)	182. (b)	183. (c)			

8

Information and Communication Technology

1. Information technology is the generic name performing the following functions
   (a) Data storage
   (b) Data retrieval
   (c) Data communication
   (d) All of the above
2. The acronym ICT stands for
   (a) Information and Communication Technology
   (b) International Communication Technology
   (c) Intra Common Technology
   (d) None of these
3. Computer cannot do anything without a
   (a) Chip (b) Memory
   (c) Output device (d) Program
4. Central Processing Unit (CPU)
   (a) is the computer's primary processing hardware which interprets and execute program instructions and manages the function of input, output and storage devices.
   (b) is considered to be heart of the computer.
   (c) may reside on a single chip on the computer's motherboard, or on a larger card inserted into a special slot on the motherboard.
   (d) All of the above.
5. Information Technology is widely used in
   (a) Telemedicines
   (b) Geographic system
   (c) Banks
   (d) All of the above
6. Information and Communication Technology means
   (a) Collection and storage of the information
   (b) Communication and processing of information
   (c) Only (a)
   (d) Both (a) and (b)
7. The word 'Computer' usually refers to the Central Processor Unit plus
   (a) External memory
   (b) Internal memory
   (c) Input devices
   (d) Output devices
8. The Arithmetic and Logic Unit (ALU)
   (a) is the component of CPU
   (b) performs arithmetic and logical operations
   (c) Both (a) and (b)
   (d) None of the above
9. The difference between 'data' and 'information' is
   (a) Data is processed as per certain rules or policies, and the resultant is called information.
   (b) Information obtained at certain level may serve as a raw data for further information at other level.
   (c) Data and information move in a vicious circle.
   (d) All of the above representing the differences.

10. Information and Communication Technology includes
    (a) Internet (b) E-commerce
    (c) E-mail (d) All of these
11. Control Unit of a digital computers is often called the
    (a) Clock (b) Nerve centre
    (c) ICs (d) All of these
12. Data
    (a) is a collection of unorganised items that can include letters, numbers, symbols, images and sounds that computer process and organise it into meaningful information.
    (b) is a set of standards for controlling the transfer of business documents, such as purchase orders and invoices, between computers.
    (c) Both (a) and (b).
    (d) None of the above.
13. Which of the following is not an ingredient of 'MS Office'?
    (a) MS Word
    (b) MS Excel
    (c) MS Powerpoint
    (d) MS Super Power
14. The statement "Computer works like a human brain" is
    (a) Correct (b) Incorrect
    (c) Uncertain (d) None of these
15. Group of instructions that directs a computer is called
    (a) Storage (b) Memory
    (c) Logic (d) Program
16. E-Mail
    (a) stands for electronic mail.
    (b) stores purchase orders and invoices, between computers.
    (c) Both (a) and (b).
    (d) None of the above.
17. Normative value of information refers
    (a) The value obtained by theoretical procedures of decision-making.
    (b) The value obtained by taking the behavioural dimensions under consideration.
    (c) The value obtained by using the initiative guess.
    (d) None of the above.
18. The main program that runs the computer is
    (a) MS-Office
    (b) Operating system
    (c) MS-DOS
    (d) Unix
19. Which kind of hardware is used the most in the input phase of a computer-based information system?
    (a) Keyboard (b) Printer
    (c) Monitor (d) Hard disk
20. EDI
    (a) stands for Electronic Data Interchange (EDI).
    (b) is a set of standards for controlling the transfer of business documents, such as purchase orders and invoices, between computers.
    (c) Both (a) and (b).
    (d) None of the above.
21. The need requirement for information in an enterprise is due to
    (a) Opportunities before the organisation and formalizing the short term/long term policy for the growth of the organisation.
    (b) Resource allocation in an optimal way in order to attain the basic goals of an organisation.
    (c) Adjusting with new and rapid changes due to technological advancement and opening new vistas for overall progress.
    (d) All of the above.

22. A keyboard has at least
    (a) 95 keys (b) 100 keys
    (c) 101 keys (d) 105 keys
23. Which kind of device allows the user to add components and capabilities to a computer system?
    (a) System boards
    (b) Storage devices
    (c) Input devices
    (d) Expansion slots
24. Hardware is
    (a) the physical components of a computer.
    (b) includes—processors, memory chips, input/output devices, tapes, disks, cables, modems.
    (c) Both (a) and (b).
    (d) None of the above.
25. Aim of Information and communication technology is
    (a) To process, store and retrieve the data.
    (b) To create cyber space Age in present time.
    (c) To disseminate the programs of apex bodies of India.
    (d) All of the above.
26. The first electronic computer devised in 1946 was
    (a) ENIAC (b) IBM
    (c) EDSAC (d) UNIVAC
27. Where was the India's first computer installed and when?
    (a) Institute of Social Science, Agra, 1955.
    (b) Indian Institute of Statistics, Delhi, 1957.
    (c) Indian Statistical Institute, Calcutta, 1955.
    (d) Indian Institute of Science, Bangalore, 1971.
28. Input
    (a) a data or instruction that you enter into the memory of a computer.
    (b) hardware components that result in the transfer of data.
    (c) Both (a) and (b).
    (d) None of the above.
29. The importance of information and communication technology is
    (a) as an excellent tool for making learning content more comprehensible.
    (b) making educational processes more comprehensible and simple.
    (c) playing a central role in the field of distance education.
    (d) All of the above.
30. Who invented the concept of stored program?
    (a) Barden
    (b) Prof. Maurice Wilkes
    (c) Prof. John Von Neumann
    (d) Remin Rand
31. Four types of Input are
    (a) data, programs, commands and user responses
    (b) hardware components that result in the transfer of data
    (c) Both (a) and (b)
    (d) None of the above.
32. Application of information and communication technology is
    (a) To determine the objectives of the content.
    (b) To select an appropriate communication technology.
    (c) To organise the adequate techniques properly.
    (d) All of the above.
33. Central Processing Unit (CPU) is
    (a) input device
    (b) output device

(c) internal memory
(d) external memory

34. Which is a unit of measurement used with computer systems?
(a) Byte (b) Kilobyte
(c) Megabyte (d) All of these

35. The input devices are the
(a) computer hardware that accepts data and instructions from user.
(b) communication between hardware components that result in the transfer of data.
(c) Both (a) and (b).
(d) None of the above.

36. Basic application of Information and communication technology in education is
(a) In relation to active participation in sharing of information.
(b) In relation to vocational development of the teachers.
(c) In relation to accessibility of education.
(d) All of the above.

37. The Arithmetic and Logic Unit (ALU) performs
(a) only arithmetic operations
(b) only logical operations
(c) Both (a) and (b)
(d) None of these

38. Hard disks and diskettes are
(a) direct access storage devices
(b) sequential access storage devices
(c) rarely used with microcomputers
(d) Both (a) and (c) are correct

39. Input/Output devices (I/O)
(a) Communications between the user and the computer that results in transfer of data.
(b) Communication between hardware components that result in the transfer of data.
(c) Both (a) and (b).
(d) None of the above.

40. The first general purpose digital computer was called
(a) ENIAC (Electronic Numerical Integrator and Calculator)
(b) UNIVAC-1
(c) Mark-1
(d) None of the above

41. The need of information and communication technology in education is
(a) to fulfil the demand of education.
(b) to make education more interesting and comprehending.
(c) to provide support to various medium of instruction.
(d) All of these.

42. Everything computer does is controlled by its
(a) RAM (b) ROM
(c) CPU (d) Storage devices

43. Microsoft office
(a) is a suite of Microsoft primary application for Window and Macintosh.
(b) includes some combination of word, Excel, Powerpoint, Access and schedule along with a host of internet and other utilities.
(c) Both (a) and (b).
(d) None of the above.

44. The Second generation computers consist of
(a) IBM-1401 (b) Honey Bell-800
(c) IBM-1620 (d) All the above

45. Input and output devices communicate
(a) between user and the computer
(b) between hardware components
(c) Both (a) and (b)
(d) None of these

46. The heart of any computer is the
    (a) CPU (b) Memory
    (c) I/O Unit (d) Disks
47. Modem
    (a) abbreviation for modulator/demodulator.
    (b) is an Input/Output device that allows computer to communicate through telephone lines.
    (c) converts outgoing digital data into analogue signals that can be transmitted over phone lines and converts incoming audio signals into digital data that can be processed by the computer.
    (d) All of the above.
48. The third generation computers are characterised by
    (a) Vacuum tubes
    (b) Transistors
    (c) Integrated circuits
    (d) Microprocessors
49. A Scanner scan an image and transfer the image to
    (a) EBCDIC Codes
    (b) BCD Codes
    (c) EBCD Codes
    (d) ASCII Codes
50. Which of the following terms applies to communication between separate computer systems?
    (a) Computer literacy
    (b) Power supply
    (c) Applications software
    (d) Connectivity
51. Multimedia
    (a) refers to the integration of multiple media such as visual imagery, text, video, sound, and animation.
    (b) often associated with the information superhighway, or with interactive TV—that can produce videos (informaion on demand) or with hypermedia.
    (c) is a combination of software and hardware.
    (d) All of the above.
52. CPU in a computer is called
    (a) Central Processing Unit
    (b) Controlling Pressure Unit
    (c) Central Public Unit
    (d) Computer Processing Unit
53. The full form of URL is
    (a) Uniform Resource Local
    (b) Uniform Resource Locator
    (c) Unit Research Locator
    (d) None of the above
54. The following typically happens in the output phase of a computer based information system
    (a) Data is put into the computer for processing.
    (b) Information is produced in hardcopy and/or softcopy form.
    (c) Mathematical calculations are performed.
    (d) The computer is turned off.
55. RAM stands for
    (a) Random Access Memory
    (b) Reading Aid Memory
    (c) Reading and Memory
    (d) None of the above
56. Computer can pass
    (a) only digital signals
    (b) analogue signals
    (c) Both (a) and (b)
    (d) None of the above
57. Which of the following best describes a computer-based information system?
    (a) A system in which a computer is used to turn data into information

(b) Inputting data
(c) Processing data
(d) Performing complex mathematical calculations

58. Motherboard
(a) is the main circuit board, also called system board, in an electronic device which consists of sockets that accepts additional boards.
(b) is a very powerful form of communicating ideas.
(c) The interactive feature of network.
(d) None of the above.

59. Auxiliary storage devices include
(a) Magnetic tapes
(b) Magnetic Drums
(c) Hard Disk
(d) All of the above

60. "Audio conferencing" is
(a) one-sided non-verbal communication
(b) two-sided non-verbal communication
(c) one-sided verbal communication
(d) two-sided verbal communication

61. The benefit of using computers are that computers
(a) are very fast and can store huge amounts of data.
(b) produce accurate output even when the input is incorrect.
(c) are designed to the inflexible.
(d) All of the above.

62. Printers
(a) is an output device that produce text and graphics on a physical medium such as paper or transparency film.
(b) are classifieds into the following categories—Impact printers and Non-Impact printers.
(c) Both (a) and (b).
(d) None of the above.

63. The term DVD represents
(a) Digital Versatile Disk
(b) Digital Visual Disk
(c) Digital Video Disk
(d) None of the above

64. The computer pointer is connected with
(a) Modem (b) Cable
(c) UPS (d) CPU

65. Super computers are primarily useful for
(a) input-output intensive processing
(b) data-retrieval operations
(c) mathematical-intensive scientific applications
(d) All of the above

66. A program
(a) is a sequence of instructions or actions.
(b) must have mechanisms for carrying out processing operations (like arithmetical operations or moving information around) and for handling input and output.
(c) Both (a) and (b).
(d) None of the above.

67. Which one of the following is not a advantage of a computer?
(a) High speed and unfatiguable.
(b) Large storage and retrieval capacity.
(c) Versatility in application.
(d) Requires rigorous training on the part of user.

68. One byte is equal to
(a) 2 bit. (b) 16 bit.
(c) 14 bit. (d) 8 bit.

69. The instructions for starting the computer are housed on
(a) random-access memory
(b) CD-ROM
(c) read-only memory chips
(d) All of these

70. Output
    (a) is the data that has been processed into a useful form and can be seen on VDU or can be taken on paper by using printer or listen to it through speakers or a headset.
    (b) can be saved on a floppy disk or CD for future use.
    (c) can be generated in the form of text, graphics, audio, video.
    (d) All of the above.
71. The important objective of ERNET is
    (a) To establish a country-wide network involving premier institutions in the country in order to foster academic and industrial research.
    (b) To develop informatics infrastructure in the country.
    (c) To promote Human resource development by providing education and training to increase awareness of information resources available through the internet.
    (d) All of the above.
72. Protable computers are called
    (a) Calculator
    (b) Microprocessor
    (c) Laptop PCs
    (d) Parallel computer
73. Which of the following is the fastest?
    (a) CPU
    (b) Magnetic tapes and disks
    (c) Video terminal
    (d) Sensors, mechanical controllers
74. Office Automation System
    (a) Automate routine office tasks
    (b) are classifieds into the following categories—Impact and Non-Impact
    (c) Both (a) and (b)
    (d) None of the above
75. A dot matrix printer is a
    (a) chain printer (b) drum printer
    (c) serial printer (d) None of these
76. A disadvantage of the laser printer is that
    (a) it is quieter than an impact printer
    (b) it is very slow
    (c) the output is of a lower quality
    (d) None of these.
77. The Information System (IS) department
    (a) Supports organisation's information systems and also support organisation's overall mission.
    (b) The IS department provide technical support for hardware and software, but may be involved in the design and implementation of an organisation's entire information system.
    (c) IS professionals also ensure that systems generate all the appropriate types of information and reports required by the organisation's manager and workers.
    (d) All of the above.
78. The function of Information and Communication Technology is
    (a) Collection and storage of the informations
    (b) Communication of informations
    (c) Processing of informations
    (d) All of the above
79. Which of the following is not a language?
    (a) COBOL (b) PASCAL
    (c) UNIX (d) FORTRAN
80. Data entry can be performed with all of the following except
    (a) OCR
    (b) OMR
    (c) COM
    (d) Voice-recognition systems

81. Programming language
    (a) is a higher level language than machine code for writing programs
    (b) use a variety of basic English
    (c) Both (a) and (b)
    (d) None of the above

82. Data and information are
    (a) Similar concepts
    (b) Data retains information in it
    (c) The information takes birth from data
    (d) Cannot say

83. The high level language which is easy to learn and useful to the beginners is
    (a) FORTRAN (b) BASIC
    (c) COBOL (d) None of these

84. Magnetic tape can serve as
    (a) input media
    (b) output media
    (c) secondary-storage media
    (d) All of these

85. Low level languages
    (a) are machine dependent, i.e. they are designed to run on a particular computer and in the form of 0's and 1's.
    (b) are also easier to learn and are not dependent on a particular type of computer.
    (c) need interpreter or compiler to convert into low level language so that computer can understand.
    (d) All of the above.

86. The objective of information and communication technology is
    (a) To propagate more and more the material related to education and research
    (b) To usher the present generation in Cyber Age
    (c) To disseminate and propagate the informal education
    (d) All of the above.

87. The memory unit which can perform only to read operation is
    (a) ROM (b) RAM
    (c) Both (a) and (b) (d) None of these

88. The most economical way to process data is
    (a) batch processing
    (b) transaction processing
    (c) distributed processing
    (d) realtime processing

89. High level languages
    (a) are English type languages where a single statement may correspond to severals instructions in machine language and human being can understand easily.
    (b) are also easier to learn and are not dependent on a particular type of computer.
    (c) need interpreter or compiler to convert into low level language so that computer can understand.
    (d) All of the above.

90. The need of information and communication technology in education is
    (a) To satisfy the growing demand of education and to form knowledge-based society.
    (b) To make educational material more interesting and comprehending.
    (c) To give support to various mediums of instruction.
    (d) All of the above.

91. In memory, the address of a word is stored in a register called
    (a) MDR (b) PROM
    (c) MAR (d) ROM

92. The amount of a cheque is recorded in magnetic ink, using an
    (a) Encoder (b) Embosser
    (c) Inscriber (d) Imprinter

93. Pipelining
   (a) is a technique that enable a processor to execute more instructions in a given time.
   (b) the control unit begins executing a new-instruction before the current instruction is completed.
   (c) Both (a) and (b).
   (d) None of the above.

94. The first step of preparing multimedia kit is
   (a) To determine the content and its objectives.
   (b) To select the appropriate communication techniques.
   (c) To follow the instructions to apply the above techniques.
   (d) All of the above.

95. WWW means
   (a) World Wide Work
   (b) Work World Wide
   (c) World Website Work
   (d) World Wide Web

96. MICR has made possible a
   (a) cashless society
   (b) checkless society
   (c) creditless society
   (d) None of these

97. Ports
   (a) external devices such as a keyboard, monitor, printer, mouse and microphone often are attached by a cable to the system unit the interface.
   (b) point of attachment to the system unit is called a port. Most of the time ports are located on the back of the system unit, but they also can be placed on the front.
   (c) Both (a) or (b)
   (d) None of the above.

98. The role of information and communication technology in education is
   (a) To give face-to-face counselling
   (b) To give counselling through telephone
   (c) To use audio-visual cassettes in counselling
   (d) All of the above

99. Which of the following is not a operating system?
   (a) EXCE (b) UNIX
   (c) DOS (d) WINDOWS

100. Optical character readers can read
   (a) machine printed data
   (b) machine printed letters and numbers, and hand printed numbers
   (c) both machine and hand printed letters, but not handwriting
   (d) machine

101. Application software
   (a) any computer program used to create or process data such as text documents, spreadsheets, graphics, etc.
   (b) programs to operate only mouse functions.
   (c) a type of program designed to handle very small instruction sets.
   (d) None of the above.

102. The present age is called the age of information revolution therefore the informations are treated as
   (a) Commodity
   (b) Article of economic development
   (c) Article of National progress and development
   (d) All of the above.

103. PASCAL, C, C++ and COBOL are the examples of
   (a) secondary memory device
   (b) external parts of a computer
   (c) internal parts of a computer
   (d) programming language

104. A floppy disk can contain approximately
(a) 2,500 bytes (b) 25,000 bytes
(c) 1,440,000 bytes (d) 2,500,000 bytes

105. Desktop Publishing programs
(a) belongs to Application software
(b) used to literate individuals in computing
(c) a type of program designed to handle very small instruction sets
(d) None of the above

106. MODEM is used for communicating data
(a) in LAN (b) in WAN
(c) in MAN (d) All of these

107. What are the two major types of computer chips?
(a) External memory chip
(b) Primary memory chip
(c) Microprocessor chip
(d) Both (b) and (c)

108. ASCII
(a) is 7 bit binary code.
(b) developed by American National Standards Institute (ANSI).
(c) represent symbolic, numeric and alphanumeric characters.
(d) All of the above.

109. The term computer is generally used for CPU and
(a) External memory
(b) Internal memory
(c) Input device
(d) Output device

110. Which of the following is a low level language?
(a) Machine language
(b) Assembly language
(c) Both (a) and (b)
(d) None of the above

111. The monitor of a computer is connected to it by a
(a) Cable (b) Wire
(c) Bus (d) Modem

112. Assembler
(a) is a computer program that converts assembly language instructions into machine language.
(b) developed by American National Standards Institute (ANSI).
(c) represent symbolic, numeric and alphanumeric characters, voice.
(d) All of the above.

113. The Control Unit in a digital computer is called
(a) Clock (b) IC's
(c) Nerve centre (d) All the above

114. Addition subtraction operation has been carried out in
(a) CPU (b) ALU
(c) UPS (d) RAM

115. In a computer system, which device is functionally opposite to a Keyboard?
(a) Mouse (b) Trackball
(c) Printer (d) Joystick

116. ATM
(a) stands for Asynchronous Transfer Mode.
(b) is a network protocol designed to send voice, video and data transmission over a single network.
(c) provides differtent kinds of connections and bandwidth on demand, depending on the type of data being transmitted.
(d) All of the above.

117. The group of instructions which directs computer, is called
(a) Storage (b) Logic
(c) Memory (d) Program

118. In a digital computer
(a) CPU is clock (b) CPU is processor
(c) CPU is IC's (d) All of these

119. A monitor looks like a TV set but it does not
(a) receive TV signals
(b) give a steady picture
(c) display graphics
(d) give a clear picture

120. Backup means
(a) To create a duplicate set of program or data files in case the originals become damaged.
(b) Provides different kinds of connections and bandwidth in computers.
(c) The type of data transmission.
(d) None of the above.

121. Which type of Hardware input is being used in computer supported information system?
(a) Keyboard (b) Printer
(c) Monitor (d) Hard Disk

122. Which of the following items is not used in Local Area Networks (LANs)?
(a) Computer (b) Modem
(c) Printer (d) Cable

123. Computers are now used in
(a) restaurants, automobile companies
(b) offices and homes
(c) research areas
(d) All of the above

124. In a computer which type of the devices are extending the facility to join components and capabilities in it?
(a) System boards (b) Storage devices
(c) Input devices (d) Expansion slots

125. Charles Babbage is called the father of
(a) Computer (b) E-mail
(c) E-commerce (d) Internet

126. A modem is connected in between a telephone line and a
(a) network
(b) computer
(c) communication adapter
(d) serial port

127. Information
(a) is the summarisation of data.
(b) implies data that is organised and is meaningful to the person who is receiving it.
(c) should be meaningful, brief, accurate and help us to our knowledge and decision-making.
(d) All of the above.

128. Which of the following statement is false?
(a) A byte is equal to 8 bits.
(b) Super computer are used for data retrieval operations.
(c) HTML is a computer language.
(d) DNS stands for dependent name system.

129. When a group of computers is connected together in a small area without the help of telephone lines, it is called
(a) Remote Communication Network (RCN)
(b) Local Area Network (LAN)
(c) Wide Area Network (WAN)
(d) Value Added Network (VAN)

130. Data
(a) can be defined as fact, observation, assumption or occurrence and is a plural of "datum".
(b) in general refers to raw facts gathered from different sources.
(c) denotes any or all facts, numbers, letters, symbols, etc. that can be processed or manipulated by a computer.
(d) All of the above.

131. A communication network which is used by large organisations over regional, national or global area is called
(a) LAN (b) WAN
(c) MAN (d) VAN

132. Data and Information are
(a) often used interchangeably
(b) not used interchangeably
(c) not used by people to make decisions
(d) None of the above

133. Which of the following measuring unit is applied in reference to computer system?
(a) Byte (b) Kilobyte
(c) Megabyte (d) All of these

134. Computer programs means
(a) list of information
(b) information stored in ROM
(c) information processed in RAM
(d) external design of computer

135. Logical data refers
(a) to the way in which the data are recorded on the storage medium.
(b) in general refers to processed facts gathered from different sources.
(c) can be defined as fact, observation, assumption or occurrence and is a plural of "datum".
(d) None of the above.

136. Which of the following statement does describe best the computer based information system?
(a) A system is which computer is used to change data into informations.
(b) Input data.
(c) Processing data.
(d) To analyse the complex mathematical calculations.

137. Storage capacity of the computer is measured in
(a) Kilogram (b) Bites
(c) Bytes (d) Both (b) and (c)

138. 1 KB (kilobyte) and 1 MB (megabyte) are respectively equal to
(a) 1024 bytes and 1000 kilobytes
(b) 1000 bytes and 100 kilobytes
(c) 1000 bytes and 10000 bytes
(d) 1024 bytes and 100 kilobytes

139. Data item
(a) is a basic or individual element of data.
(b) is identified by a name and is assigned a value.
(c) is something referred to as a field.
(d) All of the above.

140. The advantage of using the computer is
(a) The computer calculates with fast pace and more and more data can be stored in it.
(b) If your input may be wrong but output is correct.
(c) Computer is an unfatiguable machine.
(d) All of the above.

141. A computer's 'clock-speed' is measured in
(a) megabytes and gigabytes
(b) nanoseconds and picoseconds
(c) bits and megabits
(d) megahertz and gigahertz

142. Smallest addressable unit in computer is
(a) Byte—an arbitrary set of eight bits that represents a character
(b) FM
(c) TPM
(d) None of the above

143. Generally Super Computers are used
(a) for intensive processing of input and output.
(b) for data Retrieval operations.
(c) in Mathematical intensive scientific Application.
(d) All of the above.

144. In LAN, there is no need of
(a) Computer (b) Modem
(c) Printer (d) Calse

145. The computer performs all mathematical and logical operations inside its

(a) Central Processing Unit
(b) Memory Unit
(c) Output Unit
(d) Visual Display Unit

146. File
(a) is a collection of related records
(b) is a automated processing system
(c) TDM
(d) None of the above

147. For booting a computer related informations are stored in
(a) Random Access Memory
(b) CD-ROM
(c) Read only Memory
(d) All of the above

148. MODEM means
(a) Modulator-Demodulator
(b) Input/Output device
(c) Convert digital data into analog of signals
(d) All of the above

149. In electronic form, data refers to
(a) data fields, records, files and databases
(b) word processing documents, graphics, images
(c) digitally coded voice and video
(d) All of the above

150. In the following the fastest computer constituent is
(a) CPU
(b) Magnetic Tape
(c) Video Terminal
(d) Sensors and Mechanical controllers

151. Which of the following statement is false?
(a) Printer is a output device.
(b) Keyboard is a input device.
(c) Tally is a language.
(d) JAVA is a language.

152. Which of the following are examples of input devices?
(a) Visual display unit, dot matrix printer, laser printer.
(b) Keyboard, mouse, optical mark reader.
(c) Arithmetic and logic unit, control unit.
(d) RAM, ROM, PROM.

153. Data processing is the
(a) process of converting data from physical format to logical format.
(b) digitally coded voice and video.
(c) Both (a) and (b).
(d) None of the above.

154. The great disadvantage of the Laser Printing is
(a) It is comparatively silent (Noiseless).
(b) It is working with very slow speed.
(c) Its output is of low quality.
(d) None of the above.

155. In Recycle bin deleted files are
(a) stored (b) access
(c) never store (d) None of these

156. The term 'Program' refers to
(a) a sequence of instructions
(b) the computer's internal design
(c) any information stored in the memory
(d) any information processed by the computer

157. Electronic mail is the
(a) transmission of letters, messages and memos over a communications network.
(b) distribution of all information functions in the office.
(c) Both (a) and (b)
(d) None of the above

158. By which one of the following Data Entry cannot be carried out?
(a) KOM
(b) OCR
(c) OMR
(d) Voice identification system

159. Control Box consists of
(a) maximise button
(b) minimise button
(c) close button
(d) All of the above

160. The backbone of an E-mail system is a communication network that connects remote terminals to a
(a) central system or local area network that interconnect personal computers.
(b) digitally coded voice and video.
(c) Both (a) and (b).
(d) None of the above.

161. The advantage of the application of MICR is
(a) evolving cashless social structure.
(b) making chequeless society.
(c) evolving creditless society.
(d) None of the above

162. MS-DOS stands for
(a) Microsoft data operating system
(b) Microsoft disk operating system
(c) Microprocessor software data operating system
(d) None of the above

163. Unix, DOS, Windows are examples of
(a) application programs.
(b) operating systems.
(c) word processors.
(d) commercial computer brands.

164. FAX or Facsimile
(a) is the communication of a printed page between remote locations.
(b) terminals scan a paper form and converts its image into analogue code for transmission over private lines/ public dial-up telephone system.
(c) receiving terminal reconverts the codes into images and prints a "facsimile" of the original page.
(d) All of the above.

165. Optical Character Reader (OCR) can read
(a) the data printed by machine only.
(b) the numbers printed by machine and hand only.
(c) Both of the above except handwritten material.
(d) the machine.

166. On Desktop we can
(a) add items (b) remove items
(c) rearrange items (d) All of these

167. Multimedia devices enable the use of computers for
(a) automation (b) defense use
(c) entertainment (d) medical use

168. Data processing cycle consists of
(a) three basic steps—Input cycle, Processing cycle, Output cycle.
(b) terminals which scan a paper form and converts its image into analogue code for transmission.
(c) receiving terminal reconverts the codes into images and prints a "facsimile" of the original page.
(d) All of the above.

169. Magnetic Tape can work
(a) As an input media
(b) As an output media
(c) As an secondary storage media
(d) All of the above

170. GIF, JPG and TIF are the formats of
(a) word document
(b) excel document
(c) image document
(d) None of the above

171. The operation of adding two numbers is done in the
(a) program (b) ALU
(c) control unit (d) output unit

172. An Input operation performs two functions, they are

(a) It causes an input device to physically read data, and transmits the data from the Input device to an Input area of CPU.
(b) It causes an input device to transmits the data, convert into image form.
(c) It causes an input device to physical read data, transmits the data to printer.
(d) None of the above.

173. The best economic method of Data processing is
(a) Batch processing
(b) Transaction processing
(c) Distributed processing
(d) Real time processing

174. The collection of computer networks that connects millions of computers around the world is called
(a) Intranet (b) Internet
(c) Interpreter (d) All of these

175. Registers are high speed memory elements, situated in the
(a) Memory
(b) CPU
(c) I/O Unit
(d) ROM or EPROM

176. During processing cycle, a computer performs operations of
(a) data transfer, ALU operations that operate on Input data.
(b) sends data to an output area lies within the CPU (which is setup by each program).
(c) Both (a) and (b).
(d) None of the above.

177. Which of the following are Indian ISP?
(a) VSNL (b) MTNL
(c) Rolta Net (d) All of these

178. An output operation causes
(a) information to be transmitted from the output area lies within the CPU to an output device such as printer.
(b) CPU to record/display information on some medium.
(c) Both (a) and (b).
(d) None of the above.

179. Browser is a
(a) software by which we access on the web.
(b) hardware.
(c) language used to communicate in Internet.
(d) set of instructions.

180. TCP/IP is necessary if one is to connect to the
(a) Phone lines (b) LAN
(c) Internet (d) Server

181. Computers
(a) help you with your banking by using automatic teller machines (ATM) used to deposit or withdraw money.
(b) are present in every aspect of daily living-in workplace, home and in the classroom.
(c) an electronic machine operating under the control of instructions stored in its own memory that can accept data (Input), manipulate the data according to specified rules (process), produce results (output) and store this result for future use.
(d) All of the above.

182. Two main types of Computer Chips are
(a) External Memory Chip
(b) Primary Memory Chip
(c) Microprocessor Chip
(d) Both (b) and (c)

183. Which of the following is the example of output device?

(a) RAM, ROM, UPS
(b) Keyboard, Mouse, OMR
(c) ALU, CPU, UPS
(d) Monitor, printer, laser printer

184. HTML is an abbreviation for
(a) hotmail—an e-mail facility.
(b) a language in which Webpages are written.
(c) the modulation level of a Modem.
(d) the high tension requirement of a computer.

185. A person that communicates with a computer or uses the information it generates is called
(a) User (b) Processor
(c) Commentator (d) None of these

186. The Computer Monitor is joined with
(a) A Cable (b) A Buss
(c) A Wire (d) A Modem

187. At the time of booting informations are stored in
(a) ROM (b) RAM
(c) CPU (d) All of these

188. Primary memory of computer
(a) stores the necessary programs of system software.
(b) determines the size and the number of programs that can be held within the computer at same time.
(c) Both (a) and (b).
(d) None of the above.

189. Which of the following device is just against the Keyboard in a computer system?
(a) Printer (b) Trackball
(c) Joystick (d) Mouse

190. In Excel we can
(a) draw pie graph
(b) make slides
(c) Both (a) and (b)
(d) None of the above

191. An organisation's introductory webpage is called its
(a) Portal (b) Vortal
(c) Homepage (d) Website

192. As technology advances and computer extend into every facet of daily living, it
(a) is essential for everybody to gain some level of computer literacy.
(b) is not essential for everybody to gain some level of computer literacy.
(c) can create problems.
(d) None of the above.

193. The computer monitor is appeared like a TV set but cannot perform the function of
(a) Receiving of TV signals
(b) An immediate picture
(c) Display graphics
(d) Clear picture

194. POP3 and IMAP are e-mail accounts in which
(a) one automatically gets one's mail everyday.
(b) one has to be connected to the server to read or write one's mail.
(c) one only has to be connected to the server to send and receive the mail.
(d) one does not need any telephone lines.

195. The main memory of computer
(a) can be divided in two parts—RAM and ROM.
(b) is not essential for computer.
(c) can be loaded from storage media.
(d) None of the above.

196. To store word document we use the extension
(a) .doc. (b) .exl.
(c) .jpg. (d) .xlm.

197. The term 'DNS' stands for
 (a) Domain Name System
 (b) Defense Nuclear System
 (c) Downloadable New Software
 (d) Dependent Name Server

198. Generally Modem is connected with Telephone line and
 (a) In middle of Network
 (b) Communication Adopter
 (c) Serial port
 (d) Computer

199. Which of the following is not a part of Hardware?
 (a) Input device (b) CPU
 (c) Output device (d) All of these

200. Computers
 (a) uses cache memory to improve their processing times.
 (b) uses main memory for temporary storage.
 (c) uses secondary memory, which is non-volatile to store bulk data.
 (d) All of the above.

201. When in a small area, we joined a number of computers in a group and do not use telephone line in it, then it is called?
 (a) Local Area Network
 (b) Remote Communication Network
 (c) Wide Area Network
 (d) Value Aided Network

202. Which of the following is primary memory storage?
 (a) ROM, RAM and Hard Disk
 (b) ROM, RAM and C: Drive
 (c) ROM, RAM and CACHE
 (d) ROM, RAM and Floppy Disk

203. Video conferencing is a meeting between two or more geographically separated individuals who
 (a) use a network or the Internet to transmit audio and video data
 (b) use a satellite to transmit audio and video data
 (c) Both (a) and (b)
 (d) None of the above

204. Such a Network which helps in communicating regional, national and global informations through Large institutions is called
 (a) MAN (b) LAN
 (c) WAN (d) VAN

205. A set of programs which is written to do specific task is called
 (a) application s/f. (b) utility s/f.
 (c) system s/f. (d) None of these

206. CD-ROM
 (a) stands for Compact Disk Read Only Memory.
 (b) is a silver coloured compact disk that uses the laser technology.
 (c) Both (a) and (b).
 (d) None of the above.

207. The function of compiler is
 (a) to translate high level language to machine language.
 (b) to translate machine language to high level language.
 (c) to communicate between CPU and ROM.
 (d) None of the above.

208. UNIX
 (a) is a multiuser, multitasking operating system.
 (b) was developed in early 1970s by scientists at Bell Laboratories.
 (c) Both (a) and (b).
 (d) None of the above.

209. Which of the following is incorrect?
 (a) FORTRAN—used as a scientific application language.
 (b) COBOL—developed for business application.

(c) C/C++—used to develop system s/f.
(d) Java—operating system.

210. Virus
(a) is a computer program that copies itself into other programs and spreads through multiple computers.
(b) are often designed to damage a computer intentionally by destroying or corrupting its data.
(c) Both (a) and (b).
(d) None of the above.

211. Which of the following is incorrect in context of E-mail?
(a) E-mail is the short form of electronic mail.
(b) It is used to transmit text message.
(c) E-mail is very fast as compared to conversational mail.
(d) E-mail cannot allow us to send graphical images.

212. A template
(a) is a document that contains the formatting necessary for a specific document type.
(b) usually exists for documents such as memos, fax cover sheets and letters.
(c) Both (a) and (b).
(d) None of the above.

213. The memory unit that communicates directly with the CPU is called
(a) Primary memory
(b) RAM
(c) Hard disk
(d) UPS

214. The drawing tools available in MS WORD
(a) Line, rectangle, ellipse, text box, fill colour
(b) Line style and select drawing objects
(c) Both (a) and (b)
(d) None of the above

215. EEPROM Stands for
(a) Electrically Erasable Program Real Over Memo
(b) Electrically Erasable Program Randam Only Memory
(c) Electrically Erasable Programmable Read Only Memory
(d) None of these

216. In MS WORD a title bar
(a) is a bar displayed at the top of the document that displays the name of the current document.
(b) locate below the menu bar.
(c) Both (a) and (b).
(d) None of the above.

217. Which of the following is the example of input device?
(a) Visual Display unit, Dotmatrix Printer, Laser Printer
(b) Key board, Mouse, OMR
(c) RAM, ROM, PROM
(d) Arithmetic and Logic unit, Control unit

218. The diameter of the floppy disks may be
(a) 3.5 inches (b) 5.25 inches
(c) 8 inches (d) All of these

219. The mail merge in MS Word
(a) automatically creates 'unique, multiple versions of a customised form letter, when sending out a specific letter to a different person.
(b) merges two cell contents in one cell.
(c) Both (a) and (b).
(d) None of the above.

220. Which of the following is not a Boolean operator?
(a) AND (b) GOT
(c) OR (d) NOT

221. MS Excel
(a) is a replacement for the accountants columnar pad, sharp pencil and calculator.

(b) allows users to create colourful charts, print transparencies or hard copy reports, add clip arts and company logo, etc.
(c) Both (a) and (b).
(d) None of the above.

222. The difference between SORT and INDEX command
(a) Sort after sorting generates output file whereas Index does not.
(b) Sort cannot sort on expressions whereas Index can.
(c) Both (a) and (b).
(d) None of the above.

223. Which of the following is an example of printer?
(a) Dot matrix printer
(b) Inkjet printer
(c) Laser printer
(d) All of the above

224. Operating System is
(a) a collection of hardware components.
(b) a collection of input-output devices.
(c) a collection of software routines.
(d) None of the above.

225. The computer is used through multimedia devices for
(a) Automation (b) Entertainment
(c) Military use (d) Medicinal use

226. To get connected with internet we require
(a) Telephone line (b) Computer
(c) Modem (d) All of these

227. Backups should be done
(a) daily for most installations.
(b) weekly for most installations.
(c) as several image copies, followed by an incremental.
(d) as several incrementals, followed by an image copy.

228. The operation for adding two numbers has been carried out in
(a) Programme (b) ALU
(c) Control unit (d) Output unit

229. Multimedia is used in
(a) Education (b) Advertisement
(c) Both (a) and (b) (d) None of these

230. DOS, etc. are called disk operating systems because
(a) they are memory resident.
(b) they are initially stored on disk.
(c) they are available on magnetic tapes.
(d) they are partly in primary memory and partly on disk.

231. Registers—the elements of fast pace are located in
(a) Memory (b) CPU
(c) I/O Devices (d) ROM

232. Which is of the following is incorrect about web page?
(a) It is a document on the WWW.
(b) It consists of HTML file.
(c) It is identifiable by MODEM.
(d) It is identifiable by URL.

233. Which of the following is not an operating system?
(a) UNIX (b) MS-DOS
(c) PASCAL (d) CP/M

234. Machine language and Assembly language are the examples of
(a) High level language
(b) Low level language
(c) Both of the above
(d) None of the above

235. Website is a collection of
(a) web pages
(b) world document
(c) Both (a) and (b)
(d) None of these

236. User-Friendly Systems are
(a) required for object-oriented programming.

(b) easy to develop.
(c) common among traditional main frame operating system.
(d) becoming more common.

237. HTML is a briefname given to
(a) HOTMAIL—for the convenience of e-mail.
(b) A computer language which assists in preparation of web page.
(c) For the modulation level of MODEM.
(d) For the high-tension requirement of the computer.

238. An E-mail address is composed of
(a) two parts (b) three parts
(c) four parts (d) All of these

239. Address Bus is
(a) A set of wires connecting the computer's CPU and RAM, across which memory addresses are transmitted. The amount of memory that can be addressed at one time depends on the number of wires used in the bus.
(b) A set of nodes connectings the computer network.
(c) Both (a) or (b).
(d) None of the above.

240. http://www.examination.com—It is the example of
(a) URL (b) HTML
(c) AML (d) LAN

241. DBMS stands for
(a) Data Base Memory Storage
(b) Data Base Memory System
(c) Data Base Management System
(d) None of the above

242. Algorithm is
(a) A set of ordered steps or procedures needed to solve a specific problem.
(b) A set of circuit helps in connecting the computer network.
(c) Both (a) and (b).
(d) None of the above.

243. The first webpage of any organisation is called
(a) Portal (b) Home page
(c) Vortal (d) Website

244. What is going 'on-line'?
(a) Connection with a LAN.
(b) To get news connection of PTI and REUTERS.
(c) Getting access to various infromations over internet connection.
(d) To buy a Modem to connect with PC.

245. Coprocessors
(a) is a special processor chip or circuit board designed to assist the processor in performing specific tasks.
(b) can be used to increase the performance of the computer.
(c) Both (a) and (b).
(d) None of the above.

246. MODEM was invented by
(a) AT & T Information system, USA
(b) IBM
(c) Wans Laboratories Ltd.
(d) None of these

247. Control Unit (CU)
(a) The component of the CPU that contains the instruction set.
(b) gives the computer its ability to decode and then execute a stored program.
(c) directs the flow of data throughout the computer system.
(d) All of the above.

248. The abbreviation DNS stands for
(a) Domain Name System
(b) Dependent Name Server
(c) Defense Nuclear System
(d) Downloadable New Software

249. Modulation and Demodulation are performed by

(a) Modem (b) UPS
(c) Multimedia (d) Satellite

250. Transaction Processing systems
(a) store information about individual events.
(b) provide information that is useful in running an organisation, such as inventory status, billing, etc.
(c) Both (a) and (b).
(d) None of the above.

251. The mechanical digital calculator was invented by
(a) Herman Hollerith
(b) Blaize Pascal
(c) Charles Babbage
(d) Howard Icons

252. Which of the following is false?
(a) WAN - Wide Area Networks
(b) ROM - Random Only Memory
(c) LAN - Local Area Networks
(d) IT - Information Technology

253. Management Information Systems
(a) produce reports for different types of managers.
(b) automate routine office tasks.
(c) Both (a) and (b).
(d) None of the above.

254. Which generation of computer have we entered today?
(a) Fifth (b) Sixth
(c) Fourth (d) Seventh

255. Decision Support systems
(a) produce highly detailed, customised reports based on the information in an organisation's transaction processing system and based on information from other sources.
(b) these systems are used to assist managers in making critical decisions.
(c) Both (a) and (b).
(d) None of the above.

256. Expert systems
(a) include the knowledge of human experts in a specific subject area in a knowledge-base.
(b) They analyse requests from users and assist the users in developing a course of action.
(c) Both (a) and (b).
(d) None of the above.

257. Which of the following is measured in Bits and Bytes?
(a) Computer Memory
(b) Computer Speed
(c) Computer Storage Capacity
(d) None of the above

258. A large IS department include
(a) IS managers, computer scientists, system analysts, programmers, database specialists.
(b) user assistance architects, purchasing agents, technical writers, system or network managers.
(c) trainers, hardware maintenance technicians.
(d) All of the above.

259. Which of the following Network had developed first of all in the field of Education?
(a) NICNET (b) MAN
(c) WAN (d) None of these

260. 64 MB has
(a) 64,000,000 bytes for storing memory
(b) 640,000 bytes for storing memory
(c) 6,400,000 bytes for storing memory
(d) None of the above

261. Automated machine tools
(a) operate from instructions in a program through numerical control.

(b) digitally coded voice and video.
(c) Both (a) and (b).
(d) None of the above.

262. For joining gateways one uses
(a) Two similar networks.
(b) Two different networks.
(c) Best channels available for communication.
(d) Best networks of communication.

263. The version of Window is
(a) Window - 95 (b) Window - 98
(c) Window - 2000 (d) All of these

264. E-mail programs often
(a) come with local area network software or add-on options or they are independent programs designed to work with a specific network.
(b) operate as dependent programs designed to work with a specific network.
(c) Both (a) and (b).
(d) None of the above.

265. MODEM is used for communicating data
(a) In LAN (b) In MAN
(c) In WAN (d) None of these

266. What is true about smart card?
(a) It is an enhanced version of cards with magnetic stripes.
(b) It contains a microprocessor.
(c) It contain personal data in its memory.
(d) All of the above.

267. Public Data Service (PDS) is a service bureau, is an organisation that
(a) provides data processing and time sharing services to its customers and customers pay for their processing.
(b) offers wide variety of software packages, as well as customised programming.
(c) charge a monthly rental for each byte of online disk storage reserved for customer's programs and databases.
(d) All of the above.

268. Which of the following topology is considered best among the following?
(a) Ring Topology (b) Star Topology
(c) Bus Topology (d) None of these

269. Which is not a type of scanner
(a) Hand held label scanner
(b) Page scanner
(c) Word scanner
(d) Stationary label scanner

270. Two basic types of RAM exists
(a) dynamic RAM, static RAM
(b) natural RAM, static RAM
(c) dynamic RAM, virtual RAM
(d) None of the above

271. The advantage of internet to a teacher is
(a) He can modernise his knowledge and enrich it.
(b) He can counsel the students.
(c) He can prepare teaching aid material.
(d) All of the above.

272. The SORT command in FOXPRO
(a) is used to sort the records of a database file in ascending or descending order.
(b) takes records for sorting from currently opened database file and the sorted records are written in another file—output file.
(c) physically rearranges the records in the database in a new file and new file occupies the same amount of space as unsorted file occupies.
(d) All of the above.

273. The instrument which helps in receiving the web page matter through internet is called

(a) Client (b) Browser
(c) Server (d) None of these

274. Microsoft Office consists
(a) MS-Access (b) MS-Paint
(c) Coral (d) Both (a) and (b)

275. The INDEX command in DBASE III plus
(a) is used to index the records of a database file and contains only the key values and record numbers.
(b) takes records for indexing from currently opened database file but no output file is generated.
(c) Both (a) and (b).
(d) None of the above.

276. Web client is called
(a) Web server
(b) Web browser
(c) Both of the above
(d) None of the above

277. A Sell represent
(a) symbolic character
(b) numeric and alphanumeric character
(c) Both (a) and (b)
(d) None of the above.

278. Presentation graphics/softwares
(a) allow you to create presentations to communicate ideas, messages and other information to a group.
(b) incorporates some of the features of word processing software.
(c) can incorporate slides with text, graphics, movie, sound, etc.
(d) All of the above.

279. MS Word is an example of
(a) Application software
(b) System software
(c) Operating system
(d) Translating program

280. The linking of computer with communication system is called
(a) Assembling (b) Networking
(c) Multimedia (d) Internet

281. Powerpoint
(a) has tools with which you can use drawing tools to add these objects on a slide.
(b) allows you to insert sound, music, video clips on a slide.
(c) allows you to give animation effect to each object introduced in the slide.
(d) All of the above.

282. The advantage of MS Word is in
(a) Letter writing
(b) Preparing lecture
(c) Preparing question paper
(d) All of the above

283. A binary code is a combination of
(a) 0's and 1's
(b) 0's and 2's
(c) natural number
(d) alpha numeric characters

284. To maximize a Window
(a) click on the maximize button in the Window you want to maximize.
(b) double click on the maximize button in the Window you want to maximize.
(c) Both (a) and (b).
(d) None of the above.

285. A teacher can develop a Question Bank with the help of
(a) MS Word (b) Excel
(c) Powerpoint (d) All the above

286. Data within the computer is represented in
(a) binary number system
(b) decimal number system
(c) octal number system
(d) All of the above

287. You can use scroll bar
(a) to browse through the information in the Window.

(b) when Window is not large enough to display all information it contains.
(c) Both (a) and (b).
(d) None of the above.

288. In MS Word last action can be reversed by
(a) 'Repeat' (b) 'UNDO'
(c) 'REDO' (d) All the above

289. The main features of MS Word are
(a) editing (b) for mating
(c) creating tables (d) All of these

290. When you have finished working with a Window, you can
(a) close the Window to remove it from your screen. To do so click on (x) in the Window you want to close.
(b) scan the Window. To do so click on (x) in the Window you want to close.
(c) Both (a) and (b).
(d) None of the above.

291. Headers and Footers are exhibited
(a) in print layout
(b) in normal view
(c) in web layout
(d) in all the above

292. Which of the following is not a object oriented language?
(a) JAVA (b) C / C++
(c) COBOL (d) All of these

293. Frame
(a) is the part of an on-screen Window (title bar and other elements) that is controlled by operating system rather than by the application running in the Window.
(b) is used when Window is not large enough to display all information it contains.
(c) Both (a) and (b).
(d) None of the above.

294. The computer display which is generally used for typing, editing and formatting is
(a) Normal view (b) Web layout
(c) Print layout (d) All of these

295. The main function of internet is
(a) it allows people to send message to another.
(b) it stores files to access.
(c) it connects people to the main computer to do thing as if they were actually at site.
(d) All of the above.

296. Start button
(a) provides quick access to programs, files and help with Windows.
(b) provides slow access to programs, files and help with Windows.
(c) is not used now-a-days.
(d) None of the above.

297. The presentation package and slides are prepared by
(a) Powerpoint (b) Excel
(c) MS Word (d) All the above

298. A micro floppy can store data upto
(a) 1044 Mega byte
(b) 14.4 Mega byte
(c) 144 Mega byte
(d) 44.4 Mega byte

299. Recycle bin
(a) stores deleted files and allows you to recover them later
(b) provides slow access to programs, files and help with Windows
(c) is not used now-a-days
(d) None of the above

300. A person can make out presentations for
(a) Sales promotion
(b) Teaching
(c) Orientation training of employees
(d) All of the above

301. Which of the following is not a peripherals?
(a) CPU (b) Floppies
(c) Speakers (d) Printer

302. Memory protection is normally done by
(a) the processor and the associated hardware
(b) the operating system
(c) the compiler
(d) the user program

303. For preparing new presentation one should use the following command
(a) Auto content wizard
(b) MS outlook
(c) Command Prompt
(d) MS Access

304. The size of the virtual memory depends on
(a) the size of the data bus.
(b) the size of the main memory.
(c) the size of the address bus.
(d) None of the above.

305. Which of the following stages of compilation produces a syntax tree?
(a) Code generation
(b) Lexical analysis
(c) Parsing
(d) Semantic analysis

306. PASCAL, COBOL are
(a) low level languages
(b) high level languages
(c) assembly language
(d) None of the above

307. Which of the following types of software should you use if you often need to create, edit, and print documents?
(a) Word processing
(b) Spreadsheet
(c) UNIX
(d) Desktop publishing

308. Which of the following command would you like to follow to change the slide order?
(a) Replace (b) Paste
(c) Duplicate (d) Slide sorter

309. One kilobyte means
(a) 210 bytes (b) 1024 bytes
(c) both (a) and (b) (d) None of these

310. Which are the most important features of Microsoft Windows program?
(a) Windows
(b) Pull-down menus
(c) Icons
(d) All of the above

311. Font size can be changed through
(a) Insert menu (b) Tools menu
(c) Format menu (d) Edit menu

312. The standard CD-ROM capacity is
(a) 500 - 800 megabytes
(b) 600 - 900 megabytes
(c) 550 - 800 megabytes
(d) 400 - 700 megabytes

313. Which of the following requires a device driver?
(a) Register (b) Cache
(c) Main memory (d) Disk

314. We can prepare Report card through
(a) MS Word (b) Powerpoint
(c) Excel (d) All the above

315. The capacity of CD-ROM is
(a) Less than floppy disk
(b) More than floppy disk
(c) Nearly equal to floppy disk
(d) None of the above

316. What is the name of the operating system that read and reacts in terms of actual time?
(a) Batch system
(b) Quick response system

(c) Real time system
(d) Time sharing system

317. We can draw a pie-graph in
(a) Excel
(b) Powerpoint
(c) Both of the above
(d) None of the above

318. Which is the following is a type of ROM
(a) PROM (b) EPROM
(c) EEPROM (d) All of these

319. The term "operating system" means
(a) a set of programs which controls computer working.
(b) the way a computer operator works.
(c) conversion of high level language into machine code.
(d) the way a floppy disk drive operates.

320. When in a work sheet there are 256 columns, the number of rows in it should be
(a) 55555 (b) 56565
(c) 55536 (d) 65356

321. The first Super computer build by the Indian scientists is
(a) PARAM (b) SUPER
(c) PALMTOP (d) None of these

322. Data encryption
(a) is mostly used by public networks.
(b) is mostly used by financial networks.
(c) cannot be used by private installations.
(d) is not necessary, since data cannot be intercepted.

323. MICR system helps in
(a) processing information
(b) processing
(c) communication with other computers
(d) All of the above

324. A communication network which is used by large organisation over regional, national or global area is called
(a) LAN (b) WAN
(c) MAN (d) VAN

325. Which is true about Web Browser?
(a) It reads and interprets web pages.
(b) Microsoft internet explores is a popular web browser.
(c) NCSA Mosaic was first graphical web browser.
(d) All of the above.

326. If you want to execute more than one program at a time, the systems software you are using must be capable of
(a) word processing
(b) virtual memory
(c) compiling
(d) multitasking

327. The limitation of a traditional computer is
(a) The handling of the text
(b) The handling of numbers
(c) Effective communication
(d) None of the above

328. LOGO stands for
(a) Logic Oriented Graphic Oriented
(b) Local Operating Graphic Operating
(c) Locator Operating Generation Oriented
(d) None of these

329. UNIX operating system
(a) is multiuser
(b) is multitasking
(c) can run on PCs and larger systems
(d) All of the above

330. In multimedia the following range of CD-ROM is employed
(a) 150-500 Megabyte
(b) 200-600 Megabyte
(c) 250-700 Megabyte
(d) 300-800 Megabyte

331. The advantage of assembly language is

(a) programs written in the language are easy to use.
(b) programs are highly efficient.
(c) knowledge of hardware is not required.
(d) All of the above.

332. Can you name of the major Operating System used in computers?
(a) MS DOS (b) OS/2
(c) UNIX (d) All of the above

333. The Father of the Linear Programming is
(a) B.F. Skinner
(b) Sydney Pressy
(c) Norman A. Crowder
(d) Thomas F. Gilbert

334. Spreadsheet in MS Excel can have
(a) 260 columns (b) 256 columns
(c) 156 columns (d) 356 columns

335. Which of the following is always resident in machinery?
(a) Batch System
(b) Time Sharing System
(c) Operating system
(d) Controlling system

336. Computer Assisted Instruction (CAI) is generally used to fulfil
(a) Cognitive objectives
(b) Affective objectives
(c) Psycho-motor objectives
(d) Both (a) and (b)

337. MS-Power point is used to work with
(a) text
(b) pictures
(c) sound and video
(d) All of the above

338. Paging
(a) is a method of memory allocation by which the program is subdivided into equal portions or page and core is subdivided into equal portions or blocks.
(b) consists of those addresses that may be generated by a processor during execution of a computation.
(c) is a method of allocating processor time.
(d) allows multiple programs to reside in separate areas of core at the time.

339. Using Expansion card we can
(a) record sound (b) play sound
(c) Both (a) and (b) (d) None of these

340. Which of the following is necessary to work on a computer
(a) compiler
(b) operating system
(c) assembly
(d) interpreter of the above

341. CAI is a model of
(a) Hardware approach
(b) Software approach
(c) System analysis
(d) All of the above

342. Super computers are used
(a) for intensive processing of I/o.
(b) for intensive mathematical and scientific application.
(c) for data retrieval operations.
(d) All of the above.

343. Advantage(s) of using assembly language rather than machine language is (are)
(a) It is mnemonic and easy to read.
(b) Addresses any symbolic, not absolute.
(c) Introduction of data to program is easier.
(d) All of the above.

344. The advantage of the laser printing is
(a) it is working with very slow speed.
(b) it is comparatively silent.
(c) Both (a) and (b).
(d) None of the above.

345. With round-robin CPU scheduling in a time-shared system:
   (a) Using very large time slices (quantas) degenerates into FCFS (First-Come First-Served) algorithm.
   (b) Using very small time slices (quantas) degenerates into LIFO) Last-In First-Out) algorithm.
   (c) Using extremely small time slices improves performance.
   (d) Using medium sized time slices leads to SRTF (Shortest Remaining Time First) scheduling policy.

346. Which of the following is not contained in a system description?
   (a) Internal Data flows
   (b) Flows leaving and entering the system
   (c) Relationships between external entities
   (d) Internal components or process

347. Modem is connected with communication adopter and
   (a) in middle of network
   (b) Telephone line
   (c) Serial port
   (d) Computer

348. A sequence of instructions, in a computer language, to get the desired result, is known as
   (a) Algorithm (b) Decision Table
   (c) Program (d) All of the above

349. A memory chip has 8 data address lines. How many bytes on it?
   (a) 356 (b) 511
   (c) 512 (d) 256

350. HTML stands for
   (a) Hyper technology memory language
   (b) Hyper text make up language
   (c) Hyper text make up locator
   (d) None of the above

351. A characteristic of an on-line real-time system is
   (a) More than one CPU
   (b) No delay in processing
   (c) Offline batch processing
   (d) All of the above

352. Magnetic Tape can work
   (a) as an output device
   (b) as an input device
   (c) as an secondary storage device
   (d) All of the above

353. DOS is
   (a) a software
   (b) a hardware
   (c) a data organisation system
   (d) None of the above

354. To select new site which part of menu bar will you open
   (a) File (b) View
   (c) Edit (d) Insert

355. Which of the following performs modulation and demodulation?
   (a) Fiberoptic (b) Satellite
   (c) Coaxial cable (d) Modern

356. CAI is a model of
   (a) s/w approach (b) h/w approach
   (c) Both (a) and (b) (d) None of these

357. A local area network
   (a) that connects thirty personal computers can provide more computing power than a minicomputer.
   (b) cannot become bogged down like mainframe would if the load is too high.
   (c) Both (a) and (b).
   (d) All of the above.

358. Which class of the software packages allow people to send electronic mail along a network of computer and workstations?
   (a) Memory resident package
   (b) Project management package
   (c) Data communication package
   (d) Electronic mail package

359. My computer icon allow us to know the details of
(a) Hard disk (b) CD-ROM
(c) Floppy disk (d) All of these

360. We can receive data either through our television aerial or down our telephone lines and display this data on our television screen. What is the general name given to this purpose?
(a) Viewdata (b) Teletext
(c) Tele software (d) Video text

361. NET is a
(a) Program file
(b) Language
(c) Software
(d) Operation system

362. The economics of computing data is
(a) sharing peripherals and.
(b) giving processors to processing time.
(c) Both (a) and (b).
(d) All of the above.

363. MAYA is related to
(a) Animation
(b) Computer language
(c) Operating system
(d) All of the above

364. The word telematics is a combination of
(a) Computer
(b) Telecommunication
(c) Informatics
(d) Both (a) and (b)

365. EDSAC in 1949 was the first
(a) Super-computer
(b) Mini-computer
(c) Stored-program
(d) None of the above

366. The application layer of a network
(a) establishes, maintains, and terminates virtual circuits.
(b) defines the user's port into the network.
(c) consists of software being run on the computer connected to the network.
(d) All of the above.

367. A tray on a printer for holding blank paper or preprinted forms called
(a) Printer (b) Bin
(c) Window (d) None of these

368. What was the first Network that was made available
(a) DEC Net 1980
(b) Novell Netware
(c) IBMm Token Ring 1985
(d) IBM PC Network 1984

369. A/D converter converts
(a) analogue to digit
(b) digit to analogue
(c) Both (a) and (b)
(d) None of the above

370. What does the acronym (ISDN) stand for?
(a) Indian Standard Digital Network
(b) Integrated Services Digital Network
(c) Intelligent Services Digital Network
(d) Integrated Services Data Network

371. CD Caddy is plastic container that holds a
(a) WAN (b) LAN
(c) CD-ROM (d) All of these

372. Internet is
(a) network run by the US Government.
(b) a network run by the United Nations Organisation.
(c) a loose network not owned by any body but used by all universities and governments around the globe.
(d) a commercial information service run by Ziff Davis Co., in US.

373. A graphic design formed by patterns of dots is called
(a) computer graphic
(b) line graphic
(c) paint graphic
(d) dot graphic

374. If the dot pitch is smaller than the image is
(a) sharper (b) longer
(c) greater (d) None of these

375. Working of the WAN generally involves
(a) telephone lines (b) microwaves
(c) satellites (d) All of the above

376. Draft Quality is a measure of
(a) quality for input
(b) quality for printed output
(c) Both (a) and (b)
(d) None of the above

377. Video is a combination of
(a) Television
(b) Communication
(c) Computertechnology
(d) All of the above

378. FTP Stands for
(a) File Transforming Protocol
(b) File Transfer Protocol
(c) File Protocol
(d) File Transfer Protocol

379. Communication between computers is almost always
(a) Serial (b) Parallel
(c) Series parallel (d) Direct

380. BS stands for
(a) bits per second
(b) bits per sound
(c) binary per second
(d) None of these

381. Error, detection at a data link level is achieved by?
(a) Bit stuffing
(b) Hamming codes
(c) Cyclic redundancy code
(d) Equalisation

382. In a Hard Disk there are
(a) 3 to 4 platters (b) 2 to 3 platters
(c) 1 to 2 platters (d) None of these

383. The linking of computers with a communication system is called
(a) Networking (b) Pairing
(c) Interfacing (d) Assembling

384. The ZIP drive unit is
(a) 18 × 3 × 4 cm
(b) 18 × 13 × 14 cm
(c) 18 × 13 × 19 cm
(d) None of the above

385. Which of the following items is not used in Local Area Networks (LANs)?
(a) Computer (b) Modem
(c) Printer (d) Cable

386. The advantages of ZIP drive are
(a) portable (b) easy to use
(c) fast (d) All of these

387. During networking, the processor of the CPU asking each terminal whether it wants to send a message is called
(a) Querying (b) Sharing
(c) Communicating (d) Polling

388. WORM stands for
(a) Write Once Read Many
(b) Write Once Read More
(c) Write on Read More
(d) None of the above

389. DVDs first use was for
(a) playing colour movies
(b) playing black movies
(c) playing games
(d) All of the above

. All the parts in a computer talk to each other by sending
(a) digital signal
(b) analogne signals
(c) smoothly varying signal waves
(d) Both (a) and (b)

. CD-ROMS typically hold about
(a) 750 mb of data
(b) 550 mb of data
(c) 650 mb of data
(d) None of the above

. What is going 'on-line'?
(a) Buying a MODEM and connecting it to your computer.
(b) Getting a PTI or REUTERS news wire connection.
(c) Connecting your computer to a LAN.
(d) Getting access to the various commercial and other information services over the dial-up lines or I-Net connection.

. Disk's long format time take about
(a) 20 minutes (b) 25 minutes
(c) 15 minutes (d) None of these

. Which of the following is an important characteristic of LAN?
(a) Application independent interfaces.
(b) Unlimited expansion.
(c) Low cost access for bandwidth channels.
(d) None of the above.

. Algorithm is never written in
(a) programming language
(b) executing language
(c) software language
(d) All of the above

. What is a spam?
(a) Electronic junk mail
(b) Mail service
(c) Internet connection
(d) None of these

397. Who is a Technophobe?
(a) One who look after technology.
(b) One who is afraid of technological advances, especially computers.
(c) One who loves computer operation.
(d) One who likes to make computer.

398. Software can be seen in the form of
(a) icons on the Desktop
(b) icon on the Windows
(c) icon on Adobe
(d) All of the above

399. The disadvantages of the Internet are
(a) in secure information
(b) allows access to indecent information
(c) junk mails
(d) All of the above

400. Word Star has no features for
(a) text (b) graphics
(c) Both (a) and (b) (d) None of these

401. What is Hot-mail?
(a) A website on the worldwide web providing free e-mail facility.
(b) The process of sending letters through e-mail.
(c) Both (a) and (b).
(d) None of the above.

402. The user of computer is called
(a) a base (b) live ware
(c) icon (d) Logo

403. "Circa 1996", the first wireless cyber cafe in India, has been set up in
(a) Chennai (b) Bangalore
(c) Chandigarh (d) Kochi

404. dBase is an
(a) output device
(b) input device
(c) interpreter based programming language
(d) None of the above

405. The first airline to allow flyers to surf the net was

(a) Air Canada
(b) Singapore Airline
(c) Emirates Airlines
(d) Limited Airlines

406. Important parameters which influence the selection of storage device include
(a) speed and capacity
(b) cost of storage
(c) reliability and performance
(d) All of the above

407. Which of the following is form of virus?
(a) Boost-sector virus
(b) File virus
(c) Worm and Trojan horse
(d) All of the above

408. Plotter is a
(a) output device (b) input device
(c) processor (d) None of these

409. Multidimensional Array is an array with
(a) only two dimensions
(b) two or more dimensions
(c) more than two dimensions
(d) None of the above

410. The interface of source program is/are
(a) Compiler (b) Interpreter
(c) Assembler (d) All of these

411. A process of processing a single program by two or more CPUs is known as
(a) multiprocessing
(b) multitasking
(c) multiprogramming
(d) None of the above

412. Which of the following software used to publish a document?
(a) Adobe's Page Maker
(b) Quark Publisher
(c) Ready, Set Go
(d) All of the above

413. Multiprogramming is designed as technique for handing
(a) more than two independent programs simultaneously.
(b) two or more than two independent programs simultaneously.
(c) graphical programming.
(d) None of the above.

414. The world's largest database software company is
(a) Middleware (b) Oracle
(c) Microsoft (d) Solaris

415. Which of the following is an example of computer crime?
(a) Theft of Hardware
(b) Theft of Software
(c) Theft of Time and Service
(d) All of the above

416. The drawback of computer are
(a) they cannot think as human being.
(b) they do not respond to situations very flexibly.
(c) they are prone to attacks.
(d) All of the above.

417. Computer viruses do not
(a) infect files on write-protected disks
(b) infect files
(c) floppy
(d) None of the above

418. Computer virus passed via
(a) an infected diskette
(b) a network
(c) Both (a) and (b)
(d) None of the above

419. Anti-Virus software are the program designed to
(a) detect a computer virus
(b) remove a computer virus
(c) Both (a) and (b)
(d) None of the above

420. File names in powerpoint are of the Z form

(a) file name .ppp
(b) file name .ppt
(c) file name .ppi
(d) file name .pip

421. Re-writable compact discs
(a) cannot be erased
(b) can be erased
(c) depend upon type
(d) None of the above

422. Using Sort option in MS Word we can arrange the data in
(a) ascending order
(b) descending order
(c) ascending or descending order
(d) All of the above

423. BASIC, COBOL, PASCAL languages are
(a) machine dependent
(b) machine independent
(c) Both (a) and (b)
(d) None of the above

424. A file compression program that runs on PCs is known as
(a) Winsock (b) Wintel
(c) Wireframe (d) Win zip

425. Compiler is a program which translates a
(a) high level language program into a machine language program.
(b) low level language program into a machine language program.
(c) high level language program into a low level language program.
(d) None of the above.

426. To restore compressed data back to its original size is known as
(a) Decompress (b) Decollate
(c) Decryption (d) Decrement

427. Assembly language was developed in
(a) 1960 (b) 1951
(c) 1950 (d) 1970

428. Some popular Anti-virus software are
(a) Mc Affee
(b) Smart Dog
(c) Norton Anti-virus
(d) All of the above

429. The program written in high-level language is known as
(a) Object program
(b) Source program
(c) Compile program
(d) High program

430. Virus can't infect
(a) Monitor (b) Keyboard
(c) Software (d) Both (a) and (b)

431. Wizard helps users
(a) to perform a task
(b) to save a file
(c) to run a computer
(d) to detect a virus

432. In Excel a formal begins with
(a) = sign (b) – sign
(c) : sign (d) .sign

433. Windows XP is a updated version of
(a) Window XP 2000
(b) Windows 2000
(c) Window 98
(d) None of the above

434. TCP/IP is made up of
(a) internet protocol
(b) transmission control protocol
(c) internet processor
(d) Both (a) and (b)

435. Windows 95 is a
(a) 64 bit operating system
(b) 36 bit operating system
(c) 32 bit operating system
(d) 40 bit operating system

436. The smallest individual unit in a program is known as

(a) Toggle (b) Token ring
(c) Toner (d) Token

37. VAN stands for
(a) Value Added Noting
(b) Volume Allowed Network
(c) Value Audio Network
(d) Value Added Network

38. IBM mini-comptuer series introduced in 1988 is
(a) AS 1800 (b) AS 1400
(c) AS 1500 (d) AS 1700

39. Method of creating graphic images in Logo is called
(a) turtle graphics
(b) tutorial graphic
(c) logging graphics
(d) turn key

40. VOL is
(a) a internal command
(b) external command
(c) not a command
(d) None of these

441. Assertion is a Boolean statement whose evaluation is
(a) undetermine (b) true or false
(c) false (d) true

442. The tasks of determining the cause of a problem is known as
(a) Trillon (b) Truncate
(c) Troubleshooting (d) TSR

443. Batch program is a
(a) interactive program
(b) non-interactive program
(c) application program
(d) None of the above

444. Instructions in a program that actually process data is known as
(a) application code
(b) application control
(c) application instruction
(d) application generator

445. The measure of the amount of information that a particular communication medium can carry is
(a) Ball grid (b) Bar code
(c) Banner ad (d) Bandwidth

446. A feature of keyboards that allows a key to repeat automatically when hold down is known as
(a) Automation (b) Auto-radio
(c) Auto repeat (d) None of these

447. A program that allow user to access documents on the World Wide Web (WWW) is known as
(a) Brownout (b) Browser
(c) Brush (d) Broadcast

448. Scanning a list in the VDU in reverse direction is called
(a) Back tracking (b) Back slash
(c) Back up (d) Both (a) and (b)

449. The extension of a Batch File in a DOS / Window environment is
(a) .bat (b) .doc
(c) .batch (d) .tch

450. Backing up means
(a) making additional copies of any information
(b) represent the root directory
(c) store large amount of data
(d) All of these

451. An enhancement of HTML is
(a) HTMLD (b) DML
(c) DHTML (d) XML

452. If your mail cannot be delivered and come back to you then it said a
(a) Bounced message
(b) Bounced neck

(c) Bounced mail
(d) None of the above

453. Portable microcomputer that fits in a briefcase is known as
(a) Bridges computer
(b) Micro computer
(c) Broadband computer
(d) Briefcase computer

454. CGI stands for
(a) Common Gateway Interface
(b) Command Generate Interface
(c) Command Going Input
(d) None of the above

455. EBCDIC is an IBM developed
(a) 16 bit code (b) 8 bit code
(c) 4 bit code (d) 32 bit code

456. Buffer is a temporary location to store c group information in
(a) Hardware (b) Software
(c) Both (a) and (b) (d) None of these

457. Corel Draw is a popular
(a) text program
(b) illustration program
(c) programming language
(d) None of the above

ANSWERS

1. (d)	2. (a)	3. (d)	4. (d)	5. (d)	6. (d)
7. (b)	8. (c)	9. (d)	10. (d)	11. (b)	12. (a)
13. (d)	14. (a)	15. (d)	16. (a)	17. (a)	18. (b)
19. (a)	20. (a)	21. (d)	22. (c)	23. (d)	24. (c)
25. (d)	26. (a)	27. (c)	28. (a)	29. (d)	30. (a)
31. (a)	32. (d)	33. (c)	34. (d)	35. (a)	36. (d)
37. (c)	38. (a)	39. (c)	40. (a)	41. (d)	42. (c)
43. (c)	44. (d)	45. (c)	46. (a)	47. (d)	48. (c)
49. (d)	50. (d)	51. (d)	52. (a)	53. (b)	54. (b)
55. (a)	56. (a)	57. (a)	58. (a)	59. (d)	60. (d)
61. (a)	62. (c)	63. (a)	64. (b)	65. (c)	66. (c)
67. (d)	68. (d)	69. (c)	70. (d)	71. (d)	72. (c)
73. (a)	74. (a)	75. (c)	76. (d)	77. (d)	78. (a)
79. (c)	80. (c)	81. (c)	82. (c)	83. (d)	84. (d)
85. (a)	86. (d)	87. (d)	88. (a)	89. (d)	90. (d)
91. (c)	92. (a)	93. (c)	94. (d)	95. (d)	96. (a)
97. (c)	98. (d)	99. (a)	100. (d)	101. (a)	102. (d)
103. (d)	104. (c)	105. (a)	106. (b)	107. (d)	108. (d)
109. (b)	110. (c)	111. (a)	112. (a)	113. (d)	114. (b)
115. (c)	116. (d)	117. (c)	118. (d)	119. (a)	120. (a)

121. (a) 122. (b) 123. (d) 124. (d) 125. (a) 126. (c)
127. (d) 128. (d) 129. (d) 130. (d) 131. (b) 132. (a)
133. (d) 134. (a) 135. (a) 136. (a) 137. (d) 138. (a)
139. (d) 140. (d) 141. (d) 142. (a) 143. (d) 144. (b)
145. (a) 146. (a) 147. (c) 148. (a) 149. (d) 150. (a)
151. (c) 152. (b) 153. (a) 154. (d) 155. (a) 156. (a)
157. (a) 158. (a) 159. (d) 160. (a) 161. (a) 162. (a)
163. (b) 164. (d) 165. (d) 166. (d) 167. (c) 168. (a)
169. (d) 170. (c) 171. (b) 172. (a) 173. (a) 174. (b)
175. (b) 176. (a) 177. (d) 178. (a) 179. (a) 180. (c)
181. (d) 182. (d) 183. (d) 184. (b) 185. (a) 186. (a)
187. (b) 188. (c) 189. (a) 190. (a) 191. (c) 192. (a)
193. (a) 194. (c) 195. (a) 196. (a) 197. (a) 198. (b)
199. (d) 200. (d) 201. (a) 202. (c) 203. (a) 204. (c)
205. (a) 206. (c) 207. (a) 208. (c) 209. (d) 210. (c)
211. (c) 212. (c) 213. (a) 214. (c) 215. (c) 216. (b)
217. (b) 218. (d) 219. (a) 220. (b) 221. (c) 222. (c)
223. (c) 224. (d) 225. (b) 226. (d) 227. (a) 228. (b)
229. (c) 230. (b) 231. (b) 232. (c) 233. (c) 234. (b)
235. (a) 236. (d) 237. (b) 238. (b) 239. (a) 240. (a)
241. (c) 242. (a) 243. (b) 244. (c) 245. (c) 246. (a)
247. (d) 248. (a) 249. (a) 250. (c) 251. (b) 252. (b)
253. (a) 254. (a) 255. (c) 256. (c) 257. (c) 258. (d)
259. (c) 260. (a) 261. (a) 262. (b) 263. (d) 264. (a)
265. (c) 266. (d) 267. (d) 268. (c) 269. (c) 270. (a)
271. (d) 272. (d) 273. (c) 274. (d) 275. (c) 276. (b)
277. (c) 278. (d) 279. (a) 280. (b) 281. (d) 282. (d)
283. (a) 284. (a) 285. (a) 286. (d) 287. (c) 288. (b)
289. (d) 290. (a) 291. (a) 292. (c) 293. (a) 294. (a)
295. (d) 296. (a) 297. (a) 298. (a) 299. (a) 300. (d)
301. (a) 302. (a) 303. (a) 304. (c) 305. (c) 306. (b)
307. (a) 308. (d) 309. (b) 310. (d) 311. (a) 312. (b)
313. (d) 314. (b) 315. (d) 316. (c) 317. (a) 318. (a)
319. (a) 320. (c) 321. (a) 322. (b) 323. (b) 324. (b)

325. (d)	326. (d)	327. (c)	328. (c)	329. (d)	330. (b)
331. (d)	332. (d)	333. (a)	334. (c)	335. (c)	336. (d)
337. (b)	338. (a)	339. (b)	340. (b)	341. (a)	342. (d)
343. (d)	344. (d)	345. (a)	346. (c)	347. (a)	348. (c)
349. (c)	350. (b)	351. (b)	352. (d)	353. (a)	354. (b)
355. (d)	356. (a)	357. (a)	358. (c)	359. (b)	360. (d)
361. (a)	362. (c)	363. (c)	364. (d)	365. (d)	366. (c)
367. (a)	368. (a)	369. (b)	370. (b)	371. (b)	372. (c)
373. (a)	374. (c)	375. (d)	376. (b)	377. (d)	378. (d)
379. (a)	380. (a)	381. (c)	382. (b)	383. (a)	384. (c)
385. (b)	386. (c)	387. (d)	388. (b)	389. (d)	390. (a)
391. (b)	392. (d)	393. (a)	394. (a)	395. (a)	396. (b)
397. (b)	398. (b)	399. (b)	400. (c)	401. (d)	402. (a)
403. (d)	404. (a)	405. (a)	406. (a)	407. (c)	408. (a)
409. (d)	410. (d)	411. (d)	412. (a)	413. (c)	414. (d)
415. (d)	416. (b)	417. (d)	418. (a)	419. (b)	420. (b)
421. (c)	422. (a)	423. (b)	424. (d)	425. (a)	426. (b)
427. (a)	428. (d)	429. (d)	430. (a)	431. (a)	432. (b)
433. (a)	434. (c)	435. (c)	436. (c)	437. (b)	438. (a)
439. (d)	440. (d)	441. (a)	442. (a)	443. (c)	444. (d)
445. (b)	446. (a)	447. (b)	448. (b)	449. (d)	450. (c)
451. (c)	452. (a)	453. (c)	454. (a)	455. (b)	456. (b)
457. (b)					

9

People and Environment

1. Synecology is the study of interrelation between
   (a) organisms and its sub-organisms
   (b) organisms and their environment
   (c) various cultures of community
   (d) None of the above
2. Pollution is
   (a) release of undesirable/toxic substances in the environment.
   (b) removal of topsoil.
   (c) conservation of energy.
   (d) All of these.
3. The study of interrelations between organisms and their environment is known as
   (a) Biosphere (b) Autecology
   (c) Synecology (d) Ecology
4. Sericulture is
   (a) a/an science of the various kinds of serum.
   (b) artificial rearing of fish.
   (c) art of silkworm breeding.
   (d) study of various cultures of a community.
5. Acid deposition causes
   (a) acid indigestion in humans.
   (b) lakes and forests to die.
   (c) the Greenhouse effect to lessen.
   (d) All of these.
6. Spoiling of biotic and abiotic environment by physical/chemical factors is termed as
   (a) Contamination (b) Adulteratior
   (c) Pollution (d) Ionosphere
7. Who among the following is known
   "Father of Ecology in India"?
   (a) P. Maheshwari
   (b) S.K. Kashyap
   (c) B.P. Pal
   (d) Ramdeo Mishra
8. Tides in the oceans are caused by
   (a) Gravitational pull of the moon on earth's sufrace including sea wate
   (b) Gravitational pull of the sun on earth's surface only and not on sea water.
   (c) Gravitational pull of the moon the sun on the earth's surface incluc the sea water.
   (d) None of these.
9. A normal component of environm which becomes pollutant when its c centration crosses a threshold valu called
   (a) Quantitative pollutant
   (b) Qualitative pollutant
   (c) Degradable pollutant
   (d) Physical pollutant
10. Who first of all coined the term 'Ecolo
    (a) Reiter (b) Haeckel
    (c) Odum (d) Clement
11. Nagarjuna Sagar Project is situated the river

(a) Tungabhadra (b) Cauvery
(c) Krishna (d) Godavari

12. The 'IUCN Red List' was initiated in
(a) 1954 (b) 1963
(c) 1993 (d) 1995

13. Pollution can bring about change in
(a) biogeochemical cycling
(b) abiotic environment
(c) biotic environment
(d) All of the above

14. "Ecosystem is the system resulting from the integration of all the living and non-living factors of the environment." This statement was of
(a) Haeckel (b) Tansley
(c) Mishra (d) Odum

15. The difference between the Indian Standard Time and the Greenwich Mean Time is
(a) –3½ hours (b) +3½ hours
(c) –3½ hours (d) +5½ hours

16. A biosphere cannot consist of
(a) Buffer zone
(b) Transition zone
(c) Core zone
(d) None of these

17. Loss of relative biological equilibrium is due to
(a) low temperature
(b) high temperature
(c) radiation
(d) pollution

18. Which of the following is the basic unit of study in ecology?
(a) Population (b) Environment
(c) Biosphere (d) Organisms

19. Which of the following dams is not on Narmada river?
(a) Indira Sagar Project
(b) Maheshwar Hydel Power Project
(c) Jobat Project
(d) Koyna Power Project

20. National parks are also known as
(a) Ecosystem
(b) Biosphere Reserve
(c) Woodlands
(d) None of these

21. Pollution can be
(a) natural
(b) manmade
(c) Both (1) and (2)
(d) None of these

22. In which of the following plants a*Rhizobium* bacteria involved in fixin atmospheric nitrogen?
(a) Tomato (b) Rice
(c) Bean (d) Potato

23. Which of the following statements is n true about the availability of water c the earth, the crisis for which is going t increase in the years to come?
(a) About 97.5 percent of the total volun of water available on the earth salty.
(b) 80 percent of the water availab to us for use comes in bursts monsoons.
(c) About 2.5 percent of the total wat available on the earth is pollute water and cannot be used for huma activities.
(d) Possibility is that some big glacie will melt in the coming ten-fiftee years and sea level will rise by 3- meters all over the earth.

24. Which region in South America is th world's richest and most varied biologic reservoir?
(a) Amazon Rainforest
(b) The Prairies
(c) The Coniferous Forest
(d) None of these

25. Qualitative pollutants are
   (a) Added by man
   (b) Naturally occurring
   (c) Present in the high concentration
   (d) None of these

26. The wet forests of Amazon basin are known as which one of the following?
   (a) Pampas (b) Selvas
   (c) Campos (d) Lianos

27. Through which States does Cauvery River flow?
   (a) Gujarat, M.P., Tamil Nadu
   (b) Karnataka, Kerala, Tamil Nadu
   (c) Karnataka, Kerala, Andhra Pradesh
   (d) M.P., Maharashtra, Tamil Nadu

28. Laterite soil develops due to
   (a) leaching
   (b) deposition of fossil fuel
   (c) deposition of acid
   (d) None of these

29. The country which hosted first World Earth Summit (June 1992) on conservation of environment was
   (a) India (b) Brazil
   (c) Peru (d) Spain

30. A population is a group of
   (a) Communities in an ecosystem
   (b) Individuals in a family
   (c) Species in a community
   (d) Individuals in a species

31. The biggest reserves of thorium are in
   (a) India
   (b) China
   (c) The Soviet Union
   (d) U.S.A.

32. Which of the following is the most harmful pollutant?
   (a) CO_2 (b) SO_4
   (c) SO_2 (d) S_2O_2

33. Ecological backlash (ecological boomerang) is
   (a) production of adverse ecological effect by a previously useful chemical.
   (b) production of useful ecological effect by a previously useful chemical.
   (c) heat emission due to bomb explosion.
   (d) None of the above.

34. The geographic limits within which a population exists is its
   (a) Range (b) Habitat
   (c) Niche (d) Territory

35. Photosphere is described as the
   (a) lower layer of atmosphere.
   (b) visible surface of the sun from which radiation emanates.
   (c) wavelength of solar spectrum.
   (d) None of the above.

36. B.O.D. test is related to
   (a) Water pollution
   (b) Noise pollution
   (c) Air pollution
   (d) Soil pollution

37. When was the Air prevention and control of pollution act enforced in India?
   (a) 1980 (b) 1981
   (c) 1982 (d) 1984

38. Exponential growth occurs when there is
   (a) sexual reproduction only.
   (b) no inhibition from crowding.
   (c) asexual reproduction only.
   (d) a fixed carrying capacity.

39. Different seasons are formed because
   (a) Sun is moving around the earth.
   (b) of revolution of the earth around the Sun on its orbit.
   (c) of rotation of the earth around its axis.
   (d) All of the above.

40. Which of the following is function of Biosphere Reserves?
(a) Scientific research and education
(b) Development of ecological aspects
(c) Conservation
(d) All of these

41. When did the water (Prevention and control of pollution) Act came into operation in India?
(a) 1969 (b) 1972
(c) 1976 (d) 1974

42. Population dispersion is the
(a) Mixing of two populations
(b) Spatial distribution of individuals
(c) Movement from one fixed point to another and back again
(d) Movement away from a natal site

43. The world is divided into
(a) 12 time zones (b) 20 time zones
(c) 24 time zones (d) 36 time zones

44. Soil conservation can be best achieved by
(a) low rainfall
(b) good plant covers
(c) high rainfall
(d) wind screens

45. Ganga Action Plan to restore the quality of the river Ganga was launched in
(a) 1988 (b) 1992
(c) 1985 (d) 1981

46. Which of the following organisms is interoparous?
(a) Bacterium (b) Pacific salmon
(c) Human (d) Annual plant

47. The term 'Regur' refers to
(a) Laterite soils
(b) Black Cotton soils
(c) Red soils
(d) Deltaic Alluvial soils

48. When was NEPA (National Environmental Policy Act) enforced in India?
(a) 1968 (b) 1969
(c) 1970 (d) 1959

49. Most interacting populations are
(a) Coevolved (b) Mutualistic
(c) Parasitic (d) Symbiotic

50. Location of sugar industry in India is shifting from north to south because of
(a) cheap labour.
(b) expanding regional market.
(c) cheap and abundant supply of power.
(d) high yield and high sugar content in sugarcane.

51. Which of the following combinations is correct?
(a) Burning of biomass — O_2 given off
(b) Solar energy — H_2O given off
(c) Nuclear power — radioactive wastes
(d) Burning of fossil fuel — N_2O given off.

52. The newspaper contains one of the following toxic materials
(a) Cd (b) Pb
(c) Mg (d) Hg

53. An ecological community is an assemblage of
(a) Food webs
(b) Closely related species
(c) Family units
(d) Interacting populations

54. Consider the following statements.
1. Ozone is found mostly in the Stratosphere.
2. Ozone layer lies 55-75 km above the surface of the earth.
3. Ozone absorbs ultraviolet radiation from the Sun.
4. Ozone layer has no significance for life on the earth.

Which of the above statements are correct?
(a) 1 and 3 (b) 2 and 4
(c) 2 and 3 (d) 1 and 4

55. The rate of growth of population is
   (a) inversely proportional to generation time.
   (b) directory proportional to generation time.
   (c) inversely proportional to age structure.
   (d) None of these.

56. The first indoor pollutant from furniture of which the masses became aware?
   (a) CO_2 (b) Formaldehyde
   (c) Radon (d) Ozone

57. The habitat of a population is the
   (a) geographic area it covers.
   (b) set of conditions and resources it uses.
   (c) set of interactions it has with other populations.
   (d) places where it lives.

58. Atmosphere exists because
   (a) The Gravitational force of the Earth.
   (b) Revolution of the Earth.
   (c) Rotation of the Earth.
   (d) Weight of the gases of atmosphere.

59. 'Hot Spots' concept was developed by
   (a) Norman Myers in 1988
   (b) Norman Myers in 1920
   (c) P.R. Bush in 1988
   (d) R.R. Iyengar in 1988

60. Ceramic crockery of substandard quality could become a source of pollutant if food taken in it. This pollutant is
   (a) Cd (b) Pb
   (c) Cr (d) Hg

61. About how much of the solar energy that falls on the leaves of a plant is converted to chemical energy by photosynthesis?
   (a) 30% (b) 90%
   (c) 1% (d) 75%

62. Where are most of the earth's ac volcanoes concentrated?
   (a) Europe (b) Pacific Ocea
   (c) Africa (d) South Amer

63. In 2000 Red List, how many species listed as threatened?
   (a) 1244 (b) 11046
   (c) 1434 (d) 700

64. Sometimes secondary pollutants ozone, PAN (Peroxy acyl nitrate), HN H_2SO_4 formed from primary polluta are more toxic than primary polluta This phenomenon of increased toxicit pollutants is called
   (a) Biomagnification
   (b) Eutrophication
   (c) Synergism
   (d) Greenhouse effect

65. About how much of the chemical ene within producer tissues becomes chem energy within herbivore tissues?
   (a) 10% (b) 1%
   (c) 30% (d) 50%

66. Which of the following is a endotherm animal?
   (a) Man (b) Lion
   (c) Snake (d) All of these

67. Which one is not produced as exhaus vehicle?
   (a) SO_2 (b) CO_2
   (c) CO (d) Flyash

68. An ecological pyramid of energy flo often an inverted pyramid in which of following ecosystems?
   (a) Tundra (b) Ocean
   (c) Desert (d) Rainforest

69. The natural vegetation of Savana con of
   (a) Tall grass (b) Scrub jungl
   (c) Short grass (d) Trees

. Which of the following is a dam on Narmada river?

(a) Indira Sagar Project
(b) Goi Dam
(c) Maheshwar Hydel Power Project
(d) All of these

. In air pollution, industries are

(a) line sources (b) point sources
(c) area sources (d) diffuse sources

. Consider the components of a food chain: Producers → herbivores → carnivores → top carnivores. Which level contains the most energy?

(a) Herbivores (b) Carnivores
(c) Top carnivores (d) Producers

. The zone of excessively dry climate with very cold temperature throughout the year correspond to

(a) Arctic deserts (b) Tundra
(c) Alpine meadows (d) Antarctica

. Carbon monoxide is a pollutant as it

(a) inactivates nerves and cause numbness.
(b) inhibits Glycolysis.
(c) combine with oxygen and shift oxygen dissociation curve.
(d) combines with Haemoglobin and cause haemolysis.

. Which of the following is a true statement?

(a) Since gases not derived from fossil fuel combustion are involved, reduction in fossil fuel burning will not help the greenhouse effect.
(b) Global warming is so imminent that nothing can be done.
(c) Global warming is of no immediate concern.
(d) Reduction in fossil fuel burning will lessen the greenhouse effect.

. The fertility of the soil can be increased by growing

(a) Cereals (b) Fibre Crops
(c) Legumes (d) Root Crops

77. Which of the following statements is correct?

(a) Acid deposition causes lakes and forests to alive.
(b) Coevolved are most interacting population.
(c) In 1997 U.G.C. have launched career orientation program.
(d) All of these.

78. Which of the following pollutant forms a toxic and stable substance in blood by combining with haemoglobin?

(a) CO_2 (b) CO
(c) CH_4 (d) O_2

79. Which of the following is mismatched?

(a) Biomass burning — CO_2 given off
(b) Fossil fuel burning — CO_2 given off
(c) Solar energy — Greenhouse effect
(d) Nuclear power — Radioactive wastes

80. India's Oil bearing areas are mostly associated with the

(a) Plutonic rocks
(b) Volcanic rocks
(c) Sedimentary rocks
(d) Metamorphic rocks

81. Carbon monoxide is harmful for man because

(a) it is carcinogenic
(b) it damages kidney
(c) it competes with oxygen in blood
(d) it changes pH of body

82. Water is a renewable resource, and

(a) It is still subject to pollution.
(b) There will always be a plentiful supply.
(c) Primary sewage treatment plants assure clean drinking water.
(d) The oceans can never become polluted.

83. The much discussed Tehri Dam Project is located in which of the following states?
(a) Madhya Pradesh (b) Rajasthan
(c) Haryana (d) Uttarakhand

84. In tropical and subtropical regions
(a) the growth of human population is least.
(b) the growth of human population is most rapid.
(c) the growth of human populations stable.
(d) None of these.

85. CO_2 contents in air is about
(a) 0.34% (b) 4%
(c) 3.34% (d) 0.034%

86. Tropical rainforest destruction is extremely serious because
(a) Large tracts of forest absorb CO_2, reducing the treatment of global warming.
(b) It will lead to a severe reduction in biological diversity.
(c) Tropical soils cannot support agriculture for long.
(d) All of the above are correct.

87. Laterite soil develop as a result of
(a) deposits of alluvial
(b) deposition of loess
(c) leaching
(d) continued vegetation cover

88. The example of negative pollution is
(a) grazing (b) grassing
(c) Both (a) and (b) (d) None of these

89. One of the important effects of SO_2 and its transformation products on plants is
(a) Plasmolysis
(b) Destruction of Chlorophyll
(c) Destruction of Golgi bodies
(d) Destruction of Cell wall

90. Acid deposition causes
(a) The greenhouse effect to lessen
(b) Lakes and forests to die
(c) Acid indigestion in humans
(d) All of the above are correct

91. The coldest place on the earth is
(a) Halifax (b) Chicago
(c) Siachen (d) Verkhoyansk

92. Which of the following statement is false?
(a) The basic unit of study in Ecology is population.
(b) The wet forests of Amazon basin are known as Pampas.
(c) A population is a group of species in a community.
(d) All of these.

93. Taj Mahal is threatened due to the effect of
(a) Chlorine (b) Sulphur dioxide
(c) Oxygen (d) Hydrogen

94. Approximately how many people are alive today?
(a) 1 billion
(b) 2 billion
(c) 4 billion
(d) More than 6 billion

95. Which one of the following pairs is not correctly matched?
(a) Kota — Chambal
(b) Bhubaneshwar — Mahanadi
(c) Jabalpur — Narmada
(d) Surat — Tapti

96. Lichen deserts indicate
(a) Air pollution due to CO
(b) Air pollution due to SO_2
(c) Pollution due to smoke
(d) Noise pollution

97. The human population first began to grow exponentially at the time of the
(a) Agricultural revolution
(b) First World War

(c) Tool-using revolution
(d) Industrial revolution

98. Which of the following is the biggest freshwater lake in India?
(a) Dal Lake (b) Sukhna Lake
(c) Loktak Lake (d) None of these

99. Lichens are best ecological indicator of
(a) Air pollution
(b) Water pollution
(c) Noise pollution
(d) All of these

100. The growth of human population is most rapid in the
(a) Temperate regions
(b) Asia
(c) North America
(d) Tropical and subtropical regions

101. Which of the following rivers is not a tributary of the Indus?
(a) Sutlej (b) Jhelum
(c) Bhagirathi (d) Chenab

102. The land provided to the global diversity in India is
(a) 7% (b) 8%
(c) 9% (d) 10%

103. Lichens have disappeared from cities because they are highly susceptible to
(a) CO_2 (b) O_3
(c) NO_2 (d) SO_2

104. The carrying capacity of a population is determined by its
(a) Birth rate
(b) Death rate
(c) Limiting resource
(d) Population growth rate

105. Which of the following pairs of the river dam project and the State in which it is located, is not correct?
(a) Gandhi Sagar — Madhya Pradesh
(b) Tungabhadra — Tamil Nadu
(c) Bhakra Nangal — Punjab
(d) Hirakud — Orissa

106. In which of the following states scared forests are located?
(a) Kerala (b) Meghalaya
(c) Maharashtra (d) All of these

107. Most inhabitants of Kolkata suffer from bronchitis/asthma. It is due to excess of SO_2 pollutants in
(a) Air (b) Water
(c) Soil (d) Adulterated food

108. The population growth rate V is inversely related to
(a) Generation time
(b) Age structure
(c) Clutch size
(d) Number of clutches per lifetime

109. Match List I and List II and select the correct answer using the codes given below the Lists.

List I (Rivers)	List II (Dams)
A. Cauvery	1. Alamatti
B. Krishna	2. Mettur
C. Narmada	3. Gandhi Sagar
D. Chambal	4. Sardar Sarovar

Codes:	A	B	C	D
(a)	1	4	2	3
(b)	2	1	4	3
(c)	2	1	3	4
(d)	1	3	4	2

110. Which of the following not include in extinction of species?
(a) Natural extinction
(b) Artificial extinction
(c) Mass extinction
(d) All of these

111. Death while sleeping in closed room with burning coal furnace is due to
(a) CO_2 (b) CO
(c) CCl_4 (d) SO_2

12. Most agriculture makes use of plants from
(a) Early secondary succession
(b) Late secondary succession
(c) Early primary succession
(d) Late primary succession

13. What is approximately the percentage of forest cover in India?
(a) 10 percent (b) 8.5 percent
(c) 25 percent (d) 19.5 percent

14. Which of the following statements is correct?
(a) Aerosols particles in airs less than 1 μ.
(b) Cyanosis is caused by nitrate concentration.
(c) Amphyseme disease is caused by photochemical smog.
(d) All of these.

15. Air pollution is not caused by
(a) pollen grains
(b) automobiles
(c) industries
(d) hydro-electric power

16. Humans interfere with the natural phosphorus cycle by
(a) Causing erosion of land.
(b) Adding phosphate fertilizers to agricultural soils.
(c) Dumping sewage into rivers and lakes.
(d) All of the above.

17. When does the moon come between the sun and the earth?
(a) Lunar eclipse (b) Solar eclipse
(c) Sidereal day (d) Full moon day

18. Which of the following pairs is not correct?
(a) Panna-Diamond
(b) Carbon-Diamond
(c) Graphite-Carbon
(d) Iron-Steel

119. The major source of pollution (upto 80% of total air pollution) in metropolitan cities is
(a) automobiles (traffic/transportation)
(b) coal based industries
(c) pesticides
(d) radioactivity and noise

120. Which of the following atoms typically cycles within the most localised area?
(a) Sulphur (b) Phosphorus
(c) Carbon (d) Nitrogen

121. The latitude of a place is expressed by its angular distance in relation to
(a) Equator
(b) South Pole
(c) Axis of the Earth
(d) North Pole

122. Major air pollutant is
(a) CO_2 (b) N_2
(c) SO_2 (d) CO

123. Cultural eutrophication is caused by the addition of too many
(a) Ammonium (b) Nitrate
(c) Phosphate (d) All of these

124. The southern tip of India is
(a) Cape Comorin
(b) Point Calimere
(c) Indira Point in Nicobar Islands
(d) Kovalam in Trivandrum

125. Laos is the capital of
(a) Libya (b) Ankara
(c) Vientiane (d) Thailand

126. Which one of the following is usually not considered a pollutant?
(a) SO_2 (b) CO_2
(c) Hydrocarbons (d) CO

127. The burning of fossil fuels includes
(a) Coal (b) Oil
(c) Gas (d) All of these

128. During winter, the northern half of India is warmer than areas of similar latitudinal location by 3° to 8° because
(a) India is essentially a tropical country
(b) The surface wind blows in a particular direction in one season
(c) The Great Himalayas check the penetration of cold polar air into India effectively
(d) Of winter rains

129. Which of the following pairs is not correctly matched?
(a) Largest island — Madagascar
(b) Peso is the currency of — Cuba
(c) Manchester of India — Surat
(d) None of these

130. Taj Mahal is being damaged by
(a) air pollution from Mathura refinery
(b) Yamuna flood
(c) nuclear pollution and railway yard
(d) Both (a) and (b)

131. Turpentine oil used in medicine is obtained from
(a) Acacia (b) Chirpin
(c) Myrobalans (d) Kusum

132. The Indian Standard Time is the local time of
(a) East longitude
(b) 82° East longitude
(c) 83° East longitude
(d) 86° East longitude

133. Particulates in air cause
(a) permanent opening of stomata
(b) closure of stomata
(c) coiling of leaves
(d) yellowing of leaves

134. Noise pollution is created if noise is in excess to
(a) 80-100 dB (b) 70-75 dB
(c) 50-60 dB (d) 40-65 dB

135. Which country is known for the most frequent earthquakes?
(a) Italy (b) Japan
(c) China (d) Iran

136. Solar eclipse occurs when
(a) moon comes between sun and earth.
(b) earth comes between sun and moon.
(c) sun comes between earth and moon.
(d) None of these.

137. What is it that smoking produces in the largest amount?
(a) NO_2 (b) CO_2
(c) CO (d) Particulates

138. Ozone layer depletion or hole in ozone layer is being chiefly found in
(a) Russia (b) South pole
(c) North pole (d) None of these

139. In determining the Indian climate, major role played by Himalayas is/are
(a) The east-west extension of the Great-Himalayas does not permit the summer monsoon to cross it and thus keeps its sojourn restricted to India.
(b) They direct the summer monsoon towards the north-west.
(c) During the winter they stop the southward penetration of the cold and dry polar air.
(d) All of the above.

140. The common tree species in Nilgiri hills is
(a) Sal (b) Pine
(c) Eucalyptis (d) Teak

141. Coal burning hearths or stoves produce a hazardous gas which suffocates living beings even to death
(a) SO_2 (b) CO_2
(c) CO (d) H_2S

142. Aerosols are particles in air less than
(a) 1 μ (b) 6 μ
(c) 100 μ (d) 150 μ

143. Which river is flowing near Ayodhya?
(a) Ganga (b) Yamuna
(c) Saryu (d) Krishna

144. The SO_2 mainly affects
(a) nucleus (b) cell membranes
(c) cell wall (d) ribosomes

145. Cyanosis is caused by
(a) Copper
(b) Chromium
(c) Nitrate concentration
(d) Carbon dioxide

146. Which of the following is cold stream?
(a) Curasia (b) Labrador
(c) Gulf of Stream (d) Hakuna Hatata

147. A mutagenic pollutant is
(a) chlorinated hydrocarbons
(b) organophosphates
(c) nitrogen oxides
(d) resins

148. Amphysema disease is caused by
(a) Carbon dioxide
(b) Sulphur dioxide
(c) Mercury
(d) Photochemical smog

149. High velds are the temperate grasslands of
(a) Africa (b) South Australia
(c) Europe and Asia (d) South America

150. Loss of minerals on the hills is due to
(a) Strip mining
(b) Terracing
(c) Soil erosion by water
(d) Contour-strip cropping

151. The rock material carried by a glacier is called
(a) Alluvium (b) Meanders
(c) Nodules (d) Moraines

152. The example of natural pollution is
(a) Volcanoes (b) SO_2
(c) DDT (d) Smoke

153. The process of laterisation results into
(a) Mineralisation of humus
(b) Degradation of soil
(c) Formation of soil
(d) Formation of humus

154. Environmental problems caused by human activities are
(a) deforestation and soil erosion
(b) thinning of Ozone layer and Global warming
(c) salinisation
(d) All of these

155. Match List I and List II and find out the correct answer from the codes given below the Lists.

List I (Thermal Power Plants)	List II (Locations)
A. Kahalgaon	1. West Bengal
B. Farakka	2. Bihar
C. Ramagundam	3. Gujarat
D. Gandhar	4. Andhra Pradesh

Codes:	A	B	C	D
(a)	1	2	3	4
(b)	4	3	1	2
(c)	2	1	4	3
(d)	3	2	1	4

156. It is advised not to have brick kiln near fruit orchard to
(a) save trees from soil erosion.
(b) safeguard trees from large labour population.
(c) protect the orchard from operation of Trucks and Carts used for transporting fruits.
(d) save trees from poisonous fumes of smoke from brick kiln chimneys.

157. Water pollution can be stopped best by
(a) Spraying DDT
(b) Treating effluents to remove injurious chemicals
(c) Cultivating useful water plants
(d) Rearing more fishes

158. Which of following is not a type of ecosystems?
(a) Natural ecosystem
(b) Artificial ecosystem
(c) Micro ecosystem
(d) Food chain ecosystem

159. The congress grass/carrot grass that causes allergy arrived in India in 1956. It is
(a) Parthenium hysterophorous
(b) Eichhornia crassipes
(c) Opuntia dilleni
(d) Sorghum halepens

160. Which of the following is the most stable ecosystem?
(a) Ocean (b) Desert
(c) Forest (d) Mountain

161. The Suez Canal connects
(a) Baltic Sea and the Caspian Sea.
(b) Mediterranean Sea and the Red Sea.
(c) Red Sea and the Caspian Sea.
(d) Mediterranean Sea and North Sea.

162. The process of converting ammonia to nitrate is known as
(a) Ammonification
(b) Nitrification
(c) Dinitrification
(d) None of these

163. Which pollutant gas is released by cud-chewing cattle/ruminants?
(a) CH_4 (b) CO_2
(c) CO (d) NO_2

164. Krishna Raja Sagar Dam is built across the river
(a) Cauvery (b) Tungabhadra
(c) Krishna (d) Godavari

165. If N is number of individuals of a species and S is unit of space occupied at a specific time, then population density P is equal to
(a) N × S (b) N / S
(c) S / N (d) S + N

166. When did the Bhopal disaster occur?
(a) Dec. 3, 1982 (b) Dec. 3, 1984
(c) Dec. 3, 1986 (d) Dec. 3, 1980

167. When huge amount of sewage is dumped into a river, the biological oxygen demand will
(a) Decrease
(b) Increase
(c) Remain unchanged
(d) Slightly decrease

168. Which of the following States has rich forests of sandalwood?
(a) Andhra Pradesh (b) Karnataka
(c) Kerala (d) Madhya Pradesh

169. The study of communities in relation to their environment is known as
(a) Synecology
(b) Population ecology
(c) Human ecology
(d) Animal cology

170. Leakage of Methyl Isocyanate (MIC) caused the biggest industrial disaster of the recent times in 1984 (Bhopal Tragedy). What did the industrial plant manufacture where the leakage occurred?
(a) Fertilizer (b) Explosives
(c) Pesticides (d) Cement

171. Salinity of the soil is often caused due to
(a) Excessive addition of rainwater.
(b) Excessive leaching.
(c) Rapid evaporation of surface water.
(d) Accumulation of soluble minerals near or in the surface in arid region.

172. Which of the following is the smallest ocean of the world?
(a) Pacific (b) Indian
(c) Atlantic (d) Arctic

173. The disease caused by the prolonged inhalation of coal dust is called
(a) Silicosis (b) Asbestosis
(c) Pneumoconiosis (d) None of these

174. 60% of SO_2 pollution is due to
(a) burning of coal
(b) burning of oil
(c) automobile
(d) industries

175. Which of the following is the most harmful pollutant?
(a) CH_4 (b) NO_2
(c) CO_2 (d) SO_2

176. Light Year is a unit of
(a) Intensity of light
(b) Distance
(c) Time
(d) Planetary motion

177. Which gas was liberated in Bhopal gas tragedy?
(a) Ethyl isothiocyanate
(b) Sodium isothiocyanate
(c) Methy isocyanate
(d) Phenyl isocyanate and phosgene

178. A dental disease characterised by mottling of teeth is due to the presence of certain chemical element in drinking water. The element responsible for this is
(a) Mercury (b) Fluorine
(c) Molybdenum (d) Lead

179. Persistent exposure to even low levels of environmental chemicals, sometimes induce mutagenic, teratogenic or carcinogenic effects on various organisms; such mutagens may
(a) cause cell death
(b) induce chromosomal abnormalities
(c) induce gene mutation
(d) cause all the above

180. Match List I and List II and select the correct answer using the codes given below the Lists.

List I	List II
A. Troposphere	1. Dust particles
B. Stratosphere	2. Ozone layer
C. Ionosphere	3. Meteors
D. Exosphere	4. Aurora

Codes:	A	B	C	D
(a)	1	2	4	3
(b)	1	2	3	4
(c)	2	1	4	3
(d)	2	1	3	4

181. Man engineered ecosystem is
(a) Forest (b) Cropland
(c) Marine (d) Fluorides

182. The stratospheric ozone depletion leads to
(a) Forest fires
(b) Global warming
(c) Increase in the incidence of skin cancer
(d) All of the above

183. Which of the following are producers?
(a) Animals (b) Plants
(c) Both (a) and (b) (d) None of these

184. Which is the gas that produces the most damaging acid rains?
(a) SO_2 (b) NO_2
(c) CO_2 (d) H_2

185. Lead (Pb) causes
(a) Radioactive pollution
(b) Soil and water pollution
(c) Air pollution
(d) All of the above

186. The planets are kept is motion in their respective orbits by the
(a) rotation of the sun on its axis.
(b) gravitation and centrifugal forces.
(c) great size and spherical shape.
(d) rotation and the density of the planets.

187. A fairly vast wild land for the preservation and protection of flora and fauna of a country in their natural form is called
(a) Wildlife Sanctuary
(b) Biosphere Reserve
(c) Harvesting
(d) National Park

188. Recent reports of acid rains in big industrial cities are due to the effect of atmospheric pollution by
(a) more release of SO_2 and NO_2 by burning of fossil fuels.
(b) more release of CO_2 by burning of coal/wood, cutting of forests and increasing population.
(c) excessive release of NH_3 by coal gas/ industries.
(d) excessive release of CO by incomplete combustion of carbonaceous fuels.

189. Ultraviolet radiation from sunlight cause the reaction that produces
(a) Fluorides (b) SO_2
(c) Ozone (d) CO

190. All vital atmospheric processes leading to various climatic and weather conditions take place in the
(a) Troposphere (b) Ionosphere
(c) Exosphere (d) Stratosphere

191. Which one of the following trees have the largest areal coverage in India?
(a) Chir (b) Teak
(c) Deodar (d) Sal

192. In India, acid rains are not common due to
(a) less SO_2 in air
(b) factories with long chimneys
(c) dust in air
(d) rural areas

193. Which of the following is/are the chief source(s) of soil and water pollution?
(a) Thermal power station's waste product
(b) Agro-industry
(c) Mining
(d) All of the above

194. The greatest diversity of animal and plants species occurs in
(a) temperate deciduous forests
(b) tropical moist forests
(c) heavily polluted rivers
(d) desert lands

195. Population refers to the total number of
(a) people living in a country at a given point of time.
(b) people living in a particular area.
(c) animals, including man, living in a particular area.
(d) None of these.

196. A rain is called acid rain when its pH is
(a) Less than 7
(b) Less than 5.6 (generally between 3-5)
(c) Less than 4.6 (generally between 2-4)
(d) Less than 2

197. The cold oceanic current passing through the coast of North America is known as
(a) Kuroshic Current
(b) Gulf Stream
(c) Labrador Current
(d) Falkland Current

198. The energy relationships in an ecosystem can be studied with the help of
(a) Pyramid of biomass
(b) Pyramid of energy

(c) Pyramid of numbers
(d) None of these

199. Acid rain is caused by sulphur oxides, nitrogen oxides and hydrochloric acid which are produced by industries, automobiles and thermal power plants using fossil fuels. It causes
(a) defoliation, chlorosis, necrosis of plant foliage.
(b) leaching of mineral salts in soil and decolourisation of coloured stone.
(c) death of fishes due to clogging of their gills by exudation of large amount of mucus caused by solubility and availability of toxic metal like Aluminium.
(d) All the above.

200. Smog is a common pollutant in places having
(a) Excessive ammonium in the air
(b) High temperature
(c) Excessive SO_2 in the air
(d) Low temperature

201. Which of the following soil is very hard to cultivate?
(a) Alluvial (b) Red
(c) Black (d) Sandy

202. The flow of energy in ecosystem is
(a) bi-directional
(b) multi-directional
(c) uni-directional
(d) None of these

203. Smog is a combination of
(a) air and water vapour
(b) water and smoke
(c) smoke and fog
(d) fire and water

204. Grazing is an example of
(a) Positive pollution
(b) Negative pollution
(c) Gully erosion
(d) Sheet erosion

205. The Hirakud Project is on which of the following rivers?
(a) Godavari (b) Mahanadi
(c) Damodar (d) Kosi

206. Phagotrophs are
(a) micro-consumers
(b) macro-consumers
(c) decomposers
(d) All of these

207. Term Smog was given in 1905 by
(a) des Voeux (b) Hult
(c) Canon (d) Le Chatelier

208. Water pollution is caused by
(a) Hydrocarbon gases and growth of phyto-planktons
(b) Industrial effluents
(c) Rain
(d) Decay of aquatic animals bodies

209. What is meant by the term "cirrus"?
(a) A low cloud
(b) A rain-bearing cloud
(c) A high-cloud
(d) A hail-bearing cloud

210. Factors which contribute to the formation of soil are
(a) plants and animals
(b) local topography
(c) long period of time
(d) All of these

211. A smog that occurs due to low temperature and has reducing environment is
(a) Los Angeles smog
(b) Photochemical smog
(c) London smog
(d) All the above

212. Thermal pollution of water body is due to

(a) discharge of agricultural run off.
(b) discharge of chemicals from industries.
(c) discharge of chemicals from mining.
(d) discharge of heat (hot water) from power plants.

213. Most of the weather phenomena take place in the
(a) stratosphere (b) troposphere
(c) tropopause (d) ionosphere

214. Which of the following is not a Himalayan river systems?
(a) Indus system
(b) Ravi system
(c) Ganga system
(d) Brahmaputra system

215. Smog that occurs mainly by automobile exhausts at high temperature over cities due to still air is called
(a) London smog
(b) Classical smog
(c) Both (a) and (b)
(d) Photochemical smog

216. Atmospheric pressure exerted on earth is due to
(a) rotation of earth
(b) revolution of earth
(c) gravitational pull
(d) uneven heating of earth

217. Bio indicators are
(a) soil indicator (b) water indicator
(c) pH indicator (d) stains

218. London smog of 1952 that killed about 4000 persons, was
(a) Photochemical and rich in NO_2
(b) Coal induced and rich in SO_2
(c) Effect of nuclear accident
(d) Due to atomic explosion

219. The circulation of ocean water occurs
(a) only laterally
(b) only vertically
(c) both laterally and vertically
(d) neither laterally nor vertically

220. Some pollutants are
(i) Carbon monoxide
(ii) Nitrogen dioxide
(iii) Ethylene
(iv) Lead tetraethyl
(v) Sulphur-dioxide
(vi) Unburnt hydrocarbons
(vii) Partially oxidised products of formaldehyde and acetaldehyde

The photochemical SMOG formation takes place by
(a) (i) and (vi) (b) (vi) and (vii)
(c) (i) and (vii) (d) (i) to (vii), all

221. Which of the following is the transition layer between stratosphere and the mesosphere?
(a) Stratopause (b) Tropopause
(c) Mesopause (d) Thermopause

222. Match List I and List II and select the correct answer using the codes given below the Lists.

List I (Storm)	List II (Country of Occurrence)
A. Cyclone	1. China
B. Hurricane	2. Australia
C. Typhoon	3. India
D. Willy-Willy	4. U.S.A.

Codes:	A	B	C	D
(a)	3	4	2	1
(b)	4	3	2	1
(c)	3	4	1	2
(d)	4	3	1	2

223. 'Niche' refers to
(a) place of living
(b) type of Animal food
(c) place of living and type of food
(d) All of these

224. In a photochemical smog, which gas is an eye and mucous membrane irritant?
(a) SO_2 (b) O_3
(c) CO (d) N_2O

225. The special characteristics of plants and animals that enable them to be successful under prevailing set of environmental conditions are called
(a) Speciation (b) Adaptation
(c) Evolution (d) Ecotype

226. Which is called the "Tiger State"?
(a) Rajasthan
(b) Madhya Pradesh
(c) Uttar Pradesh
(d) Jammu & Kashmir

227. The land made unsuitable for cultivation due to soil erosion is called
(a) Badlands (b) Sadlands
(c) Chambal (d) None of these

228. The main component of photochemical smog is/are
(a) PAN (b) O_3
(c) Both (a) and (b) (d) SO_2

229. The dominant species in mangrove forests is/are
(a) *Rhizophora* (b) *Avicenia*
(c) Both (a) and (b) (d) None of these

230. Which one of the following rivers is known as "Sorow of Bihar"?
(a) Damodar (b) Gandak
(c) Kosi (d) Sone

231. How many flowering plants exist in India?
(a) 45 thousand (b) 20 thousand
(c) 15 thousand (d) 25 thousand

232. PAN Peroxyacylnitrate) is a secondary pollutant and is found in
(a) Smog (b) Fertilizer
(c) Herbicide (d) Pesticide

233. The example of endothermic animal is
(a) Man (b) Frogs
(c) Snakes (d) Both (b) and (c)

234. Given below are two statements, one labelled as Assertion (A) and the other lebelled as Reason (R).

Assertion (A): One of the movements of the surface water of ocean is known as ocean current.

Reason (R): Ocean currents are caused mainly due to planetary winds and the difference in temperature and density of water.

In the context of the above two statements, which one the following is correct?
(a) Both A and R are true and R is the correct explanation of A.
(b) Both A and R are true but R is not a correct explanation of A.
(c) A is true but R is false.
(d) A is false but R is true

235. Which of the following methods can be adopted to save soil erosion?
(a) Use trace cultivation
(b) Remove the soil
(c) Grow plants with adventitious root
(d) Use more soil

236. Which organism's case of colour change after the industrial revolution is quoted as the most striking example of Industrial mechanism and natural selection as a result of environmental change?
(a) Spotted Lady bird
(b) Speckled wood
(c) Peppered moth
(d) Dot moth

237. Which of the following is/are abiotic factor(s)?
(a) Light (b) Temperature
(a) Moisture (d) All of these

238. Tsunamis are huge sea waves caused by
(a) Earthquakes (b) Volcanoes
(c) Winds (d) Icebergs

239. Leafy trees help in preventing
(a) Noise pollution
(b) Air pollution
(c) Water pollution
(d) Land pollution

240. Most abundant pollutant in the atmosphere among hydrocarbons is
(a) Methane (b) Propane
(c) Butane (d) Benzpyrene

241. Population size may decrease as a result of
(a) Emigration (b) Mortality
(c) Both (a) and (b) (d) Zonation

242. Through which of the following countries does the river Tigris flow?
(a) Egypt (b) Iran
(c) Italy (d) Iraq

243. Living organisms are
(a) biotic factors in an ecosystem
(b) antibiotic factors in an ecosystem
(c) Both (a) and (b)
(d) None of these

244. Which of the following gases can deplete the ozone layer in the stratosphere (upper atmosphere)?
(a) Methane
(b) Carbon monoxide
(c) Ammonia
(d) Sulphur dioxide

245. Eutrophication means
(a) Nutrient dissipated
(b) Forest containing acid rain
(c) Nutrient enrichment
(d) None of the above

246. Imaginary lines drawn on a global map from pole to pole and from the perpendicular to the equator are called
(a) Contours (b) Isobars
(c) Meridians (d) Steppes

247. Around the planet earth all living organisms form a
(a) Abiotic community
(b) Biotic community
(c) Biosphere
(d) Bio reserve

248. The gas which is produced in flooded rice paddy fields, marshes and cud chewing cattle and is associated with global warming and depletion of ozone layer is
(a) CH_4 (b) Cl
(c) CO_2 (d) H_2S

249. Which of the following is the most widely used form of renewable energy?
(a) Coal (b) Fossil fuel
(c) Hydro power (d) Wood

250. The 23 South latitude is known as
(a) The Tropic of Cancer
(b) The Tropic of Capricorn
(c) The Equator
(d) The Prime Meridian

251. Green plants are
(a) secondary producers
(b) primary producers
(c) Both (a) and (b)
(d) None of these

252. Which pollutant gas does a landfill produce?
(a) Methane (b) Ammonia
(c) H_2S (d) SO_2

253. 'Equinox' means
(a) Days are longer than nights
(b) Days and nights are equal
(c) Days are shorter than nights
(d) None of these

254. Timberline shows
(a) a line of trees
(b) the limit of the ocean

(c) the limit of the forest
(d) the height of the mountains

255. The source of aerosol in upper atmosphere is
(a) sea currents
(b) petroleum based industries
(c) jet planes
(d) ruminants

256. The earth planet along with the atmosphere (i.e., air, water and land) that sustains life is called
(a) Troposphere (b) Biosphere
(c) Stratosphere (d) Ecosystem

257. Summer solstice occurs on
(a) March 21 (b) April 21
(c) May 21 (d) June 21

258. Afforestation means
(a) growing new forests
(b) go into the forest
(c) study of forests
(d) destroying the forest

259. As innocuous activity as a hair spraying can, on a large scale, drastically affects
(a) Ozone layer (b) Ionosphere
(c) Troposphere (d) Magnetosphere

260. On the basis of the type of environment being polluted, we may recognize
(a) Air pollution (b) Soil pollution
(c) Water pollution (d) All of these

261. A lunar eclipse occurs when
(a) Sun, Moon and Earth are not in the same line.
(b) Earth comes between the Sun and the Moon.
(c) Moon comes between the Sun and the Earth.
(d) Sun comes between the Earth and the Moon.

262. The age of a tree can be found by
(a) measuring the tree's height
(b) measuring of the tree's diameter
(c) analysis of annual growth
(d) counting the annual growth ring

263. The jet propulsion liberates a compound in outer atmosphere which causes air pollution. It is
(a) Fluorocarbons (b) CO_2
(c) SO_2 (d) Ozone

264. What percent of ultraviolet radiation increase with subsequent reduction of 1% ozone?
(a) 2% (b) 8%
(c) 18% (d) 28%

265. The sky appears blue because
(a) It is actually blue.
(b) The atmosphere scatters blue light more than the others.
(c) All colours interfere to produce blue.
(d) In white light, blue colour dominates.

266. The relation between crops and environment is known as
(a) Agroecology (b) Demecology
(c) Synecology (d) Autecology

267. Greenhouse gases are/is
(a) CO_2
(b) Chlorofluorocarbons (CFCs) and Halons
(c) CH_4 and N_2O
(d) All of these

268. Benzene is a
(a) Gaseous pollutant
(b) Liquid pollutant
(c) Solid pollutant
(d) All of the above

269. International Date Line passes through
(a) 0° Greenwich
(b) 180° Greenwich
(c) 90° Greenwich
(d) 270° Greenwich

270. Plants growing under normal conditions are
(a) Carnnibal (b) Mesophytes
(c) Detritivore (d) Carnivores

271. The most serious pollutant to rubber tyres is
(a) CO_2 (b) CO
(c) O_3 (d) NO_2

272. Which of the following is/are the source(s) of air pollution?
(a) Thermal power stations
(b) Industrial chimney wastes
(c) Automobiles
(d) All of the above

273. Port Blair is situated in
(a) North Andaman
(b) South Andaman
(c) Middle Andaman
(d) Little Andaman

274. Green plants produce food by
(a) Holophytic process
(b) Holozoic process
(c) Parasitic process
(d) None of these

275. Which satellite recorded the presence of an Ozone hole?
(a) TIROS-N (b) GOES
(c) NIMBUS-7 (d) LANDSAT-3

276. 'Minamata' disease in Japan was chiefly due to
(a) Lead pollution
(b) Fluoride pollution
(c) Mercury pollution
(d) Radioactive pollution

277. Which of the following passes through India?
(a) Tropic of Capricorn
(b) Tropic of Cancer
(c) Equator
(d) 0° Longitude

278. Organism that takes only raw plant products as their food is called
(a) Heterotroph (b) Herbivorous
(c) Carnivorous (d) Vegetarian

279. Peeling of ozone umbrella (which protects us from harmful UV rays) is made by
(a) CFMs/CFCs (b) CO_2
(c) Coal burning (d) PAN

280. Any substance which causes pollution is called
(a) Infection (b) Pollutant
(c) Co-factor (d) Inhibitor

281. At the Equator, the duration of a day is
(a) 10 hrs (b) 12 hrs
(c) 14 hrs (d) 16 hrs

282. Sharbati Sonora refers to
(a) a variety of rice
(b) a variety of maize
(c) a variety of sugarcane
(d) a variety of wheat

283. Ozone depletion in stratosphere Ozone hole would result in
(a) forest fires and acid rains.
(b) global warming.
(c) increased incidence of skin cancer due to reaching of UV radiations on earth.
(d) Greenhouse effect.

284. Fluorides enter plant leaves through
(a) Leafbase (b) Root
(c) Stomata (d) Stem

285. Suez navigation canal links up Mediterranean Sea with the
(a) Atlantic Ocean (b) Pacific Ocean
(c) North Sea (d) Red Sea

286. The end product of photosysnthesis is
(a) Glucose (b) Protein
(c) Vitamin (d) Ammonia

287. Ozone increases

(a) Photosynthesis (b) Transpiration
(c) Respiration (d) Both (b) and (c)

288. Pollutants like PAN and O_3 (Photo-chemical smog) cause
(a) Irritation of eye
(b) Irritation nose and eye
(c) Respiratory distress
(d) All of the above

289. Teak and Sal are the principal trees in the forests known as
(a) Tropical moist evergreen
(b) Dry deciduous
(c) Tropical moist deciduous
(d) Dry evergreen

290. The best example of an ecological community is
(a) an oak tree
(b) all the people in Mumbai
(c) all the fishes in sea
(d) a meadow

291. Today concentration of Greenhouse gases is high because of
(a) use of refrigerators
(b) deforestation
(c) increased combustion of fossil fuels
(d) All of the above

292. "The unwanted sound dumped into the atmosphere leading to health hazards" is meant for
(a) Noise pollution
(b) Water pollution
(c) Air pollution
(d) Radioactive pollution

293. When a ship crosses the International Date Line from West to East
(a) It loses one day
(b) It gains one day
(c) It loses half-a-day
(d) It gains half-a-day

294. Maximum threat to the world is from
(a) Global warming
(b) Ozone hole
(c) Water Pollution
(d) Soil erosion

295. Which of the following is not correctly matched?
(i) The Water (Prevention and Control of Pollution) Act, 1975
(ii) The Motor Vehicle Act came into force from 1st July, 1989
(iii) The Air (Prevention and Control) Pollution Act, 1981
(iv) The Environment Protection Act, 1983

Codes:
(a) Both (i) and (iv)
(b) Only (iii)
(c) Only (ii)
(d) All of the above are incorrectly matched

296. Siachen is
(a) Limiting glacier zone between India and Pakistan
(b) Limiting desert zone between India and Pakistan
(c) Limiting zone between China and Pakistan
(d) Limiting zone between India and Myanmar

297. Phytoplanktons in a pond ecosystem are
(a) Autotrophs (b) Lithotrophs
(c) Heterotrophs (d) Photoperiodism

298. 'Agenda-21' is the product of
(a) Evolution
(b) Earth Summit
(c) Speciation
(d) Both (b) and (c)

299. Which of the following people are related to T.E. Lawrence?
(a) The people of China
(b) Inhabitants of Mangol

(c) The people of Afghanistan
(d) The people of Arab

300. Preparation of food by green plants is called
(a) Photo-oxidation
(b) Photorespiration
(c) Photosynthesis
(d) Photoperiodism

301. Biodiversity is an abbreviation of
(a) Biological rhythm
(b) Abiotic factor
(c) Biotic factor
(d) Biological diversity

302. For which of the following reasons, clouds do not rain in desert?
(a) Maximum air velocity
(b) Minimum temperature
(c) Minimum air velocity
(d) Minimum humidity

303. The rate of growth of plants can be measured by a/an
(a) Manometer (b) Thermometer
(c) Photometer (d) Auxanometer

304. Greenpeace is
(a) NGO
(b) An inhibitory process
(c) Government policy for speciation
(d) All of the above

305. Which countries are joined by the Palk Strait?
(a) India and Sri Lanka
(b) North and South Korea
(c) Pakistan and China
(d) Britain and France

306. Which of the following factors is most responsible for the damage of stored food grains?
(a) Environment temperature
(b) Environmental humidity
(c) Moisture content of the green
(d) All of these

307. 'IUCN' stands for
(a) International Unity on Community and Nationality
(b) Interstate Unity of Culture Nature
(c) Indian Union Congress Nation
(d) International Union for the Conservation of Nature and Natural Resources

308. The smallest Continent is
(a) Europe (b) Australia
(c) Antarctica (d) South America

309. An ecosystem consists of
(a) all the plants and animals of an area.
(b) a living community and its environment.
(c) carnivores and herbivores of an area.
(d) producers, consumers and decomposers in a particular locality.

310. To achieve conservation of biological diversity it is usually necessary to
(a) Introduce certain species
(b) Establish protected areas
(c) Restore ecosystems
(d) All of the above

311. The longest dam in India is
(a) Bhakra Dam
(b) Nagarjuna Sagar Dam
(c) Hirakud Dam
(d) Kosi Dam

312. Plants growing in sunlight are called
(a) Hydrophytes (b) Heliophytes
(c) Holophytes (d) Xerophytes

313. Wetland conservation programs are generally based on
(a) Checking waste disposal in wetlands
(b) Preparation of wetland enveloping
(c) Reduction of excessive inflow of nutrients
(d) All of the above

314. Jawahar Tunnel, the largest in India, is located in the state of
(a) Himachal Pradesh
(b) Rajasthan
(c) West Bengal
(d) J&K

315. Pedology is the study of
(a) Rocks (b) Crops
(c) Soil (d) Animal diseases

316. The basic strategies of biodiversity conservation is/are
(a) *In situ* (on site)
(b) *Ex situ* (off site)
(c) Both (a) and (b)
(d) None of these

317. 'Jog' the highest waterfall in India is located in the state of
(a) Uttar Pradesh (b) West Bengal
(c) Karnataka (d) Maharashtra

318. The purpose of plants along river banks is to prevent
(a) siltage and foods
(b) heavy rainfall
(c) seepage of water underground
(d) pollution

319. Biosphere Reserves are also notified as
(a) Ecosystems (b) Woodlands
(c) National Parks (d) Conservation

320. Where is the Siachin Glacier situated in India?
(a) Uttar Pradesh
(b) Himachal Pradesh
(c) Jammu & Kashmir
(d) Sikkim

321. The National Bureau of Plant Genetic Research is located at
(a) New Delhi (b) Jammu
(c) Haryana (d) Punjab

322. A Biosphere Reserve consists of
(a) Core zone (b) Buffer zone
(c) Transition zone (d) All of these

323. The standard time of India is the local time of
(a) 81° East longitude
(b) East longitude
(c) 84° East longitude
(d) 86° East longitude

324. Scrub jungle is characterised by
(a) Heavy rainfall (b) Low rainfall
(c) Poor rainfall (d) No rainfall

325. The main functions of Biosphere Reserves are
(a) Conservation
(b) Scientific research and education
(c) Development of ecological aspects
(d) All of the above

326. In which South American country does one find the Atacama desert?
(a) Chile (b) Peru
(c) Brazil (d) Columbia

327. Ozone layer is essential because it absorbs most of the
(a) infrared radiations
(b) heat
(c) solar radiation
(d) ultraviolet radiation

328. Which of the following ports has a free trade zone?
(a) Kandla (b) Cochin
(c) Madras (d) Tuticorin

329. Decrease in number of trees may cause
(a) increase in rainfall
(b) decrease in rainfall
(c) decrease in temperature
(d) conservation of nutrients in soil

330. Which one of the following mountain peaks of the Himalayas is not in India
(a) Annapurna (b) Nanda Devi
(c) Mt. Kamet (d) Kanchenjunga

331. Acid rain is due to
(a) oil slick
(b) nuclear wastes
(c) combustion of fossil fuels
(d) oxides of sulphur and nitrogen

332. Biodiversity is of use to modern agriculture as a
(a) Source of new biodegradable pesticides.
(b) Source of new crops.
(c) Source of material for breeding improved varieties.
(d) All of the above are correct.

333. Match List I (Types of Natural Regions) with List II (Areas Associated with the Regions) and select the correct answer using the codes given below the lists.

List I (Types of Natural Regions)
A. Dry Continental
B. Humid Subtropics
C. Marine West Coast
D. Subarctics

List II (Areas Associated with the Natural Regions)
1. Brazil
2. British Isles
3. Canada
4. China
5. Mangolia

Codes:	A	B	C	D
(a)	5	4	2	3
(b)	2	3	1	5
(c)	2	4	1	3
(d)	5	3	2	4

334. UASB stands for
(a) Upflow Anaerobic Sludge Blanket
(b) Upflow Anti-Sludge Blanket
(c) Upflow Anaerobic Sludge Biomass
(d) None of these

335. Extinction of species includes
(a) Natural extinction
(b) Mass extinction
(c) Anthropogenic extinction
(d) All of the above

336. Winter rains in north and north-west India are generally associated with the phenomenon of
(a) Retreating monsoon
(b) Temperate cyclones
(c) Local thunderstorms
(d) Shift in Jet stream movement

337. Which of the following statements is correct?
(a) Green peace is N.G.O.
(b) PAN and O_3 are pollutants
(c) 'Minamata' disease occurs due to Mercury pollution
(d) All of these

338. What percentage of land area of India provides to the global diversity?
(a) 2-4% (b) 5%
(c) 8% (d) 19%

339. When the moon is near the horizon, then it appears bigger because of
(a) Atmospheric refraction
(b) Scattering of light
(c) Diffraction
(d) Total internal reflection

340. Smog is a common pollutant in places having
(a) low temperature
(b) high temperature
(c) excessive CO_2 in the air
(d) All of these

341. Who developed the 'hot spots concept' in 1988?
(a) M.S. Swaminathan
(b) P.K. Iyengar
(c) Norman Myers
(d) George Bush

342. Savanna grasslands are found in
(a) Australia (b) Africa
(c) East Asia (d) South America

343. Which one of the following is a non-biodegradable waste?
(a) Plastics (b) Manure
(c) Cow-dung (d) Kitchen waste

344. In India, sacred forests are located in
(a) Karnataka
(b) Kerala and Meghalaya
(c) Maharashtra
(d) All of the above

345. Life expectancy is highest in the world in
(a) Canada (b) Germany
(c) Japan (d) Norway

346. Bio-concentration is also known as
(a) bio-magnification of harmful chemicals
(b) bio-magnification of fossil fuel
(c) Both (a) and (b)
(d) None of these

347. The Earth Summit of 1992 at Rio de Janeiro resulted into a Convention on Biodiversity, which came into force on
(a) 5 June, 1992
(b) 19 December, 1993
(c) 29 December, 1993
(d) 1 April, 2000

348. Israel has common borders with
(a) Lebanon, Syria, Jordan and Egypt
(b) Lebanon, Syria, Turkey and Jordan
(c) Cyprus, Turkey, Jordan and Egypt
(d) Turkey, Syria, Iraq and Yemen

349. Which of the following is a occupational hazards?
(a) Silicosis (b) Asbestosis
(c) Byssionosis (d) All of these

350. Cryopreservation is the storage of material at ultra-low temperature
(a) By very rapid cooling
(b) By gradual cooling
(c) By gradual cooling and simultaneous dehydration at low temperature
(d) By all of the above

351. What is the correct sequence of the rivers—Godavari, Mahanadi, Narmada and Tapi in the descending order of their lengths?
(a) Godavari-Mahanadi-Narmada-Tapi
(b) Godavari-Narmada-Mahanadi-Tapi
(c) Narmada-Godavari-Tapi-Mahanadi
(d) Narmada-Tapi-Godavari-Mahanadi

352. Which of the following statement is correct?
(a) Water is a renewable resource.
(b) Cultural eutrophication is caused by the addition of too much nitrate.
(c) The burning of fossil fuels includes coal, oil and gas.
(d) All of these.

353. Cryopreservation involves storage of cells from embryos and shoot tips in liquid nitrogen at
(a) 0°C (b) 5°C
(c) –196°C (d) 100°C

354. Among the following cities, which one is nearest to the Tropic of Cancer?
(a) Delhi (b) Kolkata
(c) Jodhpur (d) Nagpur

355. Among the following which planet takes maximum time for one revolution around the Sun?
(a) Earth (b) Jupiter
(c) Mars (d) Venus

356. Which countries hosted the first World Earth summit on conservation of environment?
(a) UK (b) USA
(c) India (d) Brazil

357. Which one among the following languages has largest number of speakers in the world?
(a) Bengali (b) French
(c) Japanese (d) Portuguese

358. Which of the following does not affect Ozone layer?
(a) Cl_2 (b) $CFCl_3$
(c) NO (d) CH_3

359. Which one of the following is the longest glacier of India?
(a) Pindari (b) Gangotri
(c) Siachen (d) Zemu

360. The presence of which of the following pollutants in the atmosphere is affecting the marbles of which Taj Mahal is constructed?
(a) SO_2
(b) CO_2
(c) Pb Particles
(d) Radioactive disintegrations

361. In what regions can the sun be seen at midnight?
(a) The tropical zone
(b) Warm temperate regions
(c) The Arctic and Antarctic regions
(d) Anywhere at the time of lunar eclipse

362. Silviculture means
(a) to grow more and more plants
(b) to grow more and more silk worm
(c) to prevent environment pollution
(d) None of these

363. Match the rivers flowing through the cities below.

Cities	Rivers
A. Baghdad	(1) Rhine
B. Cairo	(2) Hudson
C. New York	(3) Nile
D. Rotterdam	(4) Tigris

Codes	A	B	C	D
(a)	4	3	2	1
(b)	1	2	3	4
(c)	2	1	4	3
(d)	3	4	1	2

364. Where was electricity supply first introduced in India?
(a) Kolkata (b) Darjeeling
(c) Mumbai (d) Chennai

365. Which of the following is the highest waterfall in the world?
(a) Angel (b) Ribbin
(c) Hungela (d) Quecanag

366. What percentage of ultra violet radiation increases with subsequent reduction of 1% ozone?
(a) 1 percent (b) 2 percent
(c) Nil (d) 3 percent

367. Which among the following planets intersects the orbit of Neptune?
(a) Mercury (b) Pluto
(c) Earth (d) Uranus

368. Cultivation of same crop on the same soil year after year is known as
(a) Silviculture (b) Pisciculture
(c) Horticulture (d) Monoculture

369. Nubian desert is in
(a) Ethiopia (b) Egypt
(c) Sudan (d) Somalia

370. Which of the following does not form part of particular matter?
(a) Dust (b) Fly ash
(c) Aerosols (d) Nitric oxide

371. Acid rain is the downpour of
(a) carbon dioxide in rain
(b) dust in rain
(c) sulphur dioxide in rain
(d) oxygen in rain

372. Peso is the currency of
(a) Cuba (b) Bermuda
(c) Grenada (d) Jamaica

373. Fluorides enter plant leaves through
(a) Stomata (b) Stem
(c) Leaf base (d) All of these

374. The longest highway in India runs from
(a) Kolkata to Jammu
(b) Jammu to Kanya Kumari
(c) Ambala to Nagercoil
(d) Varanasi to Kanya Kumari

375. A Biosphere reserve consists of
(a) core zone (b) transition zone
(c) buffer zone (d) All of these

376. Which of the following countries is called the "Country of white elephants"?
(a) Thailand (b) Kuwait
(c) South Africa (d) India

377. The dominant species in Mangrove forests are
(a) *Avicenia* (b) *Rhizophora*
(c) Both (a) and (b) (d) None of these

378. Which among the following is the most dangerous non-biodegradable waste?
(a) Plastic articles
(b) Cow-dung
(c) Garbage
(d) Radioactive waste

379. Which city was known as the 'Manchester of India'?
(a) Mumbai (b) Surat
(c) Ahmedabad (d) Ludhiana

380. Number of National Parks in India is
(a) 50 (b) 20
(c) 36 (d) 86

381. Where is the famous shore temple located?
(a) Puri (b) Visakhapatnam
(c) Mamallapuram (d) Chennai

382. Number of Tiger reserves in India is
(a) 16 (b) 12
(c) 25 (d) 19

383. Which of the following is the largest island?
(a) Sumatra (b) Madagascar
(c) Honshu (d) Cuba

384. Where are Nanda Devi and Nokrek Biosphere reserves situated?
(a) Nanda Devi in the Himalayas and the Nokrek in Meghalaya
(b) Mt. Everest in the Himalayas and the Nongraim in Meghalaya
(c) Mt. Kanchenjunga in the Himalayas and the Garo Hills Meghalaya
(d) None of these

385. The new alluvial deposits found in the Gangetic plain are known as
(a) Bhabar (b) Bhangar
(c) Khadar (d) Terai

386. Where was the first biosphere reserve set up?
(a) Nilgiri
(b) Karakoram Ranges
(c) Himalayan Range
(d) Kanchenjunga

387. Kodaikanal, the famous hill-station of South India is situated on
(a) Palni Hills
(b) Annamalai Mountain
(c) Nilgiri Mountain
(d) Cardamon Hills

388. Number of endangered species of plants animals is
(a) 1300/20 (b) 1200/20
(c) 1300/10 (d) None of these

389. The largest continent in the world is
(a) North America (b) Africa
(c) Asia (d) Europe

390. Number of Zoological parks till March 31, 2002 in India was
(a) 25 (b) 35
(c) 45 (d) 75

391. Which water body separates Australia from New Zealand?
(a) Cook Straits
(b) Tasman Sea

(c) McMunro Sound
(d) Great Barrier Reef

392. The sanctuary for preserving birds is established in
(a) Bangalore (b) Mumbai
(c) Delhi (d) None of these

393. 'Radcliff Line' is a boundary line between
(a) India and Bangladesh
(b) India and Bhutan
(c) India and China
(d) India and Pakistan

394. Number of sanctuaries in India till 31st March, 2002 was
(a) 490 (b) 260
(c) 480 (d) 520

395. Till March 31st, 2002 there were only 02
(a) Rhinoceros project
(b) Tiger project
(c) Bird project
(d) None of these

396. Which of the following States is abundant in camels?
(a) West Bengal (b) Rajasthan
(c) Assam (d) Gujarat

397. Which of the following district is on the international border of India
(a) Gorakhpur
(b) West Khasi Hills
(c) Kinnaur
(d) Kullu

398. Where do you find wild areas in India?
(a) Gujarat (b) Kerala
(c) Maharashtra (d) Tamil Nadu

399. Which of the following pairs is not correctly matched?
(a) Panna : Diamond
(b) Neyveli : Lignite
(c) Mysore : Marble
(d) Sambhar : Salt

400. Which of the following fuels, causes minimum environmental pollution?
(a) Coal (b) Diesel
(c) Hydrogen (d) Kerosine

401. The earthquake waves which have transverse movements are known as
(a) Primary waves
(b) Secondary waves
(c) Surface waves
(d) None of the above

402. Deforestation means
(a) the process of transforming an area into forest.
(b) the planting of trees on land where a forest has previously stood, but has been destroyed e.g., by a forest fire.
(c) the process of clearing forest.
(d) None of the above

403. The first man to reach the South Pole on December 14, 1911 was
(a) Commander Robert, E. Peary of U.S. Navy.
(b) Racald Amundsen from Norway.
(c) The Navigator Ferdinand Magellan.
(d) Sir Francis Drake of England.

404. The Great Indian Bustard is a species of
(a) bird found in Kachch and Rajasthan
(b) monkey found in the Nilgiris
(c) snake found in Assam forests
(d) bear found in the Himalaya foothills of Uttarakhand

405. Which one of the following is not the vegetation in Selva forests?
(a) Epiphytes (b) Xerophytes
(c) Lianas (d) Hydrophytes

406. Which one of the following is the main culprit in the thinning of Ozone layer in the earth's stratosphere?
(a) Carbon dioxide
(b) Chlorofluorocarbons

(c) Methane
(d) Nitrogen Oxides

407. Where does the primitive community of Bushman live?
(a) Sahara desert
(b) Thar desert
(c) Kalahari desert
(d) Attacama desert

408. Freely suspended magnetic needle stands in which direction?
(a) North-West direction
(b) North-South direction
(c) North-East direction
(d) South-West direction

409. Name the leader of the Chipko movement who is also an active opponent of the Tehri Dam Project.
(a) Sunderlal Bahuguna
(b) Madanlal Jha
(c) Pankaj Jha
(d) None of these

410. Which region of India receives rainfall due to western disturbance in winter?
(a) Western region
(b) Central region
(c) Eastern region
(d) North-Western region

411. Which of the following land masses were not a part of the Gondwanaland?
(a) Asia (b) Australia
(c) Antartica (d) Europe

412. How far the axis of earth is inclined of its orbital surface?
(a) 23
(b) 66
(c) 180°
(d) It is not inclined

413. Which of the following is only star?
(a) Moon (b) Venus
(c) Earth (d) Sun

414. Difference of longitudinal of two places on the earth is 15°. What will be the difference in its local time?
(a) No difference (b) 1 hour
(c) 2 hours (d) 15 hours

415. What is the name given to intrusive ingenuous rocks formed very deep inside the earth?
(a) Plutonic (b) Laccolits
(c) Hypabyssal (d) None of these

416. Sultanpur Lake Sanctuary in Haryana is famous for
(a) Black bucks (b) Lions
(c) Antelopes (d) Birds

417. Which of the following is the main cause of major earthquakes?
(a) Collapse of roofs of mines
(b) Collapse of roof of tunnels
(c) Explosive eruption of volcanoes
(d) Tectonic forces

418. Nilgiri Biosphere Reserve is associated with three states. They are
(a) Karnataka, Kerala and Tamil Nadu
(b) Andhra Pradesh, Kerala and Karnataka
(c) Maharashtra, Andhra Pradesh and Karnataka
(d) None of these

419. What is the name given to a mountain formed due to folding of crystal rocks by compressive forces?
(a) Block mountain
(b) Horst mountain
(c) Fold mountain
(d) None of these

420. Red Panda, an endangered species, is found exclusively in
(a) Western Himalayas
(b) Southern Himalayas
(c) Siwalik Himalayas
(d) All of these

421. The Chilka and Pulicant lakes on the eastern coast of India are examples of
(a) lagoons
(b) inland salt water lakes
(c) freshwater lakes
(d) All of the above

422. Which city of India has the highest SPM (Suspended Particulate Matter) level?
(a) Mumbai (b) Kanpur
(c) Delhi (d) None of these

423. The highly heated fragmental material which are thrown into the air by the explosive action of a volcano is called
(a) Volcanic (b) Pyroclasts
(c) Pyro bomb (d) None of these

424. Which of the following rivers has not been listed as 'critically polluted' by the World Bank sponsored State Environmental Action Plan Report 2000?
(a) Sabarmati (b) Luni
(c) Narmada (d) Tapi

425. The soil which develops in site above parent bedrock is called
(a) sedentary rock (b) primary soil
(c) secondary soil (d) None of these

426. Which of the following impact is not caused by construction of dams and reservoirs?
(a) Lead poisoning
(b) Soil erosion
(c) Loss of vegetation cover
(d) All of the above

427. Which of the following waves are the fastest of all earthquake waves?
(a) Primary waves
(b) Secondary waves
(c) Surface waves
(d) Longitudinal waves

428. How was the World Wildlife Fund renamed in 1961?
(a) World Wide Fund for Nature
(b) World Fund
(c) World Life Fund
(d) None of these

429. Name the instruments used to measure the atmospheric pressure?
(a) Barometer (b) Carometer
(c) Spectrometer (d) Pyrometer

430. Which of the following cities in India has a moderate temperature throughout the year?
(a) Delhi (b) Allahabad
(c) Bangalore (d) Dehradun

431. The plants which prepare their own food are called
(a) Heterotrophs (b) Autotrophs
(c) Saprophytes (d) Parasites

432. Temperature decreases with increasing height at the rate of
(a) 6.5° per 100 m.
(b) 6° per 100 m.
(c) 7° per 100 m.
(d) 8° per 100 m.

433. Which of the following statement is true?
(a) Relative precentage of N_2 in atmosphere = 78%
(b) Relative percentage of O_2 in atmosphere = 21%
(c) Relative percentage of CO_2 in atmosphere = 0.03%.
(d) All of these

434. The deep gorges on the ocean floor are called
(a) Gayots
(b) Seamounts
(c) Submarine Canyons
(d) Reefs

435. Which of the following atmospheric layer reflects radio waves that are to transmitted from the earth again back to the earth?

(a) Stratosphere (b) Ionosphere
(c) Mesosphere (d) Troposphere

436. The aplitic zone means that the light is
(a) always present
(b) present during day
(c) always absent
(d) present during night

437. Which of the following Indian states receives the sun rays first in the morning?
(a) Tripura
(b) Meghalaya
(c) Sikkim
(d) Arunachal Pradesh

438. Spontaneous creation of living matter was proposed by
(a) Darwin (b) Ananimenes
(c) Democritus (d) Hutchinson

439. Which of the following clouds is a middle level cloud?
(a) Cirrus (b) Cirrostratus
(c) Nimbostris (d) Alto cumulus

440. Which of the following affection is caused by noise at 180 dB?
(a) Annoyance
(b) Hearing damage
(c) Nausea, vomiting, dizziness
(d) None of these

441. Monsoon winds fall in the category of
(a) local winds
(b) periodic winds
(c) planetary winds
(d) None of these

442. The horizontal movement of air is called as
(a) Jet stream (b) Air in areas
(c) Wind (d) None of these

443. Which of the following is not a food chain?
(a) Grass - Goat - Lion
(b) Grass - Frog - Snake
(c) Grass - Sheep - Man
(d) Grass - Snake - Deer

444. India has very high density of population because of the
(a) fertile soil
(b) availability of water
(c) availability of oil
(d) None of these

445. Which of the following are referred to as the 'producer' in marine ecosystem?
(a) Small fishes (b) Fungi
(c) Zooplankton (d) Phytoplanktons

446. Atmospheric pressure exerted on earth is due to
(a) rotation of earth
(b) revolution of earth
(c) gravitational pull
(d) unwoven heating of earth

447. What is the level of sound found by WHO as 'safe noise level for cities'?
(a) 20 dB (b) 10 dB
(c) 40 dB (d) 45 dB

448. How much area of the oceans is convered by the continental shelf?
(a) 7.5% (b) 10%
(c) 7% (d) None of these

449. The Himalayan-Alpine system is a
(a) Fold mountain system
(b) Fault block system
(c) Residual hill system
(d) Plateau

450. The highest waterfall in the World is at
(a) Falls Angel, Venezuela
(b) Niagara Falls, USA
(c) Victoria Falls, Africa
(d) Jog Falls, India

451. Which of the following is not a pollutant in Leather tanning industries?
(a) Lime
(b) Common salt

(c) Sodium sulphide
(d) Chlorofluorocarbons

452. Which of the following is the largest desert of the world?
(a) The Sahara (b) The Gobi
(c) The Kalahari (d) The Atacama

453. Science which deals with the study of the effects of poisonous substances on living organism is called
(a) Toxicology (b) Ecotoxicology
(c) Emetology (d) None of these

454. Which industry provides jobs to the maximum number of people?
(a) Iron and steel
(b) Sugar Industry
(c) Cotton Textile
(d) Jute Industry

455. The first sign of life made its appearance on the earth about
(a) 1 million years ago
(b) 50 million year ago
(c) 1 billion or 1000 million years ago
(d) 3 billion years ago

456. Paleontology is the study of
(a) Birds (b) Bones
(c) Fossils (d) Primates

457. What are producer organisms?
(a) Plants
(b) Animals
(c) Organisms that can trap solar energy for photosynthesis
(d) Both plants and animals

458. Watershed development program includes which of the following?
(a) Conservation of soil and its moisture
(b) Afforestation
(c) Horticulture
(d) All of these

459. Soil conservation is done through the
(a) bounding of fields
(b) construction of embankments
(c) construction of dams and plugging of breaches in canals, etc.
(d) None of these

460. Which of the following is used by green plants for the manufacture of sugar?
(a) CO_2 (b) Sunlight
(c) H_2O (d) All of these

461. Which soils are known for the cultivation of cotton?
(a) Black soils (b) Red soils
(c) Both (a) and (b) (d) None of these

462. The best method of control of a soil borne disease is by
(a) seed treatment
(b) crop rotation
(c) using fungicides
(d) None of these

463. Which of the following is not a beneficial effect of flooding?
(a) New layer of fertile soil.
(b) Decrease in percolation of water and raining the water tables.
(c) Moisture retention in the soil and so there is no need of irrigation.
(d) Ploughing and cultivation become easy.

464. The land made unsuitable for cultivation due to soil erosion is called
(a) good land
(b) bad land
(c) soil erosion land
(d) cultivate land

465. It is not advisable to sleep under a tree at night because of
(a) release of CO (b) release of CO_2
(c) release of N_2 (d) release of O_4

466. What of India's total land comes under fallow land?

(a) 5% approximately
(b) 6% approximately
(c) 10%
(d) 12%

467. Artificial light can
(a) destroy chlorophyll
(b) synthesise chlorophyll
(c) bring about photosynthesis
(d) None of these

468. The state which has highest land areas covered by forests is
(a) Orissa
(b) Kerala
(c) Andaman and Nicobar
(d) None of these

469. Radio carbon dating is used to find out the age of
(a) Buildings (b) Rocks
(c) Fossils (d) Babies

470. Which term in commonly used to describe recreational travel for the purpose of observing and experiencing natural environments?
(a) Ecotourism
(b) Biotourism
(c) Environment tourism
(d) Plant tourism

471. Which part of India experiences the highest range of temperature in a day?
(a) Bhopal
(b) Thar Desert of Rajasthan
(c) Jaipur
(d) None of these

472. The highest mountains peak of the Ande is
(a) Chimborazo (b) Huascaran
(c) Aconcagua (d) Ancohuma

473. Which of the following areas in India are frequently struck by cyclones?
(a) Godavari Delta (b) Krishna Delta
(c) Kaveri Delta (d) All of these

474. Which is the highest lake of the world?
(a) Bhimtal (India)
(b) Lake Superior (U.S.A.)
(c) The Sekuru lake (Tibet)
(d) Gaurikand (India)

475. How many seasons can be recognised in India?
(a) 4 (b) 3
(c) 2 (d) None of these

476. Which of the following countries has the highest gold stock in the world?
(a) South Africa (b) Japan
(c) India (d) U.S.A.

477. The process of minimising pollution through reuse or the process of waste treatment is from as
(a) Abiotic (b) Abiocoen
(c) Abatement (d) None of these

478. Which country is called, 'The Pearl of the East'?
(a) Sri Lanka (b) India
(c) Pakistan (d) Mauritius

479. Abiotic is a term referring to the
(a) absence of living organisms
(b) presence of living organisms
(c) Both (a) and (b)
(d) None of these

480. Which of the following is/are the factors which can change the size of population in a country?
(a) Birth rate (b) Death rate
(c) Migration (d) All of these

481. All the planets have one or more satellites except
(a) Mercury and Venus
(b) Neptune and Saturn
(c) Pluto and Jupiter
(d) Mars and Uraus

482. A symbiotic relationship between plants and mites called

(a) Acarophily (b) Acacia
(c) Acarina (d) None of these

483. A star which appears blue is
(a) cooler than the moon
(b) hotter than the sun
(c) as hot as the sun
(d) cooler than the sun

484. Name the season in which Coromandal Coast get rainfall
(a) Winter (b) Summer
(c) Rainy (d) All of these

485. Who among the following is known as the 'Bird Man' of India?
(a) Dr. M.S. Randhawa
(b) Dr. M.S. Mani
(c) Dr. Salim Ali
(d) None of these

486. Shyok is a tributary of
(a) Brahmaputra (b) Indus
(c) Chenab (d) Sutlej

487. The general name for any substance that kills of inhibits the growth of micro-organisms is
(a) Biocide (b) Biochore
(c) Bioclimatic (d) Beta vulgaris

488. Fog formation is encouraged when
(a) an inversion of temperature occurs at or near the surface.
(b) a strong surface wind blows.
(c) the sky is overcast.
(d) a thunder engulfs the area.

489. One who maintains constituent an aquarium is
(a) Aqua (b) Aquarelle
(c) Aquanist (d) Aquarius

490. Which is the river across which Almatti dam is being built?
(a) Tungabhadra (b) Godavari
(c) Krishna (d) Sharavathi

491. The most important of the nitrogen-fixing bacteria is
(a) Azobenene (b) Bacteria
(c) Azotobacter (d) Autumn

492. Which one of the following is the biggest shipping canal in the World?
(a) Kiet Canal (b) Panama Canal
(c) Soo Canal (d) Suez Canal

493. Which of the following wildlife sanctuaries is not a tiger reserve?
(a) Corbett National Park
(b) Sunderbans
(c) Ranthambhore National Park
(d) Krishna Sanctuary

494. Nagarjuna Sagar Multipurpose project uses the water of
(a) River Son (b) River Krishna
(c) River Narmada (d) River Jhelum

495. The famous lagoon lake of India is
(a) Dal Lake (b) Chilka Lake
(c) Pubicat Lake (d) Mansarovar

496. Dust burden is usually expressed in
(a) mg/m^3 (b) mg/m^2
(c) mg/m (d) None of these

497. Which of the following places in India is proud of having hatched the *Gharial* (Crocodile) eggs for the first time in captivity anywhere in the world?
(a) Dudwa (Uttar Pradesh)
(b) Shivpuri (Madhya Pradesh)
(c) Tikerpada (Orissa)
(d) None of these

498. Which planet, other than Saturn, has rings?
(a) Neptune (b) Uranus
(c) Mars (d) None of these

499. Match List I with List II and select the correct answer using the codes given below the lists.

List I

A. Namdapha B. Dachigam

C. Ghana D. Dampa

List II

1. Jammu and Kashmir
2. Mizoram
3. Arunachal Pradesh
4. Rajasthan

Codes:	A	B	C	D
(a)	3	1	4	2
(b)	1	2	3	4
(c)	3	4	2	1
(d)	1	3	2	4

500. The Ozone layer is in the
(a) Stratosphere (b) Troposphere
(c) Mesosphere (d) Thermosphere

501. Kalahari desert is located in
(a) Northern Africa
(b) South West United States of America
(c) West Central South America
(d) South Western Africa

502. The Sun belongs to the type of stars
(a) Orion (b) Red award
(c) Binary (d) Galaxy

503. Which one among the following covers the highest percentage of forest area in the world?
(a) Temperature coniferous forest
(b) Temperature deciduous forest
(c) Tropical monsoon forest
(d) Tropical rainforest

504. Expressed as a ratio in relation to world population, India's population is roughly
(a) 1/4 (b) 1/6
(c) 1/8 (d) 1/9

505. Which one of the following countries is landlocked?
(a) Albania (b) Bulgaria
(c) Greece (d) Mecedonia

506. Which of the following natural processes is prominent to avoid and semi-arid terrains?
(a) Stream erosion
(b) Chemical erosion
(c) Wind erosion
(d) Glacial erosion

507. Kaziranga Sanctuary extends to some forty kilometres along the southern bank of the
(a) Ganges (b) Mahanadi
(c) Brahmaputra (d) Godavari

508. Which of the following inland seas has the highest salinity?
(a) The Red Sea
(b) The Baltic Sea
(c) The Dead Sea
(d) The Caspian Sea

509. Which of the following animals and birds have been declared as national animal and national bird respectively of India?
(a) Tiger and Peacock
(b) Elephant and Kite
(c) Horse and Eagle
(d) Lion and Cuckoo

510. The highest plateau in the world is the
(a) Colorado Plateau
(b) Deccan Plateau
(c) Mexican Plateau
(d) Tibetan Plateau

511. The Gir forests in Saurashtra peninsula of Gujarat is unique as the only surviving habitat of
(a) Asian Lion
(b) Snow Leopard
(c) Lion tailed macaque
(d) None of the above

512. Most poisonous gas is
(a) CO (b) CO_2
(c) NH_3 (d) Chloroform

513. Sunbeam snakes are found exclusively in
(a) Australia (b) India
(c) South America (d) America

514. Which of the following is a low pressure belt on the earth?
(a) Horse latitudes (b) Doldrums
(c) Polar winds (d) None of these

515. Jaldapara National Park is situated in
(a) Assam (b) West Bengal
(c) Orissa (d) Bihar

516. Which of the following is a hypophyseal rocks?
(a) Dolerite (b) Basalt
(c) Granite (d) Sandstorm

517. Jim Corbett National Park is in
(a) Uttarakhand and is famous for tigers
(b) Rajasthan and is house of black bucks
(c) Jammu & Kashmir and is home for Kashmir State
(d) Himachal Pradesh and is famous for birds

518. The study of earthquakes comes under
(a) Mineralogy (b) Seismology
(c) Petrology (d) Paleontology

519. The average speed of the rain-bearing South-West monsoon winds is
(a) 30 km/hr (b) 38 km/hr
(c) 40 km/hr (d) 50 km/hr

520. Which of the following is a natural lake?
(a) Walur (b) Dal
(c) Nainital (d) All of these

521. The world's lowest temperature was recorded at
(a) Verkhoyansk, Siberia
(b) Floebery Bay, Canada
(c) Vostok, Antarctica
(d) South Pole, Antarctica

522. What kind of drainage pattern is formed by the Narmada river system?
(a) Dendritic pattern (b) Penins
(c) Trellis (d) Radial

523. An equatorial forest may contain all of the following trees except
(a) Ebony (b) Iron wood
(c) Baobab (d) Green hart

524. Which of the following is not a pattern of stream?
(a) Dendritic (b) Penins
(c) Trails (d) Radial

525. The important medicinal plant which is found only in India
(a) Sarpagandha (b) Taragandha
(c) Teak (d) None of these

526. The cutting of forest leads to
(a) desalting and denaturation.
(b) soil erosion and uncontrollable floods.
(c) increase of rainfall and humidity.
(d) landslides and earthquake.

527. Which of the following is a man-made lake?
(a) Gobind Sagar (b) Gandhi Sagar
(c) Hirakund (d) All of these

528. The place where the Yamuna joins the Ganges is
(a) Allahabad (b) Rudraprayag
(c) Devaprayag (d) None of these

529. The species of animals are referred to as
(a) Flora (b) Fauna
(c) Both (a) and (b) (d) None of these

530. The birth rate measure the number of births during a year per
(a) 100 of population
(b) 1000 of population
(c) million of population
(d) 10,000 of population

531. Which of the following river flows through Punjab?
(a) Ravi and Sutlej
(b) Chenab and Beas

(c) Jhelum
(d) All of the above

532. How much of the surface water drains in the Arabian sea?
(a) About 30% (b) About 20%
(c) About 45% (d) About 2%

533. Which of the following countries contribute the maximum carbon monoxide into the atmosphere?
(a) Japan (b) Russia
(c) India (d) USA

534. The largest river basin in India is
(a) Ganga Basin (b) Yamuna Basin
(c) Gomati Basin (d) Kaveri Basin

535. Rise in temperature because of increased Greenhouse effect causes
(a) decrease in precipitation and soil moisture.
(b) melting of mountain glaciers and therapy blood.
(c) oceanic acidity.
(d) None of the above.

536. Siberian Ganes birds migrate to India in
(a) Summer (b) Winter
(c) Rains (d) None of these

537. Which of the following is not a method of solid waste management?
(a) Incineration (b) Comporting
(c) Handbill sites (d) None of these

538. The first biosphere reserve of India is at
(a) Jammu (b) Bharatpur
(c) Nilgiri (d) None of these

539. Which of the following metropolitan cities of India produce the maximum solid waste?
(a) Delhi (b) Chennai
(c) Kolkata (d) Mumbai

540. Chipko movement disfavoured
(a) the cutting of trees.
(b) the buildings of multipurpose.
(c) river valley project.
(d) the buildings of nuclear power stations.

541. Keibul Lamjao National Park is situated in
(a) Manipur (b) Meghalaya
(c) Nagaland (d) Tripura

542. A sudden movement of soil and weathered rock material down the slope under the force of gravity is called
(a) Landslide (b) Avalanches
(c) Disasters (d) None of these

543. The flow of energy from one trophic level to another is called
(a) Food chain (b) Food web
(c) Energy cycle (d) None of these

544. Match the List I with List II

List I
A. Chlorofluorocarbons
B. Sulphuric Acid
C. Carbon dioxide
D. 10,000 of population

List II
1. Acid Rains
2. Smog
3. Ozone depletion
4. Greenhouse effect

Codes:	A	B	C	D
(a)	1	2	3	4
(b)	4	3	2	1
(c)	3	1	4	2
(d)	2	3	1	4

545. Many people in Rajasthan have humped back due to the concentration of in water
(a) Fluoride (b) Chloride
(c) Lead (d) All of these

546. Which year is called the Year of Great Divide?
(a) 1921 (b) 1920
(c) 1930 (d) 1940

547. Rainwater harvesting will results in which of the following?
(a) To reduce run off.
(b) To avoid flooding of lanes.
(c) To meet the increasing demand of water.
(d) None of these.

548. What is Eutrophication?
(a) Phenomenal growth of few plants in nutrinent rich water of clues or ponds.
(b) Exercise accumulation of salt content in the soil.
(c) Cutting of trees in algae in water.
(d) All of these.

549. Which of the following is not a source of methane production?
(a) Burning of fossil fuels.
(b) Enteric Fermentation in cattle sheep and other animals.
(c) Automobiles using diesel and petrol.
(d) Anaerobic situation.

550. When Mercury-rich sludges were dumped from Minamata city to Minamata Bay (Japan) it caused
(a) Minamata disease
(b) Asbestosis
(c) Fluorisis
(d) None of these

551. The extensive growth of algae in water decreases
(a) Oxygen level of water
(b) CO_2 of water
(c) Both (a) and (b)
(d) Neither (a) nor (b)

ANSWERS

1. (b)	2. (a)	3. (d)	4. (c)	5. (d)	6. (c)
7. (d)	8. (c)	9. (a)	10. (a)	11. (c)	12. (b)
13. (d)	14. (b)	15. (d)	16. (d)	17. (d)	18. (d)
19. (d)	20. (b)	21. (c)	22. (c)	23. (d)	24. (b)
25. (a)	26. (b)	27. (b)	28. (a)	29. (b)	30. (d)
31. (a)	32. (c)	33. (a)	34. (d)	35. (b)	36. (a)
37. (c)	38. (b)	39. (b)	40. (d)	41. (d)	42. (b)
43. (c)	44. (b)	45. (c)	46. (c)	47. (b)	48. (b)
49. (a)	50. (d)	51. (c)	52. (b)	53. (d)	54. (a)
55. (d)	56. (b)	57. (d)	58. (a)	59. (a)	60. (a)
61. (c)	62. (b)	63. (b)	64. (c)	65. (c)	66. (a)
67. (d)	68. (b)	69. (a)	70. (d)	71. (b)	72. (d)
73. (a)	74. (d)	75. (d)	76. (c)	77. (b)	78. (b)
79. (c)	80. (c)	81. (c)	82. (a)	83. (d)	84. (b)
85. (d)	86. (d)	87. (c)	88. (a)	89. (b)	90. (b)
91. (d)	92. (d)	93. (b)	94. (d)	95. (a)	96. (b)

97. (a) 98. (d) 99. (a) 100. (d) 101. (c) 102. (b)
103. (d) 104. (c) 105. (b) 106. (d) 107. (a) 108. (a)
109. (b) 110. (b) 111. (b) 112. (a) 113. (d) 114. (d)
115. (d) 116. (d) 117. (b) 118. (a) 119. (a) 120. (b)
121. (a) 122. (d) 123. (d) 124. (c) 125. (c) 126. (b)
127. (d) 128. (c) 129. (c) 130. (a) 131. (b) 132. (a)
133. (b) 134. (a) 135. (b) 136. (a) 137. (d) 138. (b)
139. (d) 140. (c) 141. (c) 142. (a) 143. (c) 144. (b)
145. (c) 146. (b) 147. (a) 148. (d) 149. (a) 150. (a)
151. (d) 152. (a) 153. (b) 154. (d) 155. (c) 156. (d)
157. (b) 158. (d) 159. (a) 160. (a) 161. (b) 162. (b)
163. (a) 164. (c) 165. (b) 166. (b) 167. (b) 168. (b)
169. (a) 170. (c) 171. (d) 172. (d) 173. (c) 174. (a)
175. (d) 176. (b) 177. (c) 178. (b) 179. (d) 180. (b)
181. (b) 182. (d) 183. (d) 184. (a) 185. (c) 186. (b)
187. (b) 188. (a) 189. (a) 190. (a) 191. (c) 192. (c)
193. (d) 194. (b) 195. (a) 196. (b) 197. (c) 198. (b)
199. (d) 200. (d) 201. (b) 202. (a) 203. (c) 204. (b)
205. (b) 206. (b) 207. (a) 208. (b) 209. (c) 210. (d)
211. (c) 212. (d) 213. (b) 214. (b) 215. (d) 216. (c)
217. (a) 218. (b) 219. (c) 220. (d) 221. (a) 222. (c)
223. (c) 224. (b) 225. (b) 226. (b) 227. (a) 228. (c)
229. (c) 230. (c) 231. (c) 232. (a) 233. (a) 234. (c)
235. (c) 236. (c) 237. (d) 238. (a) 239. (c) 240. (a)
241. (c) 242. (d) 243. (a) 244. (a) 245. (c) 246. (c)
247. (c) 248. (a) 249. (c) 250. (b) 251. (b) 252. (a)
253. (b) 254. (c) 255. (c) 256. (b) 257. (d) 258. (a)
259. (a) 260. (d) 261. (b) 262. (d) 263. (a) 264. (a)
265. (b) 266. (a) 267. (d) 268. (b) 269. (b) 270. (b)
271. (c) 272. (d) 273. (b) 274. (a) 275. (c) 276. (c)
277. (b) 278. (b) 279. (a) 280. (b) 281. (b) 282. (d)
283. (c) 284. (c) 285. (d) 286. (a) 287. (d) 288. (d)
289. (c) 290. (d) 291. (d) 292. (a) 293. (a) 294. (b)
295. (a) 296. (a) 297. (a) 298. (b) 299. (d) 300. (c)

301. (d)	302. (a)	303. (d)	304. (a)	305. (a)	306. (b)
307. (d)	308. (b)	309. (d)	310. (d)	311. (c)	312. (d)
313. (d)	314. (c)	315. (c)	316. (c)	317. (c)	318. (a)
319. (c)	320. (c)	321. (a)	322. (d)	323. (b)	324. (c)
325. (d)	326. (a)	327. (d)	328. (a)	329. (c)	330. (a)
331. (b)	332. (d)	333. (a)	334. (a)	335. (d)	336. (a)
337. (d)	338. (c)	339. (a)	340. (a)	341. (c)	342. (b)
343. (a)	344. (d)	345. (c)	346. (a)	347. (c)	348. (a)
349. (d)	350. (d)	351. (b)	352. (d)	353. (c)	354. (b)
355. (b)	356. (d)	357. (a)	358. (a)	359. (c)	360. (a)
361. (c)	362. (a)	363. (a)	364. (b)	365. (a)	366. (b)
367. (d)	368. (d)	369. (c)	370. (d)	371. (c)	372. (a)
373. (a)	374. (d)	375. (d)	376. (a)	377. (c)	378. (d)
379. (d)	380. (d)	381. (c)	382. (a)	383. (b)	384. (a)
385. (c)	386. (a)	387. (a)	388. (a)	389. (c)	390. (a)
391. (b)	392. (a)	393. (d)	394. (c)	395. (a)	396. (b)
397. (c)	398. (a)	399. (c)	400. (c)	401. (b)	402. (c)
403. (b)	404. (a)	405. (b)	406. (b)	407. (c)	408. (b)
409. (a)	410. (c)	411. (d)	412. (a)	413. (d)	414. (b)
415. (a)	416. (d)	417. (d)	418. (a)	419. (c)	420. (c)
421. (a)	422. (a)	423. (b)	424. (b)	425. (c)	426. (a)
427. (c)	428. (a)	429. (a)	430. (c)	431. (b)	432. (a)
433. (d)	434. (c)	435. (b)	436. (d)	437. (d)	438. (b)
439. (d)	440. (d)	441. (b)	442. (c)	443. (d)	444. (a)
445. (d)	446. (c)	447. (d)	448. (a)	449. (a)	450. (a)
451. (d)	452. (a)	453. (a)	454. (c)	455. (d)	456. (c)
457. (a)	458. (d)	459. (c)	460. (d)	461. (a)	462. (b)
463. (d)	464. (b)	465. (b)	466. (a)	467. (c)	468. (c)
469. (b)	470. (d)	471. (b)	472. (d)	473. (d)	474. (c)
475. (a)	476. (d)	477. (c)	478. (a)	479. (a)	480. (d)
481. (a)	482. (a)	483. (a)	484. (a)	485. (c)	486. (b)
487. (a)	488. (a)	489. (c)	490. (c)	491. (c)	492. (d)
493. (d)	494. (b)	495. (a)	496. (a)	497. (c)	498. (b)
499. (a)	500. (a)	501. (c)	502. (d)	503. (a)	504. (c)

505. (d)	506. (c)	507. (c)	508. (c)	509. (a)	510. (d)
511. (a)	512. (a)	513. (b)	514. (b)	515. (b)	516. (a)
517. (a)	518. (b)	519. (a)	520. (b)	521. (c)	522. (c)
523. (c)	524. (d)	525. (a)	526. (b)	527. (d)	528. (a)
529. (c)	530. (d)	531. (d)	532. (a)	533. (d)	534. (a)
535. (a)	536. (c)	537. (c)	538. (c)	539. (d)	540. (a)
541. (a)	542. (a)	543. (a)	544. (c)	545. (a)	546. (d)
547. (a)	548. (a)	549. (a)	550. (a)	551. (a)	

10

Higher Education System: Governance, Polity and Administration

1. The ultimate purpose of Comparative Education is
   (a) closely studying the patterns of education in other countries.
   (b) exploring similarities and differences between system of education in different areas.
   (c) adapting feasible educational programs by scientifically studying these other regions.
   (d) studying the educational problems of a region in comparison with those of other regions.
2. A sector plan in education indicates
   (a) overall planning.
   (b) a limited area of planning.
   (c) planning for a region.
   (d) planning for a particular level of education.
3. Who said, "There should be no difference between the words and deeds of a teacher?"
   (a) Aristotle (b) Plato
   (c) MacKinnon (d) Rousseau
4. India is a
   (a) Secular State (b) Bilingual State
   (c) Communist State (d) Capitalist State
5. How many open universities are there in India?
   (a) 14 (b) 8
   (c) 11 (d) 7
6. What is the literal meaning of secularism?
   (a) Freedom to worship any God
   (b) Death of religion
   (c) Separation of religion from the state
   (d) None of these
7. Education and socio-economic development are related with each other in
   (a) Direct proportion
   (b) Indirect proportion
   (c) Some occasions
   (d) Infinite ratio
8. Education and socio-economic development are
   (a) related in direct proportion.
   (b) related in an indirect proportion.
   (c) sometimes related and sometimes not related.
   (d) not related.
9. According to Radhakrishnan Commission the aim of Higher Education is
   (a) to preserve democratic values and develop peace and harmony between individual and society.
   (b) to create a generation who respects old beliefs and develop intellectually having new faith in beliefs and ideologies and their coordination with old ones.
   (c) to develop and nourish young generation who can contribute towards politics, administration, profession, industry and commerce.
   (d) All of the above.

10. The Tenth Schedule to the Constitution of India relates to
    (a) Panchayati Raj Institutions.
    (b) Anti-defection Act.
    (c) List of languages recognised by the Constitution.
    (d) Procedure for amendment to the Constitution.
11. The aim of social reform is reflecting in the change of
    (a) Basic values of a society
    (b) Norms in the group
    (c) Religious practices
    (d) Habits of the individuals
12. Social reform aims at
    (a) changing basic values of society.
    (b) changing the norms of the group.
    (c) changing the religious practices.
    (d) changing the habits of the individuals.
13. Universities having central campus for imparting education are called
    (a) Central Universities
    (b) Deemed Universities
    (c) Residential Universities
    (d) Open Universities
14. The real powers in the Central Government are enjoyed, according to the Constitution of India by the
    (a) President of India
    (b) Vice-President of India
    (c) Prime Minister of India
    (d) Council of Ministers
15. Which of the following alternative reflects the traditional conception of aesthetic philosophy?
    (a) Beauty is the main theme in traditional aesthetics.
    (b) Architectural beauty never attained the artistic greatness.
    (c) Aesthetic philosophy is determined by the technical qualities of the art.
    (d) Love of wisdom supersedes the love of beauty.
16. The State in India spending the largest amount on primary education is
    (a) Maharashtra (b) Kerala
    (c) Gujarat (d) Tamil Nadu
17. In 1994-95 the UGC have launched the following programme
    (a) environmental sciences.
    (b) career orientation program.
    (c) Non-conventional energy studies program.
    (d) environment awareness program.
18. The Council of Ministers is responsible to the
    (a) President (b) Lok Sabha
    (c) Vice-President (d) Supreme Court
19. Poor enrolment of students in primary education in the rural areas is more because
    (a) Girls in villages have their marriages at an early age.
    (b) Boys within the range of age-group 6 to 9 are used to work in agricultural works instead of being admitted them to schools.
    (c) Generally students are having school-phobia.
    (d) Both (a) and (b).
20. The total number of Central Universities in India is
    (a) 41 (b) 30
    (c) 14 (d) 16
21. The Prime Minister is
    (a) nominated by the President.
    (b) elected by the Chief Ministers of States.

(c) is the leader of the majority party of Lok Sabha.
(d) is not elected; it is a hereditary post.

22. Education and population are related as follows
(a) Expansion of education leads to developing trends of small size family among educated males and females.
(b) Expansion of education can control growth-rate of population.
(c) Expansion of education makes population more qualitative.
(d) All of the above.

23. The quorum of the Parliament is fixed at
(a) one-tenth of the membership of the House.
(b) one-third of the membership of the House.
(c) one-half of the membership of the House.
(d) four-fifths of the membership of the House.

24. Which of the following methods do you employ in order to create social attitude among students?
(a) Teacher-centred approach
(b) Input-output method
(c) Collective processing method
(d) All the above

25. Individual differences in democracy are encouraged because
(a) of the guarantee of all kinds of freedom as a right provided by the constitution.
(b) in the long run individuals will act and think alike.
(c) they make diverse beneficial contributions to a common cause.
(d) political leaders want to achieve their selfish ends.

26. The organisation where a university has a separate campus for teaching purposes and there are many autonomous and constituent colleges affiliated to it are called
(a) a unitary university
(b) a centralised university
(c) a federal university
(d) All of the above

27. Why are the Fundamental Rights considered fundamental?
(a) Necessary for the successful working of democratic institution.
(b) Basic to the welfare, dignity and happiness of the individual.
(c) Constitution is based on these.
(d) Both (a) and (b).

28. The relationship between education and population can be described as
(a) Expansion of education leads to developing trends of small size family among educated males and females.
(b) Expansion of education can control growth rate of population.
(c) Expansion of education makes population more qualitative.
(d) All of the above.

29. Which categories of the following women appear in greater proportion in profession of nursing?
(a) Christian
(b) Hindu
(c) Muslim
(d) No pattern is reported

30. 'Complex of Colleges' is called
(a) Unitary University
(b) State University
(c) Federal University
(d) None of these

31. The Judges of the Supreme Court are appointed by the
    (a) Prime Minister of India
    (b) Speaker of the Lok Sabha
    (c) President of India
    (d) Ministry of Law and Justice
32. Educational process can be considered in relation to
    (a) Political system (b) Social system
    (c) Economic system (d) All the above
33. From the point of view of population control through family planning there should be
    (a) more literacy of males than females.
    (b) more literacy of women than men.
    (c) eradication of illiteracy of the old men.
    (d) emphasis on expansion of education.
34. Which of the following is not an aim of Higher education according to Kothari Commission?
    (a) To promote social justice and equality.
    (b) To explore innate abilities in persons and develop them through training.
    (c) To explore new knowledge in context of truth and interest it in terms of ancient knowledge and beliefs in contemporary needs.
    (d) To give right leadership in all the fields of life.
35. The President's Rule is imposed in a State or in a Union Territory when the
    (a) Governor of a State or the Chief Commissioner or a Lt. Governor advises the President to do so because the Government in that State/Territory cannot be carried on in accordance with the provisions of the Constitution.
    (b) Chief Minister of a State requests to this effect.
    (c) Chief Justice of the State High Court recommends through the Governor.
    (d) President knows best.
36. The basic cause of social change is
    (a) Political power system
    (b) Progress of economy
    (c) Education and legal system
    (d) All of the above
37. For raising the educational standards of the university
    (a) students opting for higher education should be selected on the basis of intellectual tests.
    (b) occupational and industrial development is essential with higher education.
    (c) state policy should be effective.
    (d) Both (a) and (b).
38. The Directive Principles
    (a) aim at establishing welfare state of Gandhian conception.
    (b) aim at giving ideals to be incorporated at a later stage.
    (c) aim at giving support to the Fundamental Rights.
    (d) Both (a) and (b).
39. If you talk about the bridging of higher education with modern technology for encouraging growth and production in higher education, to whom you would like to extend the responsibility for it?
    (a) Educationists (b) Experts
    (c) Economists (d) Technocrates
40. Which one of the following is an important occupation of educated women?
    (a) Teaching (b) Medicine
    (c) Nursing (d) All of these
41. Agriculture, including research and education, falls in

(a) State List
(b) Union List
(c) Concurrent List
(d) None of the above

42. Which one of the following alternative has judicious co-ordination with education policy?
(a) Human Resource Management
(b) State's own policies
(c) Economic Ideologies of the state
(d) Social pressures

43. For reducing expenditure on technical education
(a) technical educational institutions should start to take donations.
(b) it is necessary to reduce expenses on instruments and equipments of technical education.
(c) it is necessary to provide apprenticeship training through companies.
(d) it is necessary to reduce the number of technical educational institutions.

44. During the 10th five year plan the UGC has reserved 10% of the total allotted budged for
(a) West-Southern universities and their constituent colleges.
(b) Boarder universities and their constituent colleges.
(c) North-Western universities and their constituent colleges.
(d) North-Eastern universities and their constituent colleges.

45. Which of the following are the ideals set forth in the Preamble?
(a) Social, economic and political justice.
(b) Equality of status and of opportunity.
(c) Liberty of thought, expression, belief, faith and worship.
(d) All of the above.

46. If you are advocating the measure of population control through family planning, which one of the following method would you like to employ?
(a) Enhancing male literacy rate than the female literacy rate.
(b) Enhancing female literacy rate than the male literacy rate.
(c) Eradication of senile illiteracy.
(d) Enhancing expansion of education.

47. The higher education is still dominated by
(a) Mother-tongue (b) English
(c) Hindi (d) All of these

48. Sustainable human development, improvement in quality of teaching are development objectives of higher education of the following five year plan
(a) 1st five year plan
(b) 10th five year plan
(c) 9th five year plan
(d) 2nd five year plan

49. Fundamental Rights of the citizens are
(a) non-justiciable.
(b) justiciable.
(c) justiciable if the highest court feels it should be.
(d) some rights are justiciable while others are not.

50. In which one of the following areas a hearing-impaired child demonstrates inferiority incomparison than a normal children?
(a) Scholastic Achievement
(b) Linguistic Development
(c) Intellectual Development
(d) Emotional Development

51. The new education policy envisages major modifications in the system of education. It is implied that

(a) present education system is not consistent with national objectives and needs.
(b) present education system requires a great change.
(c) present education system is outdated.
(d) Both (a) and (b).

52. How many agricultural education institutes are there in India?
(a) 40 (b) 38
(c) 39 (d) 28

53. In India the executive is responsible directly to the
(a) Legislature (b) President
(c) Judiciary (d) People

54. The individual differences are promoted in Democratic system because
(a) It provides all sorts of guarantee to an individual as per Constitutional provisions.
(b) All individuals think and work uniformly after a certain period of life.
(c) They make diverse beneficial contributions to a common cause.
(d) It fulfils the vested interests of politicians.

55. Which one of the following difficulties occur in the rural area for continuing secondary education of girls?
(a) Parents do not desire to give co-education to their daughters along with boys.
(b) Poverty of parents.
(c) Help of girls in household work and work in agriculture.
(d) All of the above.

56. The project education method of teaching is associated with
(a) Frobel (b) Dewey
(c) Armstrong (d) Rousseau

57. Fundamental Rights of the Indian citizens are contained in the 'Indian Constitution'
(a) Part I (b) Part II
(c) Part III (d) Part IV

58. Which one of the following discoveries does not appear to be fulfilled through medical sciences?
(a) Eradication of infectious diseases like cholera and malaria, etc.
(b) Prevention of Small-Pox and Polio.
(c) Control over T.B.
(d) All of the above.

59. Political parties in democracy should not be banned because
(a) democracy cannot exist without political parties.
(b) if they are banned, there will be violation of the constitutional right of freedom of people.
(c) political parties mobilise the public opinion in an organised way.
(d) All of the above.

60. "School is life, not a preparation for life". It is an important aspect of the educational philosophy of
(a) Robert Hutchins
(b) Dr. Radhakrishnan
(c) Mortimer Adler
(d) John Dewey

61. Of which fundamental right is a foreigner in India deprived of?
(a) To seek justice in court.
(b) To seek security of life.
(c) To criticise policies of government.
(d) To vote at the time of Parliamentary election.

62. Which women's community is having largest share in nursing profession?
(a) Anglo-Indians (b) Christian
(c) Hindu (d) Both (a) and (b)

63. The main problem for determining educational policy in India is that
   (a) people having higher technical education do not have employment opportunities at all.
   (b) people of higher technical education have unemployment.
   (c) people with higher technical education do not find enough opportunity in India.
   (d) All of the above.
64. Find out the intelligence test which is individually administrated from the choices given below.
   (a) Kuhlman-Anderson
   (b) Pinter-Cunningham Primary
   (c) WISC
   (d) Army Alpha
65. Freedom of the Press as such
   (a) has been guaranteed by the Constitution.
   (b) has not been expressly guaranteed by the Constitution.
   (c) has been given only to selected institutions.
   (d) None of the above.
66. If you are interested in the progress of University Education which one of the following measures would you like to employ?
   (a) Students for university education should be selected through intellectual tests.
   (b) University education should be integrated with industrial and vocational development.
   (c) State policies must be implemented in effective manner.
   (d) Both (a) and (b).
67. Which one of the following are the effects of the World War II on trends of education?
   (a) Increase in technological training.
   (b) Schools as stronger base for national policy of education.
   (c) Improvement in the articulation between high school and college.
   (d) Both (b) and (c).
68. Learning, work and play have equal importance in
   (a) Wennetka plan
   (b) Garry's plan
   (c) Dalton scheme of education
   (d) Montessori method
69. The Rajya Sabha is
   (a) dissolved once in two years.
   (b) dissolved after every four years.
   (c) adjourned every six months.
   (d) not subject to dissolution.
70. In the rural sector the responsibility of primary education lies on
   (a) Gram Panchayat
   (b) District Council
   (c) Co-operative Societies
   (d) Both (a) and (b)
71. The workload on the teacher is very high in the following education technique
   (a) Kindergarten method
   (b) Hebert's five-stage method
   (c) Project education technique
   (d) Play-way technique
72. Administrative Law means
   (a) law passed by the Union
   (b) law or rules made by the executive
   (c) laws relating to administration of non-Governmental institutions
   (d) All of the above.
73. What is your opinion about modern popular system of education?
   (a) It imparts education according to social status (Strata).
   (b) It imparts common education to all strata of society.

(c) It sponsors the general nature of teaching.
(d) A number of stratification are available in education system in vogue.

74. Open learning institutions differ from the formal education institutions in that
(a) the former offers more courses than the latter.
(b) the former offers more flexibility in choice of course.
(c) the latter implements more-flexible evaluation pattern.
(d) the teaching process is given more importance than the learning by open learning institutions.

75. The scheme used for knowledge lessons is
(a) Dalton's scheme
(b) Hebert's five-stage system
(c) Glover's scheme
(d) Garry's scheme

76. The Legislative Council of a State is a
(a) temporary body
(b) permanent body
(c) semi-permanent body
(d) chamber of the nominated members

77. It is said about India that the Educational Revolution is delayed. The major reason of it is
(a) apathy of Indian Govt. towards it.
(b) the expenditure incurred by the Government on education is supposed to be expenditure on consumption.
(c) a major proportion of society does not have zeal for education.
(d) All of the above.

78. The education of primitive man was concerned with
(a) vocational element
(b) religious element
(c) moral element
(d) All of the above

79. Five-year plan in India is finally approved by
(a) Union Cabinet
(b) President on the advice of Prime Minister
(c) Planning Commission
(d) National Development Council

80. The Lok Sabha and the Rajya Sabha sit jointly when
(a) they like.
(b) there is a disagreement between the two (Houses).
(c) the President summons both the Houses.
(d) they must meet when two years have lapsed after the last meeting.

81. If you are thinking that the expenditure on technical education should be curtailed, which of the following measure do you feel suitable for it?
(a) Technical Institutes should receive donations against admissions from the students.
(b) Technical Institutes should curtail a large expenditures on their workshop, instruments and apparatuses.
(c) Technical Institutes should make efforts for providing Apprenticeship training to her students in selected comparison.
(d) It is better to reduce the number of technical institutes in India in order to control academic devaluation in the name of quantitative progress of the institutions.

82. In India we are facing a problem of quantitative growth of higher education. The best solution could be to
(a) use satellites to teach all the courses.
(b) accept the facts and maintain the status quo.

(c) make higher education costlier so as to prevent students going for higher education.
(d) provide alternative opportunities for lifelong learning.

83. Who put forward the principle of "Pupil activity"?
(a) Montague (b) Rousseau
(c) Binet (d) Comenius

84. Ministers in the Union Cabinet are appointed by the
(a) Prime Minister
(b) President
(c) President of India on the advice of the Prime Minister
(d) Prime Minister on the advice of the Chief Justice of the Supreme Court of India

85. During post-independence era there was a huge expansion in public and private sectors. Which one of the following view is appeared to be relevant about the growth in employment opportunities in these sectors?
(a) The employment opportunities are governing for the young people coming from the old educated upper class on a large scale.
(b) The employment opportunities are growing for the young people coming from the new educated backward class on a large scale.
(c) The employment opportunities are declined for the young people coming from the old educated upper class.
(d) The employment opportunities are rising for the young people coming from the newly literate backward class.

86. What is your opinion about religious studies in educational institutions?
(a) It should be prevented.
(b) It should be discouraged.
(c) It must be such that it should nourish humanitarian values.
(d) Educational institutes should be non-secular.

87. Herbert is known as
(a) the father of philosophy
(b) the father of teaching
(c) the father of educational psychology
(d) the father of child psychology

88. Who administers the Union Territories?
(a) The President through the Administrators appointed by him.
(b) The Prime Minister of India.
(c) The Law Minister, Government of India.
(d) The Attorney-General of India.

89. What is your opinion about the super educated class?
(a) This class is not committed for his social commitments at all
(b) This class is fully committed for his social commitments
(c) This class is quite aware about his social commitments
(d) All of the above

90. Which of the following bodies grants funds for higher education?
1. UGC
2. State Government
3. Municipal Corporation and Zila Parishad
4. Central Government
(a) Only (1)
(b) Both (3) and (4)
(c) (1), (2) and (4)
(d) All of the above

91. Which of the following is not the federal feature of the Indian Constitution?

(a) There is distribution of Powers in accordance with 2 lists
(b) Written and rigid constitution
(c) Independent Judiciary
(d) All of the above

92. During independence the main aim of Indian National Congress is to uplift the disadvantaged group of population in India because
(a) The leaders of Indian National Congress had great respect to this feeling propagated by Mahatma Gandhi.
(b) The leaders of Indian National Congress were quite aware about it.
(c) It was the result of the effects of Dr. Bhimrao Ambedkar and Mahatma Phule on INC's ideologies.
(d) All of the above.

93. The formal education
(a) makes man well civilized.
(b) is not that it makes man well civilized.
(c) may develop bad trends.
(d) Any of these.

94. How many Indian Institutes of Technology are their in India?
(a) One (b) Four
(c) Sixteen (d) Nine

95. Directive Principles of State Policy aim at
(a) ensuring individual liberty.
(b) ensuring and strengthening the country's independence.
(c) protecting the depressed classes.
(d) providing social and economic base for genuine democracy in the country.

96. The barrier to female education is
(a) no adequate facilities of schooling to girls.
(b) a large number of dropouts in case of girls recruited in the school.
(c) parents not willing to send their daughters to school.
(d) Both (a) and (b).

97. The main drawback in today's education system that promotes 'educated unemployed' is that
(a) the objective of education is not void.
(b) education gives theoretical knowledge only.
(c) professional education is not a part of education.
(d) None of these.

98. The Council of Ministers, headed by the Prime Minister is responsible to
(a) Prime Minister (b) President
(c) Parliament (d) Speaker

99. Generally from time to time the debate has been raised that the historians distort the historical events. What is your opinion in this context?
(a) Generally the people in a society have faith in the truth excavated by the historians.
(b) It is great confusion to expect truths in historical events discovered by the established historians.
(c) Both of the above.
(d) None of the above.

100. Women are not willing to work in rural areas because of
(a) nuisance by ruling people in villages.
(b) increasing trend of rowdiness.
(c) unfavourable attitude of rural society to working women.
(d) All of the above.

101. Who stated "In school, provisions must be made for free and natural expressions of a child?"
(a) Lyndon (b) Ryebum
(c) T. Remont (d) Montessori

102. Usually a Gram Panchayat is not responsible for
   (a) construction of village roads and tanks.
   (b) sanitation, maternity and child welfare.
   (c) financing of agriculturists.
   (d) agricultural production.

103. The New Education Policy 1986 envisages major reforms in the existing education system. It comprises of
   (a) Existing Education System is not consistent with National objectives and needs
   (b) Existing Education System requires a great change
   (c) Existing Education System is outdated
   (d) Both (a) and (b)

104. You are pressurised by the colleagues to accept membership of the Teachers' union. What decision will you take?
   (a) You will not accept membership to avoid enmity with the management.
   (b) You will accept membership for promoting the strength and interest of the Teaching community.
   (c) You do not like politics of any kind. So you will not accept membership.
   (d) For maintaining day-to-day relations with your colleagues, you accept membership.

105. Mainstreaming is a term associated with
   (a) education for the handicapped.
   (b) education of environment.
   (c) career consultation.
   (d) inter-age class groupings.

106. Which one of the following provides constitutional guarantee of personal freedom?
   (a) Quo Warranto (b) Mandamus
   (c) Certiorari (d) Habeas Corpus

107. The problem of juvenile delinquency is basically associated with
   (a) The children belong to low SES in society.
   (b) The children reared in problematic houses.
   (c) The children of NRTs.
   (d) A number of complicated problems.

108. In medieval universities the students mostly learned by
   (a) listening to libraries
   (b) laboratory experimentation
   (c) reading *Bible*
   (d) listening to lecturers

109. What does the Panchayati Raj System signify?
   (a) Single-tier structure of local Government.
   (b) Double-tier system of self Government.
   (c) Three-tier structure of local Govt. at the village, block and district level.
   (d) None of the above.

110. In present context, the correct statement about the primary education appears to be associated with
   (a) Child-centred approach in education.
   (b) Curriculum-centred approach in education.
   (c) Subject-oriented approach in education.
   (d) All of the above.

111. The most prominent difference between Informal Education and Non-formal Education is that
   (a) The former is organised, the latter is not organised.
   (b) The former is not organised, the latter is organised.
   (c) The former occurs within the institution, the latter occurs outside the institution.
   (d) The former is subjective, the latter is objective.

112. Following term refers to the education of the handicaps
(a) protective testing
(b) mainstreaming
(c) least restrictive environment
(d) inkblot

113. Out of the following, in which lesson, a geneal rule is explained first and then, knowledge is accumulated on the basis of that rule?
(a) Deductive lesson
(b) Inductive lesson
(c) Developing lesson
(d) Knowledge lesson

114. Which one of the following responsibilities must be fulfilled by the school personnel in your opinion?
(a) The personnel should maintain harmony between the needs of the child and the demands of the society.
(b) The personnel should adjust the child to conform to the demands of the society.
(c) The personnel should change the human nature according to social norms.
(d) All of the above.

115. The phrase, "equal educational opportunity" means
(a) Providing equal opportunity to have the type of education for which one is suited.
(b) Provision of the same type of education for all.
(c) Providing opportunity for all to get education at any level.
(d) Ensuring admission to all for the desired stream of education.

116. National institute of immunology is situated in
(a) Hyderabad (b) Chennai
(c) Chandigarh (d) Delhi

117. For knowledge lessons
(a) Glover's scheme is used.
(b) Herbart's five-stage system is used.
(c) Garry's scheme is used.
(d) None of the above.

118. The fundamental goal of modern school is
(a) To develop adequate behaviour of students.
(b) To develop ethical values in students.
(c) To develop socially acceptable behaviour in students.
(d) To develop creativity and individuality in students.

119. Which is not an important aim of educational guidance?
(a) To help the students to find out their physical, mental and education handicaps.
(b) To help the students to know about further educational channels available.
(c) To give speed coaching to selected students in various subjects.
(d) To help the students to adjust themselves to the curriculum, the college and the social life connected with it.

120. When a pupil fails in a test for which he did not study and tells that he failed because his teacher is partial then he utilises
(a) Conversion (b) Rationalisation
(c) Compensation (d) Sympathies

121. Generally the language is supposed to be
(a) A nomenclature for categorising experiences.
(b) A medium of self-development.
(c) A medium for social communication.
(d) A system of symbols for problem-solving effectively.

122. Permanent change in pupil behaviour can be brought about by
(a) Teaching procedures
(b) Learning experiences
(c) Physical activities
(d) Recitation

123. Recreational reading should be
(a) an integral part of the language arts curriculum.
(b) an integral part of the science curriculum.
(c) an integral part of homework.
(d) an assignment to be done at library.

124. "This methodology trains the child to search for facts, rules and principles by his own efforts, organise the set of knowledge gained and delineate general rules." The aforementioned statement is about the following methodology of teaching
(a) Montessory (b) Kindergarten
(c) Heuristic (d) Play-way

125. Industry and Commerce both have the common objective of
(a) Welfare of the masses
(b) National progress
(c) Satisfaction of consumers
(d) Wealth and profit

126. Education as an investment aims at
(a) Enhancing productivity
(b) Cultural development
(c) Development of democratic outlook
(d) Satisfaction of learners

127. The Gestalt learning theory embodies that
(a) learning takes place through stimulus response.
(b) learning takes place through writing.
(c) learning takes place through insight.
(d) learning takes place through cramming.

128. In the project education technique, the workload on the teacher is
(a) very high
(b) comparatively low
(c) low
(d) nil

129. Curriculum planning is a part of the sub-system of
(a) educational management
(b) educational facilities
(c) educational communication
(d) educational activity

130. Full form of NAAC is
(a) National Assessment and Accreditation Council
(b) National Aeronautics and Aeroplane Council
(c) All of these
(d) None of these

131. In Garry's Plan
(a) work is important
(b) play is important
(c) learning is important
(d) all these three have equal importance

132. What is your opinion about enrichment of university courses through Distance Education?
(a) It should be enriched to its maximum so that the people gets its maximum advantage.
(b) It should not be enriched because it brings down the qualitative education to a great extent.
(c) Both of the above statements are correct.
(d) Both of the above statements are incorrect.

133. Extension Education is understood as
(a) extending new knowledge to the doorstep of those who need it.
(b) extending educational opportunities to the deprived.

(c) a program for educating the farmers.
(d) education meant to spread knowledge among villagers.

134. Under the Wennetka Plan
(a) the diversity of interests of the students is recognised.
(b) the diversities of abilities are accepted.
(c) the diversities of needs are accepted.
(d) All of these are recognised.

135. What is your opinion about teacher's strike in teaching profession?
(a) The strikes in teaching profession should be banned completely because it causes great harm of student community.
(b) The strikes in teaching profession should be abolished because it is against the professional ethics of teaching.
(c) The strikes should be recognised in teaching profession because it fulfils the demands of the teachers like other personnel in the society.
(d) None of the above.

136. If something a new or original is noticed in the activities of a learner, then which of the following terms can describe him best?
(a) Intelligent (b) Creative
(c) Critical (d) Motivated

137. Vigyan Prasar, New Delhi is a/an
(a) unit of the CSIR
(b) unit of the ICCR
(c) autonomous institute set up by the development of science and technology
(d) department of IGNOU

138. The Dalton Scheme of education is useful for which one of the following?
(a) For infants
(b) For little children
(c) For older children
(d) For all of these

139. The most effective impression can be provided to learners by
(a) charts and maps
(b) black board presentations
(c) sound film projector
(d) meaningful verbal explanation

140. A Sport's University which is Asia's first of its kind functions in
(a) Kochi (b) Pune
(c) Wardha (d) Gandhinagar

141. Why do you not support the five-stage method of Herbart?
(a) In this, there is no scope for the individual diversity of students.
(b) Under this, it is difficult to make coordination between various subjects.
(c) Under this, generalisation is not required to be done while teaching subjects like language, history, geography, etc.
(d) All of the above.

142. In order to listen effectively, we have to guard against the tendency of skipping over ideas which we dislike to hear. The statement from this information can be concluded as follows. Point out the correct alternative.
(a) Some people have tendency of skipping over ideas and dislikes.
(b) Skipping over unwanted ideas leads to effective learning.
(c) Listening only to favourite ideas is the tendency of people.
(d) People should not have likes and dislikes in order to have effective listening.

143. The most important factor in teaching in higher education is to
(a) Supply the relevant information to students

(b) Prepare students for the various competitive examinations
(c) Lead students to the sources of information
(d) Develop a spirit of competition for higher achievement in students

144. Aligarh Muslim University was founded by
(a) Jinnah
(b) Syed Ahmed Khan
(c) Abdul Kalam Azad
(d) Bhutto

145. "In the school, provisions must be made for free and natural expressions of a child." Who give this statement?
(a) T. Remont (b) Ryeburn
(c) Montessori (d) Lyndon

146. The existing system of education has the following defects. Which one of them appears to be most significant?
(a) The inability to access the informations given to the children, whether those are correct or incorrect.
(b) Emphasis on Essay type examination of long duration.
(c) Improper assessment of the students.
(d) Emphasis on fulfilling the students, brain with the informations like a storehouse.

147. In higher education, students are better motivated through
(a) Competition
(b) Personal achievements
(c) Co-operation
(d) Individual attention

148. The Chancellor of the West Bengal National University of Juridical Sciences is the
(a) Chief Justice of India
(b) Union Law Minister
(c) Governor of West Bengal
(d) Chief Justice of Kolkata High Court

149. According to Dewry, education is a
(a) Social need
(b) Personal need
(c) Psychological need
(d) Theoretical need

150. Social workers can have the following good approach to deal with a group of delinquent children. Which one?
(a) To develop friendly relations before trying to reform them.
(b) To make them fully busy with some constructive activity.
(c) To praise them for their good behaviour.
(d) To advise them in different ways.

151. Earlier Indian Mathematicians had taught that x/0 = x, who proved that it was infinity?
(a) Brahmagupta (b) Lilavati
(c) Bhaskara (d) Mahavira

152. In the context of education, some views of Gandhiji have been appended below. Which one of them is incorrect?
(a) In education, experimentation, work and research must be given due places.
(b) Education must be self-dependent.
(c) Literacy is education.
(d) Education must be such as to develop all the powers and inherent qualities of children.

153. Which one of the following is regarded as an immediate need of an educational organisation?
(a) To focus on Employment opportunities.
(b) To ensure self-employment capabilities in the students.

(c) To make provision of maximum service opportunities.
(d) To enrich the knowledge of future generation.

154. Many individuals accept employment in educational fields, because of
(a) their zeal for imparting knowledge.
(b) lack of job opportunities elsewhere.
(c) considering teaching profession as their aim.
(d) lively interest in acquisition of knowledge.

155. The Dravidian University is located at
(a) Hoskota (Karnataka)
(b) Kuppam (Andhra Pradesh)
(c) Kaladi (Kerala)
(d) Kumbakonam (Tamil Nadu)

156. Who is known as the father of educational psychology?
(a) Pestology (b) Devy
(c) Herbart (d) Spencer

157. The main difficulties in determining the education policy in India is that
(a) People having higher technical education do not have employment opportunities at all.
(b) People with higher technical education have unemployment.
(c) People with higher technical education do not find enough opportunity in India.
(d) All of the above.

158. Approach towards education should be
(a) Imparting knowledge
(b) Investment in human resources
(c) Sacred mission
(d) Employment-oriented

159. The youngest unit of CSIR, the Institute of Genomics and Integrative Biology (IGIB), is located at
(a) Ahmedabad (b) Bangalore
(c) Chandigarh (d) New Delhi

160. "There should be no difference between the words and deeds of a teacher." Who gave this statement?
(a) Mckennan (b) John Locke
(c) Rousseau (d) Aristotle

161. Which of the following was not consisted in the recommendations of National Policy on Education, 1986.
(a) Redesigning courses
(b) Expansion of institutions
(c) Training of teachers
(d) Training of guardians

162. Which among the following National Institutes, has been wrongly matched?
(a) National Institute of Homeopathy — Kolkata
(b) National Institute of Naturopathy — Pune
(c) National Institute of Medicine — Hyderabad
(d) National Institute of Unani Medicine — Bangalore

163. Generally it is observed that as the Government has attempted to strengthen the Panchayati Raj System in rural India, it becomes more and more negligent towards primary education. What is the reason of this state in your opinion?
(a) The rural folk takes it as the germinating ground of their own leadership.
(b) The villagers treat it as their power-mongering system.
(c) The villagers should not be given the administrative and financial rights.
(d) The Village Panchayats are generally governed by illiterates therefore they do not have any bearing upon education.

164. The National Policy of Education, 1986 recommended for
   (a) Reorganisation of education
   (b) Use of English in wide range
   (c) Use of Sanskrit in wide range
   (d) None of the above

165. The first fully literate district north of the Vindhyas is
   (a) Ajmer (b) Ahmedabad
   (c) Mau (d) North Parganas

166. Personalised system of education
   (a) does not inculcate a feeling of socialisation in students.
   (b) does not inculcate a feeling of competition in students.
   (c) leads to wastage of time and energy.
   (d) All of these are true.

167. The responsibility of primary education in rural region is lying with
   (a) Village Panchayat
   (b) Zila Samiti
   (c) Cooperative Societies
   (d) Both (a) and (b)

168. The Indira Gandhi National Open University came into existence in
   (a) April, 1985
   (b) September, 1985
   (c) April, 1977
   (d) September, 1977

169. The National Museum in New Delhi is
   (a) attached to the Delhi University
   (b) a Deemed University
   (c) a subordinate office of the J.N.U.
   (d) part of Ministry of Tourism and Culture

170. The educational system of today promotes "educated unemployment". The reason is that
   (a) education gives theoretical knowledge only.
   (b) professional education is not a part of education.
   (c) the objective of education is not vivid.
   (d) All of the above.

171. The main point of distinction between open learning and the formal education is
   (a) The former offers more courses than the later
   (b) The former offers more flexibility in choice of courses
   (c) The later implements more flexible evaluation pattern
   (d) The teaching process is given more importance than the learning by open learning institutions

172. Who among the following gave particular attention to establishment of comprehensive institutions for the rural people starting at the early childhood level going upto the highest?
   (a) Mahatma Gandhi
   (b) Rabindranath Tagore
   (c) Vivekananda
   (d) Both (a) and (b)

173. The National Centre for Nuclear Science and Mathematics is located at
   (a) Kalpakkam (Near Chennai)
   (b) Colaba (Mumbai)
   (c) Kota (Rajasthan)
   (d) Karwar (Karnataka)

174. The teacher ought to know about the problems prevalent in the field of education. The reason is that
   (a) only a teacher can do something about solving them.
   (b) he can tell about the same to another teacher.
   (c) teachers can tell the government about it.
   (d) with this knowledge, the teacher can have information about education.

175. The Plato's Theory of Education includes
   (a) Education is for physical fitness and unfit should be eliminated.
   (b) Education is for life but not for its preparation.
   (c) Unacceptance of mental discipline.
   (d) Plato's science for workers and dialects for rulers.

176. In the year 1947-48, the number of technical institutions at degree level was
   (a) 38 (b) 35
   (c) 40 (d) 70

177. The college of Combat (of the Indian Army) has been renamed as
   (a) Army War College
   (b) National Defence College
   (c) Army Defence Institute
   (d) College of Military Intelligence

178. In the wake of serious shortages of resources and rising population of our nation, you have the following views about the programs for improving the standards of education (under the aegis of national policy of education).
   (a) They are impractical.
   (b) They are courageous and laudable efforts.
   (c) They are new forms of traditional programs.
   (d) They increase the workload of teachers.

179. The phrase Education according to nature has the following meaning
   (a) Back to nature.
   (b) Study of Natural laws and their application to process of education.
   (c) To educate according to the law of nature of human development.
   (d) All of the above.

180. Value education should help in
   (a) Increasing states income.
   (b) Increasing teachers income.
   (c) Controlling guardian's expenditure on child's schooling.
   (d) Eliminating violence fanaticism.

181. The specific objective of Higher Education as mentioned by the Ministry of Human Resource Development Report (2002-2003) is
   (a) emphasis on quality evaluation and accreditation.
   (b) emphasis on research and development.
   (c) emphasis on relevance of higher Education.
   (d) All of the above.

182. In your view, arrangement for "education on environment" in the school
   (a) is important for creating an awareness among students about the environment.
   (b) is likely to put more burden on students.
   (c) is a mode of entertainment for students.
   (d) is like giving work to teachers.

183. The meaning of Equal Educational opportunities is lying in the following alternative
   (a) Equality of type of education to all children.
   (b) Equality of standards of education for every child.
   (c) Equal opportunity of the type of education of which one has studied.
   (d) Equality in education opportunity to all the children.

184. Which of the followings can be included under the group of ultimate values
   (a) Goodness (b) Truth
   (c) Beauty (d) All of the above

185. The total number of Women's University is
(a) 4 (b) 3
(c) 5 (d) 2

186. In the school, "education on environment" can be imparted by
(a) Lectures
(b) Articles
(c) Sports
(d) Adopting it ourselves

187. The education of primitive man was related with
(a) Vocational development
(b) Religious development
(c) Moral development
(d) All of the above

188. Hedonism is a theory which believes in
(a) happiness as the ultimate value.
(b) liberation of the soul.
(c) ignorance is the cause of suffering.
(d) None of the above.

189. The total number of PhD's awarded till 2003 throughout the country is
(a) 11,450 (b) 11,400
(c) 10,450 (d) 2000

190. The major objective of education is
(a) reforming the society.
(b) making students discipline.
(c) developing inherent abilities/powers of students.
(d) making students followers of teachers.

191. Generally it is assumed that in India we are facing a problem of quantitative growth of higher educations. What will the best solution for it in your opinion?
(a) Application of satellite instruction throughout country.
(b) Blindly accept the pitfalls and maintain the *status quo*.
(c) Raise the cost of higher education in order to prevent the access of everyone.
(d) Provide alternative opportunities for lifelong learning.

192. The philosophy of materialism has been derived from
(a) the World (b) Matter
(c) God (d) Soul

193. Rev. P.T. Chandi was associated with
(a) Affiliating University's Standardisation Committee.
(b) Federal University Standard Committee.
(c) the Committee for University Administrative Legislation.
(d) the Committee for College Administrative Legislation.

194. Adult education should be under the authority of the following
(a) The government
(b) Non-government organisations
(c) Educated persons
(d) All of the above

195. In case of implementation of Religious education in the institutes of higher learning what is your own point of view in this regard?
(a) It should be checked immediately.
(b) It is quite essential in present context.
(c) It is upto such extent that it should strengthen the human values.
(d) The institutes of higher learning should be secular in nature.

196. Two ways of imparting value education are
(a) Incidental and accidental
(b) Systematic and non-systematic
(c) Direct and indirect
(d) None of the above

197. The Chairman of the UGC Committee 1969 who was appointed for

Administrative Legislation of University was
(a) Dr. P.B. Gajendragadkar
(b) Dr. Zakir Hussain
(c) None of the above
(d) All of these

198. Education not only conserves the culture of a nation, but also it
(a) makes the latter rich.
(b) defines the latter.
(c) makes the latter spiritual.
(d) makes the latter mass-oriented and popular.

199. The difference between the university and the deemed university is that the former
(a) is much bigger in size.
(b) is established by the act of legislature.
(c) is established by the central government.
(d) looks after only affiliated colleges.

200. Sri Prakash committee was set up in
(a) 1970-71 (b) 1965-66
(c) 1984-85 (d) 1959-60

201. Total No. of Teachers employed for Higher Education in India are
(a) 4.75 Lakh (b) 2.35 Lakh
(c) 6.05 Lakh (d) None of these

202. Indian Institute of Advanced studies is located in
(a) Shimla (b) Solan
(c) Dharmshala (d) Chandigarh

203. Which of the following agency grants aid to Higher education?
(a) UGC
(b) State government
(c) Municipal corporation
(d) Central government

204. Which of the following is not recommended by Sri Prakash Committee
(a) teaching moral values
(b) silent meditation
(c) co-curricular activities
(d) None of the above

205. According to Radhakrishnan Commission, the aim of Higher Education is
(a) to preserve the democratic values and develop peace and harmony.
(b) to develop great personalities who can give their contributions in politics, administration and Industry and commerce.
(c) Both (a) and (b).
(d) None of the above.

206. All India Institute of Medical Sciences (AIIMS) is located in
(a) Lucknow (b) Delhi
(c) Mumbai (d) Chennai

207. The Formal Education is
(a) making a man civilized.
(b) making a devil out of a man.
(c) developing bad behaviour in a man.
(d) None of the above.

208. The period of Indian Education Commission was
(a) 1965-66 (b) 1945-46
(c) 1964-66 (d) 1945-47

209. The most important area of school supervision should be
(a) developmental aspects.
(b) school environment.
(c) instructional work.
(d) pupil growth.

210. NASA is the name of space agency of
(a) Netherlands (b) Britain
(c) America (d) India

211. Generally it has been observed that the females are not interested for serving in rural areas. What is the reason of it in your opinion?

(a) The misbehaviour of rural population towards the working women.
(b) Generally the working women's are the prey of eve-teasing and filthy advancements of rural population.
(c) Generally rural folks have gender discrimination.
(d) All of the above.

212. The Indian Education Commission recommended for
(a) time-table
(b) suitable teachers
(c) methods of moral teaching
(d) All of the above

213. The George-Deen Act provided mainly for federal aid to
(a) agricultural college.
(b) industrial education.
(c) distributive occupational training.
(d) public service occupations.

214. National Defence Academy (NDA) is situated at
(a) Khadakwasla (Pune)
(b) Dehradun
(c) Allahabad
(d) Chennai

215. The biggest obstacle in the way of women's education is
(a) Inadequate facilities for schooling of girls.
(b) Highest rate of wastage and stagnation in girl's education.
(c) Parental unwillingness to send their daughters to school.
(d) Both (a) and (b).

216. Health value develops
(a) Physical aesthetics
(b) Mental aesthetics
(c) Spiritual power
(d) All of the above

217. Which of the following is not a basic problem faced by vocational education since World War II?
(a) The lack of a constant pattern in types of vocational training.
(b) The extent and nature of federal aid for vocational education.
(c) The length of time and amount of training needed for economic, etc.
(d) The extent to which the vocational school should train for specific skills.

218. Air Force Administrative College is situated in
(a) Hyderabad (b) Coimbatore
(c) Bidar (d) Agra

219. Suppose you are forced to seek membership of the teacher's union. What decision you would like to take under these conditions?
(a) You will not accept the membership because you feel that it develops enmity with the management.
(b) You will accept the membership because you feel that it enhances the moral support to teacher's community.
(c) You will not accept membership because you have develop feelings of hatredness towards political parties.
(d) You will accept membership because you feel that it enhances sweet relationship with your colleagues.

220. Patriotic values are included under the groups of
(a) social values (b) moral values
(c) health values (d) ultimate values

221. A Vestibule school was a
(a) correspondence school
(b) public trade school
(c) school for apprentices
(d) school run by a factory

222. Educating health values includes
(a) Schools should have first aid box
(b) Medical inspection of the students
(c) Ventilation in schools
(d) All of the above

223. Historically, vocational education in the West was introduced by
(a) the industrial revolution
(b) progressive educational scheme
(c) the middle class capitalistic system
(d) renaissance

224. Indian Institute of Science (IISc) is located in
(a) Chennai (b) Kolkata
(c) Bangalore (d) Mumbai

225. The Ishwarbhai Patel Committee was set up in
(a) 1977 (b) 1985
(c) 1967 (d) 1992

226. The educational philosophy of Swami Dayananda suggests
(a) a non-formal approach to pre-primary education.
(b) a formal approach to pre-primary education.
(c) a non-formal approach to co-education.
(d) a formal approach to education at all stages.

227. Bhabha Atomic Research Centre (BARC) is situated at
(a) Hyderabad
(b) Bangalore
(c) Delhi
(d) Trombay (Mumbai)

228. The meaning of the popular phrase 'Educational Equal Opportunity' is
(a) Providing equal opportunities to have the type of education for which one is suited.
(b) Provision of the same type of education for all.
(c) Providing opportunities for all to get education at any level.
(d) Ensuring admission to all for the desired stream of education.

229. The Ishwarbhai Patel Committee recommended for
(a) work experience
(b) value oriented education
(c) women legislation
(d) None of the above

230. Health education is synonymous with
(a) Hygiene (b) Physiology
(c) Health (d) None of these

231. Indian School of Mines is situated at
(a) Patna (Bihar)
(b) Dhanbad (Jharkhand)
(c) Kolkata (W. Bengal)
(d) Guwahati (Assam)

232. Which one of the following is not an important aim of guidance?
(a) To help the students in order to find out their physical, mental and educational handicaps.
(b) To help the students to know about further educational streams available.
(c) To give special coaching to selected students in various subjects.
(d) To help the students to adjust themselves to the curriculum, the college, and the social life connected with it.

233. Value oriented education develops
(a) cultural values
(b) vocational efficiency
(c) character
(d) All of the above

234. The 1947 UNESCO Seminar centred around the caption

(a) educational and the changing societies.
(b) national and international problems in education.
(c) education for internationalism.
(d) All of the above.

235. How many Indian Institutes of Management (IIM) are there in India?
(a) Thirteen (b) Seven
(c) Five (d) Eight

236. If you are interested to bring the desirable and permanent change in the behaviour of your students, what type of measures would you like to accept?
(a) By changing teaching processes.
(b) By changing learning experience.
(c) Through physical activities.
(d) Through method of recitation.

237. The total number of Central Universities in India on 31st December, 2009 was
(a) 10 (b) 41
(c) 25 (d) 31

238. Ancient Indian Educational Centres were located in Jungles, away from society as Rousseau had suggested in his time
(a) was not naturalistic because they cared more for morality and social welfare.
(b) was dominated by the requirements of the rich or the rulers
(c) was more in conformity with the philosophy
(d) was not free social influences, but was definitely naturalistic.

239. Indian Institute of Foreign Trade is situated in
(a) Lucknow (b) Dehradun
(c) New Delhi (d) Mumbai

240. Education as an investment aimed at
(a) Enhancing productivity
(b) Promoting cultural development
(c) Developing democratic outlook
(d) Satisfying the learners

241. The total number of Deemed Universities in India upto December, 2009 is
(a) 130 (b) 99
(c) 69 (d) 97

242. With regard to Environment, the forty-second chapter of fundamental duties in our constitution, brought in a new chapter of fundamental duties in our constitution with effect from January, 1977. According to clause (g) of Article 51A of the amended constitution reads as under: "It shall be the duty of every citizen of India—(g) to protect and improve the natural environment including forests, river and wild life, and to have compassion for living creatures." Which is correct?
(a) Constitutional duties should be propagated in school.
(b) Should be part of education.
(c) Practice of duties should be part of extra curriculum activities.
(d) All of the above.

243. Birla Institute of Technology is situated at
(a) Ranchi (b) Jaipur
(c) Kota (d) Hardwar

244. Generally curriculum planning is considered as a subsystem of
(a) Educational management
(b) Education infrastructural facilities
(c) Educational communication
(d) Educational innovation

245. The number of Argicultural Education Institutes in India till today is
(a) 37 (b) 45
(c) 39 (d) 38

246. The amendment of the constituion has imposed a special duty upon the citizens

of the country to protect and improve the natural environment. Therefore, education now aims at keeping the problems of environment in the courses of B.Ed and M.Ed classes and teachers are expected to inculcate in the students the spirit of fundamental duties including the duty under Article 51A (g) of the constitution to protect the environment.

(a) Students at school should not be burdened with duties.
(b) Only primary schools should do the above.
(c) Only colleges should concern with the duties.
(d) All are wrong.

247. What is the full form of MCA?
(a) Ministry of Commerce and Agriculture
(b) Master of Computer Application
(c) Member Chartered Accountant
(d) Master of Commerce and Arts

248. The National approach towards education should be
(a) Imparting knowledge
(b) Investment in human resource development
(c) Sacred mission
(d) Creating/Generating employment

249. The number of State Universities in India is
(a) 258 (b) 216
(c) 225 (d) 230

250. The main objective of Adult Education is to
(a) enable the adults to read and write.
(b) teach adults to be able to understand what they read.
(c) help adults achieve literacy along with personal development.
(d) socialise the adults to move about freely.

251. Institute of Nuclear Medicine and Allied Sciences is situated in
(a) Mumbai (b) Chennai
(c) Delhi (d) Kolkata

252. A educational guidance worker should employ the following strategy in order to bring out the desirable changes in the behaviour of the delinquent children
(a) To develop friendly support before trying to reform their behaviour.
(b) To make them busy with some constructive activities.
(c) To praise them for their good behaviour.
(d) To advise them in different way.

253. The committee that recommended socially useful and productive work at all stages of education in our country was
(a) The Kher Committee.
(b) The National Policy Committee.
(c) Secondary Education Commission Committee.
(d) Ishwarbhai Patel Committee.

254. The students in higher classes should be better motivated through
(a) Competition
(b) Personal achievement
(c) Co-operation
(d) Individual attention

255. What amount has been provided in the Eleventh Five-Year Plan for Education Mission through ICT?
(a) ₹ 5000 crore (b) ₹ 550 crore
(c) ₹ 6000 crore (d) ₹ 650 crore

256. What is now-a-days termed as non-formal education, is really
(a) a substitute for formal education.
(b) not a substitute for formal education.
(c) non-technical education.
(d) a substitute for higher education.

257. Central Forensic Science Laboratory is situated in
(a) Chandigarh (b) Patna
(c) Patiala (d) Ludhiana

258. The medium of effective communication among the students is
(a) Charts and Maps
(b) Blackboard presentation
(c) Sound film projector
(d) Meaningful verbal expression

259. The Development objective of Higher Education during Tenth Five-Year Plan (2002-07) was
(a) Sustainable Human Development
(b) Relevance in World Context
(c) Improvements in Quality of Teaching
(d) All of the above

260. The term co-curricular in education means
(a) language subjects and skills.
(b) science and mathematics, integrated.
(c) knowledge is well as skills for further education and life.
(d) public examination subjects for certification.

261. Immediate feedback is an essential characteristic of
(a) team teaching
(b) teaching machines
(c) the Dalton Plan
(d) the project method

262. The effective method of teaching of the students at higher level is
(a) To supply relevant information to the students.
(b) To prepare the students for various competitive examinations.
(c) To lead the students to the sources of information.
(d) To develop in students a spirit of competition for higher achievements.

263. Which of the following are included in main feature of the UGC XIth Five-Year Plan (2007-12)?
(a) Incentives for resource mobilisation.
(b) Universities with potential for excellence.
(c) Basic facilities for women.
(d) All of the above.

264. Educational Administration is concerned with
(a) the 'what' of educational program.
(b) the 'why' of educational processes.
(c) the 'goals' of educational practices.
(d) the 'how' of achieving educational objectives.

265. The most accurate statement about teaching machines is that
(a) B.F. Skinner began the movement for their use.
(b) they were designed as an economy measure to replace teachers.
(c) they are not as efficient as teachers in reinforcing responses.
(d) they can be used for all learning programs.

266. If you observe a new or original activity in your student's behaviour by which of the following alternative do you explain it?
(a) Creativity (b) Motivation
(c) Intelligence (d) Specificity

267. Which of the following University will be set up as a Central University during Eleventh Five-Year Plan (2007-12)?
(a) Indira Gandhi National Tribal University
(b) Hyderabad University
(c) Patna University
(d) L.N. Mishra University

268. Vocationalisation of education has the object of

(a) preparing students for a vocation along with knowledge.
(b) converting liberal education into vocational education.
(c) giving more importance to vocation than general education.
(d) creating an educational bias among vocational people.

269. A set of test papers from a class of 29 students has been arranged in order from the highest to the lowest scores. The mark on the fifteenth paper is known as the
(a) Median (b) Mean
(c) Mode (d) Norm

270. Extension education is primarily understood as
(a) Extending of the new knowledge to the doorstep of those who need it.
(b) Extending educational opportunities to the deprived.
(c) To prepare a program for educating farmers.
(d) To propagate knowledge in illiterate rural population.

271. The UGC reserved 10 percent of the total allotted Budget during Tenth Five Year Plan for
(a) North-Eastern Universities and their Constituent Colleges.
(b) East-Western Universities and their Constituent Colleges.
(c) North-Southern Universities and their Constituent Colleges.
(d) Border Universities and their Constituent Colleges.

272. The Montessori schools insist on
(a) the principle of sense training.
(b) complete discipline and supervision.
(c) creativeness, the main objective of education.
(d) well equipped school buildings.

273. In a class of ten pupils the grades in a spelling test were: 97-97-97-92-92-85-76-73-65-60. The mode of those scores is
(a) 92
(b) 97
(c) 97 minus 60 divided by 2
(d) the sum of the scores divided by 10

274. It has been observed that many individuals seek employment in educational fields, because of
(a) lack of job opportunities elsewhere.
(b) their zeal for imparting knowledge.
(c) considering teaching profession as their aim.
(d) lively interest in acquisition of knowledge.

275. The total number of Colleges till December, 2009 was
(a) 18000 (b) 6500
(c) 6600 (d) 6815

276. Mahatma Gandhi's Basic Education Scheme was characterised by
(a) strict discipline and punishment for wrongs.
(b) opposition to strict control and punishment.
(c) strict supervision and control of activities.
(d) education of children through sense training.

277. Of the following objectives of an elementary music program, the one of lowest priority is
(a) to expose children to a variety of musical compositions.
(b) to prepare children for wise use of leisure time.
(c) to develop a group of performers for the holiday assemblies.
(d) to provide children with emotional outlets.

278. The primary characteristics of Higher Education is a field of
   (a) a field of specialisation.
   (b) a formal and institutionalised system.
   (c) research orientation.
   (d) All of the above.

279. The National Institute of Education Planning and Administration has been converted into a Deemed University and is now called the
   (a) NUEPA (b) ERNET
   (c) CIEFL (d) INDEST

280. Which of the following statements would be correct in comparing the educational methods of Froebel and Montessori?
   (a) There is scope for development of imagination in both.
   (b) Froebal favours development of imagination while Montessori provides no scope for this.
   (c) Both favour classroom instructional approach.
   (d) There is greater scope for social development in the Montessori method as compared to Froebel's method.

281. A culturally disadvantaged child is best served by the school system that
   (a) places him/her in a class with other culturally disadvantaged children.
   (b) gives him/her an annual intelligence test.
   (c) trains teachers to understand his/her impoverished home background.
   (d) assesses his/her strengths and needs and provide for an individualised learning plan.

282. According to Kothari Commission the aim of university education is
   (a) To seek and cultivate new knowledge, to engage vigorously and fearlessly in the pursuit of truth and to interpret old knowledge and beliefs in the light of new needs and discoveries.
   (b) To provide the right kind of leadership in 8 all walks of life by helping the individuals to develop their potential.
   (c) To provide society with competent men and women trained in all professions who as cultivated individuals, are inclined with a sense of social purpose.
   (d) None of the Above.

283. The UGC INFONET network is run and managed as
   (a) ERNET (b) NUEPA
   (c) INFLIBNET (d) None of these

284. John's Dewey's experimental school was called as
   (a) the free school
   (b) the progressive school
   (c) the activity school
   (d) the community school

285. Recreational reading should be
   (a) reserved for the school library period.
   (b) assigned as homework.
   (c) a responsibility of the home, not the school.
   (d) an integral part of the language arts curriculum.

286. Vision of India on Higher Education 1998 reflects
   (a) Education aims at liberation from bondages and ignorance
   (b) Education aims at developing a new type of humanity in mankind
   (c) Education aims at transmitting to the new generations the lessons of the accumulated experiences
   (d) All of the above

287. At the end of Tenth Five Year Plan, the total number of Deemed Universities in India was

(a) 110 (b) 115
(c) 117 (d) 119

288. The following was the main recommendation of the Sadler Commission appointed in our country in 1917
(a) intermediate colleges would intervene between the University and Education courses.
(b) the dividing line between the University and the Secondary.
(c) the intermediate colleges should be attached to Universities.
(d) the intermediate colleges should provide instruction.

289. Of the following intelligence tests, the one which is individually administered is the
(a) WISC
(b) Pintner-Cunningham Primary
(c) Army Alpha
(d) Kuhlman-Anderson

290. The developmental objectives of Higher education in Tenth Five-Year Plan include
(a) Relevance of Higher education
(b) Emphasis on quality, evaluation and accreditation
(c) Knowledge and use of new information and communication technology
(d) All of the above

291. The UGC have launched Career Orientation Program in
(a) 1994-95 (b) 2009-10
(c) 1986-87 (d) 1992

292. The progressive education movement in U.S.A. was the direct outcome of
(a) naturalism in education.
(b) experimentalism of education.
(c) pragmatism in education.
(d) socialism in education.

293. With regard to readiness to read, all of these statements are true except that
(a) some psychologists believe that a child is not ready to begin reading until he/she has achieved a mental age of about six years.
(b) a strong desire to read is a determining factor.
(c) a reading readiness programme may begin for some children in kindergarten.
(d) physical maturation is a crucial factor.

294. On the basis of organisational structure the universities can be divided into
(a) Residential, Affiliating and Residential-cum Affiliating universities
(b) Central and State universities
(c) Unitary and Federal universities
(d) None of the above

295. The main aim of Vocationalisation in Higher Education is
(a) To control the enrolment of students in Post-graduation Courses
(b) To create repulsion towards Higher Education
(c) To shift the students' attention from the problem of Unemployment
(d) To guard the students from continuing higher education without purpose

296. Regarding co-education at the secondary stage, the 1952-53 Education Commission has suggested that
(a) to start, resource, in several states could not afford.
(b) to maintain separate schools for boys and girls.
(c) there should be objection to extend co-educational school.
(d) the situation in our country warrants establishment of more boys schools than co-educational school.

297. All of the following tend to erode local control of education in favour of national control, except the
(a) National Science Foundation
(b) National Institute of Mental Health
(c) College Entrance Examination Board
(d) National Defence Education Act

298. Jawahar Lal University, New Delhi has
(a) State University Status
(b) Central University Status
(c) Federal University Status
(d) None of the above

299. What else did National Educational Policy of 1979, recommended also about the public schools
(a) they should be brought under laws and regulations of the government public education system.
(b) their uniqueness and traditions have to preserved the interests of the best talents of the country.
(c) they must be allowed the autonomy that was bestowed on them by the past system of education.
(d) suitable ratio has to be maintained for admission of middle class and poor students also.

300. When Jeewan receives his failing test mark, he tells the teacher, "You don't like me." This is an example of:
(a) identification (b) transference
(c) egocentrism (d) projection

301. Deemed Universities are formed under the special Act of
(a) UGC (b) Constitution
(c) Both of the above (d) None of the above

302. The aim of UGC's Standing Committee of Vocational Education is
(a) To identify such-institutions where vocational courses can be implemented.
(b) To impart training to the teachers for vocational education.
(c) To prepare study material for vocational courses.
(d) All of the above.

303. The 1979, Draft National Policy Education recommended the language formula as follows for the non-Hindi speaking areas
(a) English as a link language alone with mother tongue and a modern Indian language.
(b) a modern Indian language along with a regional languages and English.
(c) Hindi as a link language along with mother tongue and English.
(d) regional language and English in addition to Hindi.

304. With respect to the development of skills, all of the following are correct except that
(a) pupils of the same mental age should learn at the same rate.
(b) group instruction facilitates the learning process.
(c) individual instruction is often required.
(d) workbooks can be an invaluable learning aid.

305. The universities having their fixed campus along with teaching faculties are called
(a) Unitary Teaching Universities
(b) Federal Teaching Universities
(c) State Universities
(d) None of the above

306. The UGC submitted a proposal to the World Bank for seeking grant in 2001-02 for the following plan
(a) To implement Vocational Courses in Higher Education.
(b) To Co-ordinate the Vocational Courses in Intermediate classes.

(c) To implement Scheme of Vocationalisation in Primary Education.
(d) To match the Vocationalisation with the process of globalisation.

307. Dr. Radhakrishnan's University Education Commission's report said the following about religious education
(a) religious education should lead to spiritual education.
(b) moral and religious education are the two poles of social education.
(c) religious education is must at the higher education stage.
(d) we do not want religious education, but education about religious.

308. If you were reading a series of articles about the teaching of reading, you would expect to be reading an article by
(a) Paul McKee (b) Albert Harris
(c) Arthur Gates (d) Frank Reissman

309. IGNOU has
(a) State Status (b) Central Status
(c) Federal Status (d) Deemed Status

310. The Secondary Education Commission's suggestion about negligence of education in school, favoured
(a) religious instruction as an integral part of regular school work without appointing special teaches for the purpose.
(b) religious instruction only on voluntary basis outside school hours with the consent of parents and management.
(c) combination of religious instruction with moral education relating to it the context of contents different curricular courses.
(d) limiting free religious instruction to only, those who wanted it, by creating the required facilities within the school timetable itself.

311. A student fails a test for which he did not study. By ascribing his failure to the fact that the teacher does not like him he is utilizing
(a) Conversion (b) Sympathism
(c) Rationalisation (d) Compensation

312. Gnanam Committee Report (1990) is entitled as
(a) Alternative Models of Management.
(b) Models of University Management.
(c) Working Models for University management.
(d) Fuzzy Model for University Management.

313. During the days of informal education children used to get
(a) some kinds of education first through the process of living.
(b) professional education through nonprofessional people.
(c) education without any specific purpose.
(d) education only at an advanced age through schools.

314. Of the following learning theories, the one that embodies the idea that learning takes place through insight is known as
(a) Gestalt
(b) stimulus-response
(c) connectionist
(d) pragmatic

315. Gnanam Committee Report find out the important lacuna in a university's administration is
(a) The Board of Studies are not broad-based and it is difficult to induct representatives from industries.
(b) It is not possible to establish regional and national facilities within the framework of the existing Acts and the universities.

(c) Acts of the most of the universities do not specifically provide for extension programs.
(d) All of the above.

316. 'CARE' is an abbreviation for
(a) Care for Adult Recreation and Employment.
(b) Committee for American Relief Everywhere.
(c) Compulsory attendance at rural Education.
(d) Contacts of American Representatives Everywhere.

317. The pair of terms incorrectly associated is
(a) IQ—relationship between MA and CA.
(b) Validity—measure of consistency in testing.
(c) Inkblot—projective testing.
(d) Median—the middle score.

318. How many times the growth has been recorded in Higher Education (Especially in the number of Universities) during the year 2007-08?
(a) 10 times (b) 9 times
(c) 20 times (d) 31 times

319. Delhi University is a
(a) Central University
(b) State University
(c) Deemed University
(d) Cannot say

320. CHEER stand for
(a) Children Enrichment Education Through Radio.
(b) Child Health Education Electronic Recording.
(c) Children for Engineers and Energy Requirement.
(d) None of these.

321. Of the following, the author of a widely used intelligence test is
(a) David Wechsler
(b) BF Skinner
(c) William Cruikshank
(d) Bruno Bettelheim

322. The total number of Deemed Universities in India upto 2009 is
(a) 128 (b) 99
(c) 69 (d) 97

323. The Residential Universities are the universities having
(a) Central Campus for Imparting Education.
(b) Many Campuses for Imparting Education.
(c) Both of the above are correct.
(d) None of the above are correct.

324. Televised educational program is useful because
(a) it can present the natural phenomenon of the world in natural form.
(b) it can magnify the microscopic forms of life and can be presented and TV.
(c) it affords the opportunity for large audience in the same auditorium or in different locations to view it clearly.
(d) All of the above.

325. The project method of teaching is best associated with the philosophy of
(a) John Dewey (b) MaxRafferty
(c) Robert Hutchins (d) B.F. Skinner

326. The number of Agricultural Education Institutes in India till today is
(a) 37 (b) 38
(c) 39 (d) 40

327. When a university has its separate campus for teaching purposes and there are many autonomous and constituent colleges affiliated to it, then this organisational pattern is called
(a) A Federal University.
(b) A Decentralised University.

(c) A Unitary University.
(d) None of the above.

328. The main purpose of the first degree in our Universities should be
(a) bring students to frontiers of knowledge and from there should be research.
(b) prepare students for social service and bring them to the threshold of knowledge.
(c) equip students with necessary competencies for different work experiences.
(d) bring to the frontiers of research with necessary equipment of knowledge.

329. Overlearning tends to strengthen an individual's
(a) powers of retention
(b) endurance
(c) feeling of boredom
(d) motivation

330. When a university runs some courses in its Central Campus and some other courses in its affiliating colleges, such University is called as
(a) Residential-Affiliating University
(b) Affiliating University
(c) Unitary Teaching University
(d) None of the above

331. The Indian Education Commission (1964-66) has recommended compulsory social service for school children as follows
(a) 10 days for the primary stage and 30 days for the secondary stage.
(b) 20 days for the lower secondary stage and 20 days for the higher secondary stage.
(c) 30 days for the lower secondary and 20 days for the higher secondary stage.
(d) 10 days for the lower secondary stage and 20 days for the higher secondary stage.

332. "School is life, not a preparation for life." This statement summarises one important aspect of the educational philosophy of:
(a) John Dewey (b) Robert Hutchins
(c) Mortimer Adler (d) S.I. Hayakawa

333. In India, total number of Women's Colleges during 2008-09 is
(a) 2166 (b) 2235
(c) 2350 (d) 2450

334. On the basis of teaching process, the universities can be categorised as
(a) Traditional and Open Universities
(b) Central and State Universities
(c) Residential and Affiliating Universities
(d) None of the above

335. The nationalist movement in India took the credit of recommending of
(a) public schools
(b) private schools
(c) vocational education
(d) mass education

336. A frequency distribution is best defined as the
(a) number of scores above the median score.
(b) number of pupils scoring above the median score.
(c) number of test items answered correctly by a majority of the class.
(d) number of pupils who received each score on a test.

337. The total outlay projected for XIth Plan in respect of adult education is
(a) ₹ 34,946 crores
(b) ₹ 34,900 crores

(c) ₹ 35,000 crores
(d) ₹ 38,000 crores

338. Open Universities are treated as Non-traditional Universities because
(a) Innovative methods of teaching and learning are used in these Universities.
(b) Innovative methods of admission, curriculum and evaluation are followed in these universities.
(c) Modern Communication Techniques are used in these universities.
(d) All of the above.

339. The term "Manpower Needs" in any country refers that the
(a) People should be educated in accordance with specified jobs requirements.
(b) Capacities of men should be fully utilised for education and training.
(c) Enrolments in educational institutions should be decided accordingly.
(d) Education at all stages should be geared to promote the powers of the educates.

340. Mainstreaming is a term associated with
(a) career education
(b) education for the handicapped
(c) interage class groupings
(d) environmental education

341. The Development objective of Higher Education during Tenth Five-Year Plan (2002-07) is
(a) Sustainable Human Development
(b) Relevance in World Context
(c) Improvements in Quality of Teaching
(d) All of the above

342. The term "Co-curricular activities" is popular one for all educational institutions. Which of the following would you regard a co-curricular activity?
(a) Debating competitions
(b) Football matches
(c) Collection of funds for school building
(d) Tournaments.

343. Of great importance in determining the amount of transference that occurs in learning is the
(a) IQ of the learner
(b) knowledge of the teacher
(c) use of appropriate materials
(d) presence of identical elements

344. Ministry of Human Resource Development Report (2002-03) mentioned the specific objective of Higher Education as
(a) Emphasis on relevance of Higher Education.
(b) Emphasis on Quality, Evaluation and Accreditation.
(c) Emphasis on Research and Development.
(d) All of the above.

345. Generally in Federal type of Universities, the Organisational Pattern of Courses is
(a) Postgraduate courses in university campus and graduate courses in constituent college.
(b) Postgraduate and graduate courses in university campus while graduate courses are only in its constituent colleges.
(c) Special postgraduate courses in university campus and in constituent colleges both types of the courses.
(d) None of the above.

346. The 1968, National Policy on Education in our country stressed
(a) the need for spread of literacy and adult education.
(b) the need for expansion of correspondence courses of education.

(c) the importance of continuing educational programmes for the needy.
(d) the need of functional literacy at the elementary and secondary levels.

347. Of the following, the educator who is not an advocate of radical educational reform is
(a) Postman (b) Illich
(c) Bestor (d) Kozol

348. The XIth Five Year Plan outlay for Higher Education is
(a) ₹ 85,000 crores (b) ₹ 86,000 crores
(c) ₹ 87,000 crores (d) ₹ 88,000 crores

349. Which of the following is not related to Indian Education Commission's (1964-66) recommendations?
(a) University's Autonomy and Income-Expenditure.
(b) Role and Appointment of Vice-Chancellor.
(c) University Legislation.
(d) Role of Registrar.

350. 'Children's House' is the name given to a school by
(a) Montessori (b) Russean
(c) Froebel (d) Pestalozzi

351. With regard to standardised testing, which of the following statements is correct?
(a) The testing of intelligence began in Germany.
(b) The Wechsler Intelligence Scale for Children (WISC) is a group test.
(c) The Rorschach test uses inkblots.
(d) The Thematic Apperception Test (TAT) is easy to interpret.

352. The scheme implemented during the above budgeting year is
(a) General Development of Universities and Colleges.
(b) Enhancing Access and Equity.
(c) Promotion of Relevant Education.
(d) All of the above.

353. In 1969 the UGC had appointed a committee for
(a) Administrative of Universities.
(b) Administrative Legislation of Colleges.
(c) Administrative Legislation for both of the above.
(d) None of the above.

354. Which of the following should be regarded as the main advantage of residential schools?
(a) To provide educational facilities for the homeless students in the school area.
(b) They can provide better education for social behaviour and community life.
(c) They remove the inconveniences of accommodation for the schools.
(d) They provide for education of orphans and for children of illiterate parents.

355. The Adiseshaiah National Review Committee in our country has recommended the following time allocation, for the vocationalised spectrum at the higher secondary stage
(a) language foundation and SUPW 30% and electives 70%.
(b) general foundation and language courses 30% and education subjects, 70%.
(c) education subjects, 30% languages and SUPW 70%.
(d) SUPW and languages and general foundation courses 30%.

356. The term least restrictive environment refers to the education of the
(a) handicapped
(b) gifted

(c) early childhood youngsters
(d) retarded

357. The total enrollment of Students in Universities and College till 2007-08 was
(a) 116.13 lakh (b) 88.00 lakh
(c) 80.21 lakh (d) 98.21 lakh

358. With which committee, the name of Rev. P.T. Chandi was associated?
(a) The Committee for College Administrative Legislation
(b) The Committee for University Administrative Legislation
(c) Affiliating University's Standardisation
(d) Federal University's Standard Committee

359. The UGC in our country was established under the act of parliament on the recomendations of
(a) the Secondary Education Commission.
(b) the University Education Commission.
(c) the Central Board of Secondary Education.
(d) the National Board of University Education.

360. All of the following are correctly paired except
(a) Froebel—progressivism
(b) Dewey—pragmatism
(c) Skinner—Gestalt
(d) Herbart—apperception

361. The proportion of the girls in reference to boys seeking higher education upto 2002-03 was
(a) 39.84% (b) 39.00%
(c) 39.64% (d) 39.79%

362. The suggestion given by Dr. Gajendragadkar committee was
(a) To review the organisation structures of universities on regular basis.
(b) To bring timely change in the University's organisation.
(c) To bring change in Administrative wings of Universities.
(d) All of the above.

363. IIMC is situated at
(a) Mumbai (b) Delhi
(c) Chennai (d) Kolkata

364. Heterogeneous grouping best serves the aims of a democratic society because
(a) parents prefer it
(b) pupils prefer it
(c) it minimises class distinctions
(d) it is the best environment for learning

365. During 2002-03 the State having highest Enrollment number of girl students in Higher Education was
(a) Meghalaya (b) Assam
(c) Kerala (d) West Bengal

366. A high level committee was set up in April 2009, headed by former UGC, Chairman Yash Pal for
(a) restructuring higher education in the country.
(b) formation of new universities.
(c) salary revision.
(d) None of the above.

367. We learn from newspapers and reports that the national average of the literacy rate in our country is
(a) about 39 percent
(b) about 36 percent
(c) about 40 percent
(d) about 45 percent

368. All of the following are advantages of teaching machines except
(a) the control of cheating
(b) the tracking of errors
(c) the insurance of attention
(d) their universal use for different kinds of programs

369. The total number of PhD's awarded during 2005-06 throughout the country was
(a) 18,730 (b) 11,400
(c) 10,450 (d) 10,150

370. The President of India is elected by
(a) Parliament
(b) State legislatures
(c) By the people directly
(d) By an electoral college consisting of the elected members of the Lok Sabha, the Rajya Sabha and the State Legislative Assemblies

371. The 1952-53 Secondary Education Commission in India recommended the following pattern of education
(a) 10 + 2 + 3 scheme
(b) 12 + 3 scheme
(c) 11 + 2 + 3 scheme
(d) 10 + 3 + 2 scheme

372. Which among the following is not a Fundamental Right now?
(a) Right to equality
(b) Right to property
(c) Right to Constitutional remedies
(d) None of these

373. According to the data 2007-08, the total number of teachers working in different universities was
(a) 0.81 lakh (b) 0.92 lakh
(c) 0.95 lakh (d) None of the above

374. What is the minimum strength of a State Legislative Assembly?
(a) 40 (b) 60
(c) 50 (d) 70

375. Which is the more desirable outcome of teaching in higher education?
(a) Increase in students achievement.
(b) Increase in the level of independent thinking of students.
(c) Higher percentage of result.
(d) Increase in the number of students who opt for the subject.

376. The most powerful Upper Chamber in the world is
(a) American Senate
(b) British House of Lords
(c) Rajya Sabha of the Indian Republic
(d) None of the above

377. The UGC has launched the pilot project of 'SAKSHAT' Program in
(a) 2006 (b) 1995-96
(c) 1986-87 (d) 1992

378. Which of the following has not been laid down by the Indian Constitution?
(a) Direct election to the Lok Sabha.
(b) Direct election to the State Legislative Assemblies.
(c) Direct election of the President of India.
(d) Creation of Supreme Court which is competent to interpret the Constitution.

379. The famous seven cordial principles of education were formulated in the U.S.A. by
(a) the progressive education association.
(b) the new education fellowship.
(c) the national education association.
(d) the national federation of education.

380. Who is legally competent under the Indian Constitution to declare war or conclude peace?
(a) The President
(b) The Prime Minister
(c) The Council of Ministers
(d) The Parliament

381. What is the age of retirement of the Supreme Court Judges?
(a) 60 years (b) 65 years
(c) 62 years (d) 70 years

382. The 1968 national policy teacher education adopted by the Indian Government laid stress on the following aspects of teachers education
(a) Adequate emoluments and academic freedom for teachers.
(b) In-service training and correspondence education for teachers.
(c) Travel allowance and family pensions for teachers.
(d) Promotion and retirement facilities for teachers.

383. Holding of elections for the village Panchayat is decided by
(a) The Collector
(b) The Election Commission
(c) The Central Government
(d) The State Government

384. The right of vote in India is given to all people on the basis of
(a) Age (b) Education
(c) Religion (d) Property

385. Educational Administration
(a) sets the goals for education
(b) tells about the role of educational objectives
(c) explains the methods of schools and class control
(d) concerned with the what of education

386. The time of gap between two sessions of Parliament is not more than
(a) 9 months (b) 1 month
(c) 3 months (d) 6 months

387. The agency which have founded SCOVE is
(a) UGC (b) NCERT
(c) ICSSR (d) CSIR

388. The most controversial amendment passed during the emergency was?
(a) 43rd (b) 41st
(c) 42nd (d) 44th

389. The second amendment of 1976 with Indian Constitution
(a) insisted on the vocationalisation of education.
(b) brought closer relationship between education and agriculture.
(c) the social aspect of knowledge to be imparted in schools.
(d) the partial considerations as aims of education.

390. The President of India is
(a) The head of the State
(b) The head of the Government
(c) The head of the State as well as Government
(d) All of these

391. The Governor of a State in India is
(a) directly elected by the people of the State.
(b) appointed by the Prime Minister.
(c) appointed by the President.
(d) appointed by the State Chief Minister.

392. Educational organisation is different from educational administration because
(a) organisation is concerned with arrangements of equipment, etc., whereas administration has to manage with tilings to be organised.
(b) administration is concerned with arrangements of things, etc., while organisation deals with the management aspects.
(c) administration is concerned with persons whereas orgnisation is concerned with equipements.
(d) organisation is concerned with the management of things and equipment, while administration is concerned with the arrangement aspects of things and equipment.

393. In the context of Panchayati Raj, which one of the following is true about Gram Sabha?
(a) This is the topmost tier of the Panchayati Raj.
(b) It consists of all the voters residing in the jurisdiction of a Village Panchayat.
(c) It is the executive body consisting of selected representative from Village Panchayat.
(d) It consists of all the adult males of the Village Panchayat.

394. How many languages have been recognised by the Constitution?
(a) 13 (b) 14
(c) 22 (d) 16

395. One of the important characteristic of successful school administration is
(a) the rational soundness.
(b) rigidity or right principles.
(c) unconcerned with the political philosophy.
(d) None of these.

396. The joint sittings of the Union Parliament may be summoned for
(a) special address of the President.
(b) annual address of the President.
(c) president's occasional messages of national significance.
(d) resolution of the deadlock between the two Houses on a non-money bill.

397. To be eligible for election as President of India a person must have completed the age of
(a) 35 years (b) 40 years
(c) 30 years (d) 25 years

398. The Hartog Committee of 1929 had recommended that
(a) diversion of children towards industrial and commercial.
(b) careers should be started at the end of the high school stage.
(c) the end of the middle school stage in the proportion for diversion into industrial and commercial avocation.
(d) the minimum qualification for starting commercial and industrial avocations should be matriculation.

399. Which one of the following High Courts has the Territorial Jurisdiction over Andaman and Nicobar islands?
(a) Andhra Pradesh (b) Kolkata
(c) Chennai (d) Orissa

400. The Union Cabinet is responsible to
(a) The Rajya Sabha and the Lok Sabha.
(b) The President of India.
(c) The Lok Sabha only.
(d) The electorate.

401. CEC program recommended by the Sixth Plan in our country into
(a) Elementary compulsory education
(b) Early Childhood Education
(c) Economic Conveniences for Education
(d) Every Child's Education

402. As per Indian Protocol, who among the following ranks highest in the order of precedence?
(a) Deputy Prime Minister
(b) Former President
(c) Governor of a State within his State
(d) Speaker of Lok Sabha

403. On the basis of organisational structure the universities can be classified as—
(a) Residential and Affiliating Universities
(b) Central and State Universities
(c) Unitary and Federal Universities
(d) None of the above

404. All the following are Fundamental Rights guaranteed by the Indian Constitution except
(a) The right to equality.
(b) The right against exploitation.

(c) The right to adequate means of livelihood.
(d) The right to freedom of religion.

405. The introduction of career courses in schools and colleges aims at
(a) developing the ability to make intelligent choice of jobs.
(b) providing professional knowledge to students.
(c) increasing G.K. in students.
(d) All of the above.

406. The Lok Sabha Secretariat comes under the control of
(a) Ministry of Home Affairs
(b) Speaker of the Lok Sabha
(c) Ministry of Parliamentary Affairs
(d) Prime Minister

407. The number of Anglo-Indians who can be nominated by the President to the Lok Sabha is
(a) 2 (b) 3
(c) 4 (d) 5

408. Kindergarten (KG) system of education means garden of small kids which is in debted to
(a) Dewey (b) Froebel
(c) Plato (d) Spencer

409. Who appoints the comptroller and Auditor-General of India?
(a) The U.P.S.C.
(b) The President
(c) The Prime Minister
(d) The Parliament

410. During 2004-05 which of the following university get a status of Central University?
(a) Allahabad University
(b) Hyderabad University
(c) Lucknow University
(d) Jauhar University

411. The Attorney General of India is appointed by
(a) The Chief Justice of India
(b) The Prime Minister
(c) The President of India
(d) The UPSC

412. The traditional school is usually associated with
(a) the activities program
(b) the great books theory
(c) the recitation of lessons
(d) the integration of subjects

413. In case of absence of President and Vice-President, which of the following acts as the president of country?
(a) Prime Minister
(b) Speaker of Lok Sabha
(c) Chief Justice of India
(d) Leader of Opposition

414. When does a Presidential Ordinance cease to operate?
(a) At the expiry of four weeks from the reassembly of Parliament or earlier if both Houses disapprove it.
(b) At the expiry of six weeks from the reassembly of Parliament or earlier if both Houses disapprove it.
(c) At the expiry of six months from the reassembly of Parliament or earlier if both Houses disapprove it.
(d) None of the above.

415. The philosophy dominating our public schools today can best be characterised by
(a) Reconstructionism
(b) Supernaturalism
(c) Programmation
(d) Essentialism

416. A bill becomes a law when
(a) Both Houses of Parliament approve it by requisite majority.

(b) The Council of Ministers approves it.
(c) The President gives his assent.
(d) The Supreme Court upholds its constitutional validity.

417. The Residential Universities are the universities having
(a) Central Campus for Imparting Education.
(b) Many Campuses for Imparting Education.
(c) Both of the above are correct.
(d) None of the above are correct.

418. The Indian Constitution has given a special status to the State of Jammu and Kashmir under Article
(a) 352 (b) 370
(c) 368 (d) 361

419. The latest educational movement started by Acharya Vinoba Bhave and having pursued by some followers even now is called
(a) the Gurukul
(b) the Sanskrit Tul
(c) the Acharyakul
(d) None of these

420. Who examines the report of the Comptroller and Auditor-General of India after it is laid before Parliament?
(a) Lok Sabha Speaker
(b) Estimates Committee
(c) Public Accounts Committee
(d) None of the above

421. Unitary Teaching College is called
(a) Residential University
(b) Affiliating University
(c) Residential-cum-Affiliating University
(d) None of the above

422. The drafting committee of the Indian Constitution was headed by
(a) Dr. Rajendra Prasad
(b) N. Gopalaswamy
(c) B.R. Ambedkar
(d) None of these

423. The 1972 International Commission on Education has entitled its report as
(a) education and national development.
(b) learning to be national development.
(c) education for development.
(d) learning as a living.

424. Consider the following statements regarding the Governor of a state in India.
(1) To be appointed as Governor, one should have completed the age of 45 years
(2) The Governor holds the office during the pleasure of the President
(3) After completing five years in office, the Governor cannot continue to hold the office even when his successor has not entered upon his office
(4) The executive power of the state is vested in the Governor

Which of the above statements are correct?
(a) 1 and 2 (b) 3 and 4
(c) 1, 2 and 3 (d) 2 and 4

425. The Supreme Commander of the Defence Forces of India is
(a) The Defence Minister
(b) The Prime Minister
(c) The Chief of the Army Staff
(d) The President of India

426. Which of the following statements would be correct with regard to the policy of non-formal education?
(a) It is not a substitute, but a supplement to formal education.
(b) It is an education of an unplanned nature to be adopted to selected situations.
(c) It is good only for lower class, unskilled and illiterate people.

(d) It does not require any theoretical basis or intellecutal preparations of trained teachers.

427. Which of the following subjects does not belong to the Union List?
(a) Atomic Energy
(b) War and Peace
(c) Post Office Savings Bank
(d) Public Health and Sanitation

428. The meaning of Affiliating University is
(a) The universities which are not having Central Campus for teaching but it is going on in Affiliating Colleges
(b) The universities which implement Curriculum only and Coordinating Examinations
(c) The Universities which work as distribution of Degrees
(d) All the above are true

429. India is a republic because
(a) Every adult of the age 18 or more has been given the right to vote.
(b) The Constitution guarantees fundamental rights of the people.
(c) The Council of Ministers is responsible to the Lok Sabha.
(d) Head of State is elected for a fixed term.

430. The idea of starting girls' University in our country started in the year 1970
(a) as a initiative of the British rulers.
(b) through the efforts of municipalities and local fund communities.
(c) with the opening of the SNDT university at Mumbai.
(d) with the political awakening in the country by the push given by Mahatma.

431. The Chairman and the members of State Public Service Commission are appointed by the
(a) President
(b) Governor
(c) Chairman of UPSC
(d) Prime Minister

432. The sanctioned strength of the Supreme Court of India is
(a) 13 (b) 31
(c) 16 (d) 26

433. According to Swami Vivekananda, teacher's success depends on
(a) his renunciation of personal gain and service to others.
(b) his professional training and creativity.
(c) his concentration on his work and duties with a spirit of obedience to God.
(d) his mastery of the subject and task in controlling the students.

434. In which of the following states was the Panchayati Raj first introduced?
(a) Rajasthan (b) Gujarat
(c) Uttar Pradesh (d) Bihar

435. Which of the following is not a Union Territory?
(a) Lakshadweep (b) Delhi
(c) Manipur (d) Daman and Diu

436. The Kothari Education Commission's report was entitled as
(a) education and National Development
(b) learning to be adventure
(c) diversification of Education
(d) education and Socialisation in Democracy

437. Open Universities are treated as Non-traditional Universities because
(a) Innovative methods of teaching and learning are used in these Universities.
(b) Innovative methods of admission, curriculum and evaluation are followed in these universities.

(c) Modern Communication Techniques are used in these universities.
(d) All of the above.

438. Article 370 of the Indian Constitution deals with
(a) The Emergency Powers of the President.
(b) The special position of the State of Jammu and Kashmir.
(c) The power to seek the advisory opinion of the Supreme Court on any matter of public importance.
(d) Distribution of taxes between the Centre and the States.

439. Mass education among people of the West originated in the
(a) Place school of Charlemagne.
(b) Court school of Vitterinolda Feltre.
(c) Cateckumenal and Catechetical schools.
(d) Protestant Vernacular reading schools.

440. President can be removed on charges of violating the Constitution by
(a) No-confidence motion.
(b) Impeachment.
(c) Electoral College of Legislative Assemblies.
(d) Prime Minister.

441. A Judge of the Supreme Court of India can be removed from office
(a) By the President of India according to his sweet will.
(b) By the Prime Minister of India.
(c) By the Chief Justice of India.
(d) By the President on an address by each House of Parliament and supported by a majority of the total membership of that house and by a majority of not less than 2/3 of the members of that House present and voting.

442. The Medieval University was dominated by
(a) Scholasticism (b) Nominalism
(c) Rationalism (d) Social realism

443. The function of the Panchayat Samiti is to
(a) deal with rural industrialisation.
(b) deal with administration of justice at the Panchayat level.
(c) implement community development project schemes.
(d) deal with financial matters of the Panchayat.

444. Generally in Federal type of Universities the Organisational Pattern of Courses is
(a) Post Graduate Courses in University Campus and Graduate Courses in Constituent College.
(b) Post Graduate and Graduate Courses in University Campus while Graduate Courses are only in its Constituent Colleges.
(c) Special Post Graduate Courses in University Campus and in Constituent Colleges both types of the courses.
(d) None of the above.

445. The vacancy in the office of the President must be filled within
(a) One year (b) Six months
(c) Four months (d) Three months

446. The 1965-66 Indian Education Commission, recommended among other things
(a) general education as distinct from vocational education.
(b) general education containing elements of vocational and technical education.
(c) complete separation between the general and vocational educational courses.
(d) general education a college preparatory courses and vocational education leading to technical course.

447. Which Writ is issued by a High Court or the Supreme Court to compel an authority to perform a function that it was not performing?
(a) Writ of certiorari
(b) Writ of Habeas Corpus
(c) Writ of Mandamus
(d) Writ of Quo Warranto

449. Which of the following is not related to Indian Education Commission's (1964-66) recommendations?
(a) University's Autonomy and Income-Expenditure.
(b) Role and Appointment of Vice-Chancellor.
(c) University Legislation.
(d) Role of Registrar.

449. The credit of planning a child's education is to achieve the divinelinity goes to
(a) Piaget (b) Montessori
(c) John Lock (d) Froebel

450. Which one of the following sets of special powers has been conferred on Rajya Sabha by the Constitution?
(a) To change the existing territory of a state and to change the name of a state.
(b) To pass a resolution empowering the parliament to make laws in the State List and creation of one or more All-India services.
(c) To amend the election procedure of the President and to determine the pension of the President after his retirement.
(d) To determine the functions of the Election Commission and to determine the number of Election Commissioners.

451. In 1969 the UGC had appointed
(a) Administration of Universities
(b) Administration of Colleges
(c) Administrative Legislation for both of the above
(d) None of the above

452. When the two Houses of Parliament differ regarding a Bill then the deadlock is resolved by
(a) A joint sitting of the two Houses
(b) President of India
(c) Prime Minister of India
(d) By a special committee formed for the purpose

453. Acculturation is the process of
(a) developing qualities which affect the culture of nation.
(b) accepting the innovations required for the development of nation's culture.
(c) being influenced by the cultural imperatives of a nation.
(d) following the latest trends of a culture as opposed to the past traditions.

454. In the Rajya Sabha, the States have been provided
(a) Equal representation
(b) Representation on the basis poupulation
(c) Representation on the basis population and size
(d) Representation on the basis of size

455. The maximum duration between two sessions of the Indian Parliament should not be more than
(a) 3 months (b) 6 months
(c) 9 months (d) one year

456. A technical educational cess was recommended to be levied in our country for the first time by
(a) the Secondary Education Commission.
(b) the University Education Commission.
(c) the International Education Commission.
(d) the Technical Education Commission.

457. The salaries of the Judges of the Supreme Court are charged on the consolidated fund of India because
(a) they may get salaries regularly every month.
(b) their salaries may be free from legislative vote.
(c) there may not be any cut in their salaries.
(d) their financial position may be secure to enable them to dispense impartial justice.

458. The maximum strength of the Lok Sabha and the Rajya Sabha is
(a) 525 and 250 respectively
(b) 550 and 250
(c) 535 and 275
(d) 500 and 250

459. The culture epoch theory of organisation of the curriculum in the 19th Century suggests that
(a) culture of a national from different epochs should find representation in the school curriculum.
(b) the curriculum should be framed in accordance with the development of human culture, epoch-wise.
(c) human beings develop through education in the order in which human culture developed in nature.
(d) there should be greater concentration in education for the cultural development in our epoch.

460. 'Judicial Review' is the power of the higher court to declare unconstitutional any
1. Law passed by legislature
2. Judgement of the lower court
3. Order of the executive

Choose the answer from the following choices
(a) 1 and 2 (b) Only 3
(c) 1 and 3 (d) 1, 2 and 3

461. The Comptroller and Auditor General of India is appointed by the
(a) Prime Minister of India
(b) President of India
(c) Finance Minister
(d) Lok Sabha

462. According to Dewey, education is a
(a) social need
(b) personal need
(c) psychological need
(d) theoretical need

463. Which of the following standing committees of Parliament has no MP from Rajya Sabha?
(a) Public Accounts Committee
(b) Estimates Committee
(c) Committee on Public Undertakings
(d) Committee on Government Assurances

464. The Yash Pal committee submitted its report on
(a) April 23, 2009 (b) May 24, 2009
(c) June 23, 2009 (d) July 25, 2009

465. The Legislative Council of a State can be abolished or created by
(a) The President of India.
(b) The Legislative Assembly of the State concerned.
(c) By Parliament accordirig to its will.
(d) By Parliament provided the State Legislative Assembly passes a resolution to that effect.

466. In the context of education, some views of Gandhiji have been appended below. Which one of them is incorrect?
(a) In education, experimentation, work and research must be given due places
(b) Education must be self-dependent

(c) Literacy is education
(d) Education must be such as to develop all the powers and inherent qualities of children

467. The Comptroller and Auditor General of India acts as the chief accountant and auditor for the
(a) Union Government
(b) State Governments
(c) Union and State Governments
(d) Neither Union nor State Governments

468. The important challenge before Open and Distance education is
(a) use of ICT on a large scale has strengthened the case for wider access to education.
(b) globalisation of education is a great challenge before these institutions.
(c) lack of Research is one of the great challenge before these institutions.
(d) All of the above.

469. The total number of members in the Legislative Council of a State cannot exceed
(a) one-fourth of the total number of members in the Legislative Assembly.
(b) one-third of the total number of members of the Legislative Assembly.
(c) one-sixth of the total members of the Legislative Assembly.
(d) no such limit has been fixed.

470. A member of the Union Public Service Commission holds office for a period of
(a) Five years
(b) Seven years
(c) Six years or sixty-five years of age whichever is more
(d) Six years or until he attains the age of sixty-five whichever is earlier

471. General support service in Distance education includes
(a) Academic and non-academic services
(b) Contractual services
(c) Software and Hardware support
(d) All of the above

472. The total number of members of the Legislative Council can in no case be less than
(a) 40
(b) 60
(c) 50
(d) No minimum strength has been fixed

473. How many types of emergency can be declared by the President of India?
(a) 2 (b) 3
(c) 4 (d) 5

474. Which one of the following instructional method is not employed in open university?
(a) Audio-Video Cassettes
(b) Radio
(c) Lecture method
(d) Satellite instruction

475. India has
(a) Parliamentary form of government
(b) Presidential form of government
(c) Both parliamentary and presidential forms of government
(d) None of these

476. Who is the custodian of fundamental rights of people?
(a) Supreme Court (b) President
(c) Prime Minister (d) State Assembly

477. Which one of the following is not an advantage of Distance education?
(a) No discrimination for getting education
(b) It liquidates illiteracy
(c) It does not give face-to-face contact in classroom conditions
(d) It is accessible in all remote regions of the country

478. If the Vice-President were to submit his resignation, he would notify to
(a) The President of India
(b) The Prime Minister
(c) The Chief justice or India
(d) The Speaker of the Lok Sabha

479. Education is a subject in the
(a) Union list (b) State list
(c) Concurrent list (d) None of the lists

480. Which of the following words were added to the Preamble of Indian Constitution under the 42nd Amendment?
(a) Democratic Republic
(b) Democratic Socialist
(c) Socialist Secular
(d) Sovereign Secular

481. Who can amend the Constitution?
(a) President (b) Parliament
(c) Prime Minister (d) Union Cabinet

482. What is internet?
(a) A global connection of computers.
(b) A global network of tele-communication links to access a whole resources of data.
(c) An international entertainment network.
(d) None of the above.

483. The Speaker of a State Assembly can be removed from his office by
(a) A resolution of the Legislative Assembly passed by a majority of all the members of the Assembly.
(b) The President of India.
(c) The Chief Minister.
(d) The Governor.

484. What is a Modem?
(a) A device which hooks a computer to the phone-line and in the usual way to hook up to the internet.
(b) A device called Modulator-demodulator and used in computer.
(c) A computer language.
(d) None of the above.

485. The Governor of a state enjoys
(a) no discretionary powers
(b) very extensive discretionary powers
(c) discretionary powers in certain matters
(d) None of the above.

486. E-mail is
(a) a feature of internet.
(b) a procedure of sending or receiving messages electronically.
(c) a system of communication through electronic network between two persons having their E-mail ID's.
(d) All of the above.

487. Chief Minister is
(a) the Head of the State.
(b) the Head of the Government.
(c) an integral part of the legislature.
(d) always a member of the Lower House.

488. The flow-chart of E-mail have the essential elements (Pathways) as following.
1. Sender's computer
2. Sender's ISP
3. Recipient ISP
4. Mail server of Recipient
5. Recipient's computer

The correct pathways is represented through the following flow-chart.

(a)

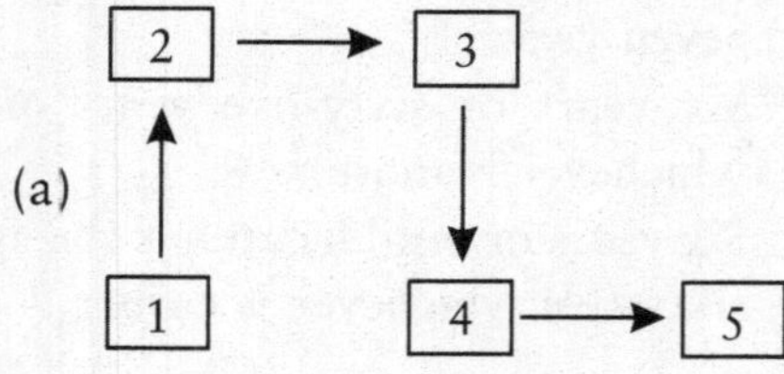

(b) 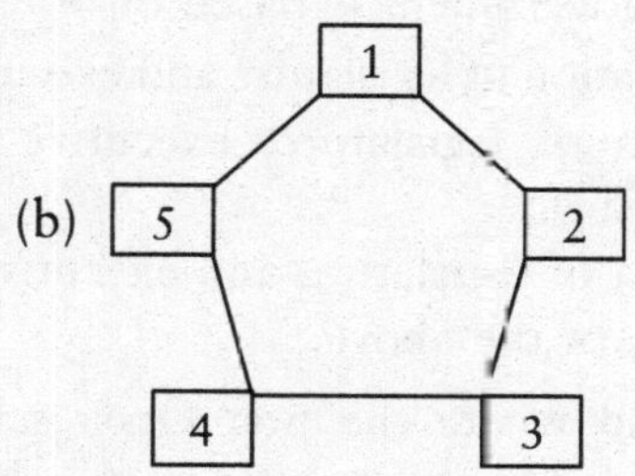

(c) 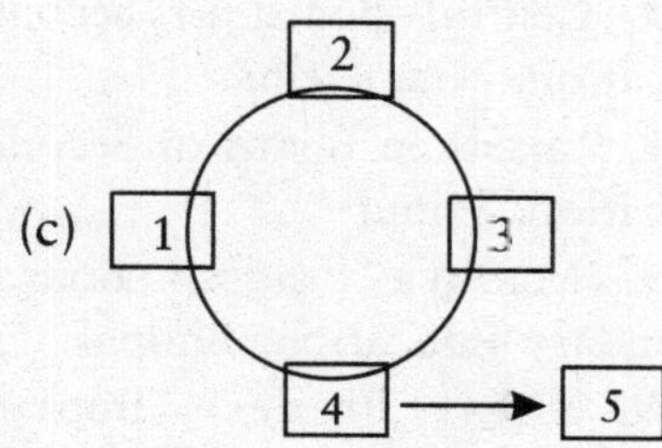

(d) 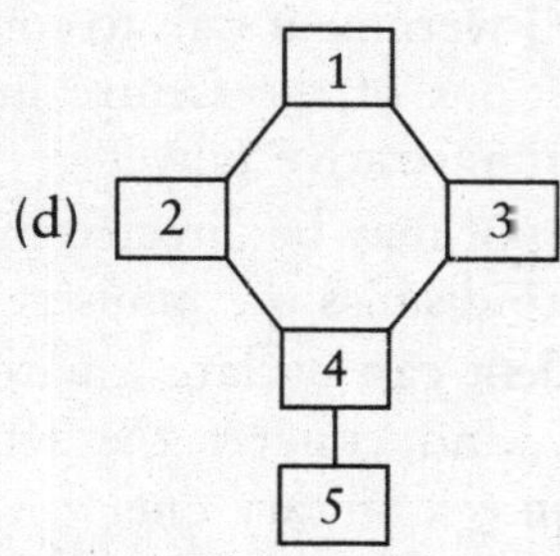

489. Collective responsibility is the hallmark of which form of Government?
(a) Parliamentary form
(b) Presidential form
(c) Military-form
(d) None of the above

490. Which of the following exercises power to promulgate ordinances during the recess of the legislative?
(a) Chief Minister (b) Governor
(c) Speaker (d) Deputy Speaker

491. Central Forensic Science Laboratory is situated at
(a) Chandigarh (b) Patna
(c) Patiala (d) Ludhiana

492. Which one of the following is not characteristic of Distance education?
(a) The speedy propagation of literacy.
(b) Formal education system.
(c) The maximum application of communicative media.
(d) The co-operation in the establishment of open universities.

493. The Contingency Fund of the State is placed under the
(a) Secretary, Finance Department
(b) State Legislature
(c) Speaker
(d) Chief Minister

494. The Distance education is
(a) a non-traditional educational process.
(b) the extension of qualitative instructional process.
(c) the application of system analysis approach.
(d) All of the above.

495. The size of the Council of Ministers of a State
(a) is fixed by the governor in accordance with the High Court's advice.
(b) is deided by the Chief Minister.
(c) is fixed by the Constitution (91st Amendment) Act, 2003.
(d) is dependent on the total strength of the assembly.

496. In Delhi University, the department of correspondence education was established in
(a) 1962 (b) 1968
(c) 1969 (d) 1970

497. Which one of the following cannot be dissolved but can be abolished any time?
(a) State Legislative Councils
(b) State Legislative Assemblies

(c) Rajya Sabha
(d) Lok Sabha

498. The first Open University in India was established by the State Government of
(a) Andhra Pradesh (b) Haryana
(c) Uttar Pradesh (d) Punjab

499. The Election Commission of a state can be removed from office
(a) only by the Governor.
(b) in the same manner and on the same grounds as a Judge of the Supreme Court.
(c) only by the President on the advice of the Chief Justice of the concerned State.
(d) in the same manner as the Vice-President of India.

500. The state Open University of Uttar Pradesh is
(a) Rajarshi Purshottam Das Tandon Open University
(b) Dr. Rajendra Prasad Open University
(c) Rajiv Gandhi Open University
(d) Indira Gandhi Open University

501. In Distance education, the students supportive activities are included as
(a) Contract service
(b) Library and study centre service
(c) Software and Hardware service
(d) All of the above

502. 'Parliamentary Supremacy' is a definite feature of the political system in
(a) UK (b) India
(c) Canada (d) Australia

503. The Distance education is not included under a specific service of the following
(a) Home assignment related service
(b) Curriculum related service
(c) Personal contract service
(d) Guidance related service

504. Cabinet government is based on
(a) separation of legislature and executive.
(b) fusion of legislature, executive and judiciary.
(c) fusion of legislature and executive.
(d) None of the above.

505. When and where the first Open school was founded in the country?
(a) 1979, Central Board of Secondary Education, New Delhi
(b) 1981, Rajasthan Board of Secondary Education, Jaipur
(c) 1979, Madhya Pradesh Board of Secondary Education, Bhopal
(d) 1979, Uttar Pradesh Board of Secondary Education, Allahabad

506. When a State Government fails to comply with the directions of the Centre in the exercise of administrative power
(a) The Governor may be directed by the President to dismiss the ministry.
(b) The President can declare a national emergency and convert the federal structure into a unitary one.
(c) A Constitutional emergency can be declared in the State and the President can assume all the powers of the State Government.
(d) The Supreme Court may be asked to intervene.

507. In National Open School, the education imparted of
(a) Foundation course only
(b) Secondary course only
(c) Senior secondary course only
(d) All the above courses

508. Open Vocational Education Program runs in
(a) National Open Schools
(b) Indira Gandhi National Open University

(c) All Common Schools
(d) Cannot say

509. ______ is the popular House of State Legislature.
(a) Legislative Assembly
(b) Legislative Council
(c) Legislative Sabha
(d) Zila Council

510. Which one of the following class of people is taking benefits from Open University?
(a) The adult person—who has left higher education due to some reasons.
(b) The working person—who are interested in enrichment of their knowledge.
(c) The adult women—who are deprived of higher education during their life.
(d) All of the above

511. Which one of the following is wrong?
(a) It is the duty of the Chief Minister to keep the Governor informed of all the decisions of the Cabinet.
(b) The Governor has the Power to ask for any information from the Chief Minister regarding the administration of the State.
(c) The Governor is the real head of the State administration.
(d) As an agent of the Central Government the Governor may have to act sometimes independently of the advice of the Council of Ministers.

512. The chief characteristic of Open University is
(a) free from campus boundation.
(b) diversification of teaching procedures.
(c) freedom from ideation.
(d) All of the above.

513. Which one of the following is not a function of the Chief Minister of a State?
(a) He allots business among his colleagues.
(b) He can ask any Minister to resign and in case of his refusal advise the Governor to dismiss him.
(c) He can dissolve the Legislative Assembly.
(d) He presides over the meetings of the Cabinet and controls the agenda thereof.

514. The main aim of Open university is
(a) To impart vocational and technical education to maximum persons
(b) To impart education to the people residing at remote places at their doorsteps
(c) To bring in contract the people through university curriculum in order to enhance national development
(d) All of the above

515. Chief Minister is not responsible for
(a) Running the entire administration of the State.
(b) The maintenance of the law and order in the State.
(c) The defence of the State.
(d) None of the above.

516. Which one of the following is not an instructional method of Open university?
(a) To learn through auto-instructional material.
(b) To teach in a face-to-face situation.
(c) To teach through satellite.
(d) To teach through computer.

517. In case of death, resignation or removal of Governor, ______ acts as the Governor.
(a) the Chief Minister
(b) the President of India
(c) the Speaker
(d) the Chief Justice of High Court

518. The meaning of Distance education is that
(a) It imparts from a distance.
(b) It imparts education through television.
(c) It propagates education in remotest areas.
(d) All the above are correct statements.

519. If a Governor wants to resign, to whom does he address his letter of resignation?
(a) Prime Minister
(b) Home Minister
(c) Chief Minister
(d) President of India

520. The advantage of Distance education is
(a) To every person, on every place, without any discrimination.
(b) An appropriate way of elimination of illiteracy.
(c) A safe education for women.
(d) All of the above.

521. A Governor can issue an ordinance
(a) whenever he likes.
(b) whenever Chief Minister advises him.
(c) whenever the State Legislature is not in Session and the Governor is satisfied that immediate action is needed.
(d) when the Union Government tells him to do so.

522. The innovative fact in Distance education is
(a) free from formal registration and enrollment.
(b) obligation of Constitutional directions.
(c) best use of leisure time.
(d) All of the above.

523. The Governor of a State can address the Legislature at the commencement of the
(a) new session after each general election
(b) first session every year
(c) Both of the above
(d) None of the above

524. The SITE program was launched by
(a) ISRO
(b) Indian TV Authority
(c) Through mutual coordination of the above agencies
(d) None of the above

525. Who appoints the Governor of a State?
(a) Home Minister of India
(b) President of India
(c) Chief Minister of that State
(d) Prime Minister of India

526. SITE has launched the program for adults which is called
(a) National News and Events
(b) Training of best instructional methods for different subjects
(c) Educational entertainment
(d) None of the above

527. In ______, the executive power of the State Government is vested.
(a) The President of India
(b) The Chief Minister
(c) The Governor
(d) The Speaker of the Legislative Assembly

528. Which of the following programs were launched by SITE?
(a) Programs for pre-primary level school going children
(b) Programs for Primary school teachers
(c) Awareness programs for masses
(d) All of the above

529. The Governor of a State holds his office only during the pleasure of
(a) Prime Minister (b) President
(c) Chief Minister (d) Home Minister

530. When INSAT 3-A was launched?
(a) 10 April, 2003 (b) 28 Sept., 2003
(c) 20 Sept., 2004 (d) 24 June, 2004

531. The right to freedom of speech and expression
(a) does not include freedom of press.
(b) includes freedom of press.
(c) includes freedom of press only in certain respects.
(d) None of the above.

532. When the Educational Programs are communicated in schools
(a) INSAT-1A (b) INSAT-1B
(c) INSAT-1C (d) INSAT-1D

533. In India freedom of press is
(a) specifically provided in the Constitution.
(b) implied in the right to freedom of expression.
(c) available to the people of India under Law of Parliament.
(d) available to the people of India under executive orders.

534. EDUSAT was projected in the orbit on
(a) 20 Sept., 2004 (b) 28 Sept., 2004
(c) 20 June, 2004 (d) 10 April, 2004

535. The grant of franchise to women on equal terms with men is assertion of the principle of
(a) Political equality
(b) Civil equality
(c) Natural equality
(d) Social equality

536. Internet is
(a) a specific tool of communication technology.
(b) a huge network among the computers.
(c) a special computer technique.
(d) None of the above.

537. The subordinate Civil Courts are headed by
(a) District Court
(b) Session Court
(c) Board of Revenue
(d) None of the above

538. The report of the Public Accounts Committee is presented to the
(a) President (b) Prime Minister
(c) Rajya Sabha (d) Lok Sabha

539. When Internet services were launched in India?
(a) January, 1997 (b) January, 1995
(c) January, 2000 (d) January, 2004

540. A Parliamentary government cannot operate without
(a) a written constitution
(b) an independent judiciary
(c) political parties
(d) a rigid constitution

541. The basic difference between Internet and Intranet is
(a) Spacing (b) Timing
(c) Technology (d) Technocrates

542. Which of the following statements is correct regarding the procedure of passing of Bills in Parliament?
(a) A bill pending in Parliament shall not lapse because of the propagation of the two Houses of Parliament.
(b) A bill pending in the Rajya Sabha which has not been passed by the Lok Sabha shall lapse on its dissolution.
(c) A bill pending in the Lok Sabha and pending in the Rajya Sabha shall not lapse on the dissolution of the Lok Sabha.
(d) A bill pending in the Rajya Sabha which has been passed by the Lok Sabha shall not lapse on the adjournment of the Rajya Sabha.

543. BITNET Network is generally used in
(a) Research and Education
(b) Commerce

(c) Trades
(d) Government offices

544. Parliamentary government was adopted in India
(a) By sheer accident.
(b) Because it was made obligatory to adopt this government under Indian Independence Act of 1947.
(c) Because of historical considerations and practical necessities.
(d) On account of all the above reasons.

545. Which one of the following statements is correct?
(a) The Chairman of the Rajya Sabha is elected by the elected members of the Rajya Sabha.
(b) The Chairman of the Rajya Sabha presides over the joint session of both the Houses of Parliament.
(c) The electoral college for the election of the Vice-President is the same as that for the election of the President.
(d) The nominated members of both the Houses of Parliament have voting right in the election of the Vice-President but not in the election of the President.

546. SDN helps in communication of
(a) Sound codes
(b) Visual codes
(c) Written informations
(d) All of the above

547. The Constitution of India is
(a) One of the smallest constitutions in the world.
(b) A medium sized constitution.
(c) One of the most elaborate constitutions of the world.
(d) None of the above.

548. The subject on which the State Government enjoys exclusive powers are given in
(a) Concurrent List (b) State List
(c) Union List (d) Residuary List

549. The Software which help in searching the information from Internet is
(a) Search Engine (b) Search Light
(c) Search Trotter (d) Search Motor

550. To which one of the following categories does the Right to Property belong?
(a) Legal Right
(b) Fundamental Right
(c) Human Right
(d) Natural Right

551. U.R.L. is stand for
(a) Universal Resource Locator
(b) Unique Research Locator
(c) Useful Research Location
(d) United Resource Laboratory

552. Decisions on question about disqualification of members of the Lok Sabha are taken by the
(a) President
(b) Prime Minister
(c) Minister for Parliamentary Affairs
(d) Secretary to Parliament

553. What is the complete version of EARN?
(a) European Academic and Research Network
(b) Eurasia Advanced Research Network
(c) English Academic Resource Network
(d) Educational Area Research Network

554. The members of Rajya Sabha are elected for a term of
(a) Three years (b) Five years
(c) Six years (d) Seven years

555. The meaning of Internet surfing is
(a) The person working with Internet
(b) The searching of required information on Internet
(c) Internet Browsing
(d) Internet Home Paging

556. Which one of the following is not an essential qualification for contesting election to Lok Sabha?
   (a) Citizenship of India
   (b) Age of 25 years
   (c) Soundness of mind
   (d) Graduation

557. Which one of the following Lok Sabhas was dissolved before the expiry of its normal term?
   (a) First Lok Sabha
   (b) Fourth Lok Sabha
   (c) Sixth Lok Sabha
   (d) None of the above

558. E-mail helps in
   (a) communication of informations.
   (b) reading of informations on other computer monitors.
   (c) preservation and Retrieval of the informations.
   (d) All of the above.

559. The Government in India is known as Parliamentary because
   (a) Parliament is elected by the people
   (b) Parliament consists of two houses
   (c) Parliament is a sovereign body
   (d) The executive is accountable to the Legislature

560. E-mail is commonly used in
   (a) Educational institutions only
   (b) Trading organisations only
   (c) Military organisations only
   (d) All of the above

561. The Rajya Sabha
   (a) is a permanent house
   (b) has a maximum life of 6 years
   (c) has a maximum life of 5 years
   (d) has no fixed life

562. E-mail brings revolution in the field of commercial business because it is
   (a) convenient in usage
   (b) economic in nature
   (c) having high speed of work
   (d) All of the above

563. How many seats have been reserved for the Union Territories in Lok Sabha?
   (a) 20 (b) 25
   (c) 30 (d) 50

564. The important E-mail companies of India are
   (a) Wipro V.T. mail (b) Global mail
   (c) X E-mail (d) All the above

565. Which one of the following statements holds good in respect of the Rajya Sabha?
   (a) One-third of its members retire after every three years.
   (b) Two-thirds of its members retire after every three years.
   (c) Two-thirds of its members retire after every two years.
   (d) One-third of its members retire after every two years.

566. The complete education services are rendered through
   (a) EDUSAT-2004 (b) INSAT-1B
   (c) INSAT-1C (d) INSAT-1E

567. Who amongst the following acts as the presiding officer of the House without being its members?
   (a) Vice-President of India
   (b) Speaker of the Lok Sabha
   (c) Chairman of the Legislative Council
   (d) Speaker of the Legislative Assembly

568. The possible lifespan of EDUSAT is
   (a) 5 years (b) 7 years
   (c) 8 years (d) 3 years

569. Who among the following is considered to the custodian of the Lok Sabha?
   (a) The Prime Minister
   (b) The Leader of the Opposition

(c) The Chief whip of the ruling party
(d) The Speaker

570. The total Number of Correspondence Course Institutes under the Distance Education Council in India during 2007-08 is
(a) 104 (b) 115
(c) 118 (d) 130

571. The Speaker of Lok Sabha has to address his letter of resignation to the
(a) Prime Minister of India
(b) Deputy Speaker of Lok Sabha
(c) President of India
(d) Vice-President of India

572. The "Fundamental Duties" of the Indian citizen have been
(a) originally provided by the constitution.
(b) included in the constitution by the 44th amendment.
(c) included in the constitution by the 42nd amendment.
(d) inserted into the constitution by a judgement of the Supreme Court.

573. How many correspondence course Institutes (CCIs) under ODL system during 2008-09?
(a) 130 (b) 135
(c) 140 (d) 145

574. The Presidential Government operates on the principle of
(a) Separation of Powers
(b) Division of Labour
(c) Fusion of Labour
(d) Centralisation of Power

575. Value can be defined in psychological terms as
(a) Individual commitment to certain goal, idea or belief
(b) Individual's affective aspect of behaviour
(c) Individual's emotions to do something for humanity
(d) None of the above

576. Consider the following statements:
The Fundamental duties
1. Have always been a part of the constitution of India
2. Have been added through an amendment
3. Are applicable to all citizens of India
Which of these statements is/are correct?
(a) 1 and 3 (b) Only 1
(c) Only 2 (d) 2 and 3

577. The dialectical hierarchy of values consists of
(a) Psycho-biological dimensions
(b) Social-ethical dimensions
(c) Spiritual-transcedent dimensions
(d) All of the above

578. Indian Constitution reserves the residuary powers to
(a) The Union (b) The States
(c) The Parliament (d) The President

579. Social ethical dimensions includes the value of
(a) Self-regulation
(b) Self-actualisation
(c) Self-transcedence
(d) None of the above

580. The Constitution amendment bills are initiated in
(a) The Lok Sabha
(b) The Rajya Sabha
(c) Either House
(d) The Lok Sabha with the prior approval of the State assemblies

581. Psycho-biological dimensions are affiliated to the dimensions of morality with
(a) Prudence (b) Loyalty
(c) Reverence (d) All of the above

582. The main feature of Presidential government is
(a) Stability
(b) Irresponsibility
(c) Checks and balances
(d) Rigidity

583. Shriprakash ji was the chairman in 1959 of the
(a) Committee on Religious and Moral Education
(b) Committee on Ethical Issues
(c) Committee on Moral Values
(d) Committee on Spiritual Values

584. Which one of the following is not concerned with the value related to life?
(a) Physical value
(b) Intellectual value
(c) Economic value
(d) Perpetual value

585. Which one of the following method cannot develop values in children?
(a) Role-playing method
(b) Interview method
(c) Lecture method
(d) Identifying method

586. The basic objective of value education is
(a) to promote in children such qualities as truthfulness co-operation, love, etc.
(b) to train them to become responsible citizens in their personal and social lines.
(c) to enable them to appreciate the national goals of socialism.
(d) All of the above.

587. On the basis of classification the temporal context value includes
(a) Perpetual and Temporary values
(b) Moral and spiritual values
(c) Cultural and Religious values
(d) Aesthetic and Political values

588. The Kothari Commission has given the following statement about Value Education
(a) To implement all the recommedations put forward by the UGC.
(b) To implement Value Education in private sector Educational Institutes.
(c) To make an hourly arrangement for delivering Value Education in the institutes.
(d) All of the above.

589. The term value is originated from
(a) Latin word *valere*
(b) Greek word *valatus*
(c) English word *valuable*
(d) None of the above

590. The Educational values are
(a) Spontaneous in value
(b) Subordinate to desires full of wisdom
(c) Aesthetic
(d) All of the above

591. Kothari Commission had recommended about the implementation of value Education through teachers as
(a) The teachers must behave in an ideal manner along with students and inculcate these feelings in their students during teaching.
(b) The teacher must do teacher-like behaviour and instruct them in a monopolise manner.
(c) The teacher must follow their duties in relation to students without any botheration.
(d) It is the pious duty of the teachers that they must do moral behaviour with their students irrespective of its any consequences.

592. 'Value' is having equivalent Sanskrit term
(a) *Isht*
(b) *Est*

(c) *Voluntary* (Echchhik)
(d) *Interest* (Ruchiatmak)

593. The essential constituents of value-oriented education is
(a) Feelings of Global Brotherhoodness
(b) Co-existence
(c) Secularity
(d) All of the above

594. Which of the following is not a characteristic of Educational value?
(a) Utility (b) Purposiveness
(c) Adequacy (d) Reliability

595. The number of *Purushartha* in Indian culture is
(a) Four (b) Two
(c) Three (d) Five

596. Values are the way of imparting education
(a) Storytelling method
(b) Direction-giving method
(c) Psychodrama method
(d) All of the above

597. The four *Purushartha's* are
(a) Artha - Kama - Dharma - Moksha
(b) Artha - Dharma - Kama - Moksha
(c) Artha - Dharma - Karma - Manna
(d) None of the above

598. Which one of the following quality is concerned with the vision of National Policy on Education - 1986 in relation to Value Education?
(a) The implementation of universal and perpetual values should be according to Indian socio-cultural milieu.
(b) The terms like—religious disbeliefs, rigidity, intolerance, violence, and luck-dependence, etc. negative ideas must be eliminated in the above Educational Values.
(c) Both of the above.
(d) None of the above.

599. The objective values are present in
(a) Objects (b) Persons
(c) Both of these (d) None of these

600. The worldly cultural value of India is
(a) Dharma - Artha - Kama
(b) Dharma - Artha only
(c) Artha and Kama only
(d) Dharma - Artha - Kama - Moksha

601. The popular point of view about the nature of values is
(a) Individualistic point of view
(b) Objective point of view
(c) Relativistic point of view
(d) All the above point of view

602. 'To describe the aims of Education is to describe its Educational value'. This statement was put forth by
(a) P.T. Nunn (b) Bertrand Russell
(c) Brubacher (d) James Ross

603. Plato's conception of value is
(a) Value is intellectually acceptable terminology not an Empirically acceptable term.
(b) Value and *Sat* have clearcut discrimination from each other.
(c) Value is absolute and perpetual subject related to *Sat*.
(d) All of the above.

ANSWERS

1. (c)	2. (d)	3. (c)	4. (a)	5. (a)	6. (c)
7. (a)	8. (a)	9. (d)	10. (b)	11. (a)	12. (a)
13. (a)	14. (c)	15. (a)	16. (b)	17. (b)	18. (b)

19. (d)	20. (a)	21. (c)	22. (d)	23. (a)	24. (a)
25. (c)	26. (c)	27. (d)	28. (d)	29. (a)	30. (c)
31. (c)	32. (d)	33. (b)	34. (b)	35. (a)	36. (d)
37. (d)	38. (d)	39. (c)	40. (d)	41. (a)	42. (a)
43. (c)	44. (d)	45. (d)	46. (b)	47. (b)	48. (b)
49. (b)	50. (b)	51. (d)	52. (b)	53. (a)	54. (c)
55. (d)	56. (b)	57. (c)	58. (a)	59. (d)	60. (d)
61. (d)	62. (d)	63. (c)	64. (c)	65. (b)	66. (d)
67. (d)	68. (b)	69. (d)	70. (d)	71. (c)	72. (b)
73. (a)	74. (c)	75. (b)	76. (b)	77. (b)	78. (d)
79. (c)	80. (b)	81. (c)	82. (d)	83. (c)	84. (c)
85. (a)	86. (c)	87. (a)	88. (a)	89. (c)	90. (c)
91. (d)	92. (d)	93. (b)	94. (c)	95. (d)	96. (d)
97. (d)	98. (c)	99. (c)	100. (d)	101. (a)	102. (c)
103. (d)	104. (b)	105. (d)	106. (d)	107. (d)	108. (c)
109. (c)	110. (a)	111. (b)	112. (d)	113. (a)	114. (a)
115. (a)	116. (b)	117. (b)	118. (a)	119. (c)	120. (a)
121. (a)	122. (b)	123. (c)	124. (c)	125. (d)	126. (a)
127. (a)	128. (a)	129. (d)	130. (a)	131. (d)	132. (d)
133. (d)	134. (d)	135. (c)	136. (a)	137. (b)	138. (c)
139. (b)	140. (b)	141. (d)	142. (d)	143. (c)	144. (b)
145. (c)	146. (b)	147. (b)	148. (c)	149. (a)	150. (a)
151. (b)	152. (c)	153. (b)	154. (b)	155. (d)	156. (c)
157. (c)	158. (b)	159. (d)	160. (a)	161. (d)	162. (b)
163. (c)	164. (a)	165. (d)	166. (d)	167. (d)	168. (b)
169. (b)	170. (b)	171. (c)	172. (d)	173. (a)	174. (a)
175. (d)	176. (a)	177. (a)	178. (b)	179. (d)	180. (d)
181. (a)	182. (a)	183. (c)	184. (d)	185. (a)	186. (d)
187. (d)	188. (a)	189. (a)	190. (c)	191. (d)	192. (b)
193. (d)	194. (b)	195. (c)	196. (c)	197. (d)	198. (a)
199. (d)	200. (d)	201. (a)	202. (a)	203. (a)	204. (d)
205. (c)	206. (b)	207. (b)	208. (c)	209. (c)	210. (c)
211. (d)	212. (d)	213. (d)	214. (a)	215. (d)	216. (d)
217. (a)	218. (b)	219. (b)	220. (a)	221. (c)	222. (d)

223. (a	224. (c)	225. (a)	226. (a)	227. (d)	228. (a)
229. (a	230. (d)	231. (b)	232. (c)	233. (d)	234. (c)
235. (a	236. (b)	237. (b)	238. (a)	239. (c)	240. (a)
241. (a	242. (d)	243. (a)	244. (d)	245. (b)	246. (d)
247. (b	248. (d)	249. (a)	250. (c)	251. (c)	252. (a)
253. (d	254. (b)	255. (a)	256. (b)	257. (a)	258. (b)
259. (d	260. (d)	261. (b)	262. (d)	263. (d)	264. (d)
265. (a)	266. (c)	267. (a)	268. (a)	269. (a)	270. (d)
271. (a)	272. (a)	273. (b)	274. (a)	275. (a)	276. (b)
277. (c)	278. (d)	279. (a)	280. (b)	281. (d)	282. (d)
283. (a)	284. (c)	285. (d)	286. (d)	287. (a)	288. (a)
289. (a)	290. (d)	291. (a)	292. (c)	293. (d)	294. (a)
295. (d)	296. (a)	297. (b)	298. (b)	299. (d)	300. (d)
301. (c)	302. (d)	303. (a)	304. (a)	305. (a)	306. (a)
307. (d)	308. (d)	309. (b)	310. (a)	311. (c)	312. (a)
313. (a)	314. (a)	315. (d)	316. (a)	317. (b)	318. (b)
319. (a)	320. (a)	321. (a)	322. (a)	323. (a)	324. (d)
325. (a)	326. (b)	327. (a)	328. (a)	329. (a)	330. (a)
331. (c)	332. (a)	333. (a)	334. (a)	335. (d)	336. (d)
337. (a)	338. (d)	339. (a)	340. (b)	341. (d)	342. (a)
343. (d)	344. (d)	345. (a)	346. (a)	347. (c)	348. (a)
349. (d)	350. (a)	351. (c)	352. (d)	353. (c)	354. (b)
355. (d)	356. (a)	357. (a)	358. (a)	359. (b)	360. (c)
361. (a)	362. (d)	363. (b)	364. (c)	365. (c)	366. (a)
367. (b)	368. (d)	369. (a)	370. (d)	371. (b)	372. (b)
373. (a)	374. (a)	375. (b)	376. (a)	377. (a)	378. (c)
379. (c)	380. (a)	381. (b)	382. (a)	383. (d)	384. (a)
385. (c)	386. (d)	387. (a)	388. (d)	389. (a)	390. (a)
391. (c)	392. (a)	393. (b)	394. (c)	395. (b)	396. (d)
397. (a)	398. (b)	399. (b)	400. (c)	401. (b)	402. (c)
403. (a)	404. (c)	405. (a)	406. (c)	407. (a)	408. (b)
409. (b)	410. (a)	411. (c)	412. (c)	413. (c)	414. (b)
415. (d)	416. (c)	417. (a)	418. (b)	419. (c)	420. (c)
421. (a)	422. (c)	423. (b)	424. (d)	425. (d)	426. (a)

427. (d)	428. (d)	429. (d)	430. (c)	431. (b)	432. (d)
433. (a)	434. (a)	435. (c)	436. (a)	437. (d)	438. (b)
439. (d)	440. (b)	441. (d)	442. (b)	443. (c)	444. (a)
445. (b)	446. (b)	447. (c)	448. (d)	449. (d)	450. (b)
451. (c)	452. (a)	453. (c)	454. (b)	455. (b)	456. (a)
457. (d)	458. (b)	459. (b)	460. (c)	461. (b)	462. (a)
463. (b)	464. (c)	465. (d)	466. (c)	467. (c)	468. (d)
469. (b)	470. (d)	471. (d)	472. (a)	473. (b)	474. (c)
475. (a)	476. (a)	477. (c)	478. (a)	479. (c)	480. (c)
481. (b)	482. (b)	483. (a)	484. (a)	485. (c)	486. (d)
487. (b)	488. (a)	489. (a)	490. (b)	491. (a)	492. (b)
493. (a)	494. (d)	495. (c)	496. (a)	497. (a)	498. (a)
499. (b)	500. (a)	501. (d)	502. (a)	503. (c)	504. (c)
505. (a)	506. (c)	507. (d)	508. (a)	509. (a)	510. (d)
511. (c)	512. (d)	513. (c)	514. (d)	515. (c)	516. (b)
517. (d)	518. (d)	519. (d)	520. (d)	521. (c)	522. (d)
523. (a)	524. (c)	525. (b)	526. (d)	527. (c)	528. (d)
529. (b)	530. (a)	531. (b)	532. (b)	533. (b)	534. (a)
535. (a)	536. (b)	537. (a)	538. (d)	539. (a)	540. (c)
541. (a)	542. (a)	543. (a)	544. (c)	545. (c)	546. (d)
547. (c)	548. (b)	549. (a)	550. (a)	551. (a)	552. (a)
553. (a)	554. (c)	555. (b)	556. (d)	557. (c)	558. (d)
559. (d)	560. (d)	561. (a)	562. (d)	563. (a)	564. (d)
565. (d)	566. (a)	567. (a)	568. (b)	569. (d)	570. (d)
571. (c)	572. (c)	573. (c)	574. (a)	575. (a)	576. (d)
577. (d)	578. (a)	579. (b)	580. (c)	581. (a)	582. (a)
583. (a)	584. (d)	585. (c)	586. (d)	587. (a)	588. (d)
589. (a)	590. (d)	591. (a)	592. (a)	593. (d)	594. (d)
595. (a)	596. (d)	597. (a)	598. (c)	599. (a)	600. (a)
601. (d)	602. (c)	603. (d)			

Model Test Papers

TEST PAPER - I

Note: This paper contains sixty multiple-choice questions, each question carrying two marks. Candidate is expected to answer any fifty questions. In case more than 50 questions are attempted, only the first 50 questions will be evaluated.

1. A teacher is called the leader of the class because
   (a) he is autocratic emperor of his class
   (b) he masters the art of oratory like a political leader
   (c) he is a maker of the future of his students
   (d) he belongs to a recognised teachers' union

2. The aim of introducing career courses in schools and colleges is to
   (a) increase G.K. in students
   (b) develop the ability to make the intelligent choice of jobs
   (c) provide professional knowledge to students
   (d) All of the above

3. The most effective attribute for a teacher is
   (a) Teaching skills (b) Knowledge
   (c) Feedback (d) Management

4. Those teachers are preferred most by students who
   (a) are themselves disciplined
   (b) give important questions before examination
   (c) dictate notes in the class
   (d) can clear their difficulties regarding subject-matter

5. The qualities of a teacher is/are:
   (i) He must not give any false promise
   (ii) He must not have any bad habits
   (iii) He should be mentally and physically fit
   (iv) He must not be superstitious about his class and students
   (a) Only (iii), (iv) and (ii)
   (b) Only (iv), (i) and (ii)
   (c) Only (i), (iii) and (iv)
   (d) All of the above

6. A teacher is more effective who can
   (a) motivate students to learn
   (b) control the class
   (c) correct the assignments carefully
   (d) give more information in less time

7. A teacher ought to know the problems prevalent in the field of education because
   (a) he can tell the government about it
   (b) with this knowledge, he can have information about education
   (c) he can tell about the same to another teacher
   (d) only he can do something about solving them

8. We can judge the quality of a research by the
   (a) experience of researcher
   (b) relevance of research

(c) depth of the research
(d) methodology followed in conducting the research

9. The theory or model developed through the fundamental research to the actual solution of the problems is applied in
(a) educational research
(b) action research
(c) applied research
(d) basic research

10. A write-up based on studies of the census data of a given area is called
(a) Research paper (b) Article
(c) Research report (d) Thesis

Direction: (11-16) Study the following passage and give answer to the questions based on it.

Knowledge creation in many cases requires creativity and idea generation. This is especially important in generating alternative decision support solutions. Some people believe that an individual's creative ability stems primarily from personality traits such as inventiveness, independence, individuality, enthusiasm, and flexibility. However, several studies have found that creativity is not so much a function of individual traits as was once believed, and that individual creativity can be learned and improved. This understanding has led innovative companies to recognise that the key to fostering creativity may be the development of an idea-nurturing work environment. Idea-generation methods and techniques, to be used by individuals or in groups, are consequently being developed. Manual methods for supporting idea generation, such as brain-storming in a group, can be very successful in certain situations. However, in other situations, such an approach is either not economically feasible or not possible. For example, manual methods in group creativity sessions will not work or will not be effective when: (a) there is no time to conduct a proper idea-generation session; (b) there is a poor facilitator (or no facilitator at all); (c) it is too expensive to conduct an idea-generation session; (d) the subject matter is too sensitive for a face-to-face session; or (e) there are not enough participants, the mix of participants is not optimal, or there is no climate for idea generation. In such cases, computerised idea-generation methods have been tried, with frequent success. Idea-generation software is designed to help stimulate a single user or a group to produce new ideas, options and choices. The user does all the work, but the software encourages and pushes, something like a personal trainer. Although idea-generation software is still relatively new, there are several packages on the market. Various approaches are used by idea-generating software to increase the flow of ideas to the user. Idea Fisher, for example, has an associate lexicon of the English language that cross-references words and phrases. These associative links, based on analogies and metaphors, make it easy for the user to be fed words related to a given theme. Some software packages use questions to prompt the user towards new, unexplored patterns of thought. This helps users to break out of cyclical thinking patterns, conquer mental blocks, or deal with bouts of procrastination.

11. The author, in this passage has focused on
(a) individual traits
(b) knowledge creation
(c) creativity
(d) idea-generation

12. Idea-generation software works as if it is a
(a) user-friendly trainer
(b) stimulant
(c) climate creator
(d) knowledge package

13. Which among the following personality traits is not believed to be a factor contributing to an individual's creative ability?
(a) Flexibility (b) Individuality
(c) Sophistication (d) Enthusiasm

14. In certain occasions, manual methods for the support of idea-generation
(a) can be less expensive
(b) do not need a facilitator
(c) require a mix of optimal participants
(d) are alternatively effective

15. Mental blocks, bouts of procrastination and cyclical thinking patterns can be won when
(a) idea-generation software prompts questions
(b) individuals acquire a neutral attitude towards the software
(c) manual methods are removed
(d) innovative companies employ electronic thinking methods

16. Fostering creativity needs an environment of
(a) decision support systems
(b) alternative individual factors
(c) idea-nurturing
(d) decision support solutions

17. For controlling noise in a classroom, the best method of communication is
(a) remaining calm and just looking at student
(b) saying 'don't talk'
(c) continue teaching without caring for noise
(d) raising one's voice above students voice

18. In India, Education TV was first introduced in the year
(a) 1978 (b) 1959
(c) 1987 (d) 1998

19. The failure of the teacher to communicate his ideas well to students may result into:
I. Classroom indiscipline.
II. Decrease in attendance in class.
III. Loss of student's interest in class.
(a) Only II (b) Only III
(c) Only I (d) All of these

20. Visualisation in the instructional process cannot increase
(a) curiosity and concentration
(b) interest and motivation
(c) stress and boredom
(d) retention and adaptation

21. Communication helps in
(a) entertainment
(b) integration of country
(c) cultural promotion
(d) All of these

22. "Because you deserve to know" is the punchline used by
(a) *Hindustan Times*
(b) *The Telegraph*
(c) *The Times of India*
(d) *India Today*

23. Find the odd man out from the following groups of letters.
(a) UlmnE (b) AbcdE
(c) ApqrL (d) IfghO

24. The ambitious computerisation program of the Government of India aimed at connecting 60,000 government schools through internet is known as
(a) Vidya Vahini (b) Gyan Vahini
(c) Kalpana project (d) Vidya Vani

25. Find the wrong number in the following sequence.
225, 336, 447, 557, 669, 771
(a) 669 (b) 557
(c) 336 (d) 771

26. In this question two words are given which have certain relationship followed by four paired lettered words. Select the paired words, that has the same relation as original pair.

ROOF : FOUNDATION

(a) Plateau : Valley
(b) Peak : Valley
(c) Mountain : Grassland
(d) Hill : Mountain

27. "Communication is a verbal process by which we understand each other and reduce uncertainty through the use of symbol." Who is the author of this statement?

(a) David K. Barlo
(b) Dance
(c) P.S.K. Serichavenko
(d) K.J. Newman

28. Find out the missing number:

8 24 12 ? 18 54

(a) 28 (b) 32
(c) 36 (d) 38

29. A D C F

C F E H

O R ? ?

(a) JK (b) RN
(c) SU (d) QT

30. 3, 12, 27, 48, 75, (?), 147.

(a) 111 (b) 108
(c) 117 (d) 122

31. In this question four words have been given, out of which three are alike in some manner and the fourth one is different. Choose the odd one out.

(a) Epigraphy (b) Ecology
(c) Archaeology (d) Palaeontology

32. Which of the following figures will represent the right relationship between, societies, societies who run schools, DPS society.

(a) 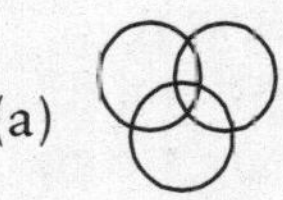 (b)

(c) (d)

33. **Statements:**

I. All students are ambitious.
II. All ambitious persons are hard working.

Conclusions:

(i) All students are hard-working.
(ii) All hardly working people are not ambitious.

Which of the following is correct?

(a) Only (i) is correct
(b) Only (ii) is correct
(c) Both (i) and (ii) are correct
(d) Neither (i) nor (ii) is correct

34. In a certain code language:

'pit dit mit' means: 'Reena went to Delhi'.
'dit ket set' means: 'Delhi is closing'.
'mit set un' means: 'Reena' is educated.

Then what is the code for 'went'?

(a) dit (b) mit
(c) pit (d) None of these

35. EDITOR : MAGAZINE

Choose the pair from the answer choices that best expresses the relationship similar to that expressed by the question pair.

(a) Novel : Writer
(b) Director : Film
(c) Poem : Poet
(d) Chair : Carpenter

36. Should education in India be made free?

Arguments:

I. Yes, this is the only way to improve the level of literacy.
II. No, this would add already heavy burden on the exchequer.

(a) Only argument I is strong
(b) Only argument II is strong
(c) Both the arguments are strong
(d) None of these

Direction: (37-41) Study the table and answer the questions:

Export of Pulses and Import of Onion (in ₹ crores)

Year	Export of Pulses (in ₹ crores)	Import of Onion (in ₹ crores)
1998-99	44	58
1999-00	45	50
2000-01	60	54
2001-02	56	60
2002-03	92	68
2003-04	100	78
2004-05	68	60

37. During which year there was a maximum fall in export?
(a) 2004-05 (b) 2001-02
(c) 2003-04 (d) None of these

38. The percent of increase of imports in 2003-04 over 2002-03 is
(a) 14.9% (b) 14.7%
(c) 18.4% (d) 18.9%

39. In 1999-2000, the ratio of export to the import is
(a) 19:11 (b) 11:9
(c) 13:17 (d) 9:10

40. During which year there was maximum increase in import over its preceding year?
(a) 2003-04 (b) 2000-01
(c) 2001-02 (d) 2002-03

41. During which year there was minimum increase in import over its preceding year?
(a) 2003-04 (b) 2002-03
(c) 2001-02 (d) None of these

42. The sum of a positive number and its reciprocal is twice the difference of the number and its reciprocal. The number is:
(c) $\sqrt{3}$ (a) $\sqrt{2}$
(b) $\frac{1}{\sqrt{2}}$ (d) $\frac{1}{\sqrt{3}}$

43. Which one of the following states has the maximum number of Wildlife Sanctuaries (National Park and Sanctuaries)?
(a) Madhya Pradesh
(b) Rajasthan
(c) Uttar Pradesh
(d) West Bengal

Directions: (44-48) Answer the following questions based on the graph given below:

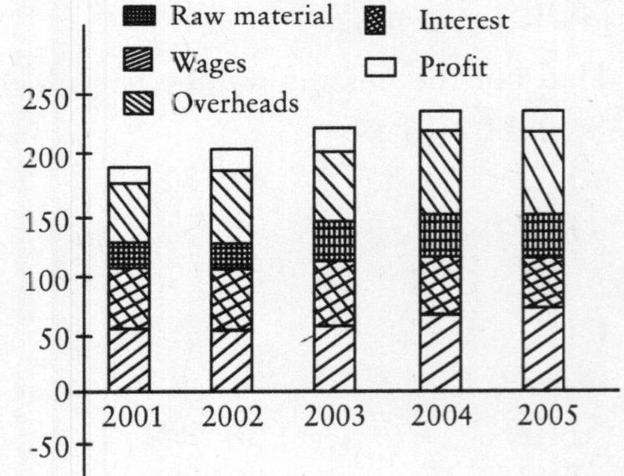

44. Which component of the cost of production has remained almost unchanged over the period 2001-2005?
(a) Wages (b) Interest
(c) Raw material (d) Overheads

45. In which year was the increase in raw material maximum?
(a) 2004 (b) 2002
(c) 2003 (d) 2001

46. What percent of costs did the profits from over the period?
(a) 7% (b) 5%
(c) 2% (d) 1%

47. In which period was the change in profit maximum?
(a) 2002-03 (b) 2001-02
(c) 2004-05 (d) 2003-04

48. If the interest component is not included in the total cost calculation, which year would show the maximum profit per unit cost?
(a) 2001 (b) 2002
(c) 2003 (d) 2005

49. How many types of emergencies have been envisaged by the constitution?
(a) One (b) Two
(c) Three (d) Four

50. Photocopying and other electrical equipments produce
(a) methane
(b) ethane
(c) ozone
(d) hydrogen dioxide

51. Which of the following is wrongly matched?
(a) Birbal Sahni Institute of Palaeobotany—Kolkata
(b) Central Institute of Cotton Research—Nagpur
(c) Indian Naval Academy—Kochin
(d) Central Leather Research Institute—Chennai

52. The most active volcanoes on earth are concentrated in
(a) South America (b) Pacific Ocean
(c) Indian Ocean (d) Atlantic Ocean

53. A set of flip-flops integrated together is called
(a) Counter (b) Register
(c) Adder (d) None of these

54. Match List I (Institutions) with List II (Functions) and select the correct answer by using the code given below.

List I (Institutions)
(A) Parliament
(B) C. & A.G.
(C) Ministry of Finance
(D) Executing Departments

List II (Functions)
(1) Formulation of Budget
(2) Enactment of Budget
(3) Implementation of Budget
(4) Implementation of Budget
(5) Justification of Income

Codes:	**A**	**B**	**C**	**D**
(a)	1	5	3	2
(b)	2	5	3	1
(c)	4	1	5	3
(d)	5	3	1	4

55. What is the sign magnitude representation of binary number +1101.011?
(a) 1100.001 (b) 1101.0110
(c) 01101.011 (d) 101001.1001

56. Green mufler is used against which type of pollution?
(a) Soil (b) Air
(c) Water (d) Noise

57. MDR (Memory Data Register) holds the
(a) Address of a memory location
(b) Segment number
(c) Register of computer controlled unit
(d) None of the above

58. Who among the following enjoys the distinction of being the first woman judge of Supreme Court of India?
(a) Kiran Bedi
(b) Hara Patnaik
(c) M. Fathima Beevi
(d) Leila Seth

59. Which of the following states is called Tiger state?
(a) Uttar Pradesh (b) Madhya Pradesh
(c) Bihar (d) West Bengal

60. During winter days, the cloudy nights are warmer compared to clear nights (without clouds), because
   (a) clouds being at great heights from earth absorb heat from the sun and send towards the earth
   (b) clouds radiate heat towards the earth
   (c) clouds prevent escaping of the heat radiation from the earth
   (d) clouds prevent cold wave from the sky, descend on earth

TEST PAPER - II

Note: This paper contains sixty multiple-choice questions, each question carrying two marks. Candidate is expected to answer any fifty questions. In case more than 50 questions are attempted, only the first 50 questions will be evaluated.

1. Minimum program of guidance includes
   (a) occupational information service
   (b) data collector service
   (c) counselling service
   (d) All of these
2. If majority of students in a class is weak, a teacher should
   (a) not care about intelligent students
   (b) keep his speed of teaching fast so that students comprehension level may increase
   (c) keep his teaching slow which can also be helpful-to bright students
   (d) keep his teaching slow along with some extra guidance to bright students
3. If the principal of your institution is not satisfied with your performance and charge you with the act of negligence of duties, how would you behave with him?
   (a) You would neglect him
   (b) You would take revenge by giving physical and mental agony to him
   (c) You would keep yourself alert and make his efforts unfruitful
   (d) You would take a tough stand against the charges
4. What makes people to undertake research?
   (a) Desire to get intellectual joy of doing some creative work
   (b) Desire to get a research degree along with its consequential benefits
   (c) Desire to face the challenge in solving the unsolved problems
   (d) All of these
5. Which of the following aims at probing into the phenomenon to formulate a more precise research problem or to develop a new hypothesis?
   (a) Descriptive research
   (b) Conclusive research
   (c) Diagnostic research
   (d) Exploratory research
6. Which of the following is not instructional material?
   (a) Transparency
   (b) Overhead projector
   (c) Printed material
   (d) Audio cassette
7. Of great importance in determining the amount of transference that occurs in the process of learning is the
   (a) knowledge of the teacher
   (b) IQ of the teacher
   (c) presence of identical elements
   (d) use of appropriate elements
8. The characteristic(s) of hypothesis is/are:
   I. It can be tested.
   II. It must consists of known facts.
   III. It must be objective and specific.
   (a) Only I and III (b) Only I and II
   (c) Only I (d) All of these
9. The guide for the research requires which of the following qualities?

(a) Interdisciplinary expertise
(b) Subject matter expertise
(c) Methodological expertise
(d) All of these

10. Which of the following indicates evaluation?
(a) Seema got 195 marks out of 200
(b) Sapna got 72 percent marks in English
(c) Asha got First Division in final examination
(d) All of the above

Direction: (11-16) Study the following passage and give answer to the questions based on it.

Much of the theoretical literature of archeology in the 1980s devotes considerable energy to bashing the 1970s, and the target often turns out to be the so-called New or Processual Archeology. While many of the attacks come from recent theorists who are attempting to replace it with post-processual archeology, some criticism comes from within what was New Archeology even from the hand of its original champion, Lewis Binford. If scholars from both outside and inside the theoretical developments of the 1970s are rejecting the New Archeology, why am I defending its importance to us today? The answer is very simple...for better or worse, it is us! As Alison Whylie has recently said the New Archeology of the 1960s quickly became everybody's archeology in the 1970s. Most of today's faculty members and senior archeologists were the people who, in one way or another, adopted the teachings of New Archeology. Although most archeologists did not claim to agree with all aspects of New Archeology nor could more than two or three people agree on what it was, virtually one rejected it outright. Typically, each one presented her or his version, often using a New Archeology text as a starting point for pedagogical purposes. Few wanted to be left out of the exciting new theoretical movement of those years, and New Archeology was passed on to the succeeding generation of students who reached maturity in the 1980s and are today's young professionals.

Criticisms now leveled against the New Archeology of the seventies do have merit, but by discounting that era as misguided, critics have overlooked its crucial importance. New Archeology has an important historical role in the developments of the field we have today and it has continuing importance because it is still guiding archeology's trajectory into the future. Equally troubling is that some critics ask us to reject the basic tenets of New Archeology and to replace them with a system often called post processualist archeology. I believe this is rhetoric that not only misrepresents the achievements of the New Archeology of the seventies, but also does not successfully articulate the potential contributions of its own position.

To put the New Archeology of the seventies into perspective, it is important to review the decades leading up to its development. In the first years following World War II, archeology was still a small field, but by the fifties and the sixties, it was expanding rapidly and taking itself quite seriously. Since the launching of Sputnik in 1957 there had emerged a frenzy in the United States to make all disciplines more scientific. Great strides were made in bringing science into archeology through new dating techniques a multidisciplinary approach, early experiments with the use of statistics, and devoting substantial attention to increasing the precision of artifact classification. The sixties provided the nation with both the optimistic Kennedy years, with an emphasis on science and the conviction that we were capable of accomplishing wondrous; things, and the cynical Vietnam era. Coming on the heels of a decade of civil rights unrest, the widespread dissatisfaction with the Vietnam conflict in the late sixties molded a generation of young Americans who were distrustful of established authority. In academic life, there was an increasing emphasis on environment, other cultures, and people oriented disciplines. Anthropology and archeology grew markedly because of these trends. Archeologists were urged to become concerned with sociological issues—the people behind the artifacts.

It was during these decades of rapid change that many of the core concepts of the New Archeology entered the literature. However, they were not, at first, assembled into a program for action that attracted a solid following. Water Taylor advocated the conjuctive approach with little effect, while Leslie White's evolutionism and Julian Styeward's cultural ecology attracted some attention, but largely among cultural anthropologists. Albert Spaulding led a one-man campaign to bring science and statistics into archeology. But the individual whose work catalyzed the New Archeology movement was Lewis Binford, who incorporated these earlier lines of thinking together with an explicit concern for scientific methods and field research designs. Much of Binford's thinking probably crystallised while he was at the University of Michigan, but was during his relatively few years at the University of Chicago that he changed the direction of modern archeology.

11. New Archeology refers to
    (a) newer techniques used in Archeology
    (b) newer inventions used in Archeology
    (c) newer theoretical foundations in Archeology
    (d) None of these

12. The author defends the Archeology of the 1970's because
    (a) he has a nostalgic feeling about it
    (b) it has research value
    (c) it paved way for newer traditions
    (d) it has historical value

13. The author suggests that
    (a) We should respect new Archeology as a movement in Archeology
    (b) We should go back to the tenets of processual Archeology
    (c) We should treat tenets of new Archeology with respect
    (d) All of the above

14. The importance of Archeology arose from
    (a) the end of World War II
    (b) an increasing scientific outlook
    (c) the launch of Sputnik in 1957
    (d) All of these

15. Which one of the following is not an area of focus for archeologist?
    (a) Study the interaction of people of small group
    (b) Studying cultures of other people
    (c) Study the social structure of the past societies
    (d) Study the man-environment relationship in the past

16. An archeologist is concerned with
    (a) classification of artefacts
    (b) maintenance of museums
    (c) digging of ancient cities
    (d) All of these

17. Rhetorics means
    (a) study of the technique and rules for using language effectively
    (b) using language effectively to please or persuade
    (c) excessive use of verbal ornamentation
    (d) All of the above

18. If a receiver replying on 'hmm-mm' or 'Isee'. This type of reply is known as
    (a) positive feedback
    (b) ambiguous feedback
    (c) negative feedback
    (d) None of these

19. Which of the following FM radio stations is owned by the Times of India group?
(a) AIR
(b) Radio Rainbow
(c) Radio Mirchi
(d) Red FM

20. Find the next number in the following sequence:
9, 8, 25, 12, 49, 18, 121, 26, ??
(a) 142, 36 (b) 169, 36
(c) 225, 36 (d) 196, 36

21. **Statement:** Should there be complete ban on pouched tobacco products (like Gutka) in India?

Arguments:
(i) Yes, it is the most important cause of mouth cancer and mouth ulcer in our country.
(ii) No, there are many people employed in this industry right from manufacturing to retailing. This ban will hamper their livelihood.
(a) Only argument (i) is strong
(b) Only argument (ii) is strong
(c) Both the arguments (i) and (ii) are strong
(d) Neither (i) nor (ii) is strong

22. The relationship between Animal, Cows, Dogs can be shown by

(a) 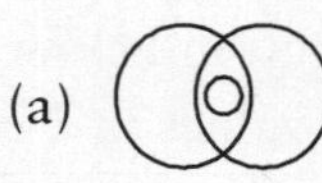 (b) 

(c) 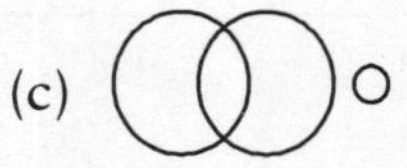 (d) 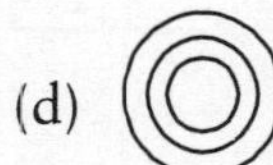

23. If in a certain code:
'nso prt kli chn' means 'sharma gets marriage gift'.
'pit lnm wop chn' means 'wife gives marriage gift'. 'tti wop nhi' means 'he gives nothing'. What would mean gives:
(a) kli (b) tti
(c) wop (d) lnm

24. Characteristics of all informal and formal communications are
(a) Same (b) Structured
(c) Different (d) None of these

25. Three of the following four are alike in a certain way and so form a group. Find the one which doesn't belong to that group?
(a) Dog (b) Tiger
(c) Horse (d) Lion

26. What is research design?
(a) The methods used in analysis and finding the final conclusion is known as research design
(b) A researcher needs to prepare a plan of action for his study which is known as research design
(c) The presentation of final data is known as research design
(d) None of these

27. Recording a television program on a Set Top Box is an example of
(a) content reference
(b) time-shifting
(c) media synchronisation
(d) mechanical clarity

28. Which of the following statements say the same thing?
(i) "I am a teacher" (said by Arvind)
(ii) "I am a teacher" (said by Binod)
(iii) "My son is a teacher" (said by Binod's father)
(iv) "My brother is a teacher" (said by Binod's sister)
(v) "My brother is a teacher" (said by Binod's only sister)
(vi) "My sole enemy is a teacher" (said by Binod's only enemy)

Choose the correct answer from the codes given below:

Codes:

(a) (v) and (vi)
(b) (i) and (ii)
(c) (ii) and (vi)
(d) (ii), (iii), (iv) and (v)

29. In this question there are two statements followed by four conclusions numbered I, II, III and IV.

Statements:

A. All books are trees.
B. All trees are lions.

Conclusions:

I. All books are lions.
II. All lions are books.
III. All trees are books.
IV. Some lions are books.

Choose the correct answer.

(a) Only I and IV follow
(b) Only II and III follow
(c) None of conclusions follow
(d) All conclusion follows

Directions: (30-34) Answer the questions based on following table.

Machines X and Y can independently produce either product P or product Q. The time taken by machines X and Y (in minutes) to produce one unit of product P and Q are given in the table below. (Each machine works 8 hours per day.)

Product	X	Y
P	10	8
Q	6	6

30. If the number of units of P is to be three times that of Q, what is the maximum idle time to maximise total units manufactured?

(a) 3 minutes (b) 0 minute
(c) 12 minutes (d) None of these

31. If X works at half its normal efficiency, what is the maximum number of units produced, if at least one unit of each must be produced?

(a) 119 (b) 135
(c) 127 (d) 136

32. What is the maximum number of units that can be manufactured in one day?

(a) 250 (b) 160
(c) 270 (d) 195

33. If equal quantities of both are to be produced, then out of four choice given below the least efficient way would be

(a) 59 of each with 8 min. idle
(b) 71 of each with 9 min. idle
(c) 53 of each with 10 min. idle
(d) 48 of each with 4 min. idle

34. What is the least number of machine hours required to produce 30 pieces of P and 25 pieces of Q respectively?

(a) 6 hr 30 min. (b) 9 hr 30 min.
(c) 6 hr 40 min. (d) 8 hr 30 min.

35. Telematic is a combination of

(a) Telecommunication and computer
(b) Telecommunication and information
(c) Television and computer
(d) All of the above

36. Following is a part of balance sheet of Timas Pvt. Ltd. Study the table and give answer to the question given below:

(All values in ₹ crore)

Year	Expenditure	Income
1990	3400	4000
1995	3800	4500
2000	4500	5400
2005	6400	8000

Which of the following conclusions is not true?

(a) There has been a steady growth in % profit of the company

(b) There is around 90% increase in expenditure of the firm from 1990 to 2005
(c) Income of the company is doubled in 15 years
(d) Percentage profit in 2000 was 18%

37. If EFGHUK is coded as VUTSRQ then LIMIT can be coded as
(a) KNRNC (b) ORNRG
(c) JKOKG (d) RSTSG

38. The more is 'Resolution Power' of a printer better is its
(a) Speed (b) Colour
(c) Memory (d) Quality

39. Laterite soil develops due to
(a) deposits of alluvial
(b) deposition of loess
(c) leaching
(d) continued vegetation cover

40. Line access and avoidance of collision are the main functions of
(a) network protocols
(b) wide area networks
(c) the CPU
(d) the monitor

41. Communication satellites are placed in
(a) Geostationary Orbit
(b) Polar Orbit
(c) Both (a) and (b)
(d) None of these

42. DLL stands for
(a) Data Deriving Language
(b) Data Definition Language
(c) Data Design Language
(d) All of the above

43. Transistors were first used in
(a) 2nd generation computers
(b) 3rd generation computers
(c) 4th generation computers
(d) None of these

44. Which of the following is not provided in the constitution?
(a) Planning Commission
(b) Election Commission
(c) Finance Commission
(d) Public Service Commission

45. The 1st satellite launched in space was
(a) Early Bird (b) Sputnik-1
(c) Skylab (d) Aryabhatta-1

46. At what time between 5.30 and 6.00 will the hands of a clock be at right angles?
(a) 45 minutes past 5
(b) $43\frac{5}{11}$ minutes past 5
(c) $43\frac{7}{11}$ minutes past 5
(d) 40 minutes past 5

47. A person can be a member of Council of Ministers without being a member of Parliament for a maximum period of
(a) 45 days (b) 90 days
(c) 180 days (d) one year

48. Many engineers and architects use a different type of pen called a
(a) Pointer pen (b) Computer pen
(c) Light pen (d) Logical pen

49. Which of the following are wrongly matched?

Name of Volcano	**Country**
(a) Mt. Spur	USA
(b) Mt. Fuego	Guatemala
(c) Mt. Ag'ung	Indonesia
(d) Mt. Lascor	Equador

50. How many types of emergency can be declared by the President of India?
(a) 1 (b) 2
(c) 3 (d) 4

51. Which species of chromium is toxic in water?

(a) Cr^{+2}
(b) Cr^{+3}
(c) Cr^{+6}
(d) Cr is non-toxic element

52. Which of the following is the binary equivalent of the octal number 13.54?
(a) 1011.101100 (b) 1101.1110
(c) 1011.1100 (d) 1100.1100

53. A — B A C — D — B C D C
— 3 — 2 — 1 — 4 ? ? ? ?
d c — — b a c b — — — —
Which of the following will come at the vacant places marked by ? ? ? ?
(a) 3, 4, 1, 4 (b) 1, 3, 4, 3
(c) 1, 4, 3, 4 (d) 2, 3, 4, 3

54. The 10th Five Year Plan covers the period
(a) 2004-09 (b) 2001-06
(c) 2002-07 (d) 2003-08

55. Find the missing term in the following series:
3, 4, 7, 7, 13, 13, 21, 22, 31, 34, ?
(a) 47 (b) 48
(c) 43 (d) 49

56. ______ is one of the oldest form of computer storage.
(a) Compact Disk
(b) Magnetic Disk
(c) Magnetic Tape
(d) Hard Disk

57. January 1, 1995 was Sunday. What day of the week lies on January 1, 1996?
(a) Tuseday (b) Monday
(c) Saturday (d) Sunday

58. What is the Gray Code for decimal 7?
(a) 111 (b) 0100
(c) 0101 (d) 0010

59. Which of the following are biodegradable pollutants?
I. Sewage
II. Domestic waste
III. Agricultural waste
IV. Lead
(a) III, IV and I (b) II, III and IV
(c) I, II and III (d) II, IV and I

60. Electoral disputes arising out of Presidential and Vice-Presidential elections are settled by
(a) Central Election Tribunal
(b) Election Commission of India
(c) Supreme Court of India
(d) Joint Committee of Parliament

TEST PAPER - III

Note: This paper contains sixty multiple-choice questions, each question carrying two marks. Candidate is expected to answer any fifty questions. In case more than 50 questions are attempted, only the first 50 questions will be evaluated.

1. In the large group communications, effectively used media is
(a) Radio
(b) Television
(c) Overhead Projector
(d) Computer

2. A child may be suffering from hearing impairment if
(a) he generally says 'please repeat' to the teacher
(b) he speaks loudly unusually
(c) he comes nearer to the speaker during conversation
(d) All of the above

3. If a student is absent from the classes for a long time
(a) Teacher should try to know the cause of his absence
(b) Teacher should try to solve his problems or help him
(c) Teacher should go to his home to meet him
(d) Both (a) and (b)

4. The telecast materials are used to
   (a) increases retention power
   (b) enhances concentration and learning
   (c) reduces the burden of the teacher
   (d) All of the above
5. The main function of educational psychology is to provide prospective teacher with
   (a) how to deal with students and everyday class situation
   (b) research procedures for evaluating current teaching procedure
   (c) insight into the needs, problems and styles of behaviour of teacher
   (d) insight into various aspects of modern teaching education
6. Which of the following is not a method of research?
   (a) Historical (b) Observation
   (c) Philosophical (d) Survey
7. The communication which transpires inside a person is known as
   (a) group communication
   (b) intrapersonal communication
   (c) interpersonal communication
   (d) mass communication
8. The word research is derived from
   (a) Greek word (b) French word
   (c) Spanish word (d) Latin word
9. Educational quality is
   (a) Only a legal right
   (b) Fundamental right
   (c) Only a customary right
   (d) None of these
10. A good teacher is one who
    (a) has genuine interest in his student
    (b) is highly intelligent
    (c) lives simple life
    (d) has mastery over his teaching subject
11. Which of the following institutions is responsible for the implemation of reforms in teaching profession?
    (a) National Institute of Educational Planning and Administration
    (b) University Grants Commission
    (c) National Council for Teacher's Education
    (d) National Council for Educational Research and Training
12. The most important characteristic of Open Book Examination system is that
    (a) it compels students to think
    (b) students become serious
    (c) it improves attendance in the classroom
    (d) it reduces examination anxiety amongst students
13. Discussion in the class will be more effective if the topic of discussion is
    (a) informed to the student well in advance
    (b) not introduced
    (c) stated before the start of discussion
    (d) written on the board without introducing it
14. A person is not a successful communicator
    (a) who presents material in a precise and clear way
    (b) who sometimes becomes informal before the receiver and developes rapport
    (c) who knows a lot but is somewhat reserve in his attitude
    (d) who is able to adapt himself according to the language of communication
15. Which of the following provides more freedom for the learners to interact actively?
    (a) Small group discussions
    (b) Lecture by experts

(c) Viewing of the TV
(d) Use of film projector

16. In this question, four words are given, out of which three are alike in some manner and one is different. Choose the odd one out.
(a) Diamond (b) Graphite
(c) Coal (d) Pearl

17. Two objects or events are related in some way. Pick out that option which has the same type of relationship stated in the given two words:
HANDS : FINGERS :: ?
(a) Competition : Victory
(b) Head : Hair
(c) Skin : Colour
(d) Machine : Tools

18. Human ear is most sensitive to noise in the range
(a) 1-2 kHz (b) 100-500 Hz
(c) 10-12 kHz (d) 13-16 kHz

Directions (19-23) Study the following passage and give answer to the questions based on it.

A recent report in *News Week* says that in American colleges, students of Asian origin outperform not only the minority group students but the majority Whites as well. Many of these students might be of Indian origin, and their achievement is something that we can be really proud of. It is unlikely that these talented youngsters will come back to India, and that is the familiar brain drain problem. However, recent statements by the nation's policy makers indicate that the perception of this issue is changing. 'Brain Bank' and not the 'Brain Drain' is the more appropriate idea, they suggest that since the expertise of Indians abroad is only deposited in other places and not lost.

This may be so, but this brain bank, like most of other banks, is one that primarily serves customers in its neighbourhood. The skills of Asians now excelling in America's colleges will mainly help the USA. No matter how significant, what non-resident Indians do for India and what their counterparts do for other Asian lands is only a by-product.

But it is also necessary to ask, or be reminded why Indians study more fruitfully when abroad. The Asians whose accomplishments *News Week* records would have probably had a very different fate if they had studied in India. In America, they found an elbow room, books and facilities not available and not likely to be available here. The need to prove themselves in their new country and the competition of an international standard they faced there must have cured mental and physical laziness. But other things helping them in America can be obtained if we achieve a change in social attitudes, especially towards youth.

We need to learn to value individuals and their unique qualities more than conformity and respectability. We need to learn the language of encouragement to add to our skill in flattery. We might also learn to be less liberal with blame and less tight-fisted with appreciation, especially to those showing signs of independence.

19. It is a general believe that the talented young Indians studying in America
(a) will not return to pursue their careers in India
(b) have a reputation for being hard-working
(c) have an opportunity to contribute in India's development
(d) can solve the brain drain problem because of recent changes in policy

20. Among the many groups of students in American colleges, Asian students

(a) have only a minority status like the blacks
(b) are often written about in magazines like *News Week*
(c) are the most successful academically
(d) have proved that they are as goods as Whites

21. There is talk of the 'Brain Bank', this idea
(a) is based on plan to utilise foreign exchange remittances to stimulate research and development
(b) is a solution to the brain drain problem
(c) is a new problem caused partly by the brain drain
(d) is a new way of looking at the role of qualified Indians living abroad

22. The students of Asian origin in America include
(a) Indians who are the most hard-working of all
(b) a fair number from India
(c) a small group from India
(d) persons from India who are very proud

23. Which of the following most appropriately sums up the intent of the author?
(a) USA has excelled just because of the contributions from talented immigrants
(b) We need to look at 'Brain Drain' in a positive way as 'Brain Bank'
(c) Indians should take pride in the fact that fellow Indians have excelled in foreign lands against all odds
(d) We need to think of the ways to help grow and retain the talent of our land

24. What should come in place of the question mark (?) in the following series?

102, 99, 104, 97, 106 ?

(a) 106 (b) 59
(c) 95 (d) 64

25. **Statement:** Let us increase the taxes to cover the deficit.

Conclusions:

I. If the taxes are not increased, the deficit cannot be met.
II. The present taxes are very low.
III. Deficit in the budget are not desirable.

Choose the correct option.
(a) Only II and III are implicit
(b) Only I and III are implicit
(c) Only I and II are implicit
(d) All are implicit

26. **Statements:**

A. Some dogs are cats.
B. None of the cats is a cow.

Conclusins:

I. Some cats are not dogs.
II. Some cats are dogs.
III. Some cows are dogs.
IV. No dog is a cow.

Choose the correct option.
(a) Only II follows
(b) Only III follows
(c) Only I and III follow
(d) Only IV follows

Directions: (27-30) Using the following table answer the questions given below.

Yearly income (in ₹ '000)

Name/Year	2008	2009	2010	2011
Mahesh	1200	1600	2000	2400
Suresh	1000	1400	1600	2000
Ganesh	900	1200	1500	2000
Seema	2000	2500	3000	3700
Sapna	1200	1200	1500	1700

27. Whose average income for all the four years is ₹ 1400000?

(a) Mahesh alone
(b) Ganesh and Sapna both
(c) Mahesh and Suresh
(d) Sapna alone

28. How high is the total average income for four years of men as compared to that of women?
(a) 2133340 (b) 3500440
(c) 4320540 (d) 5440820

29. What is the round figure, the ratio between the total income of men and that of women for all years?
(a) 16:14 (b) 14:15
(c) 15:16 (d) 23:21

30. Can we say women earn more than men?
(a) No
(b) Yes
(c) Not sure
(d) Difference is not so significant

Directions: (31-35) Using the following graph answer the questions given below.

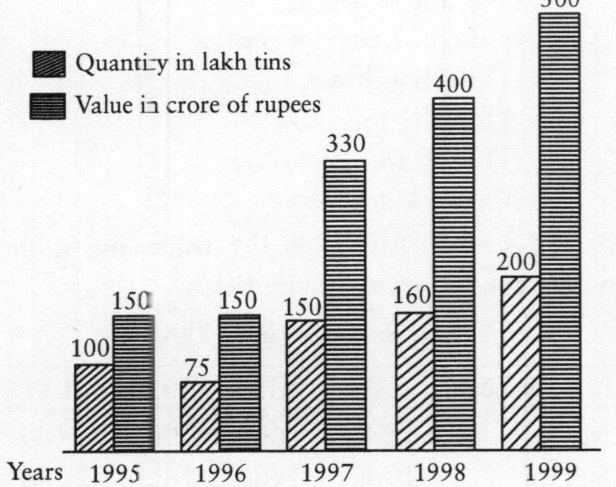

31. What was the approximate percentage increase in export value from 1995 to 1999?
(a) 435 (b) 395.5
(c) 422.8 (d) None of these

32. If in 1998, the tins were exported at the same rate per tin as that in 1997, what would be the value (in ₹ crores) of export in 1998?
(a) 375 (b) 352
(c) 395 (d) 392

33. In which year the value per tin was minimum?
(a) 1996 (b) 1998
(c) 1995 (d) 1999

34. What was the percentage drop in export quantity from 1995 to 1996?
(a) 25 (b) 46
(c) 52 (d) None of these

35. What was the difference between the tins exported in 1997 and 1998?
(a) 10 (b) 1000
(c) 100000 (d) 1000000

36. Which of the following statements is/are true about ozone layer?
(a) It is depleting due to human activities
(b) It is found in upper atmosphere, which absorbs UV rays
(c) It causes skin cancer and genetic disorder
(d) Both (a) and (b)

37. Study the figure and find the region which represents the students who study Physics and Chemistry but not Mathematics.

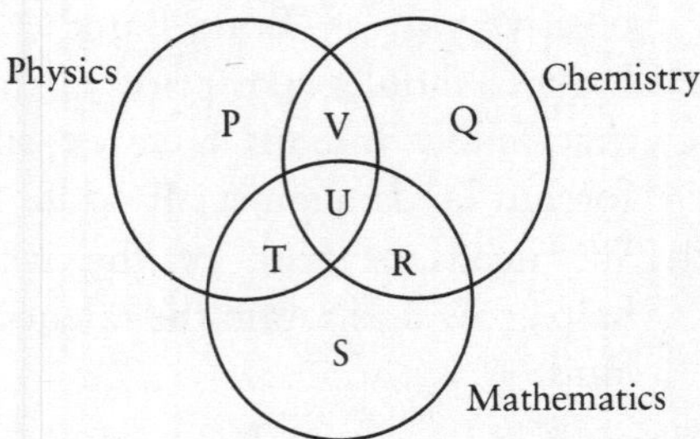

(a) P + T + S + R + U + V
(b) T

(c) P + T + S
(d) V

38. Which of the following is a non-point source of water pollution?
(a) Factories (b) Lawn
(c) Coal mines (d) None of these

39. The depletion of ozone layer causes
I. Skin cancer.
II. Damage to our immune system.
III. Damage to our eyes.
(a) Only III (b) Only I and II
(c) Only I and III (d) All of the above

40. **Statements:**
I. All the fruits are stones.
II. No tree is fruit.
III. All stones are rains.

Conclusion:
(a) Some rain is fruit
(b) No stone is a tree
(c) No rain is a tree
(d) None is true

41. Web designer is also known as
(a) Web maintainer (b) Web editor
(c) Web master (d) Web author

42. Which of the following schedule of our constitution is related to languages?
(a) Sixth (b) Eighth
(c) Seventh (d) Tenth

43. In the hypermedia database, information bits are stored in the form of
(a) Symbols (b) Signals
(c) Cubes (d) Nodes

44. Explosive volcanic eruption is caused by
(a) High water content in ground
(b) Low viscosity of magma
(c) High viscosity of magma
(d) None of these

45. The VIRUS is a
(a) Device
(b) Software program
(c) Hardware
(d) anti-piracy software

46. Appropriation Act of the General Budget is
(a) a Constitution Amendment Bill
(b) a Finance Bill
(c) a Money Bill
(d) an Ordinary Bill

47. If in a certain language, GERMANY is coded as HGUQFTF then how will you code NEOMAN?
(a) OFQQFT (b) OFQPES
(c) OGRQFT (d) None of these

48. Which of the following is biggest fresh-water lake in India?
(a) Loktak (b) Dal
(c) Sukhna (d) None of these

49. Different memories can be classified according to the concept of
(a) Transfer Rate
(b) Access mode/capacity
(c) Access Time
(d) All of the above

50. Which of the following diagrams represents the relation between red, clothes and roses most appropriately?

(c) 
(d) 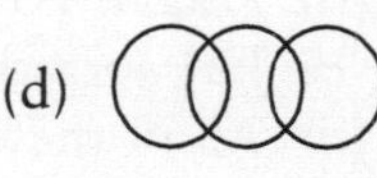

51. LAN stands for
(a) Live Area Network
(b) Local And National
(c) Local Area Network
(d) Large Area Network

52. In India the number of principle level of qualifications within the higher education system is

(a) 2 (b) 3
(c) 4 (d) 6

53. The touch pad is a ______ device.
(a) Sensitive Pointing
(b) Dynamic Pointing
(c) Stationary Pointing
(d) Temporary Pointing

54. P, Q, R, S, T, U and V are members of a family consisting of four adults and three children, two of whom U and V are girls. P and S are brothers and P is a doctor. T is an engineer married to one of the brothers and has two children. Q is married to S and V is their child. Who is R?
(a) V's brother (b) P's son
(c) T's daughter (d) U's father

55. I.C. chip used in computers is made of
(a) Copper (b) Tungsten
(c) Platinum (d) Silicon

56. The first made in India Kids channel of television is
(a) Nick Jr.
(b) Cartoon Network
(c) Walt Disney
(d) Hungama TV

57. Which of the following power plants is/are situated in Delhi?
(a) Badarpur Thermal Power Plant
(b) Pragati Power Station
(c) Indraprastha Power Plant
(d) All of these

58. A Joystick is used as
(a) Temporary pointing device
(b) Stationary pointing device
(c) Flight Stimulators
(d) None of the above

59. The main memory of a computer
(a) can be loaded from storage media
(b) can be divided in two parts—RAM and ROM
(c) is not essential for every system
(d) All of these

60. Information and Communication Technology includes
(a) Web Based Learning
(b) On-line learning
(c) Learning through the use of EDUSAT
(d) All the above

TEST PAPER - IV

Note: This paper contains sixty multiple-choice questions, each question carrying two marks. Candidate is expected to answer any fifty questions. In case more than 50 questions are attempted, only the first 50 questions will be evaluated.

1. Dewry defines education as a
(a) theoretical need
(b) social need
(c) personal need
(d) psychological need

2. All of the following statements about a teacher are correct except the one.
(a) A teacher changes his/her attitudes and behaviour according to the need of the society
(b) A teacher is a friend, guide and philosopher
(c) A teacher distinguish between students
(d) A teacher is the leader in the class

3. A person cannot be an effective teacher if he
(a) teaches moral values
(b) is a strict disciplinarian
(c) knows his subject well
(d) has no interest in teaching

4. The most important signal factor in underlying the success of a teacher is
(a) organisational ability
(b) scholarship

(c) communicative ability
(d) personality and his ability to relate to the class and to the pupils

5. If you are irritated and show rashness because of the inadequate behaviour of another teachers, what do you think about your own behaviour?
(a) Your behaviour is also a sign of maladjustment and so try to control yourself when you are maltreated
(b) It is justified because behaviours are echoice
(c) Your behaviour is not good because elders have the right to behave you in this way
(d) All of the above

6. The term 'SITE' stands for
(a) Satellite Instructional Teachers Education
(b) Satellite International Television Experiment
(c) Satellite Instructional Television Experiment
(d) Satellite Indian Television Experiment

7. Team teaching has the potential to develop
(a) highlighting the gaps in each other's teaching
(b) competitive spirit
(c) cooperation
(d) the habit of supplementing the teaching of each other

8. In any research one should
(a) not try out anything blindly but wait until a sudden flash appears in his mind
(b) know everything in the area without bothering to learn the details of any
(c) know more and more about less and less in certain specific sub area
(d) None of these

9. Determine the nature of the following definition:
'Poor' means having an annual income of ₹ 10,000.
(a) Lexical (b) Persuasive
(c) Precising (d) Stipulative

10. Which of the following methods implies the collection of information by way of investigators own examination without interviewing the respondents?
(a) Random probability sampling
(b) Observation
(c) Posting questionnaire
(d) Schedule method

11. Why do teachers use teaching aid?
(a) For students' attention
(b) To make teaching fun-filled
(c) To make students attentive
(d) To teach within understanding level of students

12. On which of the following statements there is consensus among educators?
(a) Disciplinary cases should be totally neglected in the class
(b) Disciplinary cases should be sent to the principal only when other means have failed
(c) Disciplinary cases should never be sent to principal's office
(d) None of these

13. Good evaluation of written material should not be based on
(a) Logical presentation
(b) Comprehension of subject
(c) Linguistic expression
(d) Ability to reproduce whatever is read

14. A good researcher lays his hands on
(a) any area as long as manpower and fundings are available in plenty
(b) a specific area and tries to understand in minute details

(c) several areas and tries to understand them at fundamental level
(d) None of these

15. The basis on which assumptions are formulated
(a) Universities
(b) Cultural background of the country
(c) Specific characteristics of the castes
(d) All of these

Read the following passage and answer the questions 16 to 20:

India is dedicated to free institutions and principles of democracy. We are striving to give everyone an opportunity and raise the standard of living for all. A democracy is one where people have the right to live their own lives and develop themselves in their own way under the guidance of their chosen representatives. If our political democracy is to succeed, it is essential that it be buttressed by steps towards economic equality or what has been referred to as the 'socialistic pattern of society'. Poverty and unemployment hold the biggest threat to the successful working of our democratic system.

16. One may infer from the paragraph that in a socialistic pattern of society
(a) to provide employment to all is the greatest problem
(b) the socialist party dominates
(c) all the inhabitants are treated equal
(d) None of these

17. The successful working of Indian democratic system is under a threat of
(a) economic inequality
(b) poverty
(c) unemployment
(d) All the above

18. In a democratic system
(a) commodities are freely bought and sold
(b) government serves the people
(c) the government is run by the people themselves
(d) people do not have political freedom

19. The word buttressed in the paragraph means
(a) Supported (b) Dictating
(c) Declared (d) Guided

20. Democracy can fail if there is
(a) opportunity for development
(b) a weak government
(c) economic inequality
(d) unemployment

21. Aspect ratio of TV Screen is
(a) 4:3 (b) 3:4
(c) 2:3 (d) 2:4

22. Which of the following is not a product of learning?
(a) Knowledge (b) Attitudes
(c) Maturation (d) Concepts

23. The first paper for the human beings was developed by
(a) The Aryans
(b) The Babilonians
(c) The Chinese
(d) The Sumerians

24. Which sequence in turn will lead one to face the west direction from which one starts turning?
(a) Right, right, left, right, left right
(b) Left, right, left, left, right, right
(c) Right, right left, left, right, right
(d) Left, left, right, left, right, left

25. Fill in the blank with the most appropriate choice

_____ is the supreme medium to express yesterday, today and tomorrow with its own unique language.
(a) Television (b) Cinema
(c) Radio (d) Newspaper

26. In which language the newspapers have highest circulation?
    (a) Tamil (b) English
    (c) Bengali (d) Hindi

27. Amit is the son of Rahul. Sarika, Rahul's sister has a son Sonu and a daughter Rita. Raja is the maternal uncle of Sonu. How is Rita related to Raja.
    (a) Aunt (b) Sister
    (c) Daughter (d) Niece

28. **Statements:** A man must be wise to be a good wrangler. Good wrangler's are all talkative and boring.

    Conclusions:

    I. All the wise persons are boring.
    II. All the wise persons are good wranglers.

    Choose the correct option.
    (a) Only conclusion I follows
    (b) Only conclusion II follows
    (c) Both I and II follow
    (d) None of these

29. What is the number that comes next in the sequence?
    2, 5, 9, 19, 37, ...
    (a) 74 (b) 75
    (c) 76 (d) 78

30. Match List I with List II and select the correct answer using the codes given below:

List I	List II
(A) Pandit Jasraj	(1) Hindustani vocalist
(B) Kishan Maharaj	(2) Sitar
(C) Ravi Shankar	(3) Tabla
(D) Udai Shankar	(4) Dance

Codes:	A	B	C	D
(a)	1	2	3	4
(b)	1	3	4	2
(c)	1	3	2	4
(d)	3	2	1	4

31. Who developed the ability to speak?
    (a) Aryans (b) Neanderthal
    (c) Cro-Magnon (d) Dravidians

32. In what way does communication in small group differ from that in the large group?
    (a) Large group communication provides better feedback
    (b) Small group provides far more interaction among the participants
    (c) Interaction in small group is more restrictive
    (d) Small group takes less time to convey the message

33. What is the main aim and objective of provision for feedback in communication system?
    (a) Understand more about the content
    (b) To make communication better by adjusting at both ends of Encoder and Decoder
    (c) Identify the defect of communication
    (d) Make necessary modification in communication system

34. Communications bandwidth that has the highest capacity and is used by microwave, cable and fibre optics lines is known as
    (a) Carrier wave (b) Hyper-link
    (c) Broadband (d) Bus width

35. In a certain code, CLOCK is written as KCOLC. How would STEPS be written in that code?
    (a) SPETS (b) SPEST
    (c) SPSET (d) SEPTS

36. Which one of the following is not an argument?
    (a) Ram is not at home, so he must have gone to town
    (b) Ram insulted me so I punched him in the nose

(c) If today is Tuesday, tomorrow will be Wednesday

(d) Since today is Tuesday, tomorrow will be Wednesday.

Direction: (37-41) Study the following pie chart and answer the questions based on it. Following pie chart represents the investment done by Timas Finance Ltd. in the various sectors. (All investments are in ₹ crores)

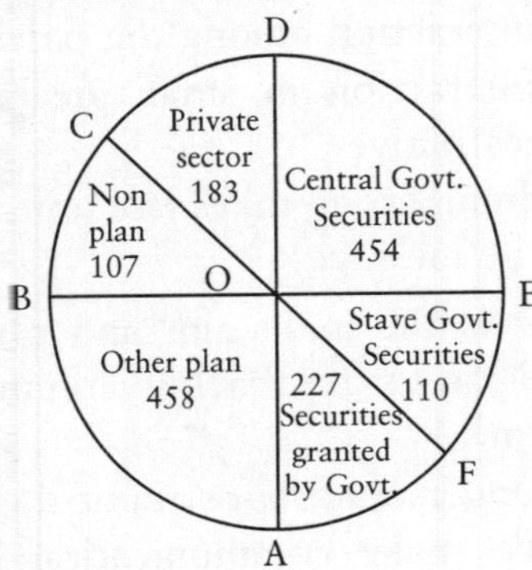

37. The percentage or gross investment in state government securities is nearly

(a) 7.1% (b) 9.2%

(c) 8.6% (d) 7.8%

38. The investment in plan and non-plan sector together is more or less than the investment in government securities (Central and State) by

(a) less, 106 crores (b) more, 4 crores

(c) more, 1 crores (d) more, 111 crores

39. The magnitude of ∠AOC is nearly

(a) 132° (b) 123°

(c) 126° (d) 115°

40. The ratio of area of the circle above ∠COF to the area of the circle below it is about

(a) 1 (b) 0.92

(c) 0.94 (d) 0.96

41. The investment in private sector is nearly what percent higher than the investment in State Government Security?

(a) 44% (b) 66%

(c) 54% (d) 46%

42. How many numbers between 100 and 300 begin or end with 2?

(a) 120 (b) 110

(c) 100 (d) 180

43. Which of the following operating system is used on mobile phones?

(a) Windows XP

(b) Windows Vista

(c) Android

(d) All of the above

44. Structure of logical argument is based on

(a) Linguistic expression

(b) Material truth

(c) Formal validity

(d) Aptness of examples

45. HTML is used to create

(a) machine language program

(b) high level program

(c) web page

(d) web server

46. Which of the following pollutants affects the respiratory tract in humans?

(a) Aerosols

(b) Sulphur di-oxide

(c) Nitric oxide

(d) Carbon monoxide

47. Which of the following sources of energy has the maximum potential in India?

(a) Wind energy

(b) Solar energy

(c) Ocean thermal energy

(d) Tidal energy

48. In a deductive argument conclusion is

(a) Additional to the premises

(b) Entailed by the premises

(c) Summing up of the premises

(d) Not necessarily based on premises

49. What is the range of the numbers which can be stored in an eight bit register?
(a) –127 to + 128 (b) –127 to + 127
(c) –128 to + 128 (d) –128 to + 127

50. Universal Product Code (UPC), a pattern of bars printed on merchandise can be read by
(a) Product Code Reader
(b) Bar Code Reader
(c) Code Reader
(d) Card Reader

51. What was the day of the week on 1st January, 2001?
(a) Sunday (b) Monday
(c) Friday (d) Wednesday

52. Which of the following figures will represent the right relationship between Women, Teachers and Doctors.

(a) 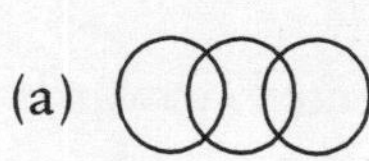 (b) 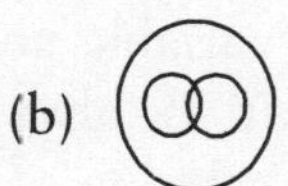

(c) 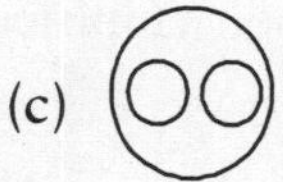 (d) 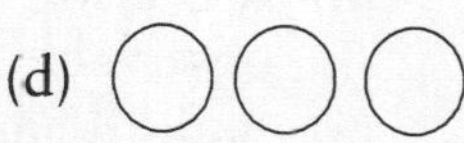

53. The processing speed of a computer is faster when the RAM size is bigger since it eliminates
(a) need for ROM
(b) need for external memory
(c) frequent disk I/Os
(d) None of the above

54. Bitumen is obtained from:
(a) underground mines
(b) forests and plants
(c) kerosene oil
(d) crude oil

55. Two ladies and two men are playing bridge and seated at North, East, South and West of a table. No lady is facing East. Persons sitting opposite to each other are not of the same sex. One man is facing South. Which direction are the ladies facing to?
(a) South and East
(b) East and West
(c) North and West
(d) None of these

56. An electronic device that takes data from 'n' number of low speed communication lines and puts on to single high speed line is
(a) channel (b) modem
(c) multiplexer (d) None of these

57. **Assertion (X):** Mentals are in molten state inside the earth.
Reason (Y): Earth absorbs sun rays.
(a) Both X and Y are true and Y correctly explains the reason for X
(b) Both X and Y are true but Y is not correct explanation of X
(c) X is true but Y is false
(d) X is false but Y is true

58. Bog is a wetland that receives water from
(a) melting
(b) sea only
(c) nearby water bodies
(d) rainfall only

59. Indicate the number of Regional Offices of University Grants Commission of India.
(a) 12 (b) 08
(c) 07 (d) 09

60. Which one of the following is not the tool of good governance?
(a) Citizens' Charter
(b) Judicial Activism
(c) Right to Information
(d) Social Auditing

TEST PAPER - V

Note: This paper contains sixty multiple-choice questions, each question carrying two marks. Candidate is expected to answer any fifty questions. In case more than 50 questions are attempted, only the first 50 questions will be evaluated.

1. Which among the following gives more freedom to the learner to interact?
   (a) Small group discussion
   (b) Lectures by experts
   (c) Use of film
   (d) Viewing country-wide classroom program on TV
2. While designing communication strategy feed-forward studies are conducted by
   (a) Media (b) Audience
   (c) Communicator (d) Satellite
3. A theory is correct because
   (a) its derivations match with most observations
   (b) its advocate has written a big volume to establish it
   (c) it is supported by a large number of scholars
   (d) it has a large number of followers
4. Which of the following are true about the concepts?
   I. Concepts have different meanings in different contents.
   II. Concepts are the blocks from which theories are built.
   III. Concepts are ideas, abstractions, that do not have meaning in themselves.
   (a) Only II (b) I and III
   (c) I and II (d) All of these
5. The most sensible idea about teaching and research is that
   (a) they interfere with each other
   (b) they are two entirely different kinds of activities
   (c) they cannot go together
   (d) they are two sides of the same coin
6. Which of the following is quality of a teacher?
   (a) He should know the child psychology
   (b) He should evoke curiosity of the pupils by presenting the subject matter in an effective manner with clear explaining leading to better understanding of the matter
   (c) He should be trained in various teaching methodologies
   (d) All of these
7. Which of the following is/are true about research?
   (i) Gives emphasis to the development of theories, principles and generalisation, which are very helpful in accurate prediction regarding the variable understudy.
   (ii) It is always directed towards the solution of a problem.
   (iii) It is always based upon empirical or observable evidences.
   (a) Both (i) and (ii)
   (b) Both (i) and (iii)
   (c) Both (ii) and (iii)
   (d) All of the above
8. Which of the following methods of teaching encourages the use of maximum senses?
   (a) Team teaching method
   (b) Problem-solving method
   (c) Laboratory method
   (d) Self-study method
9. A non-fictional literary composition that forms an independent part of a publication, as a newspaper or magazine is known as
   (a) Symposium (b) Paper
   (c) Article (d) None of these

10. Photo bleeding means
   (a) Photo placement
   (b) Photo cropping
   (c) Photo colour adjustment
   (d) Photo cutting
11. Attitudes, concepts, skills and knowledge are products of
   (a) Explanation (b) Learning
   (c) Research (d) Heredity
12. To study the relationship of family size with income a researcher classifies his population into different income slabs and then takes a random sample from each slab. Which technique of sampling does he adopt?
   (a) Systematic Sampling
   (b) Random Sampling
   (c) Stratified Random Sampling
   (d) Cluster Sampling
13. In business communication, the major obstacles arise because of the
   (a) psychological barriers
   (b) physical barriers
   (c) organisational barriers
   (d) mechanical barriers
14. The most important question that a researcher is interested to use statistical techniques in his problem then he has to see
   (a) whether worthwhile inferences could be drawn
   (b) whether the data could be quantified
   (c) whether appropriate statistical techniques are available
   (d) whether analysis of data would be possible
15. How can the objectivity of the research be enhanced?
   (a) Through its validity
   (b) Through its impartiality
   (c) Through its reliability
   (d) All of these
16. Which one of the following is not correct? A belief becomes a scientific truth when it
   (a) can be replicated
   (b) is established experimentally
   (c) is arrived by logically
   (d) is accepted by many people
17. **Statements:** All cars are ducks. All ducks are birds.

   Conclusions:
   (i) All birds are cars.
   (ii) All cars are birds.
   Choose the correct one.
   (a) Only conclusion (i) follows
   (b) Only conclusion (ii) follows
   (c) Both (i) and (ii) follow
   (d) Neither (i) nor (ii) follows
18. Research can be conducted by a person who
   (a) is a hard worker
   (b) has studied research methodology
   (c) holds a postgraduate degree
   (d) possesses thinking and reasoning ability
19. Action-research is
   (a) A longitudinal research
   (b) An applied research
   (c) A research carried out to solve immediate problems
   (d) All of the above

Read the following passage and answer the questions 20 to 24:

The genesis of service tax emanates from the ongoing structural transformation of the Indian economy, whereby presently more than one-half of GDP originates from the services sector. Despite the growing presence of the services sector in the Indian economy it remained out of the tax net prior to 1994-95, leading to a steady deterioration in tax-GDP ratio. The service tax was introduced in 1994-95 on a select category of services at a low rate of five percent. While the service tax rate and the coverage of services being taxed have increased ever since, the combined tax-GDP ratio of the Centre and States, nevertheless, deteriorated from 16.4 percent in 1985-86 to 14.1 percent in 1999-2000. It may be noted that between 1990-91 and 1998-99, the share of industrial sector in GDP dropped by 6.4 percentage points whereas almost 64 percent of the tax revenue was generated by indirect taxes for which industrial sector continues to be the principal tax base. On the other hand, during the same period, the share of services sector in GDP has increased by 10 percentage points and this sector has still remained poorly taxed.

The rationale for service tax, therefore, lies not only in arresting the falling tax-GDP ratio but also in *ipso facto* improving allocative efficiency in the economy as well as promoting equity. Against this backdrop, the service tax needs to be designed taking into account the fact that (i) the share of services in GDP is expanding; (ii) failure to tax services distorts consumer choices and encourages spending on services at the expense of goods; (iii) untaxed service traders are unable to claim Value Added Tax (VAT) on service inputs, which encourages businesses to develop in-house services, creating further distortions; and (iv) most services that are likely to become taxable are positively correlated with expenditure of high-income households and, therefore, service tax improves equity.

In the Indian context, taxation of services assumes importance in the wake of the need for improving the revenue system, ensuring a measure of neutrality in taxation between goods and services and eventually helping to evolve an efficient system of domestic trade taxes, both at the Central and the State levels.

20. What, according to the passage, was the impact of exclusion of service tax till the first half of the last decade of the past century?
    (a) Service sector used to flourish exorbitantly
    (b) There was no impact as there was no service tax
    (c) There was a steady deterioration in the GDP
    (d) Tax-GDP ratio had steadily and gradually aggravated
21. Levying service tax is most likely to achieve which of the following?
    (i) Promoting equity.
    (ii) Check on reducing tax-GDP ratio.
    (iii) Enhancement in allocative efficiency.
    (a) Both (ii) and (iii)
    (b) Both (i) and (iii)
    (c) Both (i) and (ii)
    (d) All the three
22. The origin of service tax is attributed to
    (a) metamorphosis of our country's economy
    (b) increase in Gross Domestic Product (GDP)
    (c) existence of service sector
    (d) tax of the future
23. Which of the following factors helps service tax to improve fairness across different economic strata of society?
    (a) It improves revenue system
    (b) Taxable services are mostly those that are utilised by the rich
    (c) Untaxed service traders are prevented from claiming value added tax
    (d) Encouragement to in-house services is effected

24. Which of the following is most likely to provide neutrality to various economic activities?
    (a) Consistency in tax structure and revenue buoyancy
    (b) Increase in revenue buoyancy
    (c) fairness in tax administration
    (d) Equity and efficiency in various activities
25. Which of the following is classified in the category of the developmental research?
    (a) Descriptive research
    (b) Philosophical research
    (c) Action research
    (d) All the above
26. The education aims at the fullest realisation of all the potentialities of children. It implies that
    I. it is necessary that their attitudes are helpful, encouraging and sympathetic.
    II. teacher and parents must know what children are capable of and what potentialities they possess.
    III. they should provide suitable opportunities and favourable environmental facilities which are conducive to the maximum growth of children.

    Choose the correct one.
    (a) II and III (b) I and III
    (c) I and II (d) All of them
27. How many times has the preamble of Indian constitution been amended so far?
    (a) Once (b) Twice
    (c) Thrice (d) Never
28. The relationship between earth, mountains and forests can be represented as

    (a) 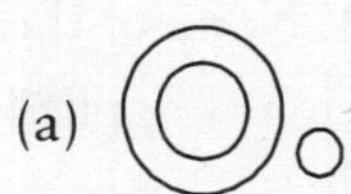 (b) 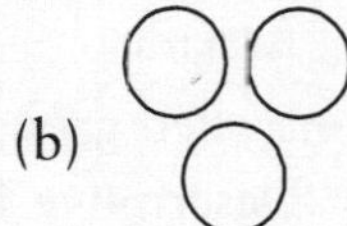

    (c)  (d) 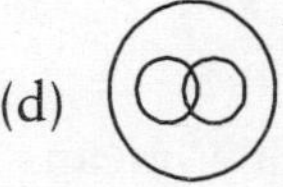
29. Central Fuel Research Institute is situated in
    (a) Pune (b) Jadugoda
    (c) Lucknow (d) Kolkata
30. The letters in the first set have certain relationship. On the basis of this relationship what is the right choice for the second set?

    AST : BRU :: NQV : ?
    (a) OPW (b) ORW
    (c) MPU (d) MRW
31. The number of students in four classes A, B, C, D and their respective mean marks obtained by each of the class are given below:

	Class A	Class B	Class C	Class D
Number of students	10	40	30	20
Arithmetic mean	20	30	50	15

    The combined mean of the marks of four classes together will be
    (a) 15 (b) 32
    (c) 50 (d) 20
32. Communication with oneself is known as
    (a) Organisational communication
    (b) Interpersonal communication
    (c) Intrapersonal communication
    (d) Grapewine communication
33. The number system which is not a positional notation system is
    (a) Binary (b) Octal
    (c) Roman (d) Decimal
34. Which of the following options will complete the series?

    AZ, GT, MN, ?, YB.

(a) TS (b) KF
(c) RX (d) SH

35. If '367' means 'I am happy'; '748' means 'You are sad' and '469' means 'Happy and sad' in a given code, then which of the following represents 'and' in that code?
(a) 4 (b) 6
(c) 3 (d) 9

36. What is the excess 3 code?
(a) self-algebraic code
(b) cyclic complimenting code
(c) cyclic algebraic code
(d) self-complimenting code

37. Which of the following is not created by the Act of Parliament?
(a) Railway Board
(b) Atomic Energy Commission
(c) Backward Class Commission
(d) University Grants Commission

38. Which of the following is radioactive pollutant?
(a) Nickel (b) Iron
(c) Chlorine (d) Thorium

39. The first Indian experimental geostationary communication satellite was
(a) Skylab (b) Apple
(c) INSAT-1A (d) INSAT-1B

40. Which one of the following is a research tool?
(a) Diagram (b) Questionnaire
(c) Graph (d) Illustration

41. Which article of the constitution provides safeguards to Naga Customary and their social practices against any act of Parliament?
(a) Article 371 B (b) Article 371 A
(c) Article 263 (d) Article 371 C

42. **Statement:** Although the city was under kneedeep water for a week in this monsoon, there is no outbreak of any water borne disease.

Assumptions:
(i) Waterborne disease usually spreads in monsoon.
(ii) Water concentration at a place leads to waterborne disease.

Choose the correct option.
(a) Only assumption (i) is implicit
(b) Only assumption (ii) is implicit
(c) Both (i) and (ii) are implicit
(d) Neither (i) nor (ii) is implicit

43. Books and records are the primary sources of data in
(a) laboratory research
(b) historical research
(c) participatory research
(d) clinical research

44. The Kothari Commission's report was entitled on
(a) Learning to be adventure
(b) Education and National Development
(c) Education and socialisation in democracy
(d) Diversification of Education

45. What is the term used for a half byte?
(a) word (b) bit
(c) nibble (d) bug

46. C-band transponder in satellites uses the frequency range
(a) 12 GHz to 14 GHz
(b) 4 GHz to 6 GHz
(c) 2 GHz to 4 GHz
(d) None of these.

47. Which of the following water pollutants is the cause of sterility in human beings?
(a) Manganese (b) Mercury
(c) Arsenic (d) None of these

48. Controlled group condition is applied in
(a) Descriptive Research
(b) Survey Research

(c) Experimental Research
(d) Historical Research

49. Match List I with List II and select the correct answer using the codes given below.

List I (Institutes)
(A) Central Arid Zone Institute
(B) Space Application Centre
(C) Indian Institute of Public Administration
(D) Headquarters of Indian Science Congress

List II (Cities)
(1) Kolkata (2) New Delhi
(3) Ahmedabad (4) Jodhpur

Codes:	A	B	C	D
(a)	4	3	2	1
(b)	4	2	1	3
(c)	3	1	2	4
(d)	1	2	4	3

The total CO_2 emissions from various sectors are 5 mmt. In the Pie Chart given below, the percentage contribution to CO_2 emissions from various sectors is indicated.

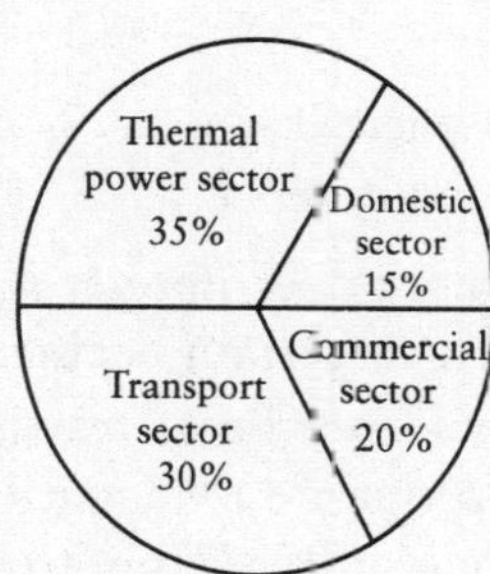

50. What is the absolute CO_2 emission from domestic sector?
(a) 1.75 mmt (b) 0.75 mmt
(c) 1.5 mmt (d) 2.5 mmt

51. What is the absolute CO_2 emission for combined thermal power and transport sectors?
(a) 1.5 mmt (b) 3.25 mmt
(c) 4 mmt (d) 2.5 mmt

52. The linking of computers with a communication system is called
(a) assembling (b) networking
(c) pairing (d) None of these

53. Malaria is caused by
(a) fungal infection
(b) parasitic infection
(c) viral infection
(d) bacterial infection

54. What is the maximum count that a 6 bit binary word can represent?
(a) 64 (b) 61
(c) 62 (d) 63

55. The OMR used is the competitive examinations stands for
(a) Optical Monitor Reader
(b) Optical Magnetic Reader
(c) Optical Mark Reader
(d) Optical Memory Reader

56. Historiography is
(a) method of gathering historical evidences
(b) method of analysing historical evidences
(c) method of historical research
(d) All of the above

57. In a college having 300 students, every student reads 5 newspapers and every newspaper is read by 60 students. The number of newspapers required is
(a) at most 20 (b) at least 30
(c) exactly 5 (d) exactly 25

58. The power to establish new states in India rests with
(a) the Home Ministry
(b) the President
(c) the Parliament
(d) Both (b) and (c) jointly

59. EEPROM stands for

(a) Entities Erasable Programmable Read Only Memory
(b) Effective Erasable Programmable Read Only Memory
(c) Electrically Erasable Programmable Read Only Memory
(d) None of the above

60. Which of the following is not a Fundamental Right?
(a) Right of free compulsory education of all children upto the age of 18
(b) Right to equality
(c) Right against exploitation
(d) Right to freedom of speech and expression

TEST PAPER - VI

Note: This paper contains sixty multiple-choice questions, each question carrying two marks. Candidate is expected to answer any fifty questions. In case more than 50 questions are attempted, only the first 50 questions will be evaluated.

1. Chlorophyll is related to chloroplast in the same way as vulture is related to
(a) Air (b) Flesh
(c) Birds (d) Wings

2. In which language the newspapers have highest circulation?
(a) Hindi (b) English
(c) Malyalam (d) Bengali

3. Factorial Analysis is used
(a) to test the hypothesis
(b) to know the difference between two variables
(c) to know the difference among the many variables
(d) to know the relationship between two variables

4. Which of the following statements is correct?
(a) Variability is the source of problem
(b) Objectives of research are stated in first chapter of the thesis
(c) Researcher must possess analytical ability
(d) All of the above

5. The best way for a teacher to introduce a new subject is by
(a) relating it to previously studied subject or course material
(b) giving a broad outline of the subject
(c) relating it to daily life situation
(d) Any of these

6. The most important function of education is
(a) Human resource development
(b) Political development
(c) Industrial development
(d) Economic development

7. Which one of the following Telephonic Conferencing with a radio link is very popular throughout the world?
(a) Telepresence
(b) TPS
(c) Video teletext
(d) Video conference

8. If a researcher does not get a satisfactory explanation to certain occurrences
(a) he would not be at rest until he gets an appropriate explanation
(b) he should give a damn to it perhaps it is not worth knowing
(c) he would wait until he comes across a right person who may explain it to him
(d) he would visit a nearby research institute to find out whether an answer could be obtained

9. Which of the following is characteristic of a hypothesis?
(a) It can be tested
(b) It must be clear in concept

(c) It must consists of known fact
(d) All of these

10. The main objective of FM station in radio is
(a) Tourism, Interaction and Entertainment
(b) Entertainment only
(c) Entertainment, Information and Interaction
(d) Information, Entertainment and Tourism

11. Inductive logic studies the way in which a premise may
(a) not support but entail a conclusion
(b) support and entail a conclusion
(c) support a conclusion without entailing it
(d) neither support nor entail a conclusion

12. The Prime Minister is the chairman of
(a) Minorities Commission
(b) Planning Commission
(c) Finance Commission
(d) None of these

13. One of the following is not a quality of researcher.
(a) His assertion to outstrip the evidence
(b) Unison with that of which he is in search
(c) He must be of alert mind
(d) Keenness in enquiry

14. Which of the following pollutants is not emitted from the transport sector?
(a) Carbon monoxide
(b) Oxides of nitrogen
(c) Chlorofluorocarbons
(d) Poly aromatic hydrocarbons

15. Ozone layer is present in the
(a) Troposphere (b) Ionosphere
(c) Mesosphere (d) Stratosphere

16. A journalist need to be ____ while covering an event.
(a) impartial (b) partial
(c) meticulous (d) None of these

17. How many types of political units existed in India at the time of independence?
(a) 1 (b) 2
(c) 3 (d) 4

18. Ecological footprint represents
(a) CO_2 emissions per person
(b) forest cover
(c) energy consumption
(d) area of productive land and water to meet the resources requirement

19. The aim of value education to include in students is
(a) the social values
(b) the political values
(c) the moral values
(d) the economic values

Read the following passage and answer the questions 20 to 24:

At one time it would have been impossible to imagine the integration of different religious thoughts, ideas and ideals. That is because of the closed society, the lack of any communication or interdependence on other nations. People were happy and content amongst themselves; they did not need any more. The physical distance and cultural barriers prevented any exchange of thoughts and beliefs. But such is not the case today. Today, the world has become a much smaller place, thanks to the adventures and miracles of science. Foreign nations have become our next-door neighbours. Mingling of population is bringing about an interchange of thought. We are slowly realising that the world is a single cooperative group. Other religions have become forces with which we have to reckon and we are seeking for ways and means by which we can live together in peace and harmony. We cannot have religious unity and peace so long as we assert that we are in possession of the light and all others are groping in the darkness. That very assertion is a challenge to a fight. The political ideal of the world is not so much a single empire with a homogeneous civilisation and single communal group as a brotherhood of free nations differing profoundly in life and mind, habits and institutions, existing side by side in peace and order, harmony and cooperation and each contributing to the world its own unique and specific best, which is irreducible to the terms of the others.

The cosmopolitanism of the eighteenth century and the nationalism of the nineteenth are combined in our ideal of a world commonwealth, which allows every branch of the human family to find freedom, security and self-realisation in the larger life of mankind. I see no hope for the religious future of the world, if this ideal is not extended to the religious sphere also. When two or three different systems claim that they contain the revelation of the very core and centre of truth and the acceptance of it is the exclusive pathway to heaven, conflicts are inevitable. In such conflicts, one religion will not allow others to steal a march over it and no one can gain ascendancy until the world is reduced to dust and ashes. To obliterate every other religion than one's own is a sort of Bolshevism in religion which we must try to prevent. We can do so only if we accept something like the Indian solution, which seeks the unity of religion not in a common creed but in a common quest. Let us believe in the unity of spirit and not of organisation, a unity which secures ample liberty not only for every individual but for every type of organised life which has proved itself effective.

20. According to the passage, the political ideal of the contemporary world is to
    (a) create a world commonwealth preserving religious diversity of all the nations
    (b) create a single empire with a homogeneous civilisation
    (c) foster the unity of all the religions of the world
    (d) None of these

21. According to the passage, religious unity and peace can be obtained if
    (a) we believe that truth does matter and will prevail
    (b) we believe that the world is a single co-operative group
    (c) we do not assert that we alone are in possession of the real knowledge
    (d) we believe in a unity of spirit and not of organisation

22. Which of the following is most opposite in meaning of the word "profoundly" as used in the passage?
    (a) Marginally (b) Meagerly
    (c) Hardly (d) Scarcely

23. Which of the following, according to the passage, is the 'Indian solution'? Unity of religions in a common
    (a) Creed (b) Belief
    (c) Organisation (d) Search

24. According to the passage, what is Bolshevism in religion?
    (a) To make changes in a religion so that it becomes more acceptable
    (b) To ridicule the views sincerely held by others
    (c) To accept others' religious beliefs and doctrines to be as authentic as ours
    (d) To adhere to rigid dogmatism in religion

25. Which is not 24 hours news channel?
    (a) Aajtak
    (b) Zee News
    (c) Lok Sabha channel
    (d) NDTV 24×7

26. Which of the following is not a source of pollution in soil?
    (a) Hydropower plants
    (b) Transport sector
    (c) Agriculture sector
    (d) Thermal power plants
27. Which institution brought co-ordination and co-operation between Union and States in the field of education?
    (a) CCCE (Council for Co-ordination and Cooperation on Education)
    (b) NCERT (National Council for Educational Research and Training)
    (c) CABE (Central Advisory Board of Education)
    (d) None of these
28. In this question four words are given, out of which three are alike and fourth one is different. Choose the odd one out.
    (a) Spectacle (b) Pageant
    (c) View (d) Display
29. Which of the following is not a natural hazard?
    (a) Tsunami
    (b) Flash floods
    (c) Nuclear accident
    (d) Earthquake
30. **Statement:** Should all electronic goods be exempted from the custom duty?

    Arguments:

    I. No, it will reduce the income of the government and development activities will be adversely affected.

    II. No, local manufacturers will be unable to compete with technology of foreign manufacturers.

    (a) Only I is strong
    (b) Only II is strong
    (c) Both are strong
    (d) None of them is strong
31. The Minimata disease of Japan in 1953 was caused by eating fish contaminated by
    (a) Nickel (b) Cadmium
    (c) Lead (d) Mercury
32. Kishanganga power project has now become the new sour point in Indo-Pak relations. This project is situated on which of the following rivers?
    (a) Indus (b) Chenab
    (c) Bias (d) Jhelum
33. In a certain code, ROUNDS is written as RONUDS. How will PLEASE will be written in the same code?
    (a) PLASEE (b) LPAESE
    (c) PLAESE (d) LPAEES
34. **Statement:** Most labourers are poor.

    Conclusions:

    (i) Some labourers are poor.

    (ii) All labourers are not poor. Which of the following is implied?

    (a) Only (i) is implied
    (b) Only (ii) is implied
    (c) Both (i) and (ii) are implied
    (d) Neither (i) nor (ii) is implied
35. One-rupee currency note in India bears the signature of
    (a) Finance Minister of India
    (b) Finance Secretary of Government of India
    (c) The President of India
    (d) Governor, Reserve Bank of India
36. Name the kind of pen used to draw directly on the digitizing tablet.
    (a) Computer Pen (b) Puck/stylus
    (c) Light Pen (d) None of these
37. FERA was changed to FEMA in 1998, FEMA stands for
    (a) Foreign Exchange Monitoring Act
    (b) Foreign Exchange Management Administration

(c) Foreign Exchange Management Act
(d) Foreign Exchange Maintenance Act

38. The Lok Sabha can be dissolved before the expiry of its normal five-year term by
(a) The Speaker of Lok Sabha
(b) The Prime Minister
(c) The President on the recommendation of the Prime Minister
(d) None of the above

39. Match the List-I with the List-II and select the correct answer from the codes given below:

List I (Commissions and Committees)
(A) First Administrative Reforms Commission.
(B) Paul H. Appleby Committee I.
(C) K. Santhanam Committee.
(D) Second Administrative Reforms Commission.

List II (Years)
(1) 2005 (2) 1962
(3) 1966 (4) 1953

Codes:	A	B	C	D
(a)	1	3	2	4
(b)	3	4	2	1
(c)	4	2	3	1
(d)	2	1	4	3

40. Internet is
(a) a commercial information service run by Zift Davis Co. in United States of America.
(b) a network owned and run by US Government.
(c) a network for education, news and entertainment run by United Nations and owned by the people of world.
(d) a network not owned by any body but used by all including governments agencies, universities, United Nations, etc. all round the globe.

41. Which of the following was created for the co-ordination and maintenance of standards in higher education?
(a) SCERT
(b) UGC
(c) NCERT
(d) Higher Education Information System Project

42. In communication chatting in internet is
(a) Non-verbal communication
(b) Verbal communication
(c) Parallel communication
(d) Grapevine communication

43. Match the following.

Institutions
A. IIMC.
B. IISC.
C. Indian School of Mines.
D. Institute of Nuclear Medicine and Allied Sciences.

Situated at
1. Dhanbad 2. New Delhi
3. Bengluru 4. Delhi.

Codes:	A	B	C	D
(a)	1	2	3	4
(b)	2	3	1	4
(c)	2	3	4	1
(d)	3	1	2	4

44. The unit kIPS (thousand instruction per second) is used to measure the speed of
(a) Tape drive (b) Processor
(c) Disk drive (d) Printer

45. Data (information) is stored in computers as
(a) Matter (b) Files
(c) Directories (d) Floppies

46. Laser Scanners are capable of scanning bar codes upto a distance of
(a) 35 cm (b) 8 cm
(c) 25 cm (d) 45 cm

47. The coldest place on earth is
(a) Siachin (b) Halifex
(c) Verkhoyansk (d) Chicago

48. The University Grants Commission was constituted on the recommendation of
(a) Kothari Commission
(b) Sargent Commission
(c) Mudaliar Commission
(d) Dr. Sarvapalli Radhakrishnan Commission

49. Pen scanner is also known as
(a) LCD scanner
(b) Wand scanner
(c) Stationary scanner
(d) Hand held scanner

50. Calculate the binary division of $(11000)_2$ + $(100)_2$
(a) 111 (b) 10
(c) 100 (d) 110

51. Memory unit is one part of
(a) Central Processing Unit
(b) Input device
(c) Control unit
(d) Output device

Study the following graph carefully and answer questions 52 to 54.

Export of Engineering Goods

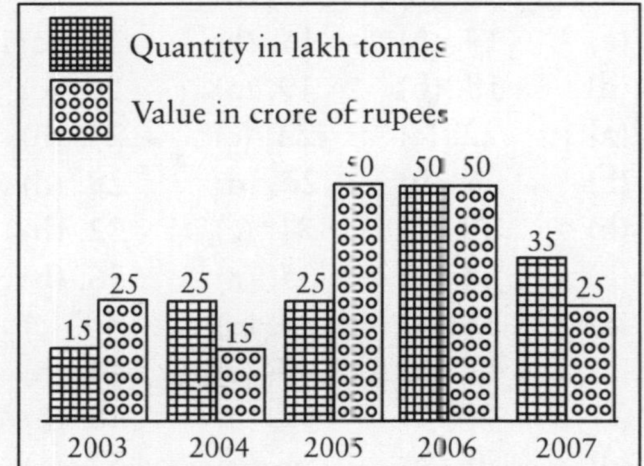

52. In which year the quantity of engineering goods' exports was maximum?
(a) 2006 (b) 2005
(c) 2007 (d) 2003

53. In which year the quantity of exports was 100 percent higher than the quantity of previous year?
(a) 2003 (b) 2007
(c) 2006 (d) 2005

54. In which year the value of engineering goods decreased by 50 percent compared to the previous year?
(a) 2006 (b) 2004
(c) 2007 (d) 2005

55. Who can amend the constitution?
(a) Council of Ministers
(b) President
(c) Parliament
(d) None of these

56. Main pollutant of the Indian coastal water is
(a) aerosols
(b) oil spill
(c) municipal sewage
(d) industrial effluents

57. Largest soil group of India is
(a) Mountain soil (b) Red soil
(c) Black soil (d) Alluvial soil

58. Which of the following is not a step of CPU
(a) Logic (b) Decode
(c) Execute (d) Fetch

59. What is the excess 3 code?
(a) self-algebraic code
(b) cyclic complimenting code
(c) cyclic algebraic code
(d) self-complimenting code

60. Environmental impact assessment is an objective analysis of the probable changes in
(a) biophysical characteristics of the environment
(b) physical characteristics of the environment

(c) socio-economic characteristics of the environment
(d) All of the above

ANSWER SHEET

TEST PAPER - I

1. (c)	2. (c)	3. (a)	4. (d)
5. (d)	6. (a)	7. (d)	8. (b)
9. (c)	10. (b)	11. (d)	12. (a)
13. (c)	14. (c)	15. (a)	16. (c)
17. (a)	18. (b)	19. (a)	20. (c)
21. (d)	22. (a)	23. (c)	24. (a)
25. (b)	26. (b)	27. (b)	28. (c)
29. (d)	30. (b)	31. (b)	32. (c)
33. (a)	34. (c)	35. (b)	36. (b)
37. (a)	38. (b)	39. (d)	40. (a)
41. (d)	42. (c)	43. (a)	44. (b)
45. (c)	46. (b)	47. (d)	48. (b)
49. (c)	50. (c)	51. (a)	52. (b)
53. (b)	54. (b)	55. (c)	56. (d)
57. (d)	58. (c)	59. (b)	60. (c)

TEST PAPER - II

1. (d)	2. (d)	3. (c)	4. (d)
5. (d)	6. (a)	7. (b)	8. (d)
9. (d)	10. (d)	11. (d)	12. (c)
13. (c)	14. (b)	15. (a)	16. (d)
17. (d)	18. (b)	19. (c)	20. (b)
21. (a)	22. (b)	23. (c)	24. (c)
25. (c)	26. (b)	27. (b)	28. (c)
29. (b)	30. (b)	31. (a)	32. (b)
33. (c)	34. (a)	35. (b)	36. (d)
37. (b)	38. (d)	39. (c)	40. (a)
41. (a)	42. (b)	43. (a)	44. (a)
45. (b)	46. (c)	47. (c)	48. (c)
49. (d)	50. (c)	51. (c)	52. (a)
53. (c)	54. (c)	55. (c)	56. (c)
57. (b)	58. (b)	59. (c)	60. (c)

TEST PAPER - III

1. (c)	2. (d)	3. (d)	4. (b)
5. (a)	6. (c)	7. (b)	8. (d)
9. (d)	10. (a)	11. (a)	12. (d)
13. (a)	14. (c)	15. (b)	16. (d)
17. (b)	18. (a)	19. (a)	20. (c)
21. (d)	22. (b)	23. (d)	24. (c)
25. (b)	26. (a)	27. (b)	28. (a)
29. (a)	30. (c)	31. (d)	32. (b)
33. (c)	34. (a)	35. (d)	36. (d)
37. (d)	38. (b)	39. (d)	40. (d)
41. (d)	42. (b)	43. (d)	44. (c)
45. (b)	46. (c)	47. (c)	48. (d)
49. (d)	50. (d)	51. (c)	52. (b)
53. (c)	54. (b)	55. (d)	56. (d)
57. (d)	58. (c)	59. (b)	60. (d)

TEST PAPER - IV

1. (b)	2. (c)	3. (d)	4. (d)
5. (a)	6. (c)	7. (d)	8. (c)
9. (c)	10. (b)	11. (b)	12. (b)
13. (a)	14. (b)	15. (b)	16. (c)
17. (d)	18. (b)	19. (a)	20. (c)
21. (a)	22. (c)	23. (c)	24. (b)
25. (b)	26. (b)	27. (d)	28. (d)
29. (b)	30. (c)	31. (c)	32. (b)
33. (b)	34. (c)	35. (a)	36. (b)
37. (a)	38. (c)	39. (a)	40. (c)
41. (b)	42. (b)	43. (c)	44. (b)
45. (c)	46. (c)	47. (b)	48. (b)
49. (d)	50. (b)	51. (b)	52. (a)
53. (b)	54. (d)	55. (c)	56. (c)
57. (b)	58. (c)	59. (c)	60. (b)

TEST PAPER - V

1. (a)	2. (c)	3. (a)	4. (d)
5. (d)	6. (d)	7. (d)	8. (c)
9. (b)	10. (c)	11. (b)	12. (c)
13. (c)	14. (b)	15. (d)	16. (b)
17. (a)	18. (d)	19. (c)	20. (d)
21. (d)	22. (a)	23. (b)	24. (a)
25. (d)	26. (d)	27. (a)	28. (d)
29. (b)	30. (a)	31. (b)	32. (c)
33. (c)	34. (d)	35. (d)	36. (d)
37. (a)	38. (d)	39. (b)	40. (b)
41. (b)	42. (c)	43. (b)	44. (b)
45. (c)	46. (b)	47. (a)	48. (c)
49. (a)	50. (b)	51. (b)	52. (b)
53. (b)	54. (d)	55. (c)	56. (d)
57. (d)	58. (c)	59. (c)	60. (a)

TEST PAPER - VI

1. (c)	2. (b)	3. (c)	4. (d)
5. (d)	6. (a)	7. (a)	8. (a)
9. (d)	10. (c)	11. (c)	12. (b)
13. (a)	14. (c)	15. (d)	16. (b)
17. (b)	18. (d)	19. (c)	20. (d)
21. (c)	22. (a)	23. (d)	24. (b)
25. (c)	26. (a)	27. (c)	28. (c)
29. (c)	30. (a)	31. (d)	32. (a)
33. (c)	34. (c)	35. (b)	36. (b)
37. (b)	38. (c)	39. (b)	40. (d)
41. (b)	42. (a)	43. (b)	44. (b)
45. (b)	46. (c)	47. (c)	48. (b)
49. (b)	50. (d)	51. (a)	52. (a)
53. (c)	54. (c)	55. (c)	56. (b)
57. (d)	58. (a)	59. (d)	60. (d)

Previous Years' Papers

DECEMBER-2011 (PAPER-I)

1. Photo bleeding means
   (a) Photo cropping
   (b) Photo placement
   (c) Photo cutting
   (d) Photo colour adjustment

2. While designing communication strategy feed-forward studies are conducted by
   (a) Audience (b) Communicator
   (c) Satellite (d) Media

3. In which language the newspapers have highest circulation?
   (a) English (b) Hindi
   (c) Bengali (d) Tamil

4. Aspect ratio of TV Screen is
   (a) 4 : 3 (b) 3 : 4
   (c) 2 : 3 (d) 2 : 4

5. Communication with oneself is known as
   (a) Organisational Communication
   (b) Grapevine Communication
   (c) Interpersonal Communication
   (d) Intrapersonal Communication

6. The term 'SITE' stands for
   (a) Satellite Indian Television Experiment
   (b) Satellite International Television Experiment
   (c) Satellite Instructional Television Experiment
   (d) Satellite Instructional Teachers Education

7. What is the number that comes next in the sequence?
   2, 5, 9, 19, 37, ___
   (a) 76 (b) 74
   (c) 75 (d) 50

8. Find the next letter for the series MPSV.....
   (a) X (b) Y
   (c) Z (d) A

9. If '367' means 'I am happy'; '748' means 'you are sad' and '469' means 'happy and sad' in a given code, then which of the following represents 'and' in that code?
   (a) 3 (b) 6
   (c) 9 (d) 4

10. The basis of the following classification is 'animal', 'man', 'house', 'book', and 'student':
    (a) Definite descriptions
    (b) Proper names
    (c) Descriptive phrases
    (d) Common names

11. **Assertion (A):** The coin when flipped next time will come up tails.
    Reason (R): Because the coin was flipped five times in a row, and each time it came up heads.
    Choose the correct answer from below:
    (a) Both (A) and (R) are true, and (R) is the correct explanation of (A).
    (b) Both (A) and (R) are false, and (R) is the correct explanation of (A).

(c) (A) is doubtful, (R) is true, and (R) is not the correct explanation of (A).
(d) (A) is doubtful, (R) is false, and (R) is the correct explanation of (A).

12. The relation 'is a sister of' is
(a) non-symmetrical (b) symmetrical
(c) asymmetrical (d) transitive

13. If the proposition "Vegetarians are not meat eaters" is false, then which of the following inferences is correct? Choose from the codes given below:
1. "Some vegetarians are meat eaters" is true.
2. "All vegetarians are meat eaters" is doubtful.
3. "Some vegetarians are not meat eaters" is true.
4. "Some vegetarians are not meat eaters" is doubtful.

Codes:
(a) 1, 2 and 3 (b) 2, 3 and 4
(c) 1, 3 and 4 (d) 1, 2 and 4

14. Determine the nature of the following definition:
'Poor' means having an annual income of ₹ 10,000.
(a) persuasive (b) precising
(c) lexical (d) stipulative

15. Which one of the following is not an argument?
(a) If today is Tuesday, tomorrow will be Wednesday.
(b) Since today is Tuesday, tomorrow will be Wednesday.
(c) Ram insulted me so I punched him in the nose.
(d) Ram is not at home, so he must have gone to town.

16. Venn diagram is a kind of diagram to
(a) represent and assess the truth of elementary inferences with the help of Boolean Algebra of classes.
(b) represent and assess the validity of elementary inferences with the help of Boolean Algebra of classes.
(c) represent but not assess the validity of elementary inferences with the help of Boolean Algebra of classes.
(d) assess but not represent the validity of elementary inferences with the help of Boolean Algebra of classes.

17. Inductive logic studies the way in which a premise may
(a) support and entail a conclusion
(b) not support but entail a conclusion
(c) neither support nor entail a conclusion
(d) support a conclusion without entailing it

18. Which of the following statements are true? Choose from the codes given below.
1. Some arguments, while not completely valid, are almost valid.
2. A sound argument may be invalid.
3. A cogent argument may have a probably false conclusion.
4. A statement may be true or false.

Codes:
(a) 1 and 2 (b) 1, 3 and 4
(c) Only 4 (d) 3 and 4

19. If the side of the square increases by 40%, then the area of the square increases by
(a) 60% (b) 40%
(c) 196% (d) 96%

20. There are 10 lamps in a hall. Each one of them can be switched on independently. The number of ways in which hall can be illuminated is
(a) 10^2 (b) 1023
(c) 2^{10} (d) 10!

21. How many numbers between 100 and 300 begin or end with 2?
(a) 100 (b) 110
(c) 120 (d) 180

22. In a college having 300 students, every student reads 5 newspapers and every newspaper is read by 60 students. The number of newspapers required is
(a) at least 30 (b) at most 20
(c) exactly 25 (d) exactly 5

The total CO_2 emissions from various sectors are 5 mmt. In the Pie Chart given below, the percentage contribution to CO_2 emissions from various sectors is indicated.

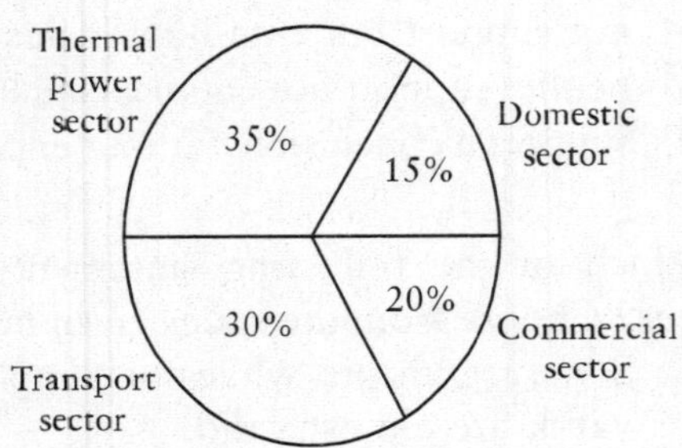

23. What is the absolute CO_2 emission from domestic sector?
(a) 1.5 mmt (b) 2.5 mmt
(c) 1.75 mmt (d) 0.75 mmt

24. What is the absolute CO_2 emission for combined thermal power and transport sectors?
(a) 3.25 mmt (b) 1.5 mmt
(c) 2.5 mmt (d) 4 mmt

25. Which of the following operating system is used on mobile phones?
(a) Windows Vista
(b) Android
(c) Windows XP
(d) All of the above

26. If $(y)_x$ represents a number y in base x, then which of the following numbers is smallest of all?
(a) $(1111)_2$ (b) $(1111)_8$
(c) $(1111)_{10}$ (d) $(1111)_{16}$

27. High level programming language can be converted to machine language using which of the following?
(a) Oracle (b) Compiler
(c) Mat lab (d) Assembler

28. HTML is used to create
(a) machine language program
(b) high level program
(c) web page
(d) web server

29. The term DNS stands for
(a) Domain Name System
(b) Defense Nuclear System
(c) Downloadable New Software
(d) Dependent Name Server

30. IPv4 and IPv6 are addresses used to identify computers on the internet. Find the correct statement out of the following:
(a) Number of bits required for IPv4 address is more than number of bits required for IPv6 address.
(b) Number of bits required for IPv4 address is same as number of bits required for IPv6 address.
(c) Number of bits required for IPv4 address is less than number of bits required for IPv6 address.
(d) Number of bits required for IPv4 address is 64.

31. Which of the following pollutants affects the respiratory tract in humans?
(a) Carbon monoxide
(b) Nitric oxide
(c) Sulphur di-oxide
(d) Aerosols

32. Which of the following pollutants is not emitted from the transport sector?
(a) Oxides of nitrogen
(b) Chlorofluorocarbons
(c) Carbon monoxide
(d) Poly aromatic hydrocarbons

33. Which of the following sources of energy has the maximum potential in India?
(a) Solar energy
(b) Wind energy
(c) Ocean thermal energy
(d) Tidal energy

34. Which of the following is not a source of pollution in soil?
(a) Transport sector
(b) Agriculture sector
(c) Thermal power plants
(d) Hydropower plants

35. Which of the following is not a natural hazard?
(a) Earthquake (b) Tsunami
(c) Flash floods (d) Nuclear accident

36. Ecological footprint represents
(a) area of productive land and water to meet the resources requirement
(b) energy consumption
(c) CO_2 emissions per person
(d) forest cover

37. The aim of value education to inculcate in students is
(a) the moral values
(b) the social values
(c) the political values
(d) the economic values

38. Indicate the number of Regional Offices of University Grants Commission of India.
(a) 10 (b) 07
(c) 08 (d) 09

39. One-rupee currency note in India bears the signature of
(a) The President of India
(b) Finance Minister of India
(c) Governor, Reserve Bank of India
(d) Finance Secretary of Government of India

40. Match the List I with the List II and select the correct answer from the codes given below:

List I (Commissions and Committees)
A. First Administrative Reforms Commission
B. Paul H. Appleby Committee I
C. K. Santhanam Committee
D. Second Administrative Reforms Commission

List II (Year)
1. 2005 2. 1962
3. 1966 4. 1953

Codes:	A	B	C	D
(a)	1	3	2	4
(b)	3	4	2	1
(c)	4	2	3	1
(d)	2	1	4	3

41. Constitutionally the registration and recognition of political parties is the function performed by
(a) The State Election Commission of respective States
(b) The Law Ministry of Government of India
(c) The Election Commission of India
(d) Election Department of the State Governments

42. The members of Gram Sabha are
(a) Sarpanch, Upsarpanch and all elected Panchas
(b) Sarpanch, Upsarpanch and Village level worker
(c) Sarpanch, Gram Sevak and elected Panchas
(d) Registered voters of Village Panchayat

43. By which of the following methods the true evaluation of the students is possible?
(a) Evaluation at the end of the course
(b) Evaluation twice in a year

(c) Continuous evaluation
(d) Formative evaluation

44. Suppose a student wants to share his problems with his teacher and he visits the teacher's house for the purpose, the teacher should
(a) contact the student's parents and solve his problem
(b) suggest him that he should never visit his house
(c) suggest him to meet the principal and solve the problem
(d) extend reasonable help and boost his morale

45. When some students are deliberately attempting to disturb the discipline of the class by making mischief, what will be your role as a teacher?
(a) Expelling those students
(b) Isolate those students
(c) Reform the group with your authority
(d) Giving them an opportunity for introspection and improve their behaviour

46. Which of the following belongs to a projected aid?
(a) Blackboard (b) Diorama
(c) Epidiascope (d) Globe

47. A teacher is said to be fluent in asking questions, if he can ask
(a) meaningful questions
(b) as many questions as possible
(c) maximum number of questions in a fixed time
(d) many meaningful questions in a fixed time

48. Which of the following qualities is most essential for a teacher?
(a) He should be a learned person
(b) He should be a well dressed person
(c) He should have patience
(d) He should be an expert in his subject

49. A hypothesis is a
(a) law (b) canon
(c) postulate (d) supposition

50. Suppose you want to investigate the working efficiency of nationalised bank in India, which one of the following would you follow?
(a) Area Sampling
(b) Multi-stage Sampling
(c) Sequential Sampling
(d) Quota Sampling

51. Controlled group condition is applied in
(a) Survey Research
(b) Historical Research
(c) Experimental Research
(d) Descriptive Research

52. Workshops are meant for
(a) giving lectures
(b) multiple target groups
(c) showcase new theories
(d) hands on training/experience

53. Which one of the following is a research tool?
(a) Graph (b) Illustration
(c) Questionnaire (d) Diagram

54. Research is not considered ethical if it
(a) tries to prove a particular point.
(b) does not ensure privacy and anonymity of the respondent.
(c) does not investigate the data scientifically.
(d) is not of a very high standard.

Read the following passage carefully and answer the questions (55 to 60):

The catalytic fact of the twentieth century is uncontrollable development, consumerist society, political materialism, and spiritual devaluation. This inordinate development has led to the transcendental 'second reality' of sacred perception that biologically transcendence is a part of human life. As the century closes, it dawns with imperative vigour that the 'first reality' of enlightened rationalism and the 'second reality' of the Beyond have to be harmonised in a worthy state of man. The *de facto* values describe what we are, they portray the 'is' of our ethic, they are *est* values (Latin *est* means is). The ideal values tell us what we ought to be, they are *esto* values (Latin *esto* 'ought to be'). Both have to be in the ebb and flow of consciousness. The ever new science and technology and the ever-perennial faith are two modes of one certainty, that is the wholeness of man, his courage to be, his share in Being.

The materialistic foundations of science have crumbled down. Science itself has proved that matter is energy, processes are as valid as facts, and affirmed the non-materiality of the universe. The encounter of the 'two cultures', the scientific and the humane, will restore the normal vision, and will be the bedrock of a 'science of understanding' in the new century. It will give new meaning to the ancient perception that quantity (measure) and quality (value) coexist at the root of nature. Human endeavours cannot afford to be humanistically irresponsible.

55. The problem raised in the passage reflects overall on
    (a) Consumerism
    (b) Materialism
    (c) Spiritual devaluation
    (d) Inordinate development

56. The *de facto* values in the passage means
    (a) What is
    (b) What ought to be
    (c) What can be
    (d) Where it is

57. According to the passage, the 'first reality' constitutes
    (a) Economic prosperity
    (b) Political development
    (c) Sacred perception of life
    (d) Enlightened rationalism

58. Encounter of the 'two cultures', the scientific and the human implies
    (a) Restoration of normal vision
    (b) Universe is both material and non-material
    (c) Man is superior to nature
    (d) Co-existence of quantity and quality in nature

59. The contents of the passage are
    (a) Descriptive (b) Prescriptive
    (c) Axiomatic (d) Optional

60. The passage indicates that science has proved that
    (a) universe is material
    (b) matter is energy
    (c) nature has abundance
    (d) humans are irresponsible

ANSWERS

1. (d)	2. (b)	3. (a)	4. (a)
5. (d)	6. (c)	7. (c)	8. (b)
9. (c)	10. (d)	11. (c)	12. (d)
13. (c)	14. (b)	15. (c)	16. (a)
17. (d)	18. (b)	19. (d)	20. (d)
21. (b)	22. (c)	23. (d)	24. (a)
25. (b)	26. (a)	27. (b)	28. (c)
29. (a)	30. (c)	31. (b)	32. (b)
33. (a)	34. (d)	35. (d)	36. (a)
37. (a)	38. (b)	39. (d)	40. (b)
41. (c)	42. (d)	43. (c)	44. (d)
45. (d)	46. (c)	47. (a)	48. (d)
49. (d)	50. (b)	51. (c)	52. (d)
53. (c)	54. (b)	55. (d)	56. (a)
57. (d)	58. (a)	59. (b)	60. (b)

JUNE-2011 (PAPER-I)

1. A research paper is a brief report of research work based on
   (a) Primary Data only
   (b) Secondary Data only
   (c) Both Primary and Secondary Data
   (d) None of the above
2. Newton gave three basic laws of motion. This research is categorised as
   (a) Descriptive Research
   (b) Sample Survey
   (c) Fundamental Research
   (d) Applied Research
3. A group of experts in a specific area of knowledge assembled at a place and prepared a syllabus for a new course. The process may be termed as
   (a) Seminar (b) Workshop
   (c) Conference (d) Symposium
4. In the process of conducting research "Formulation of Hypothesis" is followed by
   (a) Statement of Objectives
   (b) Analysis of Data
   (c) Selection of Research Tools
   (d) Collection of Data

Read the following passage carefully and answer questions 5 to 10:

All historians are interpreters of text if they be private letters, Government records or parish birthlists or whatever. For most kinds of historians, these are only the necessary means to understanding something other than the texts themselves, such as a political action or a historical trend, whereas for the intellectual historian, a full understanding of his chosen texts is itself the aim of his enquiries. Of course, the intellectual history is particularly prone to draw on the focus of other disciplines that are habitually interpreting texts for purposes of their own, probing the reasoning that ostensibly connects premises and conclusions. Furthermore, the boundaries with adjacent subdisciplines are shifting and indistinct: the history of art and the history of science both claim a certain autonomy, partly just because they require specialised technical skills, but both can also be seen as part of a wider intellectual history, as is evident when one considers, for example, the common stock of knowledge about cosmological beliefs or moral ideals of a period.

Like all historians, the intellectual historian is a consumer rather than a producer of 'methods'. His distinctiveness lies in which aspect of the past he is trying to illuminate, not in having exclusive possession of either a corpus of evidence or a body of techniques. That being said, it does seem that the label 'intellectual history' attracts a disproportionate share of misunderstanding.

It is alleged that intellectual history is the history of something that never really mattered. The long dominance of the historical profession by political historians bred a kind of philistinism, an unspoken belief that power and its exercise was 'what mattered'. The prejudice was reinforced by the assertion that political action was never really the outcome of principles or ideas that were 'more flapdoodle'. The legacy of this precept is still discernible in the tendency to require ideas to have 'licensed' the political class before they can be deemed worthy of intellectual attention, as if there were some reasons why the history of art or science, of philosophy or literature, were somehow of interest and significance than the history of Parties or Parliaments. Perhaps in recent years the mirror-image of this philistinism has been more common in the claim that ideas of any one is of systematic expression or sophistication do not matter, as if they were only held by a minority.

Answer the following questions:

5. An intellectual historian aims to fully understand
   (a) the chosen texts of his own
   (b) political actions
   (c) historical trends
   (d) his enquiries
6. Intellectual historians do not claim exclusive possession of
   (a) conclusions
   (b) any corpus of evidence
   (c) distinctiveness
   (d) habitual interpretation
7. The misconceptions about intellectual history stem from
   (a) a body of techniques
   (b) the common stock of knowledge
   (c) the dominance of political historians
   (d) cosmological beliefs
8. What is philistinism?
   (a) Reinforcement of prejudice
   (b) Fabrication of reasons
   (c) The hold of land-owning classes
   (d) Belief that power and its exercise matter
9. Knowledge of cosmological beliefs or moral ideas of a period can be drawn as part of
   (a) literary criticism
   (b) history of science
   (c) history of philosophy
   (d) intellectual history
10. The claim that ideas of any one is of systematic expression do not matter, as if they were held by a minority, is
    (a) to have a licensed political class
    (b) a political action
    (c) a philosophy of literature
    (d) the mirror-image of philistinism
11. Public communication tends to occur within a more
    (a) complex structure
    (b) political structure
    (c) convenient structure
    (d) formal structure
12. Transforming thoughts, ideas and messages into verbal and non-verbal signs is referred to as
    (a) channelisation (b) mediation
    (c) encoding (d) decoding
13. Effective communication needs a supportive
    (a) economic environment
    (b) political environment
    (c) social environment
    (d) multi-cultural environment
14. A major barrier in the transmission of cognitive data in the process of communication is an individual's
    (a) personality (b) expectation
    (c) social status (d) coding ability
15. When communicated, institutionalised stereotypes become
    (a) myths (b) reasons
    (c) experiences (d) convictions
16. In mass communication, selective perception is dependent on the receiver's
    (a) competence (b) pre-disposition
    (c) receptivity (d) ethnicity
17. Determine the relationship between the pair of words NUMERATOR : DENOMINATOR and then select the pair of words from the following which have a similar relationship:
    (a) fraction : decimal
    (b) divisor : quotient
    (c) top : bottom
    (d) dividend : divisor

18. Find the wrong number in the sequence 125, 127, 130, 135, 142, 153, 165
(a) 130 (b) 142
(c) 153 (d) 165

19. If HOBBY is coded as IOBY and LOBBY is coded as MOBY; then BOBBY is coded as
(a) BOBY (b) COBY
(c) DOBY (d) OOBY

20. The letters in the first set have certain relationship. On the basis of this relationship, make the right choice for the second set

K/T : 11/20 :: J/R :?
(a) 10/8 (b) 10/18
(c) 11/19 (d) 10/19

21. If A = 5, B = 6, C = 7, D = 8 and so on, what do the following numbers stand for?
17, 19, 20, 9, 8
(a) Plane (b) Moped
(c) Motor (d) Tonga

22. The price of oil is increased by 25%. If the expenditure is not allowed to increase, the ratio between the reduction in consumption and the original consumption is
(a) 1:3 (b) 1:4
(c) 1:5 (d) 1:6

23. How many 8's are there in the following sequence which are preceded by 5 but not immediately followed by 3?
5 8 3 7 5 8 6 3 8 5 4 5 8 4 7 6
5 5 8 3 5 8 7 5 8 2 8 5
(a) 4 (b) 5
(c) 7 (d) 3

24. If a rectangle were called a circle, a circle a point, a point a triangle and a triangle a square, the shape of a wheel is
(a) Rectangle (b) Circle
(c) Point (d) Triangle

25. Which one of the following methods is best suited for mapping the distribution of different crops as provided in the standard classification of crops in India?
(a) Pie diagram
(b) Chorochromatic technique
(c) Isopleth technique
(d) Dot method

26. Which one of the following does not come under the methods of data classification?
(a) Qualitative (b) Normative
(c) Spatial (d) Quantitative

27. Which one of the following is not a source of data?
(a) Administrative records
(b) Population census
(c) GIS
(d) Sample survey

28. If the statement 'some men are cruel' is false, which of the following statements/ statement are/is true?
(i) All men are cruel.
(ii) No men are cruel.
(iii) Some men are not cruel.
(a) (i) and (iii) (b) (i) and (ii)
(c) (ii) and (iii) (d) Only (iii)

29. The octal number system consists of the following symbols
(a) 0 – 7
(b) 0 – 9
(c) 0 – 9, A – F
(d) None of the above

30. The binary equivalent of $(-19)_{10}$ in signed magnitude system is
(a) 11101100 (b) 11101101
(c) 10010011 (d) None of these

31. DNS in internet technology stands for
(a) Dynamic Name System
(b) Domain Name System

(c) Distributed Name System
(d) None of these

32. HTML stands for
(a) Hyper Text Markup Language
(b) Hyper Text Manipulation Language
(c) Hyper Text Managing Links
(d) Hyper Text Manipulating Links

33. Which of the following is type of LAN?
(a) Ethernet (b) Token Ring
(c) FDDI (d) All of the above

34. Which of the following statements is true?
(a) Smart cards do not require an operating system.
(b) Smart cards and PCs use some operating system.
(c) COS is smart card operating system.
(d) The communication between reader and card is in full duplex mode.

35. The Ganga Action Plan was initiated during the year
(a) 1986 (b) 1988
(c) 1990 (d) 1992

36. Identify the correct sequence of energy sources in order of their share in the power sector in India.
(a) Thermal > nuclear > hydro > wind
(b) Thermal > hydro > nuclear > wind
(c) Hydro > nuclear > thermal > wind
(d) Nuclear > hydro > wind > thermal

37. Chromium as a contaminant in drinking water in excess of permissible levels, causes
(a) Skeletal damage
(b) Gastrointestinal problem
(c) Dermal and nervous problems
(d) Liver/Kidney problems

38. The main precursors of winter smog are
(a) N_2O and hydrocarbons
(b) NO_x and hydrocarbons
(c) SO_2 and hydrocarbons
(d) SO_2 and ozone

39. Flash floods are caused when
(a) the atmosphere is convectively unstable and there is considerable vertical wind shear
(b) the atmosphere is stable
(c) the atmosphere is convectively unstable with no vertical windshear
(d) winds are catabatic

40. In mega cities of India, the dominant source of air pollution is
(a) transport sector
(b) thermal power
(c) municipal waste
(d) commercial sector

41. The first Open University in India was set up in the State of
(a) Andhra Pradesh
(b) Delhi
(c) Himachal Pradesh
(d) Tamil Nadu

42. Most of the Universities in India are funded by
(a) the Central Government
(b) the State Governments
(c) the University Grants Commission
(d) Private bodies and Individuals

43. Which of the following organisations looks after the quality of Technical and Management education in India?
(a) NCTE (b) MCI
(c) AICTE (d) CSIR

44. Consider the following statements: Identify the statement which implies natural justice.
(a) The principle of natural justice is followed by the Courts.
(b) Justice delayed is justice denied.

(c) Natural justice is an inalienable right of a citizen.
(d) A reasonable opportunity of being heard must be given.

45. The President of India is
(a) the Head of State
(b) the Head of Government
(c) both Head of the State and the Head of the Government
(d) None of the above

46. Who among the following holds office during the pleasure of the President of India?
(a) Chief Election Commissioner
(b) Comptroller and Auditor General of India
(c) Chairman of the Union Public Service Commission
(d) Governor of a State

Questions 47 to 49 are based upon the following diagram in which there are three interlocking circles A, P and S where A stands for Artists, circle P for Professors and circle S for Sportspersons. Different regions in the figure are lettered from a to f:

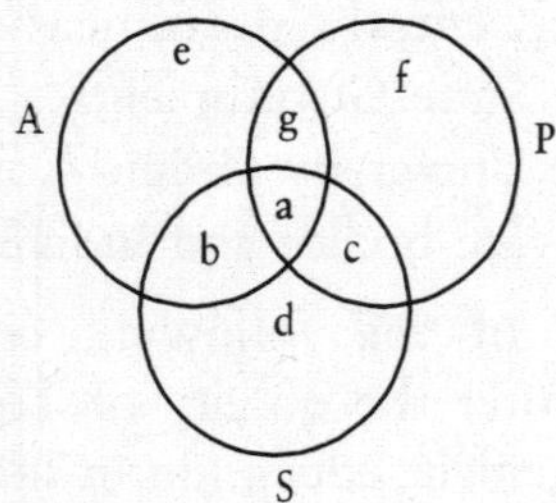

47. The region which represents artists who are neither sportsmen nor professors.
(a) d (b) e
(c) b (d) g

48. The region which represents professors, who are both artists and sportspersons.
(a) a (b) c
(c) d (d) g

49. The region which represents professors, who are also sportspersons, but not artists.
(a) e (b) f
(c) c (d) g

Questions 50 to 52 are based on the following data:

Measurements of some variable X were made at an interval of 1 minute from 10 A.M. to 10:20 A.M. The data, thus, obtained is as follows:

X: 60, 62, 65, 64, 63, 61, 66, 65, 70, 68
63, 62, 64, 69, 65, 64, 66, 67, 66, 64

50. The value of X, which is exceeded 10% of the time in the duration of measurement, is
(a) 69 (b) 68
(c) 67 (d) 66

51. The value of X, which is exceeded 90% of the time in the duration of measurement, is
(a) 63 (b) 62
(c) 61 (d) 60

52. The value of X, which is exceeded 50% of the time in the duration of measurement, is
(a) 66 (b) 65
(c) 64 (d) 63

53. For maintaining an effective discipline in the class, the teacher should
(a) Allow students to do what they like.
(b) Deal with the students strictly.
(c) Give the students some problem to solve.
(d) Deal with them politely and firmly.

54. An effective teaching aid is one which
(a) is colourful and good looking
(b) activates all faculties
(c) is visible to all students
(d) easy to prepare and use

55. Those teachers are popular among students who
(a) develop intimacy with them
(b) help them solve their problems
(c) award good grades
(d) take classes on extra tuition fee

56. The essence of an effective classroom environment is
(a) a variety of teaching aids
(b) lively student-teacher interaction
(c) pin-drop silence
(d) strict discipline

57. On the first day of his class, if a teacher is asked by the students to introduce himself, he should
(a) ask them to meet after the class
(b) tell them about himself in brief
(c) ignore the demand and start teaching
(d) scold the student for this unwanted demand

58. Moral values can be effectively inculcated among the students when the teacher
(a) frequently talks about values
(b) himself practices them
(c) tells stories of great persons
(d) talks of Gods and Goddesses

59. The essential qualities of a researcher are
(a) spirit of free enquiry
(b) reliance on observation and evidence
(c) systematisation or theorising of knowledge
(d) All of the above

60. Research is conducted to
1. Generate new knowledge
2. Not to develop a theory
3. Obtain research degree
4. Reinterpret existing knowledge

Which of the above are correct?
(a) 1, 3 & 2 (b) 3, 2 & 4
(c) 2, 1 & 3 (d) 1, 3 & 4

ANSWERS

1. (c)	2. (c)	3. (b)	4. (d)
5. (a)	6. (d)	7. (d)	8. (d)
9. (d)	10. (d)	11. (c)	12. (a)
13. (c)	14. (d)	15. (c)	16. (c)
17. (d)	18. (d)	19. (b)	20. (b)
21. (b)	22. (c)	23. (a)	24. (c)
25. (b)	26. (c)	27. (a)	28. (d)
29. (a)	30. (d)	31. (b)	32. (a)
33. (a)	34. (d)	35. (a)	36. (b)
37. (c)	38. (b)	39. (a)	40. (c)
41. (a)	42. (c)	43. (c)	44. (c)
45. (c)	46. (d)	47. (b)	48. (a)
49. (c)	50. (b)	51. (c)	52. (b)
53. (d)	54. (b)	55. (b)	56. (b)
57. (b)	58. (b)	59. (d)	60. (d)

DECEMBER-2010 (PAPER-I)

1. Which of the following variables cannot be expressed in quantitative terms?
(a) Socio-economic Status
(b) Marital Status
(c) Numerical Aptitude
(d) Professional Attitude

2. A doctor studies the relative effectiveness of two drugs of dengue fever. His research would be classified as
(a) Descriptive Survey
(b) Experimental Research
(c) Case Study
(d) Ethnography

3. The term 'phenomenology' is associated with the process of
(a) Qualitative Research
(b) Analysis of Variance
(c) Correlational Study
(d) Probability Sampling

4. The 'Sociogram' technique is used to study
(a) Vocational Interest
(b) Professional Competence

(c) Human Relations
(d) Achievement Motivation

Read the following passage carefully and answer questions from 5 to 10.

It should be remembered that the nationalist movement in India, like all nationalist movements, was essentially a bourgeois movement. It represented the natural historical stage of development, and to consider it or to criticise it as a working-class movement is wrong. Gandhi represented that movement and the Indian masses in relation to that movement to a supreme degree, and he became the voice of Indian people to that extent. The main contribution of Gandhi to India and the Indian masses has been through the powerful movements which he launched through the National Congress. Through nation-wide action he sought to mould the millions, and largely succeeded in doing so, and changing them from a demoralised, timid and hopeless mass, bullied and crushed by every dominant interest, and incapable of resistance, into a people with self-respect and self-reliance, resisting tyranny, and capable of united action and sacrifice for a larger cause.

Gandhi made people think of political and economic issues and every village and every bazaar hummed with argument and debate on the new ideas and hopes that filled the people. That was an amazing psychological change. The time was ripe for it, of course, and circumstances and world conditions worked for this change. But a great leader is necessary to take advantage of circumstances and conditions. Gandhi was that leader, and he released many of the bonds that imprisoned and disabled our minds, and none of us who experienced it can ever forget that great feeling of release and exhilaration that came over the Indian people.

Gandhi has played a revolutionary role in India of the greatest importance because he knew how to make the most of the objective conditions and could reach the heart of the masses, while groups with a more advanced ideology functioned largely in the air because they did not fit in with those conditions and could therefore not evoke any substantial response from the masses.

It is perfectly true that Gandhi, functioning in the nationalist plane, does not think in terms of the conflict of classes, and tries to compose their differences. But the action he has indulged and taught the people has inevitably raised mass consciousness tremendously and made social issues vital. Gandhi and the Congress must be judged by the policies they pursue and the action they indulge in. But behind this, personality counts and colours those policies and activities. In the case of very exceptional person like Gandhi the question of personality becomes especially important in order to understand and appraise him. To us he has represented the spirit and honour of India, the yearning of her sorrowing millions to be rid of their innumerable burdens, and an insult to him by the British Government or others has been an insult to India and her people.

5. Which one of the following is true of the given passage?
   (a) The passage is a critique of Gandhi's role in Indian movement for independence
   (b) The passage hails the role of Gandhi in India's freedom movement
   (c) The author is neutral on Gandhi's role in India's freedom movement
   (d) It is an account of Indian National Congress's support to the working-class movement

6. The change that the Gandhian movement brought among the Indian masses was
   (a) Physical (b) Cultural
   (c) Technological (d) Psychological

7. To consider the nationalist movement or to criticise it as a working-class movement was wrong because it was a
   (a) historical movement
   (b) voice of the Indian people
   (c) bourgeois movement
   (d) movement represented by Gandhi
8. Gandhi played a revolutionary role in India because he could
   (a) preach morality
   (b) reach the heart of Indians
   (c) see the conflict of classes
   (d) lead the Indian National Congress
9. Groups with advanced ideology functioned in the air as they did not fit in with
   (a) objective conditions of masses
   (b) the Gandhian ideology
   (c) the class consciousness of the people
   (d) the differences among masses
10. The author concludes the passage by
    (a) criticising the Indian masses
    (b) the Gandhian movement
    (c) pointing out the importance of the personality of Gandhi
    (d) identifying the sorrows of millions of Indians
11. Media that exist in an interconnected series of communication—points are referred to as
    (a) Networked media
    (b) Connective media
    (c) Nodal media
    (d) Multimedia
12. The information function of mass communication is described as
    (a) diffusion (b) publicity
    (c) surveillance (d) diversion
13. An example of asynchronous medium is
    (a) Radio (b) Television
    (c) Film (d) Newspaper
14. In communication, connotative words are
    (a) explicit (c) abstract
    (b) simple (d) cultural
15. A message beneath a message is labelled as
    (a) embedded text (b) internal text
    (c) inter-text (d) sub-text
16. In analogue mass communication, stories are
    (a) static (b) dynamic
    (c) interactive (d) exploratory
17. Determine the relationship between the pair of words ALWAYS : NEVER and then select from the following pair of words which have a similar relationship
    (a) often : rarely
    (b) frequently : occasionally
    (c) constantly : frequently
    (d) intermittently : casually
18. Find the wrong number in the sequence 52, 51, 48, 43, 34, 27, 16
    (a) 27 (b) 34
    (c) 43 (d) 48
19. In a certain code, PAN is written as 31 and PAR as 35, then PAT is written in the same code as
    (a) 30 (b) 37
    (c) 39 (d) 41
20. The letters in the first set have certain relationship. On the basis of this relationship, make the right choice for the second set:
    AF : IK : : LQ :?
    (a) MO (b) NP
    (c) OR (d) TV
21. If 5472 = 9, 6342 = 6, 7584 = 6, what is 9236?
    (a) 2 (b) 3
    (c) 4 (d) 5

22. In an examination, 35% of the total students failed in Hindi, 45% failed in English and 20% in both. The percentage of those who passed in both subjects is
(a) 10 (b) 20
(c) 30 (d) 40

23. Two statements I and II given below are followed by two conclusions (a) and (b). Supposing the statements are true, which of the following conclusions can logically follow?

Statements:

I. Some flowers are red.
II. Some flowers are blue.

Conclusions:

(a) Some flowers are neither red nor blue.
(b) Some flowers are both red and blue.

(a) Only (a) follows
(b) Only (b) follows
(c) Both (a) and (b) follows
(d) Neither (a) nor (b) follows

24. If the statement 'all students are intelligent' is true, which of the following statements are false?
(i) No students are intelligent.
(ii) Some students are intelligent.
(iii) Some students are not intelligent.
(a) (i) and (ii) (b) (i) and (iii)
(c) (ii) and (iii) (d) Only (i)

25. A reasoning where we start with certain particular statements and conclude with a universal statement is called
(a) Deductive Reasoning
(b) Inductive Reasoning
(c) Abnormal Reasoning
(d) Transcendental Reasoning

26. What is the smallest number of ducks that could swim in this formation—two ducks in front of a duck, two ducks behind a duck and a duck between two ducks?
(a) 5 (b) 7
(c) 4 (d) 3

27. Mr. A, Miss B, Mr. C and Miss D are sitting around a table and discussing their trades.
(i) Mr. A sits opposite to the cook.
(ii) Miss B sits right to the barber.
(iii) The washerman sits right to the barber.
(iv) Miss D sits opposite to Mr. C.
What are the trades of A and B?
(a) Tailor and barber
(b) Barber and cook
(c) Tailor and cook
(d) Tailor and washerman

28. Which one of the following methods serve to measure correlation between two variables?
(a) Scatter Diagram
(b) Frequency Distrubution
(c) Two-way table
(d) Coefficient of Rank Correlation

29. Which one of the following is not an Internet Service Provider (ISP)?
(a) MTNL
(b) BSNL
(c) ERNET India
(d) Infotech India Ltd.

30. The hexadecimal number system consists of the symbols
(a) 0 - 7 (b) 0 - 9, A - F
(c) 0 - 7, A - F (d) None of these

31. The binary equivalent of $(-15)_{10}$ is (2's complement system is used)
(a) 11110001 (b) 11110000
(c) 10001111 (d) None of these

32. 1 GB is equal to
(a) 2^{30} bits (b) 2^{30} bytes
(c) 2^{20} bits (d) 2^{20} bytes

33. The set of computer programs that manage the hardware/software of a computer is called
    (a) Compiler system
    (b) Operation system
    (c) Operating system
    (d) None of these
34. SMIME in Internet technology stands for
    (a) Secure Multipurpose Internet Mail Extension
    (b) Secure Multimedia Internet Mail Extension
    (c) Simple Multipurpose Internet Mail Extension
    (d) Simple Multimedia Internet Mail Extension
35. Which of the following is not covered in 8 missions under the Climate Action Plan of Government of India?
    (a) Solar power
    (b) Waste to energy conversion
    (c) Afforestation
    (d) Nuclear energy
36. The concentration of Total Dissolved Solids (TDS) in drinking water should not exceed
    (a) 500 mg/L (b) 400 mg/L
    (c) 300 mg/L (d) 200 mg/L
37. 'Chipko' movement was first started by
    (a) Arundhati Roy
    (b) Medha Patkar
    (c) Ila Bhatt
    (d) Sunderlal Bahuguna
38. The constituents of photochemical smog responsible for eye irritation are
    (a) SO_2 and O_3
    (b) SO_2 and NO_2
    (c) HCHO and PAN
    (d) SO_2 and SPM
39. **Assertion (A):** Some carbonaceous aerosols may be carcinogenic.

    Reason (R): They may contain polycyclic aromatic hydrocarbons (PAHs).
    (a) Both (A) and (R) are correct and (R) is the correct explanation of (A).
    (b) Both (A) and (R) are correct but (R) is not the correct explanation of (A).
    (c) (A) is correct, but (R) is false.
    (d) (A) is false, but (R) is correct.
40. Volcanic eruptions affect
    (a) atmosphere and hydrosphere
    (b) hydrosphere and biosphere
    (c) lithosphere, biosphere and atmosphere
    (d) lithosphere, hydrosphere and atmosphere
41. India's first Defence University is in the State of
    (a) Haryana
    (b) Andhra Pradesh
    (c) Uttar Pradesh
    (d) Punjab
42. Most of the Universities in India
    (a) conduct teaching and research only
    (b) affiliate colleges and conduct examinations
    (c) conduct teaching/research and examinations
    (d) promote research only
43. Which one of the following is not a Constitutional Body?
    (a) Election Commission
    (b) Finance Commission
    (c) Union Public Service Commission
    (d) Planning Commission
44. Which one of the following statements is not correct?
    (a) Indian Parliament is supreme.
    (b) The Supreme Court of India has the power of judicial review.

(c) There is a division of powers between the Centre and the States.
(d) There is a Council of Ministers to aid and advise the President.

45. Which one of the following statements reflects the republic character of Indian democracy?
(a) Written constitution
(b) No State religion
(c) Devolution of power to local Government institutions
(d) Elected President and directly or indirectly elected Parliament

46. Who among the following appointed by the Governor can be removed by only the President of India?
(a) Chief Minister of a State
(b) A member of the State Public Service Commission
(c) Advocate-General
(d) Vice-Chancellor of a State University

47. If two small circles represent the class of the 'men' and the class of the 'plants' and the big circle represents 'mortality', which one of the following figures represent the proposition 'All men are mortal?.'

(a) 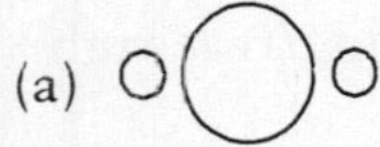 (b) 

(c) 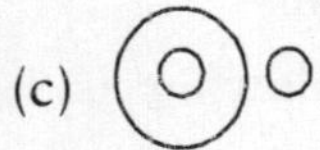 (d) 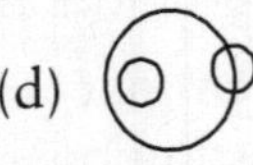

The following table presents the production of electronic items (TVs and LCDs) in a factory during the period from 2006 to 2010. Study the table carefully and answer the questions from 48 to 52:

Year	2006	2007	2008	2009	2010
TVs	6000	9000	13000	11000	8000
LCDs	7000	9400	9000	10000	12000

48. In which year, the total production of electronic items is maximum?
(a) 2006 (b) 2007
(c) 2008 (d) 2010

49. What is the difference between averages of production of LCDs and TVs from 2006 to 2008?
(a) 3000 (b) 2867
(c) 3015 (d) None of these

50. What is the year in which production of TVs is half the production of LCDs in the year 2010?
(a) 2007 (b) 2006
(c) 2009 (d) 2008

51. What is the ratio of production of LCDs in the years 2008 and 2010?
(a) 4:3 (b) 3:4
(c) 1:3 (d) 2:3

52. What is the ratio of production of TVs in the years 2006 and 2007?
(a) 6:7 (b) 7:6
(c) 2:3 (d) 3:2

53. Some students in a class exhibit great curiosity for learning. It may be because such children
(a) Are gifted
(b) Come from rich families
(c) Show artificial behaviour
(d) Create indiscipline in the class

54. The most important quality of a good teacher is
(a) Sound knowledge of subject matter
(b) Good communication skills
(c) Concern for students' welfare
(d) Effective leadership qualities

55. Which one of the following is appropriate in respect of teacher-student relationship?
(a) Very informal and intimate
(b) Limited to classroom only
(c) Cordial and respectful
(d) Indifferent

56. The academic performance of students can be improved if parents are encouraged to
(a) supervise the work of their wards
(b) arrange for extra tuition
(c) remain unconcerned about it
(d) interact with teachers frequently

57. In a lively classroom situation, there is likely to be
(a) occasional roars of laughter
(b) complete silence
(c) frequent teacher-student dialogue
(d) loud discussion among students

58. If a parent approaches the teacher to do some favour to his/her ward in the examination, the teacher should
(a) try to help him
(b) ask him not to talk in those terms
(c) refuse politely and firmly
(d) ask him rudely to go away

59. Which of the following phrases is not relevant to describe the meaning of research as a process?
(a) Systematic Activity
(b) Objective Observation
(c) Trial and Error
(d) Problem Solving

60. Which of the following is not an example of a continuous variable?
(a) Family size (b) Intelligence
(c) Height (d) Altitude

ANSWERS

1. (d)	2. (b)	3. (a)	4. (c)
5. (b)	6. (d)	7. (c)	8. (b)
9. (a)	10. (c)	11. (a)	12. (c)
13. (d)	14. (d)	15. (d)	16. (a)
17. (a)	18. (b)	19. (b)	20. (d)
21. (a)	22. (b)	23. (d)	24. (b)
25. (d)	26. (a)	27. (d)	28. (d)
29. (d)	30. (b)	31. (d)	32. (b)
33. (c)	34. (a)	35. (d)	36. (a)
37. (d)	38. (b)	39. (a)	40. (d)
41. (a)	42. (c)	43. (d)	44. (b)
45. (d)	46. (b)	47. (c)	48. (c)
49. (d)	50. (b)	51. (b)	52. (c)
53. (a)	54. (b)	55. (c)	56. (d)
57. (a)	58. (a)	59. (b)	60. (b)

JUNE-2010 (PAPER-I)

1. Which one of the following is the most important quality of a good teacher?
(a) Punctuality and sincerity
(b) Content mastery
(c) Content mastery and reactive
(d) Content mastery and sociable

2. The primary responsibility for the teacher's adjustment lies with
(a) The children
(b) The principal
(c) The teacher himself
(d) The community

3. As per the NCTE norms, what should be the staff strength for a unit of 100 students at B.Ed. level?
(a) 1 + 7 (b) 1 + 9
(c) 1 + 10 (d) 1 + 5

4. Research has shown that the most frequent symptom of nervous instability among teachers is
(a) Digestive upsets
(b) Explosive behaviour
(c) Fatigue
(d) Worry

5. Which one of the following statements is correct?
(a) Syllabus is an annexure to the curriculum.
(b) Curriculum is the same in all educational institutions.
(c) Curriculum includes both formal and informal education.
(d) Curriculum does not include methods of evaluation.

6. A successful teacher is one who is
   (a) Compassionate and disciplinarian
   (b) Quite and reactive
   (c) Tolerant and dominating
   (d) Passive and active

Read the following passage carefully and answer the questions 7 to 12.

The phrase "What is it like?" stands for a fundamental thought process. How does one go about observing and reporting on things and events that occupy segments of earth space? Of all the infinite variety of phenomena on the face of the earth, how does one decide what phenomena to observe? There is no such thing as a complete description of the earth or any part of it, for every microscopic point on the earth's surface differs from every other such point. Experience shows that the things observed are already familiar, because they are like phenomena that occur at home or because they resemble the abstract images and models developed in the human mind.

How are abstract images formed? Humans alone among the animals possess language; their words symbolise not only specific things but also mental images of classes of things. People can remember what they have seen or experienced because they attach a word symbol to them.

During the long record of our efforts to gain more and more knowledge about the face of the earth as the human habitat, there has been a continuing interplay between things and events. The direct observation through the senses is described as a percept; the mental image is described as a concept. Percepts are what some people describe as reality, in contrast to mental images, which are theoretical, implying that they are not real.

The relation of Percept to Concept is not as simple as the definition implies. It is now quite clear that people of different cultures or even individuals in the same culture develop different mental images of reality and what they perceive is a reflection of these preconceptions. The direct observation of things and events on the face of the earth is so clearly a function of the mental images of the mind of the observer that the whole idea of reality must be reconsidered.

Concepts determine what the observer perceives, yet concepts are derived from the generalisations of previous percepts. What happens is that the educated observer is taught to accept a set of concepts and then sharpens or changes these concepts during a professional career. In any one field of scholarship, professional opinion at one time determines what concepts and procedures are acceptable, and these form a kind of model of scholarly behaviour.

7. The problem raised in the passage reflects on
   (a) thought process
   (b) human behaviour
   (c) cultural perceptions
   (d) professional opinion
8. According to the passage, human beings have mostly in mind
   (a) Observation of things
   (b) Preparation of mental images
   (c) Expression through language
   (d) To gain knowledge
9. Concept means
   (a) A mental image
   (b) A reality
   (c) An idea expressed in language form
   (d) All the above
10. The relation of Percept to Concept is
    (a) Positive (b) Negative
    (c) Reflective (d) Absolute
11. In the passage, the earth is taken as
    (a) The Globe
    (b) The Human Habitat

(c) A Celestial Body
(d) A Planet

12. Percept means
(a) Direct observation through the senses
(b) A conceived idea
(c) Ends of a spectrum
(d) An abstract image

13. Action research means
(a) A longitudinal research
(b) An applied research
(c) A research initiated to solve an immediate problem
(d) A research with socio-economic objective

14. Research is
(a) Searching again and again
(b) Finding solution to any problem
(c) Working in a scientific way to search for truth of any problem
(d) None of the above

15. A common test in research demands much priority on
(a) Reliability (b) Usability
(c) Objectivity (d) All of the above

16. Which of the following is the first step in starting the research process?
(a) Searching sources of information to locate problem
(b) Survey of related literature
(c) Identification of problem
(d) Searching for solutions to the problem

17. If a researcher conducts a research on finding out which administrative style contributes more to institutional effectiveness? This will be an example of
(a) Basic Research
(b) Action Research
(c) Applied Research
(d) None of the above

18. Normal Probability Curve should be
(a) Positively skewed
(b) Negatively skewed
(c) Leptokurtic skewed
(d) Zero skewed

19. In communication, a major barrier to reception of messages is
(a) audience attitude
(b) audience knowledge
(c) audience education
(d) audience income

20. Post-modernism is associated with
(a) Newspapers (b) Magazines
(c) Radio (d) Television

21. Didactic communication is
(a) intra-porsonal (b) inter-personal
(c) organisational (d) relational

22. In communication, the language is
(a) the non-verbal code
(b) the verbal code
(c) the symbolic code
(d) the iconic code

23. Identify the correct sequence of the following:
(a) Source, channel, message, receiver
(b) Source, receiver, channel, message
(c) Source, message, receiver, channel
(d) Source, message, channel, receiver

24. **Assertion (A):** Mass media promote a culture of violence in the society.

Reason (R): Because violence sells in the market as people themselves are violent in character.
(a) Both (A) and (R) are true and (R) is the correct explanation of (A).
(b) Both (A) and (R) are true, but (R) is not the correct explanation of (A).
(c) (A) is true, but (R) is false.
(d) Both (A) and (R) are false.

25. When an error of 1% is made in the length of a square, the percentage error in the area of a square will be
(a) 0 (b) 1/2
(c) 1 (d) 2

26. On January 12, 1980, it was a Saturday. The day of the week on January 12, 1979 was
(a) Thursday (b) Friday
(c) Saturday (d) Sunday

27. If water is called food, food is called tree, tree is called earth, earth is called world, which of the following grows a fruit?
(a) Water (b) Tree
(c) World (d) Earth

28. E is the son of A, D is the son of B, E is married to C, C is the daughter of E. How is D related to E?
(a) Brother (b) Uncle
(c) Father-in-law (d) Brother-in-law

29. If INSURANCE is coded as ECNARUSNI, how HINDRANCE will be coded?
(a) CADNIHWCE (b) HANODEINR
(c) AENIRHDCN (d) ECNARDNIH

30. Find the next number in the following series: 2, 5, 10, 17, 26, 37, 50, ?
(a) 63 (b) 65
(c) 67 (d) 69

31. Which of the following is an example of circular argument?
(a) God created man in his image and man created God in his own image.
(b) God is the source of a scripture and the scripture is the source of our knowledge of God.
(c) Some of the Indians are great because India is great.
(d) Rama is great because he is Rama.

32. Lakshmana is a morally good person because
(a) he is religious (b) he is educated
(c) he is rich (d) he is rational

33. Two statements I and II given below are followed by two conclusions (a) and (b). Supposing the statements are true, which of the following conclusions can logically follow?

Statements:
I. Some religious people are morally good.
II. Some religious people are rational.

Conclusion:
(a) Rationally religious people are good morally.
(b) Non-rational religious persons are not morally good.

(a) Only (a) follows
(b) Only (b) follows
(c) Both (a) and (b) follow
(d) Neither (a) nor (b) follows

34. Certainty is
(a) an objective fact
(b) emotionally satisfying
(c) logical
(d) ontological

Questions from 35 to 36 are based on the following diagram in which there are three intersecting circles I, S and P where circle I stands for Indians, circle S stands for Scientists and circle P for Politicians. Different regions of the figure are lettered from a to g.

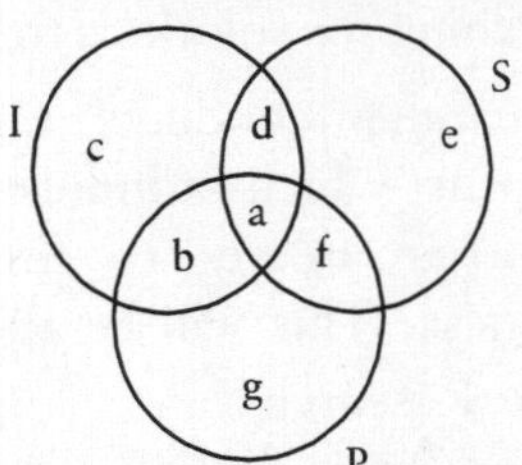

35. The region which represents non-scientists who are politicians.
(a) f (b) d
(c) a (d) c

36. The region which represents politicians who are Indians as well as scientists.
    (a) b (b) c
    (c) a (d) d

37. The population of a city is plotted as a function of time (years) in graphic form below:

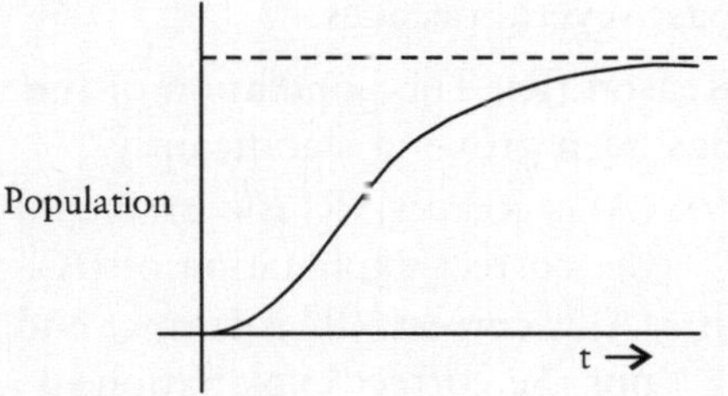

Which of the following inference can be drawn from above plot?
    (a) The population increases exponentially.
    (b) The population increases in parabolic fashion.
    (c) The population initially increases in a linear fashion and then stabilises.
    (d) The population initially increases exponentially and then stabilises.

In the following chart, the price of logs is shown in per cubic metre and that of Plywood and Saw Timber in per tonnes. Study the chart and answer the following questions 38, 39 and 40.

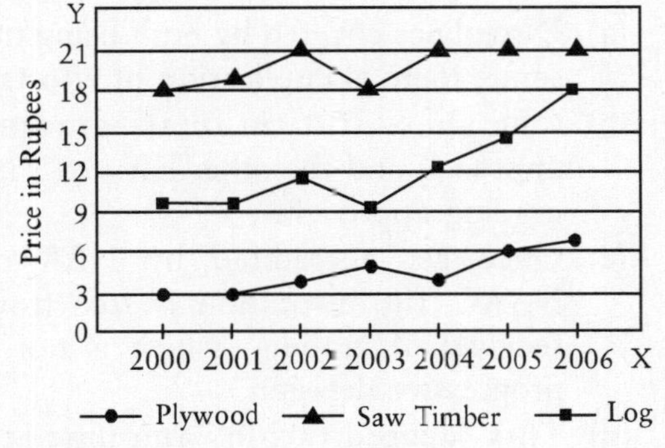

38. Which product shows the maximum percentage increase in price over the period?
    (a) Saw timber (b) Plywood
    (c) Log (d) None of these

39. What is the maximum percentage increase in price per cubic metre of log?
    (a) 6 (b) 12
    (c) 18 (d) None of these

40. In which year the prices of two products increased and that of the third increased?
    (a) 2000 (b) 2002
    (c) 2003 (d) 2006

41. Which one of the following is the oldest Archival source of data in India?
    (a) National Sample Surveys
    (b) Agricultural Statistics
    (c) Census
    (d) Vital Statistics

42. In a large random data set following normal distribution, the ratio (%) of number of data points which are in the range of (mean ± standard deviation) to the total number of data points, is
    (a) ~ 50% (b) ~ 67%
    (c) ~ 97% (d) ~ 47%

43. Which number system is usually followed in a typical 32-bit computer?
    (a) 2 (b) 8
    (c) 10 (d) 16

44. Which one of the following is an example of Operating System?
    (a) Microsoft Word
    (b) Microsoft Excel
    (c) Microsoft Access
    (d) Microsoft Windows

45. Which one of the following represent the binary equivalent of the decimal number 23?
    (a) 01011 (b) 10111
    (c) 10011 (d) None of these

46. Which one of the following is different from other members?

(a) Google (b) Windows
(c) Linux (d) Mac

47. Where does a computer add and compare its data?
(a) CPU (b) Memory
(c) Hard disk (d) Floppy disk

48. Computers on an internet are identified by
(a) e-mail address
(b) street address
(c) IP address
(d) None of the above

49. The Right to Information Act, 2005 makes the provision of
(a) Dissemination of all types of information by all Public authorities to any person
(b) Establishment of Central, State and District Level Information Commissions as an appellate body
(c) Transparency and accountability in Public authorities
(d) All of the above

50. Which type of natural hazards cause maximum damage to property and lives?
(a) Hydrological
(b) Hydro-meteorological
(c) Geological
(d) Geo-chemical

51. Dioxins are produced from
(a) Wastelands
(b) Power plants
(c) Sugar factories
(d) Combustion of plastics

52. The slogan "A tree for each child" was coined for
(a) Social forestry program
(b) Clean Air program
(c) Soil conservation program
(d) Environmental protection program

53. The main constituents of biogas are
(a) Methane and Carbon di-oxide
(b) Methane and Nitric oxide
(c) Methane, Hydrogen and Nitric oxide
(d) Methane and Sulphur di-oxide

54. **Assertion (A):** In the world as a whole, the environment has degraded during past several decades.

Reason (R): The population of the world has been growing significantly.
(a) (A) is correct, (R) is correct and (R) is the correct explanation of (A).
(b) (A) is correct, (R) is correct and (R) is not the correct explanation of (A).
(c) (A) is correct, but (R) is false.
(d) (A) is false, but (R) is correct.

55. Climate change has implications for
1. soil moisture 2. forest fires
3. biodiversity 4. groundwater

Identify the correct combination according to the code:

Codes:
(a) 1 and 3 (b) 1, 2 and 3
(c) 1, 3 and 4 (d) 1, 2, 3 and 4

56. The accreditation process by National Assessment and Accreditation Council (NAAC) differs from that of National Board of Accreditation (NBA) in terms of
(a) Disciplines covered by both being the same, there is duplication of efforts.
(b) One has institutional grading approach and the other has program grading approach.
(c) Once get accredited by NBA or NAAC, the institution is free from renewal of grading, which is not a progressive decision.
(d) This accreditation amounts to approval of minimum standards in the quality of education in the institution concerned.

57. Which option is not correct?
   (a) Most of the educational institutions of National repute in scientific and technical sphere fall under 64th entry of Union list.
   (b) Education, in general, is the subject of concurrent list since 42nd Constitutional Amendment Act 1976.
   (c) Central Advisory Board on Education (CABE) was first established in 1920.
   (d) India had implemented the right to Free and Compulsory Primary Education in 2002 through 86th Constitutional Amendment.

58. Which statement is not correct about the "National Education Day" of India?
   (a) It is celebrated on 5th September every year.
   (b) It is celebrated on 11th November every year.
   (c) It is celebrated in the memory of India's first Union Minister of Education, Dr. Abul Kalam Azad.
   (d) It is being celebrated since 2008.

59. Match List I with List II and select the correct answer from the codes given below:

List I (Articles of the Constitution)

A. Article 280 B. Article 324
C. Article 323 D. Article 315

List II (Institutions)

1. Administrative Tribunals
2. Election Commission of India
3. Finance Commission at Union level
4. Union Public Service Commission

Codes:	A	B	C	D
(a)	1	2	3	4
(b)	3	2	1	4
(c)	2	3	4	1
(d)	2	4	3	1

60. Deemed Universities declared by UGC under Section 3 of the UGC Act 1956, are not permitted to
   (a) offer programs in higher education and issue degrees
   (b) give affiliation to any institute of higher education
   (c) open off-campus and off-shore campus anywhere in the country and overseas respectively without the permission of the UGC
   (d) offer distance education programs without the approval of the Distance Education Council

ANSWERS

1. (b)	2. (c)	3. (a)	4. (b)
5. (c)	6. (a)	7. (a)	8. (a)
9. (a)	10. (c)	11. (b)	12. (a)
13. (c)	14. (c)	15. (d)	16. (c)
17. (c)	18. (d)	19. (a)	20. (d)
21. (b)	22. (b)	23. (d)	24. (d)
25. (d)	26. (b)	27. (d)	28. (d)
29. (d)	30. (b)	31. (c)	32. (d)
33. (d)	34. (b)	35. (a)	36. (c)
37. (d)	38. (b)	39. (d)	40. (c)
41. (c)	42. (b)	43. (a)	44. (d)
45. (b)	46. (a)	47. (a)	48. (c)
49. (d)	50. (b)	51. (d)	52. (d)
53. (a)	54. (b)	55. (d)	56. (b)
57. (a)	58. (a)	59. (b)	60. (b)

DECEMBER-2009 (PAPER-I)

1. The University which telecasts interaction educational programs through its own channel is
   (a) Osmania University
   (b) University of Pune
   (c) Annamalai University
   (d) Indira Gandhi National University (IGNOU)

2. Which of the following skills are needed for present day teacher to adjust effectively with the classroom teaching?
   1. Knowledge of technology
   2. Use of technology in teaching learning
   3. Knowledge of students' needs
   4. Content mastery

   (a) 1 and 3 (b) 2 and 3
   (c) 2, 3 and 4 (d) 2 and 4

3. Who has signed as MoU for Accreditation of Teacher Education Institutions in India?
   (a) NAAC and UGC
   (b) NCTE and NAAC
   (c) UGC and NCTE
   (d) NCTE and IGNOU

4. The primary duty of the teacher is to
   (a) raise the intellectual standard of the students
   (b) improve the physical standard of the students
   (c) help all-round development of the students
   (d) imbibe value system in the students

5. Micro teaching is more effective
   (a) during the preparation for teaching-practice
   (b) during the teaching-practice
   (c) after the teaching-practice
   (d) always

6. What quality the students like the most in a teacher?
   (a) Idealist philosophy
   (b) Compassion
   (c) Discipline
   (d) Entertaining

7. A null hypothesis is
   (a) when there is no difference between the variables
   (b) the same as research hypothesis
   (c) subjective in nature
   (d) when there is difference between the variables

8. The research which is exploring new facts through the study of the past is called
   (a) Philosophical research
   (b) Historical research
   (c) Mythological research
   (d) Content analysis

9. Action research is
   (a) An applied research
   (b) A research carried out to solve immediate problems
   (c) A longitudinal research
   (d) Simulative research

10. The process not needed in Experimental Researches is
    (a) Observation (b) Manipulation
    (c) Controlling (d) Content Analysis

11. Manipulation is always a part of
    (a) Historical research
    (b) Fundamental research
    (c) Descriptive research
    (d) Experimental research

12. Which correlation co-efficient best explains the relationship between creativity and intelligence?
    (a) 1.00 (b) 0.6
    (c) 0.5 (d) 0.3

Read the following passage and answer the Question Nos. 13 to 18:

The decisive shift in British Policy really came about under mass pressure in the autumn and winter of 1945 to 46—the months which Penderel Moon while editing Wavell's Journal has perceptively described as 'The Edge of a Volcano'. Very foolishly, the British initially decided to hold public trials of several hundreds of the 20,000 I.N.A. prisoners (as well as dismissing from service and detaining without trial no less than 7,000). They compounded the folly by holding the first trial in the Red Fort, Delhi in November 1945, and putting on the dock together a Hindu, a Muslim and a Sikh (P.K. Sehgal, Shah Nawaz, Gurbaksh Singh Dhillon). Bhulabhai Desai, Tejbahadur Sapru and Nehru appeared for the defence (the latter putting on his barrister's gown after 25 years), and the Muslim League also joined the countrywide protest. On 20 November, an Intelligence Bureau note admitted that "there has seldom been a matter which has attracted so much Indian public interest and, it is safe to say, sympathy...this particular brand of sympathy cuts across communal barriers". A journalist (B. Shiva Rao) visiting the Red Fort prisoners on the same day reported that 'There is not the slightest feeling among them of Hindu and Muslim.... A majority of the men now awaiting trial in the Red Fort is Muslim. Some of these men are bitter that Mr. Jinnah is keeping alive a controversy about Pakistan.' The British became extremely nervous about the I.N.A. spirit spreading to the Indian Army, and in January the Punjab Governor reported that a Lahore reception for released I.N.A. prisoners had been attended by Indian soldiers in uniform.

13. Which heading is more appropriate to assign to the above passage?
    (a) Wavell's Journal
    (b) Role of Muslim League
    (c) I.N.A. Trials
    (d) Red Fort Prisoners
14. The trial of P.K. Sehgal, Shah Nawaz and Gurbaksh Singh Dhillon symbolises
    (a) communal harmony
    (b) threat to all religious persons
    (c) threat to persons fighting for the freedom
    (d) British reaction against the natives
15. I.N.A. stands for
    (a) Indian National Assembly
    (b) Indian National Association
    (c) Inter-national Association
    (d) Indian National Army
16. 'There has seldom been a matter which has attracted so much Indian Public Interest and, it is safe to say, sympathy... this particular brand of sympathy cuts across communal barriers.' Who sympathises to whom and against whom?
    (a) Muslims sympathised with Shah Nawaz against the British
    (b) Hindus sympathised with P.K. Sehgal against the British
    (c) Sikhs sympathised with Gurbaksh Singh Dhillon against the British
    (d) Indians sympathised with the persons who were to be trialled
17. The majority of people waiting for trial outside the Red Fort and criticising Jinnah were the
    (a) Hindus
    (b) Muslims
    (c) Sikhs
    (d) Hindus and Muslims both
18. The sympathy of Indian soldiers in uniform with the released I.N.A. prisoners at Lahore indicates
    (a) Feeling of Nationalism and Fraternity
    (b) Rebellion nature of Indian soldiers
    (c) Simply to participate in the reception party
    (d) None of the above
19. The country which has the distinction of having the two largest circulated newspapers in the world is
    (a) Great Britain
    (b) The United States
    (c) Japan
    (d) China
20. The chronological order of non-verbal communication is
    (a) Signs, symbols, codes, colours
    (b) Symbols, codes, signs, colours
    (c) Colours, signs, codes, symbols
    (d) Codes, colours, symbols, signs

21. Which of the following statements is not connected with communication?
(a) Medium is the message.
(b) The world is an electronic cocoon.
(c) Information is power.
(d) Telepathy is technological.

22. Communication becomes circular when
(a) the decoder becomes an encoder
(b) the feedback is absent
(c) the source is credible
(d) the channel is clear

23. The site that played a major role during the terrorist attack on Mumbai (26/11) in 2008 was
(a) Orkut (b) Facebook
(c) Amazon.com (d) Twitter

24. **Assertion (A):** For an effective classroom communication at times it is desirable to use the projection technology.
Reason (R): Using the projection technology facilitates extensive coverage of course contents.
(a) Both (A) and (R) are true, and (R) is the correct explanation.
(b) Both (A) and (R) are true, but (R) is not the correct explanation.
(c) (A) is true, but (R) is false.
(d) (A) is false, but (R) is true.

25. January 1, 1995 was a Sunday. What day of the week lies on January 1, 1996?
(a) Sunday (b) Monday
(c) Wednesday (d) Saturday

26. When an error of 1% is made in the length and breadth of a rectangle, the percentage error (%) in the area of a rectangle will be
(a) 0 (b) 1
(c) 2 (d) 4

27. The next number in the series 2, 5, 9, 19, 37, ? will be
(a) 74 (b) 75
(c) 76 (d) None of these

28. There are 10 true-false questions in an examination. Then these questions can be answered in
(a) 20 ways (b) 100 ways
(c) 240 ways (d) 1024 ways

29. What will be the next term in the following?
DCXW, FEVU, HGTS, ?
(a) AKPO (b) ABYZ
(c) JIRQ (d) LMRS

30. Three individuals X, Y, Z hired a car on a sharing basis and paid ₹ 1,040. They used it for 7, 8, 11 hours, respectively. What are the charges paid by Y?
(a) ₹ 290 (b) ₹ 320
(c) ₹ 360 (d) ₹ 440

31. Deductive argument involves
(a) sufficient evidence
(b) critical thinking
(c) seeing logical relations
(d) repeated observation

32. Inductive reasoning is based on or presupposes
(a) uniformity of nature
(b) God created the world
(c) unity of nature
(d) laws of nature

33. To be critical, thinking must be
(a) practical
(b) socially relevant
(c) individually satisfying
(d) analytical

34. Which of the following is an analogous statement?
(a) Man is like God
(b) God is great
(c) Gandhiji is the Father of the Nation
(d) Man is a rational being

Questions from 35-36 are based on the following diagram in which there are three intersecting circles. H representing The Hindu, I representing Indian Express and T representing The Times of India. A total of 50 persons were surveyed and the number in the Venn diagram indicates the number of persons reading the newspapers.

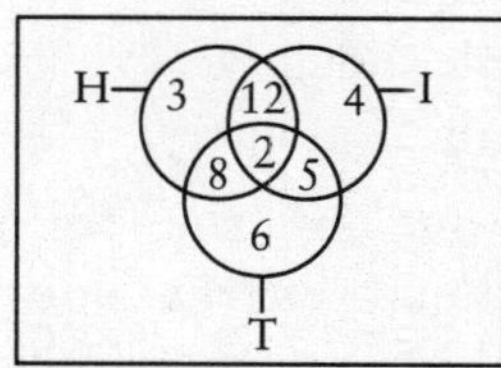

35. How many persons would be reading at least two newspapers?
(a) 23 (b) 25
(c) 27 (d) 29

36. How many persons would be reading almost two newspapers?
(a) 23 (b) 25
(c) 27 (d) 48

37. Which of the following graphs does not represent regular (periodic) behaviour of the variable f(t)?

1. 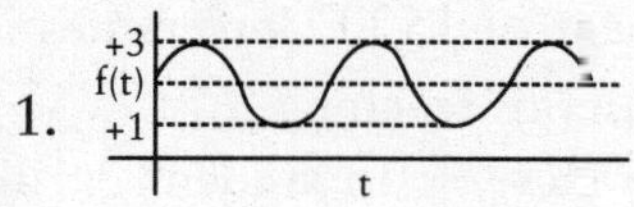

2. 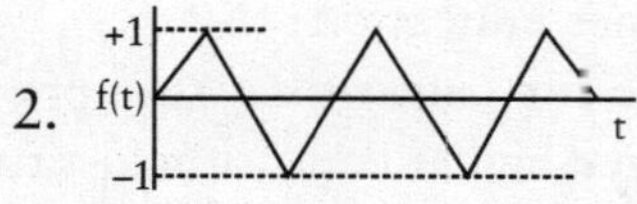

3. 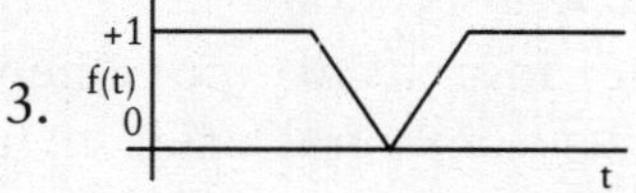

4. 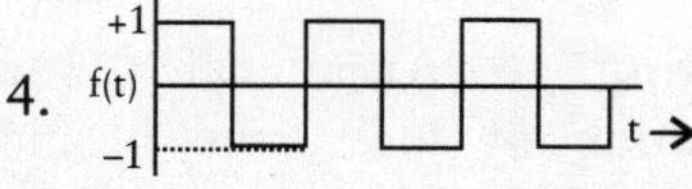

(a) 1 (b) 2
(c) 3 (d) 4

Study the following graph and answer the questions 38 to 40.

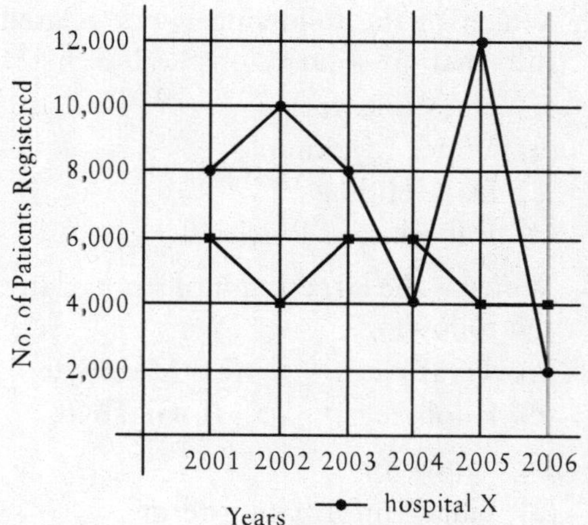

38. In which year total number of patients registered in hospital X and hospital Y was the maximum?
(a) 2003 (b) 2004
(c) 2005 (d) 2006

39. What is the maximum dispersion in the registration of patients in the two hospitals in a year?
(a) 8000 (b) 6000
(c) 4000 (d) 2000

40. In which year there was maximum decrease in registration of patients in hospital X?
(a) 2003 (b) 2004
(c) 2005 (d) 2006

41. Which of the following sources of data is not based on primary data collection?
(a) Census of India
(b) National Sample Survey
(c) Statistical Abstracts of India
(d) National Family Health Survey

42. Which of the four data sets have more dispersion?

(a)	88	91	90	92	89	91
(b)	0	1	1	0	–1	–2
(c)	3	5	2	4	1	5
(d)	0	5	8	10	–2	–8

43. Which of the following is not related to information security on the Internet?
(a) Data Encryption
(b) Water Marking
(c) Data Hiding
(d) Information Retrieval

44. Which is the largest unit of storage among the following?
(a) Terabyte (b) Megabyte
(c) Kilobyte (d) Gigabyte

45. bit stands for
(a) binary information term
(b) binary digit
(c) binary tree
(d) Bivariate Theory

46. Which one of the following is not a linear data structure?
(a) Array (b) Binary Tree
(c) Queue (d) Stack

47. Which one of the following is not a network device?
(a) Router (b) Switch
(c) Hub (d) CPU

48. A compiler is used to convert the following to object code which can be executed
(a) High-level language
(b) Low-level language
(c) Assembly language
(d) Natural language

49. The great Indian Bustard bird is found in
(a) Thar Desert of Rajasthan
(b) Malabar Coast
(c) Coastal regions of India
(d) Delta regions

50. The Sagarmanthan National Park has been established to preserve the eco-system of which mountain peak?
(a) Kanchenjunga (b) Mount Everest
(c) Annapurna (d) Dhaulavira

51. Maximum soot is released from
(a) Petrol vehicles
(b) CNG vehicles
(c) Diesel vehicles
(d) Thermal Power Plants

52. Surface Ozone is produced from
(a) Transport sector
(b) Cement plants
(c) Textile industry
(d) Chemical industry

53. Which one of the following non-conventional energy sources can be exploited most economically?
(a) Solar
(b) Wind
(c) Geo-thermal
(d) Ocean Thermal Energy Conversion (OTEC)

54. The most recurring natural hazard in India is
(a) Earthquakes (b) Floods
(c) Landslides (d) Volcanoes

55. The recommendation of National Knowledge Commission for the establishment of 1500 Universities is to
(a) create more teaching jobs
(b) ensure increase in student enrolment in higher education
(c) replace or substitute the privately managed higher education institutions by public institutions
(d) enable increased movement of students from rural areas to urban areas

56. According to Article 120 of the Constitution of India, the business in Parliament shall be transacted in
(a) Only English
(b) Only Hindi

(c) Both English and Hindi
(d) All the languages included in Eighth Schedule of the Constitution

57. Which of the following is more interactive and student centric?
(a) Seminar
(b) Workshop
(c) Lecture
(d) Group Discussion

58. The Parliament in India is composed of
(a) Lok Sabha and Rajya Sabha
(b) Lok Sabha, Rajya Sabha and Vice President
(c) Lok Sabha, Rajya Sabha and President
(d) Lok Sabha, Rajya Sabha with their Secretariats

59. The enrolment in higher education in India is contributed both by Formal System of Education and by System of Distance Education. Distance education contributes
(a) 50% of formal system
(b) 25% of formal system
(c) 10% of the formal system
(d) Distance education system's contribution is not taken into account while considering the figures of enrolment in higher education

60. **Assertion (A):** The UGC Academic Staff Colleges came into existence to improve the quality of teachers.

Reason (R): University and college teachers have to undergo both orientation and refresher courses.
(a) Both (A) and (R) are true and (R) is the correct explanation.
(b) Both (A) and (R) are correct but (R) is not the correct explanation of (A).
(c) (A) is correct and (R) is false.
(d) (A) is false and (R) is correct.

ANSWERS

1. (d)	2. (c)	3. (b)	4. (c)
5. (b)	6. (c)	7. (a)	8. (b)
9. (b)	10. (b)	11. (c)	12. (b)
13. (c)	14. (a)	15. (d)	16. (d)
17. (b)	18. (a)	19. (d)	20. (a)
21. (d)	22. (a)	23. (a)	24. (a)
25. (b)	26. (c)	27. (b)	28. (d)
29. (c)	30. (b)	31. (c)	32. (a)
33. (b)	34. (a)	35. (b)	36. (d)
37. (c)	38. (c)	39. (a)	40. (d)
41. (c)	42. (d)	43. (d)	44. (a)
45. (b)	46. (b)	47. (c)	48. (a)
49. (a)	50. (b)	51. (d)	52. (a)
53. (a)	54. (b)	55. (b)	56. (c)
57. (d)	58. (c)	59. (b)	60. (a)

JUNE-2009 (PAPER-I)

1. Good evaluation of written material should not be based on
(a) Linguistic expression
(b) Logical presentation
(c) Ability to reproduce whatever is read
(d) Comprehension of subject

2. Why do teachers use teaching aid?
(a) To make teaching fun-filled
(b) To teach within understanding level of students
(c) For students' attention
(d) To make students attentive

3. Attitudes, concepts, skills and knowledge are products of
(a) Learning (b) Research
(c) Heredity (d) Explanation

4. Which among the following gives more freedom to the learner to interact?
(a) Use of film
(b) Small group discussion

(c) Lectures by experts
(d) Viewing country-wide classroom program on TV

5. Which of the following is not a product of learning?
(a) Attitudes (b) Concepts
(c) Knowledge (d) Maturation

6. How can the objectivity of the research be enhanced?
(a) Through its impartiality
(b) Through its reliability
(c) Through its validity
(d) All of these

7. Action-research is
(a) An applied research
(b) A research carried out to solve immediate problems
(c) A longitudinal research
(d) All the above

8. The basis on which assumptions are formulated
(a) Cultural background of the country
(b) Universities
(c) Specific characteristics of the castes
(d) All of these

9. Which of the following is classified in the category of the developmental research?
(a) Philosophical research
(b) Action research
(c) Descriptive research
(d) All the above

10. We use Factorial Analysis
(a) To know the relationship between two variables
(b) To test the Hypothesis
(c) To know the difference between two variables
(d) To know the difference among the many variables

Read the following passage and answer the questions 11 to 15:

While the British rule in India was detrimental to the economic development of the country, it did help in starting of the process of modernising Indian society and formed several progressive institutions during that process. One of the most beneficial institutions, which were initiated by the British, was democracy. Nobody can dispute that despite its many shortcomings, democracy was and is far better alternative to the arbitrary rule of the rajas and nawabs, which prevailed in India in the pre-British days.

However, one of the harmful traditions of British democracy inherited by India was that of conflict instead of cooperation between elected members. This was its essential feature. The party, which got the support of the majority of elected members, formed the Government while the others constituted a standing opposition. The existence of the opposition to those in power was and is regarded as a hallmark of democracy.

In principle, democracy consists of rule by the people; but where direct rule is not possible, it's rule by persons elected by the people. It is natural that there would be some differences of opinion among the elected members as in the rest of the society.

Normally, members of any organisations have differences of opinion between themselves on different issues but they manage to work on the basis of a consensus and they do not normally form a division between some who are in majority and are placed in power, while treating the others as in opposition.

The members of an organisation usually work on consensus. Consensus simply means that after an adequate discussion, members agree that the majority opinion may prevail for the time being. Thus persons who form a majority on one issue and whose opinion is allowed to prevail may not be on the same side if there is a difference on some other issue.

It was largely by accident that instead of this normal procedure, a two-party system came to prevail in Britain and that is now being generally taken as the best method of democratic rule.

Many democratically inclined persons in India regret that such a two-party system was not brought about in the country. It appears that to have two parties in India—of more or less equal strength—is a virtual impossibility. Those who regret the absence of a two-party system should take the reasons into consideration.

When the two-party system got established in Britain, there were two groups among the rules (consisting of a limited electorate) who had the same economic interests among themselves and who therefore formed two groups within the selected members of Parliament.

There were members of the British aristocracy (which landed interests and consisting of lord, barons, etc.) and members of the new commercial class consisting of merchants and artisans. These groups were more or less of equal strength and they were able to establish their separate rule at different times.

Answer the following questions:

11. In pre-British period, when India was ruled by the independent rulers
    - (a) Peace and prosperity prevailed in the society
    - (b) People were isolated from political affairs
    - (c) Public opinion was inevitable for policy making
    - (d) Law was equal for one and all
12. What is the distinguishing feature of the democracy practiced in Britain?
    - (a) End to the rule of might is right.
    - (b) Rule of the people, by the people and for the people.
    - (c) It has stood the test of time.
    - (d) Cooperation between elected members.
13. Democracy is practiced where
    - (a) Elected members form a uniform opinion regarding policy matter.
    - (b) Opposition is more powerful than the ruling combine.
    - (c) Representatives of masses.
    - (d) None of these.
14. Which of the following is true about the British rule in India?
    - (a) It was behind the modernisation of the Indian society.
    - (b) India gained economically during that period.
    - (c) Various establishments were formed for the purpose of progress.
    - (d) None of these.
15. Who became the members of the new commercial class during that time?
    - (a) British Aristocrats
    - (b) Lord and Barons
    - (c) Political Persons
    - (d) Merchants and Artisans
16. Which one of the following Telephonic Conferencing with a radio link is very popular throughout the world?
    - (a) TPS (b) Telepresence
    - (c) Video conference (d) Video teletext
17. Which is not 24 hours news channel?
    - (a) NDTV 24×7
    - (b) ZEE News
    - (c) Aajtak
    - (d) Lok Sabha Channel
18. The main objective of FM station in radio is

(a) Information, Entertainment and Tourism
(b) Entertainment, Information and Interaction
(c) Tourism, Interaction and Entertainment
(d) Entertainment only

19. In communication chatting in internet is
(a) Verbal communication
(b) Non-verbal communication
(c) Parallel communication
(d) Grapevine communication

20. Match List I with List II and select the correct answer using the codes given below:

List I (Artists)

A. Pandit Jasraj B. Kishan Maharaj
C. Ravi Shankar D. Udai Shankar

List II (Art)

1. Hindustani vocalist
2. Sitar
3. Tabla
4. Dance

Codes:	A	B	C	D
(a)	1	2	3	4
(b)	1	3	4	2
(c)	1	3	2	4
(d)	3	2	1	4

21. Insert the missing number in the following.
3, 8, 18, 23, 33, ?, 48
(a) 37 (b) 40
(c) 38 (d) 45

22. In a certain code, CLOCK is written as KCOLC. How would STEPS be written in that code?
(a) SPEST (b) SPSET
(c) SPETS (d) SEPTS

23. The letters in the first set have a certain relationship. On the basis of this relationship mark the right choice for the second set
BDFH : OMKI :: GHIK : ?
(a) FHJL (b) RPNL
(c) LNPR (d) LJHF

24. What was the day of the week on 1st January 2001?
(a) Friday (b) Monday
(c) Sunday (d) Wednesday

25. Find out the wrong number in the sequence.
52, 51, 48, 43, 34, 27, 16
(a) 27 (b) 34
(c) 43 (d) 48

26. In a deductive argument conclusion is
(a) Summing up of the premises
(b) Not necessarily based on premises
(c) Entailed by the premises
(d) Additional to the premises

27. 'No man are mortal' is contradictory of
(a) Some man are mortal
(b) Some man are not mortal
(c) All men are mortal
(d) No mortal is man

28. A deductive argument is valid if
(a) premises are false and conclusion is true
(b) premises are false and conclusion is also false
(c) premises are true and conclusion is false
(d) premises are true and conclusion is true

29. Structure of logical argument is based on
(a) Formal validity
(b) Material truth
(c) Linguistic expression
(d) Aptness of examples

30. Two ladies and two men are playing bridge and seated at North, East, South and West of a table. No lady is facing East. Persons sitting opposite to each other are not of the same sex. One man is facing South. Which direction are the ladies facing to?

(a) East and West
(b) North and West
(c) South and East
(d) None of these

Questions 31 and 32 are based on the following venn diagram in which there are three intersecting circles representing Hindi knowing persons, English knowing persons and persons who are working as teachers. Different regions so obtained in the figure are marked as a, b, c, d, e, f and g.

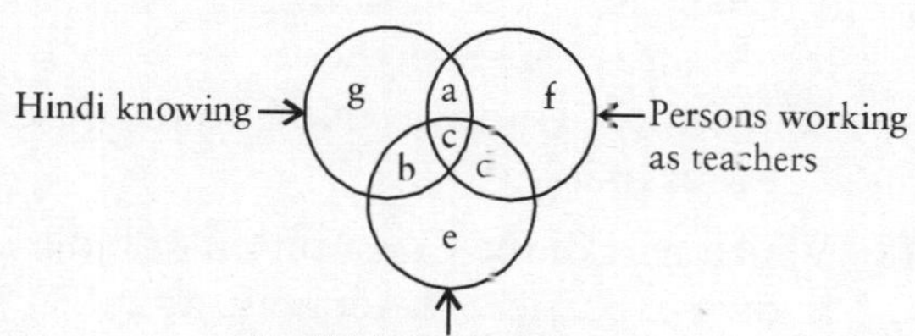

31. If you want to select Hindi and English knowing teachers, which of the following is to be selected?
(a) g (b) b
(c) c (d) e

32. If you want to select persons, who do not know English and are not teachers, which of the region is to be selected?
(a) e (b) g
(c) b (d) a

Study the following graph carefully and answer questions 33 to 35.

Export of Engineering Goods

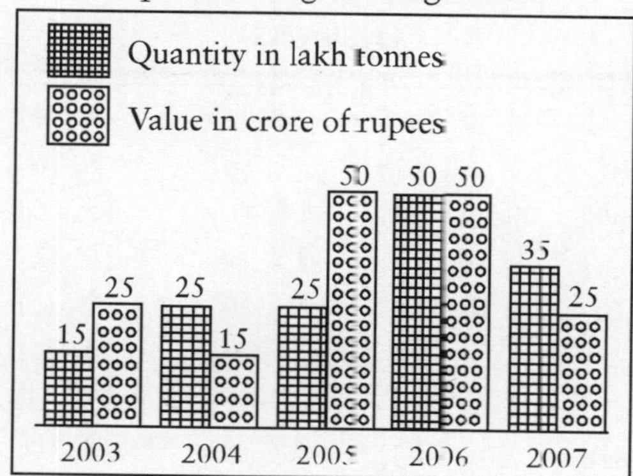

33. In which year the quantity of engineering goods' exports was maximum?
(a) 2005 (b) 2006
(c) 2004 (d) 2007

34. In which year the value of engineering goods decreased by 50 percent compared to the previous year?
(a) 2004 (b) 2007
(c) 2005 (d) 2006

35. In which year the quantity of exports was 100 percent higher than the quantity of previous year?
(a) 2004 (b) 2005
(c) 2006 (d) 2007

36. What do you need to put your web pages on the www?
(a) a connection to internet
(b) a web browser
(c) a web server
(d) All of the above

37. Which was the first company to launch mobile phone services in India?
(a) Essar (b) BPL
(c) Hutchison (d) Airtel

38. Chandrayan I was launched on 22nd October, 2008 in India from
(a) Bangalore (b) Sri Harikota
(c) Chennai (d) Ahmedabad

39. What is blog?
(a) Online music
(b) Intranet
(c) A personal or corporate website in the form of an online journal
(d) A personal or corporate Google search

40. Which is not online Indian Matrimonial website?
(a) www.jeevansathi.com
(b) www.bharatmatrimony.com
(c) www.shaadi.com
(d) www.u.k.singlemuslim.com

41. Environmental impact assessment is an objective analysis of the probable changes in
   (a) physical characteristics of the environment
   (b) biophysical characteristics of the environment
   (c) socio-economic characteristics of the environment
   (d) All the above

42. Bog is a wetland that receives water from
   (a) nearby water bodies
   (b) melting
   (c) Only rainfall
   (d) Only sea

43. Which of the following region is in the very high risk zone of earthquakes?
   (a) Central Indian Highland
   (b) Coastal region
   (c) Himalayan region
   (d) Indian desert

44. Match List I with List II and select the correct answer using the codes given below.

   List I (Institutes)
   A. Central Arid Zone Institute
   B. Space Application Centre
   C. Indian Institute of Public Administration
   D. Headquarters of Indian Science Congress

   List II (Cities)
   1. Kolkata 2. New Delhi
   3. Ahmedabad 4. Jodhpur

Codes:	A	B	C	D
(a)	4	3	2	1
(b)	4	2	1	3
(c)	3	1	2	4
(d)	1	2	4	3

45. Indian coastal areas experienced Tsunami disaster in the year
   (a) 2005 (b) 2004
   (c) 2006 (d) 2007

46. The Kothari Commission's report was entitled on
   (a) Education and National Development
   (b) Learning to be adventure
   (c) Diversification of Education
   (d) Education and socialisation in democracy

47. Which of the following is not a Dualmode University?
   (a) Delhi University
   (b) Bangalore University
   (c) Madras University
   (d) Indira Gandhi National Open University

48. Which part of the Constitution of India is known as "Code of Administrators"?
   (a) Part I (b) Part II
   (c) Part III (d) Part IV

49. Which article of the constitution provides safeguards to Naga Customary and their social practices against any act of Parliament?
   (a) Article 371 A (b) Article 371 B
   (c) Article 371 C (d) Article 263

50. Which one of the following is not the tool of good governance?
   (a) Right to Information
   (b) Citizens' Charter
   (c) Social Auditing
   (d) Judicial Activism

ANSWERS

1. (a)	2. (a)	3. (a)	4. (b)
5. (d)	6. (d)	7. (b)	8. (a)
9. (d)	10. (d)	11. (b)	12. (d)
13. (a)	14. (c)	15. (a)	16. (b)
17. (d)	18. (b)	19. (b)	20. (c)
21. (c)	22. (c)	23. (b)	24. (b)
25. (b)	26. (c)	27. (c)	28. (d)
29. (b)	30. (b)	31. (c)	32. (b)
33. (b)	34. (b)	35. (c)	36. (d)

37. (d)	38. (b)	39. (c)	40. (d)
41. (d)	42. (a)	43. (b)	44. (a)
45. (b)	46. (a)	47. (d)	48. (d)
49. (a)	50. (d)		

DECEMBER-2008 (PAPER-I)

1. According to Swami Vivekananda, teacher's success depends on
   (a) His renunciation of personal gain and service to others
   (b) His professional training and creativity
   (c) His concentration on his work and duties with a spirit of obedience to God
   (d) His mastery on the subject and capacity in controlling the students
2. Which of the following teacher will be liked most?
   (a) A teacher of high idealistic attitude
   (b) A loving teacher
   (c) A teacher who is disciplined
   (d) A teacher who often amuses his students
3. A teacher's most important challenge is
   (a) To make students do their home work
   (b) To make teaching-learning process enjoyable
   (c) To maintain discipline in the class-room
   (d) To prepare the question paper
4. Value-education stands for
   (a) making a student healthy
   (b) making a student to get a job
   (c) inculcation of virtues
   (d) all-round development of personality
5. When a normal student behaves in an erratic manner in the class, you would
   (a) pull up the student then and there
   (b) talk to the student after the class
   (c) ask the student to leave the class
   (d) ignore the student
6. The research is always
   (a) verifying the old knowledge
   (b) exploring new knowledge
   (c) filling the gap between knowledge
   (d) All of these
7. The research that applies the laws at the time of field study to draw more and more clear ideas about the problem is
   (a) Applied research
   (b) Action research
   (c) Experimental research
   (d) None of these
8. When a research problem is related to heterogeneous population, the most suitable sampling method is
   (a) Cluster Sampling
   (b) Stratified Sampling
   (c) Convenient Sampling
   (d) Lottery Method
9. The process not needed in experimental research is:
   (a) Observation
   (b) Manipulation and replication
   (c) Controlling
   (d) Reference collection
10. A research problem is not feasible only when
    (a) it is researchable
    (b) it is new and adds something to knowledge
    (c) it consists of independent and dependent variables
    (d) it has utility and relevance

Read the following passage carefully and answer the questions 11 to 15:

Radically changing monsoon patterns, reduction in the winter rice harvest and a quantum increase in respiratory diseases all part of the environmental doomsday scenario which is reportedly playing out in South Asia. According to a United Nations Environment Program report, a deadly three-kilometer deep blanket of pollution comprising a fearsome, cocktail of ash, acids, aerosols and other particles has enveloped in this region. For India, already struggling to cope with a drought, the implication of this are devastating and further crop failure will amount to a life and death question for many Indians. The increase in premature deaths will have adverse social and economic consequences and a rise in morbidities will place an unbearable burden on our crumbling health system. And there is no one to blame but ourselves. Both official and corporate India has always been allergic to any mention of clean technology. Most mechanical two wheelers roll of the assembly line without proper pollution control system. Little effort is made for R&D on simple technologies, which could make a vital difference to people's lives and the environment.

However, while there is no denying that South Asia must clean up its act, skeptics might question the timing of the haze report. The Kyoto meet on climate change is just two weeks away and the stage is set for the usual battle between the developing world and the West, particularly the Unites States of America. President Mr. Bush has adamantly refused to sign any protocol, which would mean a change in American consumption level. U.N. environment report will likely find a place in the U.S. arsenal as it plants an accusing finger towards controls like India and China. Yet the U.S.A. can hardly deny its own dubious role in the matter of erasing trading quotas.

Richer countries can simply buy up excess credits from poorer countries and continue to pollute. Rather than try to get the better of developing countries, who undoubtedly have taken up environmental shortcuts in their bid to catch up with the West, the USA should take a look at the environmental profigacy, which is going on within. From opening up virgin territories for oil exploration to relaxing the standards for drinking water, Mr. Bush's policies are not exactly beneficial, not even to America's interests. We realise that we are all in this together and that pollution anywhere should be a global concern otherwise there will only be more tunnels at the end of the tunnel.

11. Both official and corporate India is allergic to
    (a) Failure of Monsoon
    (b) Poverty and Inequality
    (c) Slowdown in Industrial Production
    (d) Mention of Clean Technology
12. If the rate of premature death increases it will
    (a) Exert added burden on the crumbling economy
    (b) Have adverse social and economic consequences
    (c) Make positive effect on our effort to control population
    (d) Have less job aspirants in the society
13. According to the passage, the two-wheeler industry is not adequately concerned about
    (a) Passenger safety on the roads
    (b) Life cover insurance of the vehicle owner
    (c) Pollution control system in the vehicle
    (d) Rising cost of the two wheelers
14. What could be the reason behind timing of the haze report just before the Kyoto meet?
    (a) United Nations is working hand-in-glove with U.S.A.
    (b) Organisers of the forthcoming meet to teach a lesson to the U.S.A.

(c) Drawing attention of the world towards devastating effects of environment degradation.
(d) U.S.A. wants to use it as a handle against the developing countries in the forthcoming meet.

15. Which of the following is the indication of environmental degradation in South Asia?
(a) Social and economic inequality
(b) Crumbling health care system
(c) Inadequate pollution control system
(d) Radically changing monsoon pattern

16. Community Radio is a type of radio service that caters to the interest of
(a) Local audience (b) Education
(c) Entertainment (d) News

17. Orcut is a part of
(a) Intrapersonal Communication
(b) Mass Communication
(c) Group Communication
(d) Interpersonal Communication

18. Match List I with List II and select the correct answer using the codes given below.

List I (Artists)
A. Amrita Shergill
B. T. Swaminathan Pillai
C. Bhimsen Joshi
D. Padma Subramaniyam

List II (Art)
1. Flute
2. Classical Song
3. Painting
4. Bharat Natyam

Codes:	A	B	C	D
(a)	3	1	2	4
(b)	2	3	1	4
(c)	4	2	3	1
(d)	1	4	2	3

19. Which is not correct in latest communication award?
(a) Salman Rushdie - Booker's Prize—July 20, 2008
(b) Dilip Sanghavi - Business Standard CEO Award, July 22, 2008
(c) Tapan Sinha - Dada Saheb Falke Award, July 21, 2008
(d) Gautam Ghosh - Osians Lifetime Achievement Award, July 11, 2008

20. Firewalls are used to protect a communication network system against
(a) Unauthorised attacks
(b) Virus attacks
(c) Data-driven attacks
(d) Fire-attacks

21. Insert the missing number in the following

$\frac{2}{7}, \frac{4}{7}, ?\ \frac{11}{21}, \frac{16}{31},$

(a) $\frac{10}{8}$ (b) $\frac{6}{10}$
(c) $\frac{5}{10}$ (d) $\frac{7}{13}$

22. In a certain code, GAMESMAN is written as AGMEMSAN. How would DISCLOSE be written in that code?
(a) IDSCOLSE (b) IDCSOLES
(c) IDSCOLES (d) IDSCLOSE

23. The letters in the first set have a certain relationship. On the basis of this relationship mark the right choice for the second set : AST : BRU :: NQV: ?
(a) ORW (b) MPU
(c) MRW (d) OPW

24. On what dates of April, 1994 did Sunday fall?
(a) 2, 9, 16, 23, 30
(b) 3, 10, 17, 24

(c) 4, 11, 18, 25
(d) 1, 8, 15, 22, 29

25. Find out the wrong number in the sequence
125, 127, 130, 135, 142, 153, 165
(a) 130 (b) 142
(c) 153 (d) 165

26. There are five books A, B, C, D and E. The book C lies above D, the book E is below A and B is below E. Which is at the bottom?
(a) E (b) B
(c) A (d) C

27. Logical reasoning is based on
(a) Truth of involved propositions
(b) Valid relation among the involved propositions
(c) Employment of symbolic language
(d) Employment of ordinary language

28. Two propositions with the same subject and predicate terms but different in quality are
(a) Contradictory (b) Contrary
(c) Subaltern (d) Identical

29. The premises of a valid deductive argument
(a) Provide some evidence for its conclusion
(b) Provide no evidence for its conclusion
(c) Are irrelevant for its conclusion
(d) Provide conclusive evidence for its conclusion

30. Syllogistic reasoning is
(a) Deductive (b) Inductive
(c) Experimental (d) Hypothetical

Study the following Venn diagram and answer questions nos. 31 to 33.

Three circles representing GRADUATES, CLERKS and GOVERNMENT EMPLOYEES are intersecting. The intersections are marked A, B, C, e, f, g and h. Which part best represents the statements in questions 31 to 33?

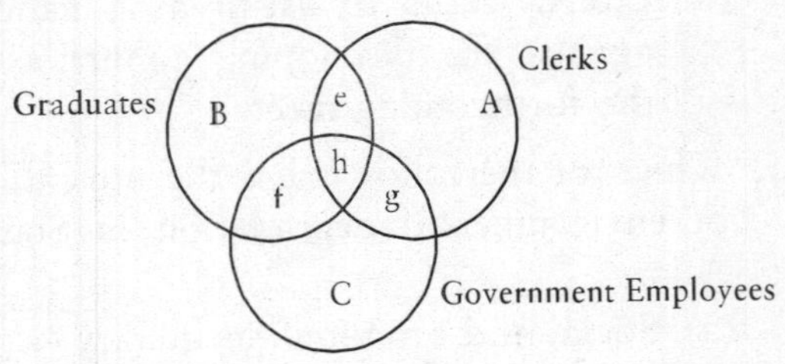

31. Some Graduates are Government employees but not as Clerks.
(a) h (b) g
(c) f (d) e

32. Clerks who are graduates as well as government employees.
(a) e (b) f
(c) g (d) h

33. Some graduates are Clerks but not Government employees.
(a) f (b) g
(c) h (d) e

Study the following graph and answer questions numbers from 34 to 35

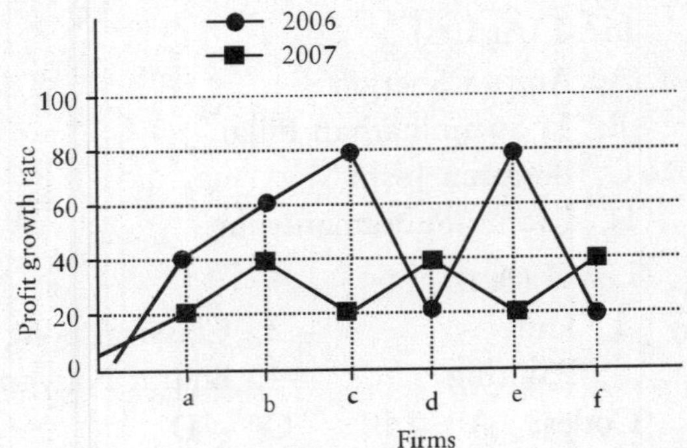

34. Which of the firms got maximum profit growth rate in the year 2006.
(a) ab (b) ce
(c) cd (d) ef

35. Which of the firms got maximum profit growth rate in the year 2007.

(a) bdf (b) acf
(c) bed (d) ace

36. The accounting software 'Tally' was developed by
(a) HCL (b) TCS
(c) Infosys (d) Wipro

37. Errors in computer programs are called
(a) Follies (b) Mistakes
(c) Bugs (d) Spam

38. HTML is basically used to design
(a) Webpage
(b) Website
(c) Graphics
(d) Tables and Frames

39. 'Micro Processing' is made for
(a) Computer
(b) Digital System
(c) Calculator
(d) Electronic Goods

40. Information, a combination of graphics, text, sound, video and animation is called
(a) Multiprogram
(b) Multifacet
(c) Multimedia
(d) Multiprocess

41. Which of the following pairs regarding typical composition of hospital wastes is incorrect?
(a) Plastic - 9-12%
(b) Metals - 1-2%
(c) Ceramic - 8-10%
(d) Biodegradable - 35-40%

42. Freshwater achieves its greatest density at
(a) –4°C (b) 0°C
(c) 4°C (d) –2.5°C

43. Which one of the following is not associated with earthquakes?
(a) Focus (b) Epicenter
(c) Seismograph (d) Swells

44. The tallest trees in the world are found in the region
(a) Equatorial region
(b) Temperate region
(c) Monsoon region
(d) Mediterranean region

45. Match List I with List II and select the correct answer from the codes given below.

List I (National Parks)
A. Periyar
B. Nandan Kanan
C. Corbett National Park
D. Sariska Tiger Reserve

List II (States)
1. Orissa
2. Kerala
3. Rajasthan
4. Uttarakhand

Codes:	**A**	**B**	**C**	**D**
(a)	2	1	4	3
(b)	1	2	4	3
(c)	3	2	1	4
(d)	1	2	3	4

46. According to Radhakrishnan Commission, the aim of Higher Education is
(a) To develop the democratic values, peace and harmony
(b) To develop great personalities who can give their contributions in politics, administration, industry and commerce
(c) Both (a) and (b)
(d) None of these

47. The National Museum at New Delhi is attached to
(a) Delhi University
(b) a Deemed University
(c) a Subordinate Office of the JNU
(d) Part of Ministry of Tourism and Culture

48. Match List I with List II and select the correct answer from the code given below.

List I (Institutions)	List II (Locations)
A. National Law Institute	1. Shimla
B. Indian Institute of Advanced Studies	2. Bhopal
C. National Judicial Academy	3. Hyderabad
D. National Savings Institute	4. Nagpur

Codes:	A	B	C	D
(a)	3	2	4	1
(b)	1	2	3	4
(c)	4	3	1	2
(d)	3	1	2	4

49. Election of Rural and Urban local bodies are conducted and ultimately supervised by
   (a) Election Commission of India
   (b) State Election Commission
   (c) District Collector and District Magistrate
   (d) Concerned Returning Officer

50. Which opinion is not correct?
   (a) Education is a subject of concurrent list of VII schedule of Constitution of India
   (b) University Grants Commission is a statutory body
   (c) Patent, inventions, design, copyright and trade marks are the subject of concurrent list
   (d) Indian Council of Social Science Research is a statutory body related to research in social sciences

ANSWERS

1. (d)	2. (c)	3. (b)	4. (c)
5. (b)	6. (d)	7. (a)	8. (b)
9. (d)	10. (b)	11. (d)	12. (b)
13. (c)	14. (c)	15. (d)	16. (a)
17. (d)	18. (a)	19. (b)	20. (a)
21. (d)	22. (a)	23. (d)	24. (b)
25. (d)	26. (b)	27. (b)	28. (a)
29. (d)	30. (a)	31. (c)	32. (d)
33. (d)	34. (b)	35. (a)	36. (b)
37. (c)	38. (a)	39. (a)	40. (c)
41. (d)	42. (c)	43. (d)	44. (b)
45. (a)	46. (c)	47. (d)	48. (d)
49. (b)	50. (c)		

JUNE-2008 (PAPER-I)

1. The teacher has been glorified by the phrase "Friend, philosopher and guide" because
   (a) He has to play all vital roles in the context of society
   (b) He transmits the high value of humanity to students
   (c) He is the great reformer of the society
   (d) He is a great patriot

2. The most important cause of failure for teacher lies in the area of
   (a) interpersonal relationship
   (b) lack of command over the knowledge of the subject
   (c) verbal ability
   (d) strict handling of the students

3. A teacher can establish rapport with his students by
   (a) becoming a figure of authority
   (b) impressing students with knowledge and skill
   (c) playing the role of a guide
   (d) becoming a friend to the students

4. Education is a powerful instrument of
   (a) Social transformation
   (b) Personal transformation
   (c) Cultural transformation
   (d) All the above

5. A teacher's major contribution towards the maximum self-realisation of the student is affected through
   (a) Constant fulfilment of the students' needs
   (b) Strict control of classroom activities
   (c) Sensitivity to students' needs, goals and purposes
   (d) Strict reinforcement of academic standards
6. Research problem is selected from the stand point of
   (a) Researcher's interest
   (b) Financial support
   (c) Social relevance
   (d) Availability of relevant literature
7. Which one is called non-probability sampling?
   (a) Cluster sampling
   (b) Quota sampling
   (c) Systematic sampling
   (d) Stratified random sampling
8. Formulation of hypothesis may not be required in
   (a) Survey method
   (b) Historical studies
   (c) Experimental studies
   (d) Normative studies
9. Field-work based research is classified as
   (a) Empirical (b) Historical
   (c) Experimental (d) Biographical
10. Which of the following sampling method is appropriate to study the prevalence of AIDS amongst male and female in India in 1976, 1986, 1996 and 2006?
   (a) Cluster sampling
   (b) Systematic sampling
   (c) Quota sampling
   (d) Stratified random sampling

Read the following passage and answer the questions 11 to 15:

The fundamental principle is that Article 14 forbids class legislation but permits reasonable classification for the purpose of legislation which classification must satisfy the twin tests of classification being founded on an intelligible differentia which distinguishes persons or things that are grouped together from those that are left out of the group and that differentia must have a rational nexus to the object sought to be achieved by the Statute in question. The thrust of Article 14 is that the citizen is entitled to equality before law and equal protection of laws. In the very nature of things the society being composed of unequals a welfare State will have to strive by both executive and legislative action to help the less fortunate in society to ameliorate their condition so that the social and economic inequality in the society may be bridged. This would necessitate a legislative application to a group of citizens otherwise unequal and amelioration of whose lot is the object of state affirmative action. In the absence of the doctrine of classification such legislation is likely to flounder on the bedrock of equality enshrined in Article 14. The Court realistically appraising the social and economic inequality and keeping in view the guidelines on which the State action must move as constitutionally laid down in Part IV of the Constitution evolved the doctrine of classification. The doctrine was evolved to sustain a legislation or State action designed to help weaker sections of the society or some such segments of the society in need of succour. Legislative and executive action may accordingly be sustained if it satisfies the twin tests of reasonable classification and the rational principle correlated to the object sought to be achieved.

The concept of equality before the law does not involve the idea of absolute equality among human beings which is a physical impossibility. All that Article 14 guarantees is a similarity of treatment contra-distinguished from identical treatment. Equality before law means that among equals the law should be equal and should be equally administered and that the likes should be treated alike. Equality before the law does not mean that things which are different shall be as though they are the same. It of course means denial of any special privilege by reason of birth, creed or the like. The legislation as well as the executive government, while dealing with diverse problems arising out of an infinite variety of human relations must of necessity have the power of making special laws, to attain any particular object and to achieve that object it must have the power of selection or classification of persons and things upon which such laws are to operate.

11. Right to equality, one of the fundamental rights, is enunciated in the constitution under Part III, Article
    (a) 12 (b) 13
    (c) 14 (d) 15
12. The main thrust of Right to equality is that it permits
    (a) class legislation
    (b) equality before law and equal protection under the law
    (c) absolute equality
    (d) special privilege by reason of birth
13. The social and economic inequality in the society can be bridged by
    (a) executive and legislative action
    (b) universal suffrage
    (c) identical treatment
    (d) None of the above
14. The doctrine of classification is evolved to
    (a) Help weaker sections of the society
    (b) Provide absolute equality
    (c) Provide identical treatment
    (d) None of the above
15. While dealing with diverse problems arising out of an infinite variety of human relations, the government
    (a) must have the power of making special laws
    (b) must not have any power to make special laws
    (c) must have power to withdraw equal rights
    (d) None of the above
16. Communication with oneself is known as
    (a) Group communication
    (b) Grapevine communication
    (c) Interpersonal communication
    (d) Intrapersonal communication
17. Which broadcasting system for TV is followed in India?
    (a) NTSE (b) PAL
    (c) SECAM (d) NTCS
18. All India Radio before 1936 was known as
    (a) Indian Radio Broadcasting
    (b) Broadcasting Service of India
    (c) Indian State Broadcasting Service
    (d) All India Broadcasting Service
19. The biggest news agency of India is
    (a) PTI
    (b) UNI
    (c) NANAP
    (d) Samachar Bharati
20. Prasar Bharati was launched in the year
    (a) 1995 (b) 1997
    (c) 1999 (d) 2001
21. A statistical measure based upon the entire population is called parameter while measure based upon a sample is known as

(a) Sample parameter
(b) Inference
(c) Statistics
(d) None of these

22. The importance of the correlation coefficient lies in the fact that
(a) There is a linear relationship between the correlated variables
(b) It is one of the most valid measure of statistics
(c) It allows one to determine the degree or strength of the association between two variables
(d) It is a non-parametric method of statistical analysis

23. The F-test
(a) is essentially a two tailed test
(b) is essentially a one tailed test
(c) can be one tailed as well as two tailed depending on the hypothesis
(d) can never be a one tailed test

24. What will be the next letter in the following series
DCXW, FEVU, HGTS, ______
(a) AKPO (b) JBYZ
(c) JIRQ (d) LMRS

25. The following question is based on the diagram given below. If the two small circles represent formal classroom education and distance education and the big circle stands for university system of education, which figure represents the university systems.

(a)

(b) 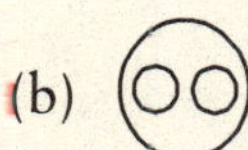

(c)

(d)

26. The statement, 'To be non-violent is good' is a
(a) Moral judgement
(b) Factual judgement
(c) Religious judgement
(d) Value judgement

27. **Assertion (A):** Man is a rational being.
Reason (R): Man is a social being.
(a) Both (A) and (R) are true and (R) is the correct explanation of (A)
(b) Both (A) and (R) are true but (R) is not the correct explanation of (A)
(c) (A) is true but (R) is false
(d) (A) is false but (R) is true

28. Value Judgements are
(a) Factual Judgements
(b) Ordinary Judgements
(c) Normative Judgements
(d) Expression of public opinion

29. Deductive reasoning proceeds from
(a) general to particular
(b) particular to general
(c) one general conclusion to another general conclusion
(d) one particular conclusion to another particular conclusion

30. AGARTALA is written in code as 14168171, the code for AGRA is
(a) 1641 (b) 1416
(c) 1441 (d) 1461

31. Which one of the following is the most comprehensive source of population data?
(a) National Family Health Surveys
(b) National Sample Surveys
(c) Census
(d) Demographic Health Surveys

32. Which one of the following principles is\ not applicable to sampling?
(a) Sample units must be clearly defined
(b) Sample units must be dependent on each other

(c) Same units of sample should be used throughout the study
(d) Sample units must be chosen in a systematic and objective manner

33. If January 1st, 2007 is Monday, what was the day on 1st January 1995?
(a) Sunday (b) Monday
(c) Friday (d) Saturday

34. Insert the missing number in the following series
4 16 8 64 ? 256
(a) 16 (b) 24
(c) 32 (d) 20

35. If an article is sold for ₹ 178 at a loss of 11%; what would be its selling price in order to earn a profit of 11%?
(a) ₹ 222.50 (b) ₹ 267
(c) ₹ 222 (d) ₹ 220

36. WYSIWYG—describes the display of a document on screen as it will actually print
(a) What you state is what you get
(b) What you see is what you get
(c) What you save is what you get
(d) What you suggest is what you get

37. Which of the following is not a Computer language?
(a) PASCAL (b) UNIX
(c) FORTRAN (d) COBOL

38. A keyboard has at least
(a) 91 keys (b) 101 keys
(c) 111 keys (d) 121 keys

39. An E-mail address is composed of
(a) two parts (b) three parts
(c) four parts (d) five parts

40. Corel Draw is a popular
(a) Illustration program
(b) Programming language
(c) Text program
(d) None of the above

41. Human ear is most sensitive to noise in which of the following ranges
(a) 1-2 KHz (b) 100-500 Hz
(c) 10-12 KHz (d) 13-16 KHz

42. Which one of the following units is used to measure intensity of noise?
(a) decible (b) Hz
(c) Phon (d) Watts/m^2

43. If the population growth follows a logistic curve, the maximum sustainable yield
(a) is equal to half the carrying capacity
(b) is equal to the carrying capacity
(c) depends on growth rates
(d) depends on the initial population

44. Chemical weathering of rocks is largely dependent upon
(a) high temperature
(b) strong wind action
(c) heavy rainfall
(d) glaciation

45. Structure of earth's system consists of the following: Match List I with List II and give the correct answer.

List I (Zone)
A. Atmosphere B. Biosphere
C. Hydrosphere D. Lithosphere

List II (Chemical Character)
1. Inert gases
2. Salt, freshwater, snow and ice
3. Organic substances, skeleton matter
4. Light silicates

Codes:	A	B	C	D
(a)	2	3	1	4
(b)	1	3	2	4
(c)	2	1	3	4
(d)	3	1	2	4

46. NAAC is an autonomous institution under the aegis of
(a) ICSSR (b) CSIR
(c) AICTE (d) UGC

47. National Council for Women's Education was established in
(a) 1958 (b) 1976
(c) 1989 (d) 2000

48. Which one of the following is not situated in New Delhi?
(a) Indian Council of Cultural Relations
(b) Indian Council of Scientific Research
(c) National Council of Educational Research and Training
(d) Indian Institute of Advanced Studies

49. Autonomy in higher education implies freedom in
(a) Administration
(b) Policy-making
(c) Finance
(d) Curriculum development

50. Match List I with List II and select the correct answer from the code given below

List I (Institutions)
A. Dr. Hari Singh Gour University
B. S.N.D.T. University
C. M.S. University
D. J.N. Vyas University

List II (Locations)
1. Mumbai 2. Baroda
3. Jodhpur 4. Sagar

Codes:	A	B	C	D
(a)	4	1	2	3
(b)	1	2	3	4
(c)	3	1	2	4
(d)	2	4	1	3

ANSWERS

1. (b)	2. (b)	3. (b)	4. (d)
5. (c)	6. (c)	7. (b)	8. (b)
9. (a)	10. (d)	11. (c)	12. (b)
13. (a)	14. (a)	15. (a)	16. (d)
17. (b)	18. (c)	19. (a)	20. (b)
21. (a)	22. (c)	23. (c)	24. (c)
25. (b)	26. (a)	27. (b)	28. (c)
29. (a)	30. (d)	31. (c)	32. (b)
33. (d)	34. (a)	35. (c)	36. (b)
37. (b)	38. (b)	39. (a)	40. (a)
41. (b)	42. (a)	43. (a)	44. (c)
45. (b)	46. (d)	47. (a)	48. (d)
49. (c)	50. (a)		

DECEMBER-2007 (PAPER-I)

1. Verbal guidance is least effective in the learning of
(a) Aptitudes (b) Skills
(c) Attitudes (d) Relationship

2. Which is the most important aspect of the teacher's rule in learning?
(a) The development of insight into what consititutes an adequate performance
(b) The development of insight into what consititutes the pitfalls and dangers to be avoided
(c) The provision of encouragement and moral support
(d) The provision of continuous diagnostic and remedial help

3. The most appropriate purpose of learning is
(a) personal adjustment
(b) modification of behaviour
(c) social and political awarness
(d) preparing oneself for employment

4. The students who keep on asking questions in the class should be
(a) encouraged to find answer independently
(b) advised to meet the teacher after the class
(c) encouraged to continue questioning
(d) advised not to disturb during the lecture

5. Maximum participation of students is possible in teaching through

(a) discussion method
(b) lecture method
(c) audio-visual aids
(d) textbook method

6. Generalised conclusion on the basis of a sample is technically known as
(a) Data analysis and interpretation
(b) Parameter inference
(c) Statistical inference
(d) All of the above

7. The experimental study is based on
(a) The manipulation of variables
(b) Conceptual parameters
(c) Replication of research
(d) Survey of literature

8. The main characteristic of scientific research is
(a) empirical (b) theoretical
(c) experimental (d) All of the above

9. Authenticity of a research finding is its
(a) Originality (b) Validity
(c) Objectivity (d) All of the above

10. Which technique is generally followed when the population is finite?
(a) Area Sampling Technique
(b) Purposive Sampling Technique
(c) Systematic Sampling Technique
(d) None of the above

Read the following passage and answer the questions 11 to 15:

Gandhi's overall social and environmental philosophy is based on what human beings need rather than what they want. His early introduction to the teachings of Jains, Theosophists, Christian sermons, Ruskin and Tolstoy, and most significantly the *Bhagavad Gita*, were to have profound impact on the development of Gandhi's holistic thinking on humanity, nature and their ecological interrelation. His deep concern for the disadvantaged, the poor and rural population created an ambience for an alternative social thinking that was at once far-sighted, local and immediate. For Gandhi was acutely aware that the demands generated by the need to feed and sustain human life, compounded by the growing industrialisation of India, far outstripped the finite resources of nature. This might nowadays appear naive or commonplace, but such pronouncements were as rare as they were heretical a century ago. Gandhi was also concerned about the destruction, under colonial and modernist designs, of the existing infrastructures which had more potential for keeping a community flourishing within ecologically-sensitive traditional patterns of subsistence, especially in the rural areas, than did the incoming Western alternatives based on nature-blind technology and the enslavement of human spirit and energies.

Perhaps the moral principle for which Gandhi is best known is that of active non-violence, derived from the traditional moral restraint of not injuring another being. The most refined expression of this value is in the great epic of the *Mahabharata*, (c. 100 BCE to 200 CE), where moral development proceeds through placing constraints on the liberties, desires and acquisitiveness endemic to human life. One's action is judged in terms of consequences and the impact it is likely to have on another. Jainas had generalised this principle to include all sentient creatures and biocommunities alike. Advanced Jaina monks and nuns will sweep their path to avoid harming insects and even bacteria. Non-injury is a non-negotiable universal prescription.

11. Which one of the following have a profound impact on the development of Gandhi's holistic thinking on humanity, nature and their ecological interrelations?
(a) Jain teachings
(b) Christian sermons
(c) *Bhagavad Gita*
(d) Ruskin and Tolstoy

12. Gandhi's overall social and environmental philosophy is based on human beings'
(a) need (b) desire
(c) wealth (d) welfare

13. Gandhiji's deep concern for the disadvantaged, the poor and rural population created an ambience for an alternative
(a) rural policy
(b) social thinking
(c) urban policy
(d) economic thinking

14. Colonial policy and modernisation led to the destruction of
(a) major industrial infrastructure
(b) irrigation infrastructure
(c) urban infrastructure
(d) rural infrastructure

15. Gandhi's active non-violence is derived from
(a) Moral restraint of not injuring another being
(b) Having liberties, desires and acquisitiveness
(c) Freedom of action
(d) Nature-blind technology and enslavement of human spirit and energies

16. DTH service was started in the year
(a) 2000 (b) 2002
(c) 2004 (d) 2006

17. National Press day is celebrated on
(a) 16th November (b) 19th November
(c) 21st November (d) 30th November

18. The total number of members in the Press Council of India are
(a) 28 (b) 14
(c) 17 (d) 20

19. The right to impart and receive information is guaranteed in the Constitution of India by Article
(a) 19(2)(a) (b) 19(16)
(c) 19(2) (d) 19(1)(a)

20. Use of radio for higher education is based on the presumption of
(a) Enriching curriculum based instruction
(b) Replacing teacher in the long run
(c) Everybody having access to a radio set
(d) Other means of instruction getting outdated

21. Find out the number which should come at the place of question mark which will complete the following series.
5, 4, 9, 17, 35, ? = 139
(a) 149 (b) 79
(c) 49 (d) 69

Questions 22 to 24 are based on the following diagram in which there are three interlocking circles I, S and P, where circle I stands for Indians, circle S for Scientists and circle P for Politicians. Different regions in the figure are lettered from a to f.

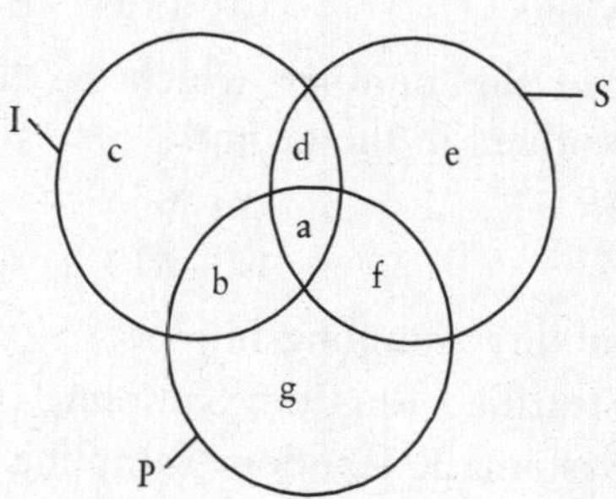

22. The region which represents Non-Indian Scientists who are Politicians.
(a) f (b) d
(c) a (d) c

23. The region which represents Indians who are neither Scientists nor Politicians.
(a) g (b) c
(c) f (d) a

24. The region which represents Politicians who are Indians as well as Scientists.

(a) b (b) c
(c) a (d) d

25. Which number is missing in the following series?
2, 5, 10, 17, 26, 37, 50, ?
(a) 63 (b) 65
(c) 67 (d) 69

26. The function of measurement includes.
(a) Prognosis (b) Diagnosis
(c) Prediction (d) All of the above

27. Logical arguments are based on.
(a) Scientific reasoning
(b) Customary reasoning
(c) Mathematical reasoning
(d) Syllogistic reasoning

28. Insert the missing number 4 : 17 : : 7 : ?
(a) 48 (b) 49
(c) 50 (d) 51

29. Choose the odd word.
(a) Nun (b) Knight
(c) Monk (d) Priest

30. Choose the number which is different from others in the group.
(a) 49 (b) 63
(c) 77 (d) 81

31. Probability sampling implies.
(a) Stratified Random Sampling
(b) Systematic Random Sampling
(c) Simple Random Sampling
(d) All of the above

32. Insert the missing number.
$\frac{36}{62}, \frac{39}{63}, \frac{43}{61}, \frac{48}{64}, ?$
(a) $\frac{51}{65}$ (b) $\frac{56}{60}$
(c) $\frac{54}{65}$ (d) $\frac{33}{60}$

33. At what time between 3 and 4 O'clock will the hands of a watch point in opposite directions?
(a) 40 minutes past three
(b) 45 minutes past three
(c) 50 minutes past three
(d) 55 minutes past three

34. Mary has three children. What is the probability that none of the three children is a boy?
(a) $\frac{1}{2}$ (b) $\frac{1}{3}$
(c) $\frac{3}{4}$ (d) 1

35. If the radius of a circle is increased by 50 percent. Its area is increased by
(a) 125 percent (b) 100 percent
(c) 75 percent (d) 50 percent

36. CD ROM stands for
(a) Computer Disk Read Only Memory
(b) Compact Disk Read Over Memory
(c) Compact Disk Read Only Memory
(d) Computer Disk Read Over Memory

37. The 'brain' of a computer which keeps peripherals under its control is called
(a) Common Power Unit
(b) Common Processing Unit
(c) Central Power Unit
(d) Central Processing Unit

38. Data can be saved on backing storage medium known as
(a) Compact Disk Recordable
(b) Computer Disk Rewritable
(c) Compact Disk Rewritable
(d) Computer Data Rewritable

39. RAM means
(a) Random Access Memory
(b) Rigid Access Memory

(c) Rapid Access Memory
(d) Revolving Access Memory

40. www represents
(a) who what and where
(b) weird wide web
(c) word wide web
(d) world wide web

41. Deforestation during the recent decades has led to
(a) Soil erosion
(b) Landslides
(c) Loss of bio-diversity
(d) All of the above

42. Which one of the following natural hazards is responsible for causing highest human disaster?
(a) Earthquakes
(b) Volcanic eruptions
(c) Snowstorms
(d) Tsunami

43. Which one of the following is appropriate for natural hazard mitigation?
(a) International AID
(b) Timely Warning System
(c) Rehabilitation
(d) Community Participation

44. Slums in metro city are the result of
(a) Rural to urban migration
(b) Poverty of the city-scape
(c) Lack of urban infrastructure
(d) Urban-governance

45. The great Indian Bustard bird is found in
(a) Thar Desert of India
(b) Coastal regions of India
(c) Temperate Forests in the Himalaya
(d) Tarai zones of the Himalayan Foot

46. The first Indian Satellite for serving the educational sector is known as
(a) SATEDU (b) INSAT-B
(c) EDUSAT (d) DMSAT-C

47. Exclusive educational channel of IGNOU is known as
(a) Gyan Darshan (b) Gyan Vani
(c) Door Darshan (d) Prasar Bharati

48. The headquarter of Mahatma Gandhi Antarrashtriya Hindi Vishwavidyalaya is situated in
(a) Sevagram (b) New Delhi
(c) Wardha (d) Ahmedabad

49. Match List I with List II and select the correct answer using the codes given below.

List I (Institutes)
A. Central Institute of English and Foreign Languages
B. Gramodaya Vishwavidyalaya
C. Central Institute of Higher Tibetan Studies
D. IGNOU

List II (Locations)
1. Chitrakoot 2. Hyderabad
3. New Delhi 4. Dharmasala

Codes:	A	B	C	D
(a)	2	1	4	3
(b)	4	3	2	1
(c)	3	4	1	2
(d)	1	2	4	3

50. The aim of vocationalisation of education is
(a) preparing students for a vocation along with knowledge
(b) converting liberal education into vocational education
(c) giving more importance to vocational than general education
(d) making liberal education job-oriented

ANSWERS

1. (b)	2. (a)	3. (b)	4. (a)
5. (a)	6. (c)	7. (c)	8. (c)
9. (d)	10. (c)	11. (c)	12. (a)
13. (b)	14. (c)	15. (a)	16. (d)
17. (a)	18. (a)	19. (d)	20. (b)
21. (d)	22. (a)	23. (b)	24. (d)
25. (b)	26. (d)	27. (d)	28. (c)
29. (b)	30. (c)	31. (d)	32. (c)
33. (c)	34. (d)	35. (a)	36. (c)
37. (d)	38. (c)	39. (a)	40. (d)
41. (d)	42. (a)	43. (b)	44. (a)
45. (a)	46. (c)	47. (a)	48. (c)
49. (a)	50. (d)		

JUNE-2007 (PAPER-I)

1. Teacher uses visual-aids to make learning
   (a) simple
   (b) more knowledgeable
   (c) quicker
   (d) interesting
2. The teacher's role at the higher educational level is to
   (a) provide information to students
   (b) promote self-learning in students
   (c) encourage healthy competition among students
   (d) help students to solve their personal problems
3. Which one of the following teachers would you like the most?
   (a) Punctual
   (b) Having research aptitude
   (c) Loving and having high idealistic philosophy
   (d) Who often amuses his students
4. Micro teaching is most effective for the student-teacher
   (a) during the practice-teaching
   (b) after the practice-teaching
   (c) before the practice-teaching
   (d) None of the above
5. Which is the least important factor in teaching?
   (a) Punishing the students
   (b) Maintaining discipline in the class
   (c) Lecturing in impressive way
   (d) Drawing sketches and diagrams on the blackboard
6. To test null hypothesis, a researcher uses
   (a) t test (b) ANOVA
   (c) x^2 (d) factorial analysis
7. A research problem is feasible only when
   (a) it has utility and relevance
   (b) it is researchable
   (c) it is new and adds something to knowledge
   (d) All of the above
8. Bibliography given in a research report
   (a) shows vast knowledge of the researcher
   (b) helps those interested in further research
   (c) has no relevance to research
   (d) All of the above
9. Fundamental research reflects the ability to
   (a) Synthesise new ideals
   (b) Expound new principles
   (c) Evaluate the existing material concerning research
   (d) Study the existing literature regarding various topics
10. The study in which the investigators attempt to trace an effect is known as
   (a) Survey Research
   (b) *Ex-post Facto* Research

(c) Historical Research
(d) Summative Research

Read the following passage and answer the questions 11 to 15:

All political systems need to mediate the relationship between private wealth and public power. Those that fail risk a dysfunctional government captured by wealthy interests. Corruption is one symptom of such failure with private willingness-to-pay trumping public goals. Private individuals and business firms pay to get routine services and to get to the head of the bureaucratic queue. They pay to limit their taxes, avoid costly regulations, obtain contracts at inflated prices and get concessions and privatised firms at low prices. If corruption is endemic, public officials—both bureaucrats and elected officials—may redesign programs and propose public projects with few public benefits and many opportunities for private profit. Of course, corruption, in the sense of bribes, pay-offs and kickbacks, is only one type of government failure. Efforts to promote "good governance' must be broader than anti-corruption campaigns. Governments may be honest but inefficient because no one has an incentive to work productively, and narrow elites may capture the state and exert excess influence on policy. Bribery may induce the lazy to work hard and permit those not in the inner circle of cronies to obtain benefits. However, even in such cases, corruption cannot be confined to 'functional' areas. It will be a temptation whenever private benefits are positive. It may be a reasonable response to a harsh reality but, over time, it can facilitate a spiral into an even worse situation.

11. The governments which fail to focus on the relationship between private wealth and public power are likely to become
    (a) Functional
    (b) Dysfunctional
    (c) Normal functioning
    (d) Good governance
12. One important symptom of bad governance is
    (a) Corruption
    (b) High taxes
    (c) Complicated rules and regulations
    (d) High prices
13. When corruption is rampant, public officials always aim at many opportunities for:
    (a) Public benefits (b) Public profit
    (c) Private profit (d) Corporate gains
14. Productivity linked incentives to public/ private officials is one of the indicatives for
    (a) Efficient government
    (b) Bad governance
    (c) Inefficient government
    (d) Corruption
15. The spiralling corruption can only be contained by promoting
    (a) Private profit
    (b) Anti-corruption campaign
    (c) Good governance
    (d) Pay-offs and kickbacks
16. Press Council of India is located at
    (a) Chennai (b) Mumbai
    (c) Kolkata (d) Delhi
17. Adjusting the photo for publication by cutting is technically known as
    (a) Photo cutting
    (b) Photo bleeding
    (c) Photo cropping
    (d) Photo adjustment
18. Feedback of a message comes from
    (a) Satellite (b) Media
    (c) Audience (d) Communicator
19. Collection of information in advance before designing communication strategy is known as

(a) Feedback (b) Feed-forward
(c) Research study (d) Opinion poll

20. The aspect ratio of TV screen is
(a) 4:3 (b) 4:2
(c) 3:5 (d) 2:3

21. Which is the number that comes next in the sequence?
9, 8, 8, 8, 7, 8, 6, __
(a) 5 (b) 6
(c) 8 (d) 4

22. If in a certain language PUNCTUAL is coded as 16598623, how would ACTUPULN be coded?
(a) 834536 (b) 29861635
(c) 834530 (d) 834539

23. The question to be answered by factorial analysis of the quantitative data does not explain one of the following
(a) Is 'X' related to 'Y'?
(b) How is 'X' related to 'Y'?
(c) How does 'X' affect the dependent variable 'Y' at different levels of another independent variable 'K' or 'M'?
(d) How is 'X' by 'K' related to 'M'?

24. January 12, 1980 was Saturday, what day was January 12, 1979?
(a) Saturday (b) Friday
(c) Sunday (d) Thursday

25. How many Mondays are there in a particular month of a particular year, if the month ends on Wednesday?
(a) 5 (b) 4
(c) 3 (d) None of these

26. From the given four statements, select the two which cannot be true but yet both can be false. Choose the right pair.
1. All men are mortal
2. Some men are mortal
3. No man is mortal
4. Some men are not mortal

(a) 1 and 2 (b) 3 and 4
(c) 1 and 3 (d) 2 and 4

27. A Syllogism must have
(a) Three terms (b) Four terms
(c) Six terms (d) Five terms

28. Copula is that part of proposition which denotes the relationship between
(a) Subject and predicate
(b) Known and unknown
(c) Major premise and minor premise
(d) Subject and object

29. "E" denotes
(a) Universal Negative Proposition
(b) Particular Affirmative Proposition
(c) Universal Affirmative Proposition
(d) Particular Negative Proposition

30. 'A' is the father of 'C' and 'D' is the son of 'B'. 'E' is the brother of 'A'. If 'C' is the sister of 'D' how is 'B' related to 'E'?
(a) Daughter (b) Husband
(c) Sister-in-law (d) Brother-in-law

31. Which of the following methods will you choose to prepare choropleth map of India showing urban density of population?
(a) Quartiles (b) Quintiles
(c) Mean and SD (d) Break-point

32. Which of the following methods is best suited to show on a map the types of crops being grown in a region?
(a) Choropleth (b) Chorochromatic
(c) Choroschematic (d) Isopleth

33. A ratio represents the relation between
(a) Part and Part
(b) Part and Whole
(c) Whole and Whole
(d) All of the above

34. Out of four numbers, the average of the first three numbers is thrice the fourth number. If the average of the four numbers is 5, the fourth number is

(a) 4.5 (b) 5
(c) 2 (d) 4

35. Circle graphs are used to show
(a) How various sections share in the whole
(b) How various parts are related to the whole
(c) How one whole is related to other wholes
(d) How one part is related to other parts

36. On the keyboard of computer each character has an "ASCII" value which stands for
(a) American Stock Code for Information Interchange
(b) American Standard Code for Information Interchange
(c) African Standard Code for Information Interchange
(d) Adaptable Standard Code for Information Change

37. Which part of the Central Processing Unit (CPU) performs calculation and makes decisions
(a) Arithmetic Logic Unit
(b) Alternating Logic Unit
(c) Alternate Local Unit
(d) American Logic Unit

38. "Dpi" stands for
(a) Dots per inch
(b) Digits per unit
(c) Dots pixel inch
(d) Diagrams per inch

39. The process of laying out a document with text, graphics, headlines and photographs is involved in
(a) Deck Top Publishing
(b) Desk Top Printing
(c) Desk Top Publishing
(d) Deck Top Printing

40. Transfer of data from one application to another line is known as
(a) Dynamic Disk Exchange
(b) Dodgy Data Exchange
(c) Dogmatic Data Exchange
(d) Dynamic Data Exchange

41. Tsunami occurs due to
(a) Mild earthquakes and landslides in the oceans
(b) Strong earthquakes and landslides in the oceans
(c) Strong earthquakes and landslides in mountains
(d) Strong earthquakes and landslides in deserts

42. Which of the natural hazards have big effect on Indian people each year?
(a) Cyclones (b) Floods
(c) Earthquakes (d) Landslides

43. Comparative Environment Impact Assessment study is to be conducted for
(a) the whole year
(b) three seasons excluding monsoon
(c) any three seasons
(d) the worst season

44. Sea level rise results primarily due to
(a) Heavy rainfall
(b) Melting of glaciers
(c) Submarine volcanism
(d) Seafloor spreading

45. The plume rise in a coal based power plant depends on
1. Buoyancy
2. Atmospheric stability
3. Momentum of exhaust gases identify

Codes:
(a) Both (1) and (2)
(b) Both (2) and (3)
(c) Both (1) and (3)
(d) (1), (2) and (3)

46. Value education makes a student
(a) Good citizen
(b) Successful businessman
(c) Popular teacher
(d) Efficient manager

47. Networking of libraries through electronic media is known as
(a) Inflibnet (b) Libinfnet
(c) Internet (d) HTML

48. The University which telecasts interactive educational programs through its own channel is
(a) B.R. Ambedkar Open University, Hyderabad
(b) I.G.N.O.U.
(c) University of Pune
(d) Annamalai University

49. The Government established the University Grants Commission by an Act of Parliament in the year
(a) 1980 (b) 1948
(c) 1950 (d) 1956

50. Universities having central campus for imparting education are called
(a) Central Universities
(b) Deemed Universities
(c) Residential Universities
(d) Open Universities

ANSWERS

1. (d)	2. (a)	3. (a)	4. (b)
5. (a)	6. (c)	7. (d)	8. (b)
9. (b)	10. (b)	11. (b)	12. (a)
13. (c)	14. (a)	15. (c)	16. (d)
17. (c)	18. (c)	19. (d)	20. (a)
21. (c)	22. (b)	23. (c)	24. (b)
25. (d)	26. (b)	27. (a)	28. (b)
29. (a)	30. (d)	31. (b)	32. (c)
33. (b)	34. (c)	35. (a)	36. (a)
37. (a)	38. (a)	39. (c)	40. (d)
41. (b)	42. (b)	43. (a)	44. (b)
45. (d)	46. (a)	47. (a)	48. (b)
49. (d)	50. (b)		